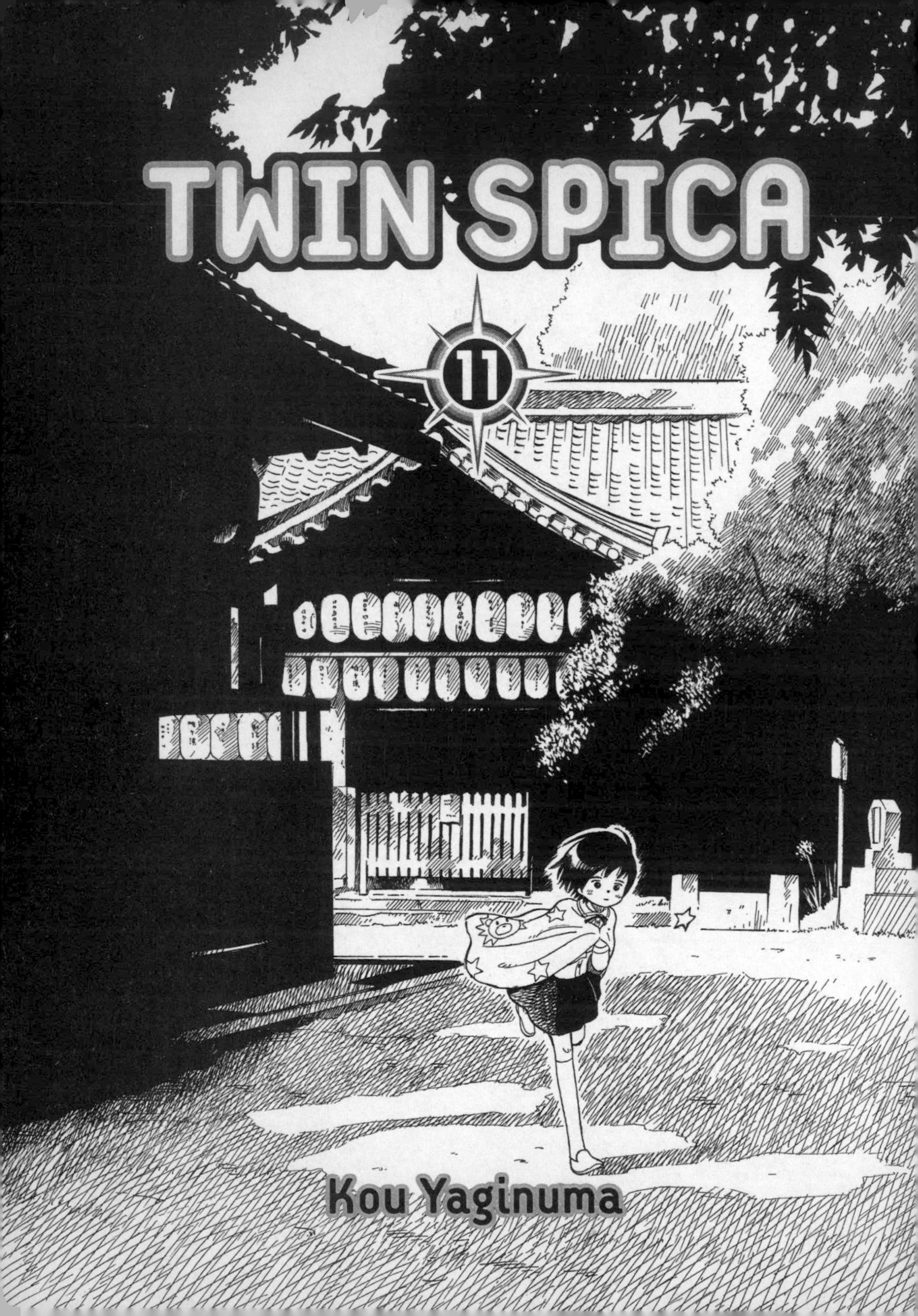
TWIN SPICA
11
Kou Yaginuma

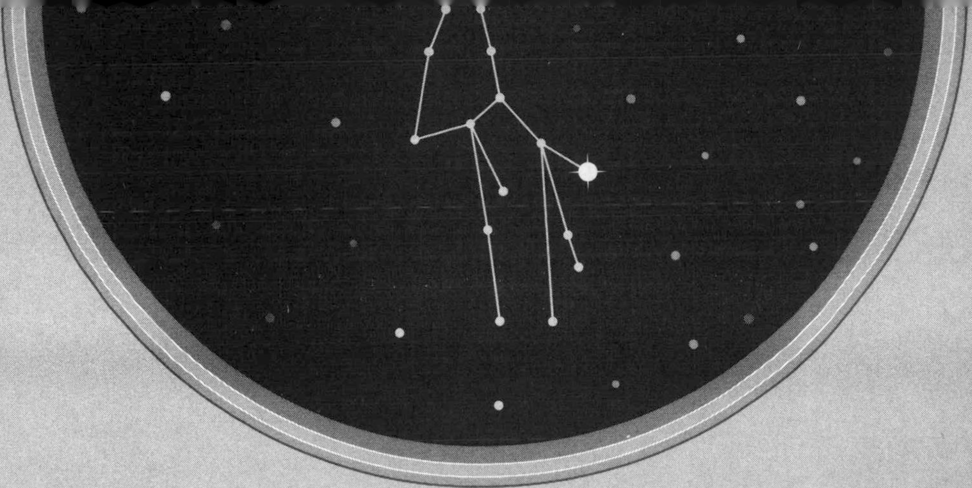

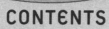

CONTENTS

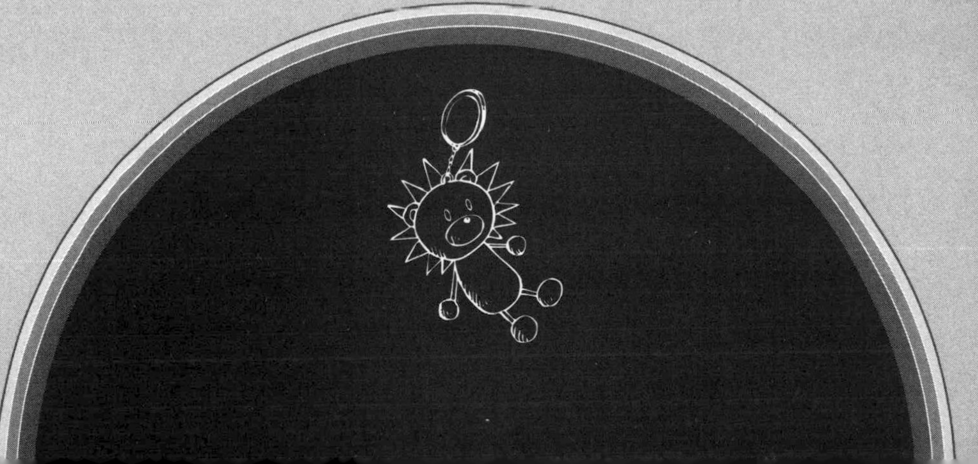

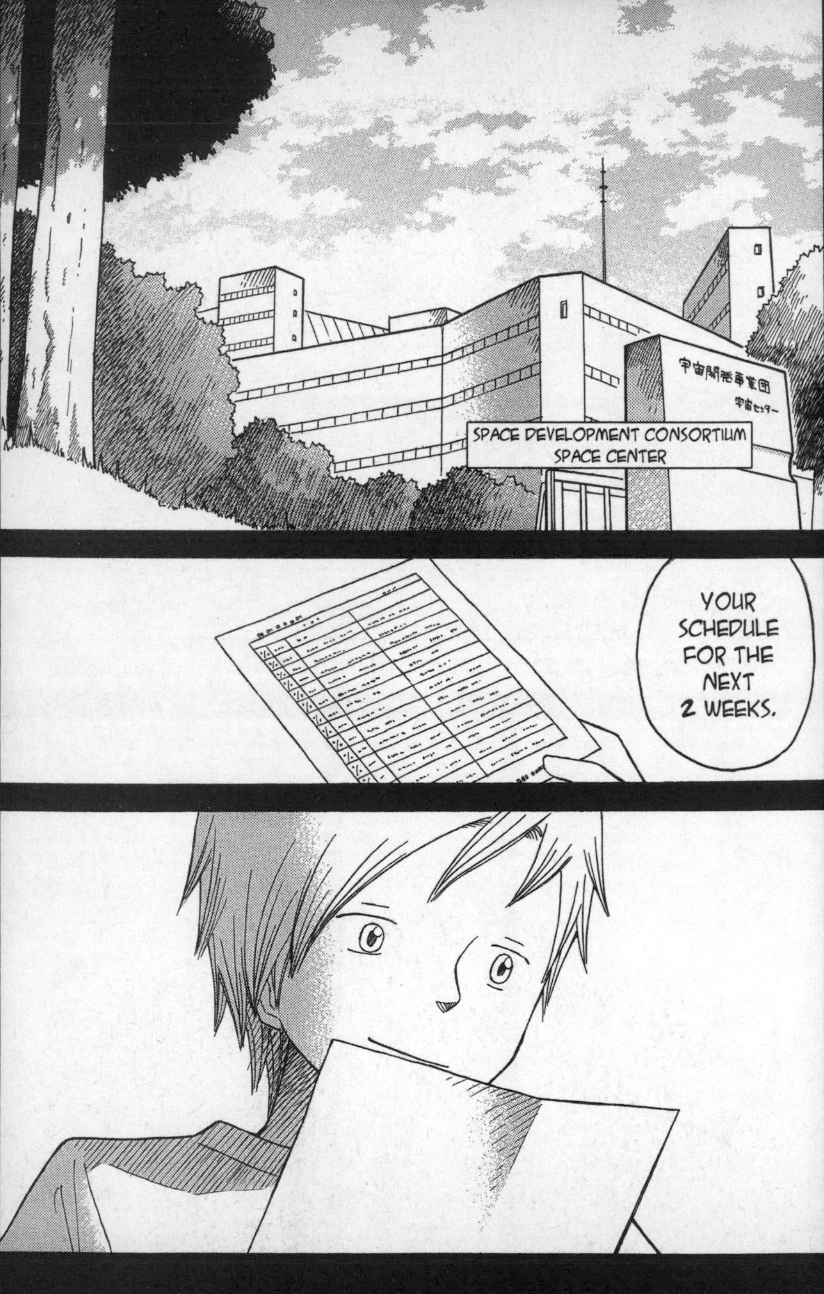
宇宙開発事業団
宇宙センター
SPACE DEVELOPMENT CONSORTIUM
SPACE CENTER
YOUR SCHEDULE FOR THE NEXT 2 WEEKS.

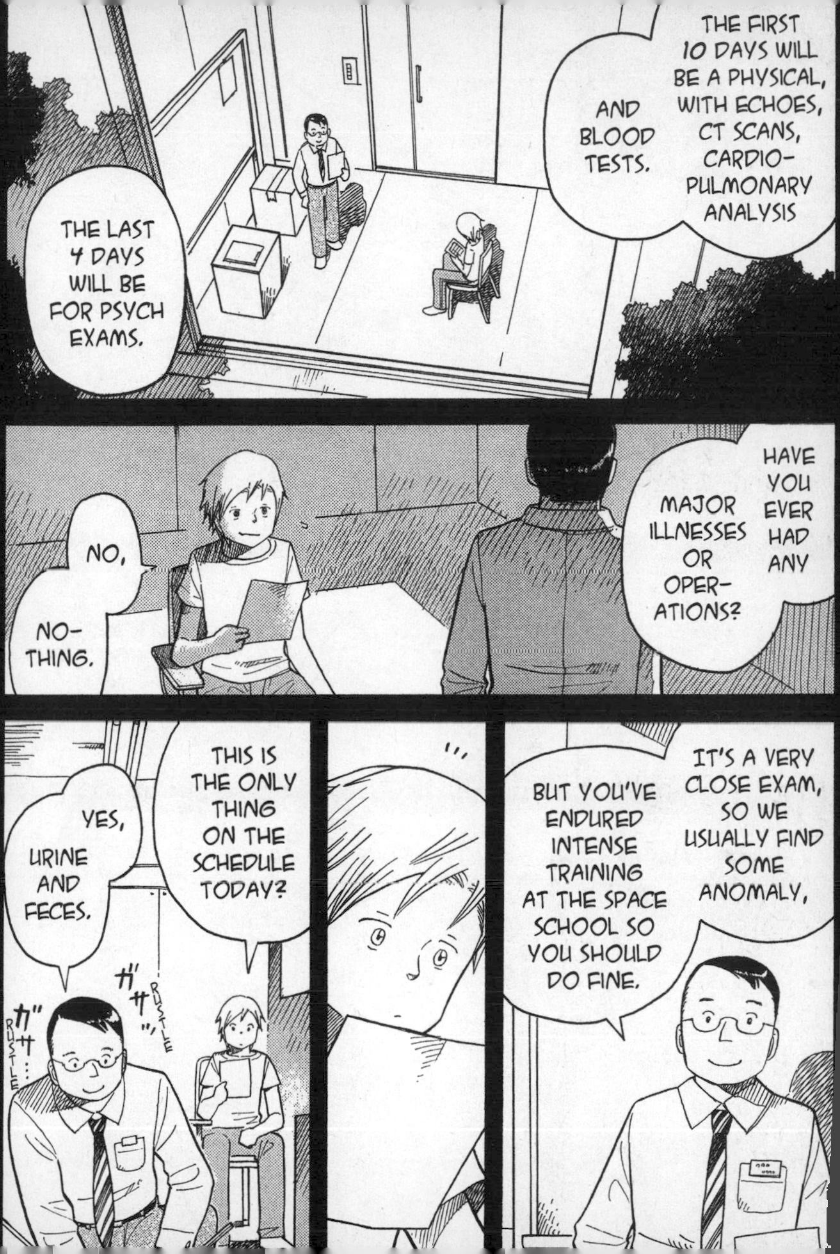
THE FIRST 10 DAYS WILL BE A PHYSICAL, WITH ECHOES, CT SCANS, CARDIO-PULMONARY ANALYSIS
AND BLOOD TESTS.
THE LAST 4 DAYS WILL BE FOR PSYCH EXAMS.
HAVE YOU EVER HAD ANY MAJOR ILLNESSES OR OPERATIONS?
NO,
NO-THING.
IT'S A VERY CLOSE EXAM, SO WE USUALLY FIND SOME ANOMALY,
BUT YOU'VE ENDURED INTENSE TRAINING AT THE SPACE SCHOOL SO YOU SHOULD DO FINE.
THIS IS THE ONLY THING ON THE SCHEDULE TODAY?
ガサ RUSTLE
YES,
URINE AND FECES.
ガサ… RUSTLE

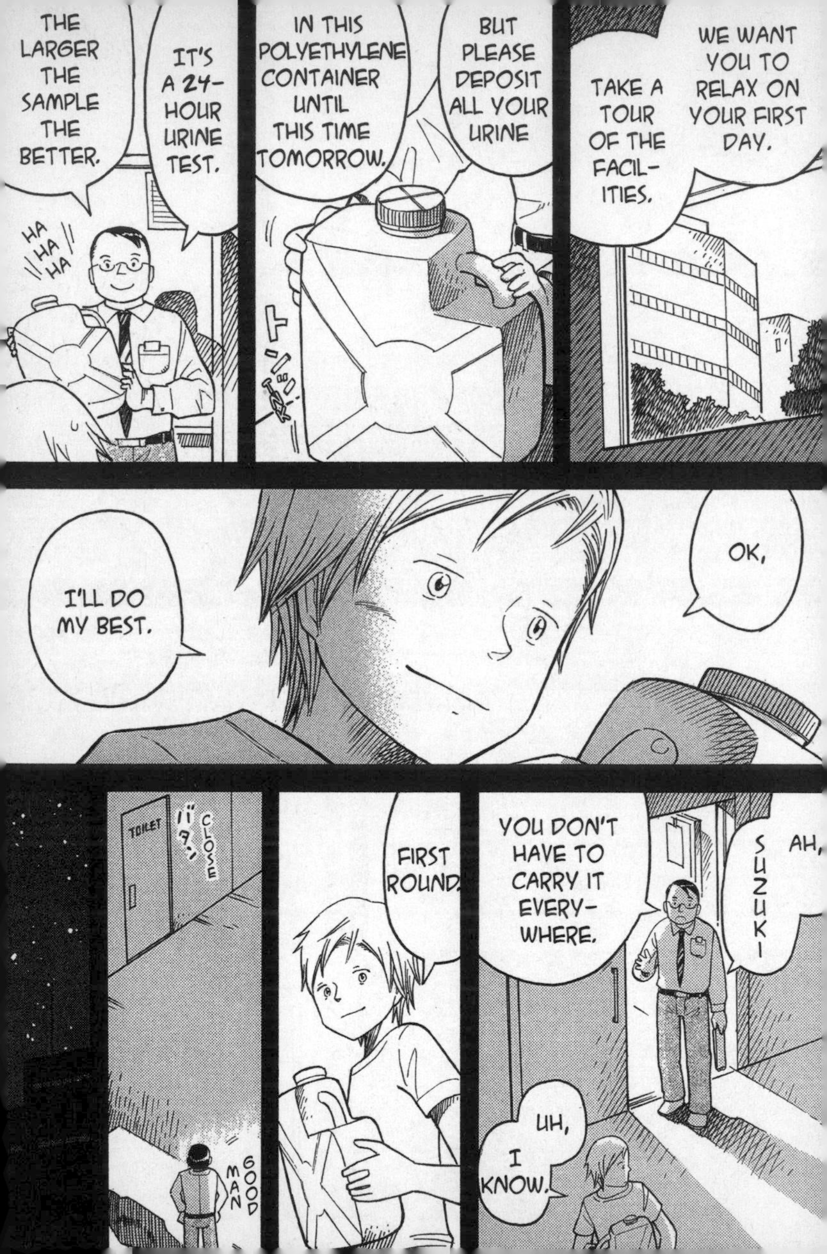
WE WANT YOU TO RELAX ON YOUR FIRST DAY.
TAKE A TOUR OF THE FACIL-ITIES.
BUT PLEASE DEPOSIT ALL YOUR URINE
IN THIS POLYETHYLENE CONTAINER UNTIL THIS TIME TOMORROW.
IT'S A 24-HOUR URINE TEST.
THE LARGER THE SAMPLE THE BETTER.
HA HA HA
OK,
I'LL DO MY BEST.
AH,
SUZUKI
YOU DON'T HAVE TO CARRY IT EVERY-WHERE.
UH, I KNOW.
FIRST ROUND!
TOILET
CLOSE
GOOD MAN

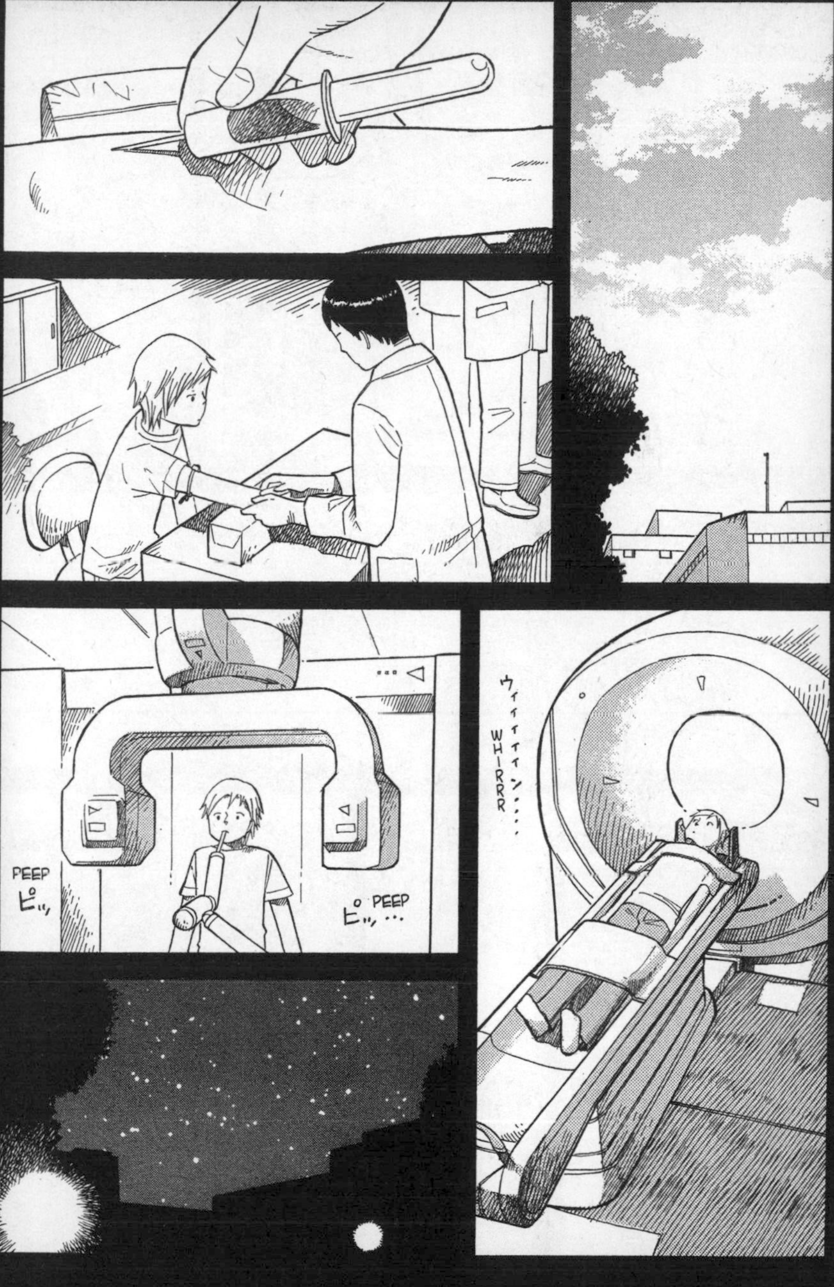

ウィィィィン…
WHIRRR...
PEEP
ピッ
ピッ…
PEEP

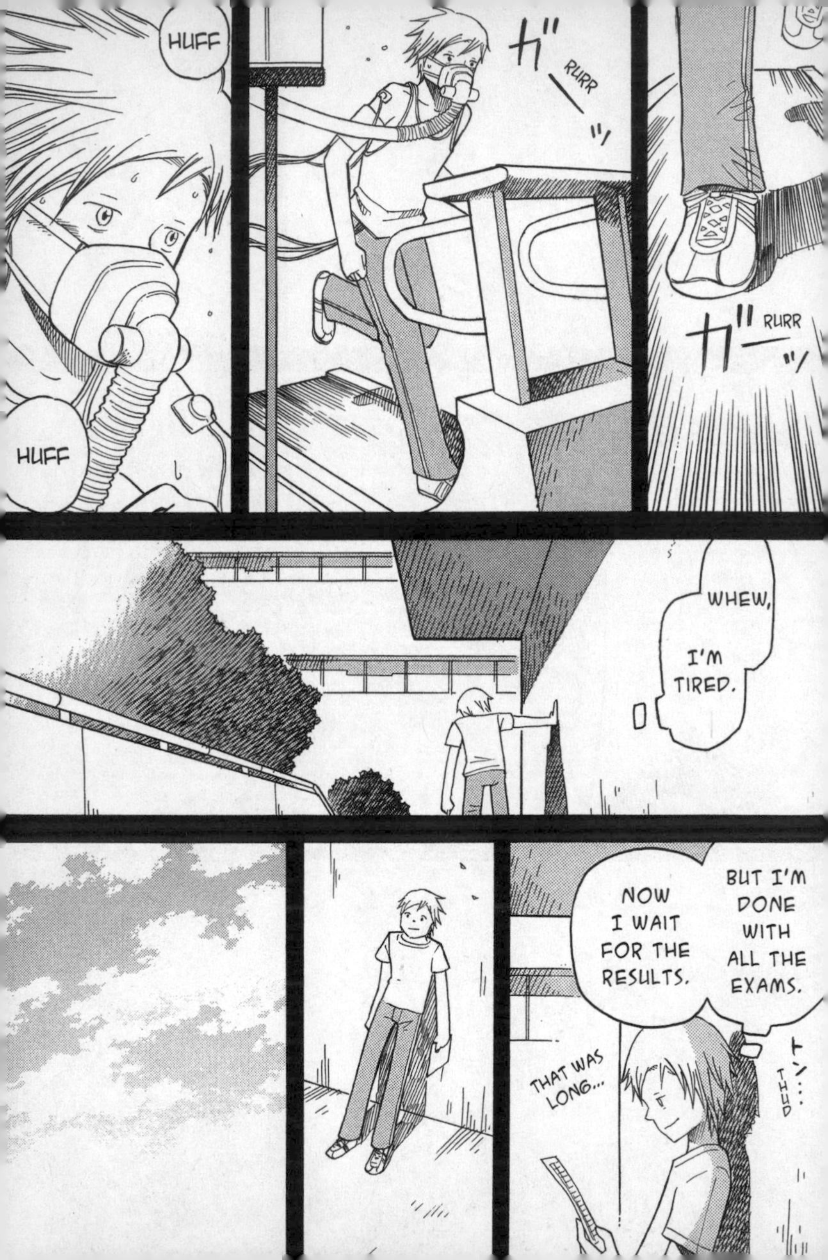
ガッ
RURR
ガッ
RURR
HUFF
HUFF
WHEW,
I'M TIRED.
BUT I'M DONE WITH ALL THE EXAMS.
NOW I WAIT FOR THE RESULTS.
THAT WAS LONG...
トン…
THUD

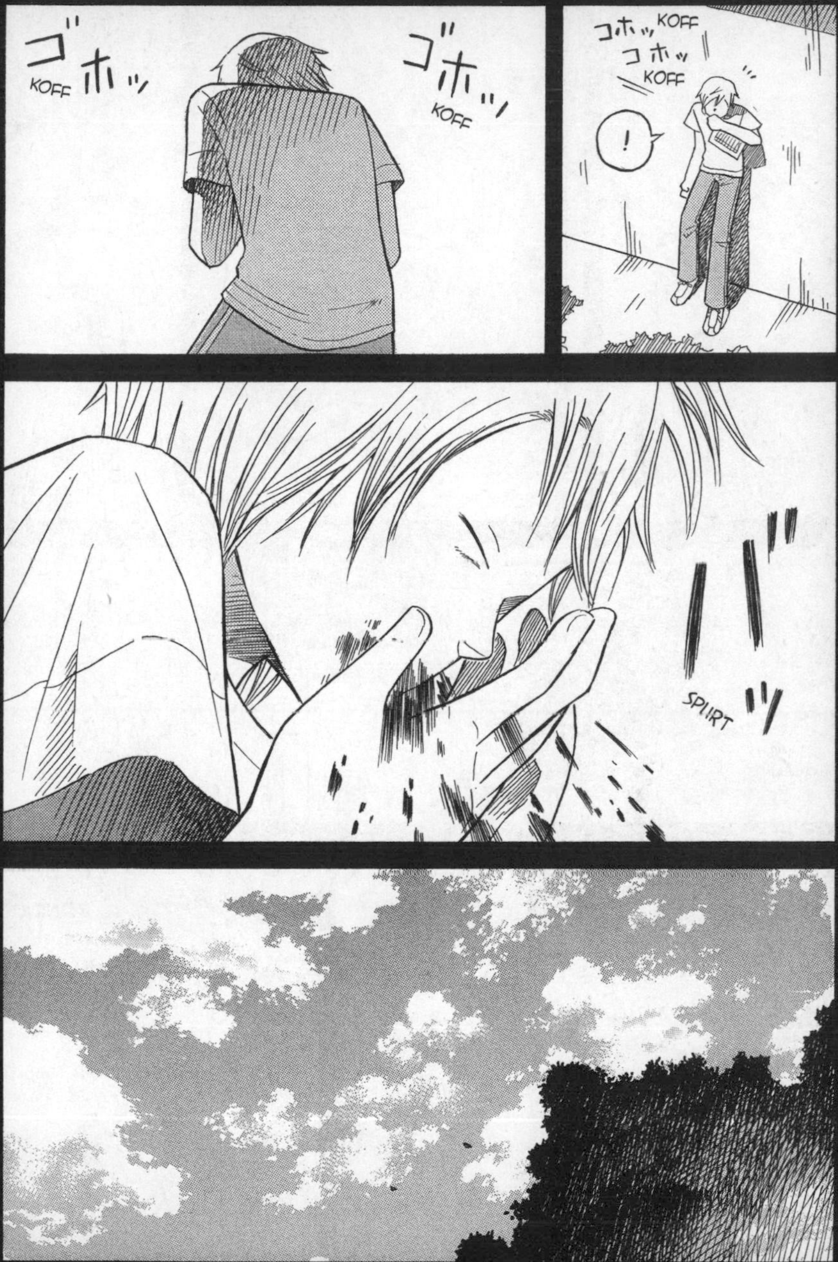
コホッ KOFF
コホッ KOFF
!
ゴホッ KOFF
ゴホッ KOFF
SPURT

MISSION:65

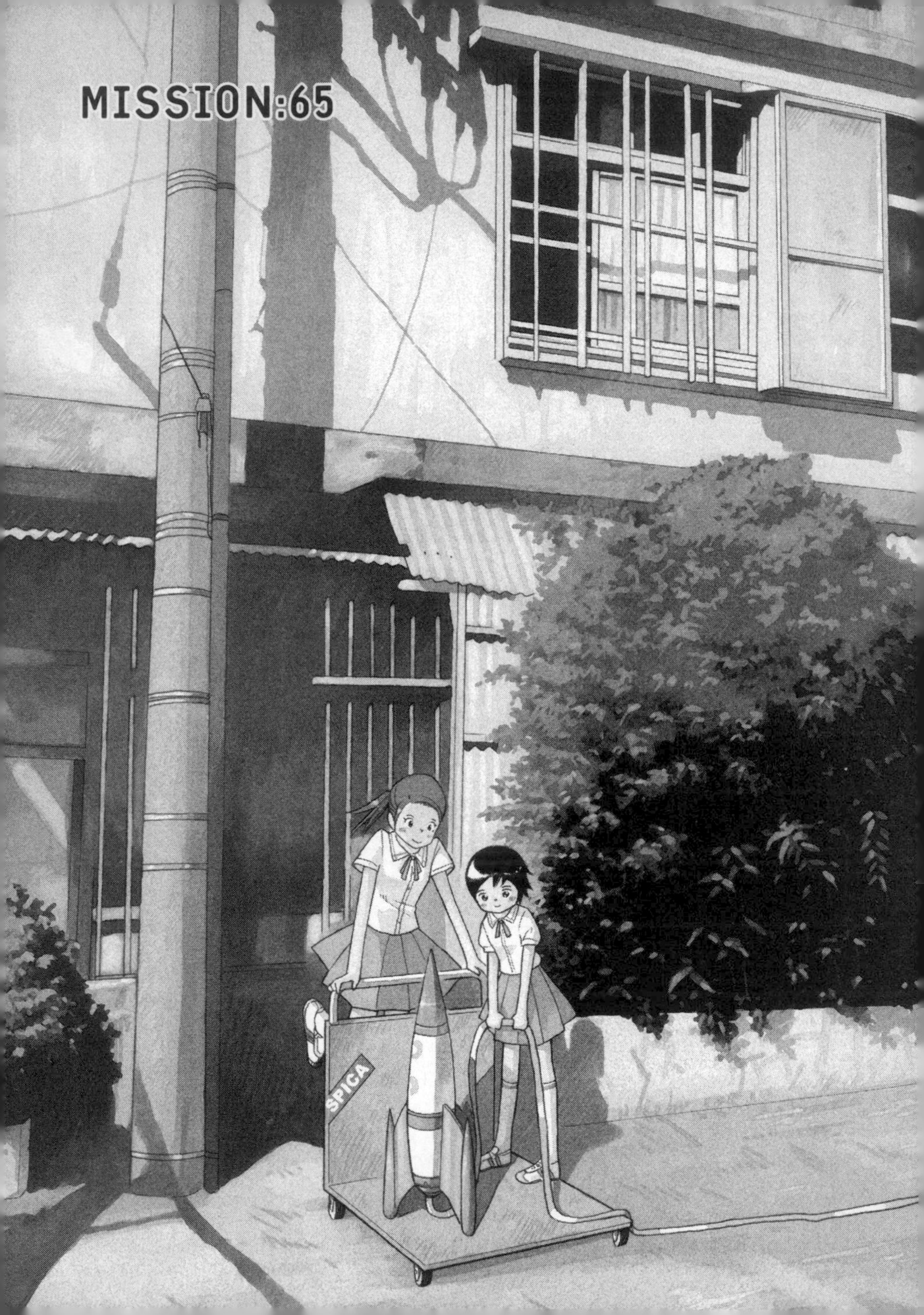
SPICA

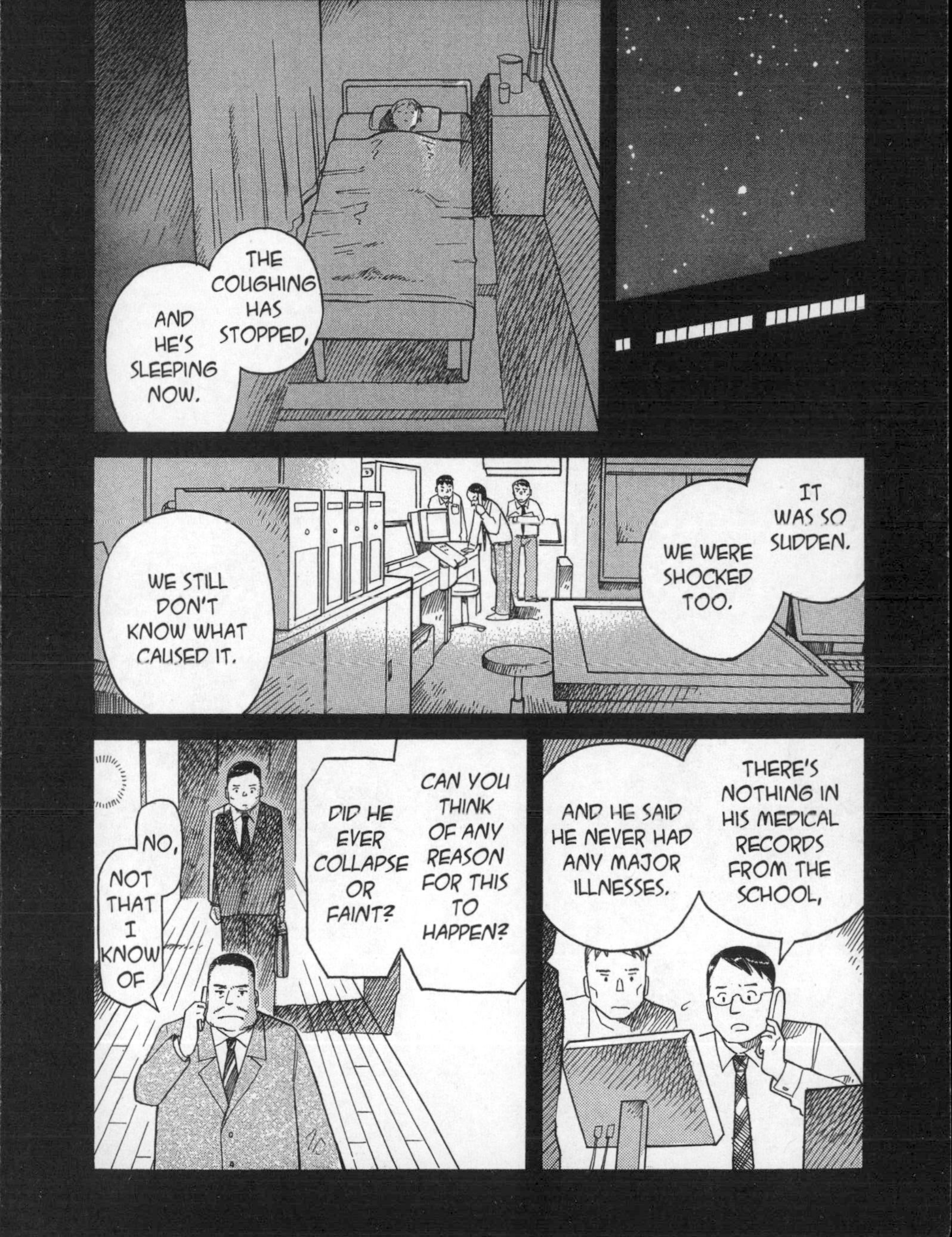
THE COUGHING HAS STOPPED,
AND HE'S SLEEPING NOW.
IT WAS SO SUDDEN.
WE WERE SHOCKED TOO.
WE STILL DON'T KNOW WHAT CAUSED IT.
THERE'S NOTHING IN HIS MEDICAL RECORDS FROM THE SCHOOL,
AND HE SAID HE NEVER HAD ANY MAJOR ILLNESSES.
CAN YOU THINK OF ANY REASON FOR THIS TO HAPPEN?
DID HE EVER COLLAPSE OR FAINT?
NO, NOT THAT I KNOW OF

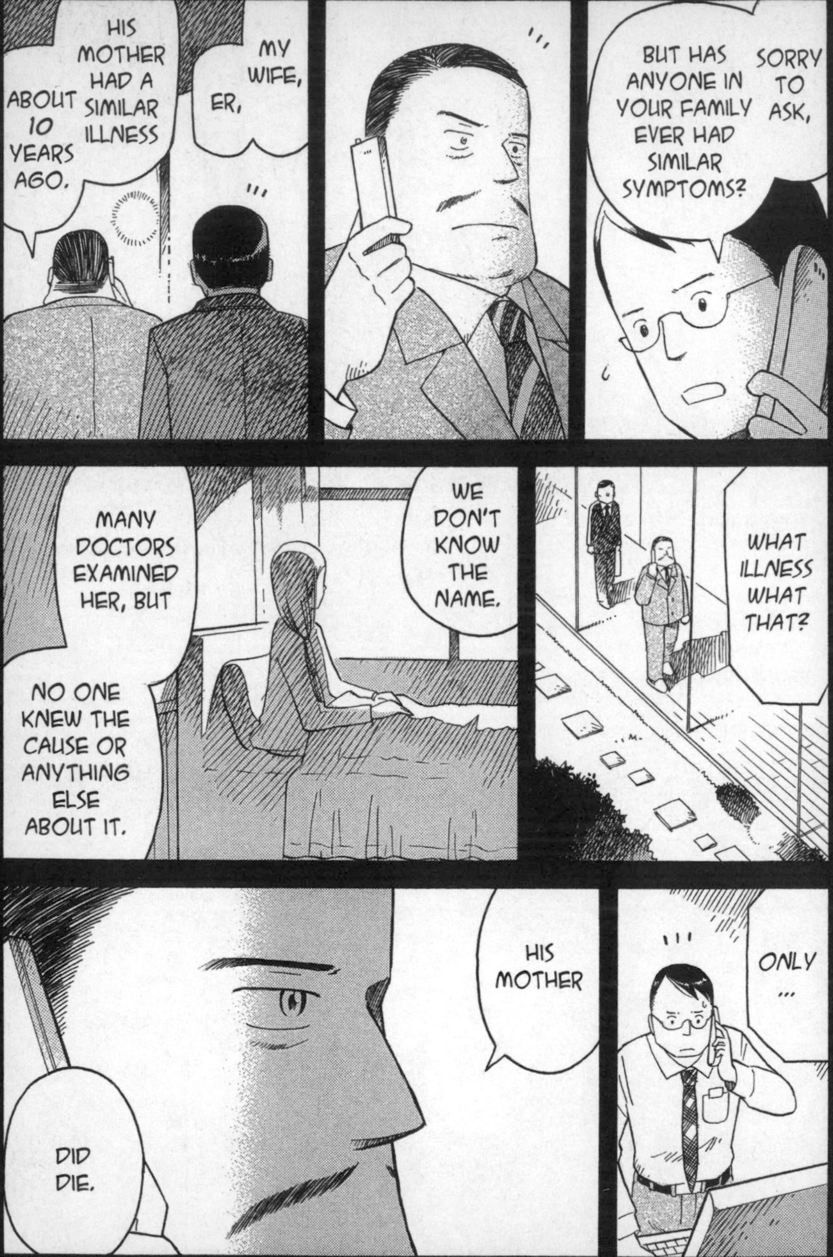
SORRY TO ASK,
BUT HAS ANYONE IN YOUR FAMILY EVER HAD SIMILAR SYMPTOMS?
MY WIFE,
ER,
HIS MOTHER HAD A SIMILAR ILLNESS ABOUT 10 YEARS AGO.
WHAT ILLNESS WHAT THAT?
WE DON'T KNOW THE NAME.
MANY DOCTORS EXAMINED HER, BUT
NO ONE KNEW THE CAUSE OR ANYTHING ELSE ABOUT IT.
ONLY ...
HIS MOTHER
DID DIE.

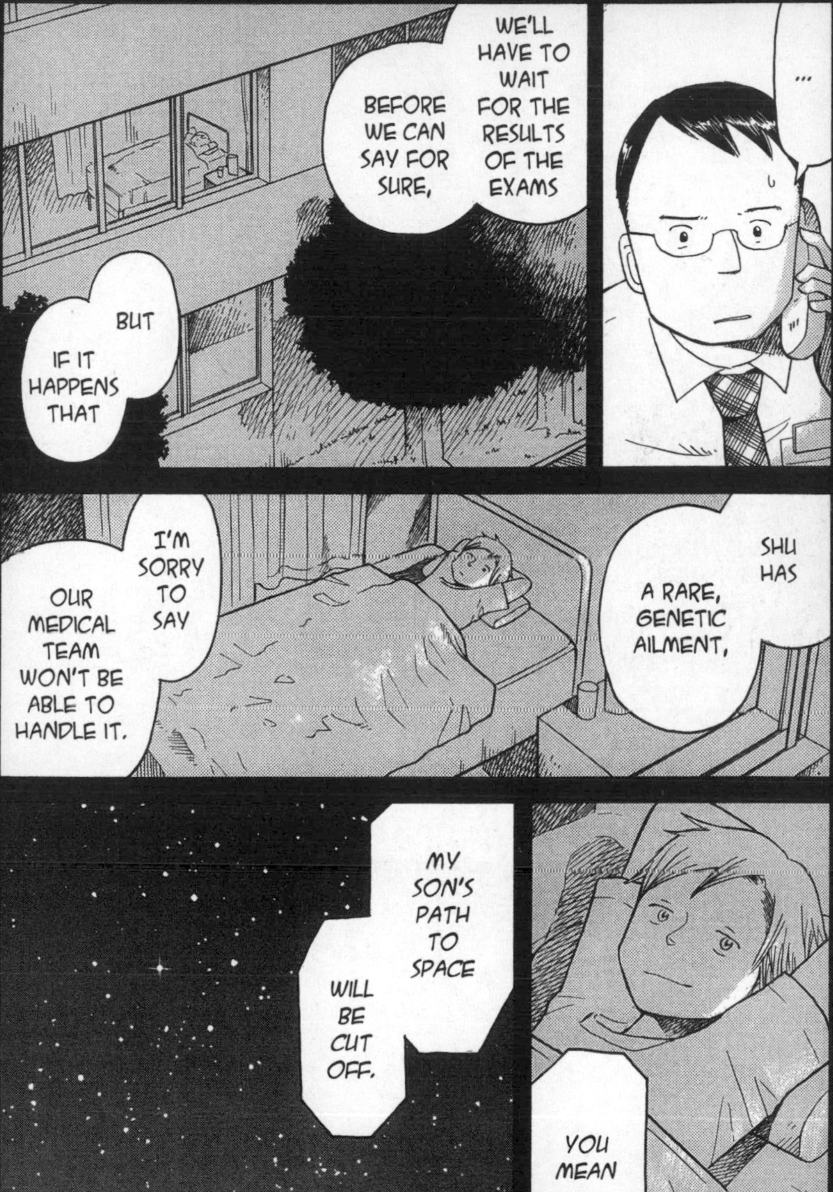
...
WE'LL HAVE TO WAIT FOR THE RESULTS OF THE EXAMS
BEFORE WE CAN SAY FOR SURE,
BUT
IF IT HAPPENS THAT
SHU HAS
A RARE, GENETIC AILMENT,
I'M SORRY TO SAY
OUR MEDICAL TEAM WON'T BE ABLE TO HANDLE IT.
YOU MEAN ...
MY SON'S PATH TO SPACE
WILL BE CUT OFF.

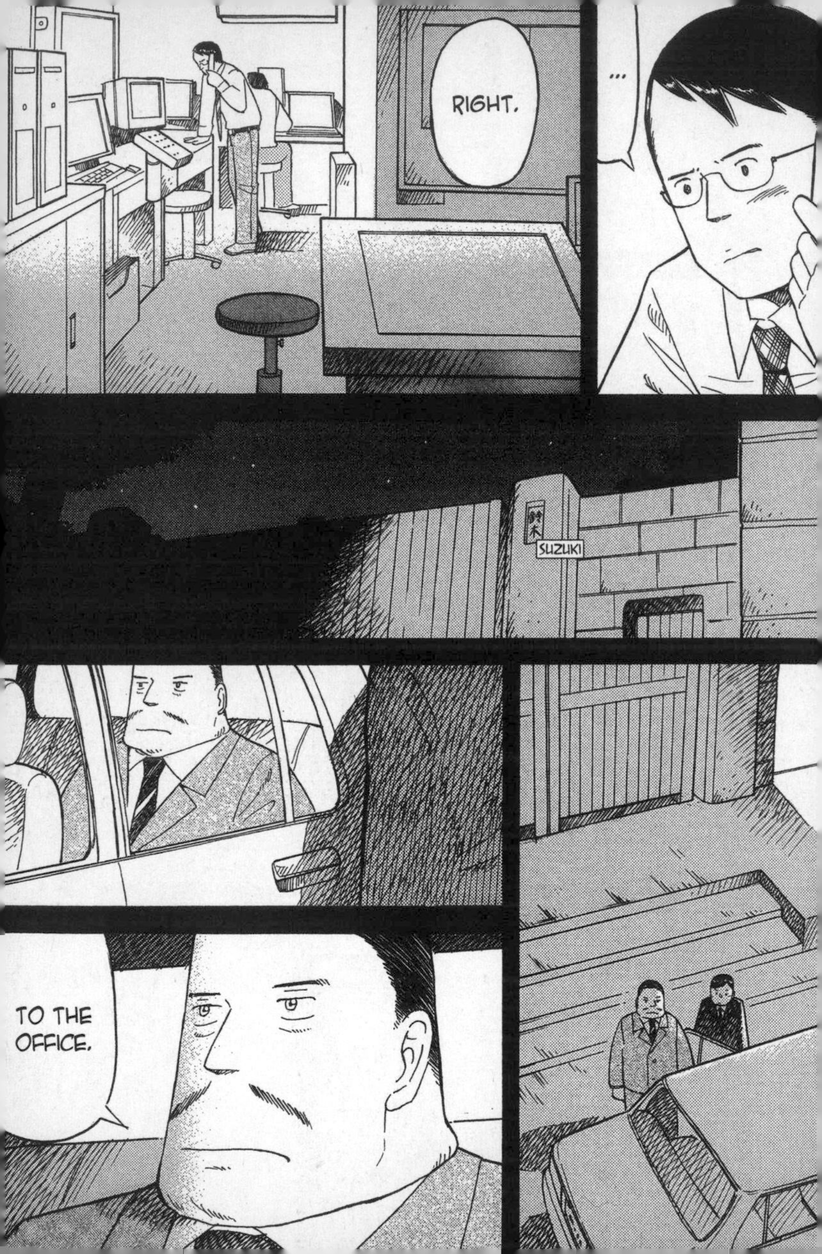
...
RIGHT.
SUZUKI
TO THE OFFICE.

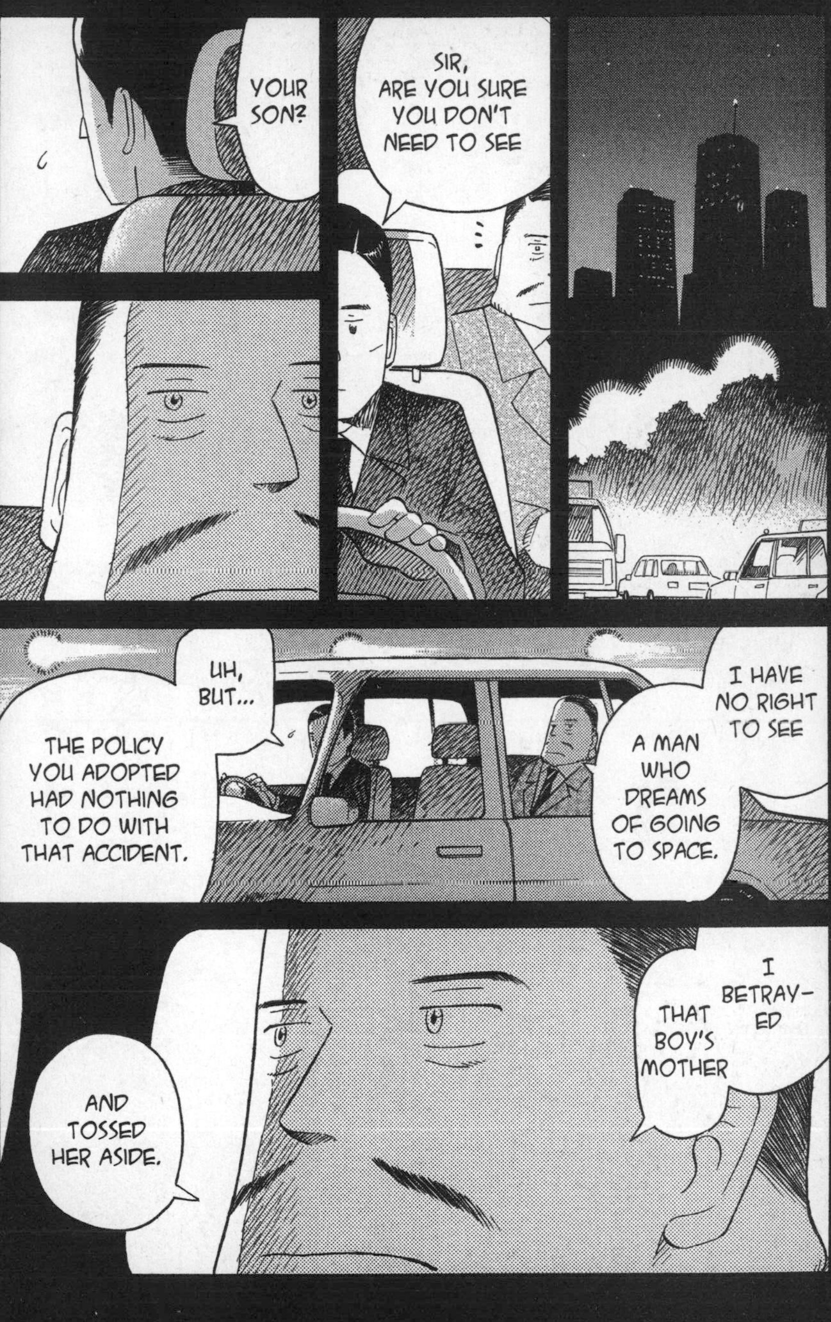
SIR, ARE YOU SURE YOU DON'T NEED TO SEE
YOUR SON?
I HAVE NO RIGHT TO SEE
A MAN WHO DREAMS OF GOING TO SPACE.
UH, BUT...
THE POLICY YOU ADOPTED HAD NOTHING TO DO WITH THAT ACCIDENT.
I BETRAY-ED
THAT BOY'S MOTHER
AND TOSSED HER ASIDE.

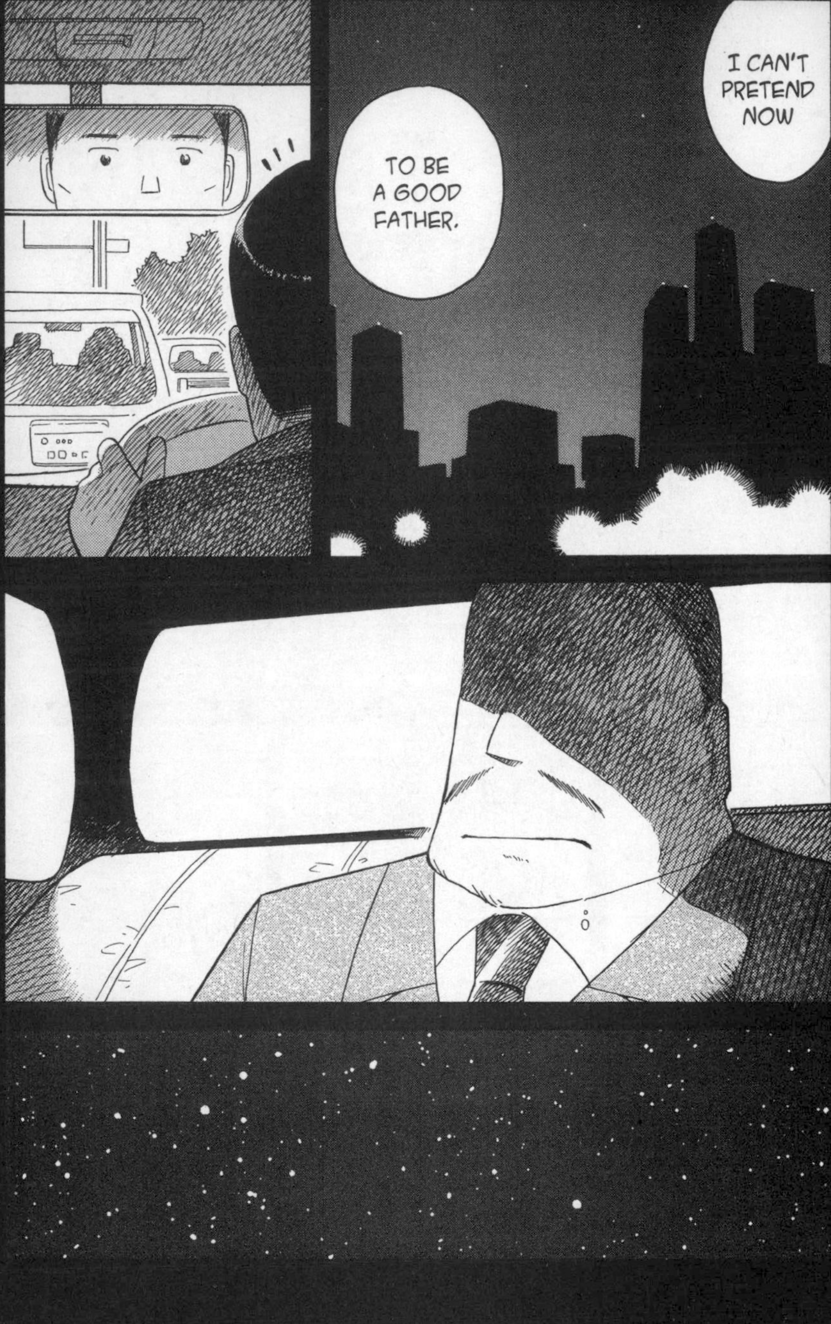
I CAN'T PRETEND NOW
TO BE A GOOD FATHER.

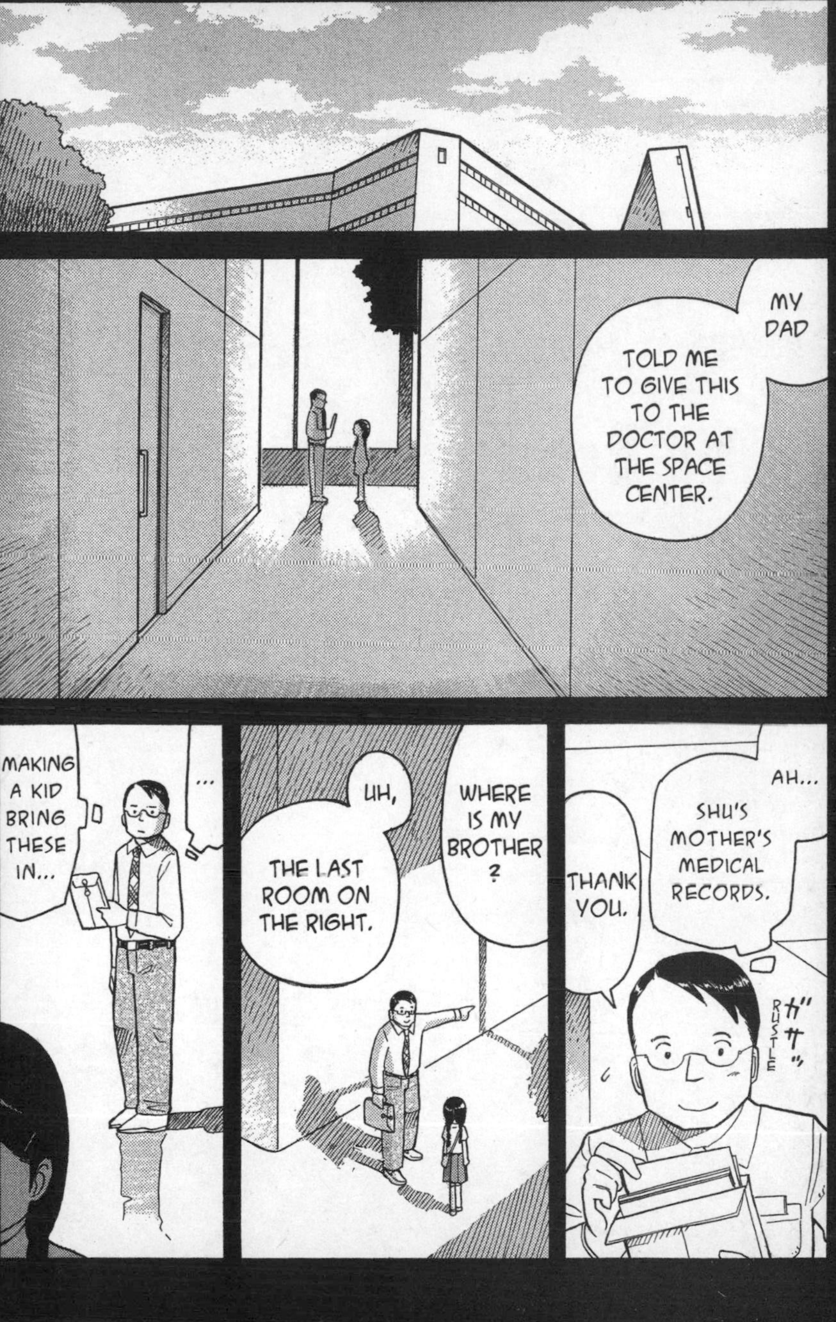
MY DAD TOLD ME TO GIVE THIS TO THE DOCTOR AT THE SPACE CENTER.
AH... SHU'S MOTHER'S MEDICAL RECORDS.
THANK YOU.
ガサッ
RUSTLE
WHERE IS MY BROTHER?
UH, THE LAST ROOM ON THE RIGHT.
...
MAKING A KID BRING THESE IN...

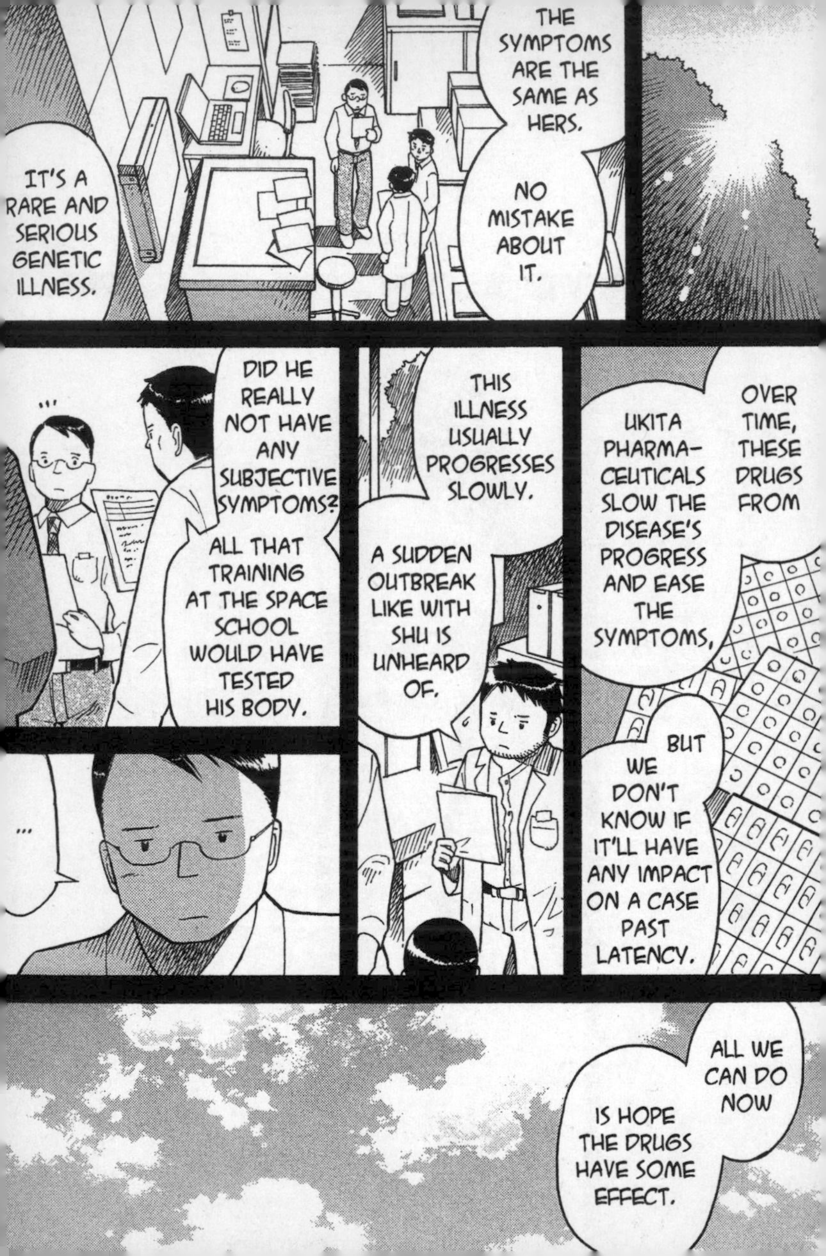
THE SYMPTOMS ARE THE SAME AS HERS.
NO MISTAKE ABOUT IT.
IT'S A RARE AND SERIOUS GENETIC ILLNESS.
OVER TIME, THESE DRUGS FROM
UKITA PHARMA-CEUTICALS SLOW THE DISEASE'S PROGRESS AND EASE THE SYMPTOMS,
BUT WE DON'T KNOW IF IT'LL HAVE ANY IMPACT ON A CASE PAST LATENCY.
THIS ILLNESS USUALLY PROGRESSES SLOWLY.
A SUDDEN OUTBREAK LIKE WITH SHU IS UNHEARD OF.
DID HE REALLY NOT HAVE ANY SUBJECTIVE SYMPTOMS?
ALL THAT TRAINING AT THE SPACE SCHOOL WOULD HAVE TESTED HIS BODY.
...
...
ALL WE CAN DO NOW
IS HOPE THE DRUGS HAVE SOME EFFECT.

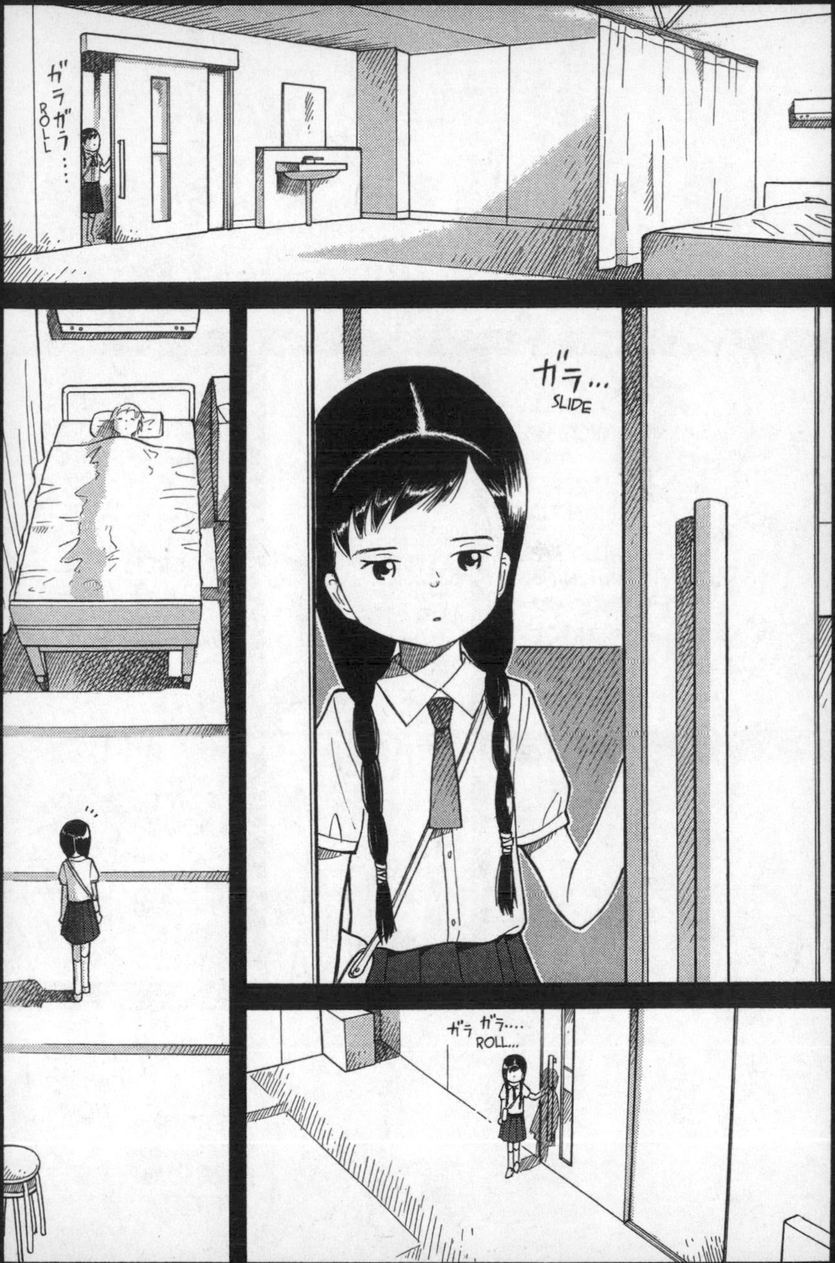
ガラガラ……
ROLL
ガラ…
SLIDE
ガラ ガラ….
ROLL…

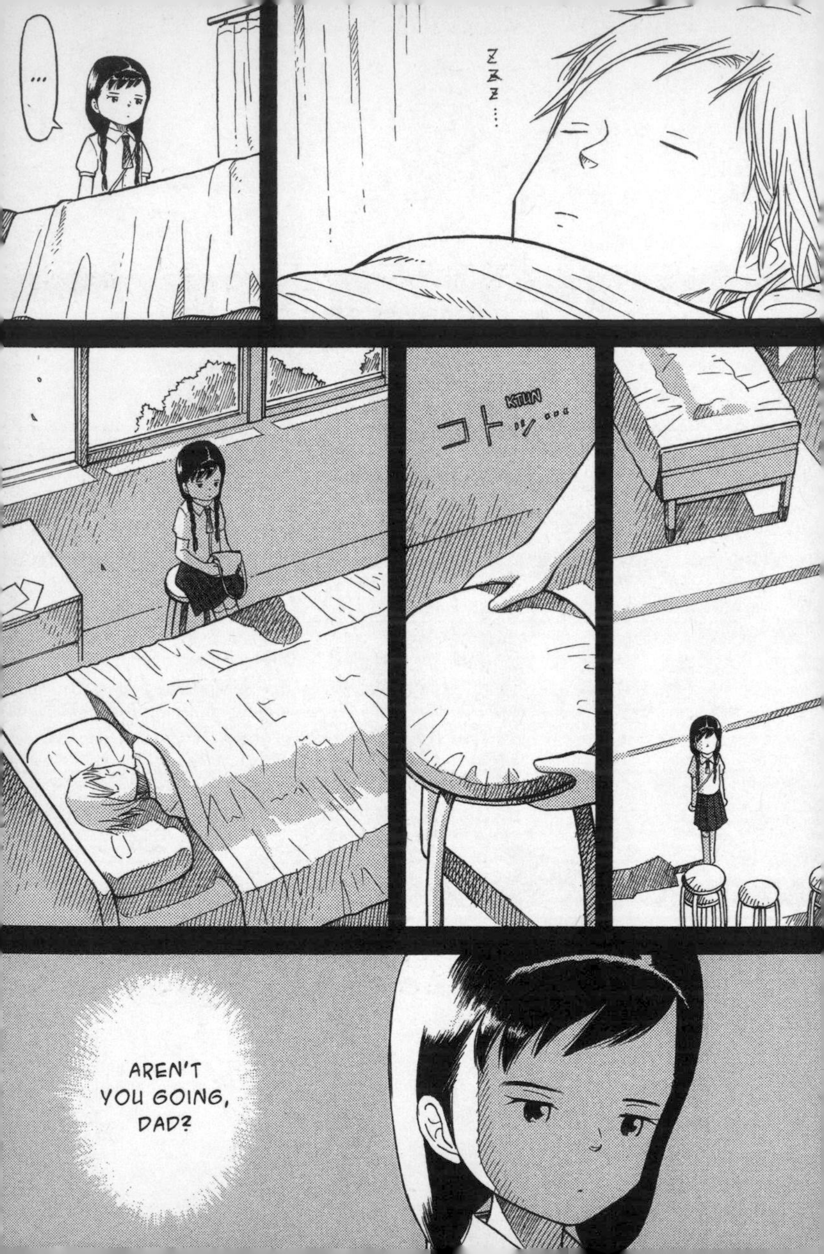
ZZZ....
...
KTUN
コトッ...
AREN'T YOU GOING, DAD?

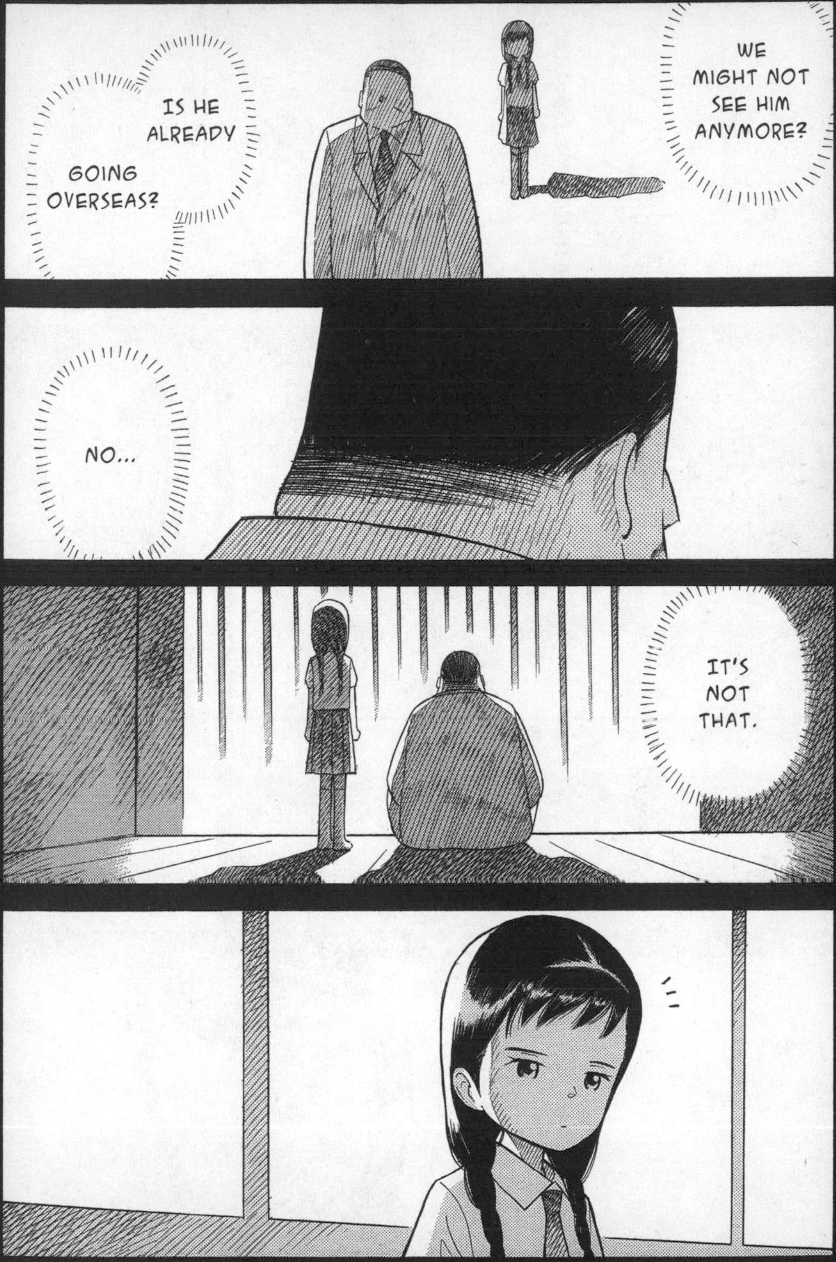
WE MIGHT NOT SEE HIM ANYMORE?
IS HE ALREADY GOING OVERSEAS?
NO...
IT'S NOT THAT.

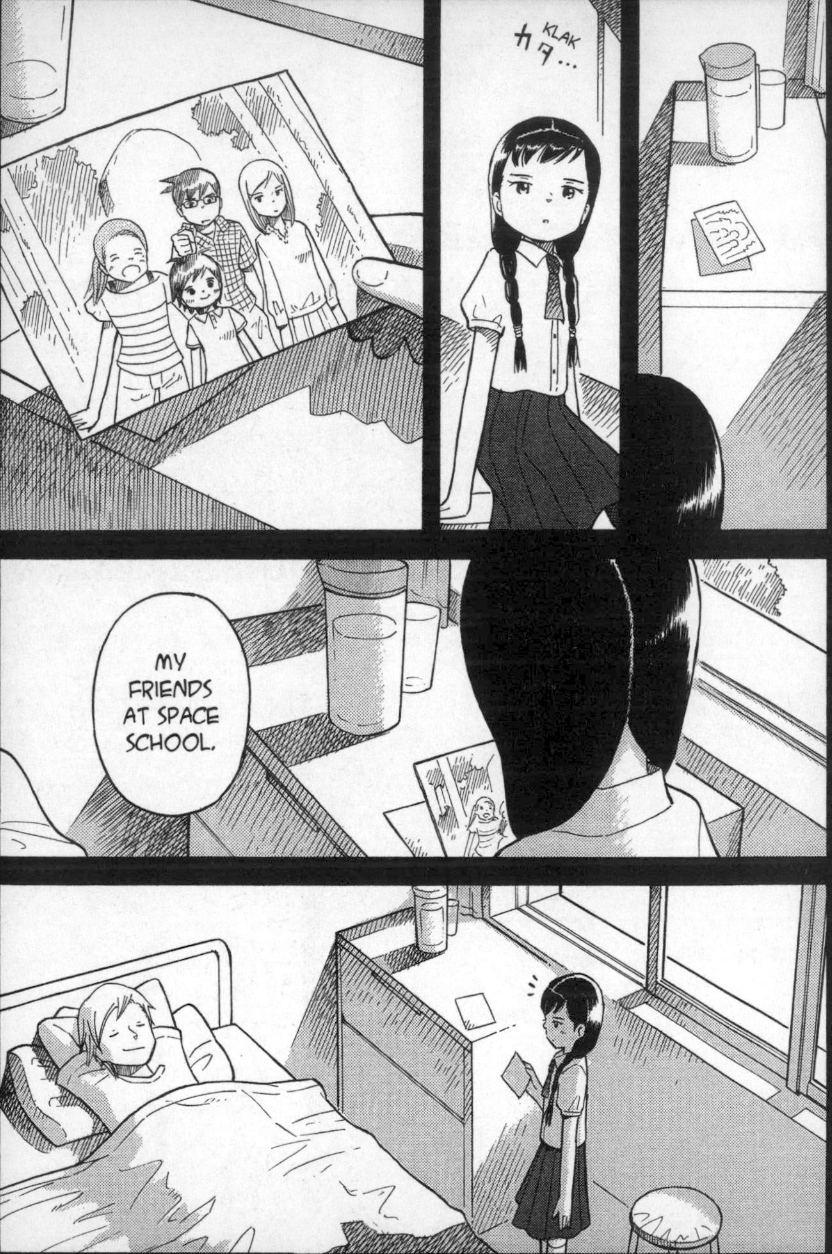
カタ… KLAK
MY FRIENDS AT SPACE SCHOOL.

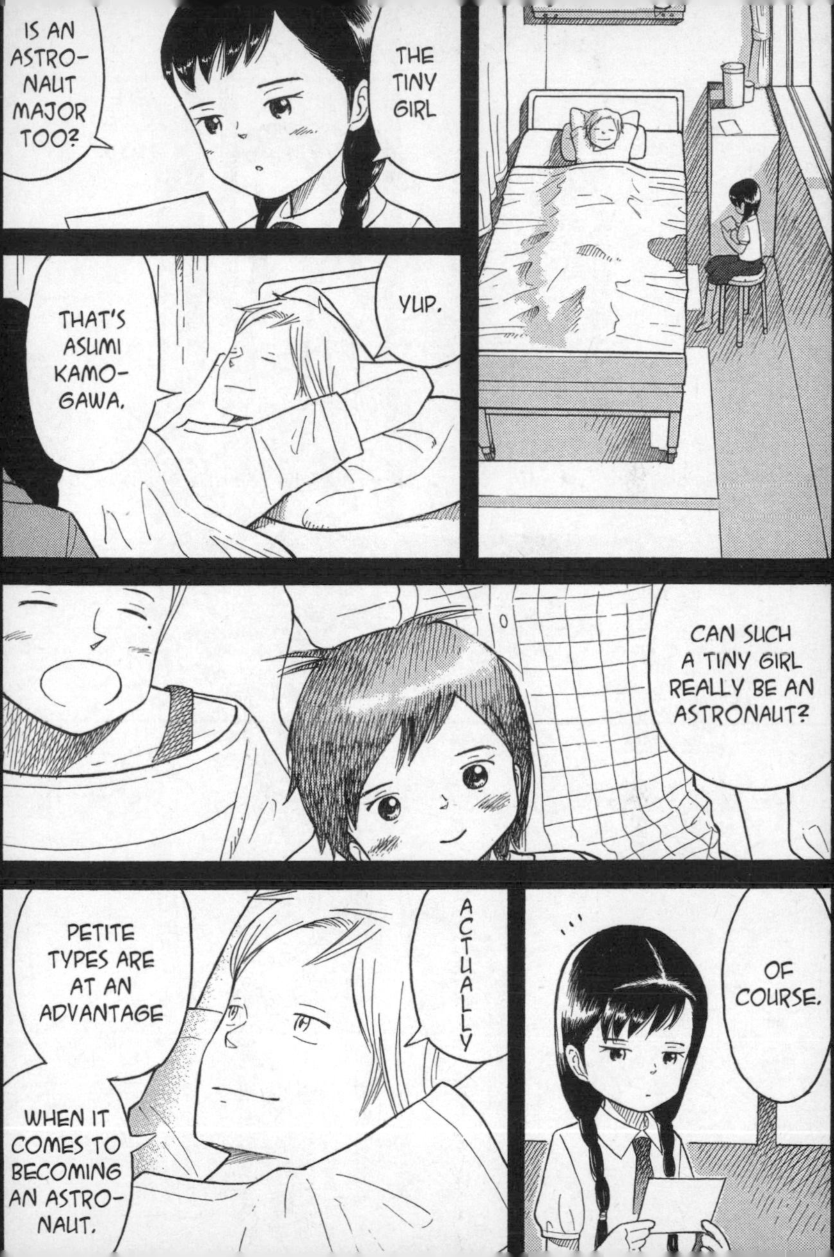
THE TINY GIRL
IS AN ASTRONAUT MAJOR TOO?
YUP.
THAT'S ASUMI KAMOGAWA.
CAN SUCH A TINY GIRL REALLY BE AN ASTRONAUT?
OF COURSE.
ACTUALLY
PETITE TYPES ARE AT AN ADVANTAGE
WHEN IT COMES TO BECOMING AN ASTRONAUT.

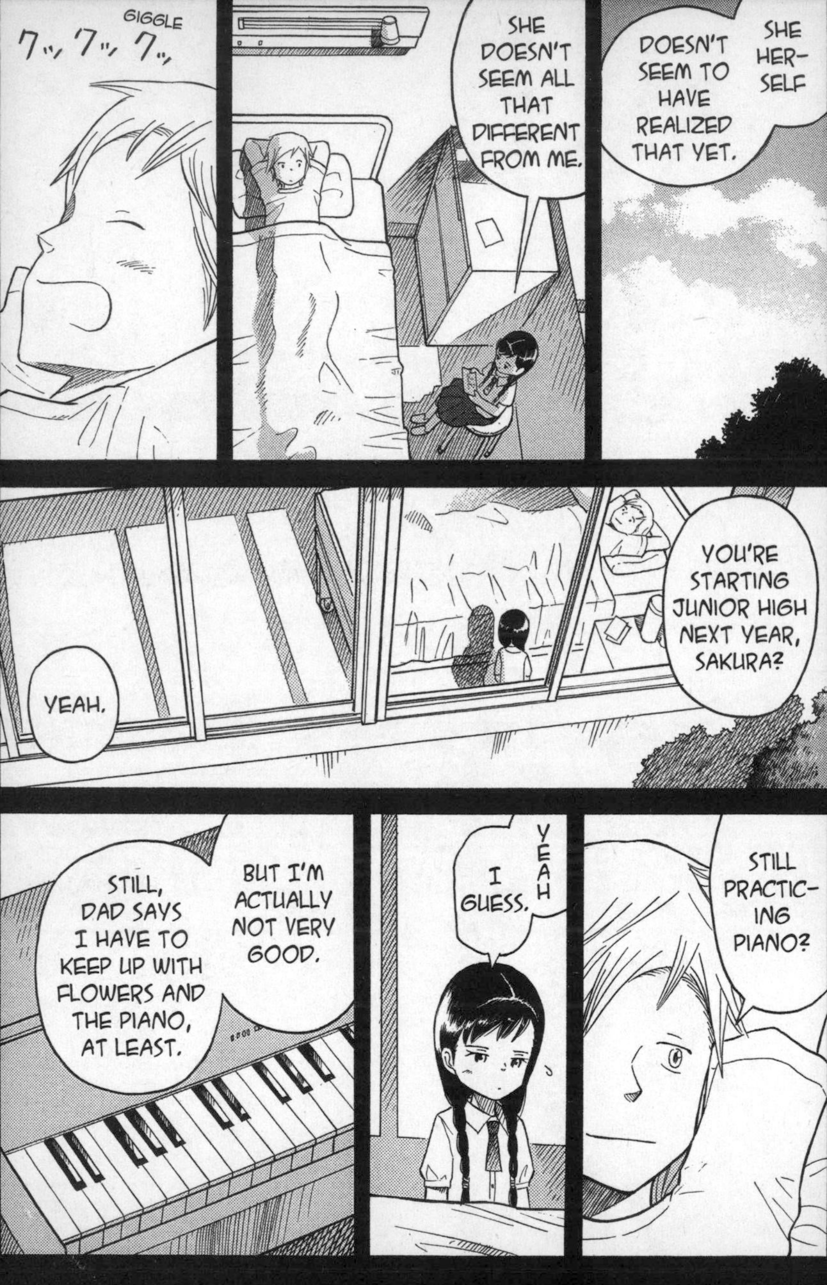
SHE HER-SELF
DOESN'T SEEM TO HAVE REALIZED THAT YET.
SHE DOESN'T SEEM ALL THAT DIFFERENT FROM ME.
GIGGLE
クッ、クッ、クッ
YOU'RE STARTING JUNIOR HIGH NEXT YEAR, SAKURA?
YEAH.
STILL PRACTIC-ING PIANO?
YEAH
I GUESS.
BUT I'M ACTUALLY NOT VERY GOOD.
STILL, DAD SAYS I HAVE TO KEEP UP WITH FLOWERS AND THE PIANO, AT LEAST.

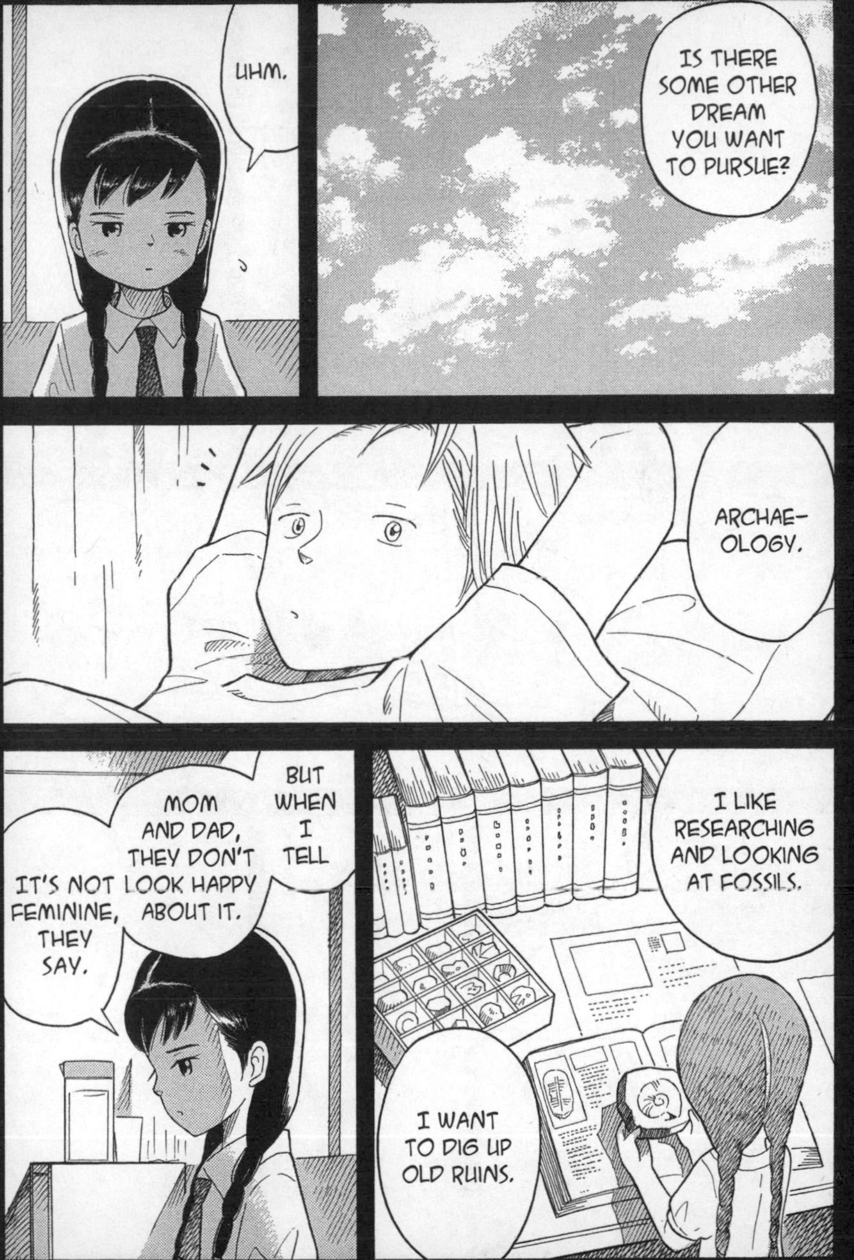
IS THERE SOME OTHER DREAM YOU WANT TO PURSUE?
UHM.
ARCHAE-OLOGY.
I LIKE RESEARCHING AND LOOKING AT FOSSILS.
I WANT TO DIG UP OLD RUINS.
BUT WHEN I TELL
MOM AND DAD, THEY DON'T LOOK HAPPY ABOUT IT.
IT'S NOT FEMININE, THEY SAY.

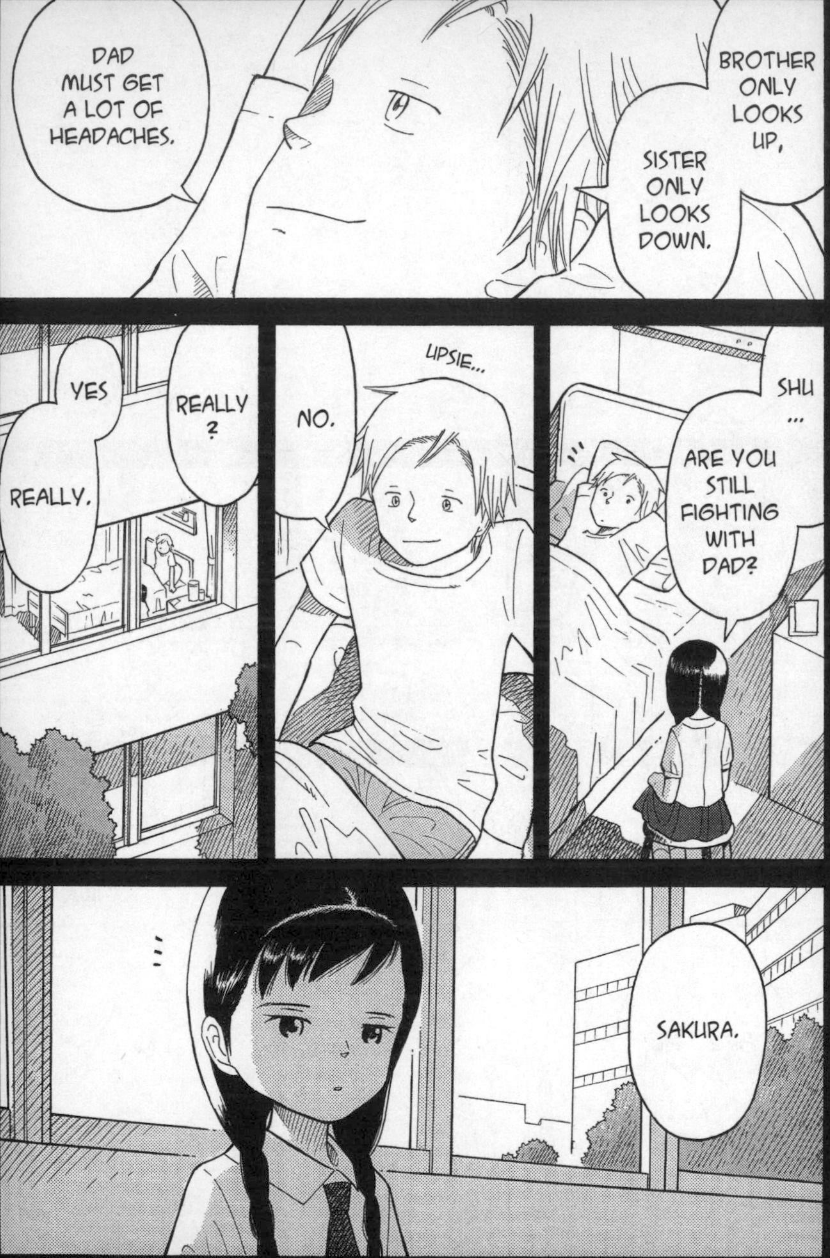
BROTHER ONLY LOOKS UP,
SISTER ONLY LOOKS DOWN.
DAD MUST GET A LOT OF HEADACHES.
SHU ...
ARE YOU STILL FIGHTING WITH DAD?
UPSIE...
NO.
REALLY ?
YES
REALLY.
SAKURA.
...

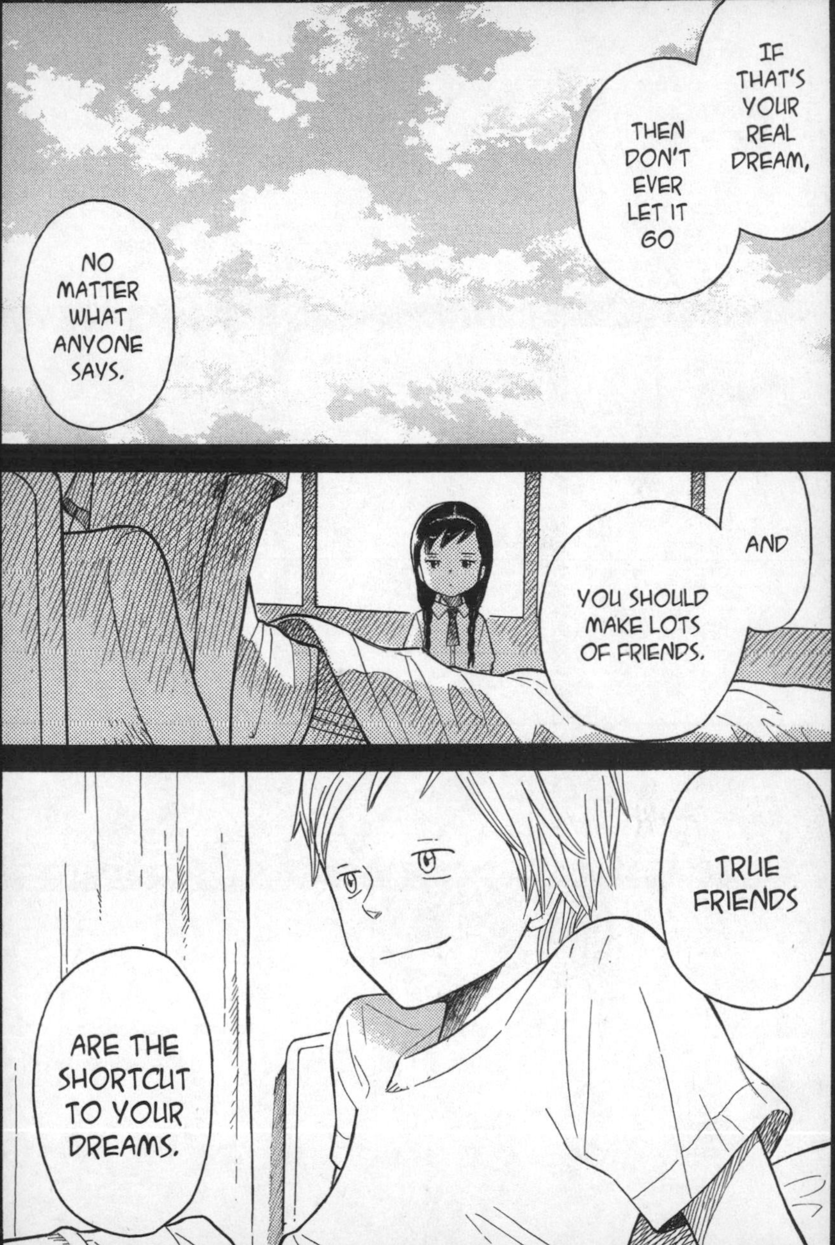
IF THAT'S YOUR REAL DREAM,
THEN DON'T EVER LET IT GO
NO MATTER WHAT ANYONE SAYS.
AND
YOU SHOULD MAKE LOTS OF FRIENDS.
TRUE FRIENDS
ARE THE SHORTCUT TO YOUR DREAMS.

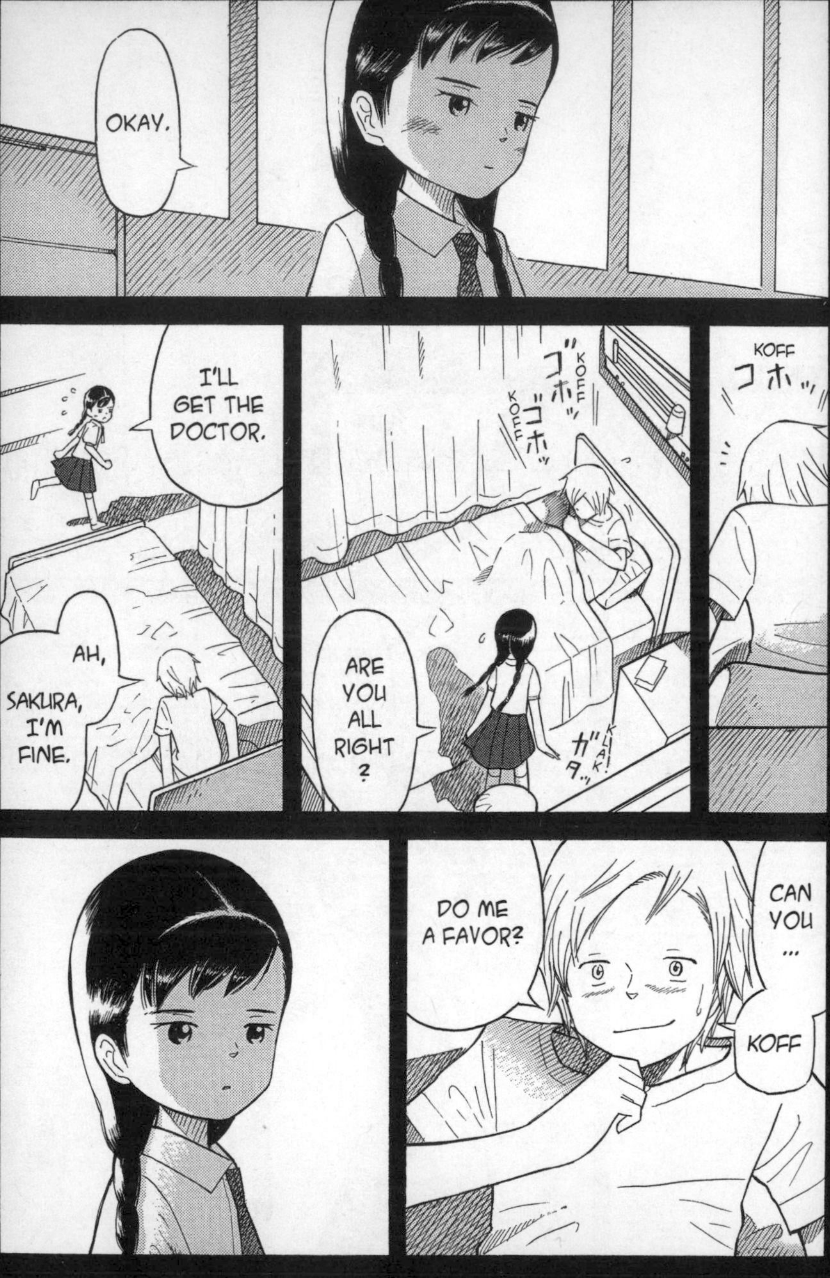
OKAY.
KOFF
コホッ
ゴホッ
KOFF
ゴホッ
KOFF
ARE YOU ALL RIGHT?
ガタッ
KLAK!
I'LL GET THE DOCTOR.
AH, SAKURA, I'M FINE.
CAN YOU ...
KOFF
DO ME A FAVOR?

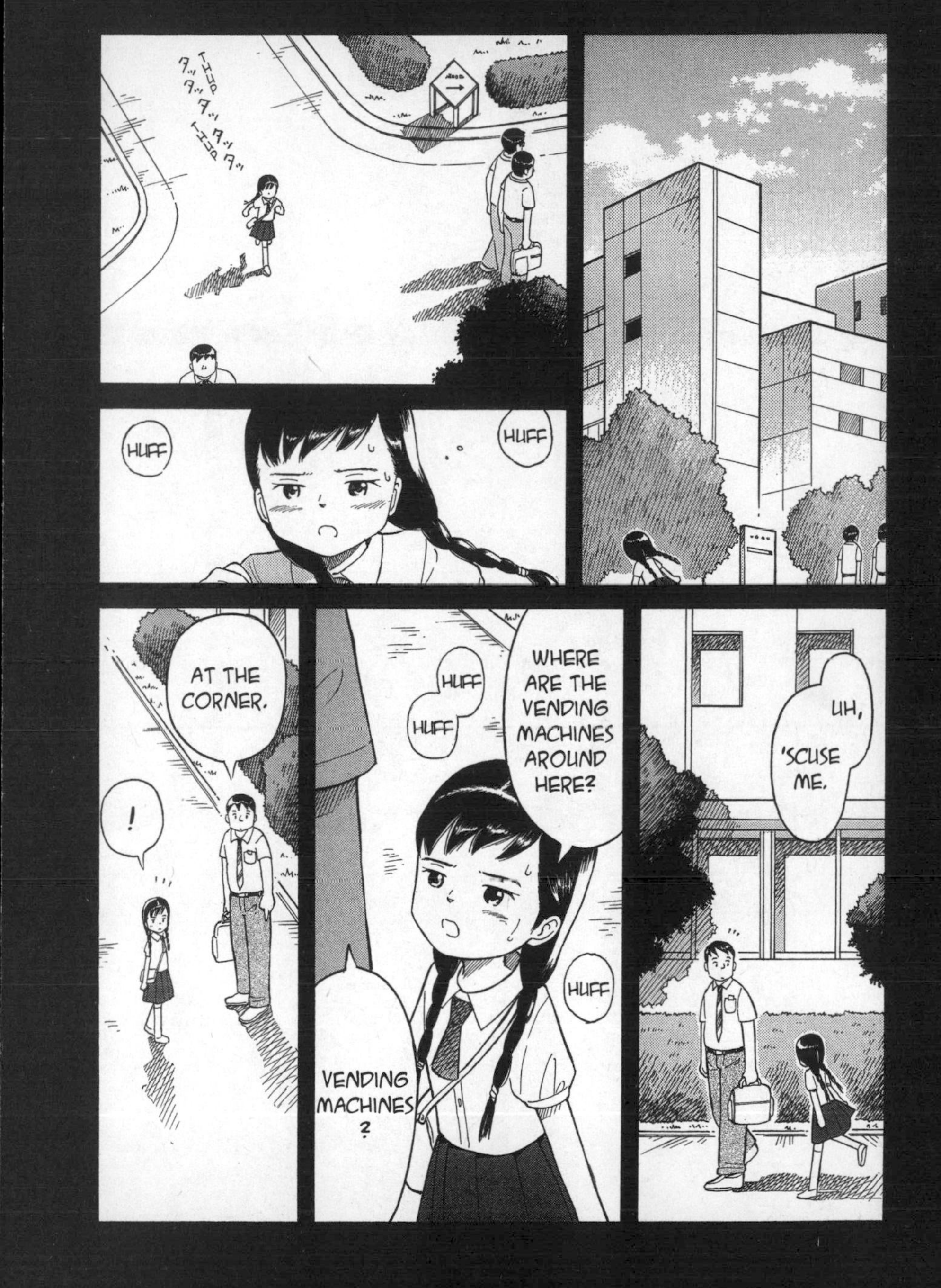
タッ THUP タッ タッ タッ THUP タッ
HUFF
HUFF
UH, 'SCUSE ME.
WHERE ARE THE VENDING MACHINES AROUND HERE?
HUFF
HUFF
HUFF
VENDING MACHINES?
AT THE CORNER.
!

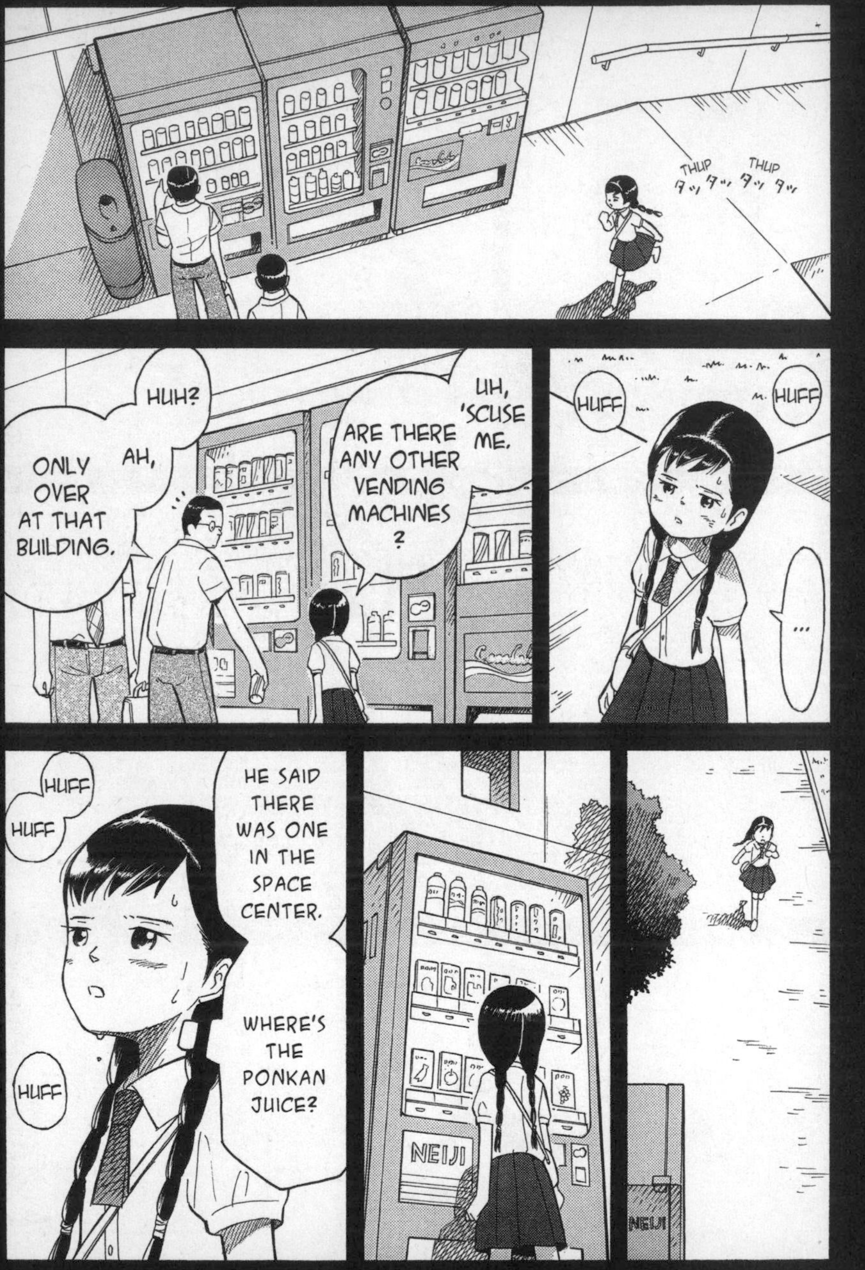
THUP
タッ タッ
THUP
タッ タッ
HUFF
HUFF
...
UH, 'SCUSE ME.
ARE THERE ANY OTHER VENDING MACHINES?
HUH?
AH,
ONLY OVER AT THAT BUILDING.
NEIJI
NEIJI
HUFF
HUFF
HE SAID THERE WAS ONE IN THE SPACE CENTER.
WHERE'S THE PONKAN JUICE?
HUFF

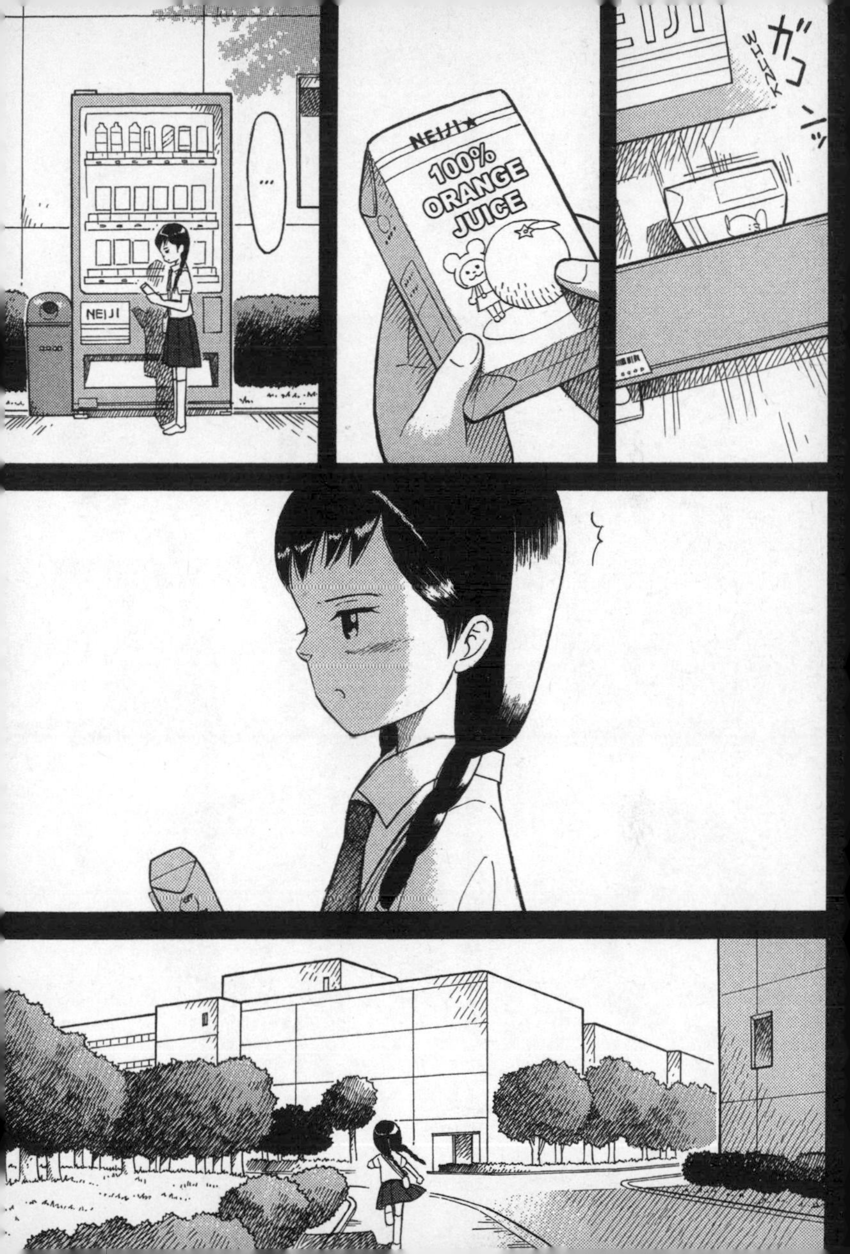
ガコーンッ
WHUNK
NEIJI★
100% ORANGE JUICE
NEIJI
...

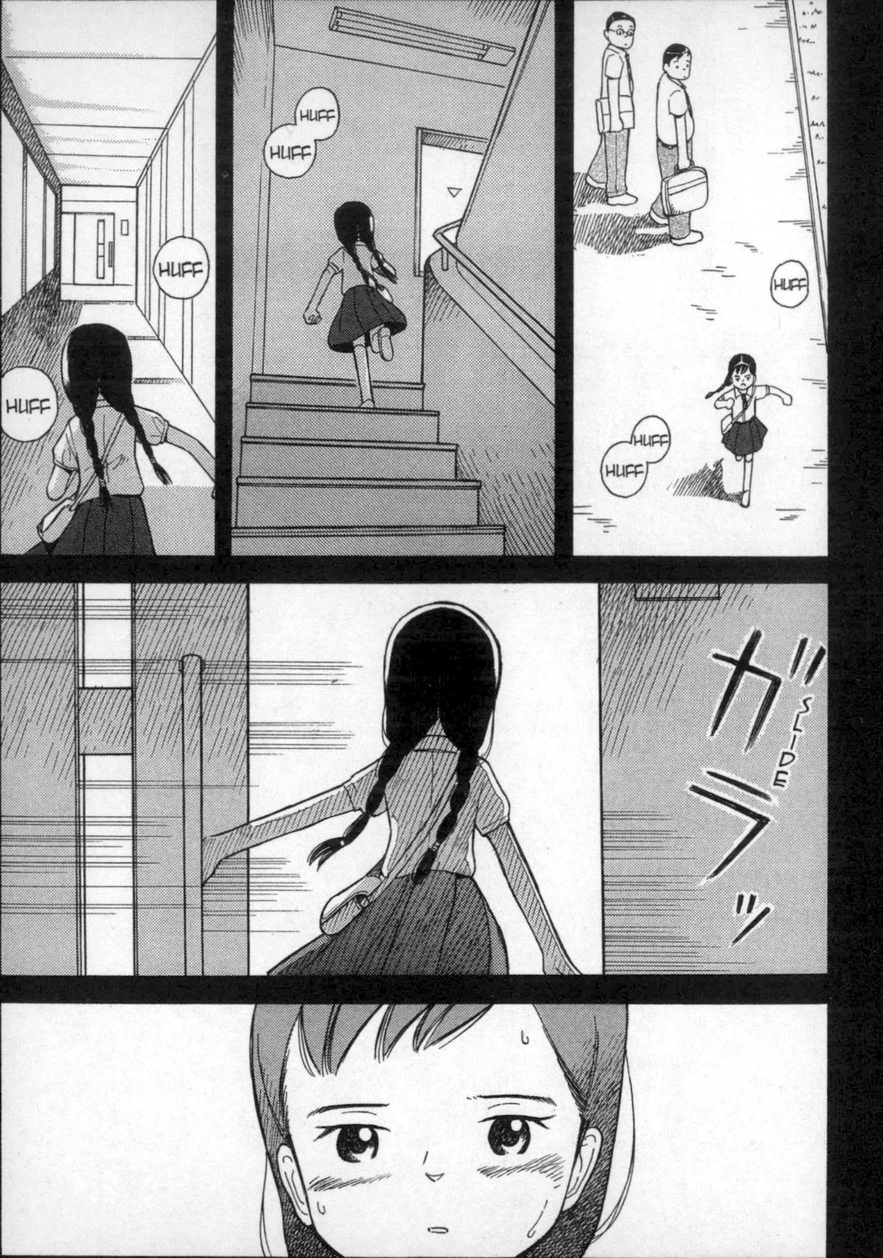
HUFF
HUFF
HUFF
HUFF
HUFF
HUFF
HUFF
ガラッ
SLIDE

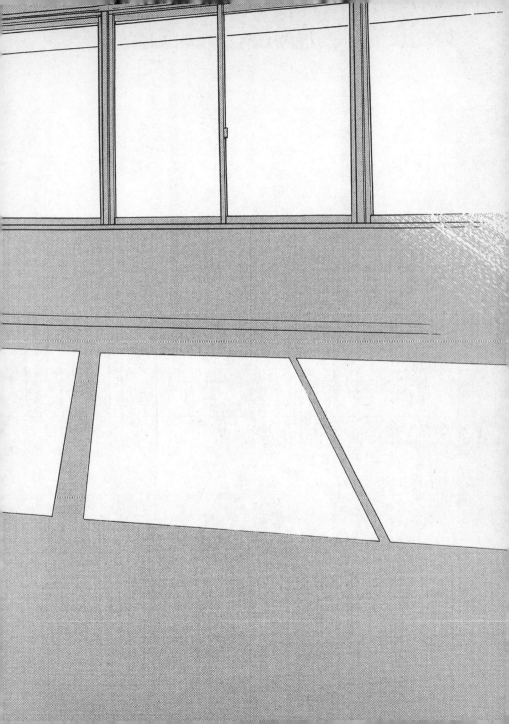

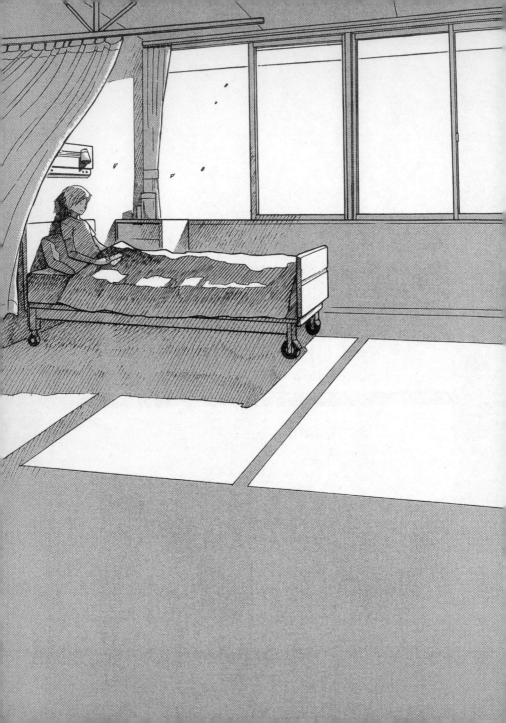

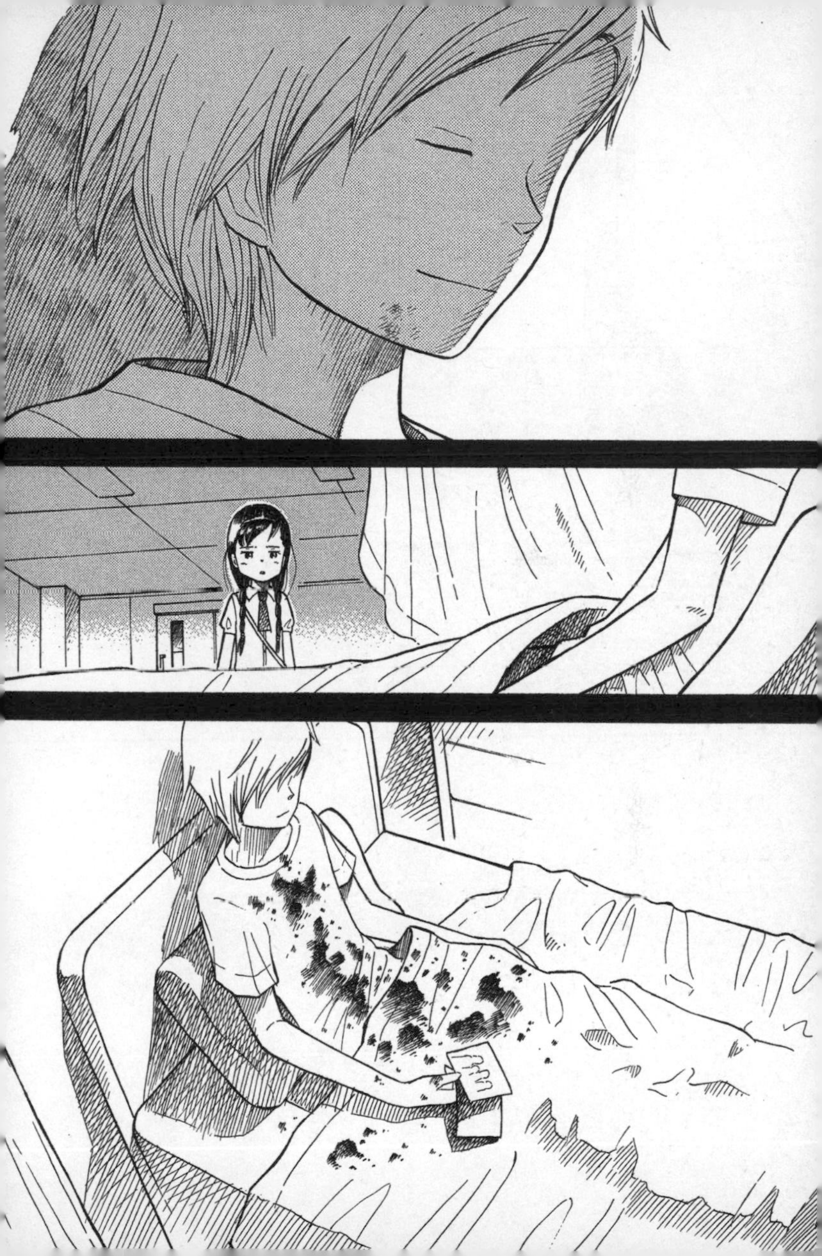

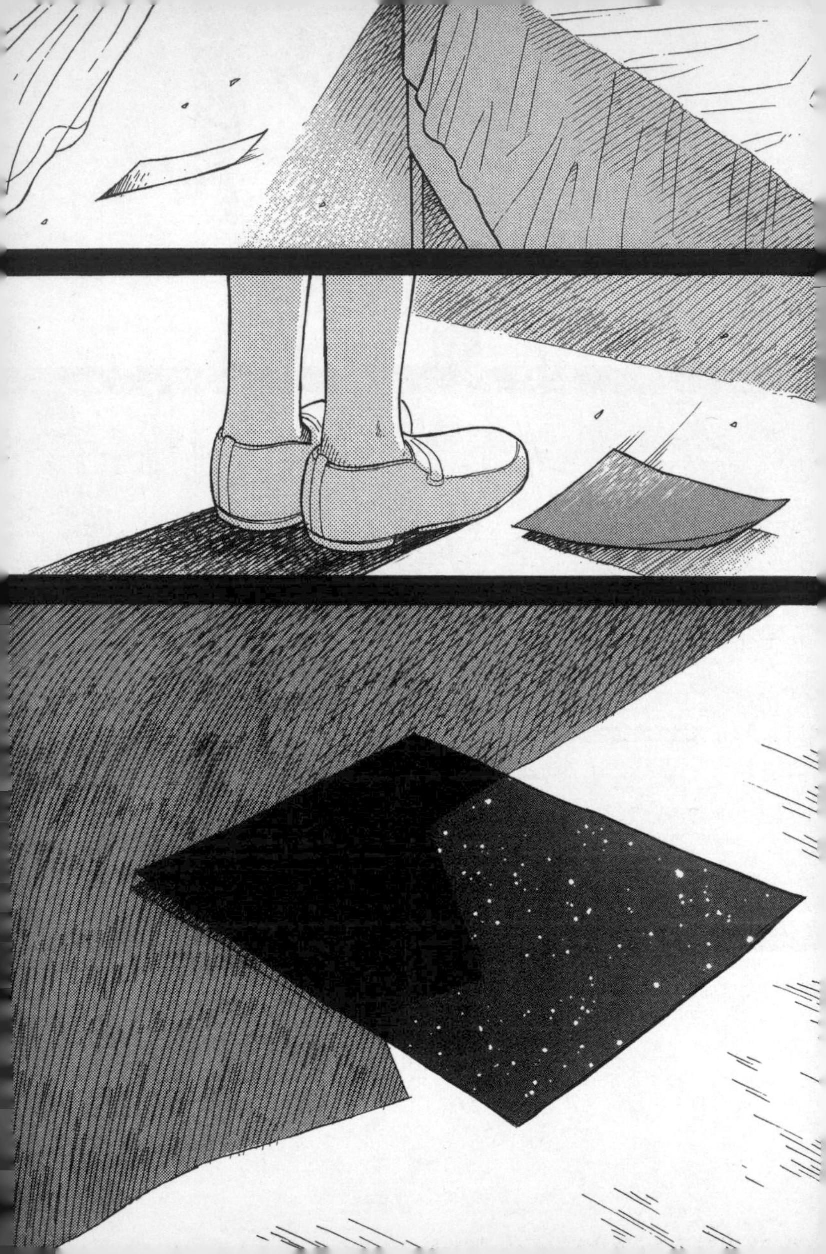

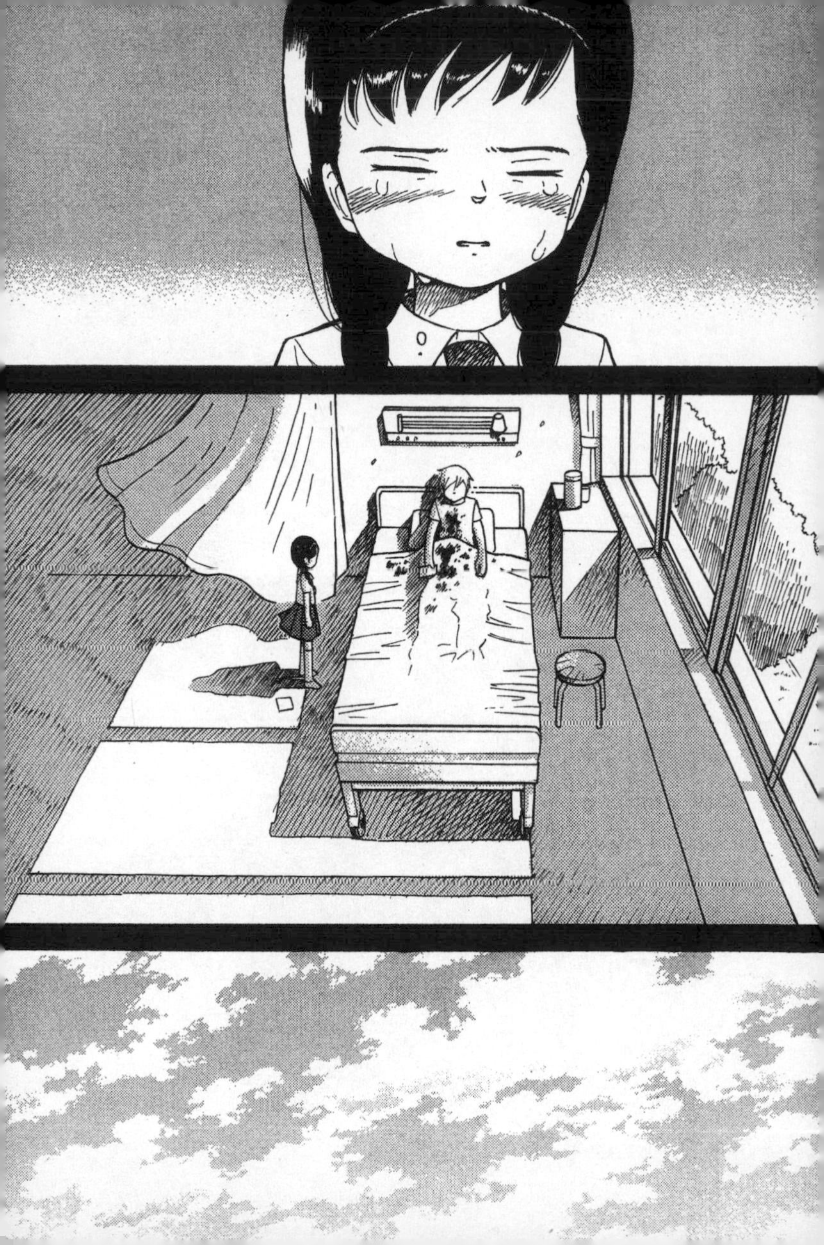

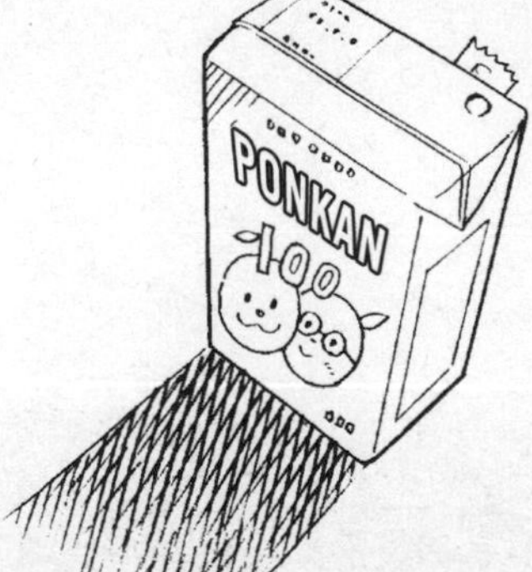
PONKAN
100

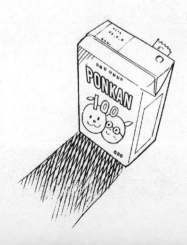

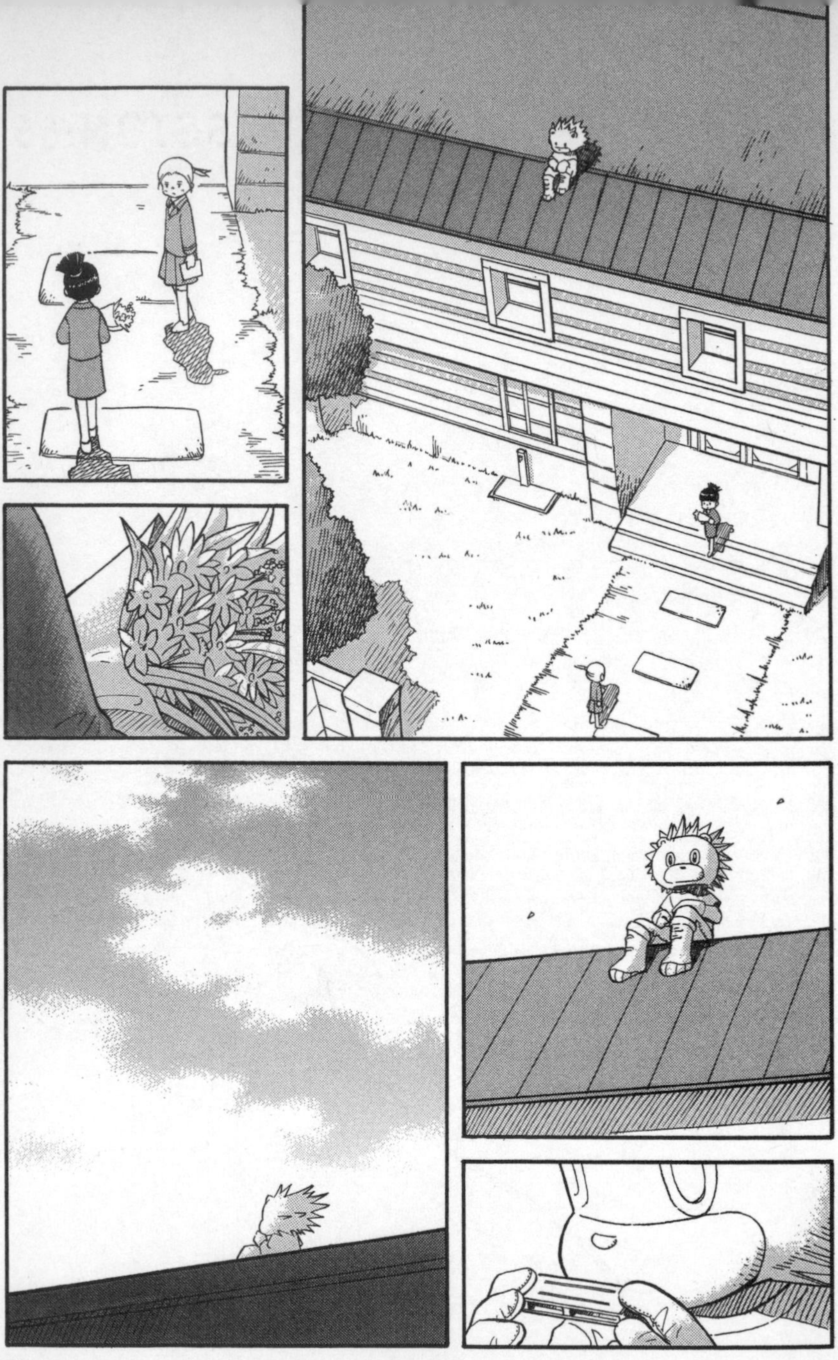

MISSION:66

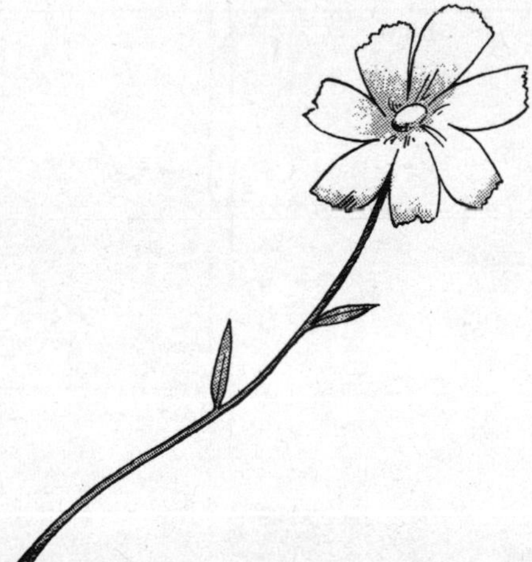

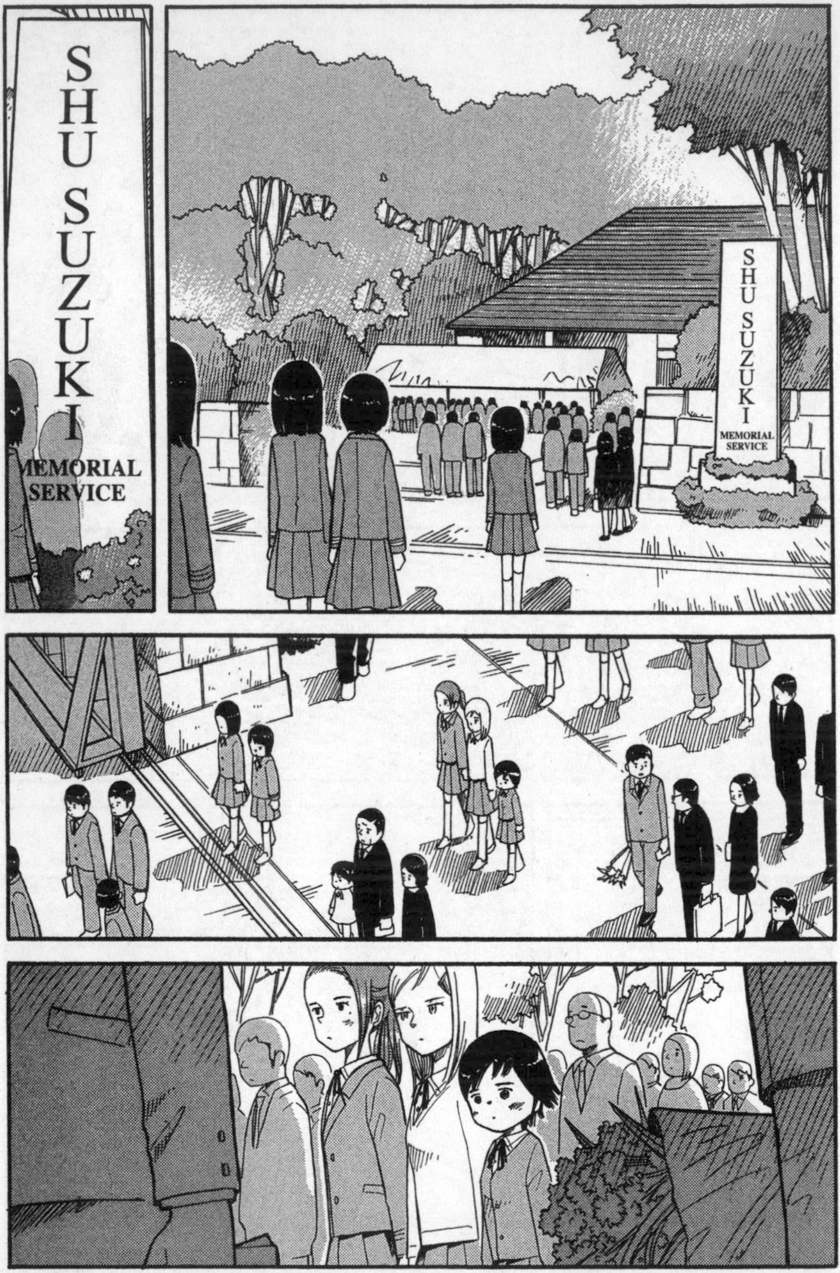
SHU SUZUKI MEMORIAL SERVICE
SHU SUZUKI MEMORIAL SERVICE

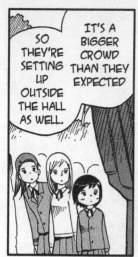

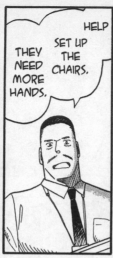

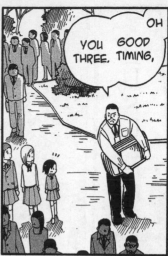

OH GOOD TIMING, YOU THREE.
HELP
SET UP THE CHAIRS.
THEY NEED MORE HANDS.
IT'S A BIGGER CROWD THAN THEY EXPECTED
SO THEY'RE SETTING UP OUTSIDE THE HALL AS WELL.
ガシャン
KLANG
THIS SHOULD BE ENOUGH, RIGHT?
I THINK SO.
ガラ ガラ ガラ…
ROLL ROLL ROLL

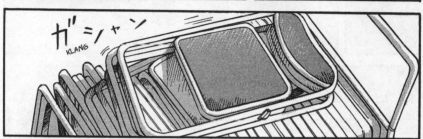

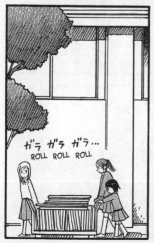

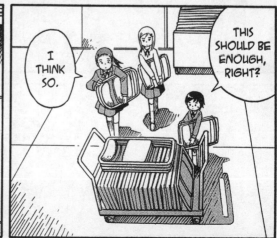

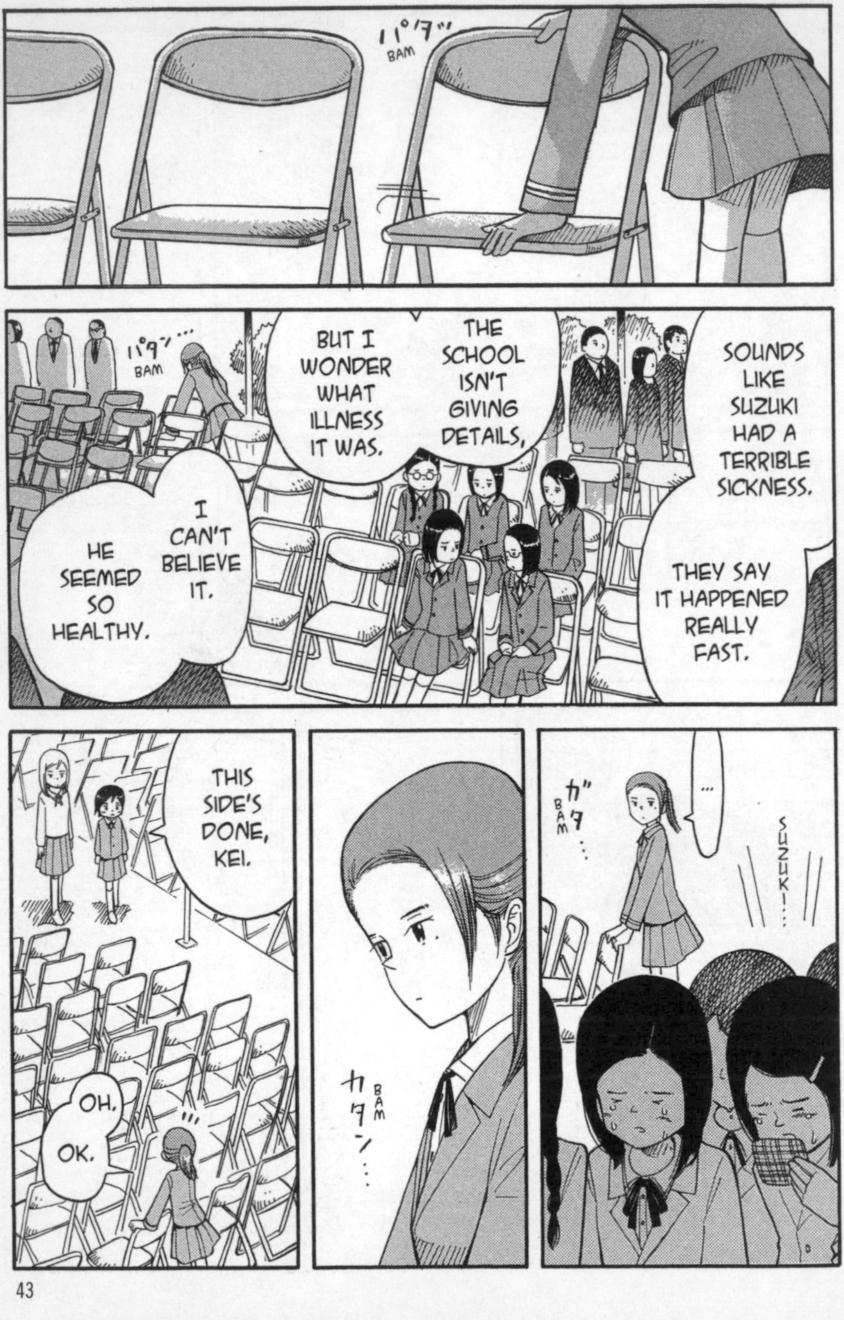
パタッ
BAM
SOUNDS LIKE SUZUKI HAD A TERRIBLE SICKNESS.
THE SCHOOL ISN'T GIVING DETAILS,
BUT I WONDER WHAT ILLNESS IT WAS.
パタン…
BAM
THEY SAY IT HAPPENED REALLY FAST.
I CAN'T BELIEVE IT.
HE SEEMED SO HEALTHY.
SUZUKI!…
…
ガタ…
BAM
カタン…
BAM
THIS SIDE'S DONE, KEI.
OH.
OK.

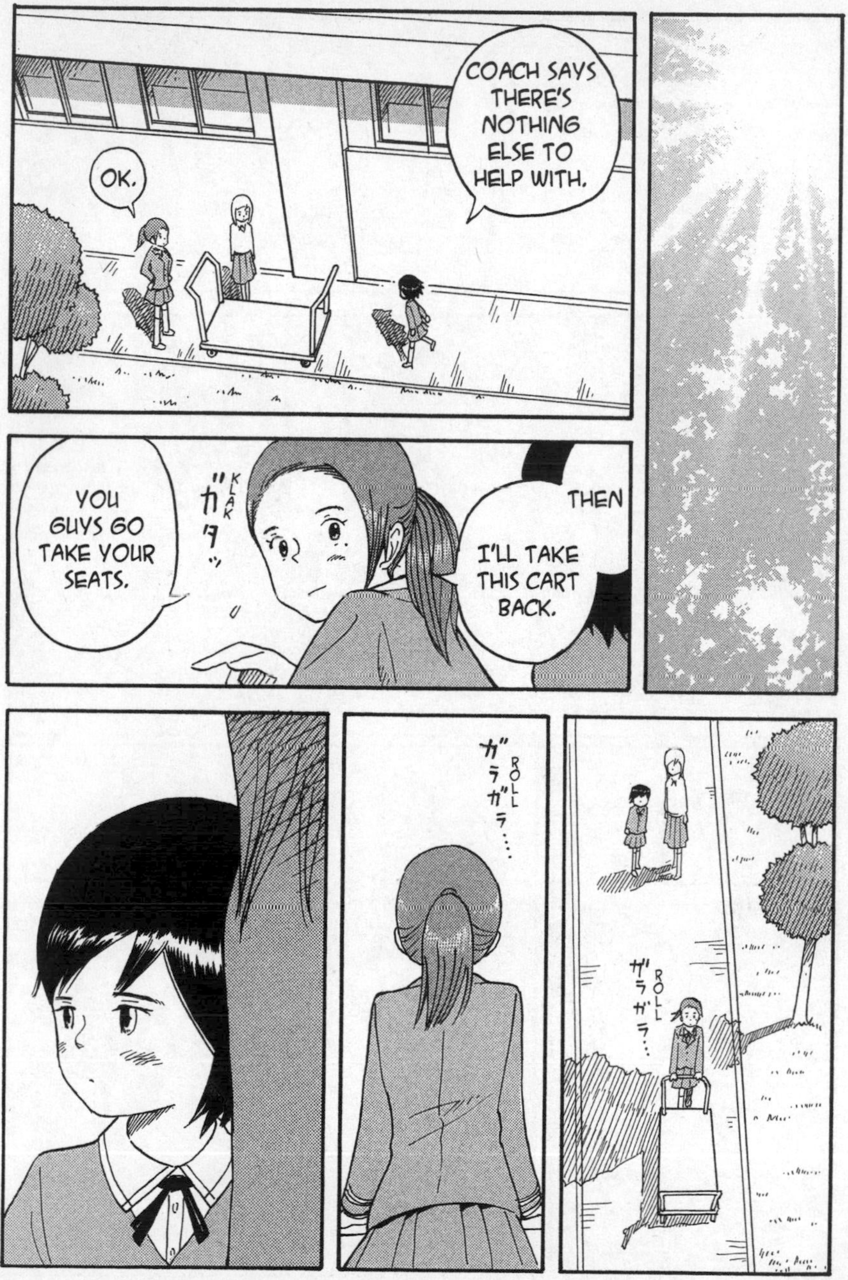
COACH SAYS THERE'S NOTHING ELSE TO HELP WITH.
OK.
THEN
I'LL TAKE THIS CART BACK.
ガタッ
KLAK
YOU GUYS GO TAKE YOUR SEATS.
ガラガラ…
ROLL
ガラガラ…
ROLL

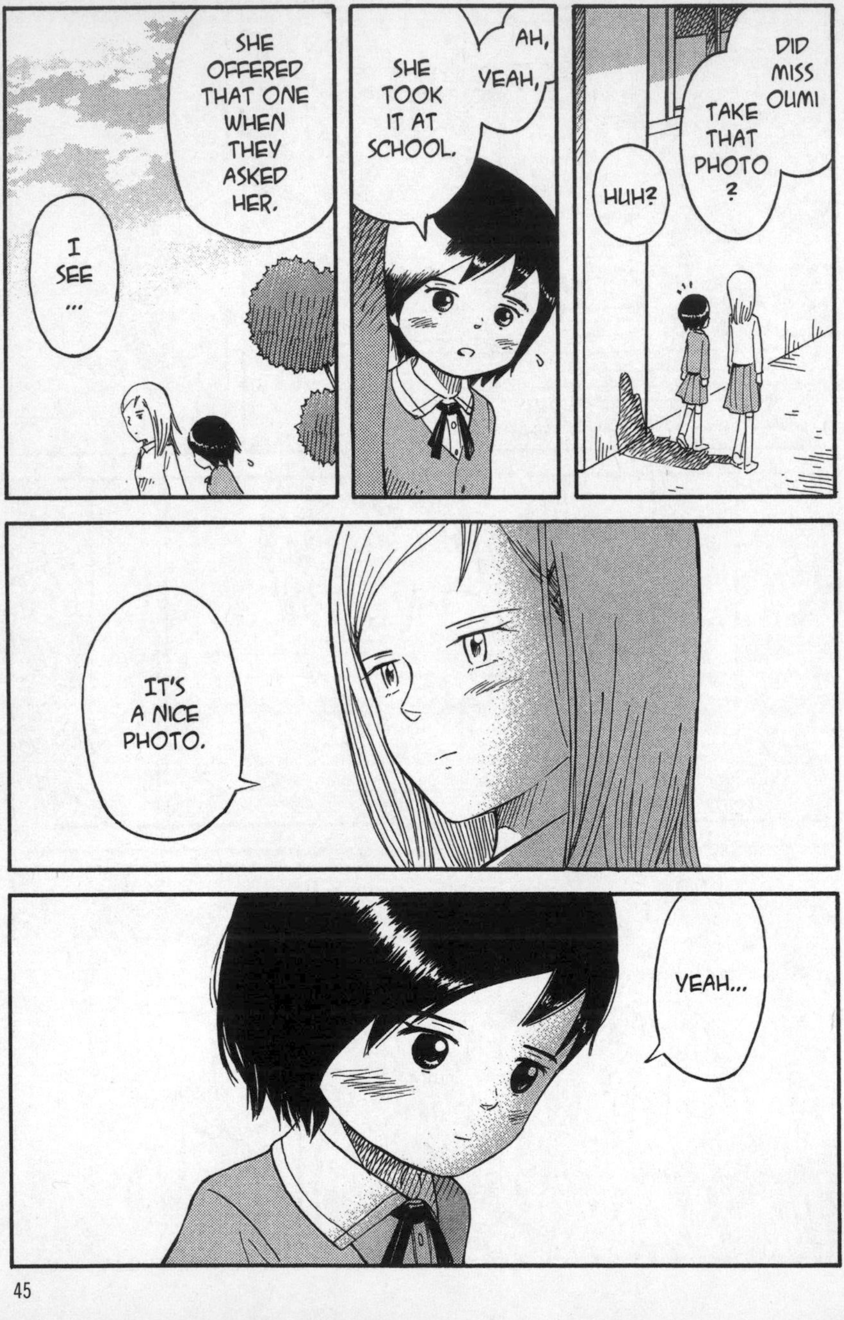
DID MISS OUMI TAKE THAT PHOTO?
HUH?
AH, YEAH,
SHE TOOK IT AT SCHOOL.
SHE OFFERED THAT ONE WHEN THEY ASKED HER.
I SEE ...
IT'S A NICE PHOTO.
YEAH...

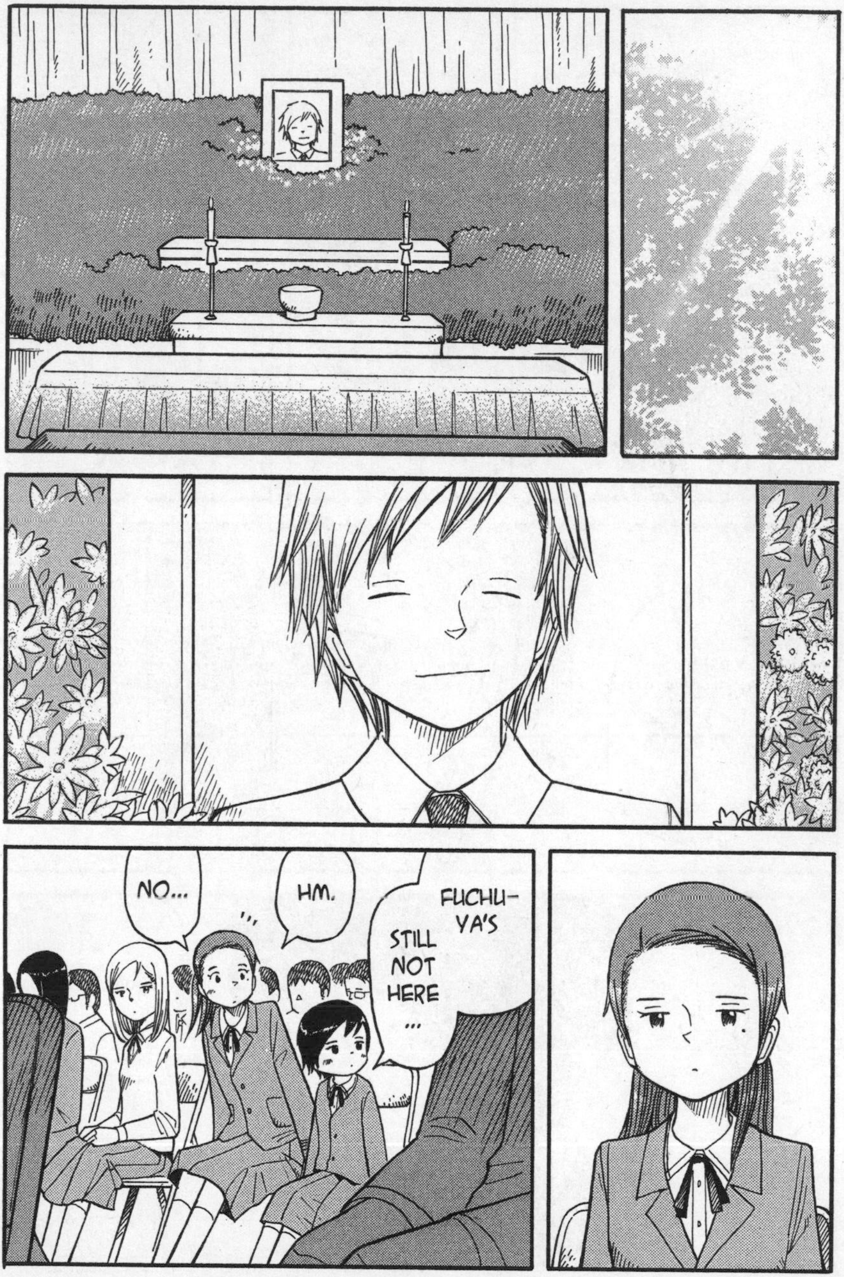
FUCHU-YA'S STILL NOT HERE ...
HM.
NO...

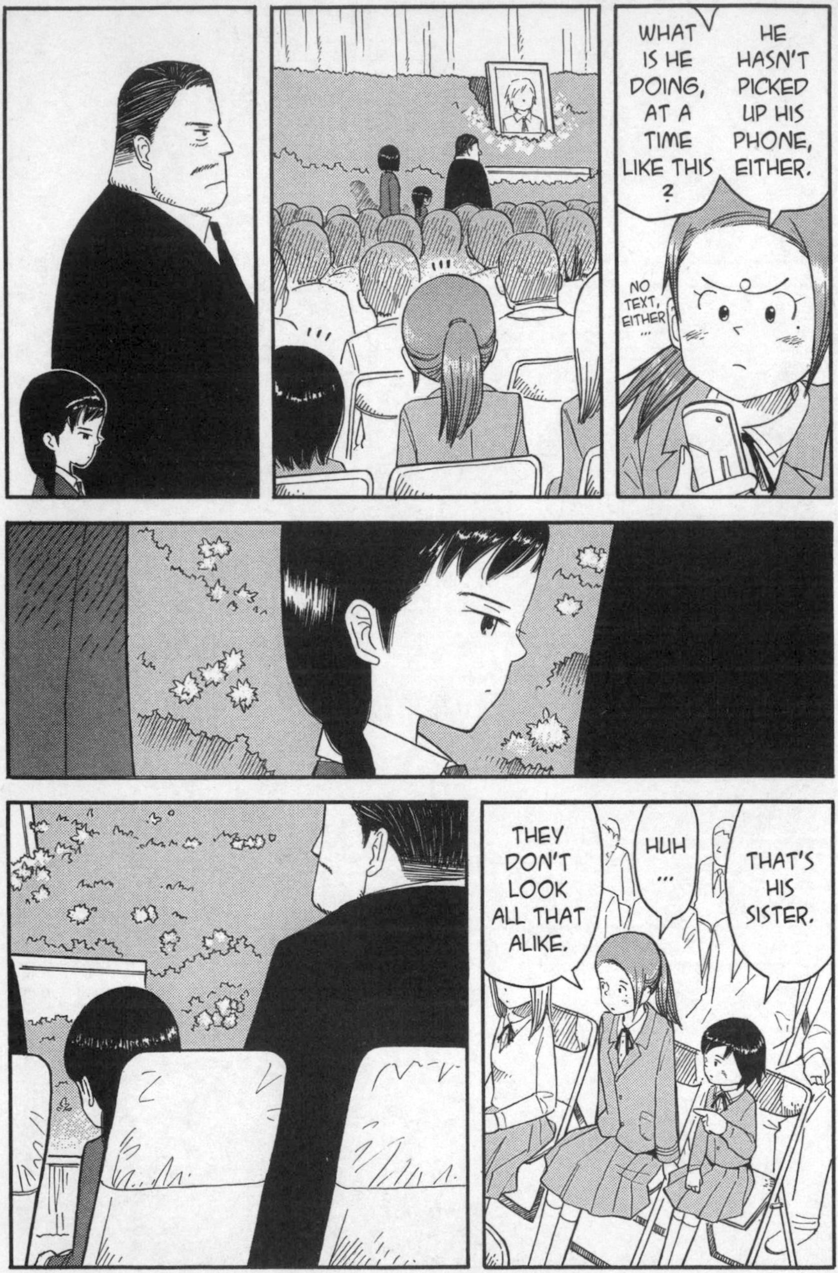
HE HASN'T PICKED UP HIS PHONE, EITHER.
WHAT IS HE DOING, AT A TIME LIKE THIS?
NO TEXT, EITHER...
THAT'S HIS SISTER.
HUH...
THEY DON'T LOOK ALL THAT ALIKE.

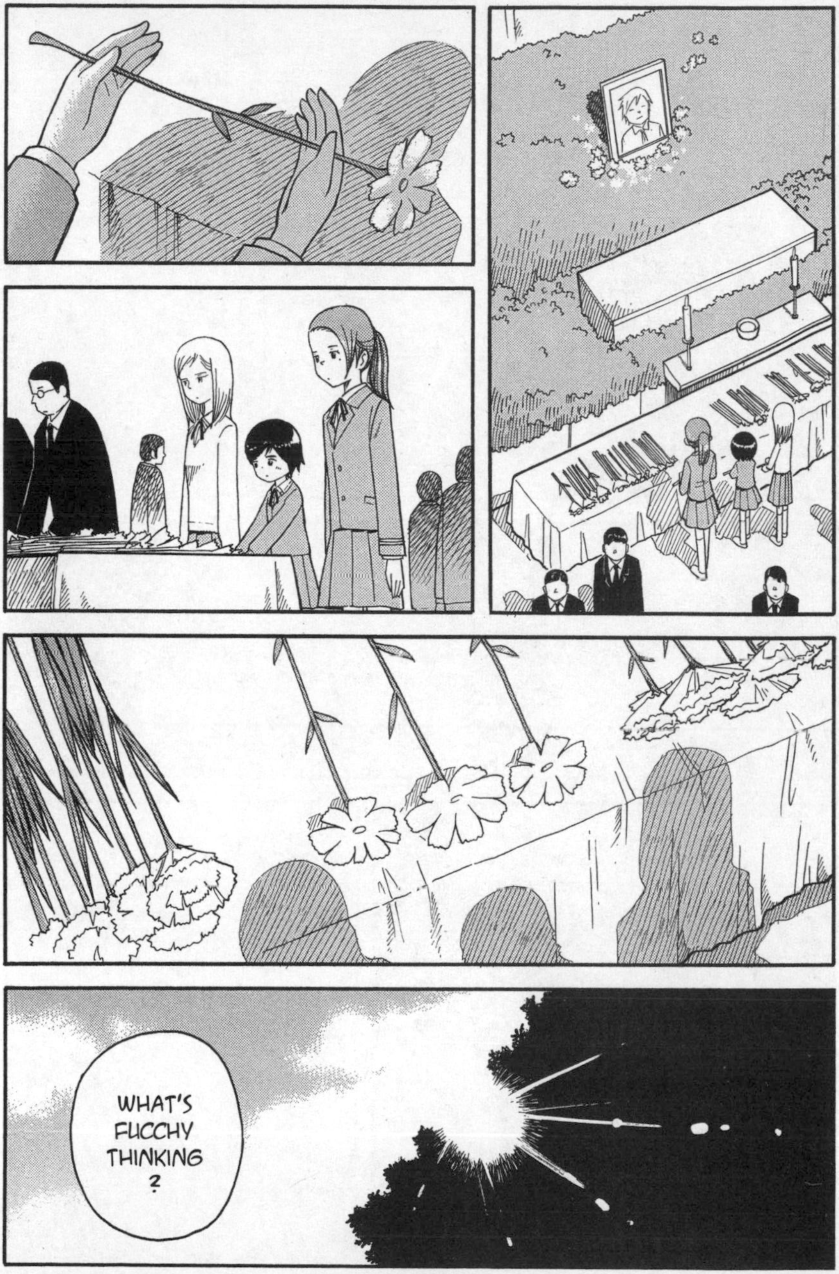
WHAT'S FUCCHY THINKING ?

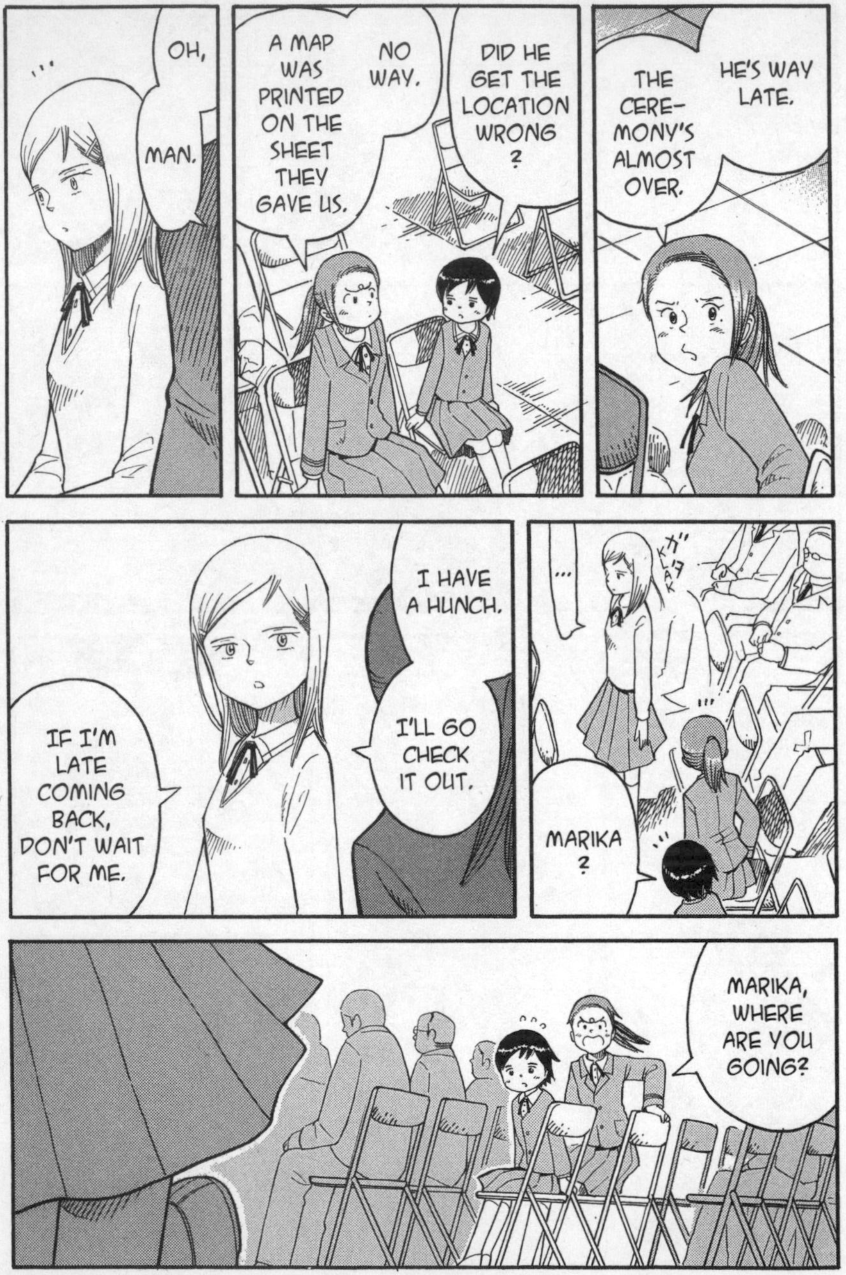
HE'S WAY LATE.
THE CEREMONY'S ALMOST OVER.
DID HE GET THE LOCATION WRONG?
NO WAY.
A MAP WAS PRINTED ON THE SHEET THEY GAVE US.
OH,
MAN.
...
...
KLAK
MARIKA?
I HAVE A HUNCH.
I'LL GO CHECK IT OUT.
IF I'M LATE COMING BACK, DON'T WAIT FOR ME.
MARIKA, WHERE ARE YOU GOING?

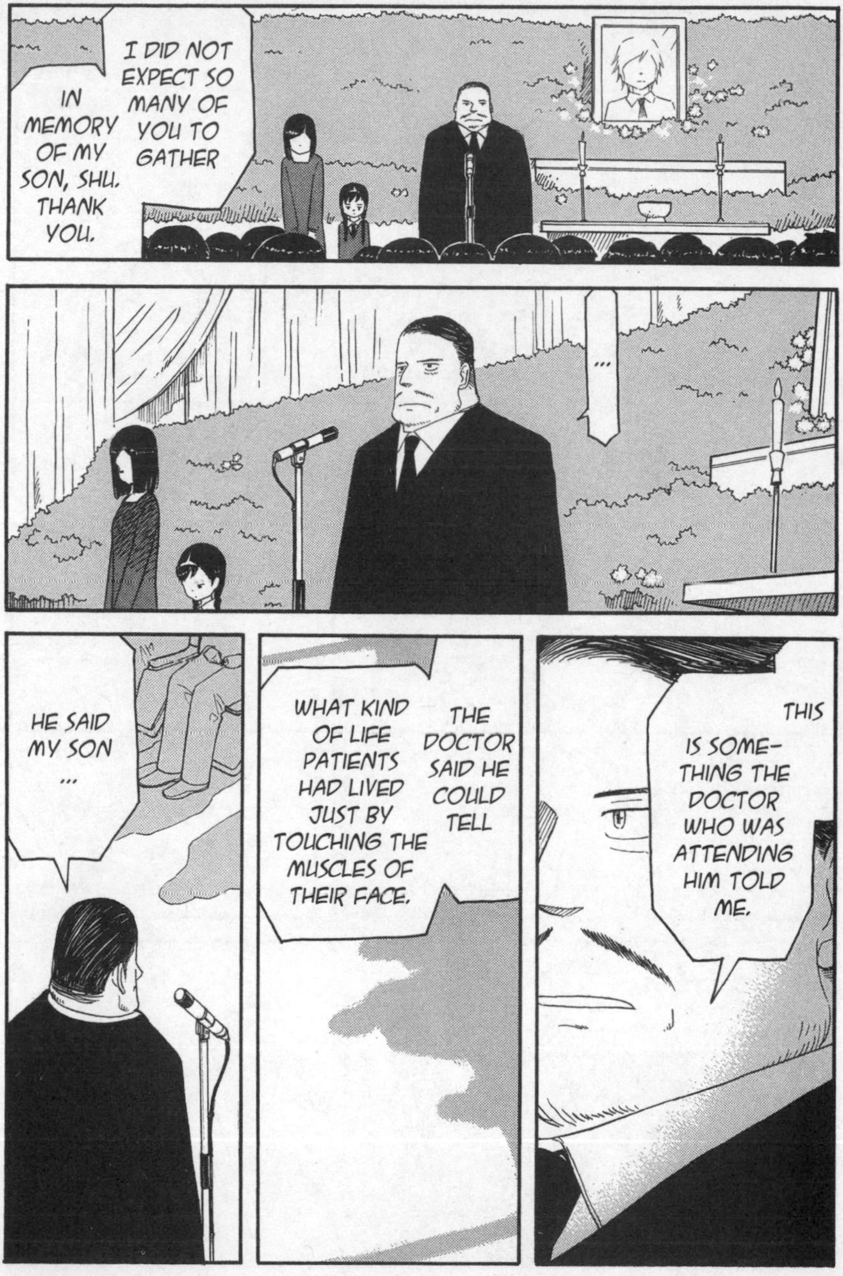
I DID NOT EXPECT SO MANY OF YOU TO GATHER
IN MEMORY OF MY SON, SHU. THANK YOU.
...
THIS IS SOME-THING THE DOCTOR WHO WAS ATTENDING HIM TOLD ME.
THE DOCTOR SAID HE COULD TELL
WHAT KIND OF LIFE PATIENTS HAD LIVED JUST BY TOUCHING THE MUSCLES OF THEIR FACE.
HE SAID MY SON ...

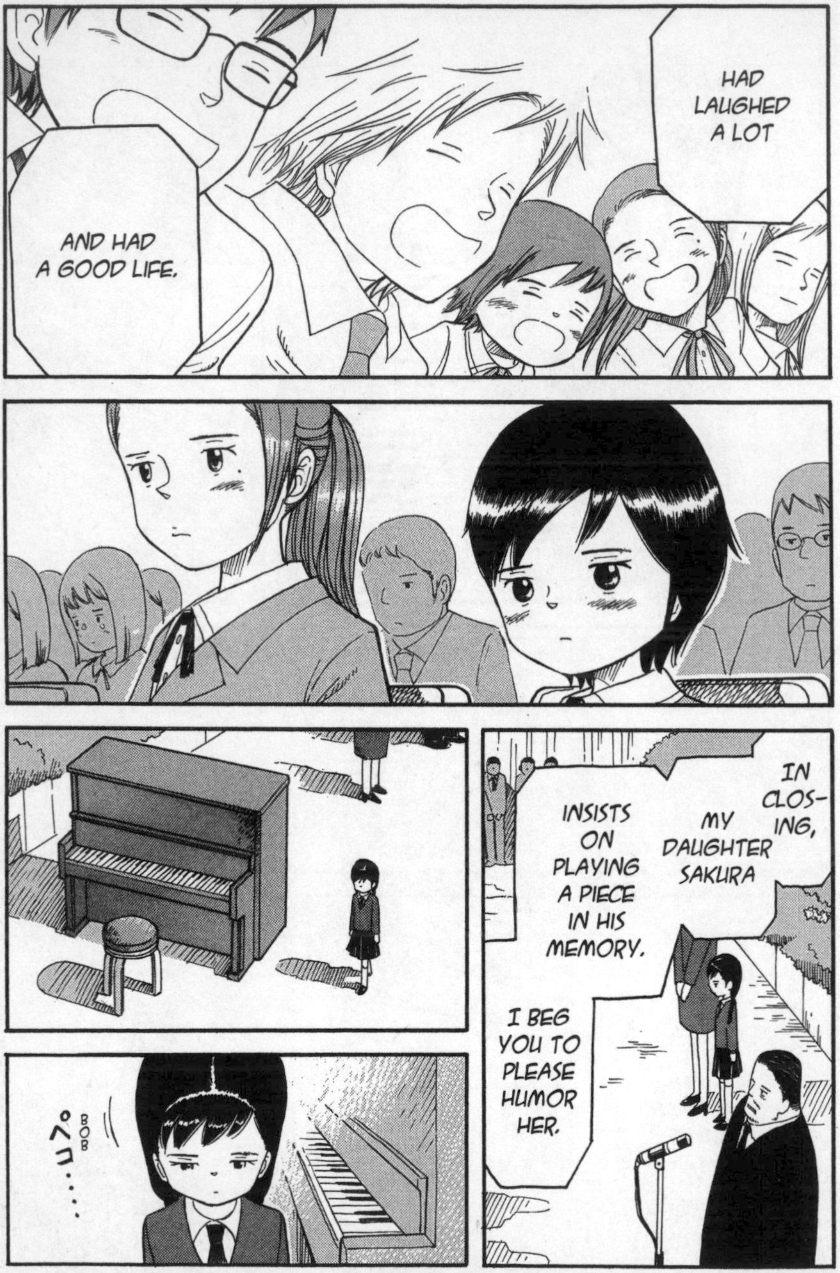
HAD LAUGHED A LOT
AND HAD A GOOD LIFE.
IN CLOSING, MY DAUGHTER SAKURA
INSISTS ON PLAYING A PIECE IN HIS MEMORY.
I BEG YOU TO PLEASE HUMOR HER.
ペコ・・・・
BOB

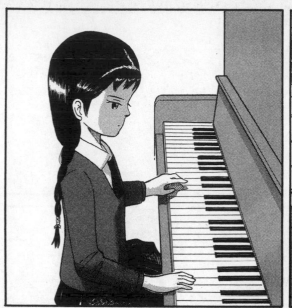
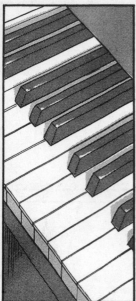

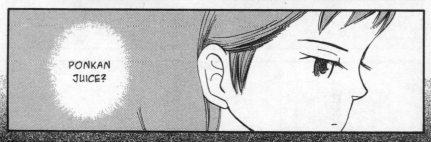

PONKAN
JUICE?

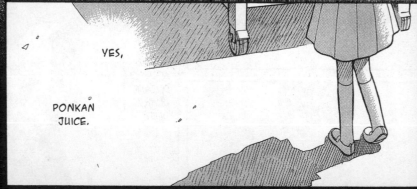

YES,

PONKAN
JUICE.

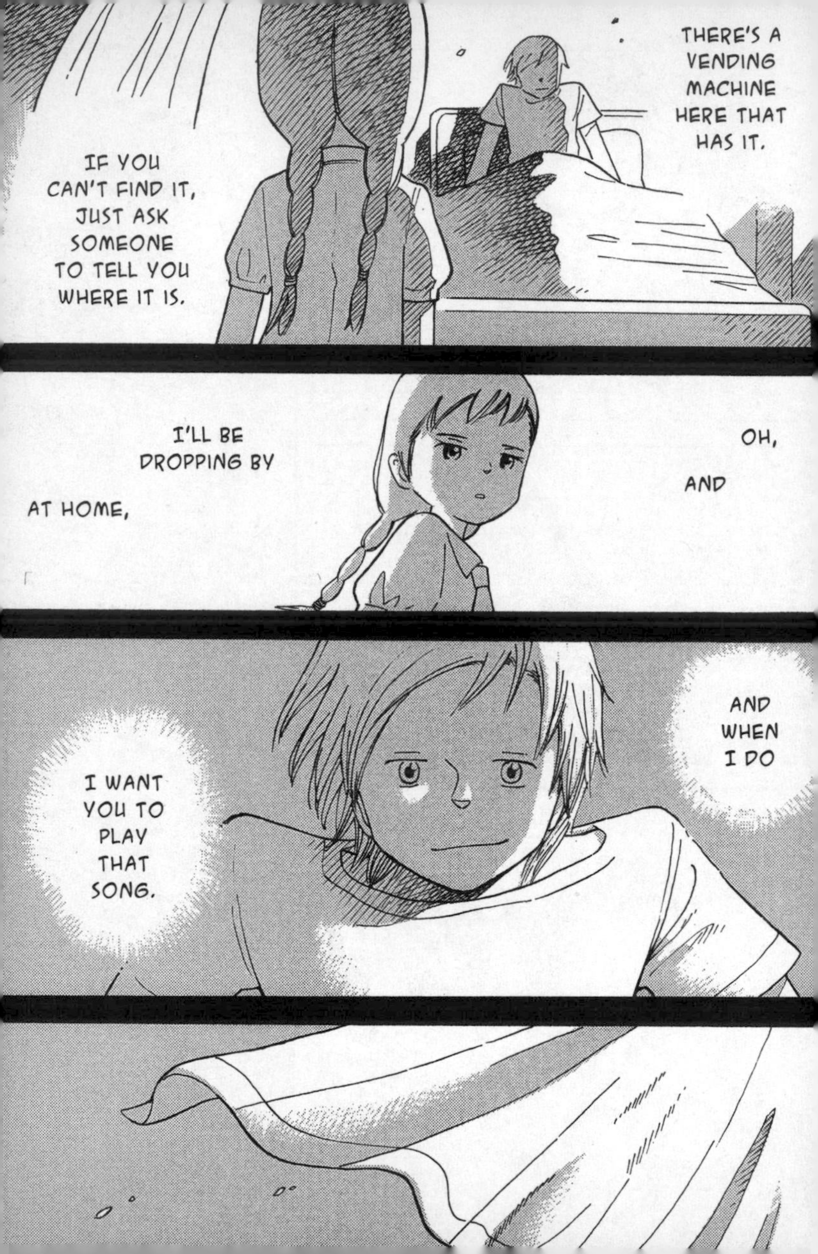
THERE'S A VENDING MACHINE HERE THAT HAS IT.
IF YOU CAN'T FIND IT, JUST ASK SOMEONE TO TELL YOU WHERE IT IS.
OH, AND
I'LL BE DROPPING BY
AT HOME,
AND WHEN I DO
I WANT YOU TO PLAY THAT SONG.

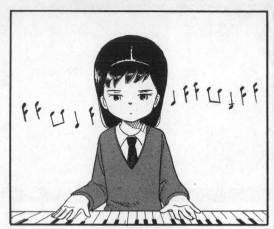

FF LJ JF J J F F LJ J FF

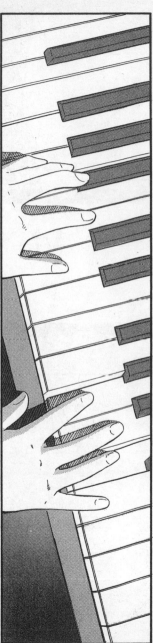

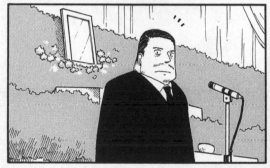

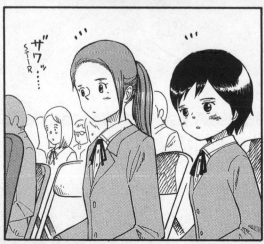

ザワ…
STIR

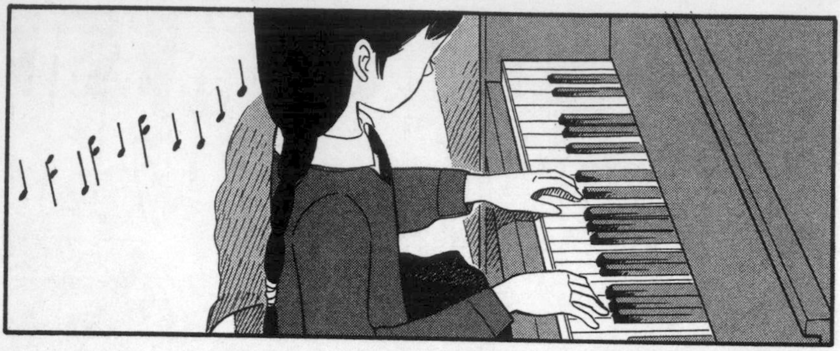

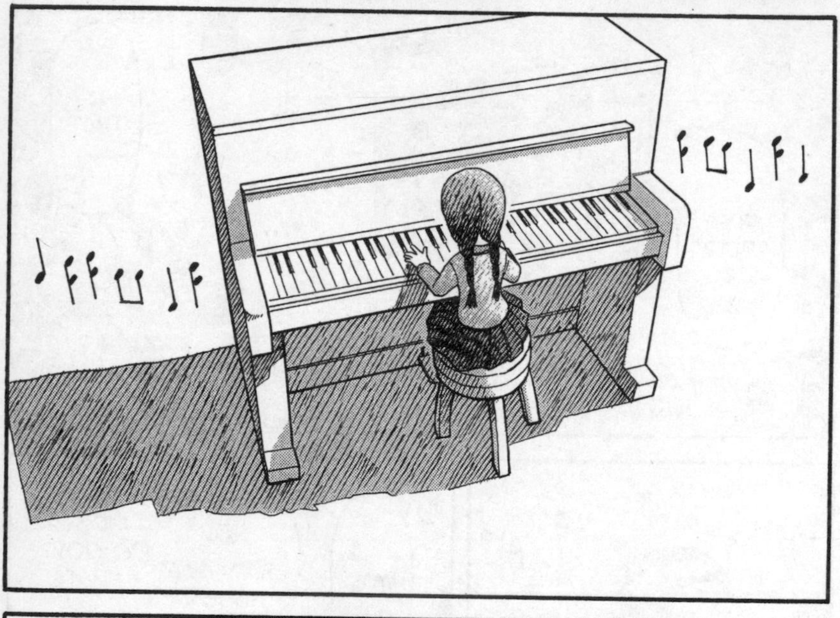

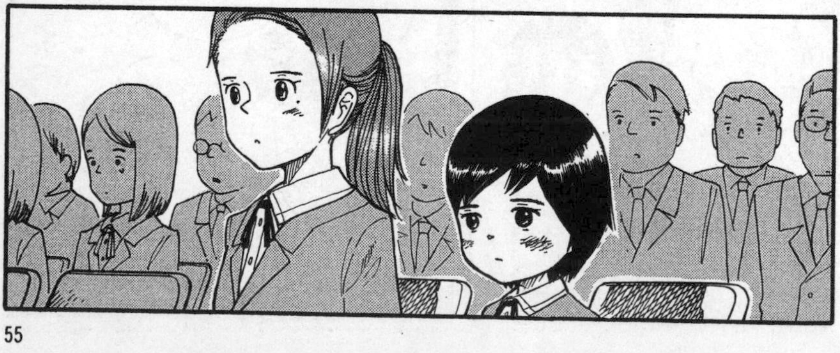

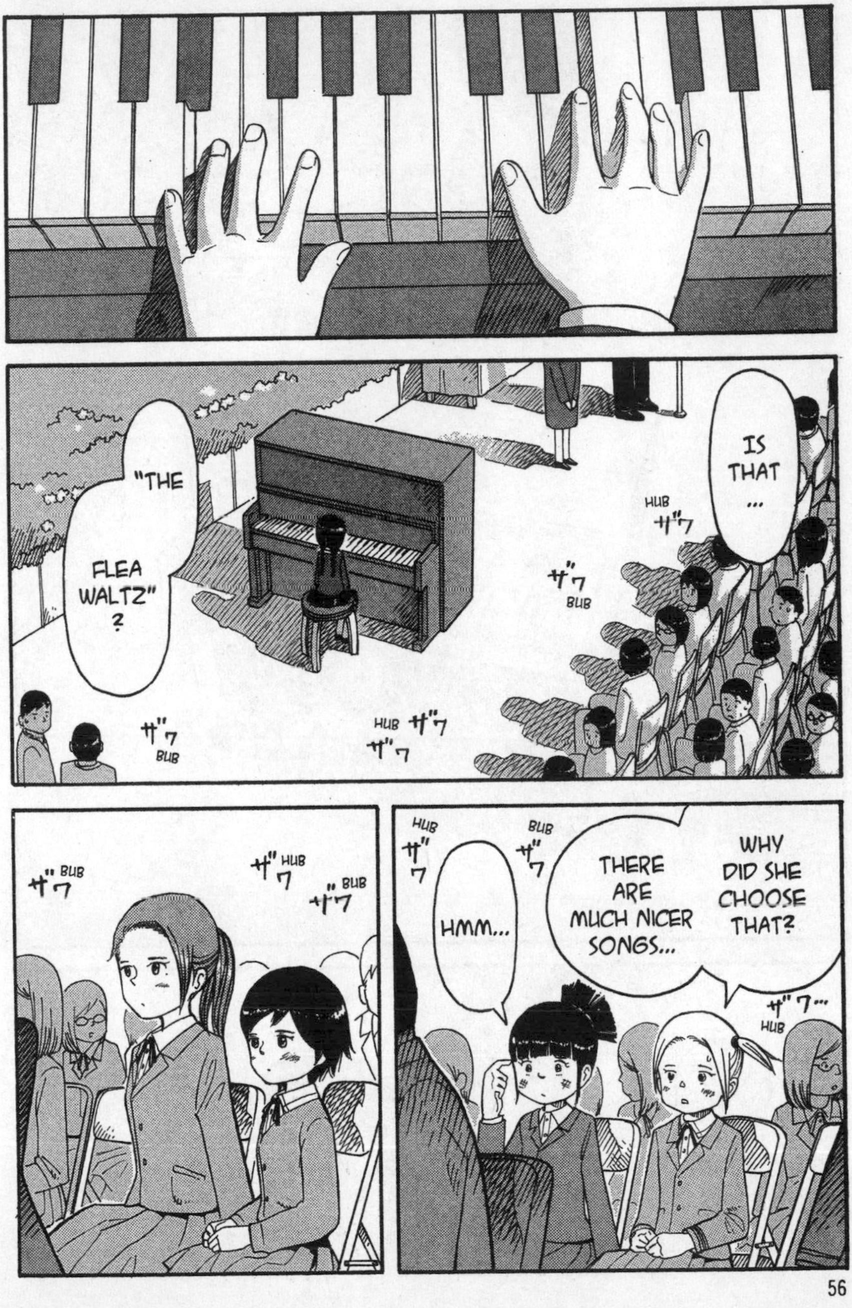
IS THAT ...
HUB ザワ
"THE FLEA WALTZ"?
ザワ BUB
HUB ザワ ザワ
ザワ BUB
WHY DID SHE CHOOSE THAT?
THERE ARE MUCH NICER SONGS...
BUB ザワ
HMM...
HUB ザワ
ザワ... HUB
ザワ HUB
ザワ BUB
ザワ BUB

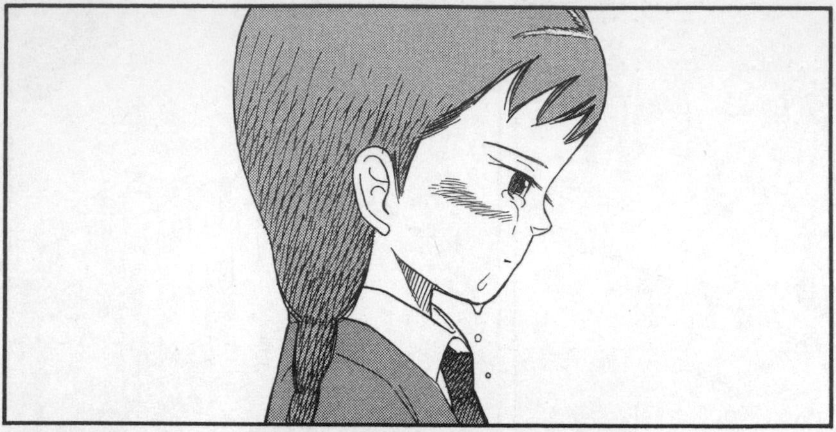
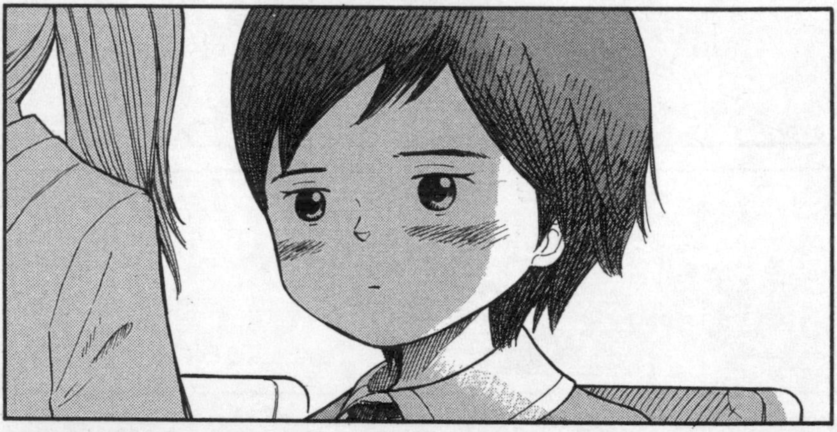
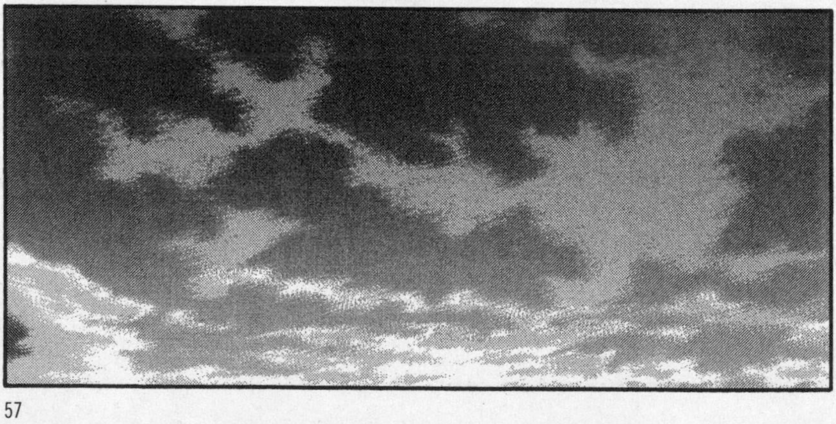

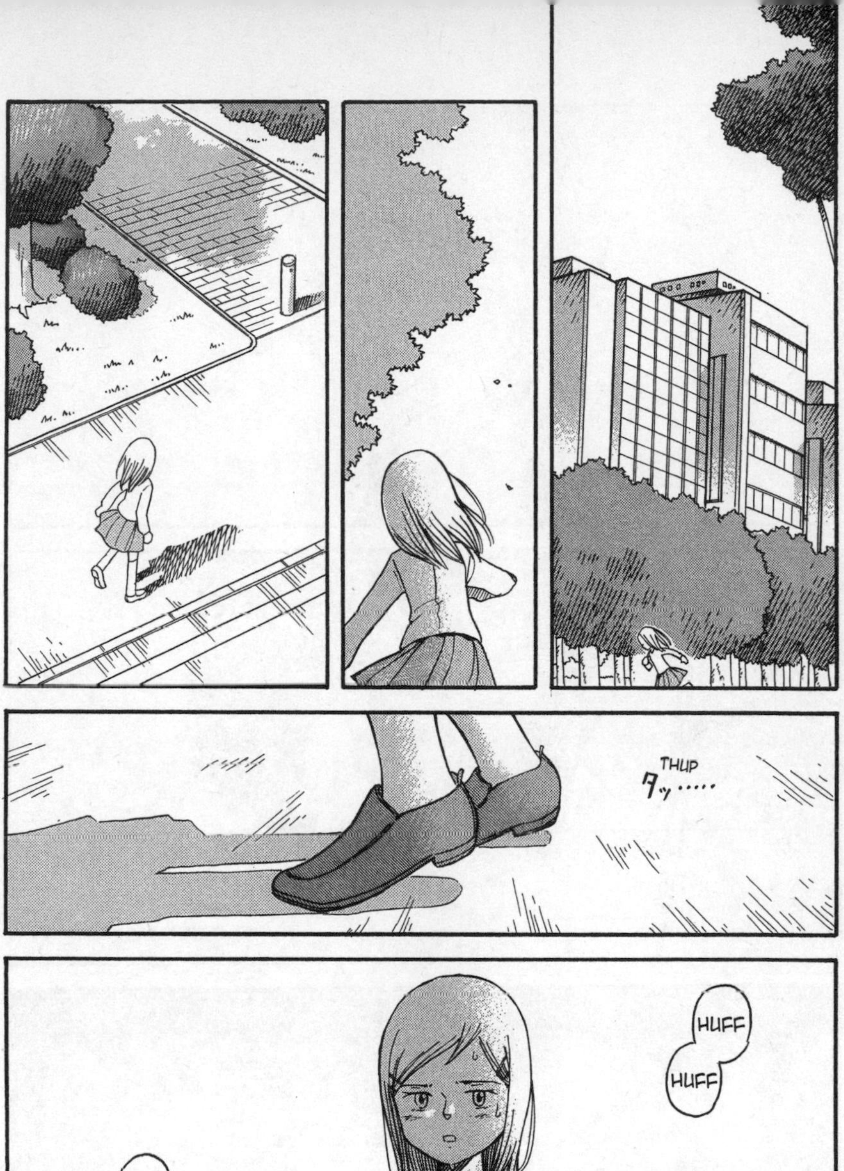
THUP
タッ.....
HUFF
HUFF
HUFF
HUFF

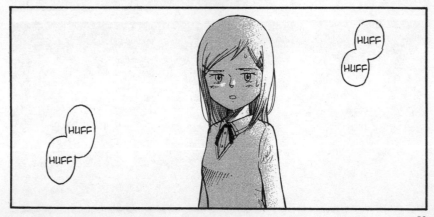

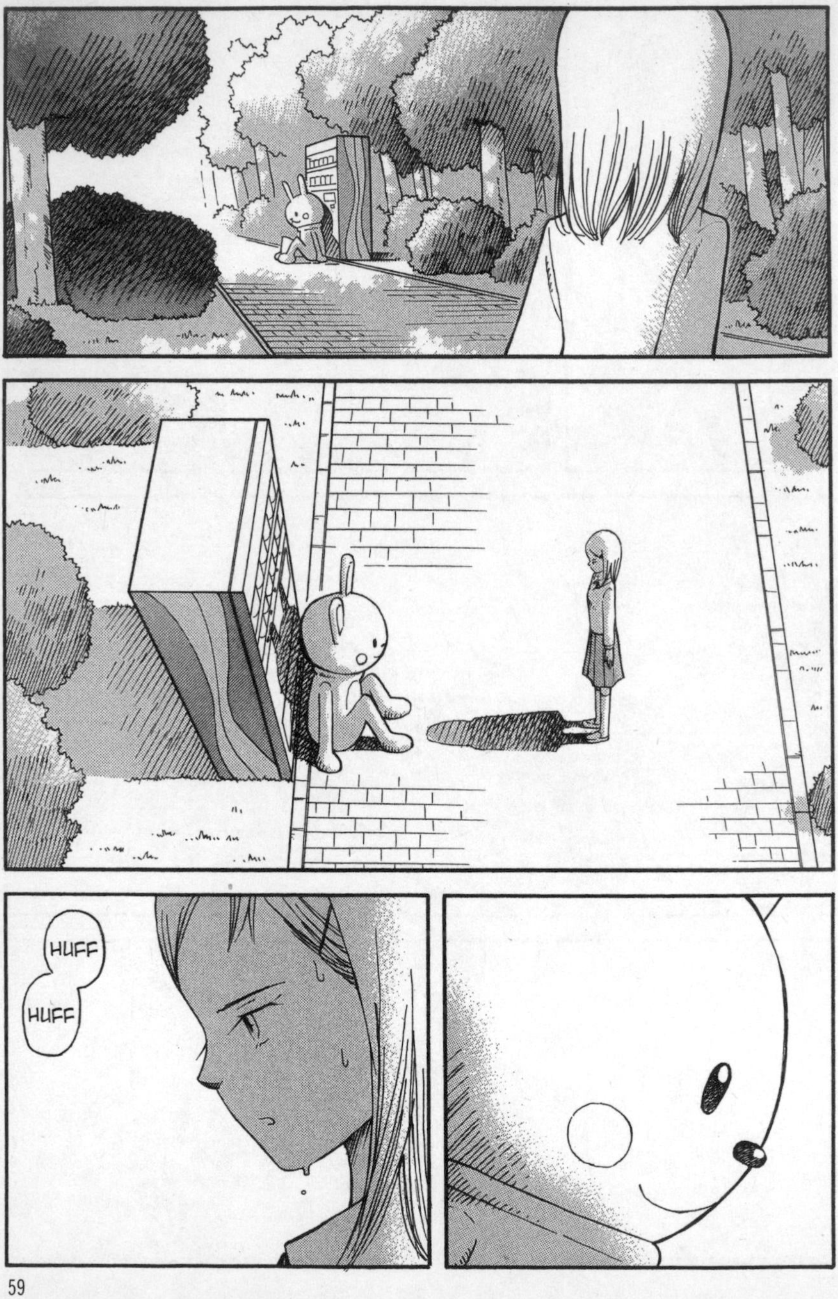
HUFF
HUFF

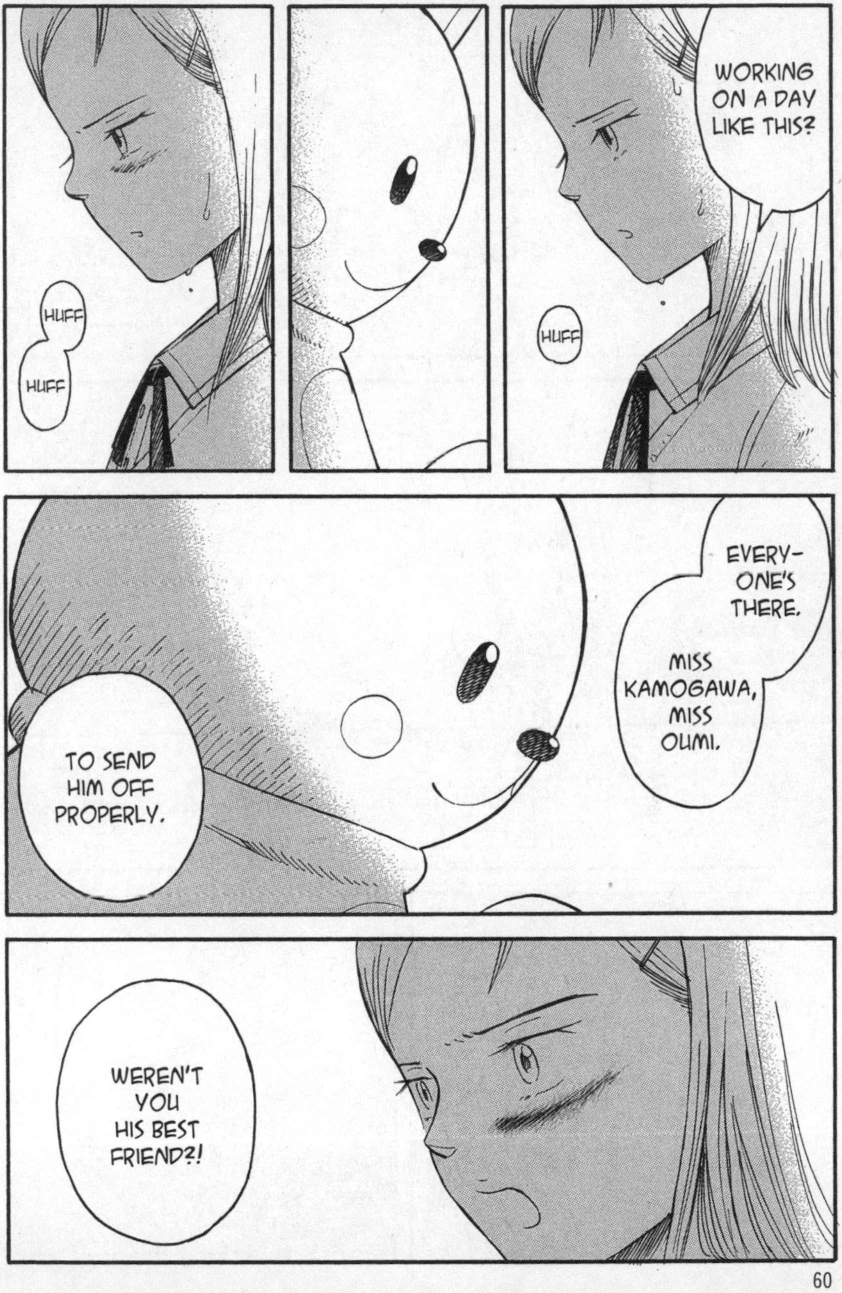
WORKING ON A DAY LIKE THIS?
HUFF
HUFF
HUFF
EVERY-ONE'S THERE.
MISS KAMOGAWA, MISS OUMI.
TO SEND HIM OFF PROPERLY.
WEREN'T YOU HIS BEST FRIEND?!

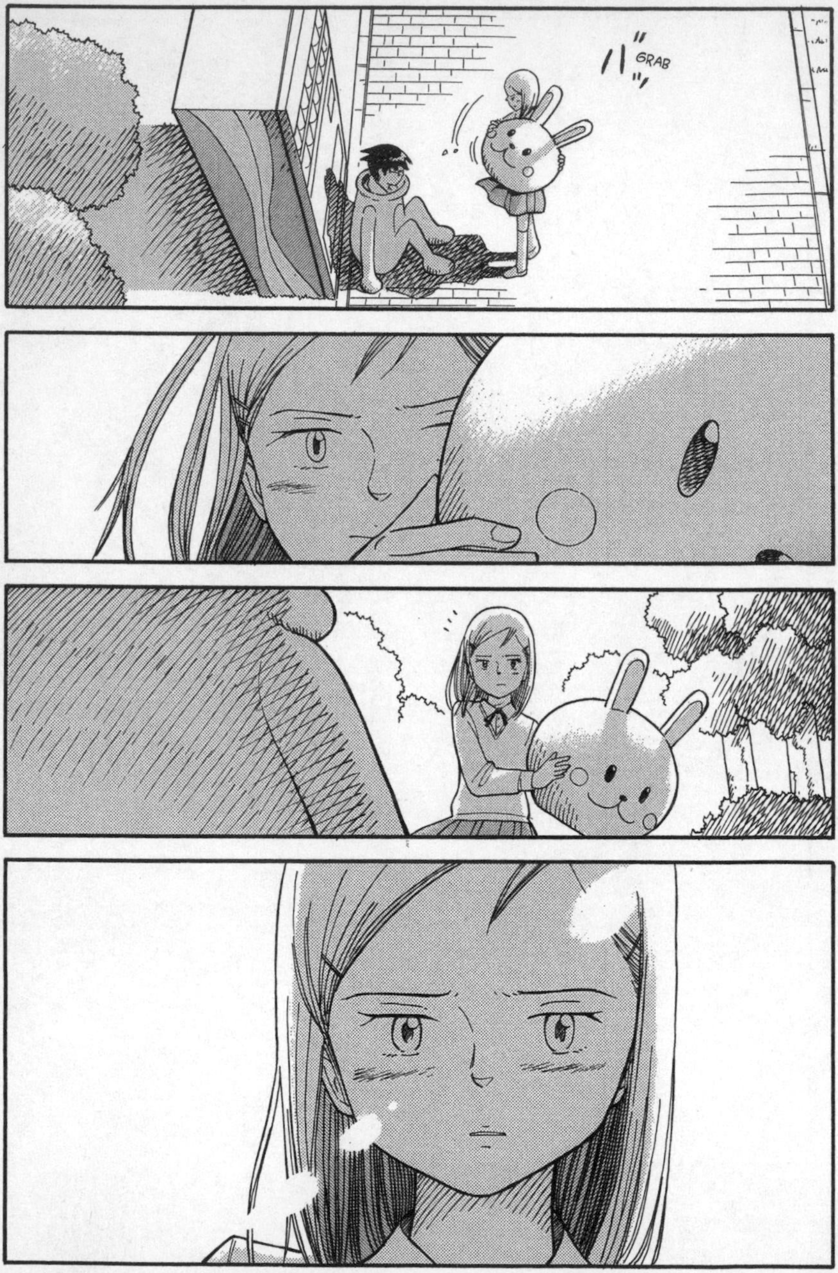
GRAB

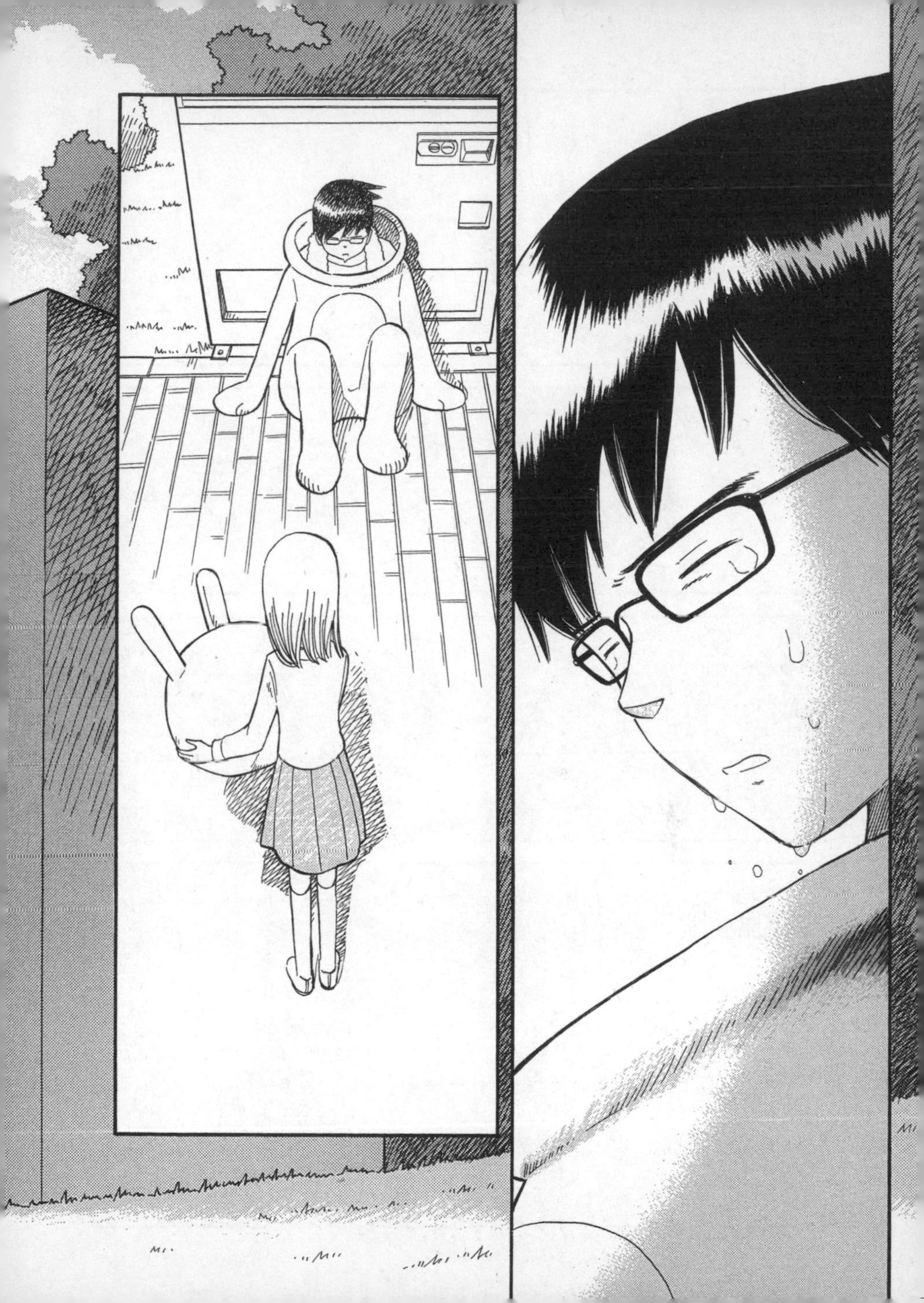

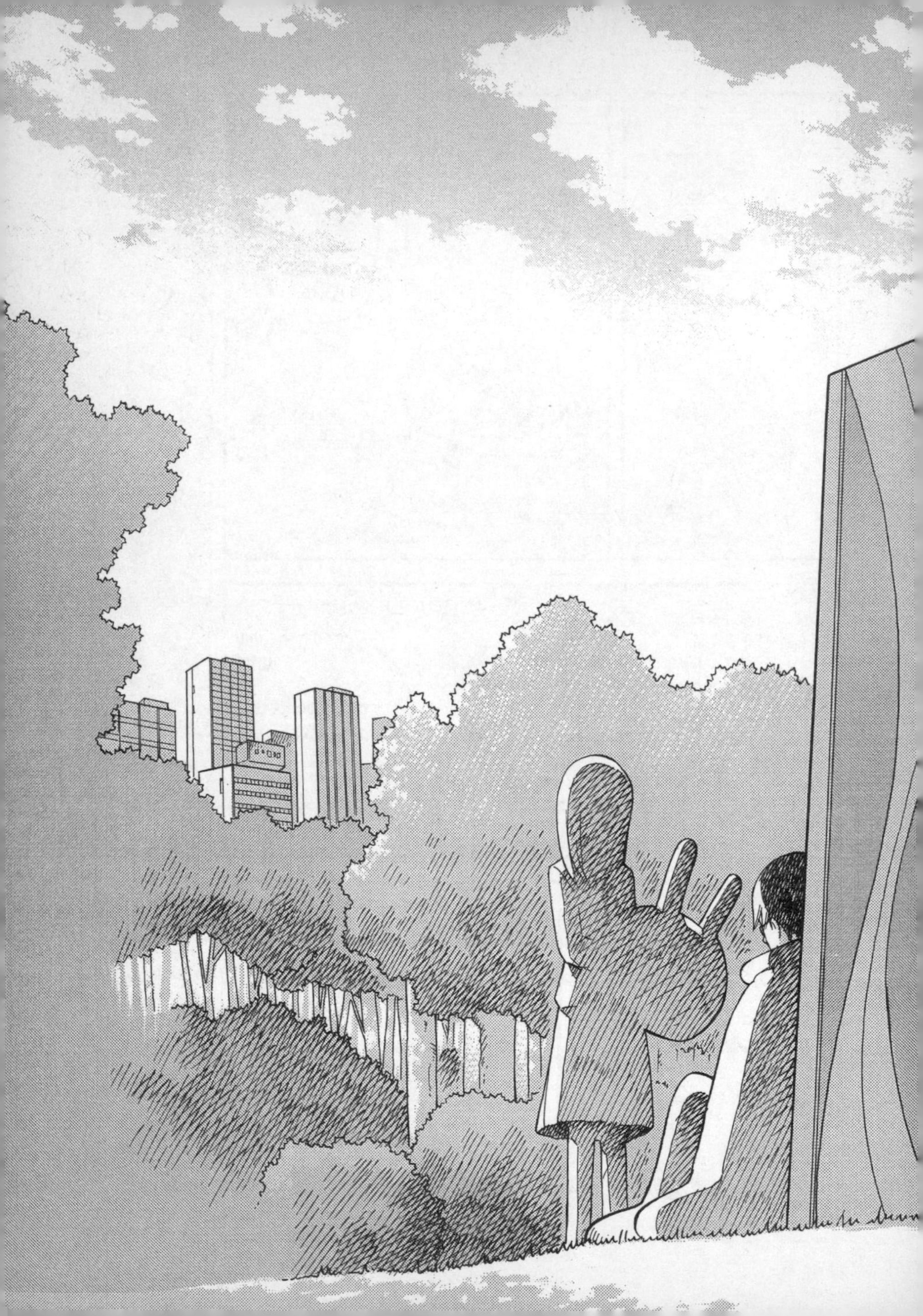

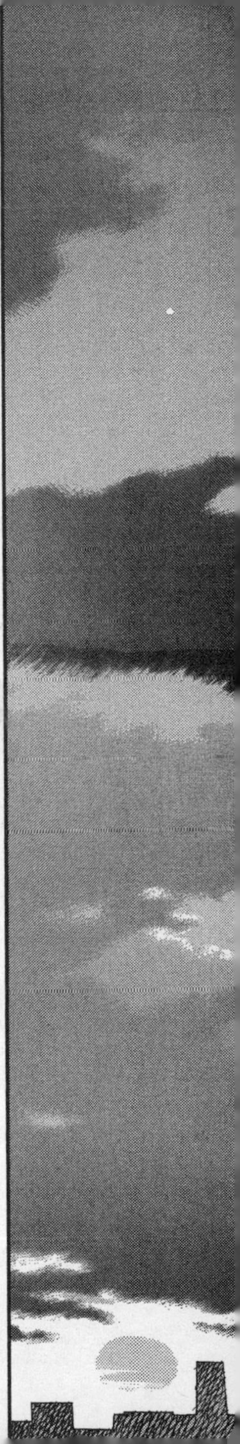

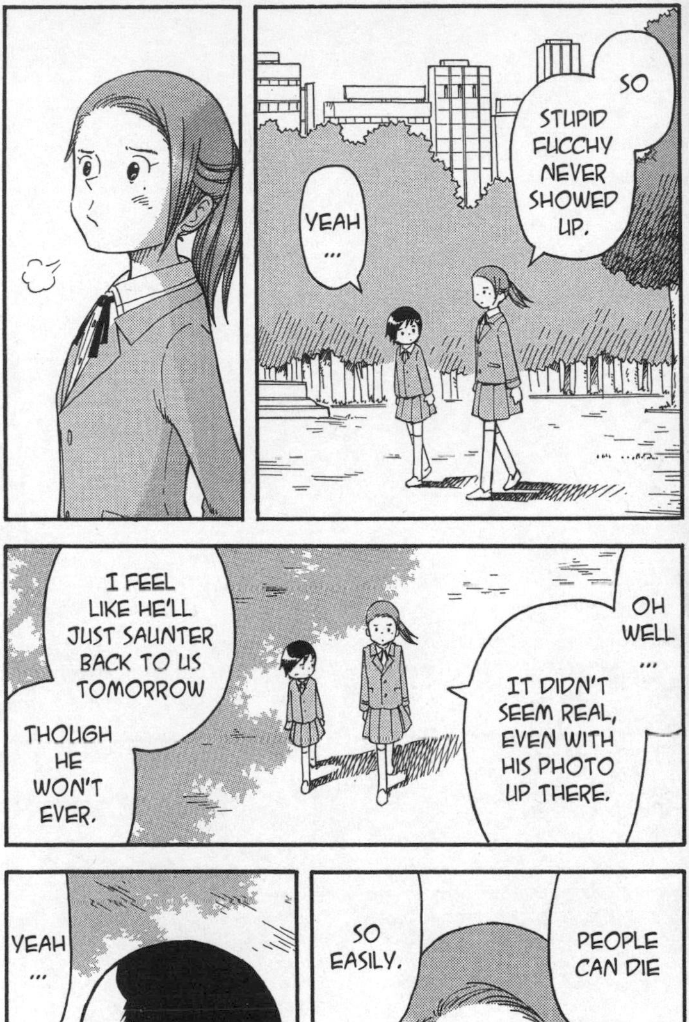
SO STUPID FUCCHY NEVER SHOWED UP.
YEAH ...
OH WELL ...
IT DIDN'T SEEM REAL, EVEN WITH HIS PHOTO UP THERE.
I FEEL LIKE HE'LL JUST SAUNTER BACK TO US TOMORROW
THOUGH HE WON'T EVER.
PEOPLE CAN DIE
SO EASILY.
YEAH ...

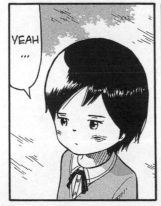

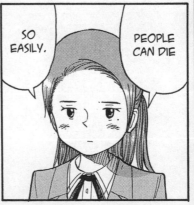

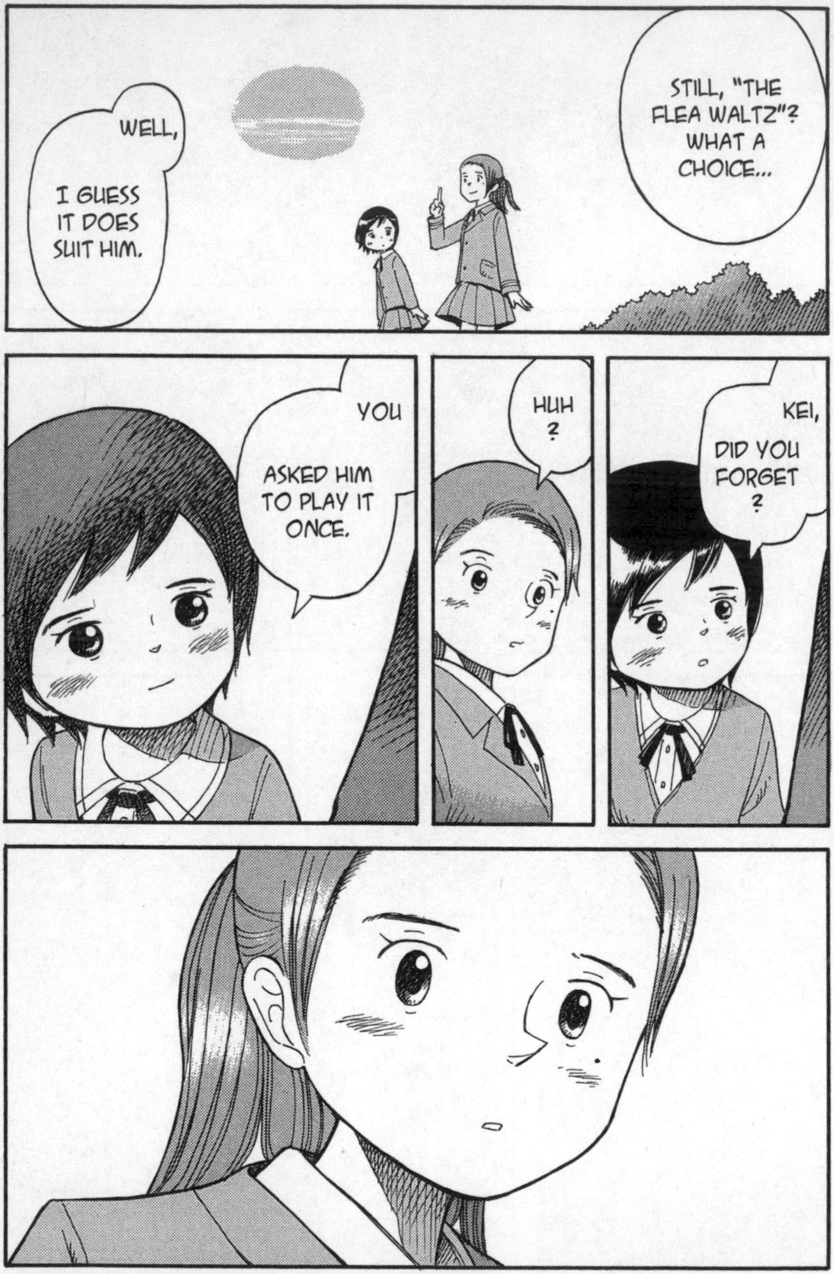
STILL, "THE FLEA WALTZ"? WHAT A CHOICE...
WELL,
I GUESS IT DOES SUIT HIM.
KEI,
DID YOU FORGET?
HUH?
YOU
ASKED HIM TO PLAY IT ONCE.

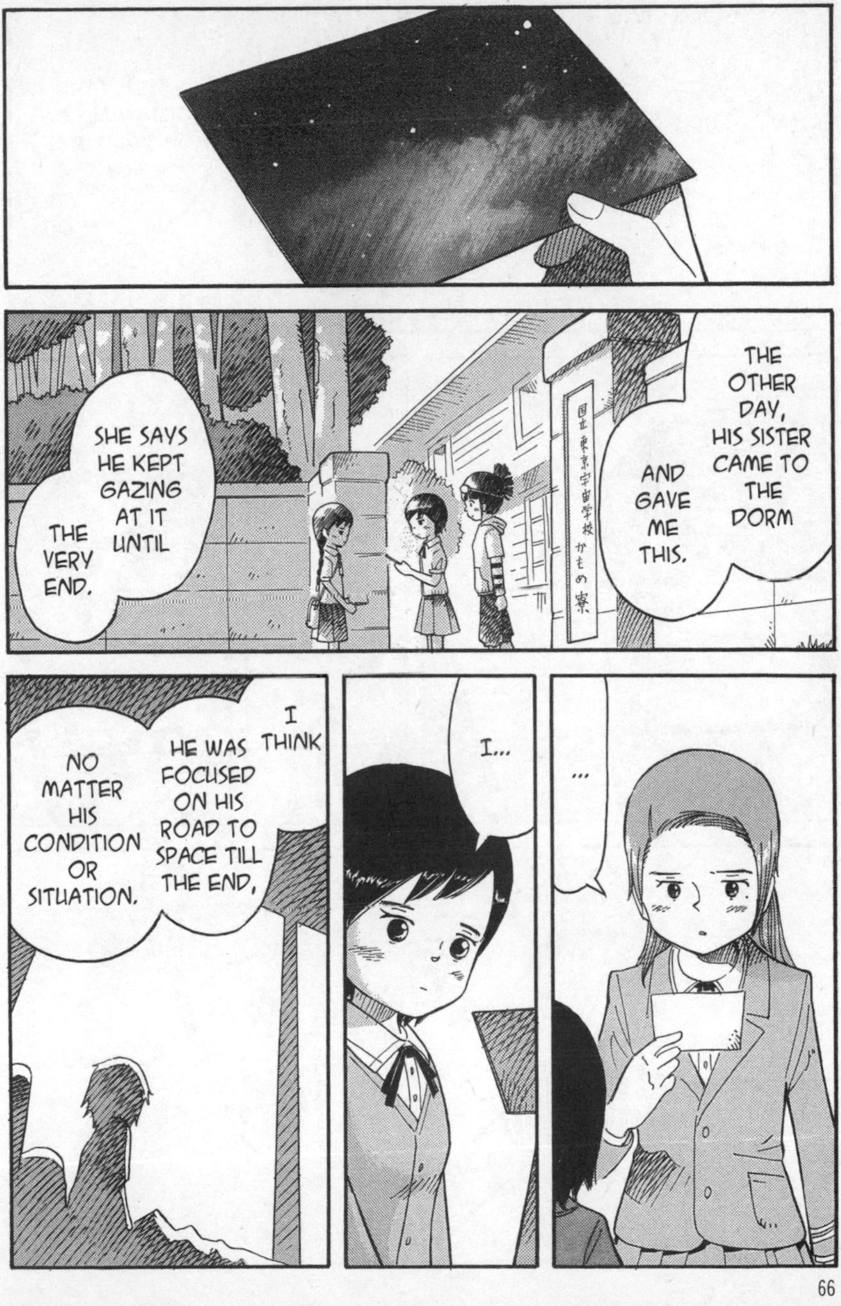
THE OTHER DAY, HIS SISTER CAME TO THE DORM
AND GAVE ME THIS.
国立東京宇宙学校 かもめ寮
SHE SAYS HE KEPT GAZING AT IT UNTIL
THE VERY END.
...
I...
I THINK
HE WAS FOCUSED ON HIS ROAD TO SPACE TILL THE END,
NO MATTER HIS CONDITION OR SITUATION.

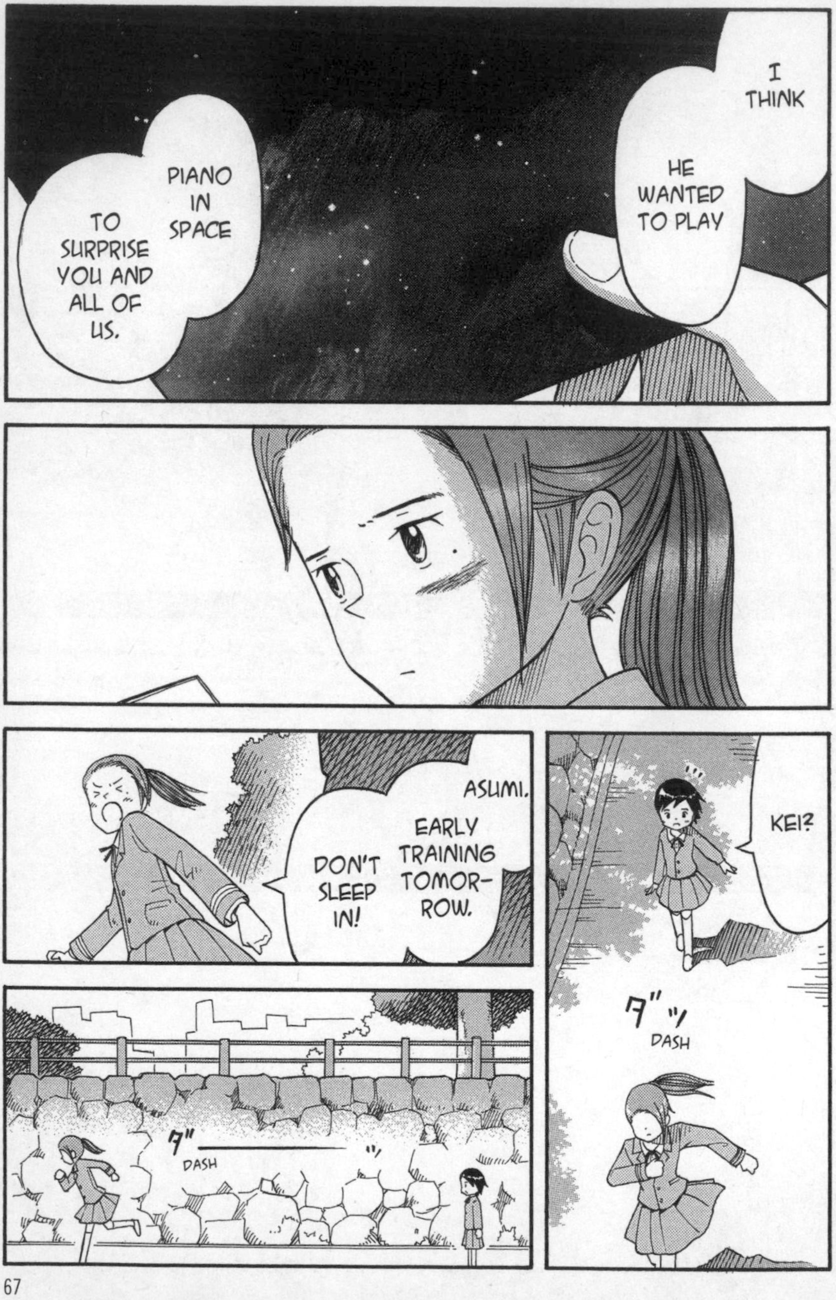
I THINK HE WANTED TO PLAY
PIANO IN SPACE TO SURPRISE YOU AND ALL OF US.
KEI?
ダッ
DASH
ASUMI. EARLY TRAINING TOMOR-ROW. DON'T SLEEP IN!
ダ——ッ
DASH

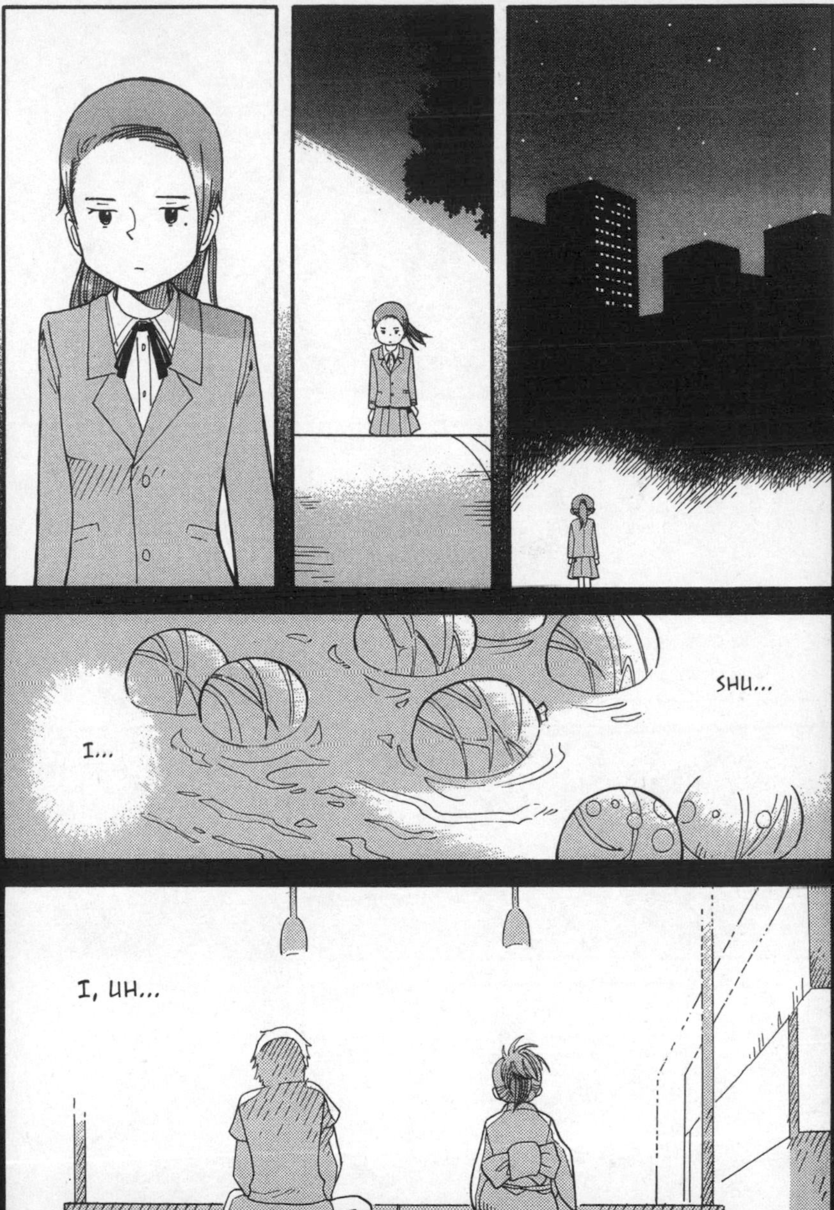
SHU...
I...
I, UH...

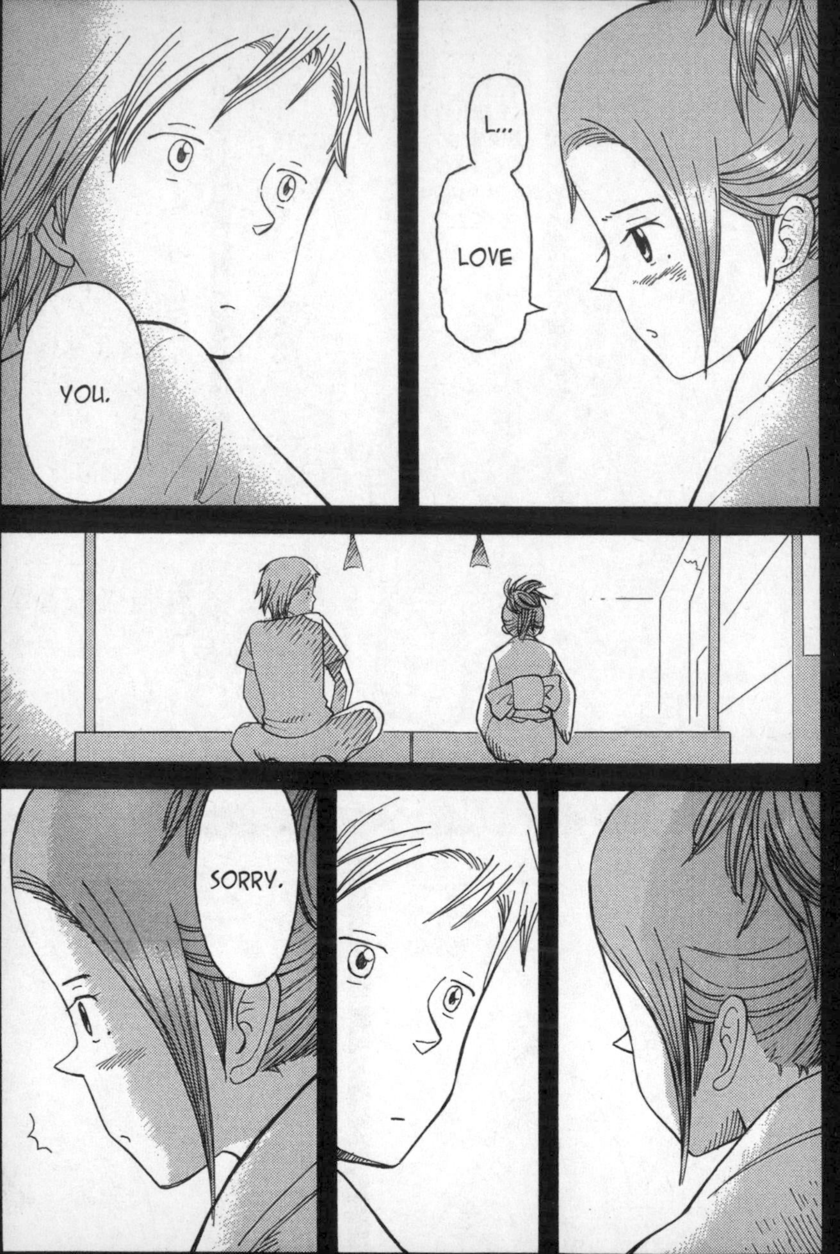
I... LOVE
YOU.
SORRY.

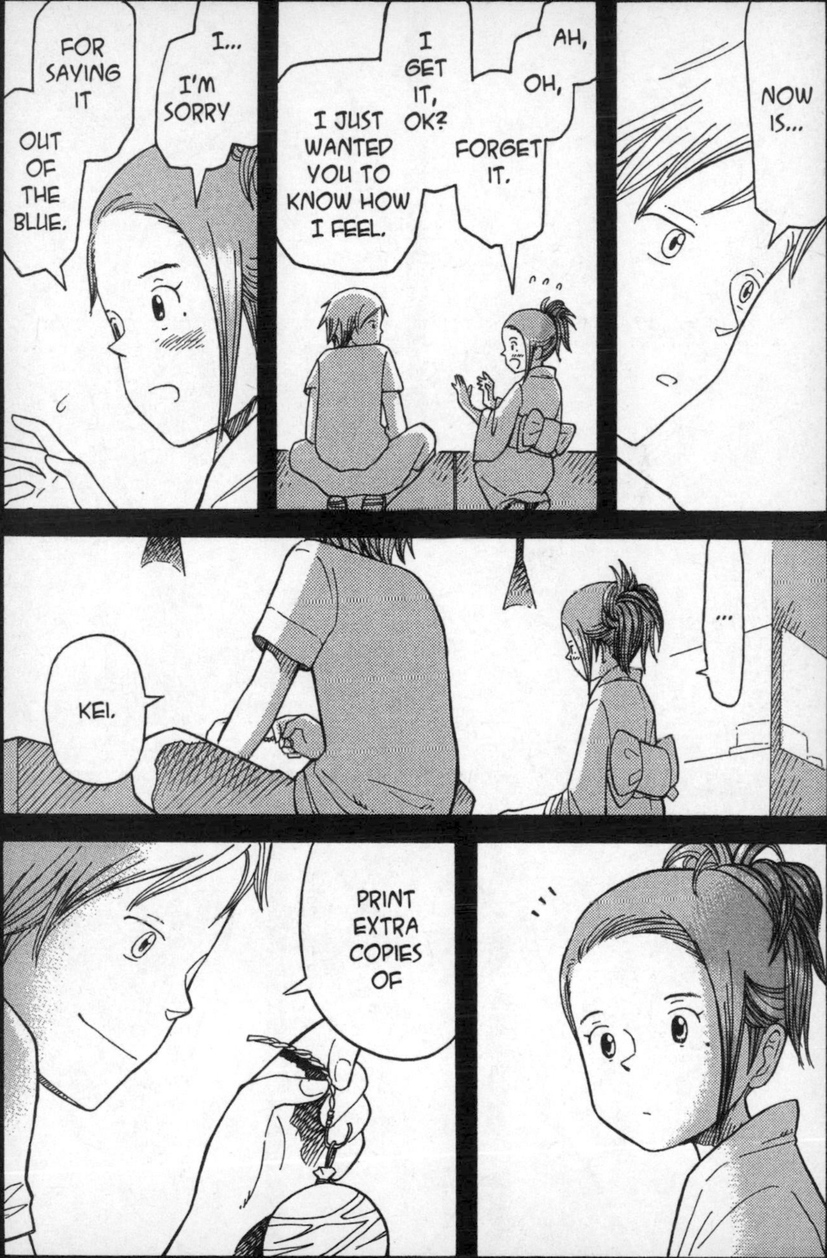
NOW IS...
AH, OH, FORGET IT.
I GET IT, OK?
I JUST WANTED YOU TO KNOW HOW I FEEL.
I... I'M SORRY
FOR SAYING IT OUT OF THE BLUE.
...
KEI.
PRINT EXTRA COPIES OF

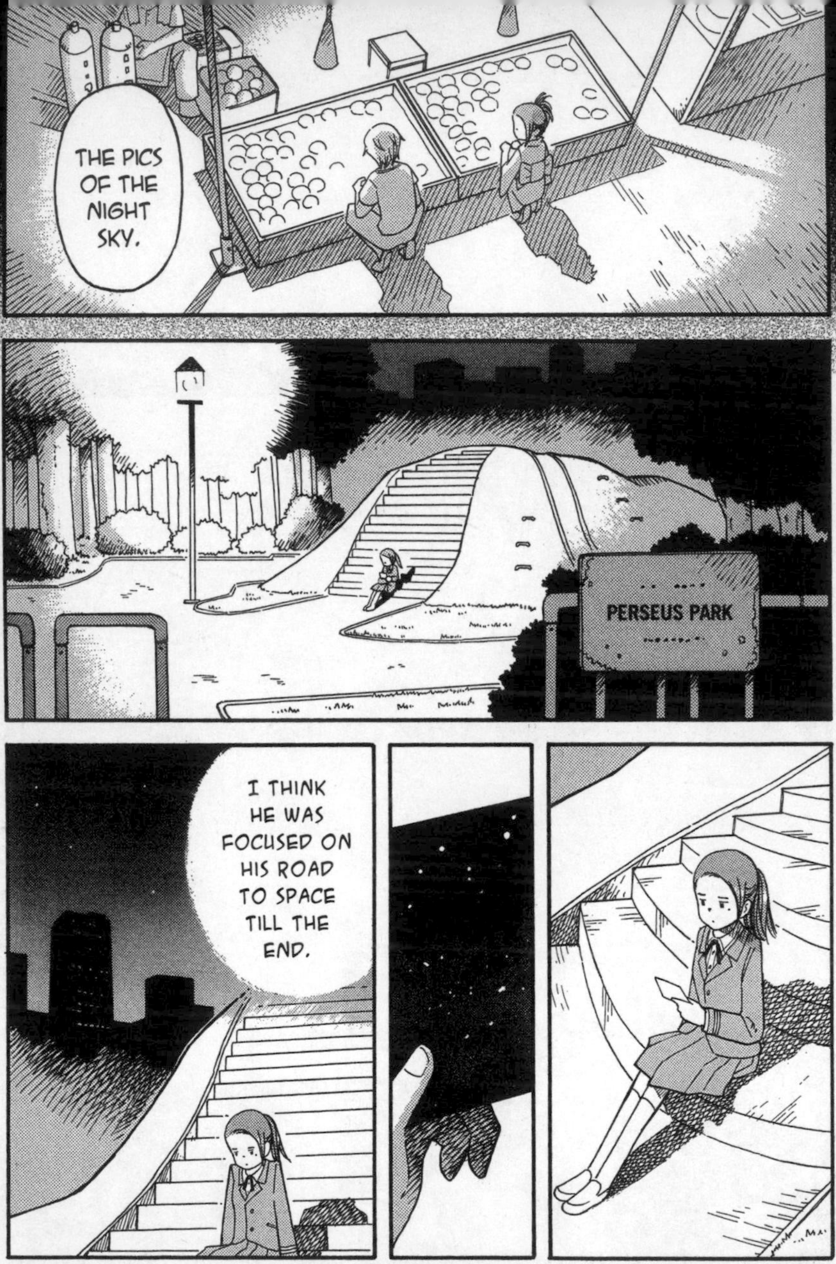
THE PICS OF THE NIGHT SKY.
PERSEUS PARK
I THINK HE WAS FOCUSED ON HIS ROAD TO SPACE TILL THE END.

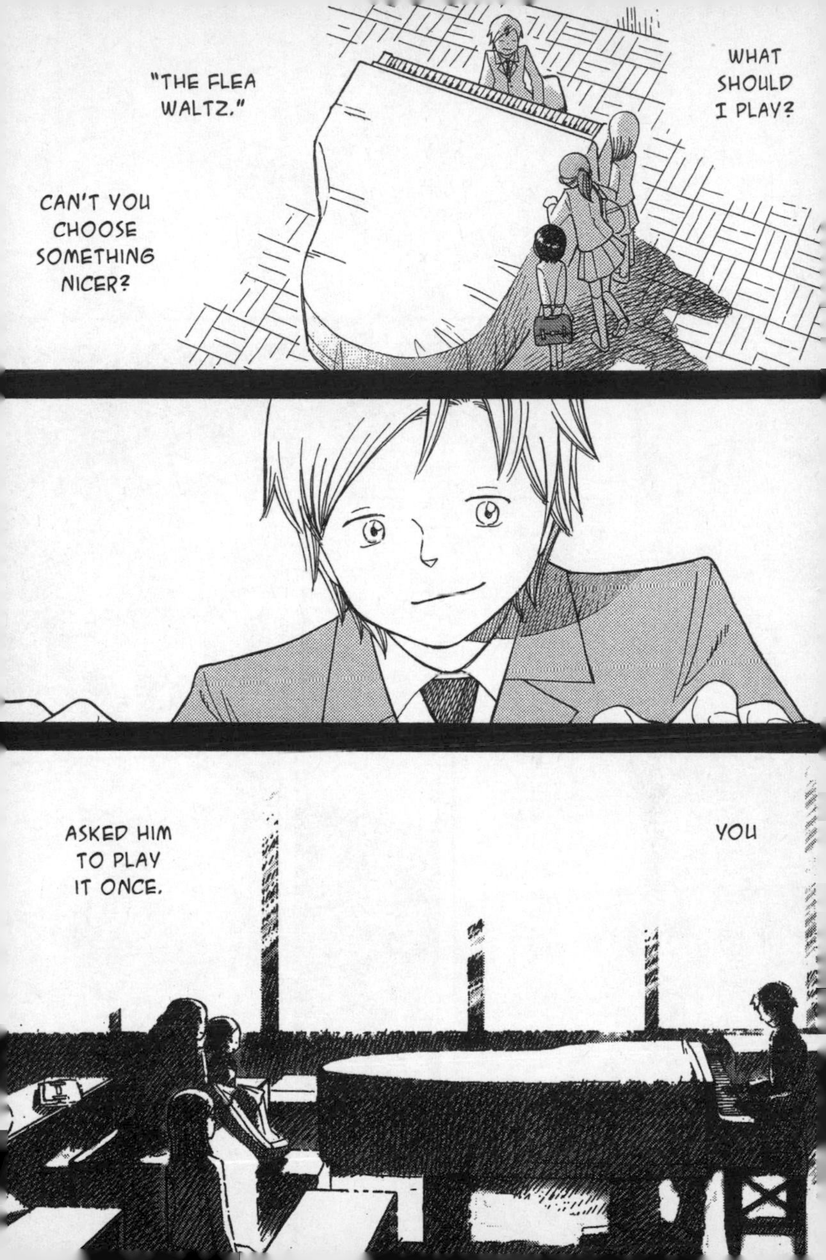
WHAT SHOULD I PLAY?
"THE FLEA WALTZ."
CAN'T YOU CHOOSE SOMETHING NICER?
YOU
ASKED HIM TO PLAY IT ONCE.

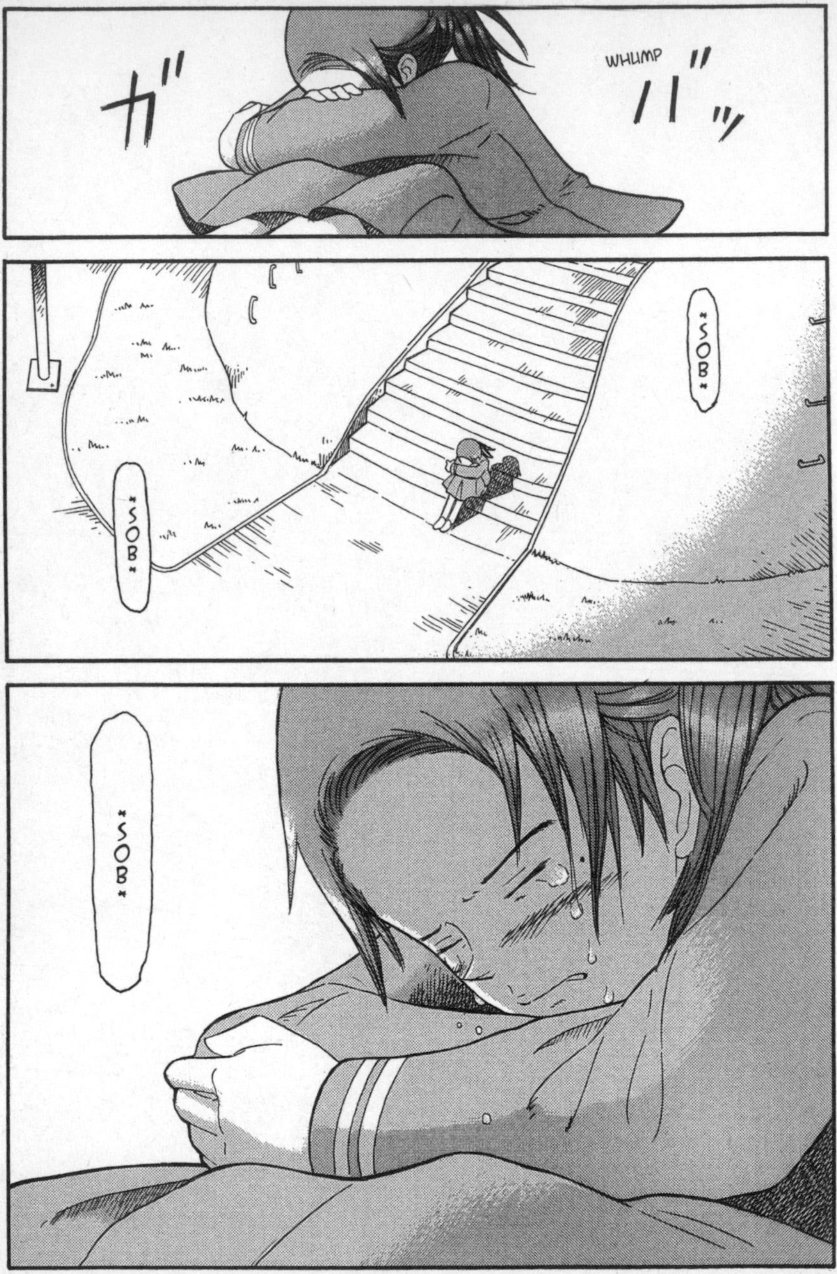
WHUMP
ガバッ
SOB
SOB
SOB

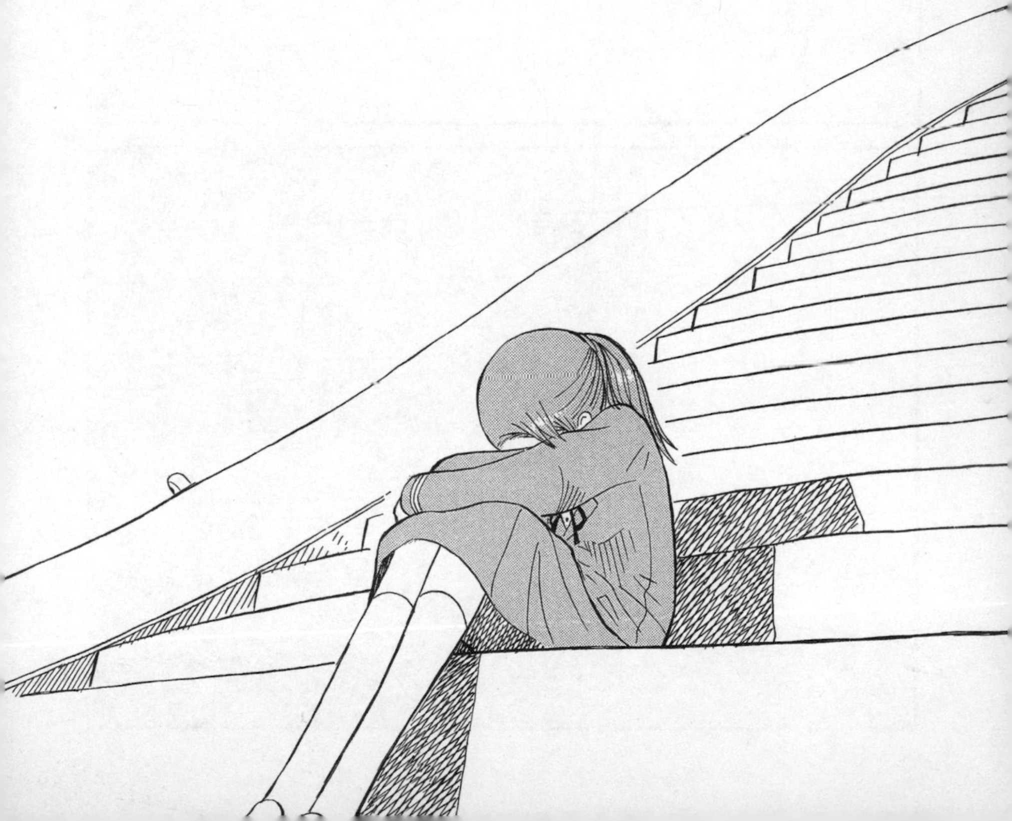

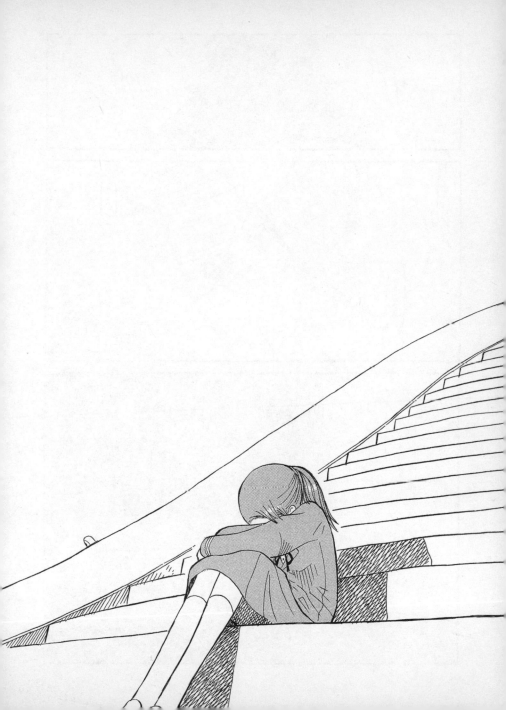

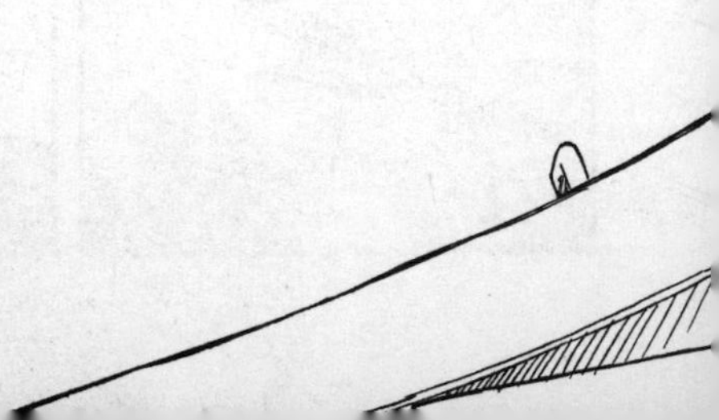

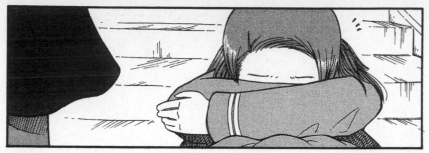

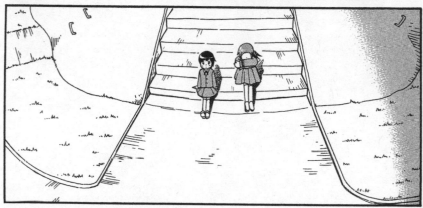

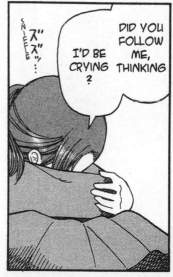

SNIFFLE ズズッ…

I'D BE CRYING?

DID YOU FOLLOW ME, THINKING

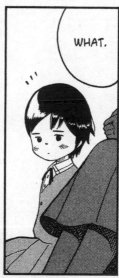

WHAT.

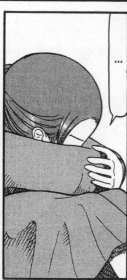

...

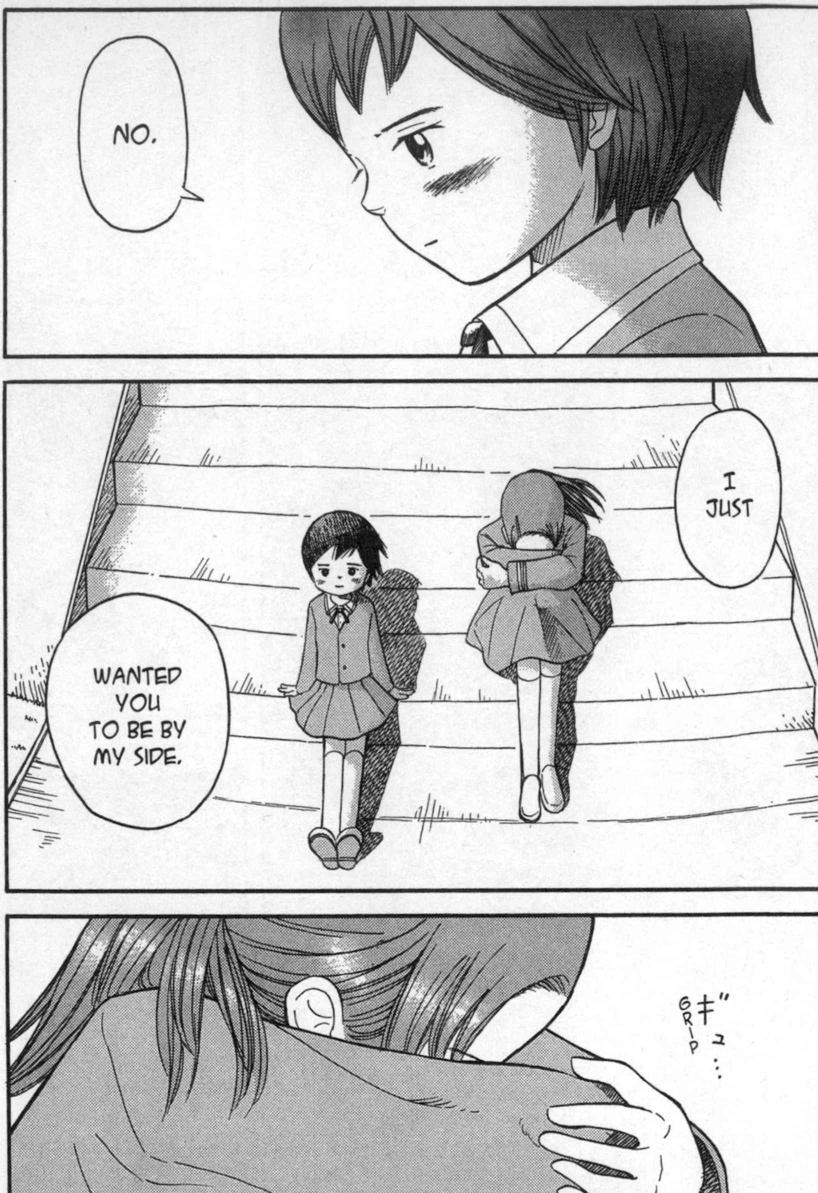
NO.
I JUST
WANTED YOU TO BE BY MY SIDE.
ギュ…
GRIP

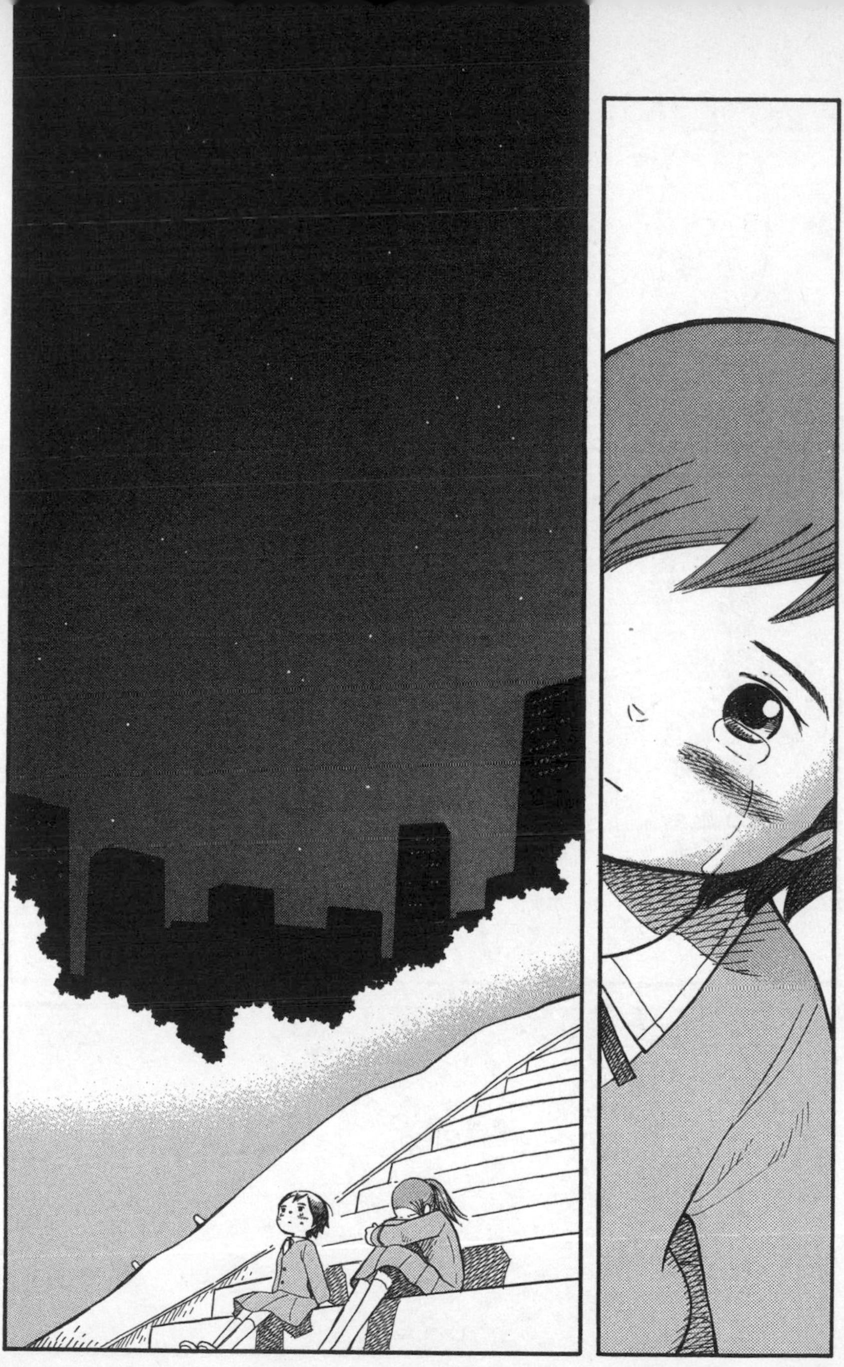

MISSION:67

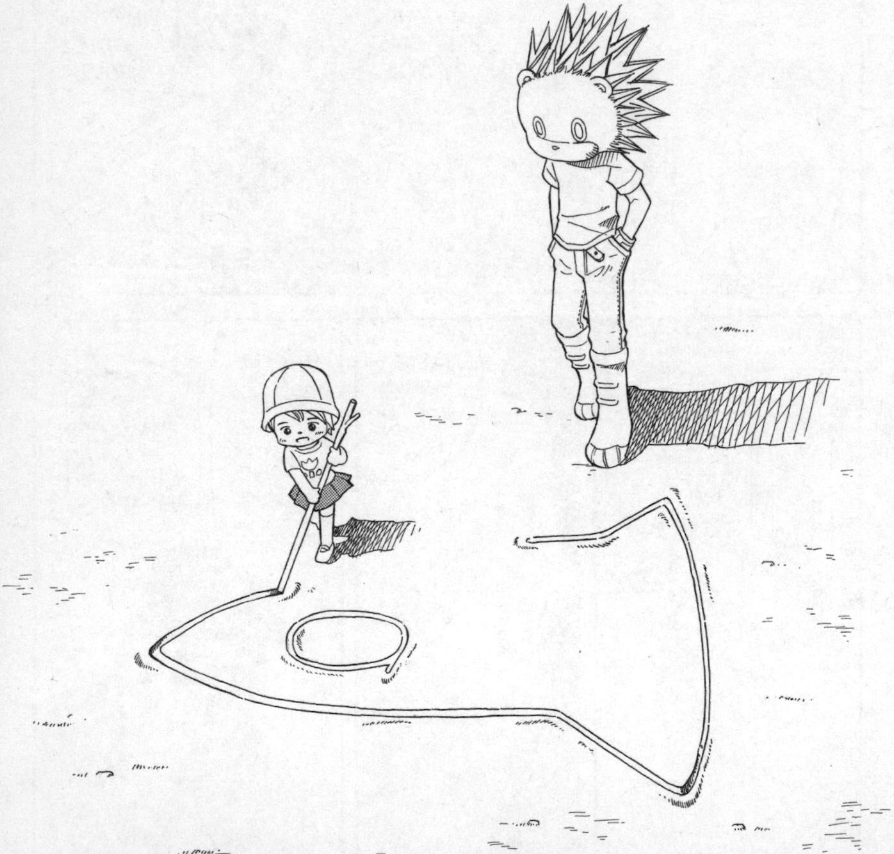

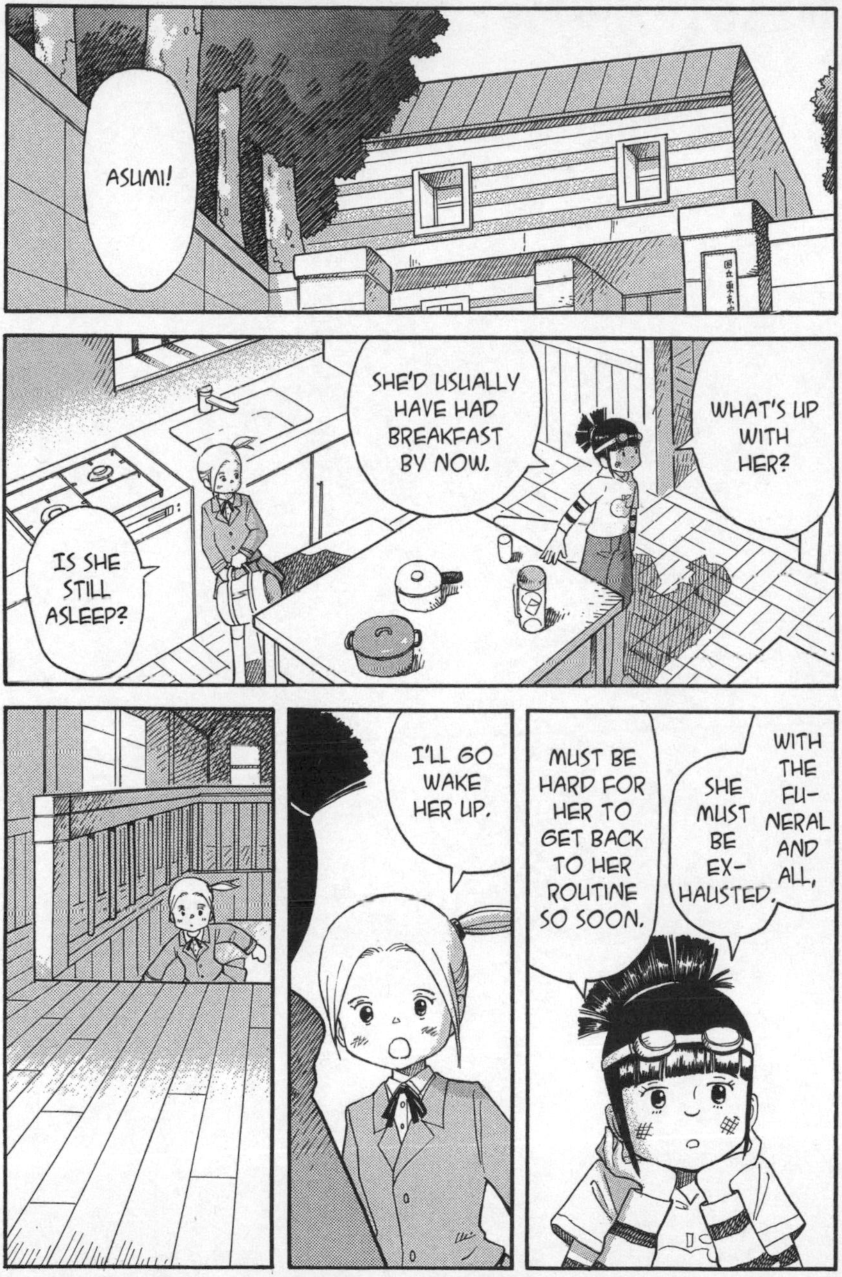
ASUMI!
WHAT'S UP WITH HER?
SHE'D USUALLY HAVE HAD BREAKFAST BY NOW.
IS SHE STILL ASLEEP?
WITH THE FU-NERAL AND ALL,
SHE MUST BE EX-HAUSTED.
MUST BE HARD FOR HER TO GET BACK TO HER ROUTINE SO SOON.
I'LL GO WAKE HER UP.

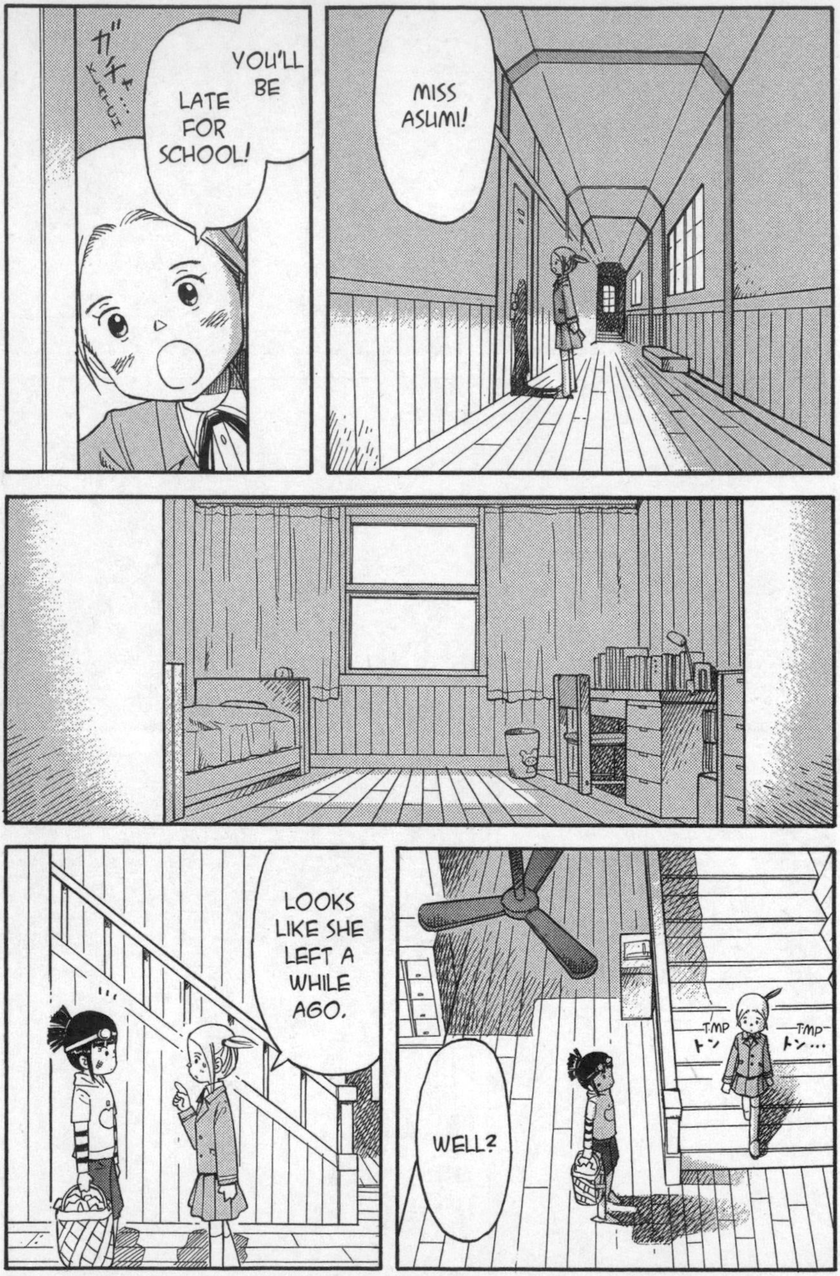
MISS ASUMI!
ガチャ…
KLACHCH
YOU'LL BE LATE FOR SCHOOL!
TMP
トン
TMP
トン…
WELL?
LOOKS LIKE SHE LEFT A WHILE AGO.
…

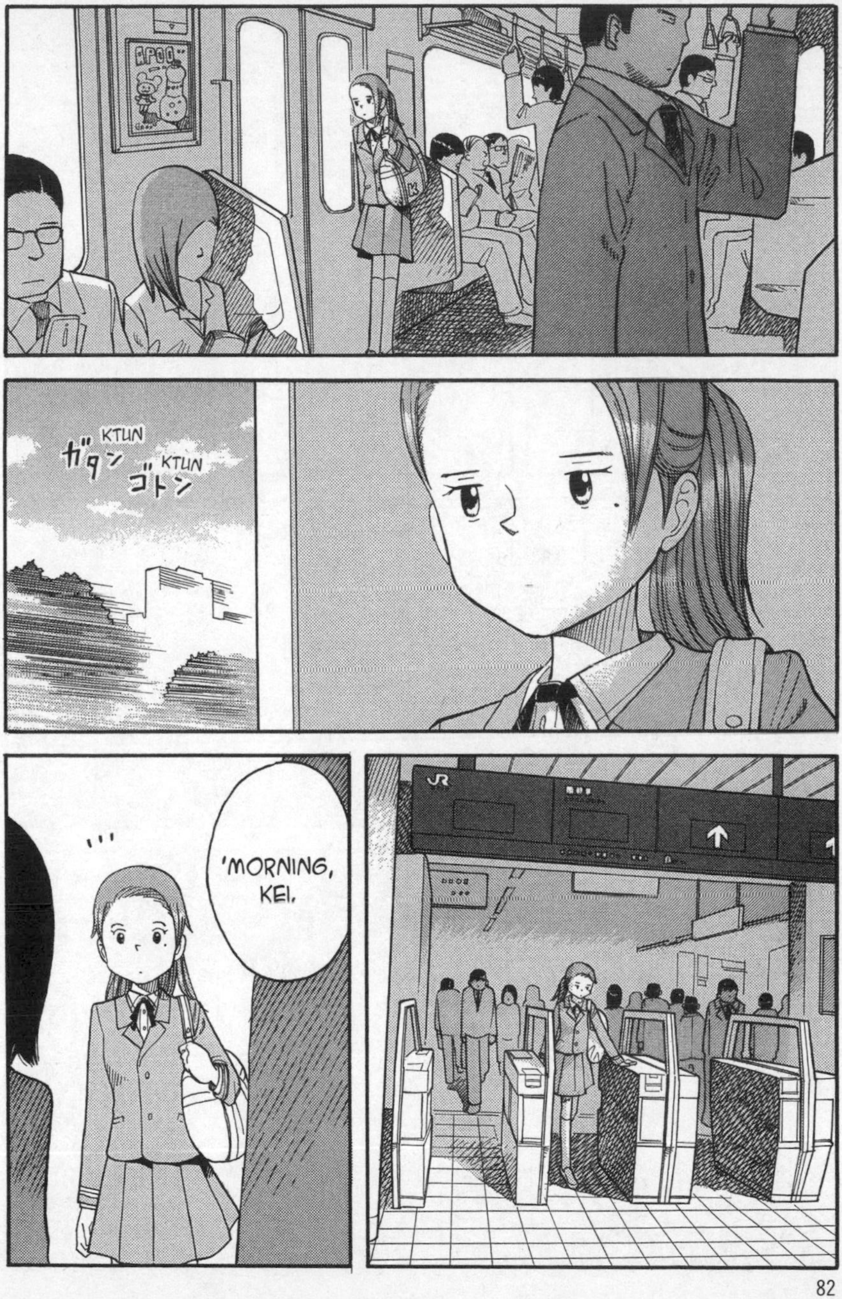
KTUN
ガタン
KTUN
ゴトン
'MORNING, KEI.
'''

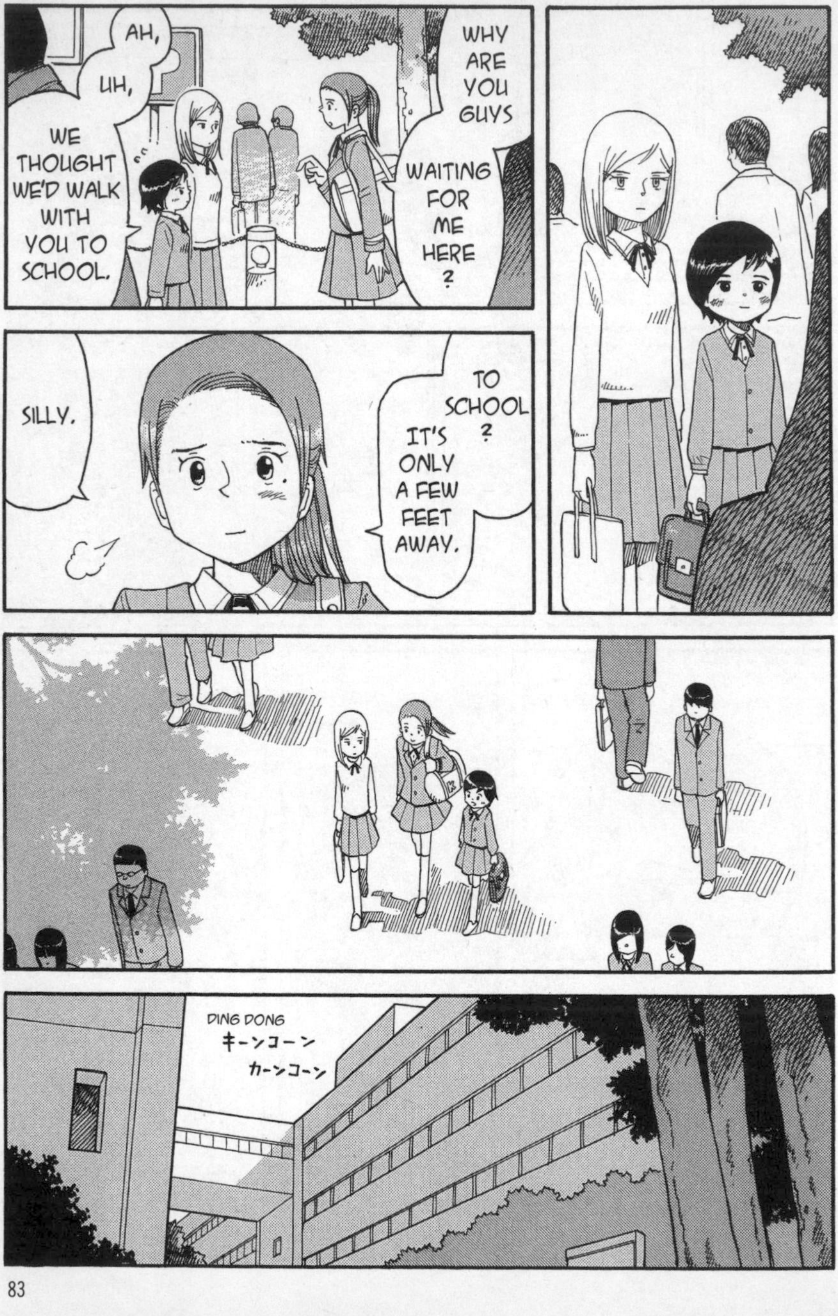
WHY ARE YOU GUYS WAITING FOR ME HERE?
AH,
UH,
WE THOUGHT WE'D WALK WITH YOU TO SCHOOL.
TO SCHOOL? IT'S ONLY A FEW FEET AWAY.
SILLY.
DING DONG
キーンコーン
カーンコーン

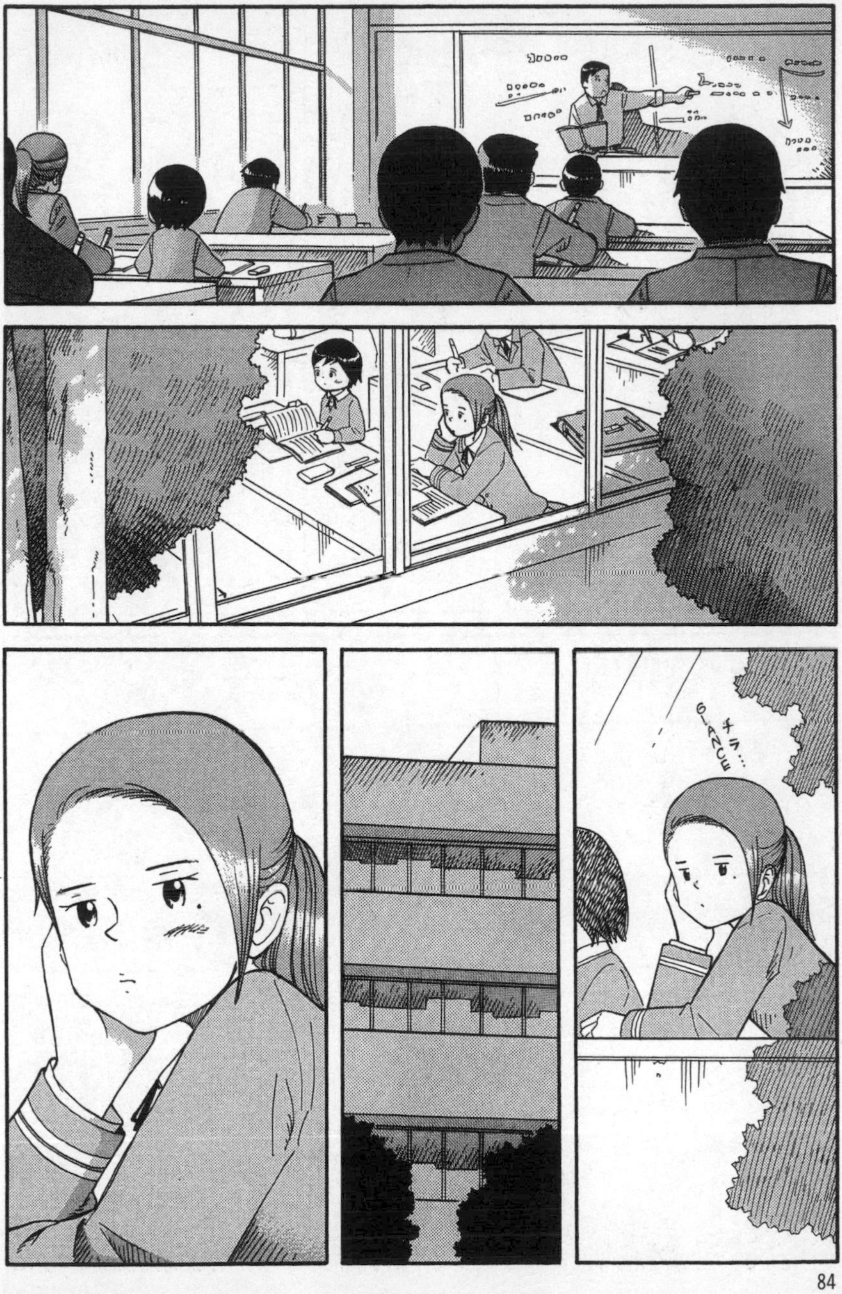
チラ…
GLANCE

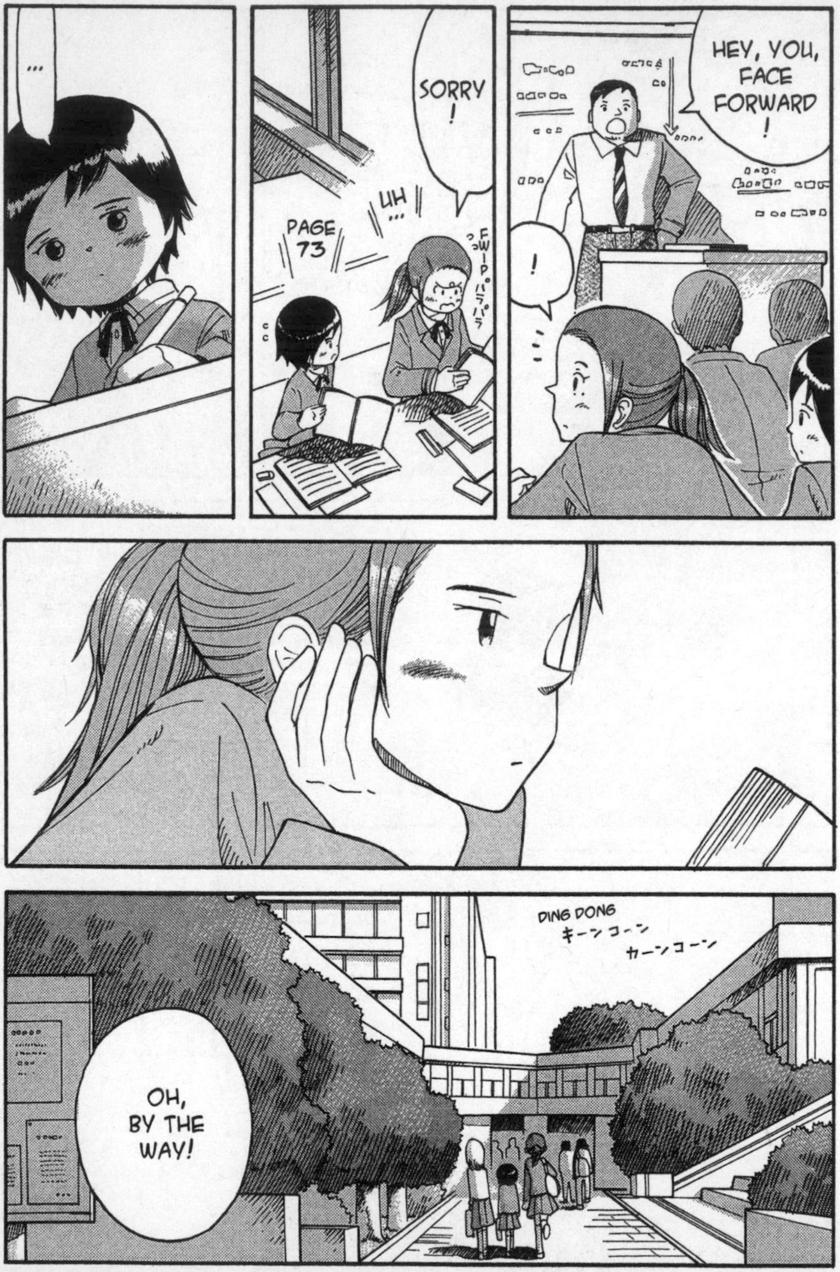
HEY, YOU, FACE FORWARD!
!
SORRY!
UH...
PAGE 73
FWIP
パラパラ
...
DING DONG
キーンコーン
カーンコーン
OH, BY THE WAY!

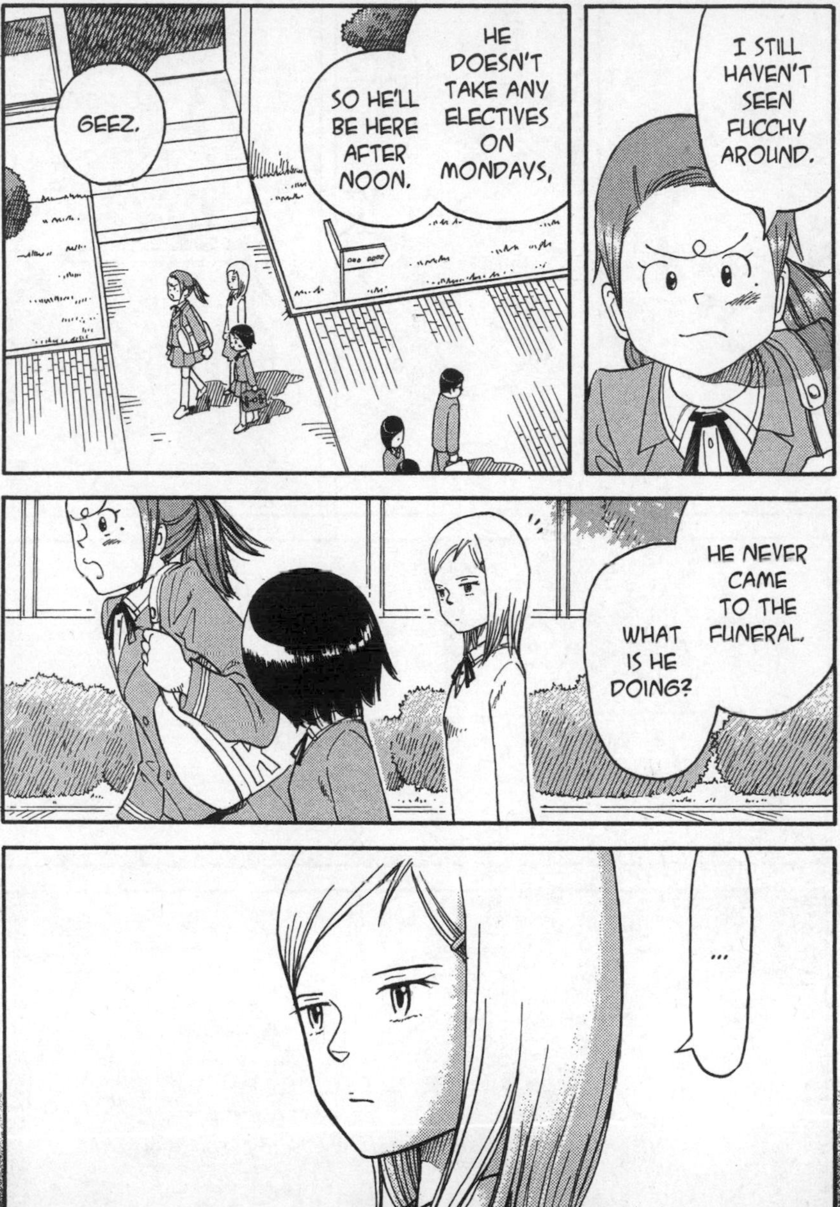
I STILL HAVEN'T SEEN FUCCHY AROUND.
HE DOESN'T TAKE ANY ELECTIVES ON MONDAYS, SO HE'LL BE HERE AFTER NOON.
GEEZ.
HE NEVER CAME TO THE FUNERAL. WHAT IS HE DOING?
...

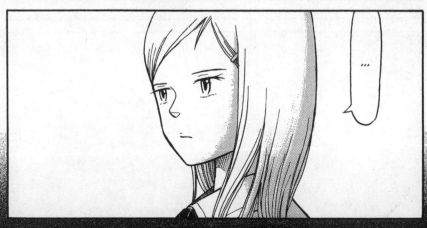

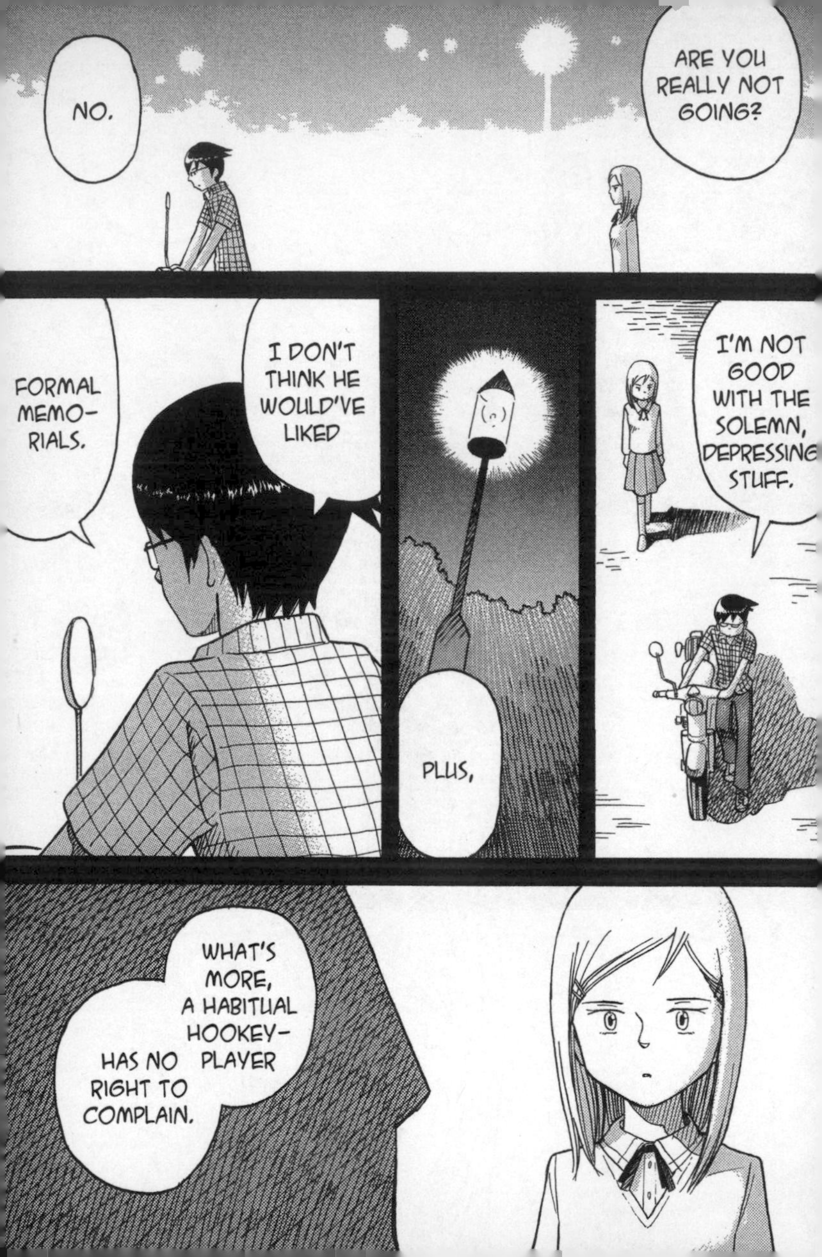
ARE YOU REALLY NOT GOING?
NO.
I'M NOT GOOD WITH THE SOLEMN, DEPRESSING STUFF.
PLUS,
I DON'T THINK HE WOULD'VE LIKED
FORMAL MEMO-RIALS.
WHAT'S MORE, A HABITUAL HOOKEY-PLAYER HAS NO RIGHT TO COMPLAIN.

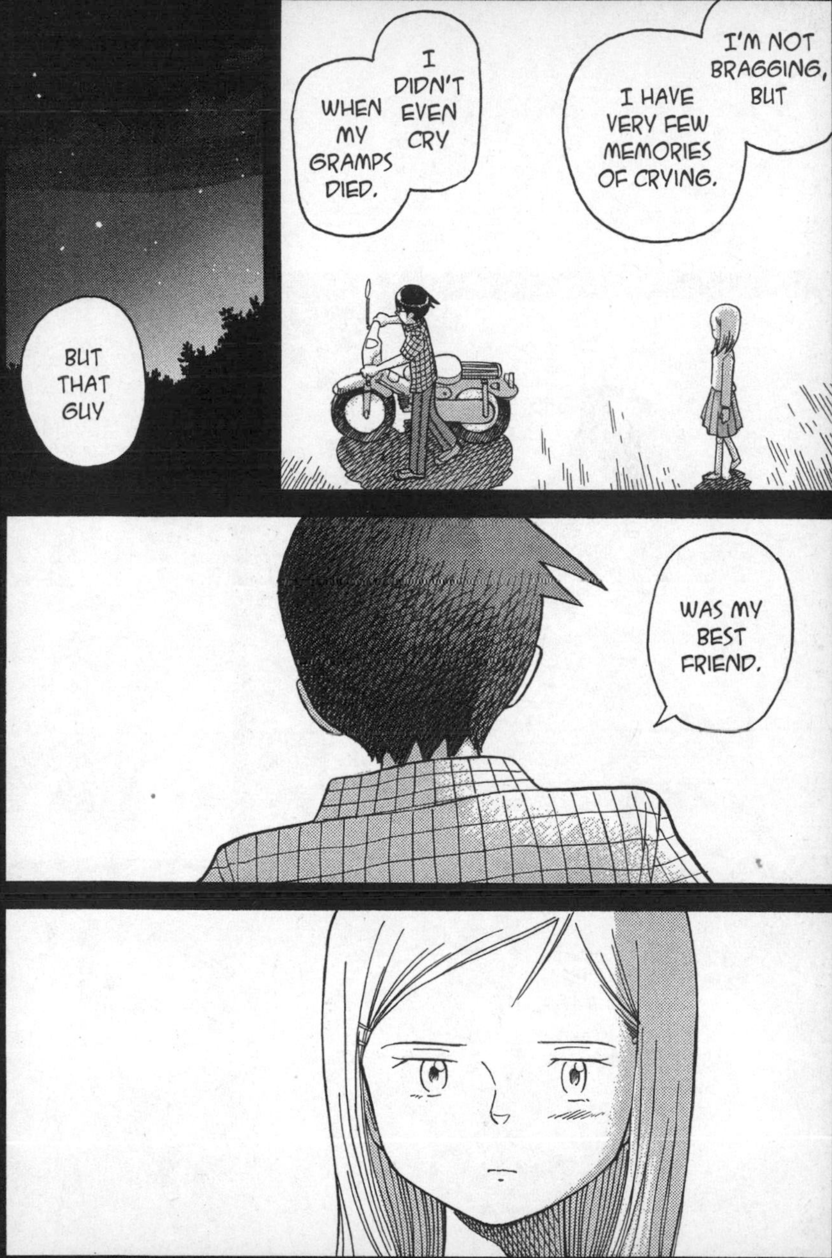
I'M NOT BRAGGING, BUT
I HAVE VERY FEW MEMORIES OF CRYING.
I DIDN'T EVEN CRY WHEN MY GRAMPS DIED.
BUT THAT GUY
WAS MY BEST FRIEND.

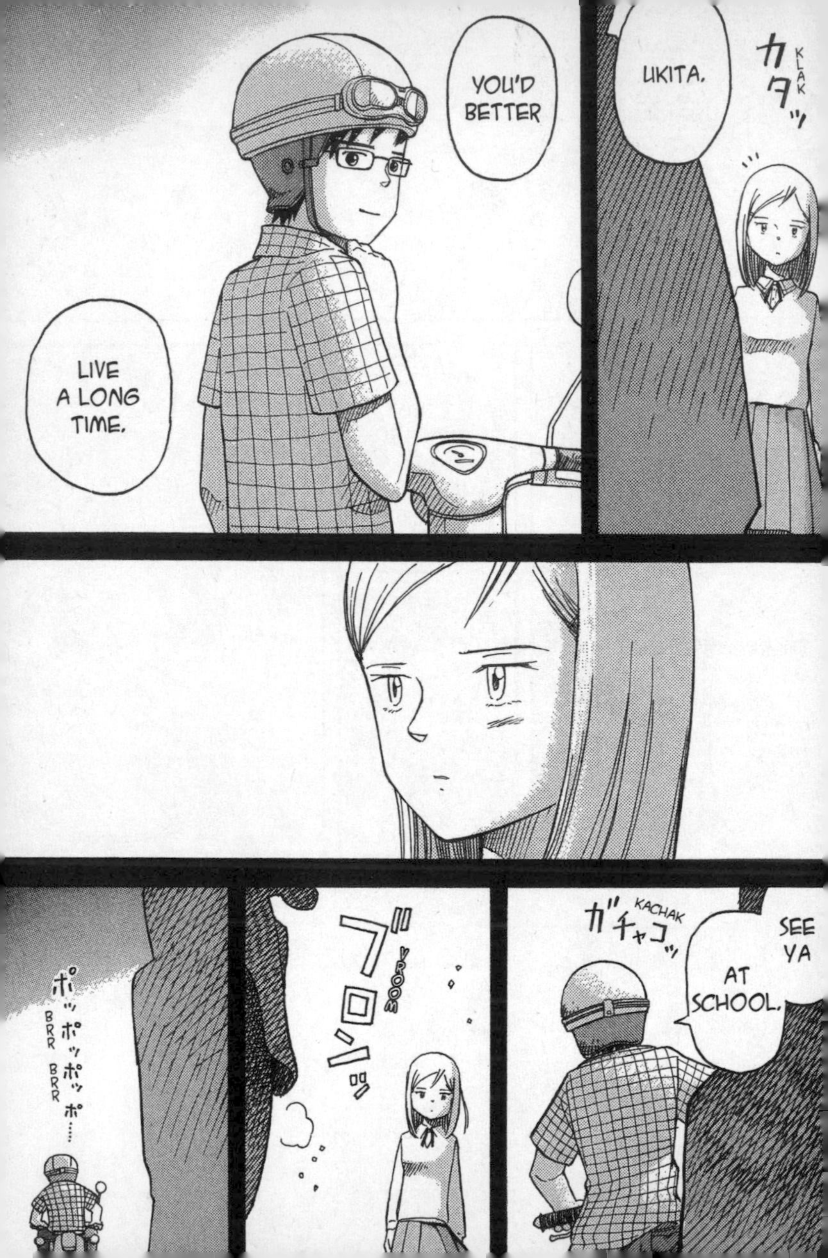
UKITA.
カタッ
KLAK
YOU'D BETTER
LIVE A LONG TIME.
ガチャコッ
KACHAK
SEE YA AT SCHOOL.
ブロン
VROOM
ポッポッポッポ……
BRR BRR

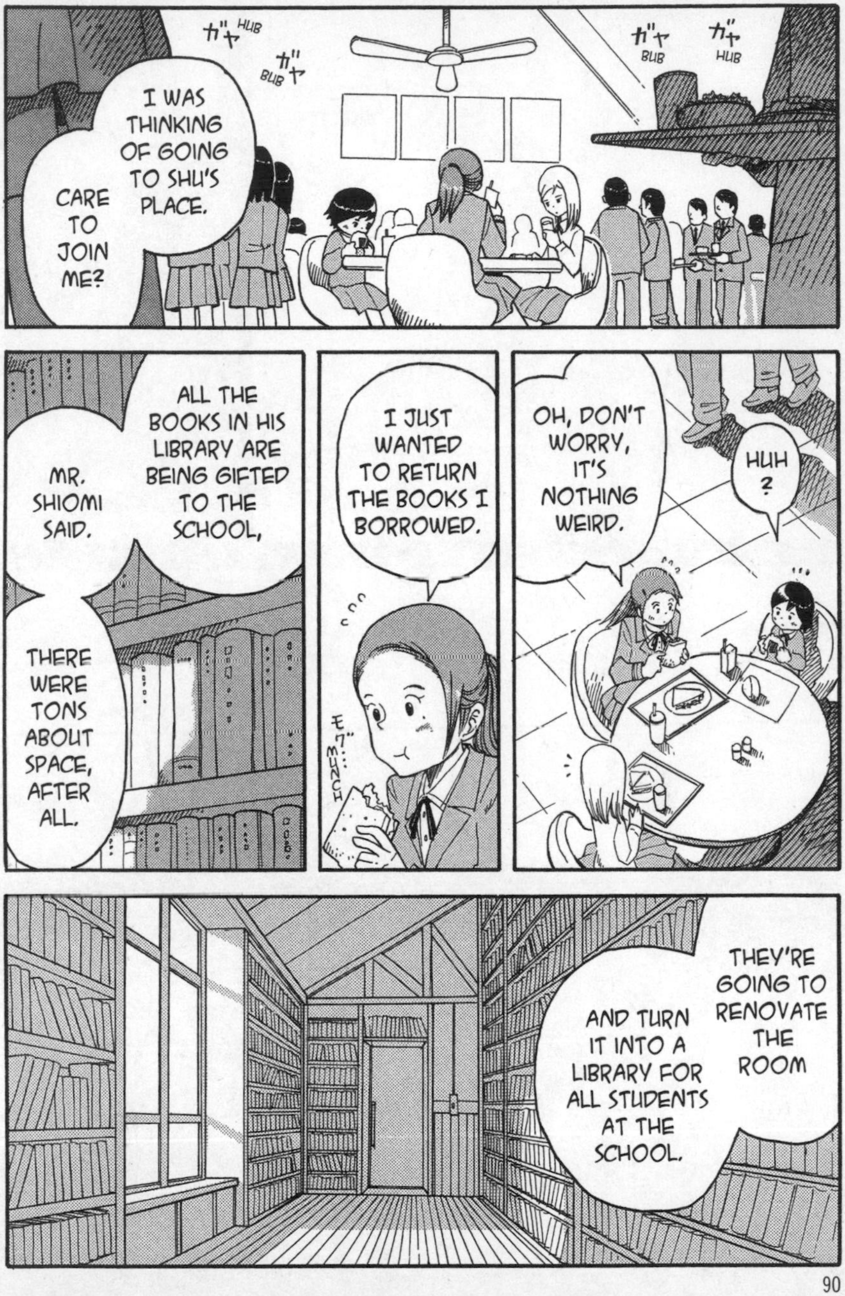
ガヤ BUB
ガヤ HUB
ガヤ HUB
ガヤ BUB
I WAS THINKING OF GOING TO SHU'S PLACE.
CARE TO JOIN ME?
HUH?
OH, DON'T WORRY, IT'S NOTHING WEIRD.
I JUST WANTED TO RETURN THE BOOKS I BORROWED.
モグ MUNCH
ALL THE BOOKS IN HIS LIBRARY ARE BEING GIFTED TO THE SCHOOL,
MR. SHIOMI SAID.
THERE WERE TONS ABOUT SPACE, AFTER ALL.
THEY'RE GOING TO RENOVATE THE ROOM
AND TURN IT INTO A LIBRARY FOR ALL STUDENTS AT THE SCHOOL.

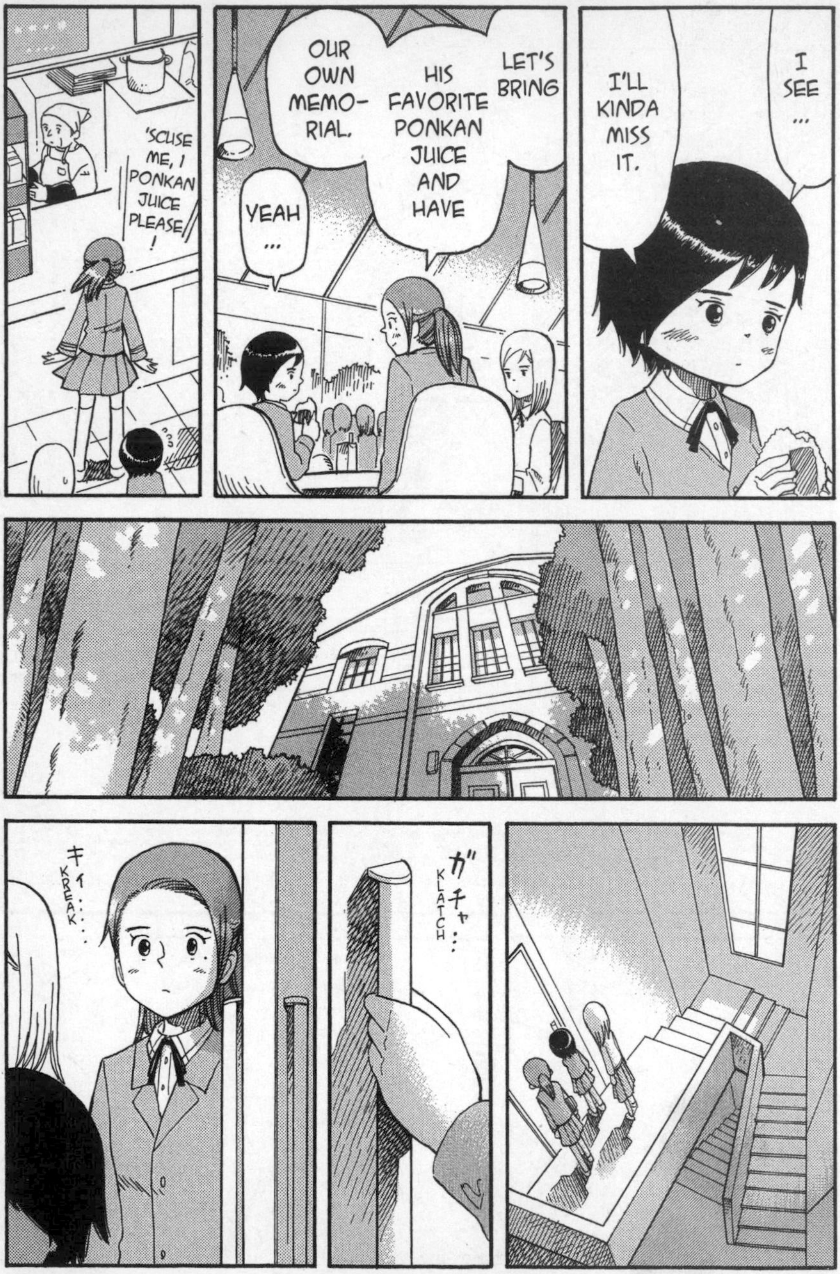
I SEE ...
I'LL KINDA MISS IT.
LET'S BRING HIS FAVORITE PONKAN JUICE AND HAVE OUR OWN MEMORIAL.
YEAH ...
'SCUSE ME, I PONKAN JUICE PLEASE!
ガチャ...
KLATCH
キィ...
KREAK

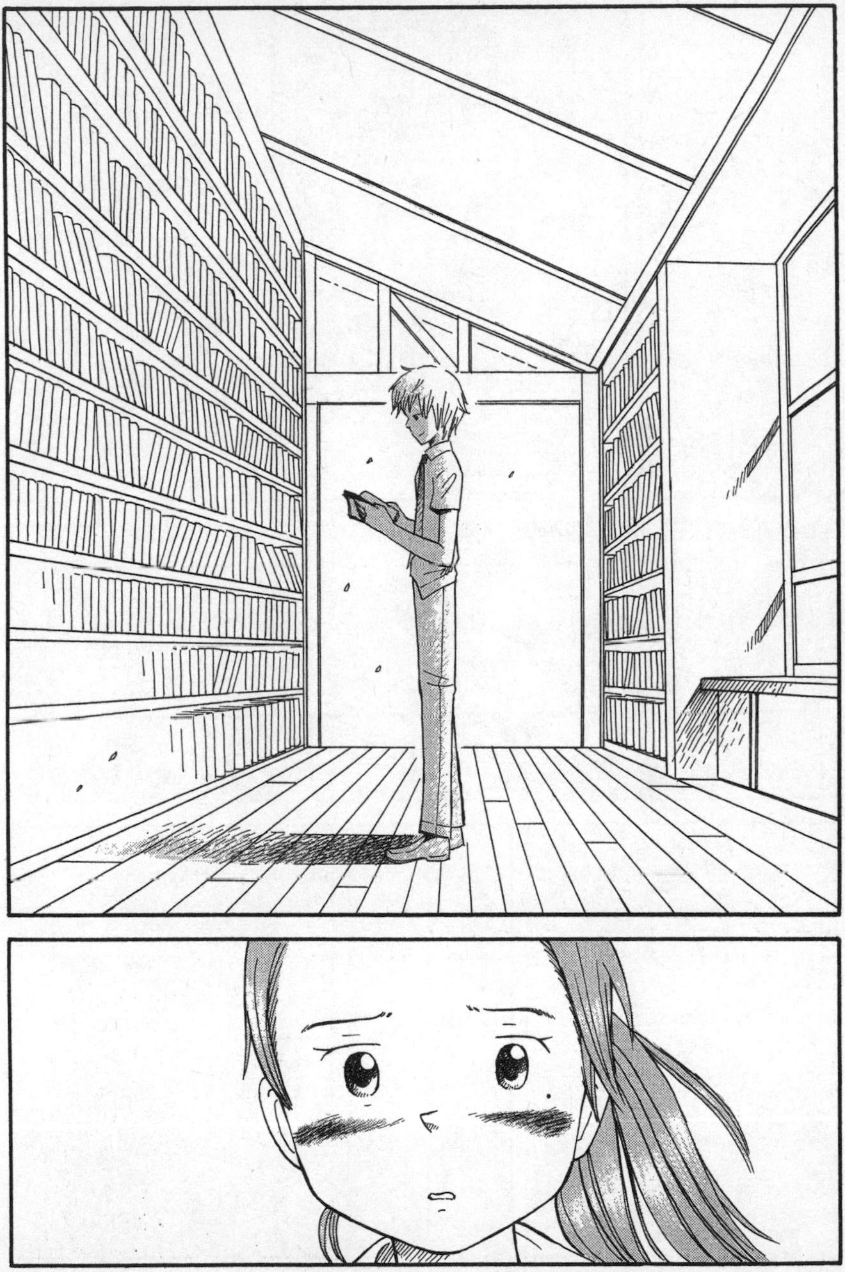

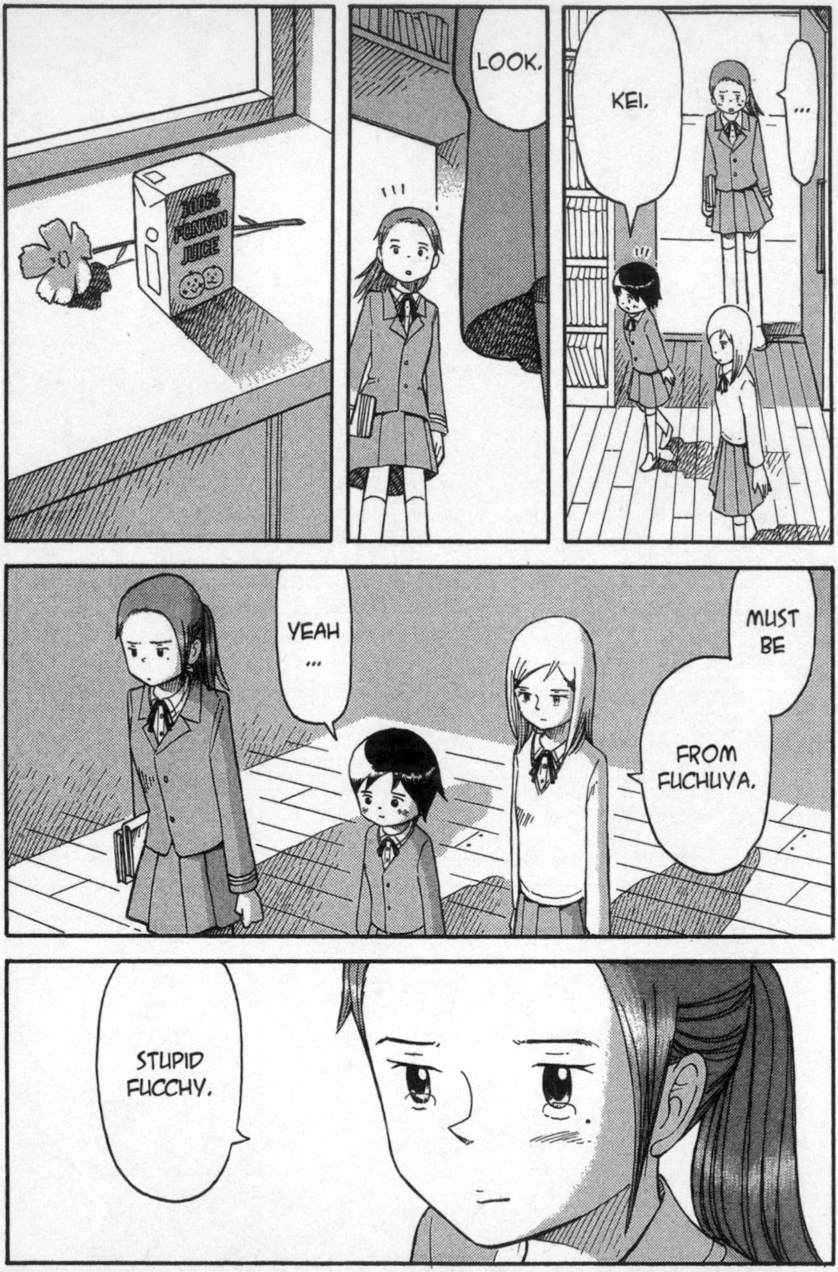
...
KEI.
LOOK.
100% PONKAN JUICE
MUST BE FROM FUCHUYA.
YEAH ...
STUPID FUCCHY.

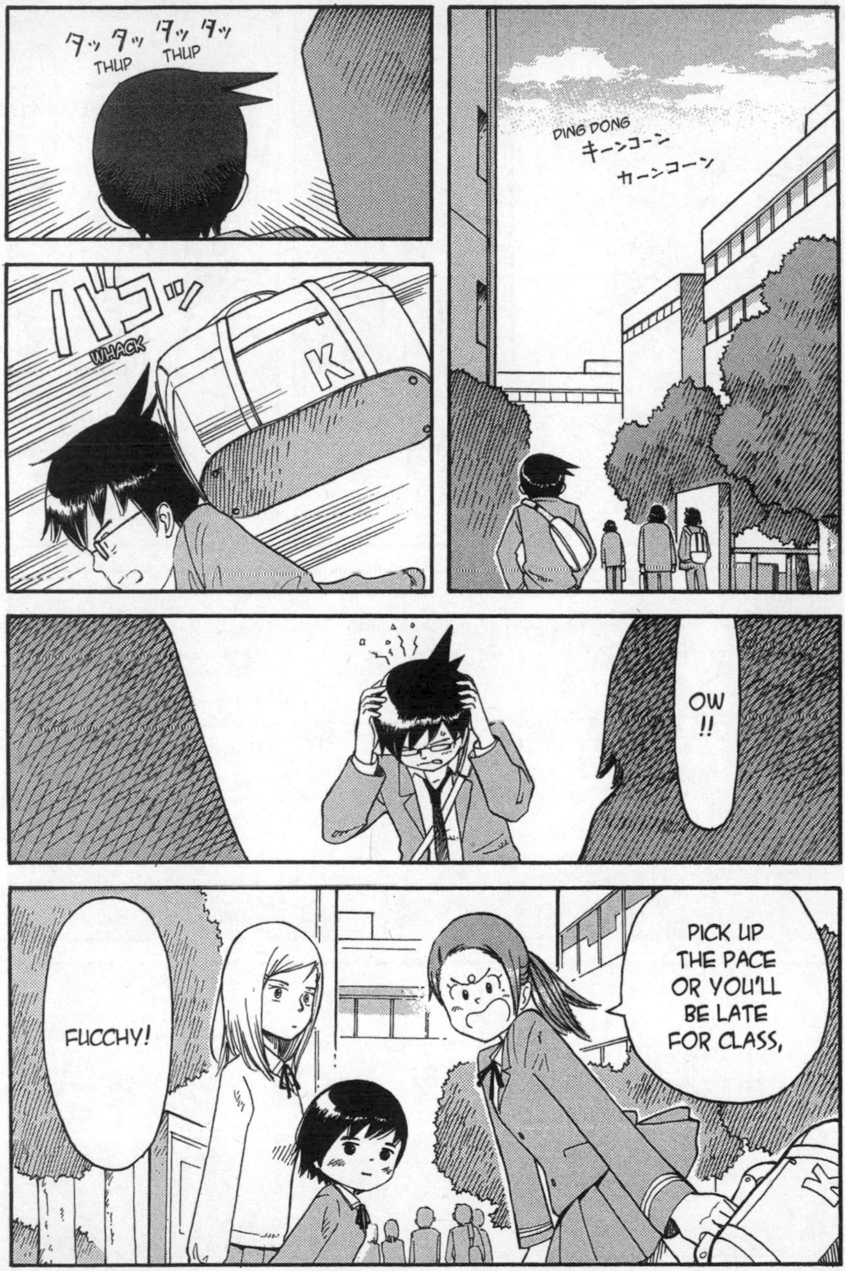
DING DONG
キーンコーン
カーンコーン
タッタッ タッタッ
THUP THUP
バコッ
WHACK
OW !!
PICK UP THE PACE OR YOU'LL BE LATE FOR CLASS,
FUCCHY!

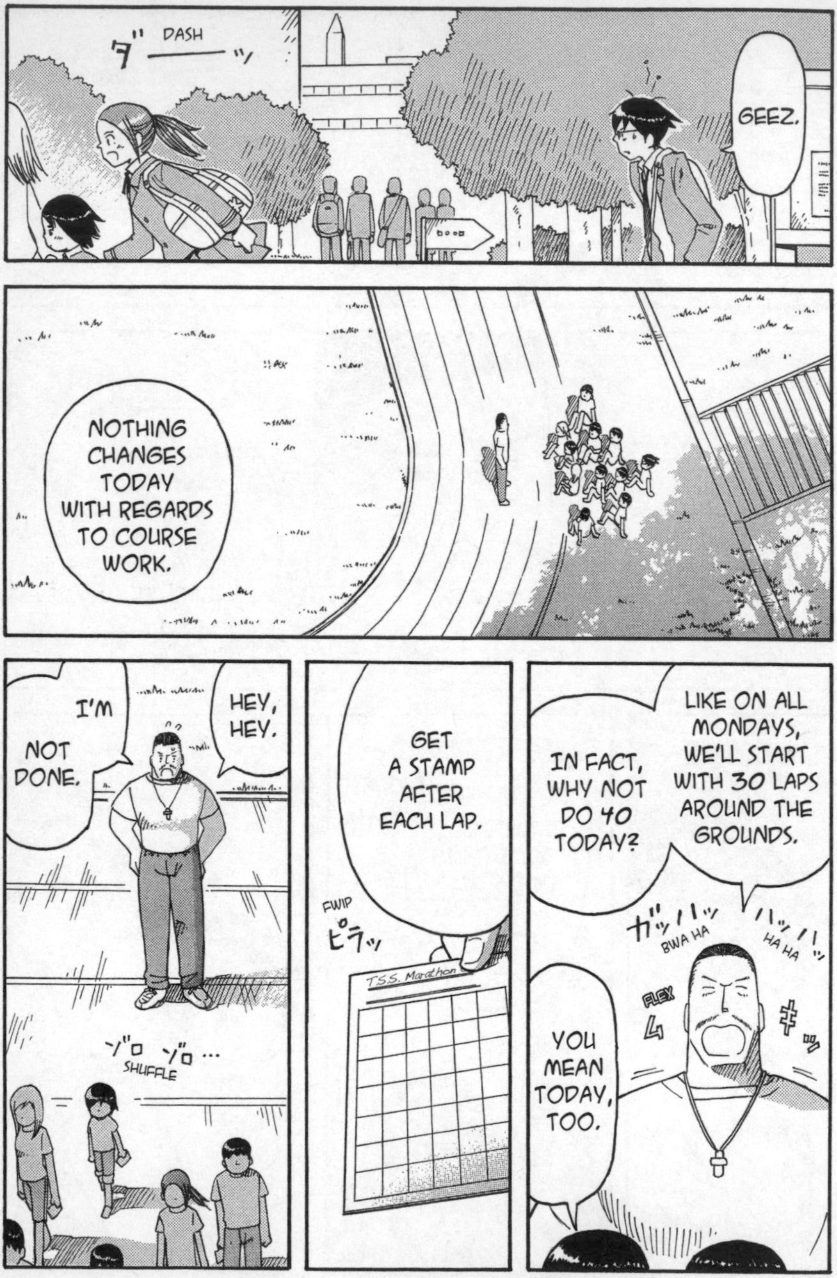
GEEZ.
ダーッ
DASH
NOTHING CHANGES TODAY WITH REGARDS TO COURSE WORK.
LIKE ON ALL MONDAYS, WE'LL START WITH 30 LAPS AROUND THE GROUNDS.
IN FACT, WHY NOT DO 40 TODAY?
ハッハッ
HA HA
ガッハッ
BWA HA
ムキッ
FLEX
YOU MEAN TODAY, TOO.
GET A STAMP AFTER EACH LAP.
ピラッ
FWIP
T.S.S. Marathon
HEY, HEY.
I'M NOT DONE.
ゾロゾロ…
SHUFFLE

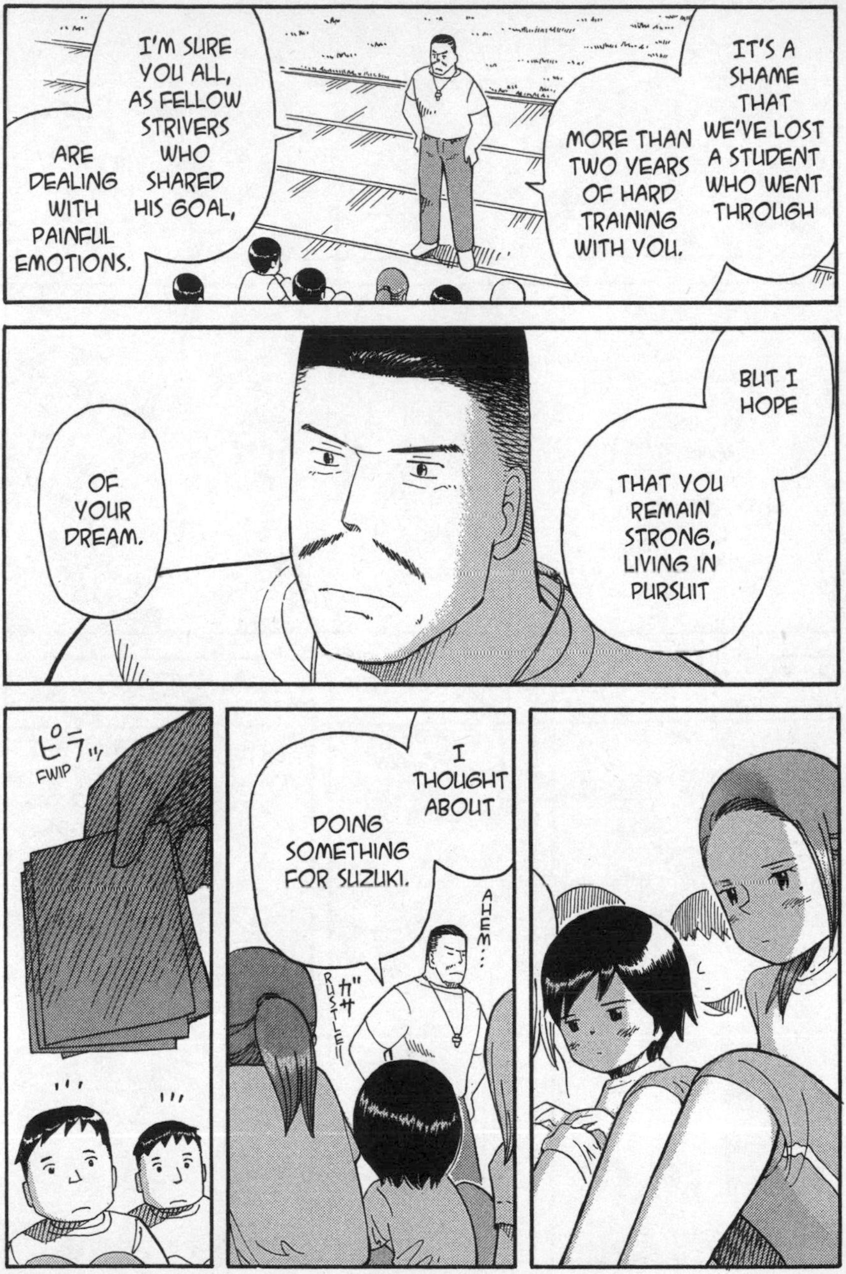
IT'S A SHAME THAT WE'VE LOST A STUDENT WHO WENT THROUGH
MORE THAN TWO YEARS OF HARD TRAINING WITH YOU.
I'M SURE YOU ALL, AS FELLOW STRIVERS WHO SHARED HIS GOAL,
ARE DEALING WITH PAINFUL EMOTIONS.
BUT I HOPE
THAT YOU REMAIN STRONG, LIVING IN PURSUIT
OF YOUR DREAM.
I THOUGHT ABOUT
DOING SOMETHING FOR SUZUKI.
AHEM...
ガサ
RUSTLE!!
ピラッ
FWIP

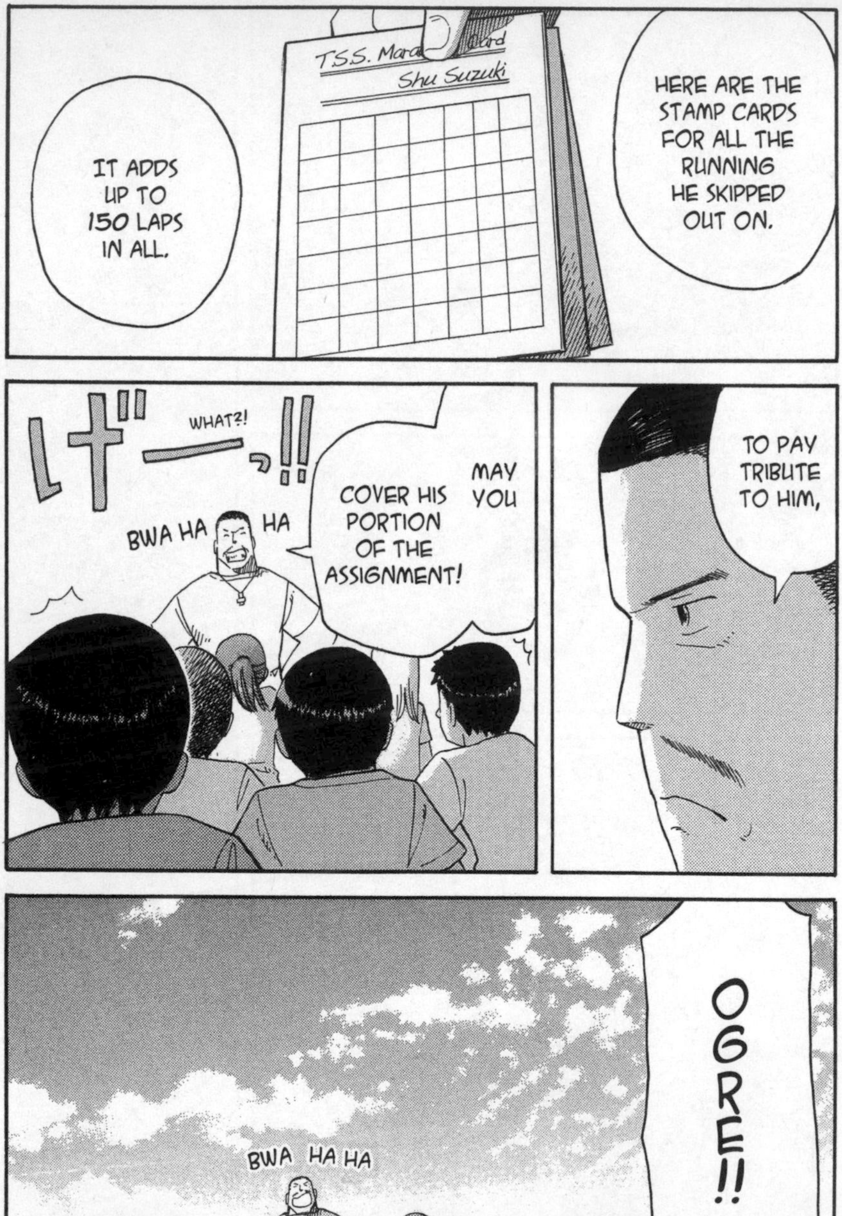
HERE ARE THE STAMP CARDS FOR ALL THE RUNNING HE SKIPPED OUT ON.
Shu Suzuki
IT ADDS UP TO 150 LAPS IN ALL.
TO PAY TRIBUTE TO HIM,
MAY YOU COVER HIS PORTION OF THE ASSIGNMENT!
BWA HA HA
げーっ!!
WHAT?!
OGRE!!
BWA HA HA

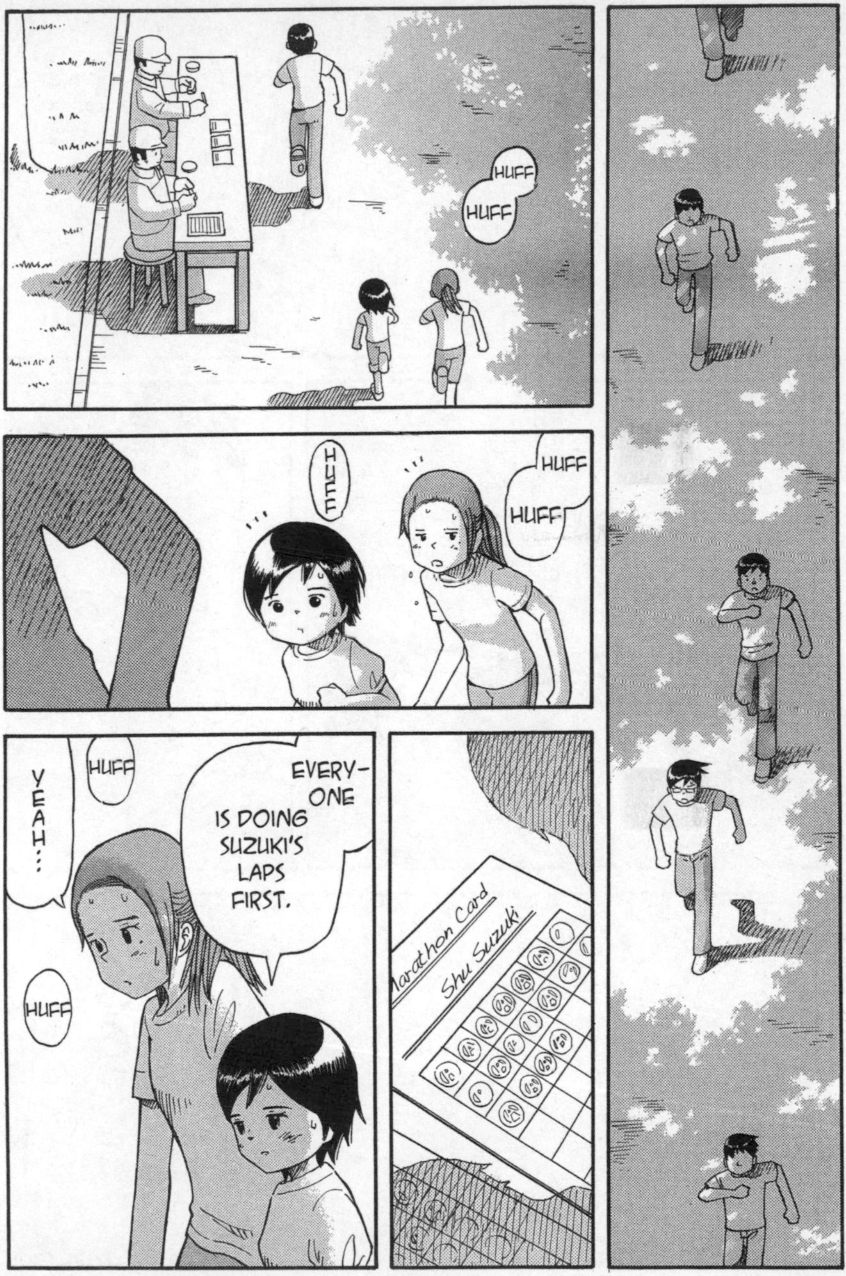
HUFF
HUFF
HUFF
HUFF
HUFF
Marathon Card
Shu Suzuki
EVERY-ONE IS DOING SUZUKI'S LAPS FIRST.
HUFF
YEAH...
HUFF

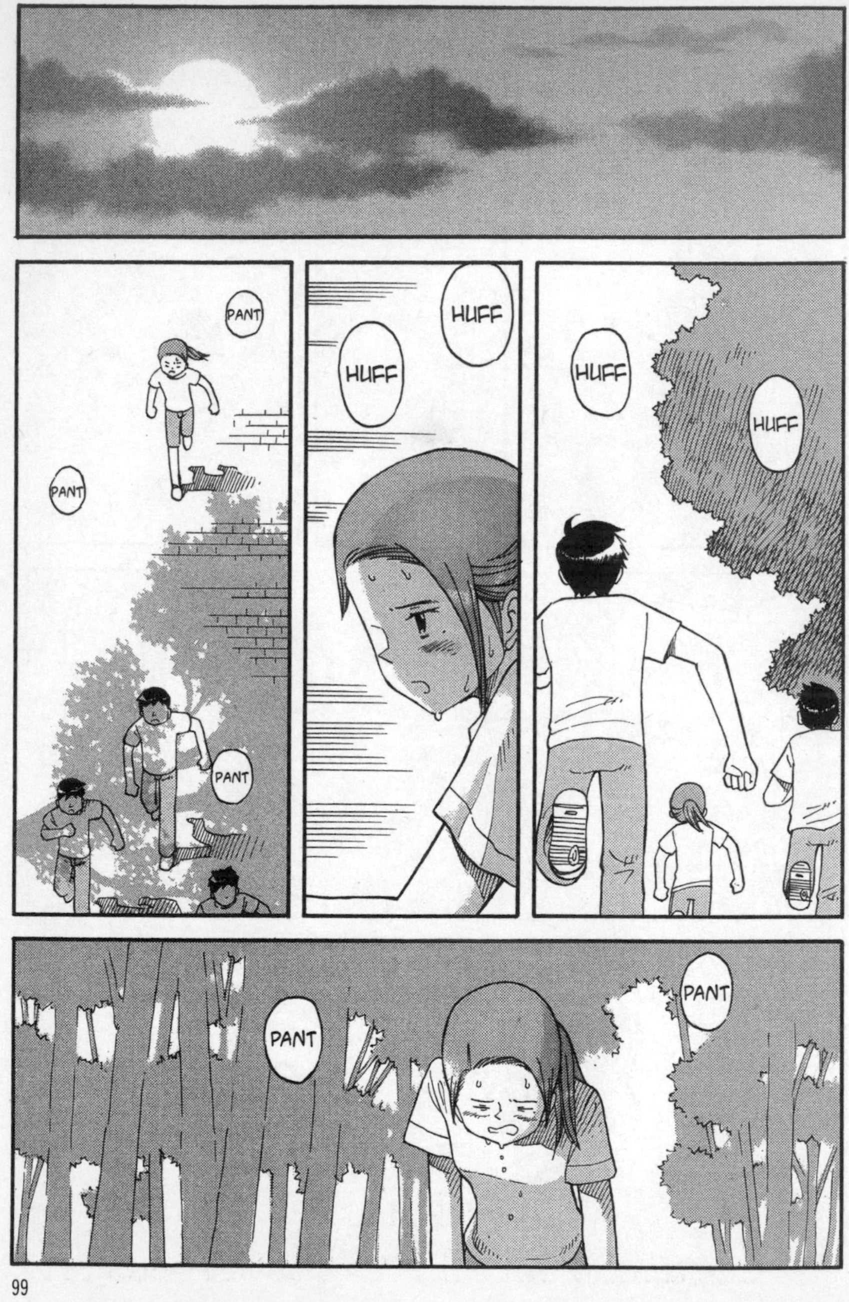
HUFF
HUFF
HUFF
HUFF
PANT
PANT
PANT
PANT
PANT

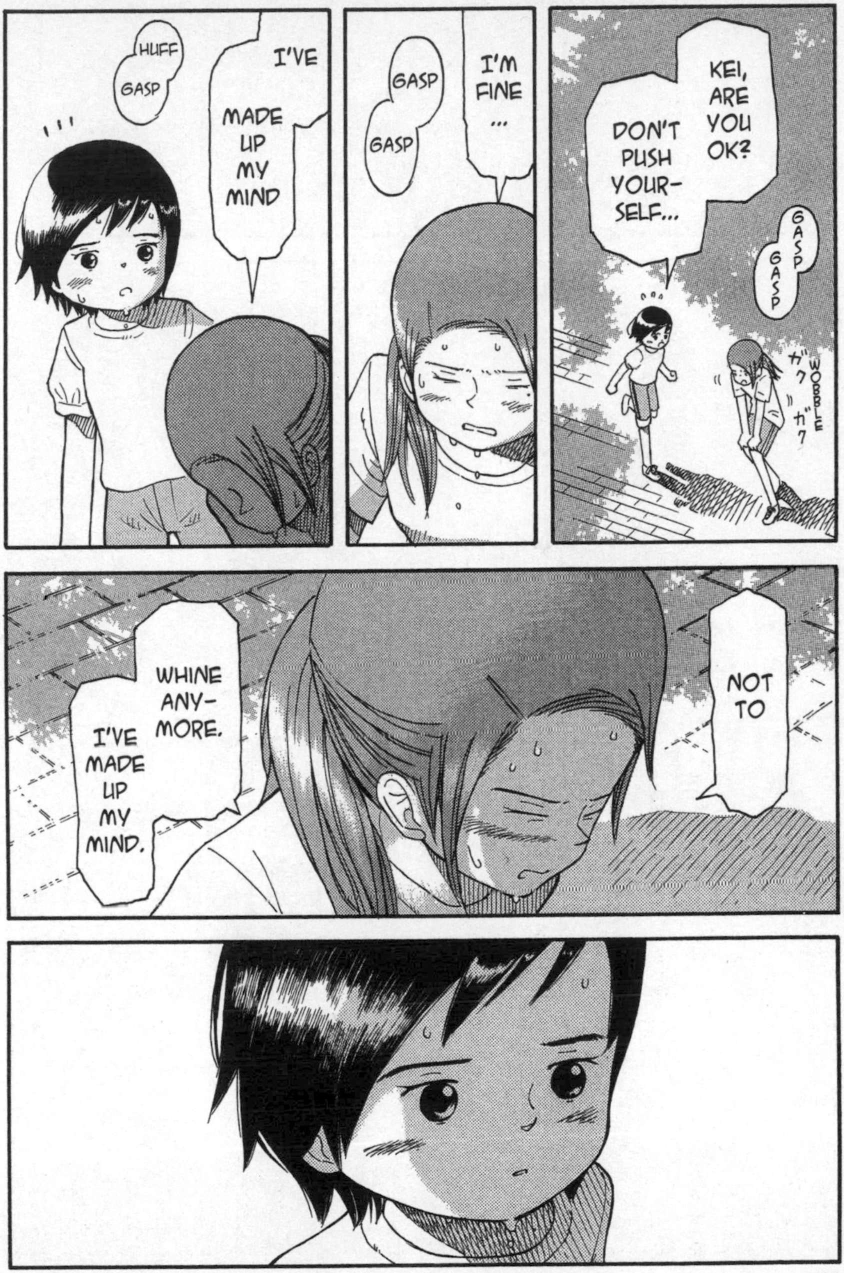
KEI, ARE YOU OK?
DON'T PUSH YOUR-SELF...
GASP GASP
ガク ガク
WOBBLE
I'M FINE ...
GASP
GASP
I'VE MADE UP MY MIND
HUFF
GASP
NOT TO
WHINE ANY-MORE.
I'VE MADE UP MY MIND.

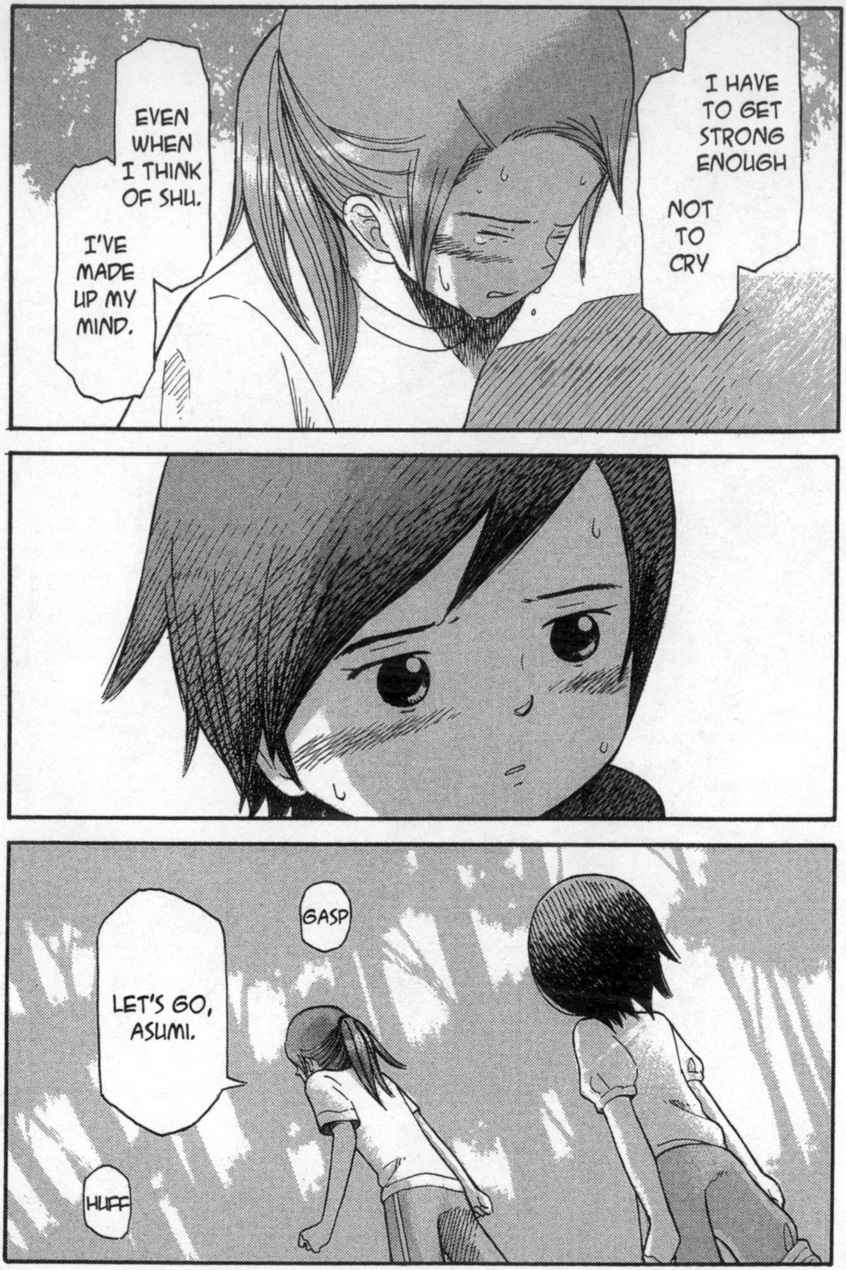
I HAVE TO GET STRONG ENOUGH
NOT TO CRY
EVEN WHEN I THINK OF SHU.
I'VE MADE UP MY MIND.
GASP
LET'S GO, ASUMI.
HUFF

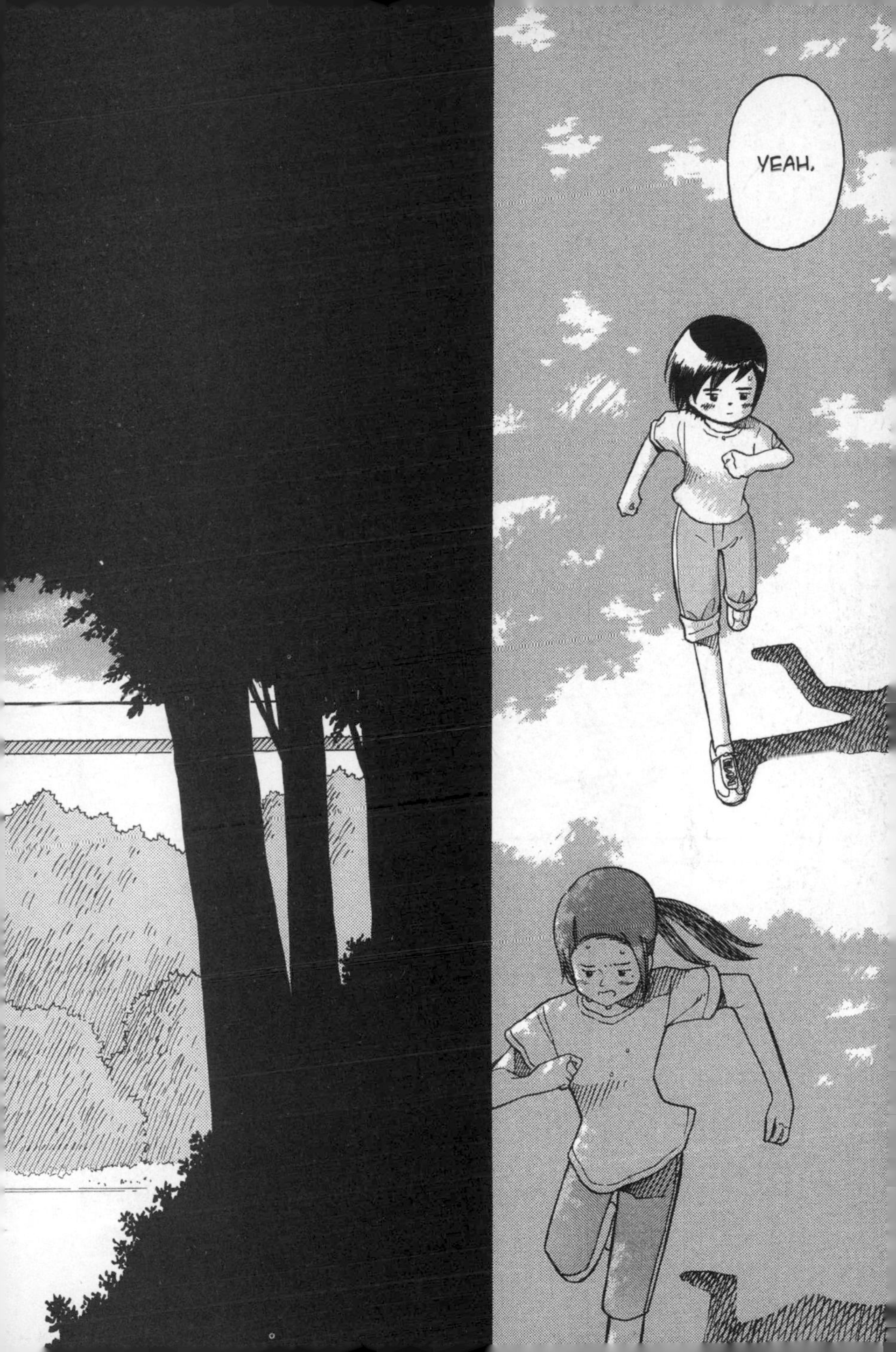
YEAH.

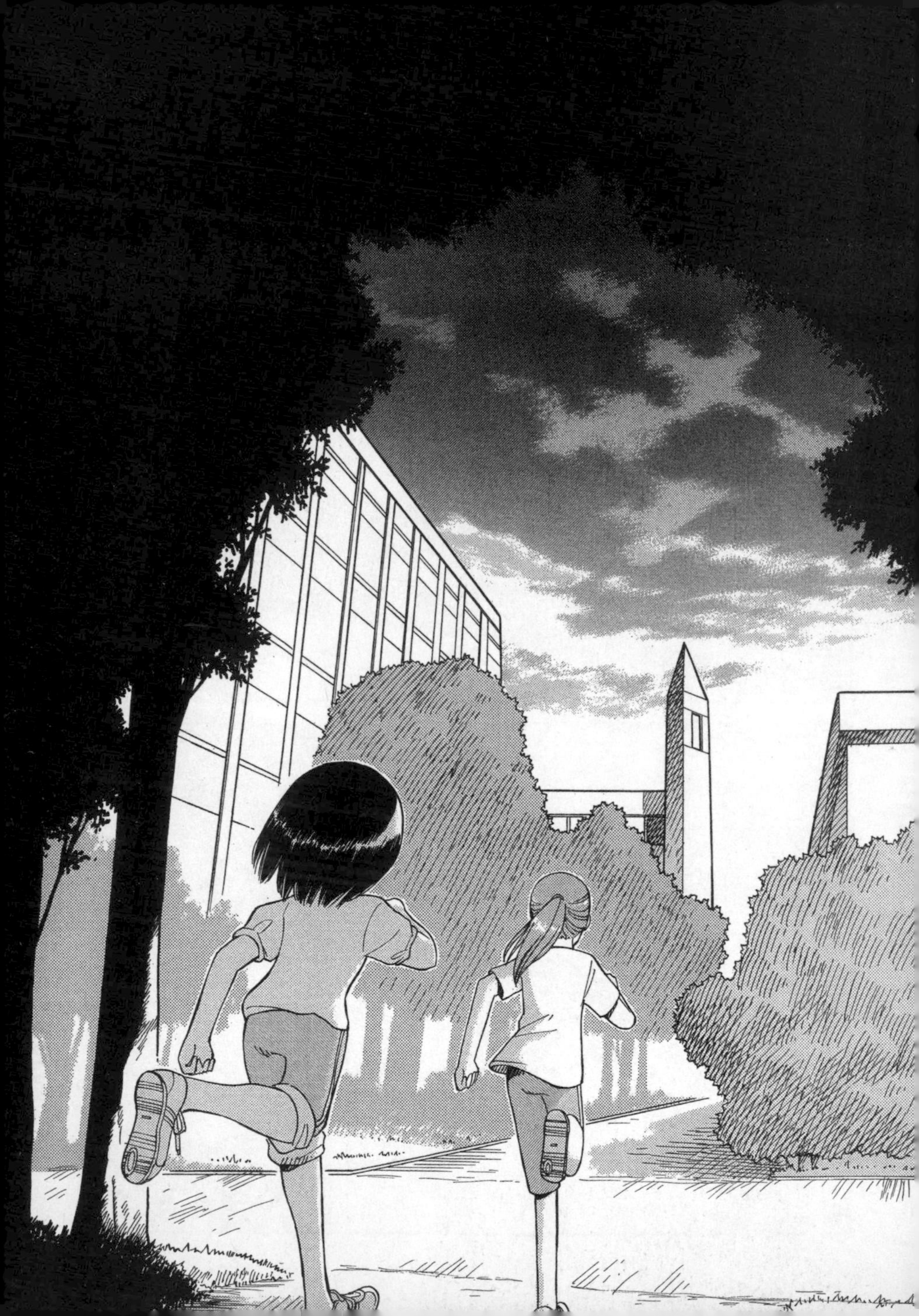

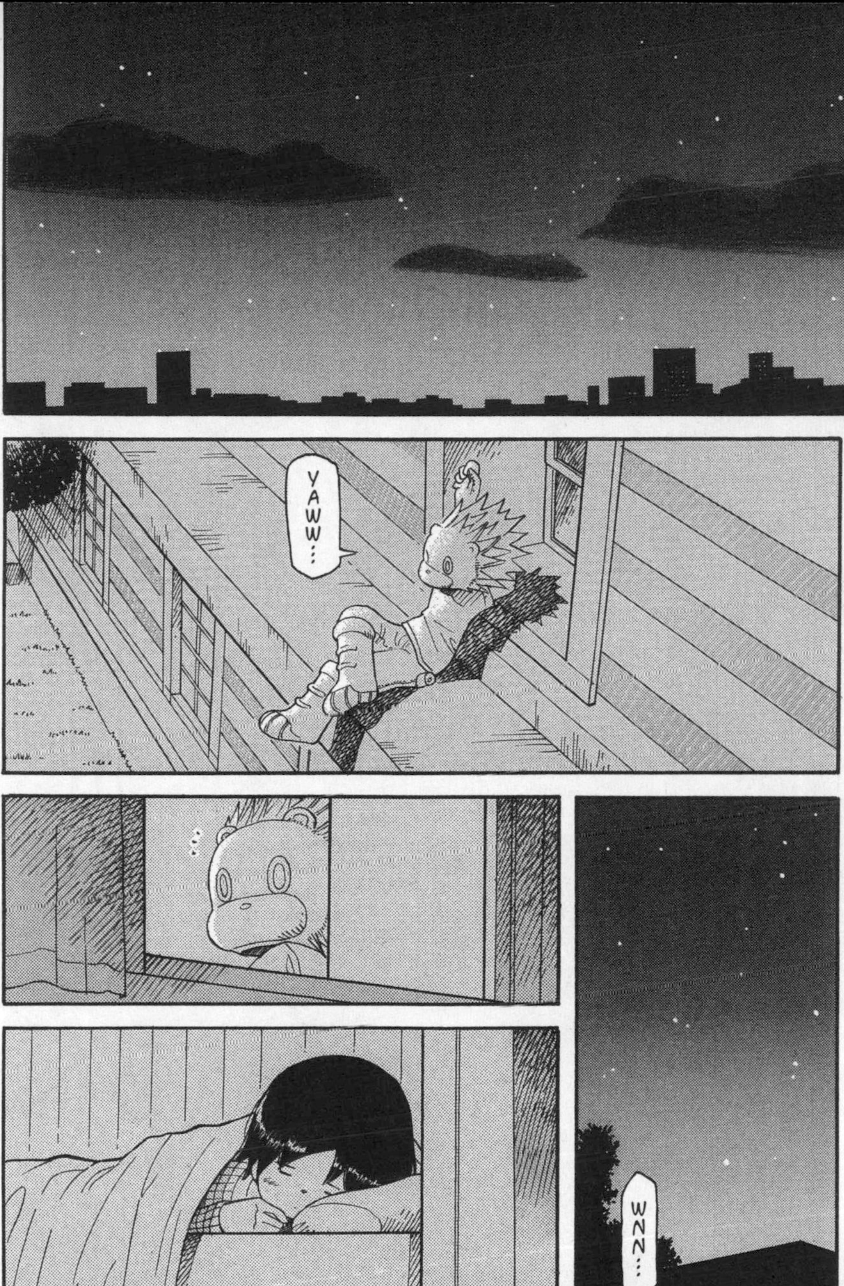
YAWW...
WNN...

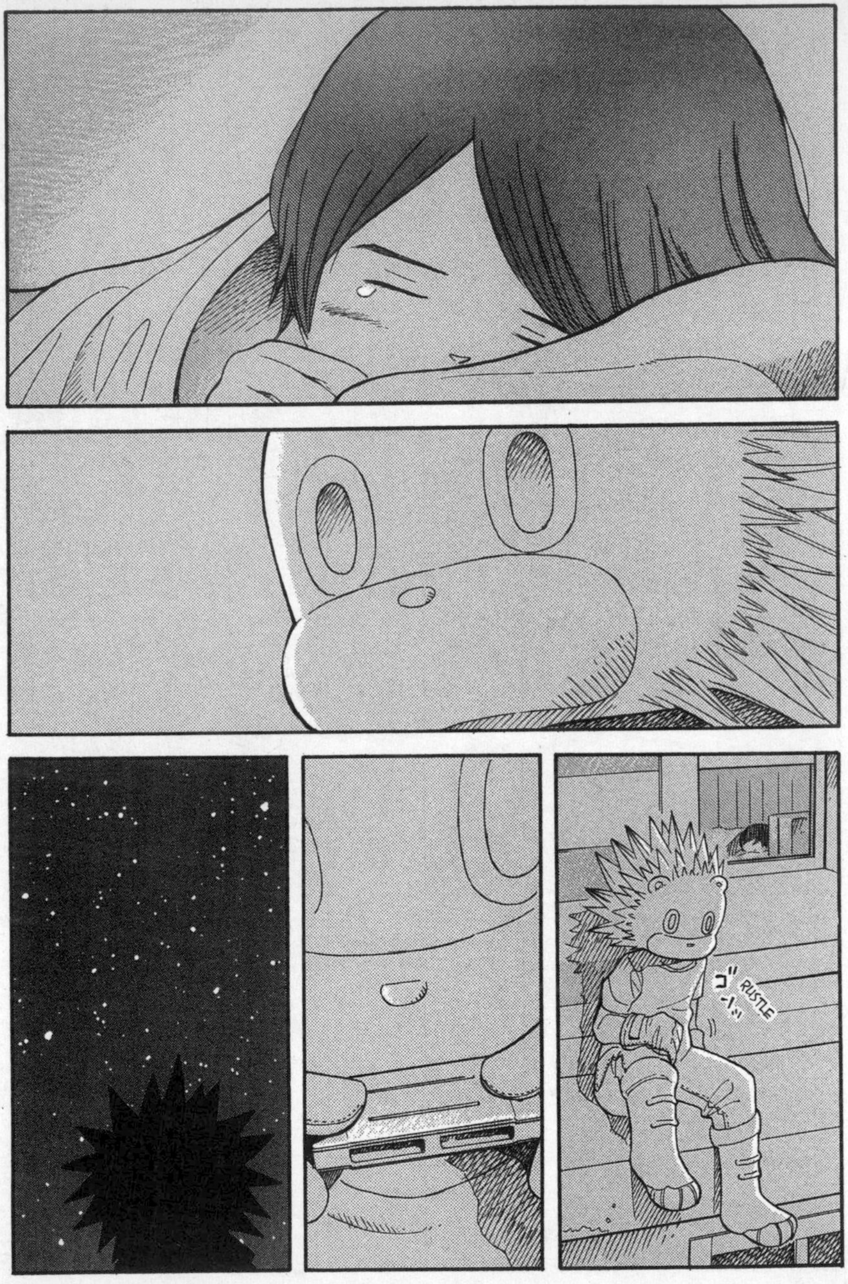
ゴソッ
RUSTLE

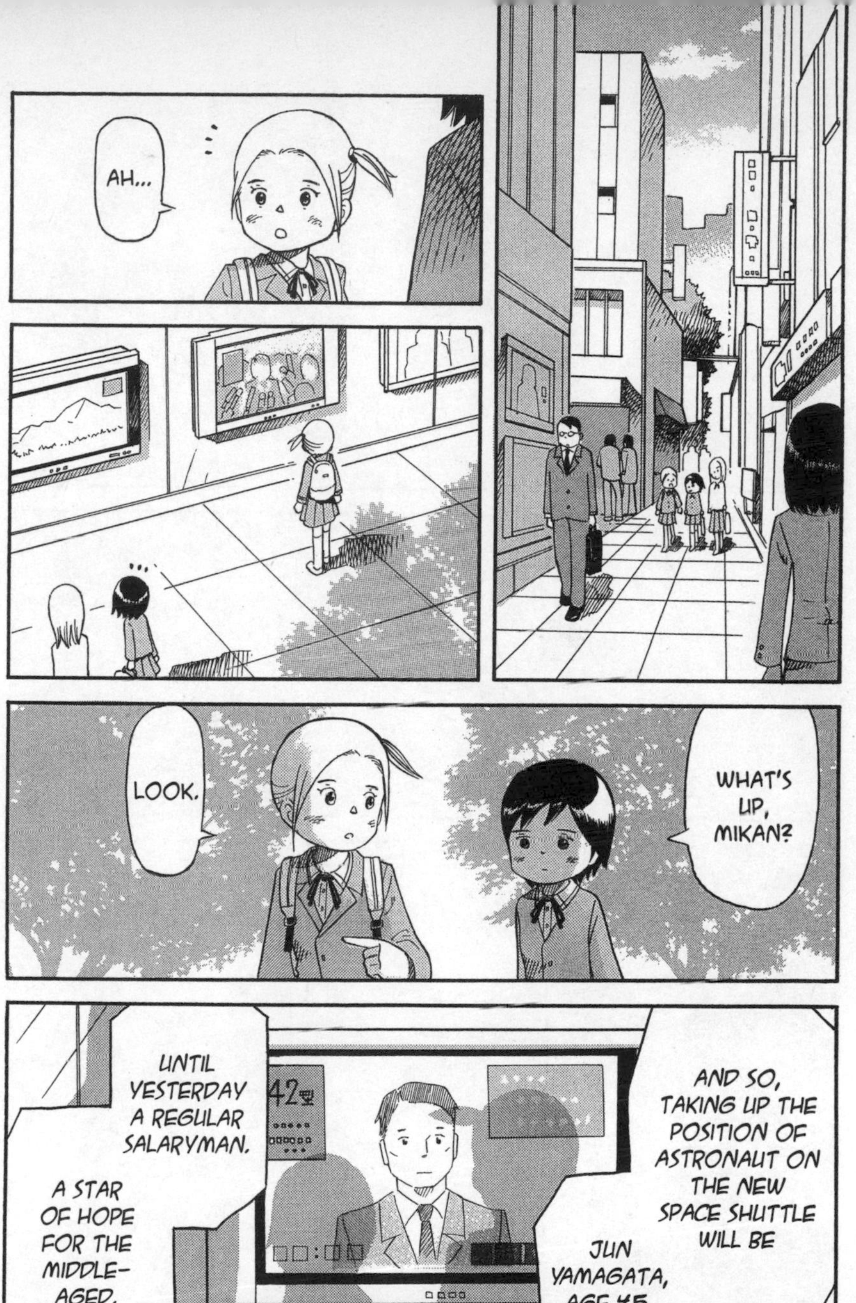
AH...
WHAT'S UP, MIKAN?
LOOK.
AND SO, TAKING UP THE POSITION OF ASTRONAUT ON THE NEW SPACE SHUTTLE WILL BE
JUN YAMAGATA, AGE 45,
UNTIL YESTERDAY A REGULAR SALARYMAN.
A STAR OF HOPE FOR THE MIDDLE-AGED.

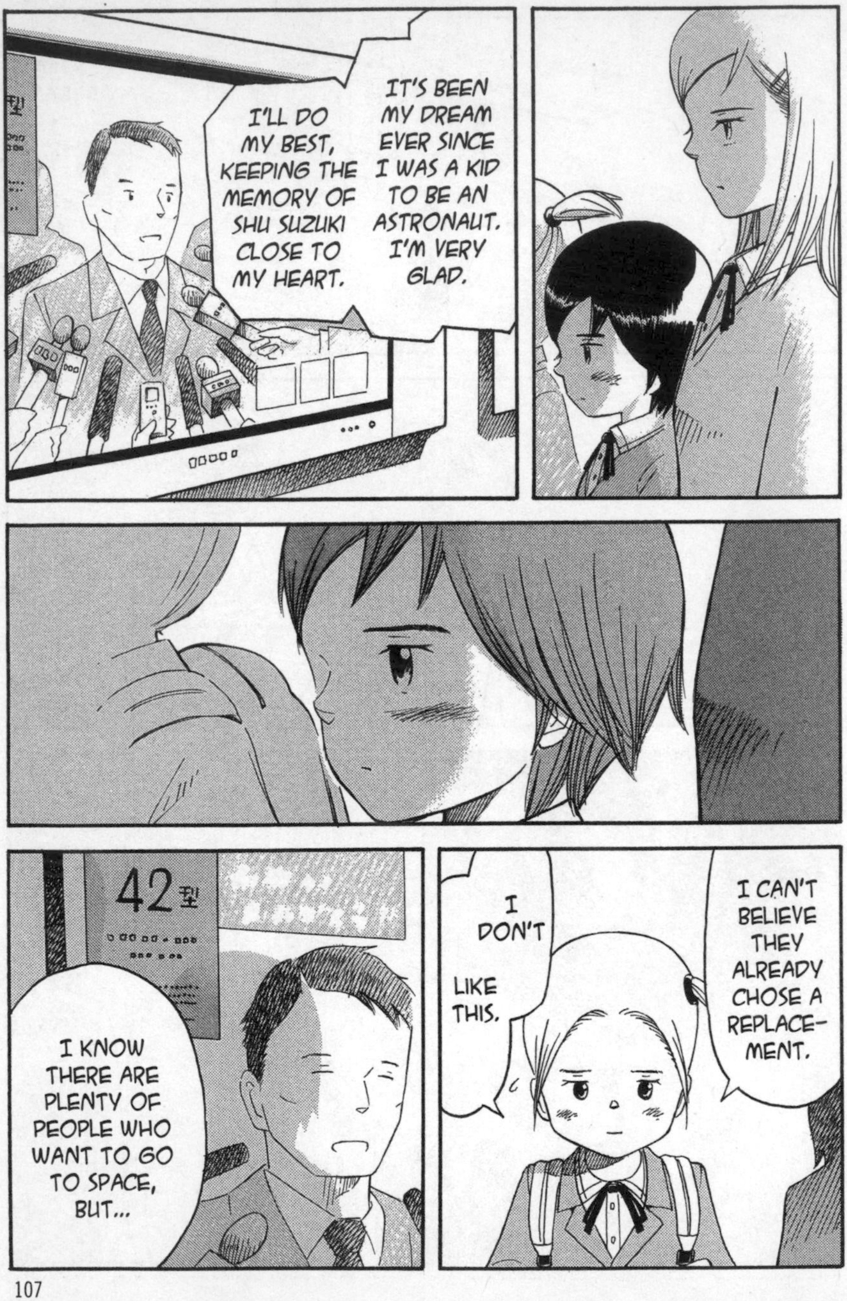
IT'S BEEN MY DREAM EVER SINCE I WAS A KID TO BE AN ASTRONAUT. I'M VERY GLAD.
I'LL DO MY BEST, KEEPING THE MEMORY OF SHU SUZUKI CLOSE TO MY HEART.
I CAN'T BELIEVE THEY ALREADY CHOSE A REPLACE-MENT.
I DON'T
LIKE THIS.
I KNOW THERE ARE PLENTY OF PEOPLE WHO WANT TO GO TO SPACE, BUT...

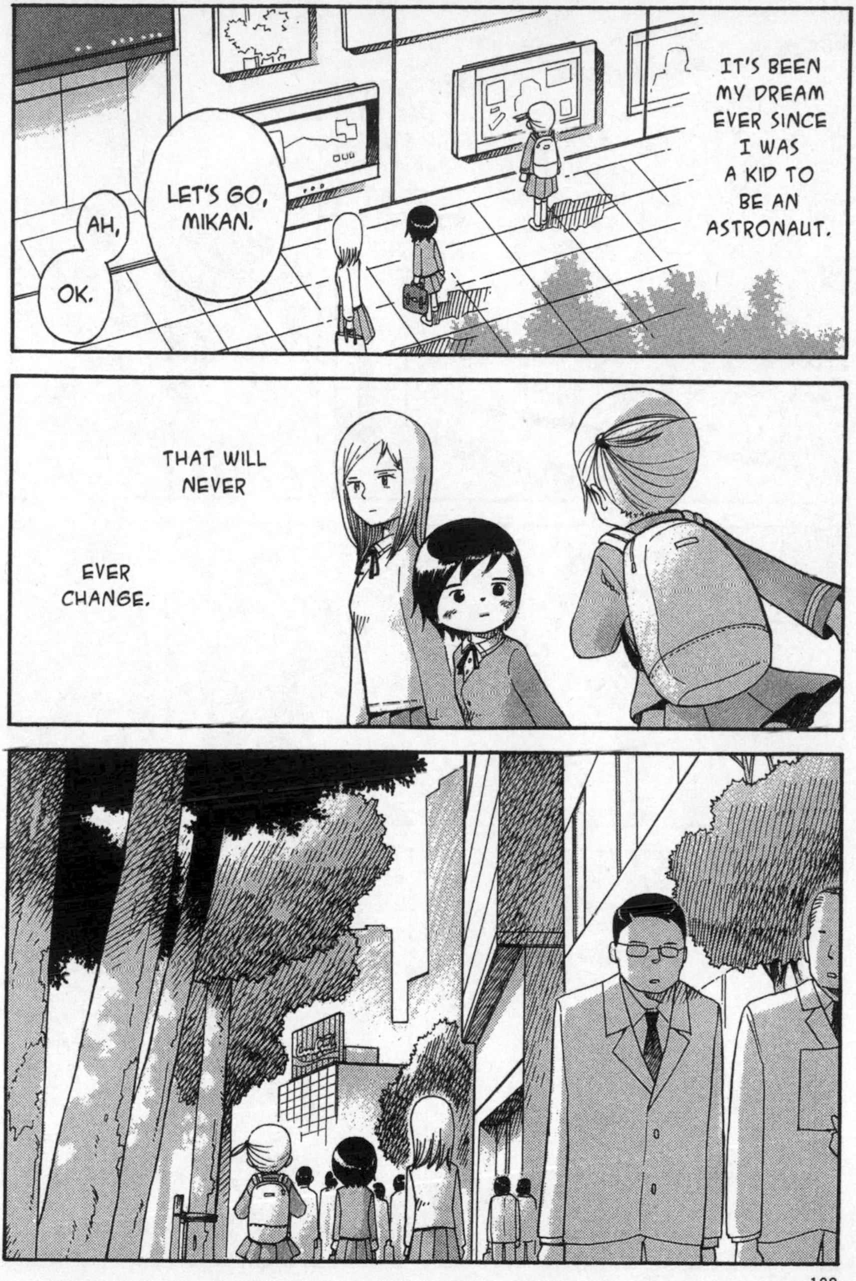
IT'S BEEN MY DREAM EVER SINCE I WAS A KID TO BE AN ASTRONAUT.
LET'S GO, MIKAN.
AH,
OK.
THAT WILL NEVER
EVER CHANGE.

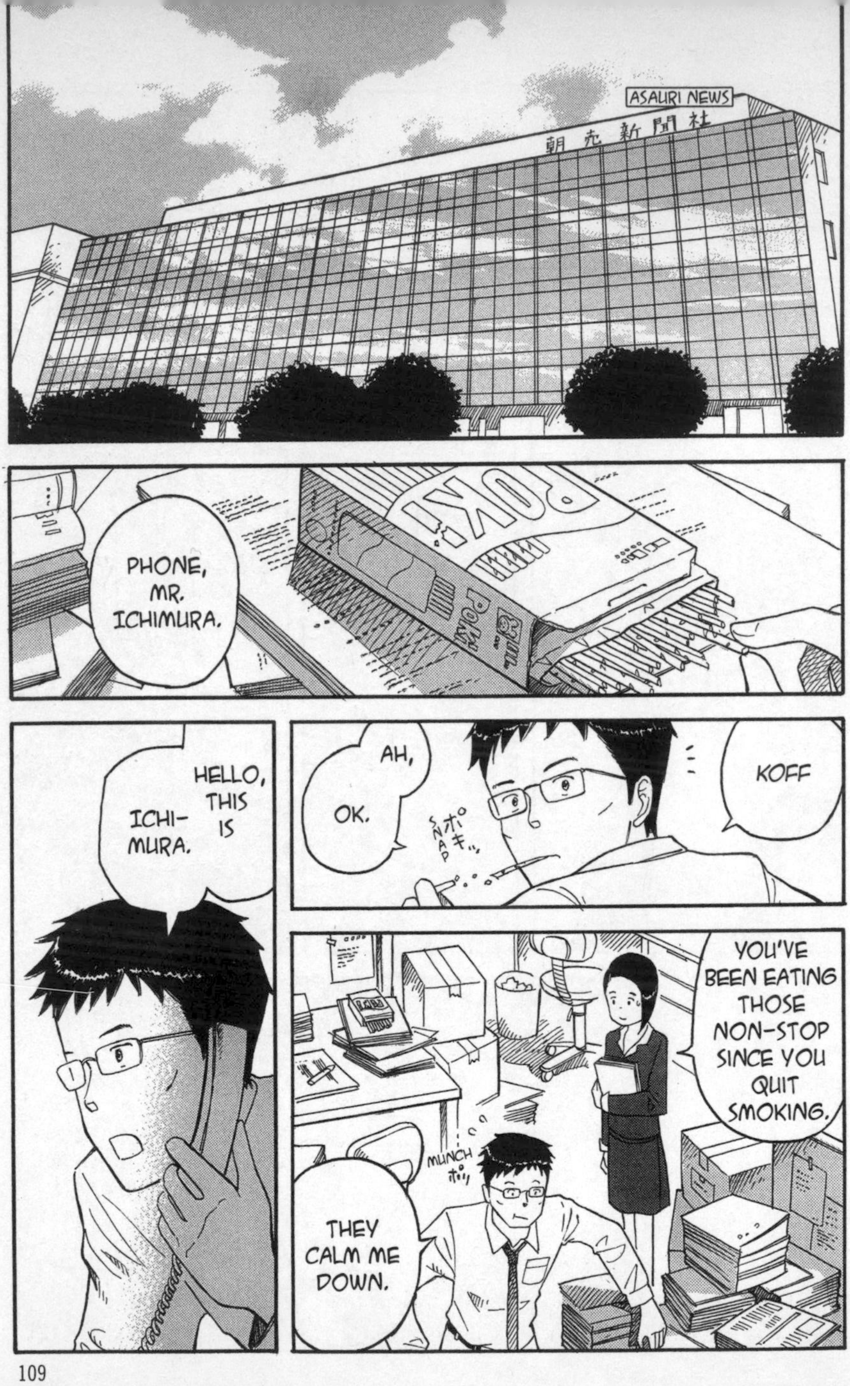
ASAURI NEWS
朝売新聞社
PHONE, MR. ICHIMURA.
POKI
POKI
KOFF
AH, OK.
SNAP ポキッ
YOU'VE BEEN EATING THOSE NON-STOP SINCE YOU QUIT SMOKING.
MUNCH ポリ
THEY CALM ME DOWN.
HELLO, THIS IS ICHIMURA.

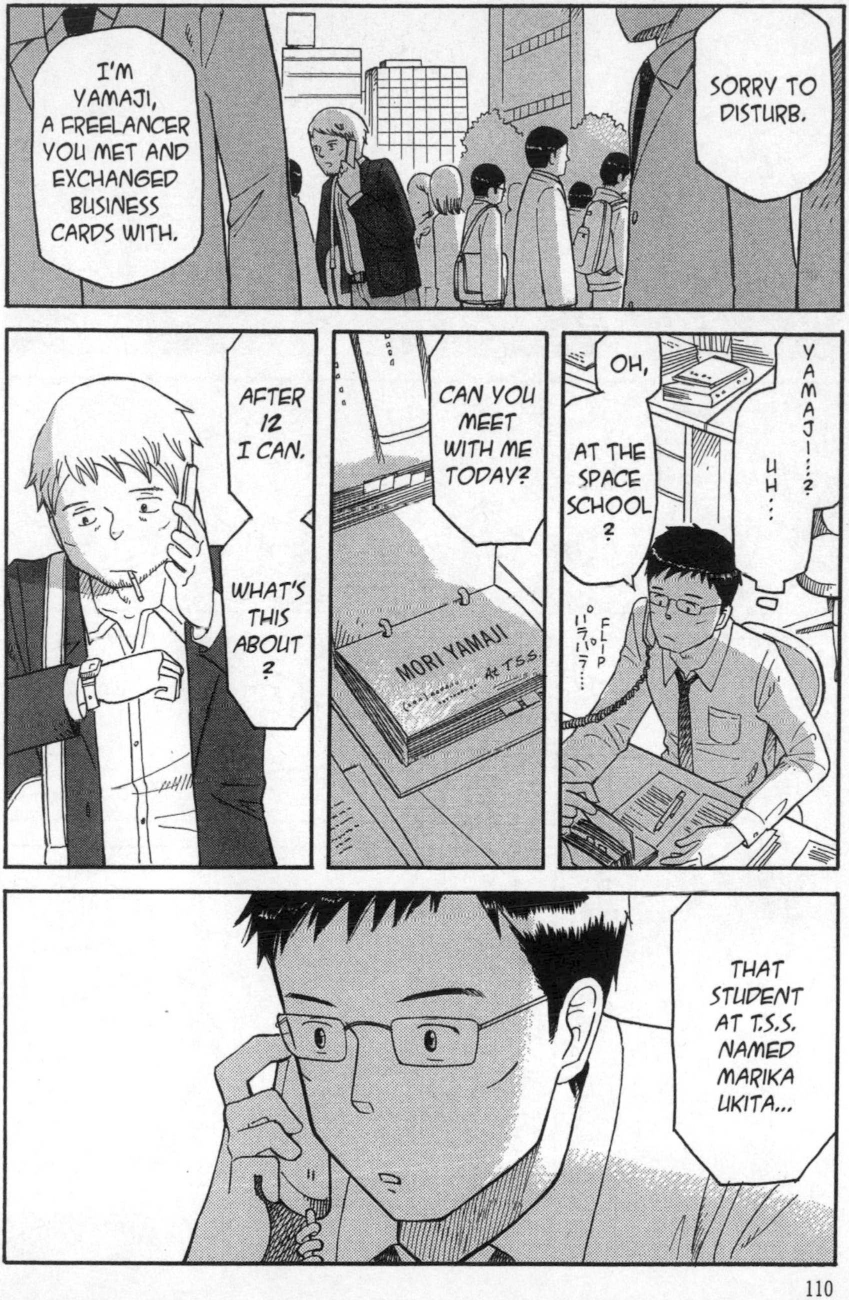
SORRY TO DISTURB.
I'M YAMAJI, A FREELANCER YOU MET AND EXCHANGED BUSINESS CARDS WITH.
YAMAJI...?
UH...
OH,
AT THE SPACE SCHOOL?
FLIP
CAN YOU MEET WITH ME TODAY?
MORI YAMAJI
At T.S.S.
AFTER 12 I CAN.
WHAT'S THIS ABOUT?
THAT STUDENT AT T.S.S. NAMED MARIKA UKITA...

MISSION:68

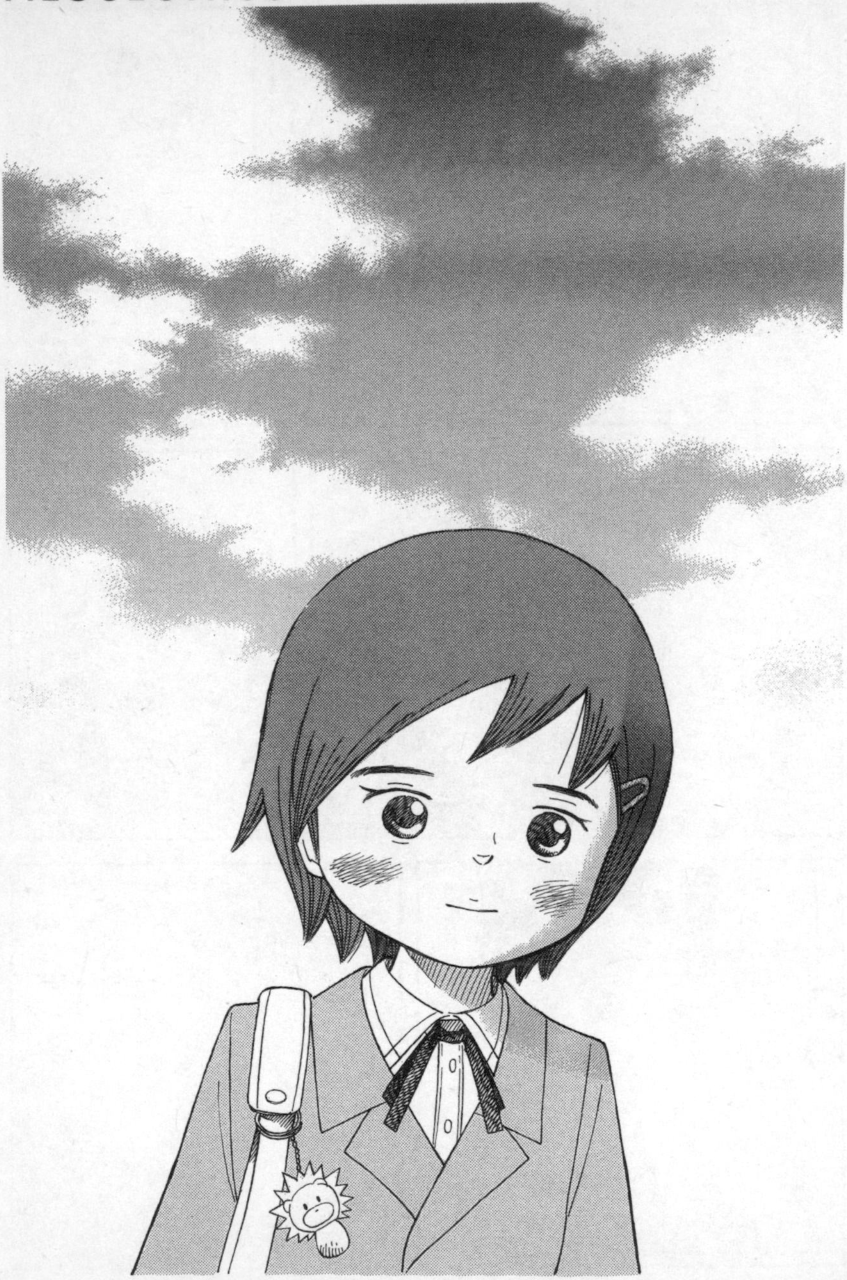

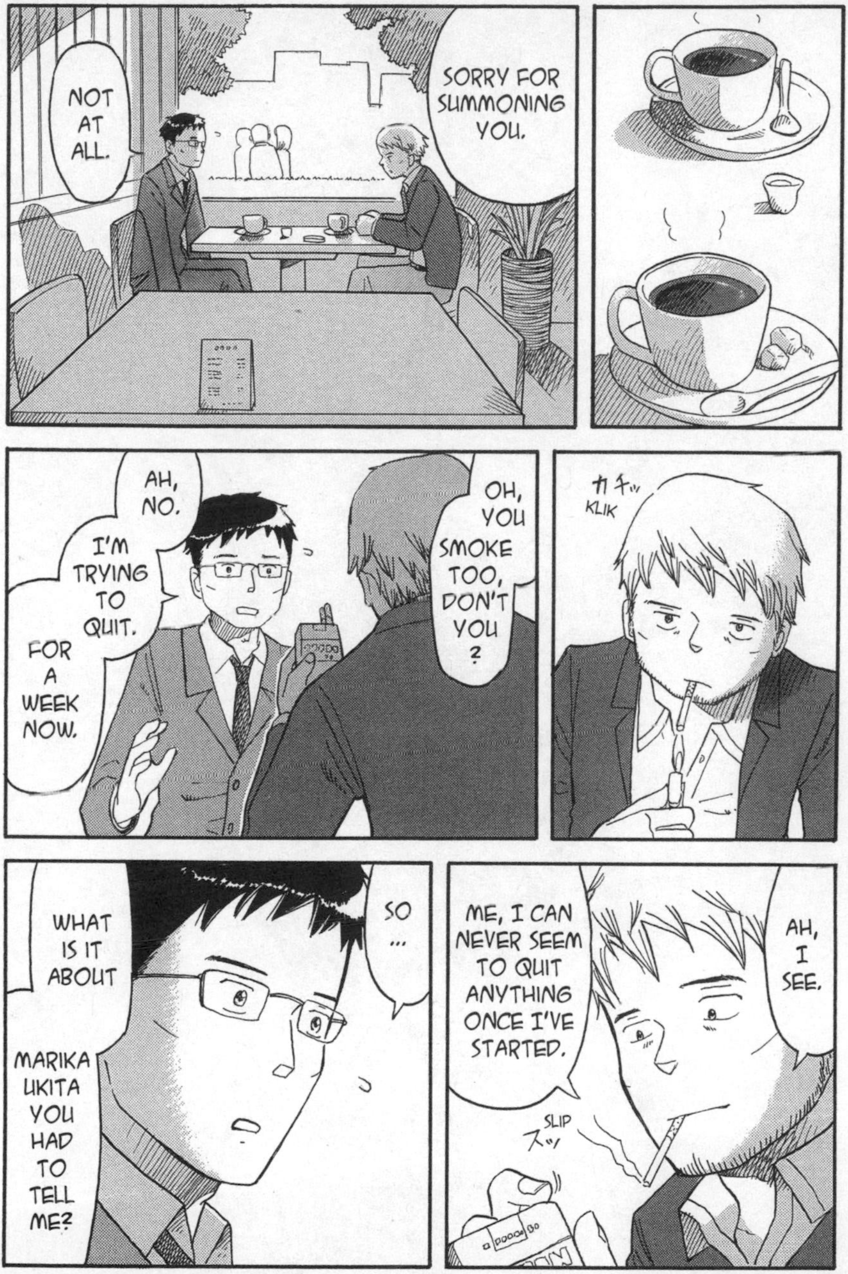
SORRY FOR SUMMONING YOU.
NOT AT ALL.
カチッ
KLIK
OH, YOU SMOKE TOO, DON'T YOU?
AH, NO.
I'M TRYING TO QUIT.
FOR A WEEK NOW.
AH, I SEE.
ME, I CAN NEVER SEEM TO QUIT ANYTHING ONCE I'VE STARTED.
SLIP
スッ
SO ...
WHAT IS IT ABOUT
MARIKA UKITA YOU HAD TO TELL ME?

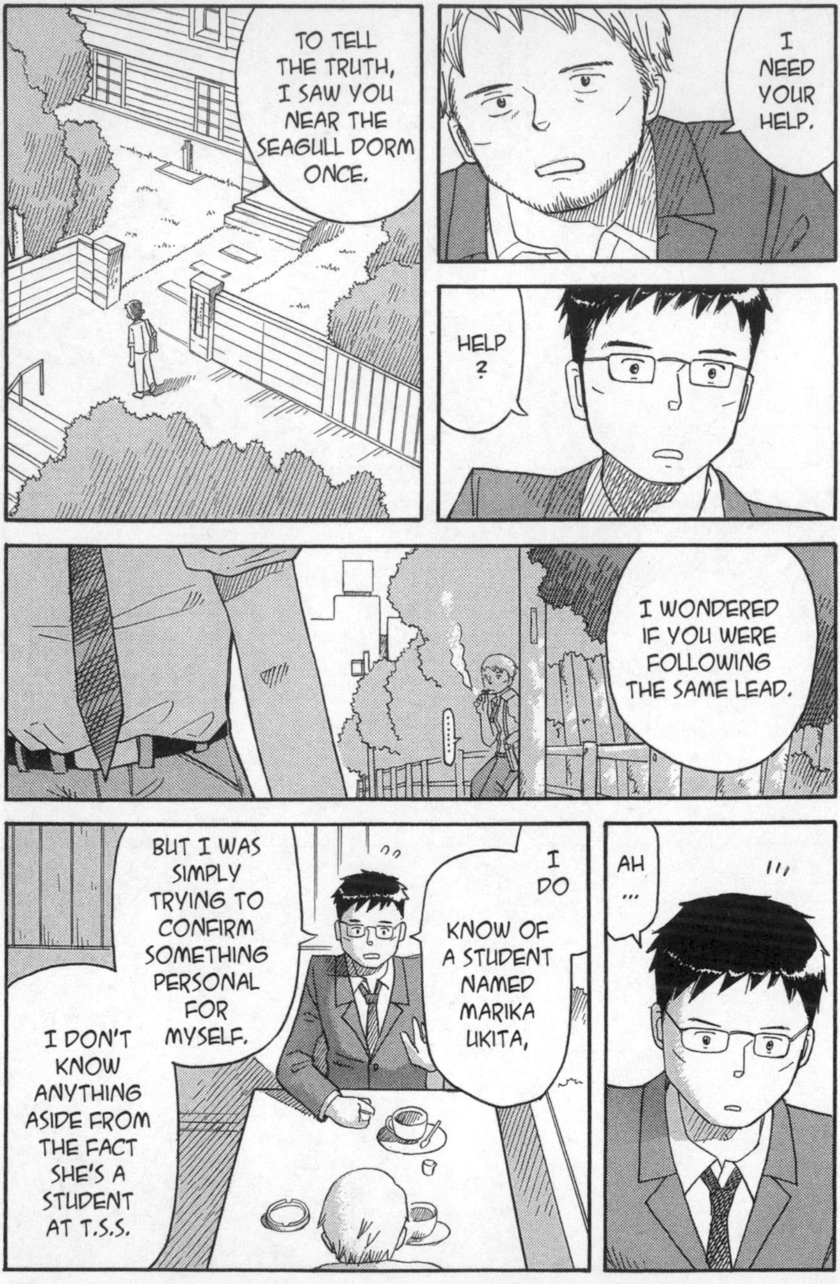

I NEED YOUR HELP.
HELP?
TO TELL THE TRUTH, I SAW YOU NEAR THE SEAGULL DORM ONCE.
I WONDERED IF YOU WERE FOLLOWING THE SAME LEAD.
......
AH...
I DO KNOW OF A STUDENT NAMED MARIKA UKITA,
BUT I WAS SIMPLY TRYING TO CONFIRM SOMETHING PERSONAL FOR MYSELF.
I DON'T KNOW ANYTHING ASIDE FROM THE FACT SHE'S A STUDENT AT T.S.S.

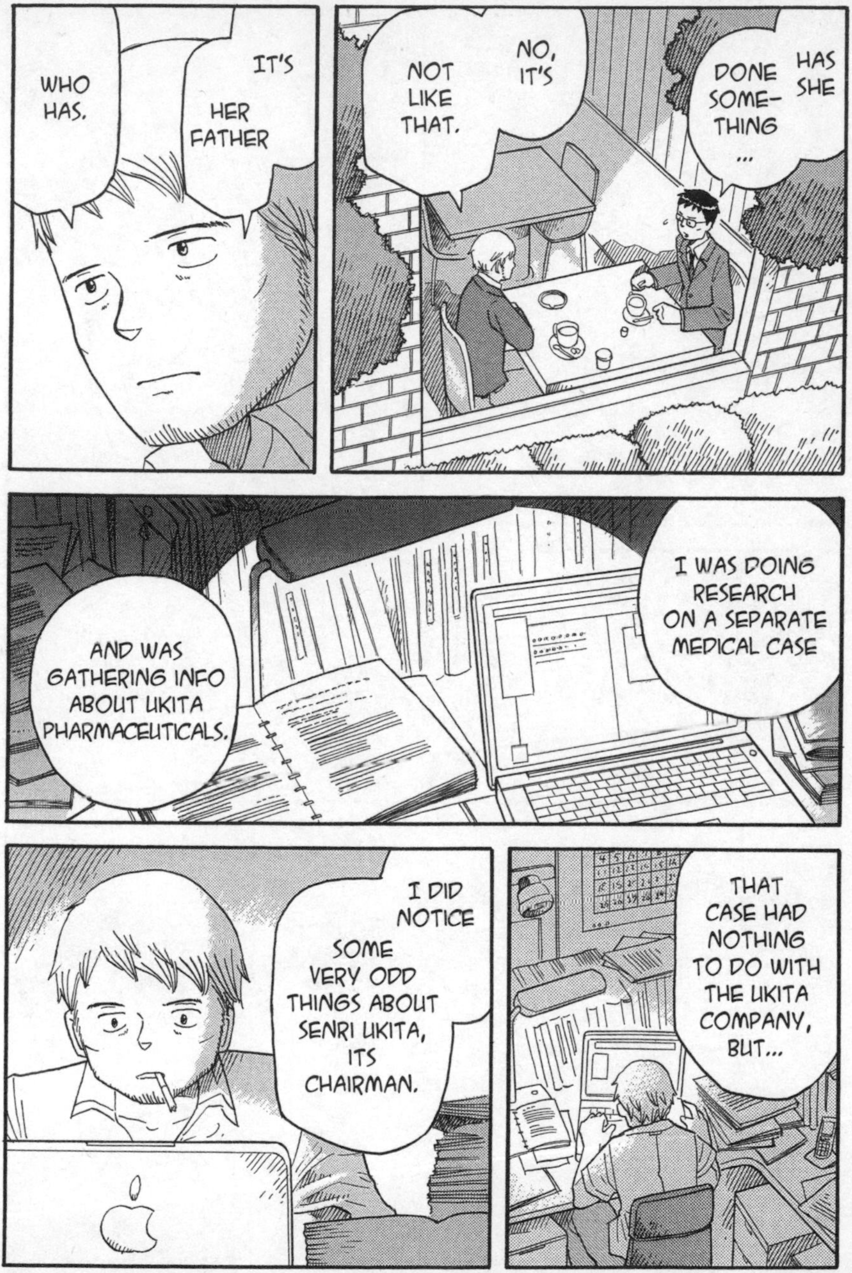
HAS SHE DONE SOMETHING...
NO, IT'S NOT LIKE THAT.
IT'S HER FATHER
WHO HAS.
I WAS DOING RESEARCH ON A SEPARATE MEDICAL CASE
AND WAS GATHERING INFO ABOUT UKITA PHARMACEUTICALS.
THAT CASE HAD NOTHING TO DO WITH THE UKITA COMPANY, BUT...
I DID NOTICE
SOME VERY ODD THINGS ABOUT SENRI UKITA, ITS CHAIRMAN.

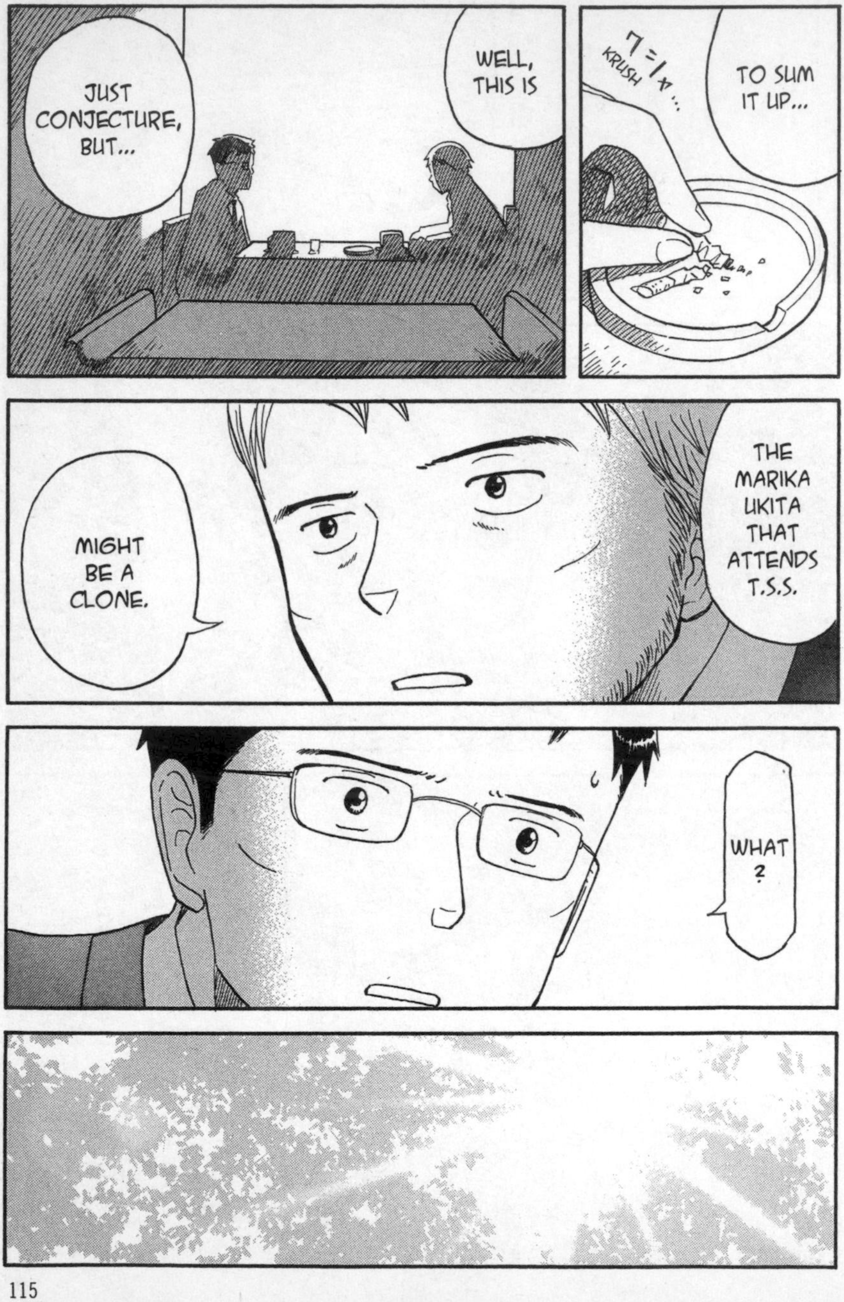
TO SUM IT UP...
KRUSH
WELL, THIS IS
JUST CONJECTURE, BUT...
THE MARIKA UKITA THAT ATTENDS T.S.S.
MIGHT BE A CLONE.
WHAT?

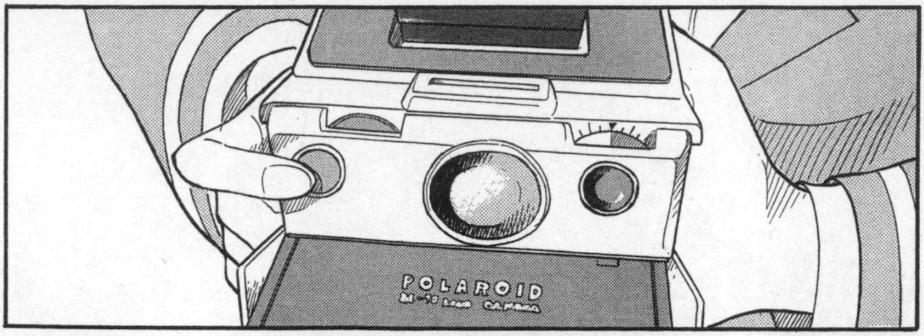
POLAROID

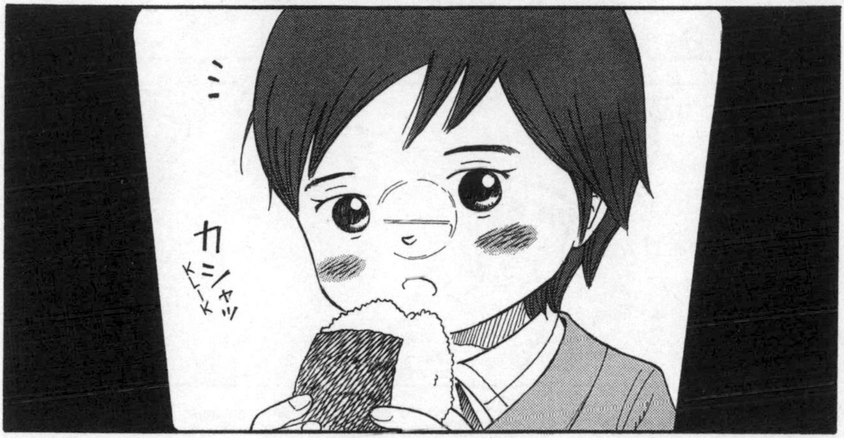
カシャッ
KLIK

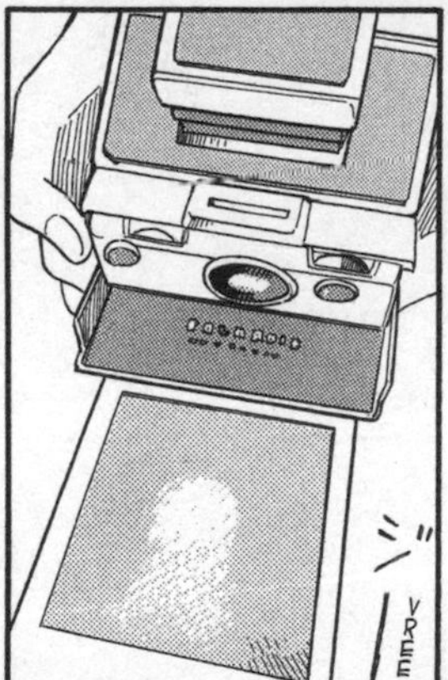
VREE

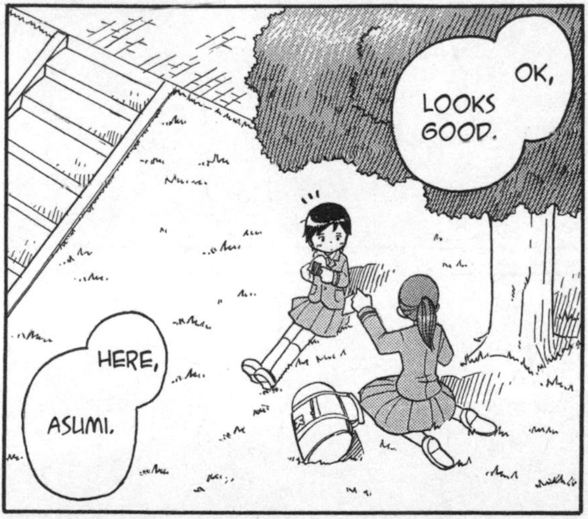
OK, LOOKS GOOD.
HERE, ASUMI.

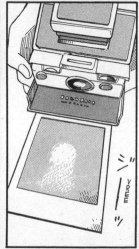

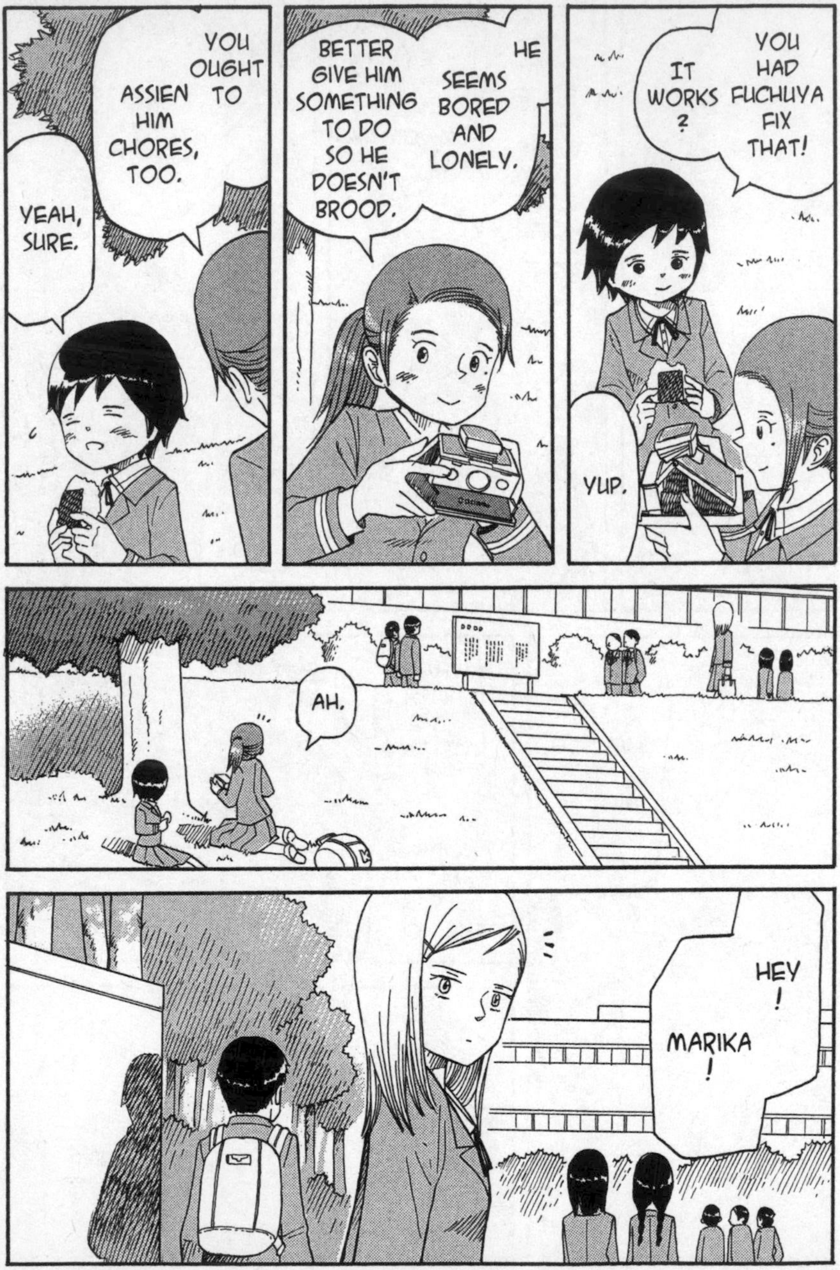
YOU HAD FUCHUYA FIX THAT!
IT WORKS?
YUP.
HE SEEMS BORED AND LONELY.
BETTER GIVE HIM SOMETHING TO DO SO HE DOESN'T BROOD.
YOU OUGHT TO ASSIEN HIM CHORES, TOO.
YEAH, SURE.
AH.
HEY! MARIKA!

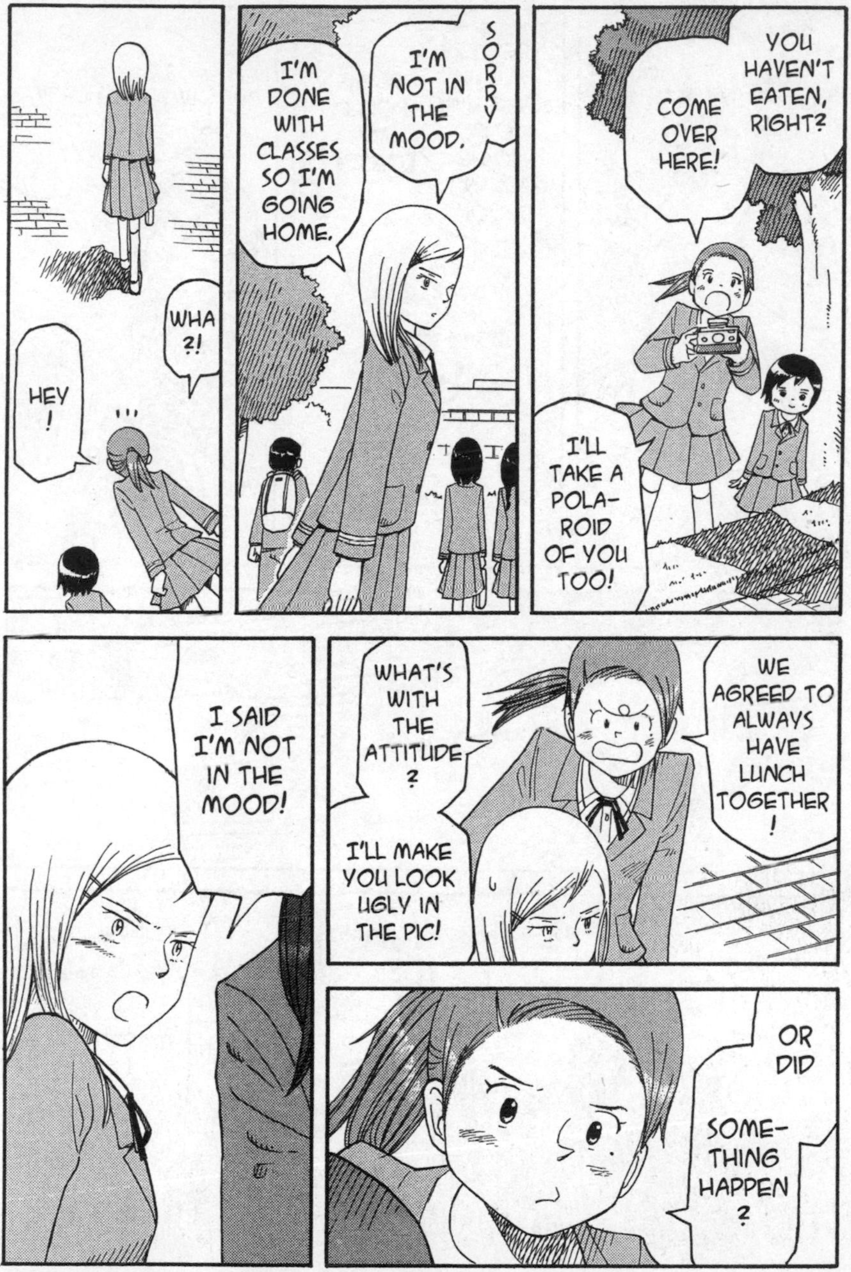
YOU HAVEN'T EATEN, RIGHT?
COME OVER HERE!
I'LL TAKE A POLAROID OF YOU TOO!
SORRY
I'M NOT IN THE MOOD.
I'M DONE WITH CLASSES SO I'M GOING HOME.
WHA?!
HEY!
WE AGREED TO ALWAYS HAVE LUNCH TOGETHER!
WHAT'S WITH THE ATTITUDE?
I'LL MAKE YOU LOOK UGLY IN THE PIC!
OR DID SOMETHING HAPPEN?
I SAID I'M NOT IN THE MOOD!

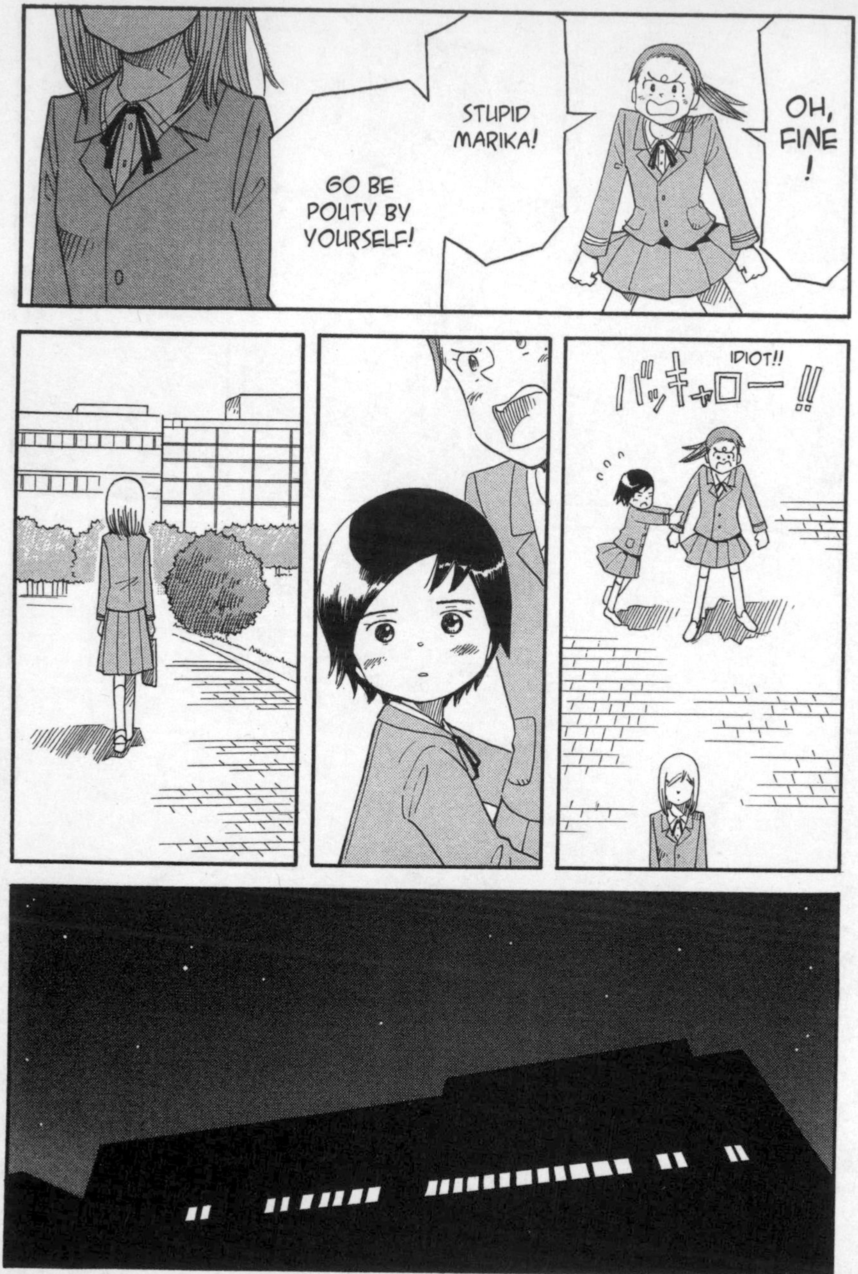
OH, FINE!
STUPID MARIKA!
GO BE POUTY BY YOURSELF!
IDIOT!!
バッキャロー!!

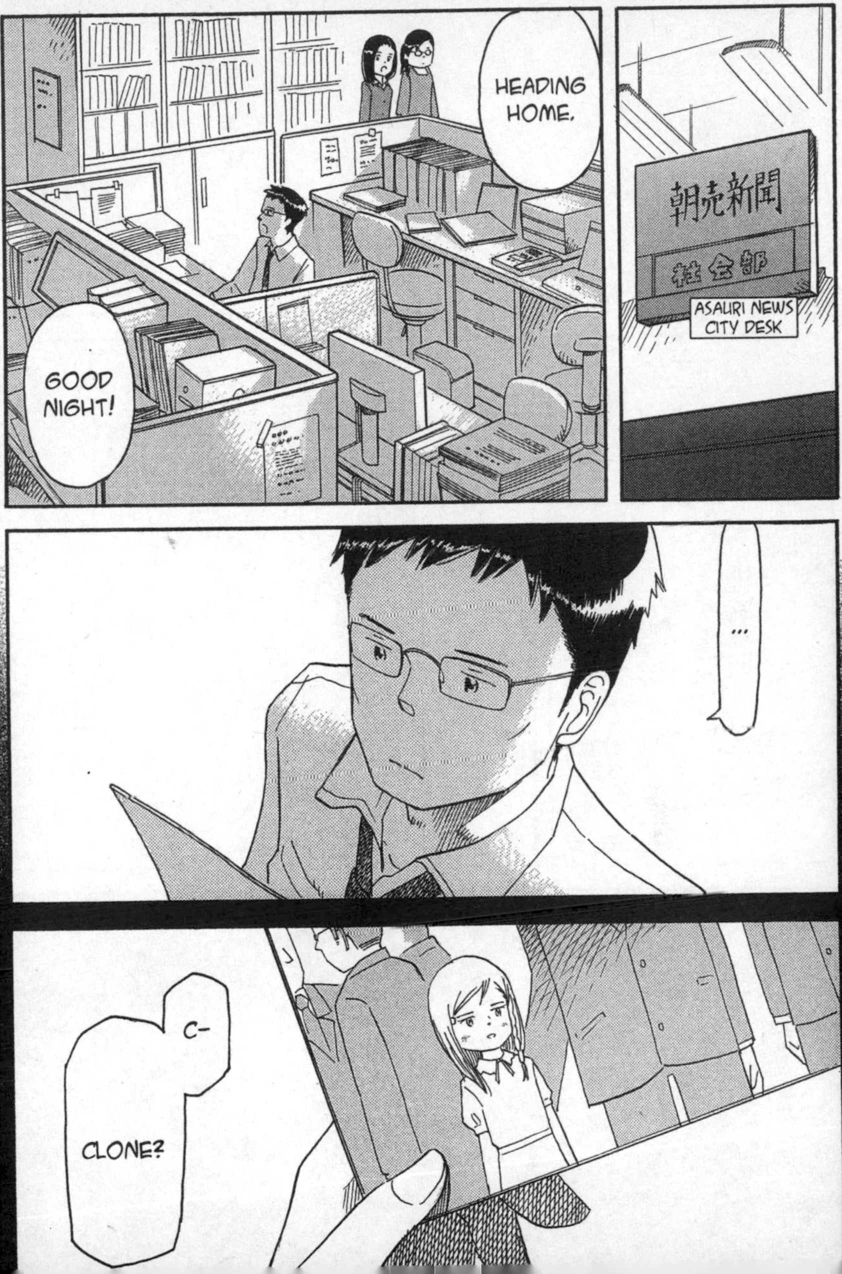

朝売新聞
社会部
ASAURI NEWS CITY DESK
HEADING HOME.
GOOD NIGHT!
...
C-
CLONE?

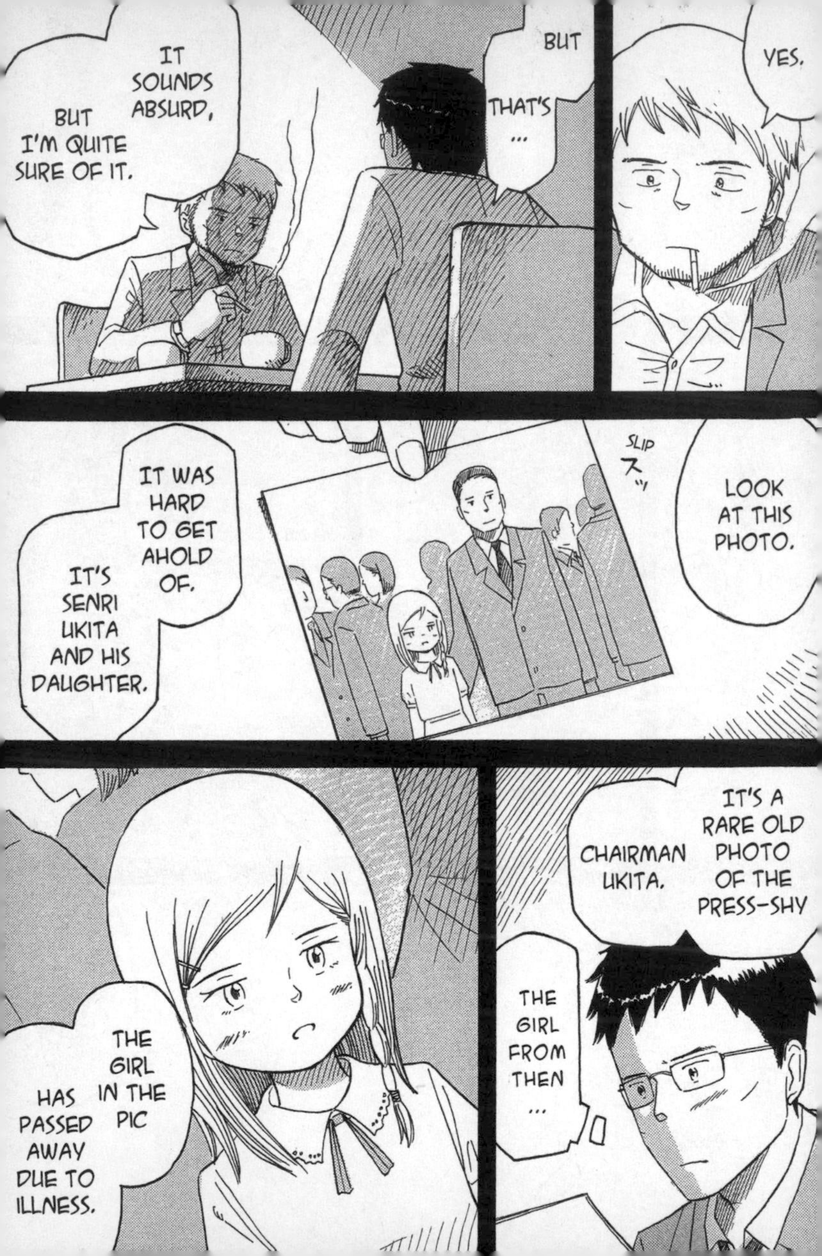
YES.
BUT THAT'S ...
IT SOUNDS ABSURD,
BUT I'M QUITE SURE OF IT.
LOOK AT THIS PHOTO.
SLIP
IT WAS HARD TO GET AHOLD OF.
IT'S SENRI UKITA AND HIS DAUGHTER.
IT'S A RARE OLD PHOTO OF THE PRESS-SHY
CHAIRMAN UKITA.
THE GIRL FROM THEN ...
THE GIRL IN THE PIC
HAS PASSED AWAY DUE TO ILLNESS.

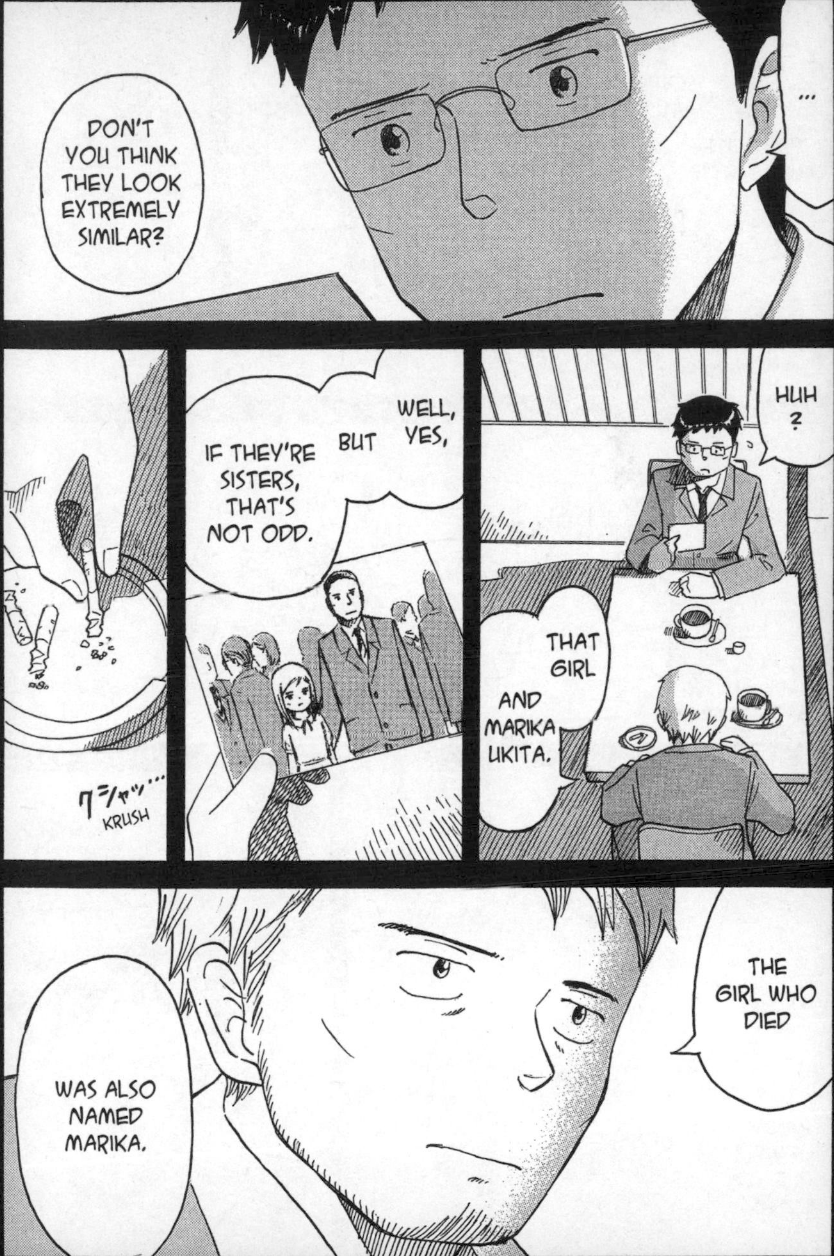
...
DON'T YOU THINK THEY LOOK EXTREMELY SIMILAR?
HUH?
THAT GIRL
AND MARIKA UKITA.
WELL, YES,
BUT
IF THEY'RE SISTERS, THAT'S NOT ODD.
グシャッ...
KRUSH
THE GIRL WHO DIED
WAS ALSO NAMED MARIKA.

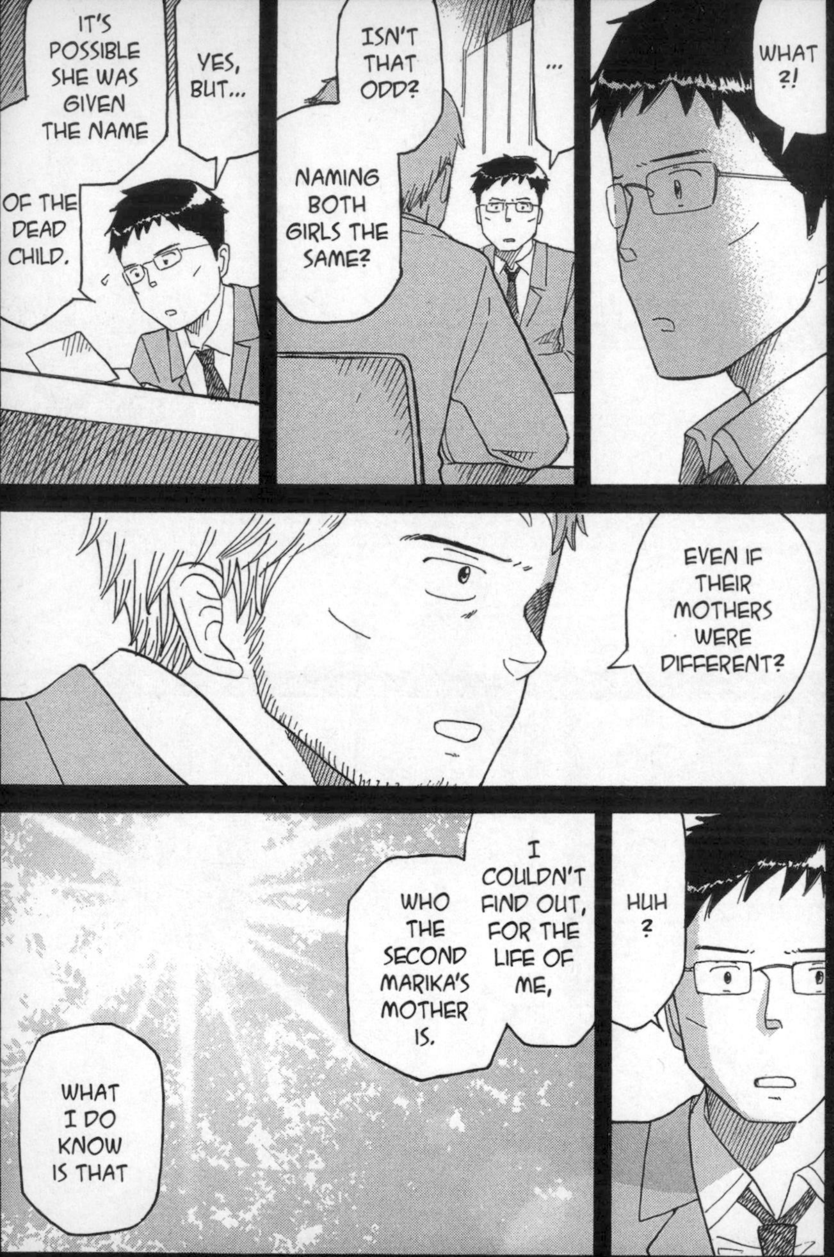
IT'S POSSIBLE SHE WAS GIVEN THE NAME
OF THE DEAD CHILD.
YES, BUT...
ISN'T THAT ODD?
NAMING BOTH GIRLS THE SAME?
...
WHAT ?!
EVEN IF THEIR MOTHERS WERE DIFFERENT?
HUH ?
I COULDN'T FIND OUT, FOR THE LIFE OF ME,
WHO THE SECOND MARIKA'S MOTHER IS.
WHAT I DO KNOW IS THAT

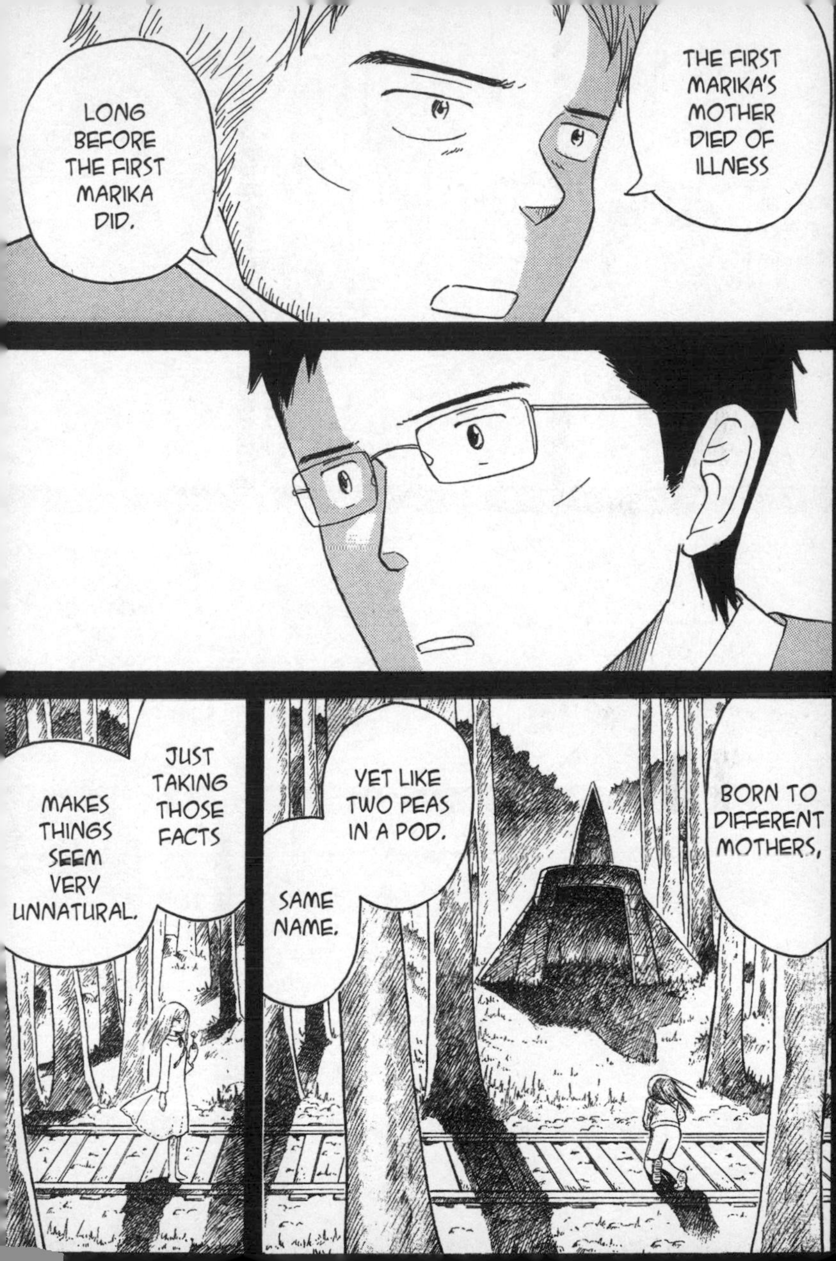
THE FIRST MARIKA'S MOTHER DIED OF ILLNESS
LONG BEFORE THE FIRST MARIKA DID.
BORN TO DIFFERENT MOTHERS,
SAME NAME.
YET LIKE TWO PEAS IN A POD.
JUST TAKING THOSE FACTS
MAKES THINGS SEEM VERY UNNATURAL.

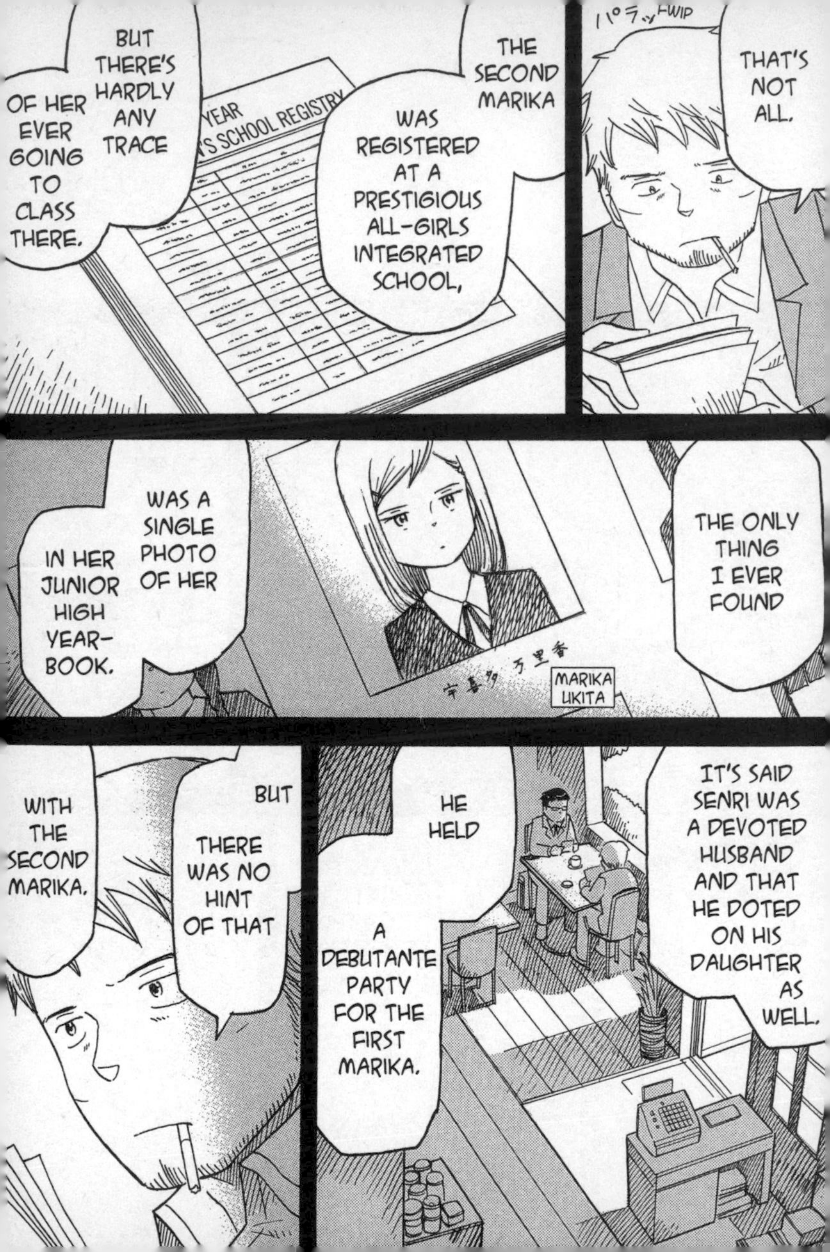
パラッ FWIP
THAT'S NOT ALL.
THE SECOND MARIKA
WAS REGISTERED AT A PRESTIGIOUS ALL-GIRLS INTEGRATED SCHOOL,
BUT THERE'S HARDLY ANY TRACE
OF HER EVER GOING TO CLASS THERE.
THE ONLY THING I EVER FOUND
WAS A SINGLE PHOTO OF HER
IN HER JUNIOR HIGH YEAR-BOOK.
宇喜多 万里香
MARIKA UKITA
IT'S SAID SENRI WAS A DEVOTED HUSBAND AND THAT HE DOTED ON HIS DAUGHTER AS WELL.
HE HELD
A DEBUTANTE PARTY FOR THE FIRST MARIKA.
BUT
THERE WAS NO HINT OF THAT
WITH THE SECOND MARIKA.

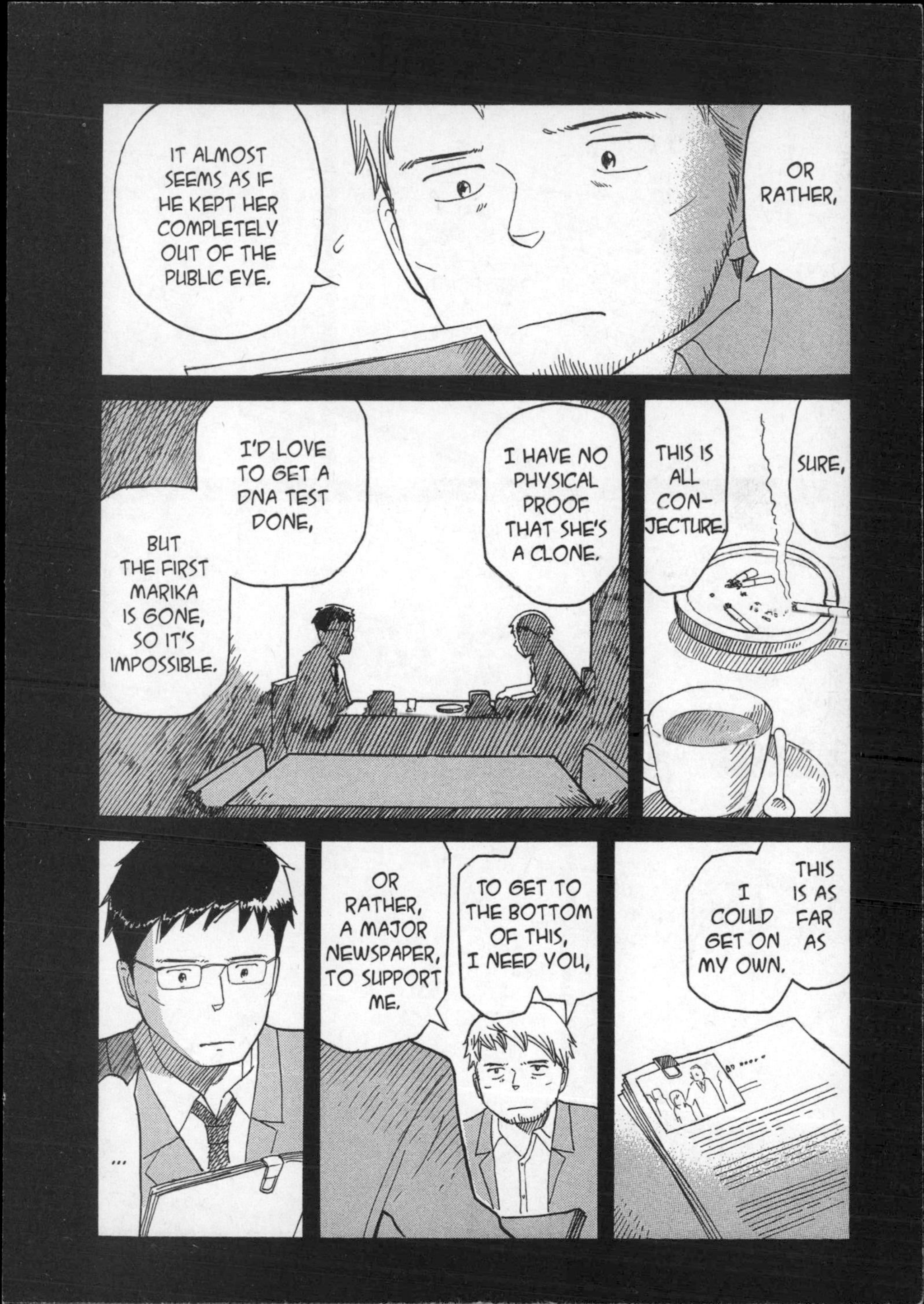
OR RATHER,
IT ALMOST SEEMS AS IF HE KEPT HER COMPLETELY OUT OF THE PUBLIC EYE.
SURE,
THIS IS ALL CON-JECTURE.
I HAVE NO PHYSICAL PROOF THAT SHE'S A CLONE.
I'D LOVE TO GET A DNA TEST DONE,
BUT THE FIRST MARIKA IS GONE, SO IT'S IMPOSSIBLE.
THIS IS AS FAR AS I COULD GET ON MY OWN.
TO GET TO THE BOTTOM OF THIS, I NEED YOU,
OR RATHER, A MAJOR NEWSPAPER, TO SUPPORT ME.
...

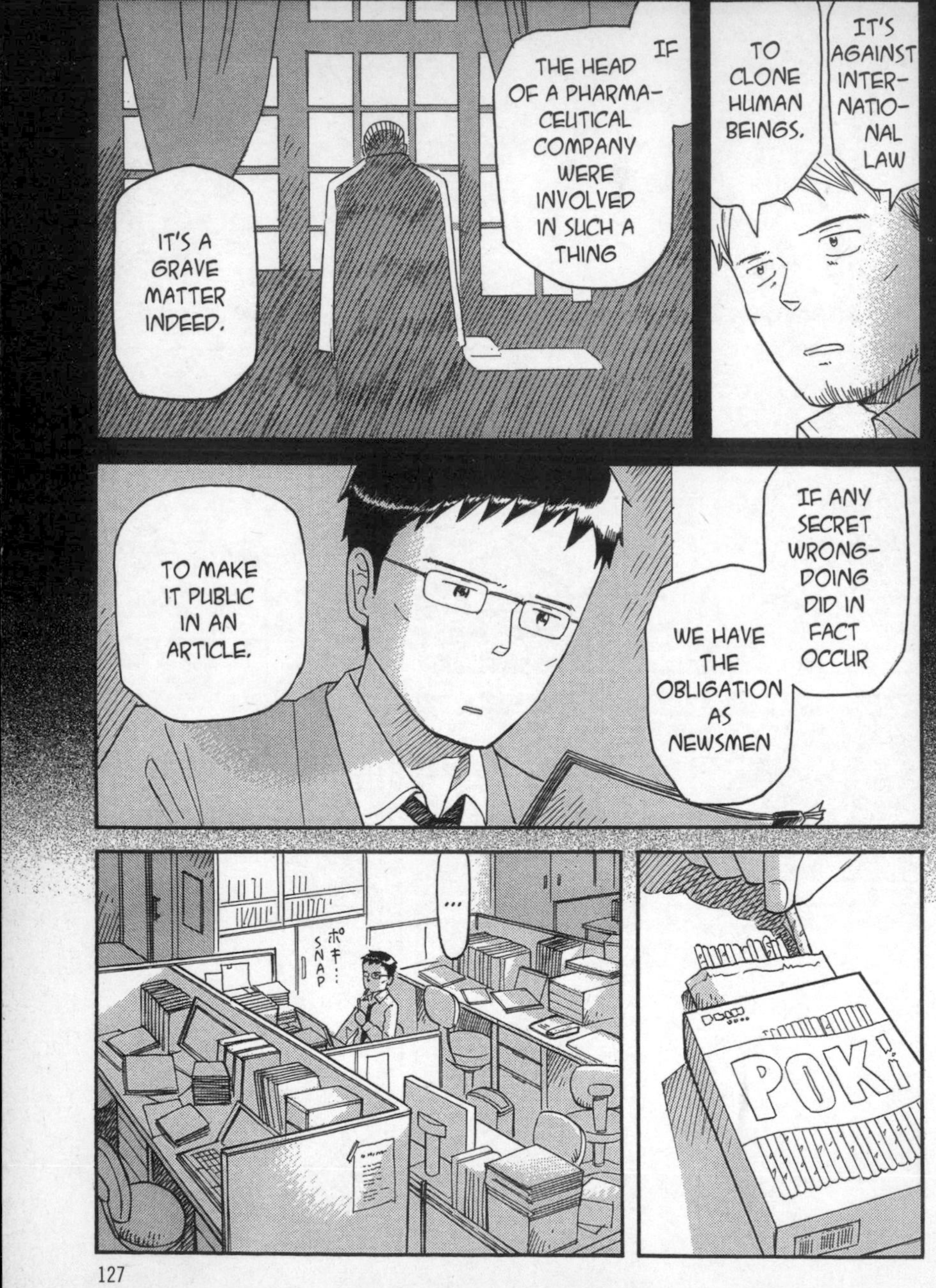
IT'S AGAINST INTER-NATIO-NAL LAW
TO CLONE HUMAN BEINGS.
IF THE HEAD OF A PHARMA-CEUTICAL COMPANY WERE INVOLVED IN SUCH A THING
IT'S A GRAVE MATTER INDEED.
IF ANY SECRET WRONG-DOING DID IN FACT OCCUR
WE HAVE THE OBLIGATION AS NEWSMEN
TO MAKE IT PUBLIC IN AN ARTICLE.
POKi
...
ポキ… SNAP

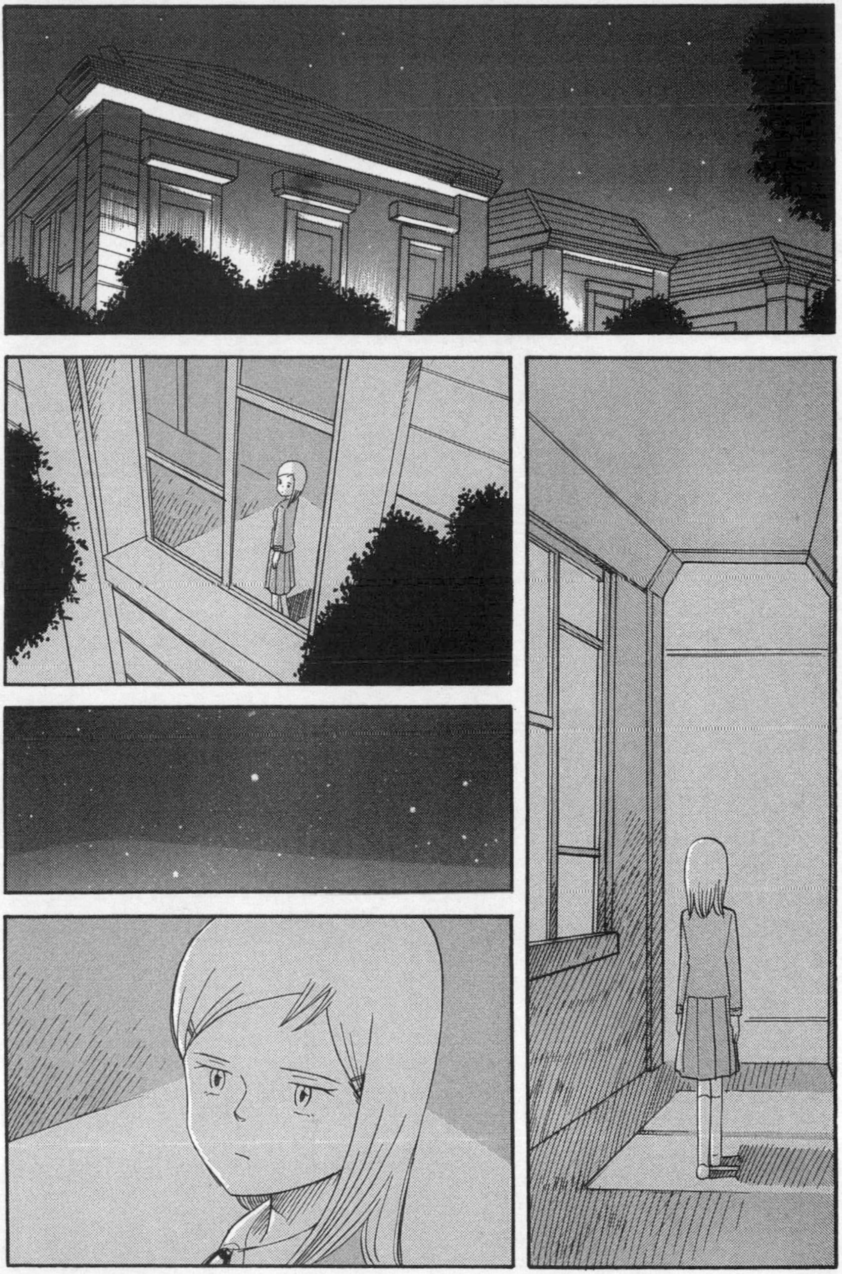

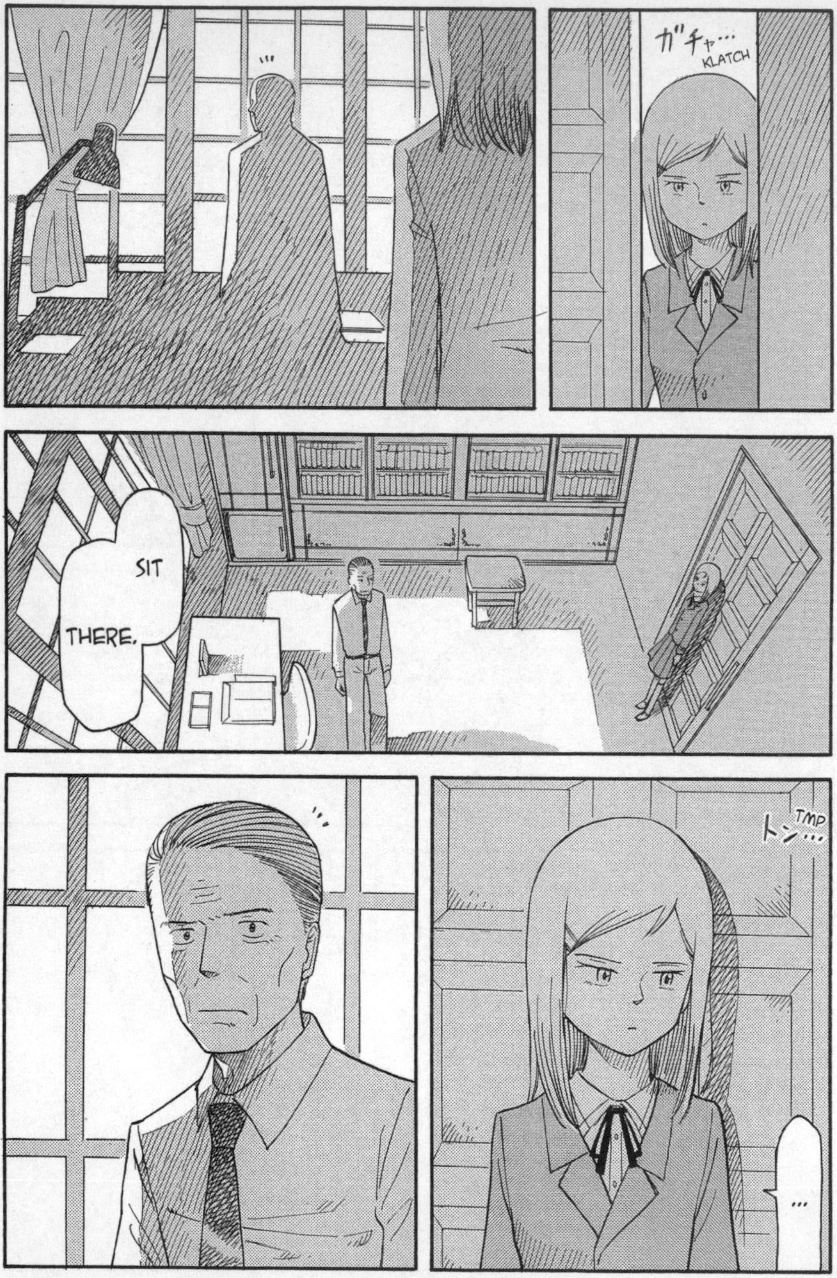
ガチャ…
KLATCH
SIT THERE.
トン…
TMP
…

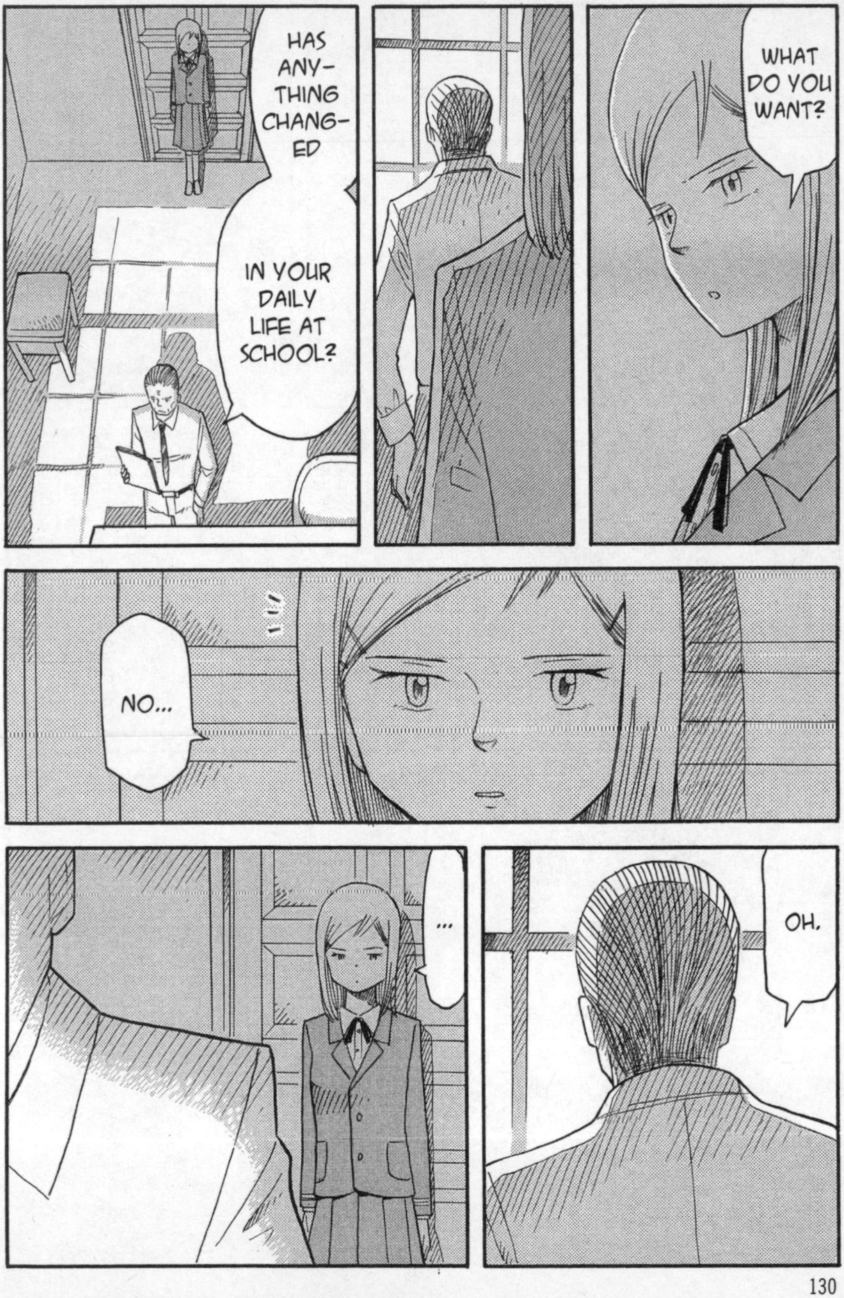
WHAT DO YOU WANT?
HAS ANY-THING CHANG-ED
IN YOUR DAILY LIFE AT SCHOOL?
NO...
OH.
...

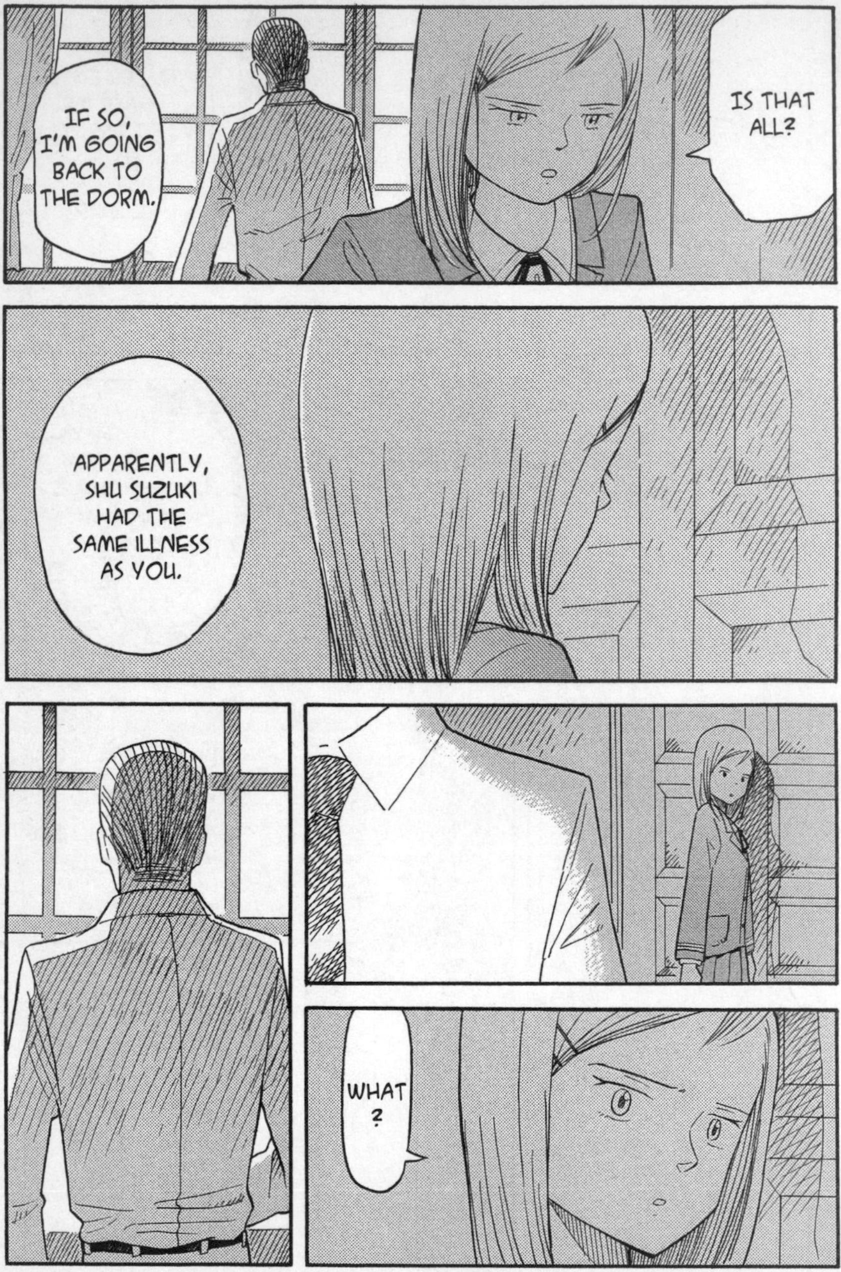
IS THAT ALL?
IF SO, I'M GOING BACK TO THE DORM.
APPARENTLY, SHU SUZUKI HAD THE SAME ILLNESS AS YOU.
WHAT?

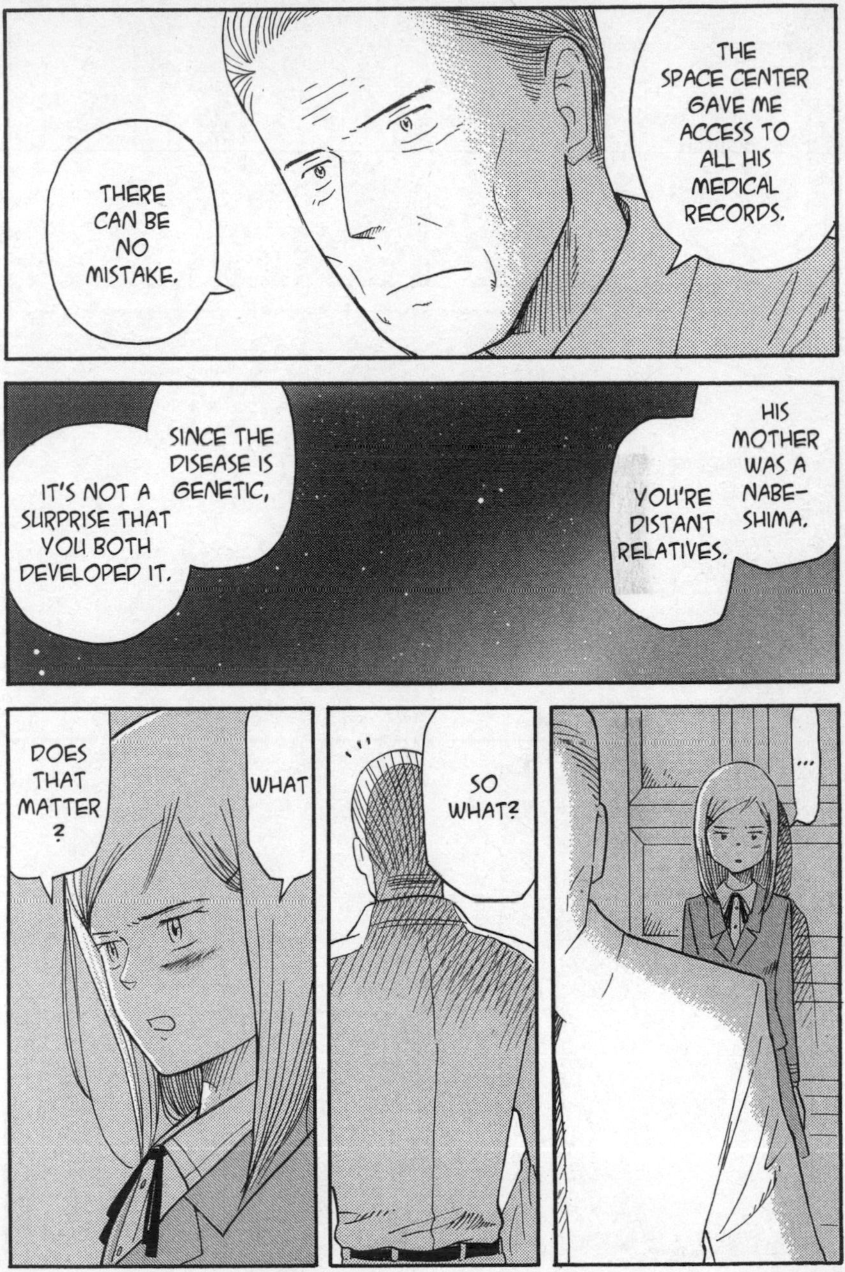
THE SPACE CENTER GAVE ME ACCESS TO ALL HIS MEDICAL RECORDS.
THERE CAN BE NO MISTAKE.
HIS MOTHER WAS A NABE-SHIMA.
YOU'RE DISTANT RELATIVES.
SINCE THE DISEASE IS GENETIC,
IT'S NOT A SURPRISE THAT YOU BOTH DEVELOPED IT.
...
SO WHAT?
WHAT
DOES THAT MATTER ?

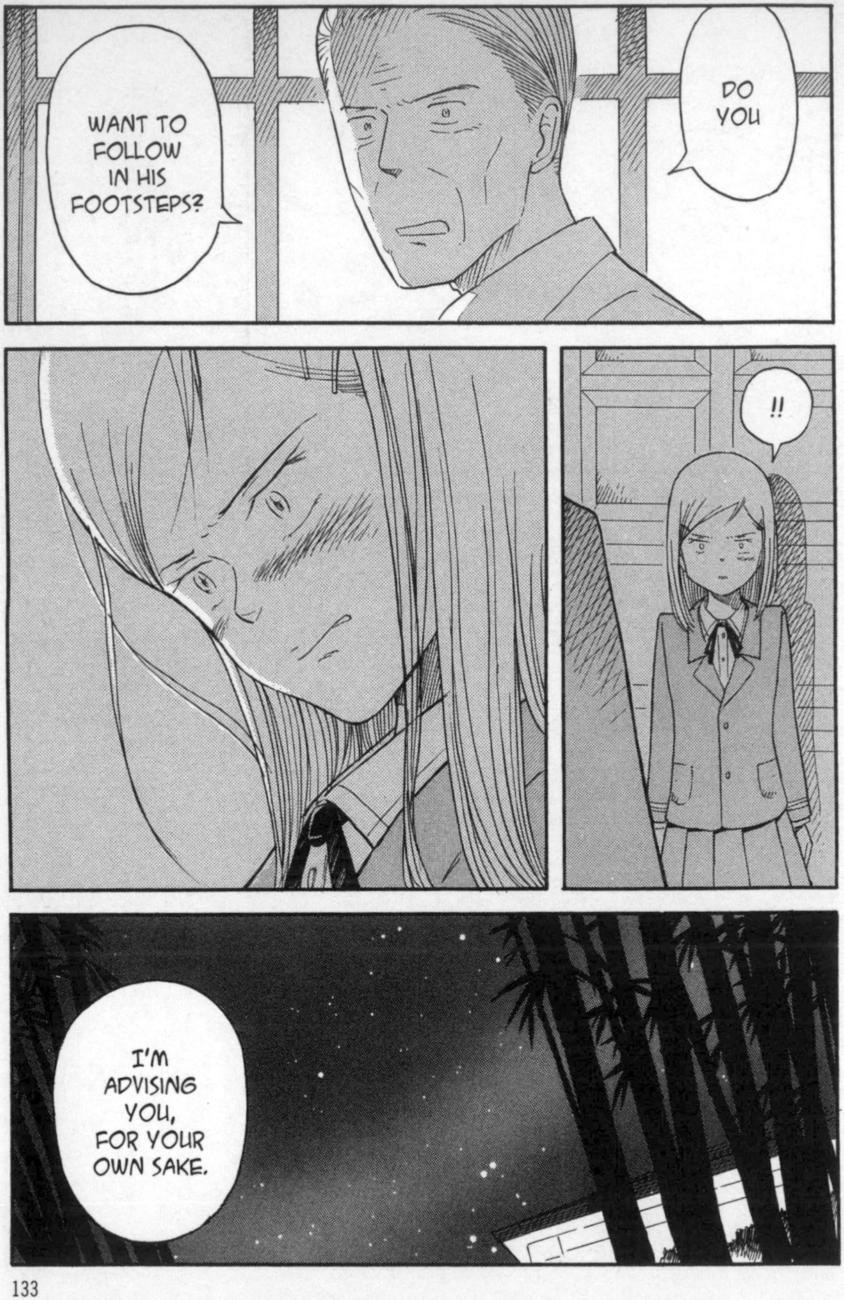
DO YOU
WANT TO FOLLOW IN HIS FOOTSTEPS?
!!
I'M ADVISING YOU, FOR YOUR OWN SAKE.

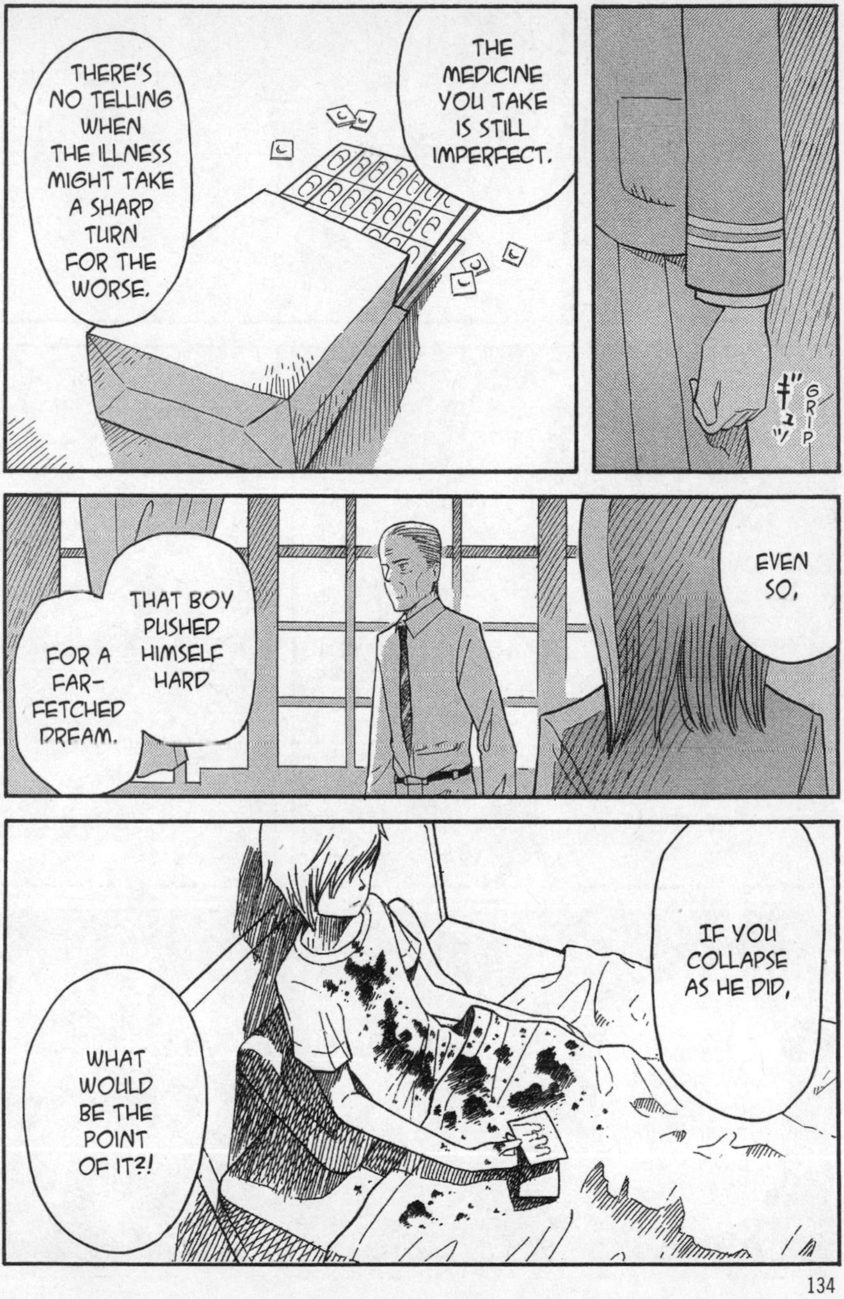
ギュッ
GRIP
THE MEDICINE YOU TAKE IS STILL IMPERFECT.
THERE'S NO TELLING WHEN THE ILLNESS MIGHT TAKE A SHARP TURN FOR THE WORSE.
EVEN SO,
THAT BOY PUSHED HIMSELF HARD
FOR A FAR-FETCHED DREAM.
IF YOU COLLAPSE AS HE DID,
WHAT WOULD BE THE POINT OF IT?!

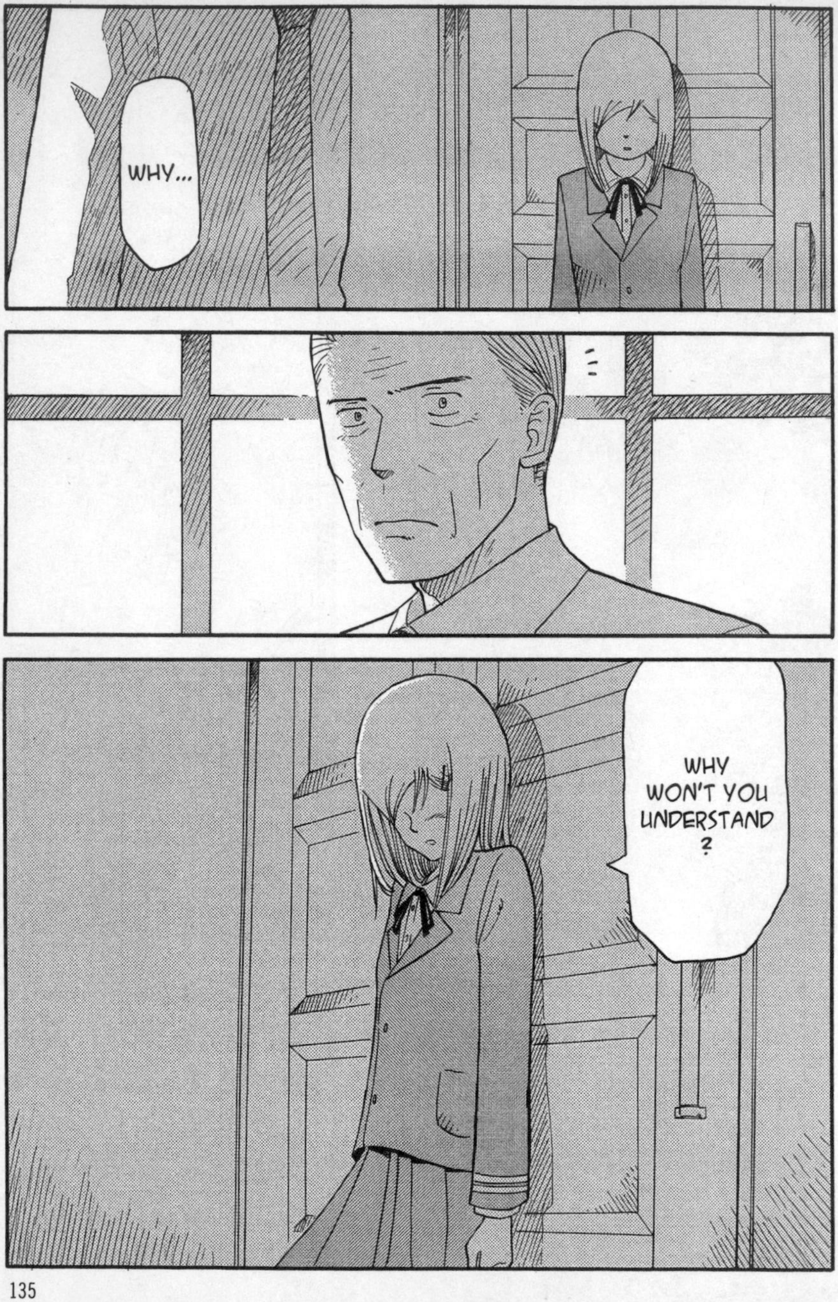
WHY...
WHY WON'T YOU UNDERSTAND?

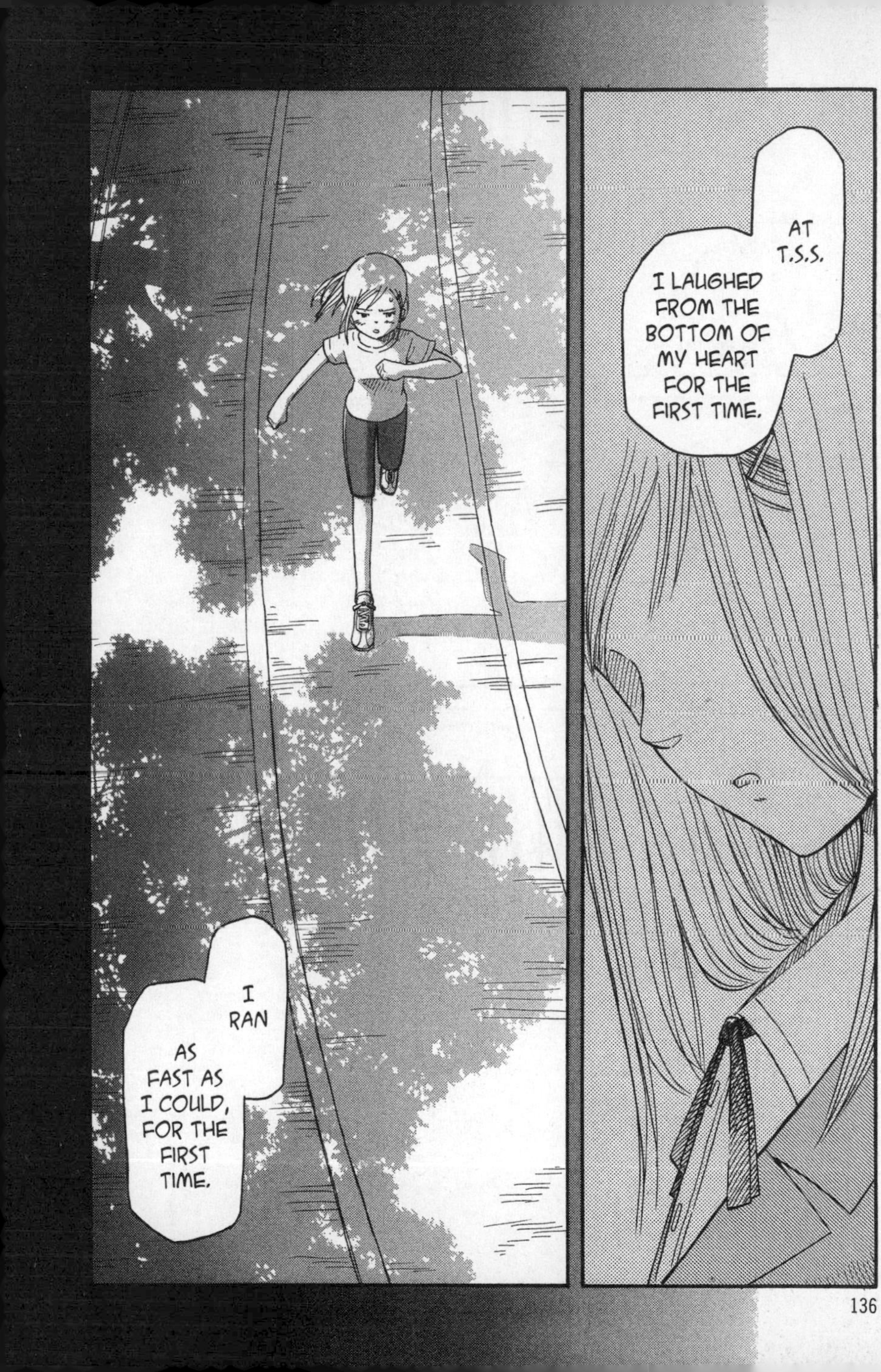
AT T.S.S. I LAUGHED FROM THE BOTTOM OF MY HEART FOR THE FIRST TIME.
I RAN AS FAST AS I COULD, FOR THE FIRST TIME.

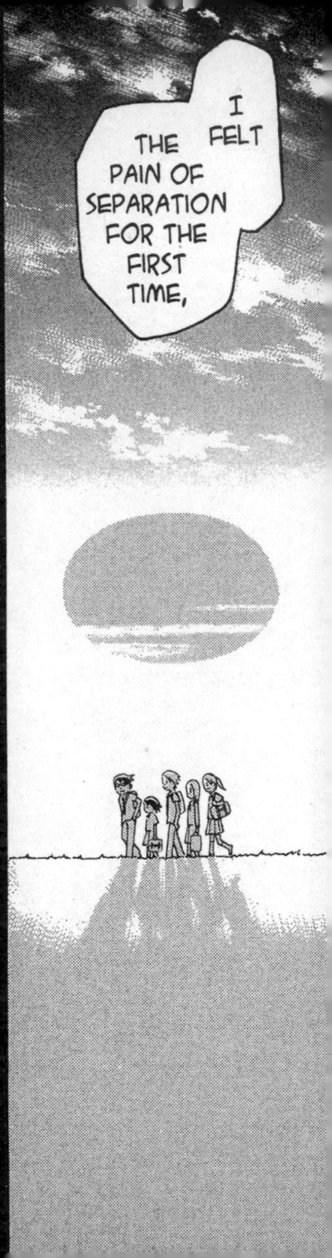
I FELT THE PAIN OF SEPARATION FOR THE FIRST TIME,
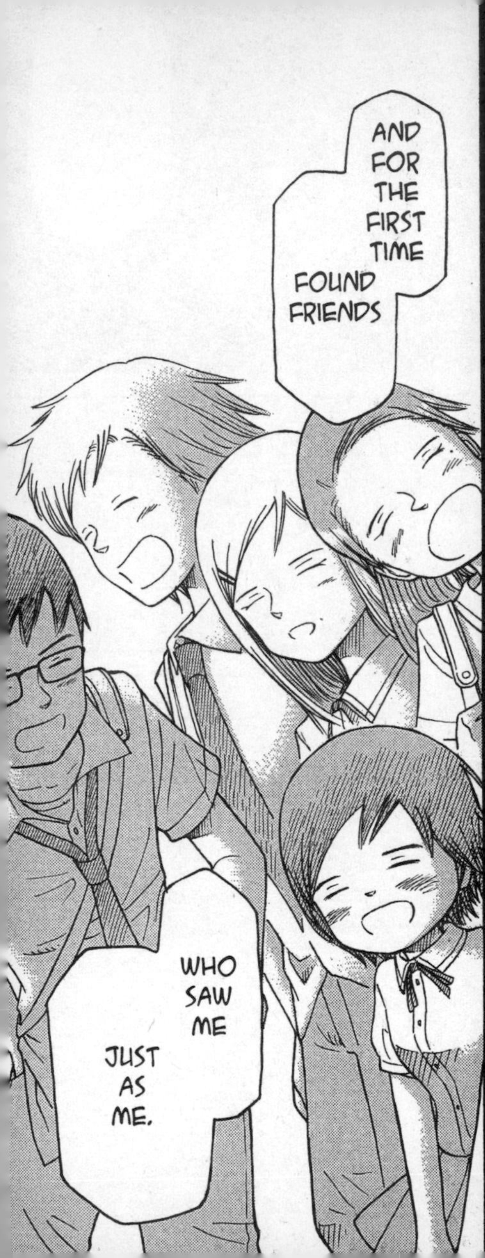
AND FOR THE FIRST TIME FOUND FRIENDS
WHO SAW ME JUST AS ME.

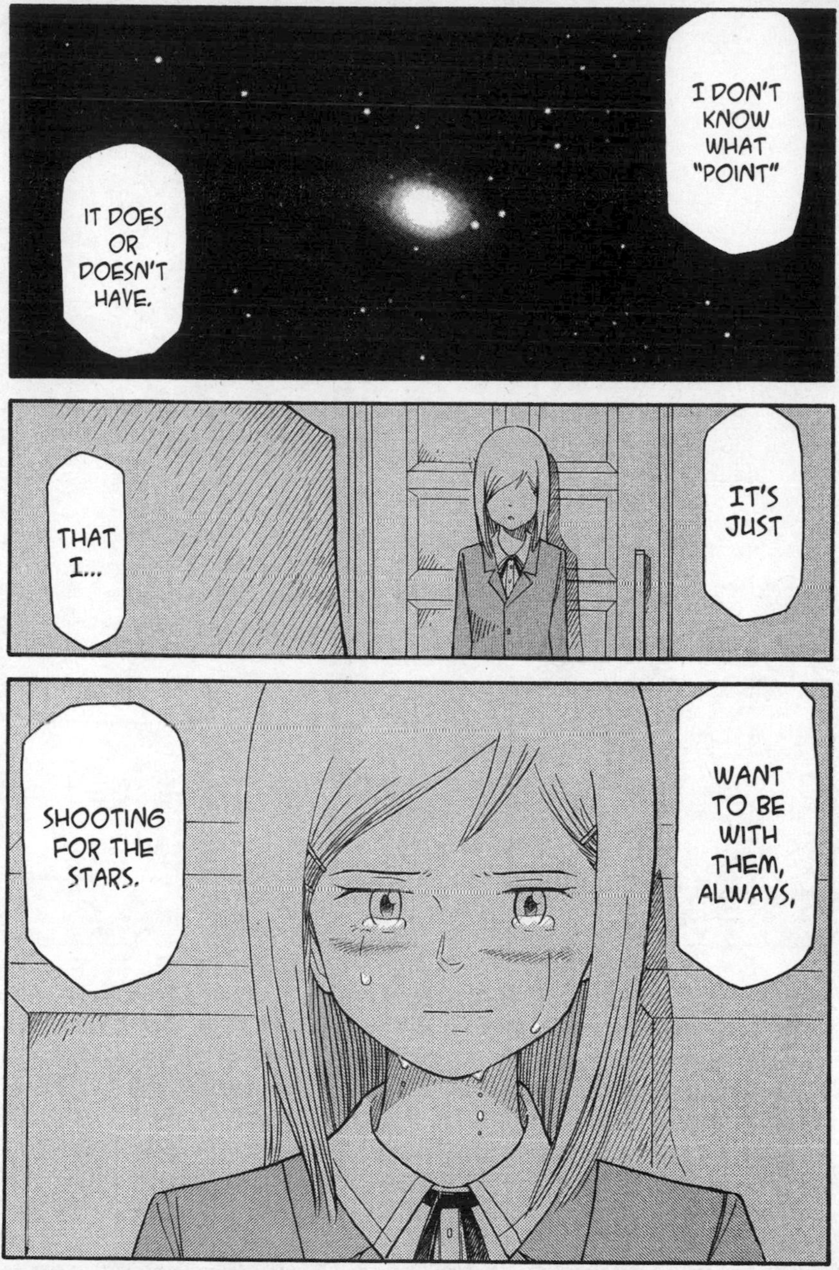
I DON'T KNOW WHAT "POINT"
IT DOES OR DOESN'T HAVE.
IT'S JUST
THAT I...
WANT TO BE WITH THEM, ALWAYS,
SHOOTING FOR THE STARS.

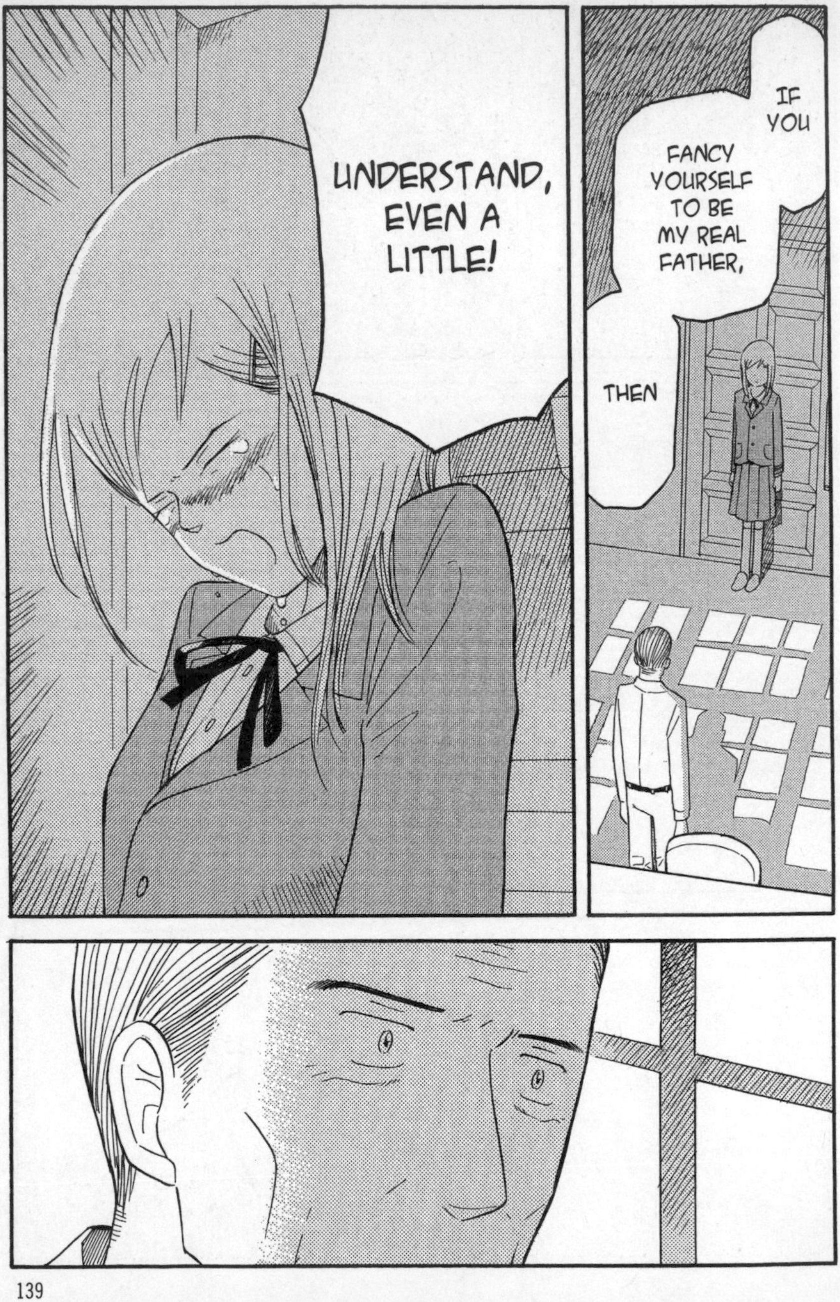
IF YOU
FANCY YOURSELF TO BE MY REAL FATHER,
THEN
UNDERSTAND, EVEN A LITTLE!

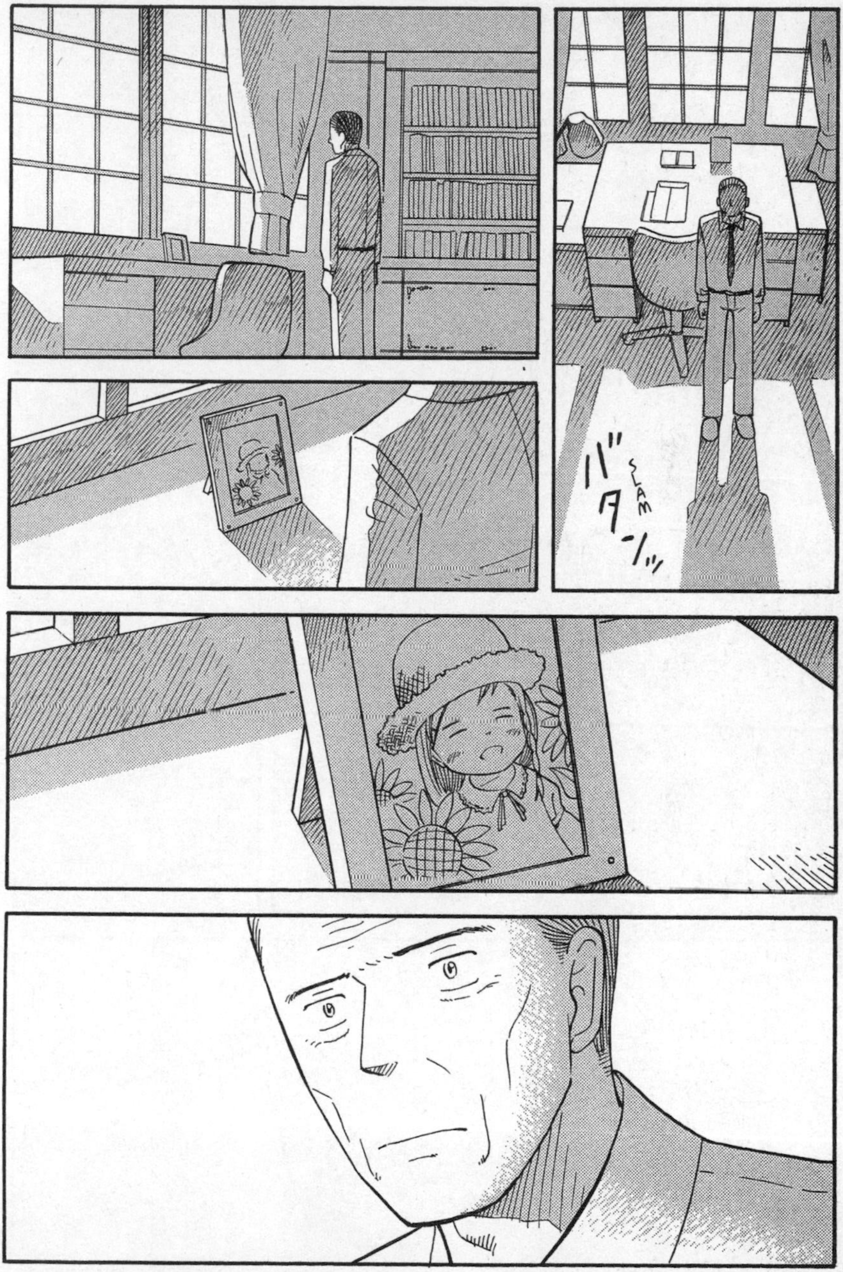
バターンッ
SLAM

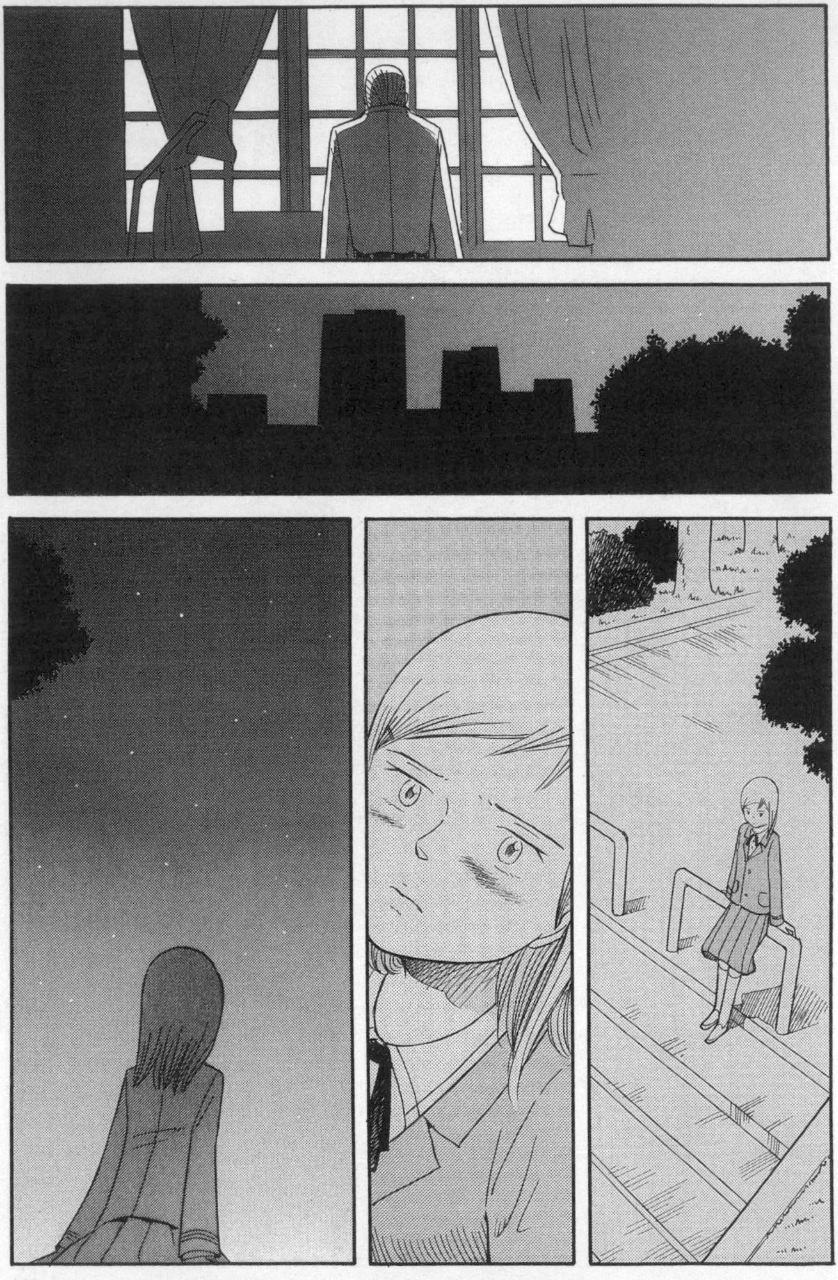

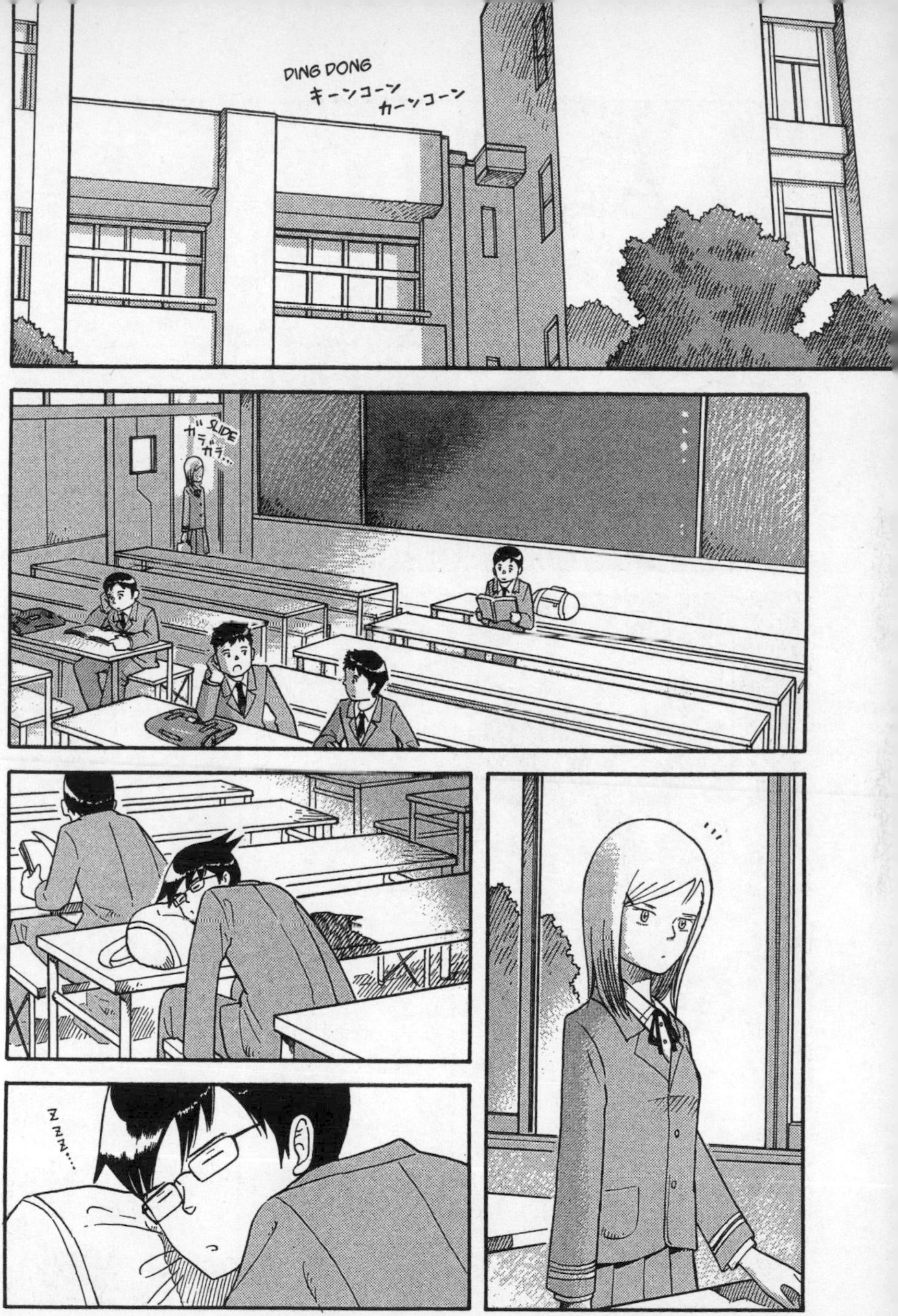
DING DONG
キーンコーン カーンコーン
SLIDE
ガラ ガラ...
ZZZ....

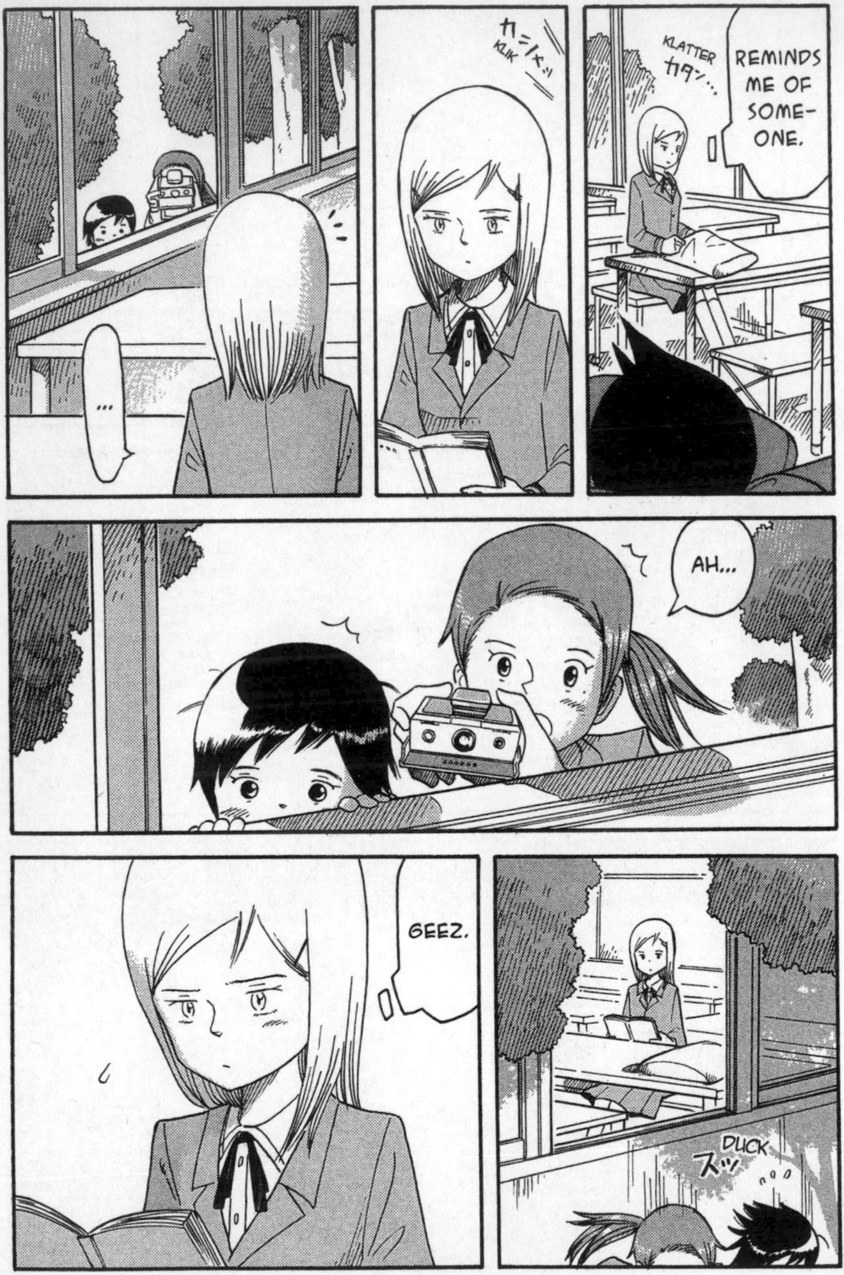
KLATTER
カタン…
REMINDS ME OF SOME-ONE.
カシャッ
KLIK
...
AH...
DUCK
ズッ
GEEZ.

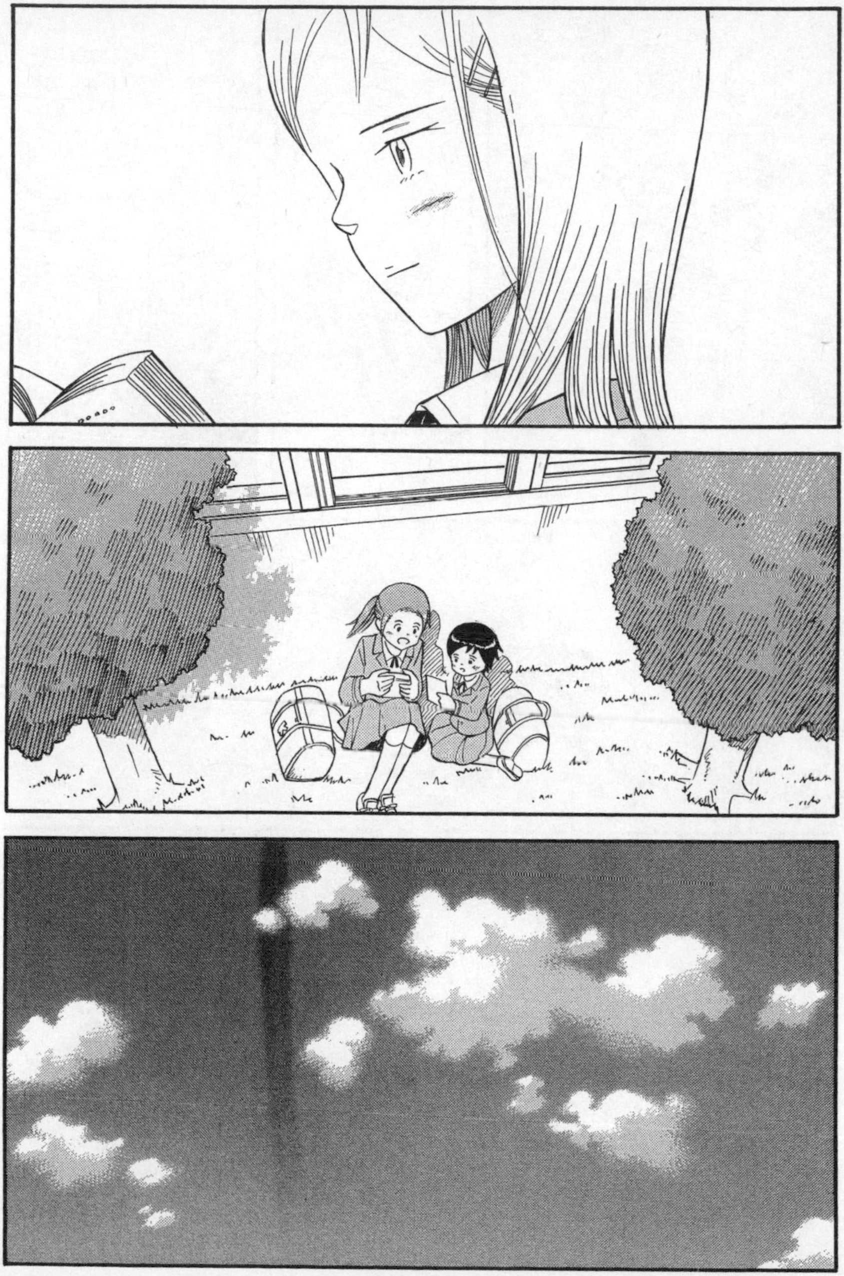

MISSION:69

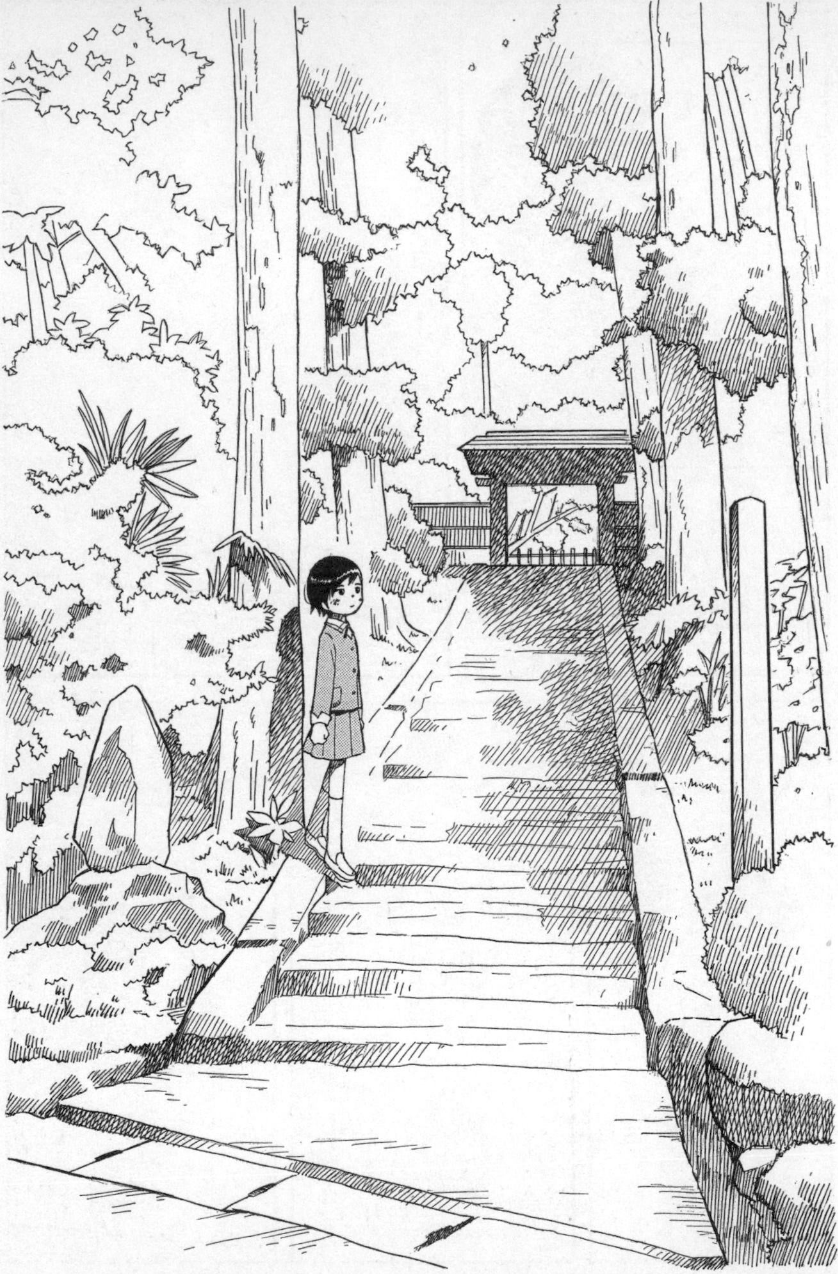

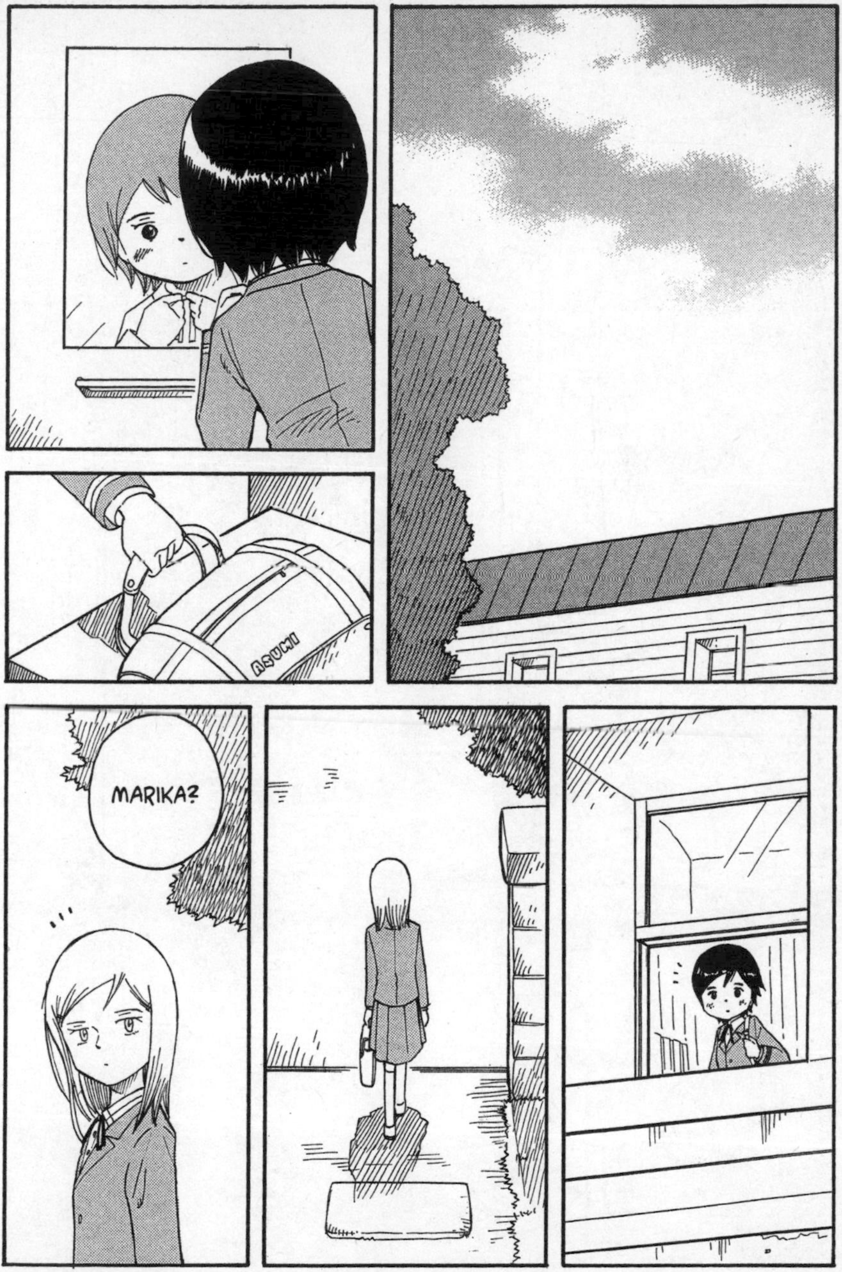
ASUMI
MARIKA?

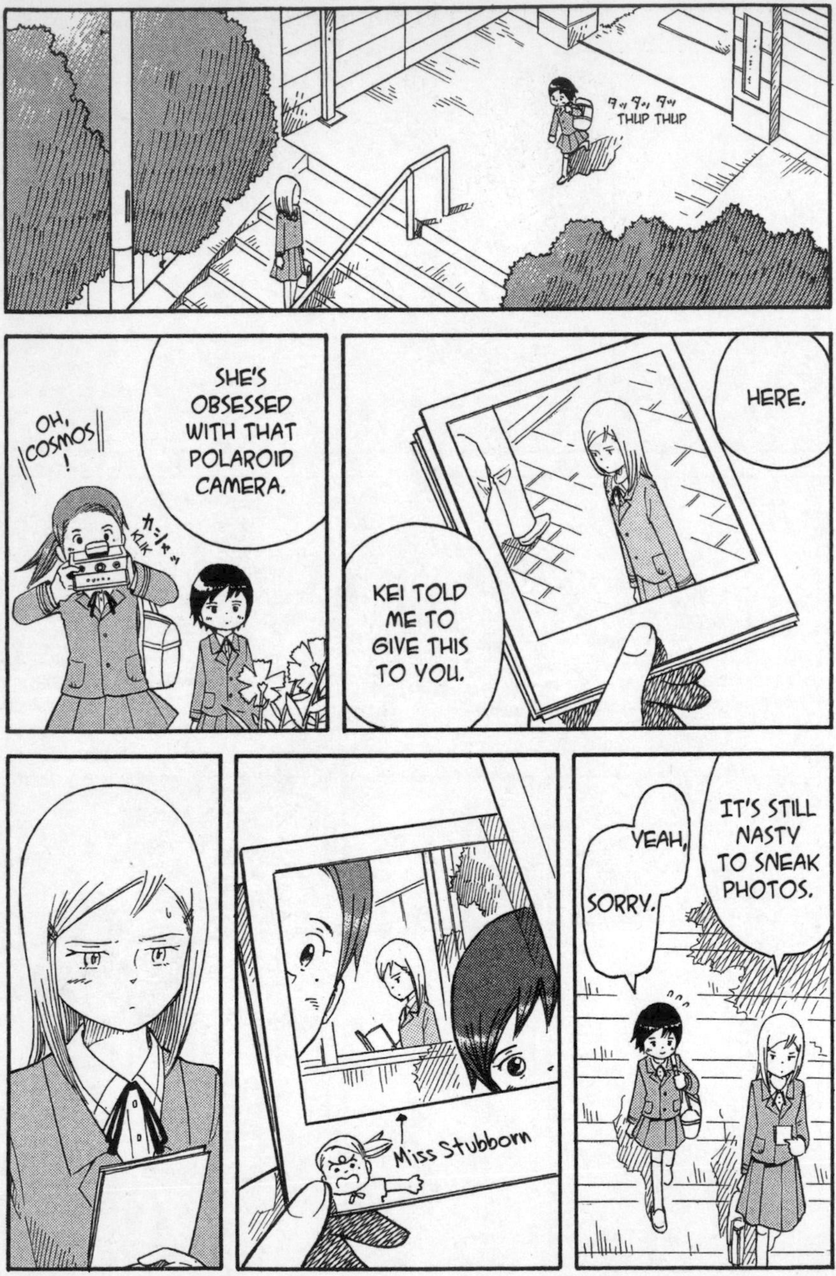
タッタッタッ
THUP THUP
HERE.
KEI TOLD ME TO GIVE THIS TO YOU.
SHE'S OBSESSED WITH THAT POLAROID CAMERA.
OH, COSMOS!
カシャッ
KLIK
IT'S STILL NASTY TO SNEAK PHOTOS.
YEAH, SORRY.
Miss Stubborn

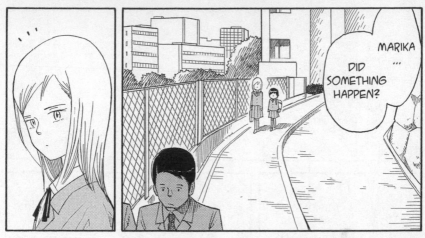

MARIKA ...
DID SOMETHING HAPPEN?
I HOPE NOT, BUT
KEI'S BEEN WORRIED TOO.
MAYBE KEI AND I
TEND TO GET TOO CONCERNED OVER THE LITTLEST THINGS.
...
I THINK KEI
WANTS TO SPEND AS MUCH TIME AS POSSIBLE WITH EVERYONE.

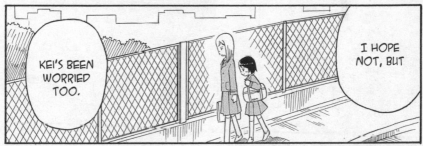

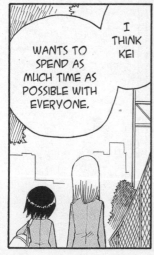

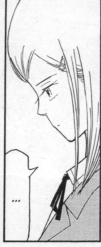

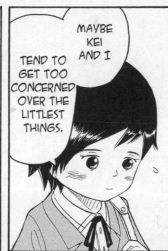

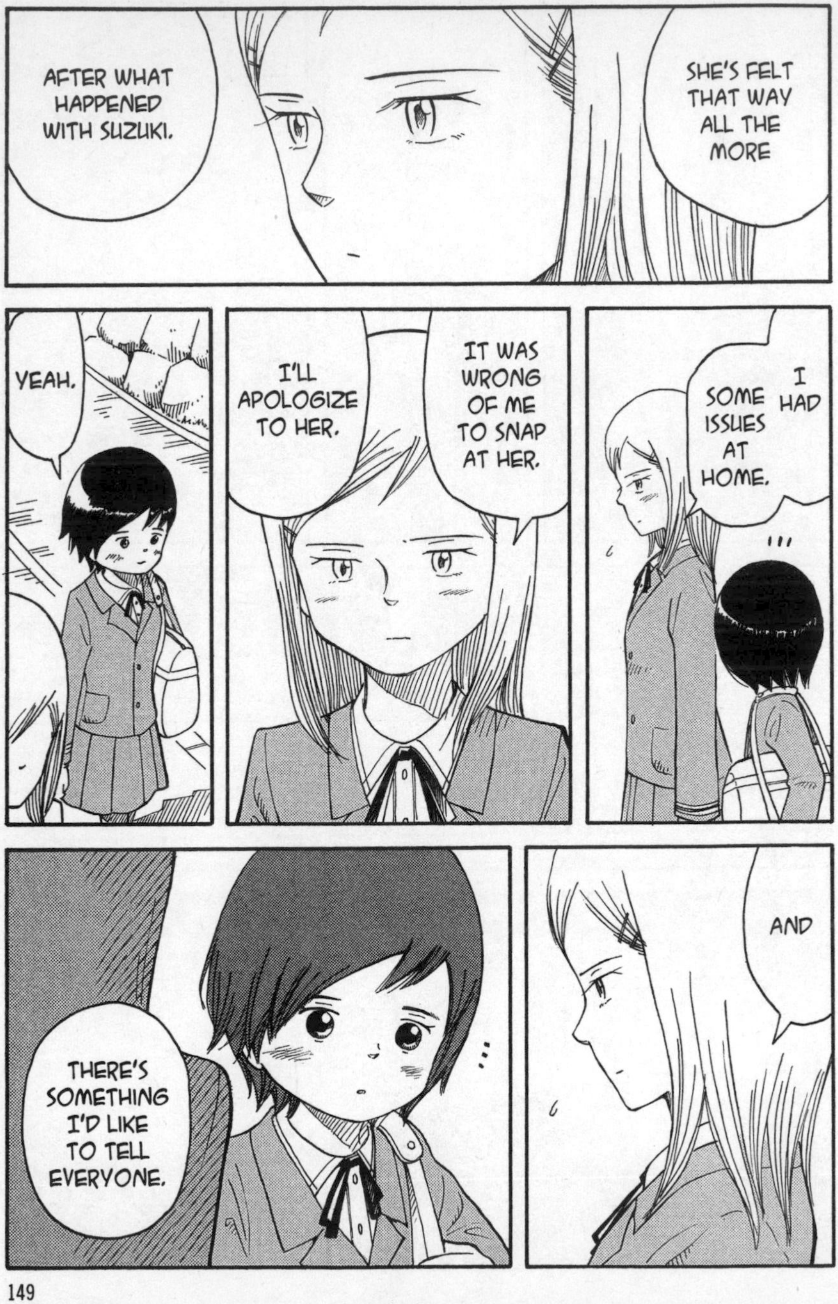
SHE'S FELT THAT WAY ALL THE MORE
AFTER WHAT HAPPENED WITH SUZUKI.
I HAD SOME ISSUES AT HOME.
IT WAS WRONG OF ME TO SNAP AT HER.
I'LL APOLOGIZE TO HER.
YEAH.
AND
THERE'S SOMETHING I'D LIKE TO TELL EVERYONE.

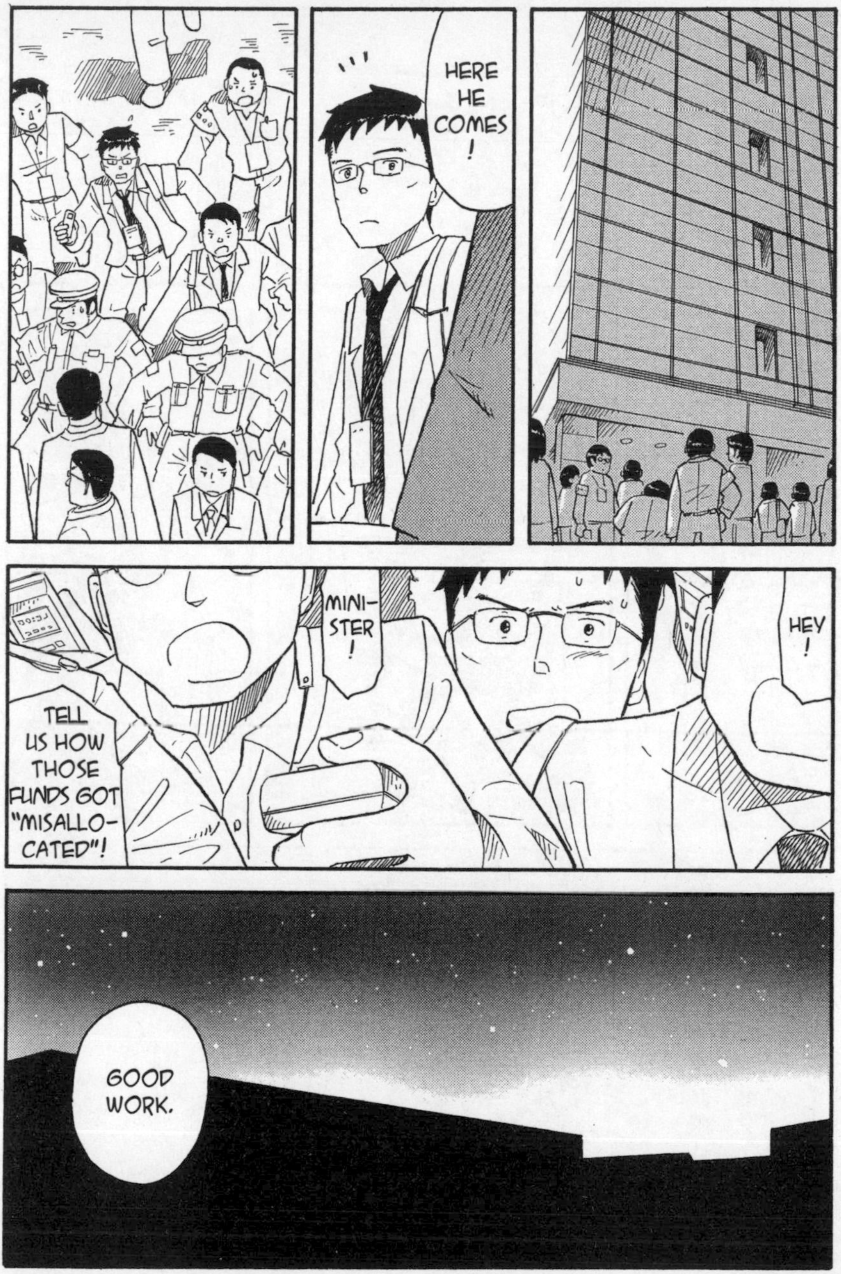
HERE HE COMES!
HEY!
MINI-STER!
TELL US HOW THOSE FUNDS GOT "MISALLO-CATED"!
GOOD WORK.

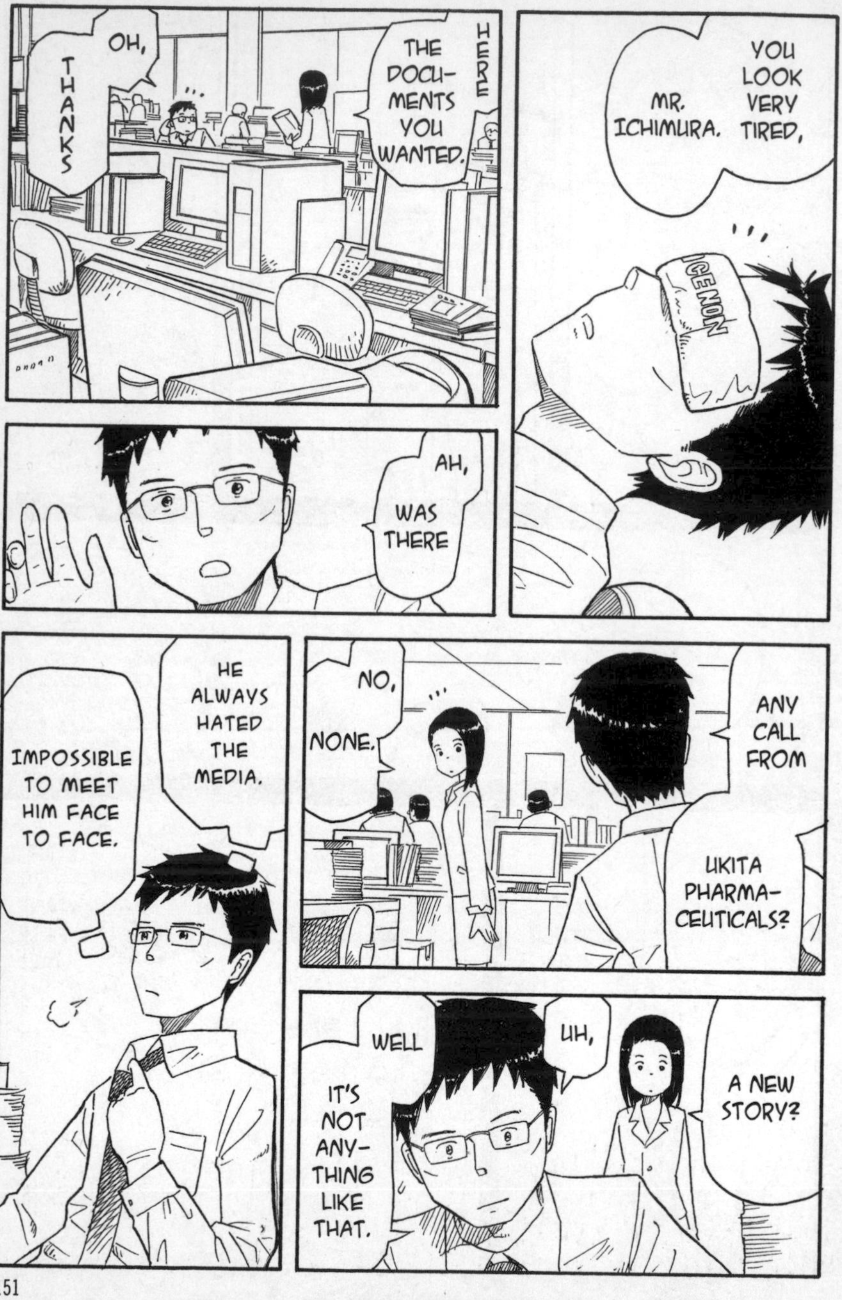
YOU LOOK VERY TIRED,
MR. ICHIMURA.
ICE NON
HERE
THE DOCU-MENTS YOU WANTED.
OH,
THANKS
...
AH,
WAS THERE
ANY CALL FROM
UKITA PHARMA-CEUTICALS?
NO,
NONE.
...
A NEW STORY?
UH,
WELL
IT'S NOT ANY-THING LIKE THAT.
HE ALWAYS HATED THE MEDIA.
IMPOSSIBLE TO MEET HIM FACE TO FACE.

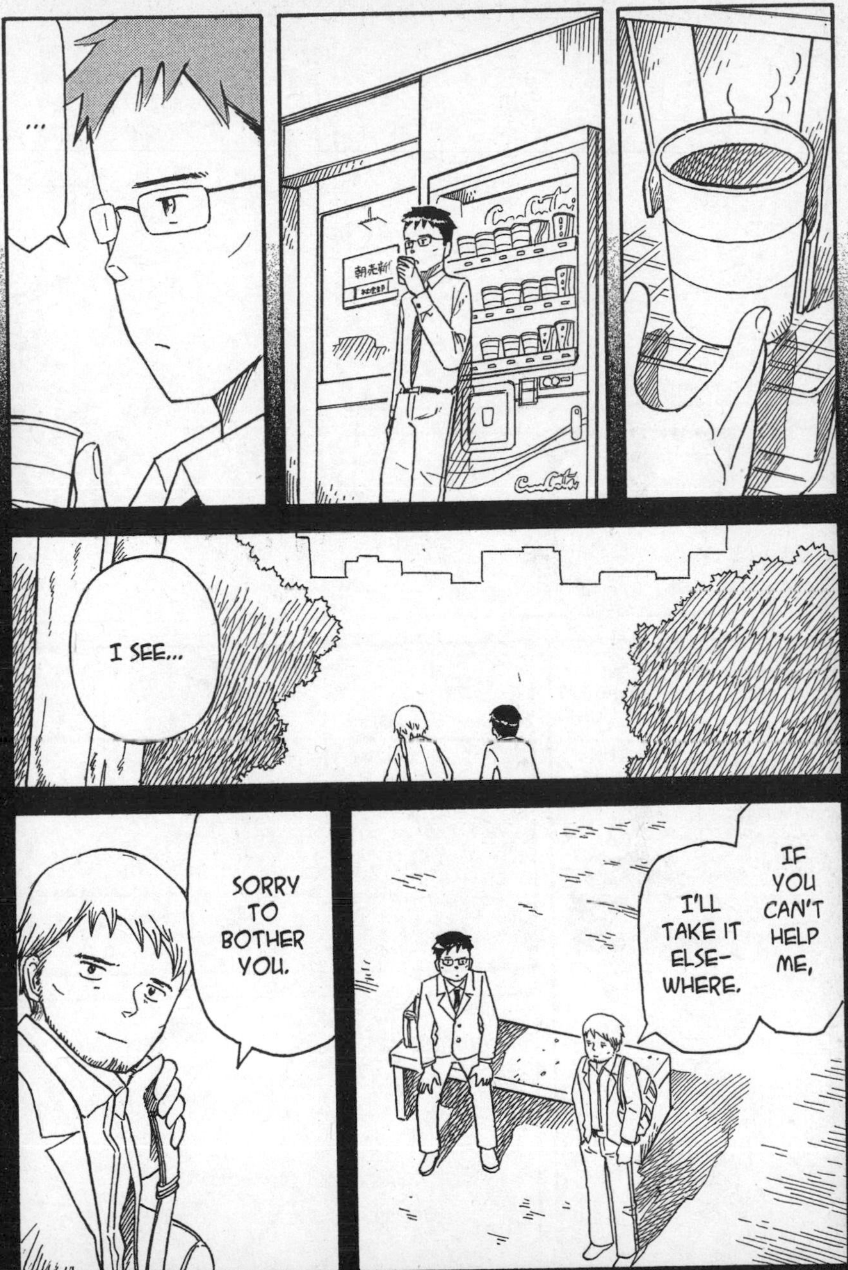
...
I SEE...
IF YOU CAN'T HELP ME,
I'LL TAKE IT ELSEWHERE.
SORRY TO BOTHER YOU.

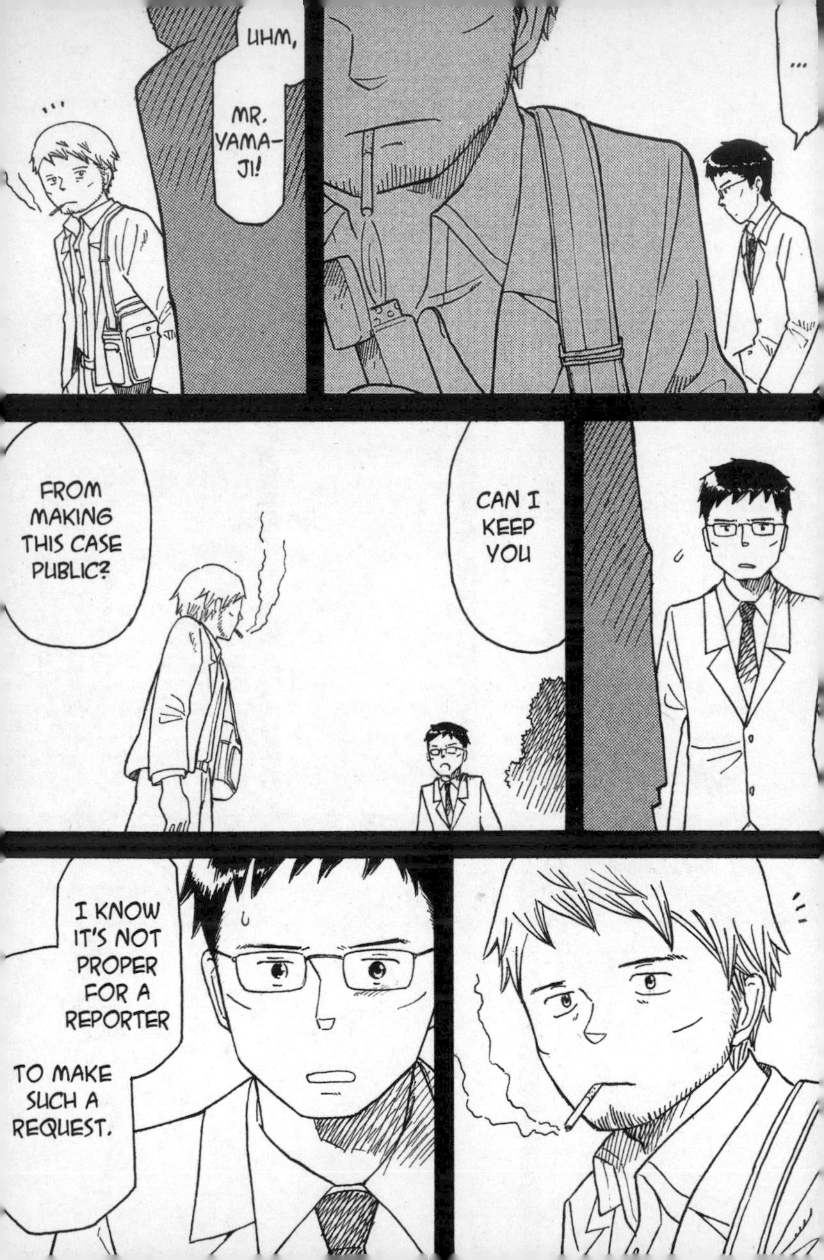
...
UHM,
MR. YAMA-JI!
...
CAN I KEEP YOU
FROM MAKING THIS CASE PUBLIC?
I KNOW IT'S NOT PROPER FOR A REPORTER
TO MAKE SUCH A REQUEST.

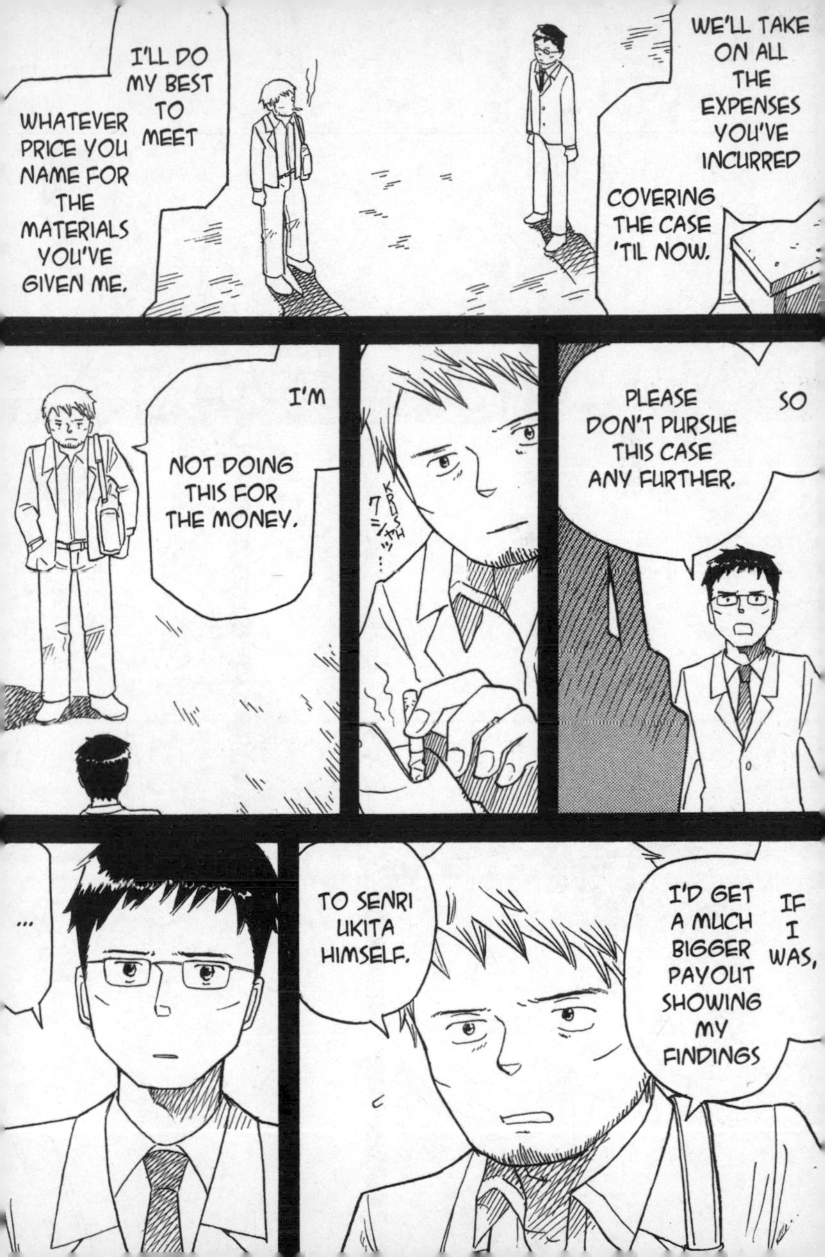
WE'LL TAKE ON ALL THE EXPENSES YOU'VE INCURRED
COVERING THE CASE 'TIL NOW.
I'LL DO MY BEST TO MEET
WHATEVER PRICE YOU NAME FOR THE MATERIALS YOU'VE GIVEN ME.
SO
PLEASE DON'T PURSUE THIS CASE ANY FURTHER.
KRUSH
I'M
NOT DOING THIS FOR THE MONEY.
IF I WAS,
I'D GET A MUCH BIGGER PAYOUT SHOWING MY FINDINGS
TO SENRI UKITA HIMSELF.
...

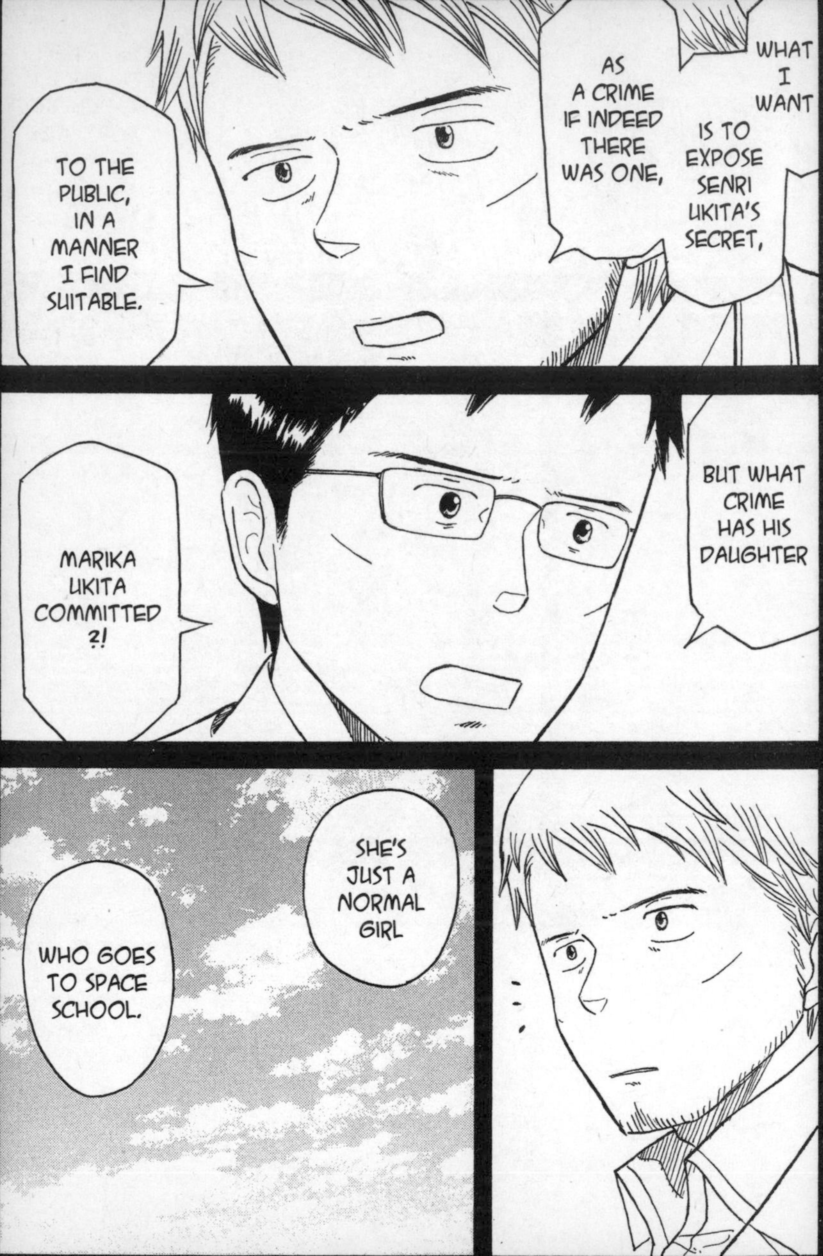
WHAT I WANT
IS TO EXPOSE SENRI UKITA'S SECRET,
AS A CRIME IF INDEED THERE WAS ONE,
TO THE PUBLIC, IN A MANNER I FIND SUITABLE.
BUT WHAT CRIME HAS HIS DAUGHTER
MARIKA UKITA COMMITTED ?!
SHE'S JUST A NORMAL GIRL
WHO GOES TO SPACE SCHOOL.

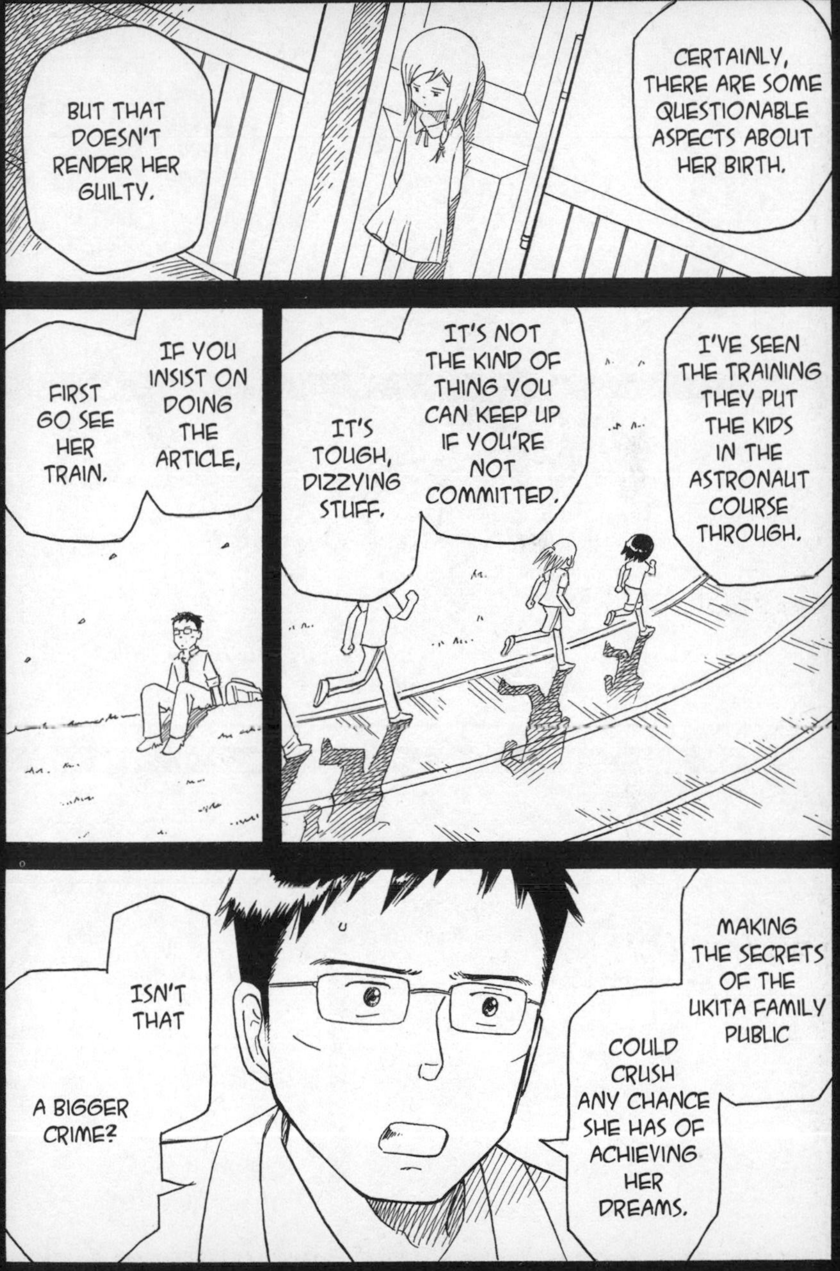
CERTAINLY, THERE ARE SOME QUESTIONABLE ASPECTS ABOUT HER BIRTH.
BUT THAT DOESN'T RENDER HER GUILTY.
I'VE SEEN THE TRAINING THEY PUT THE KIDS IN THE ASTRONAUT COURSE THROUGH.
IT'S NOT THE KIND OF THING YOU CAN KEEP UP IF YOU'RE NOT COMMITTED.
IT'S TOUGH, DIZZYING STUFF.
IF YOU INSIST ON DOING THE ARTICLE,
FIRST GO SEE HER TRAIN.
MAKING THE SECRETS OF THE UKITA FAMILY PUBLIC
COULD CRUSH ANY CHANCE SHE HAS OF ACHIEVING HER DREAMS.
ISN'T THAT
A BIGGER CRIME?

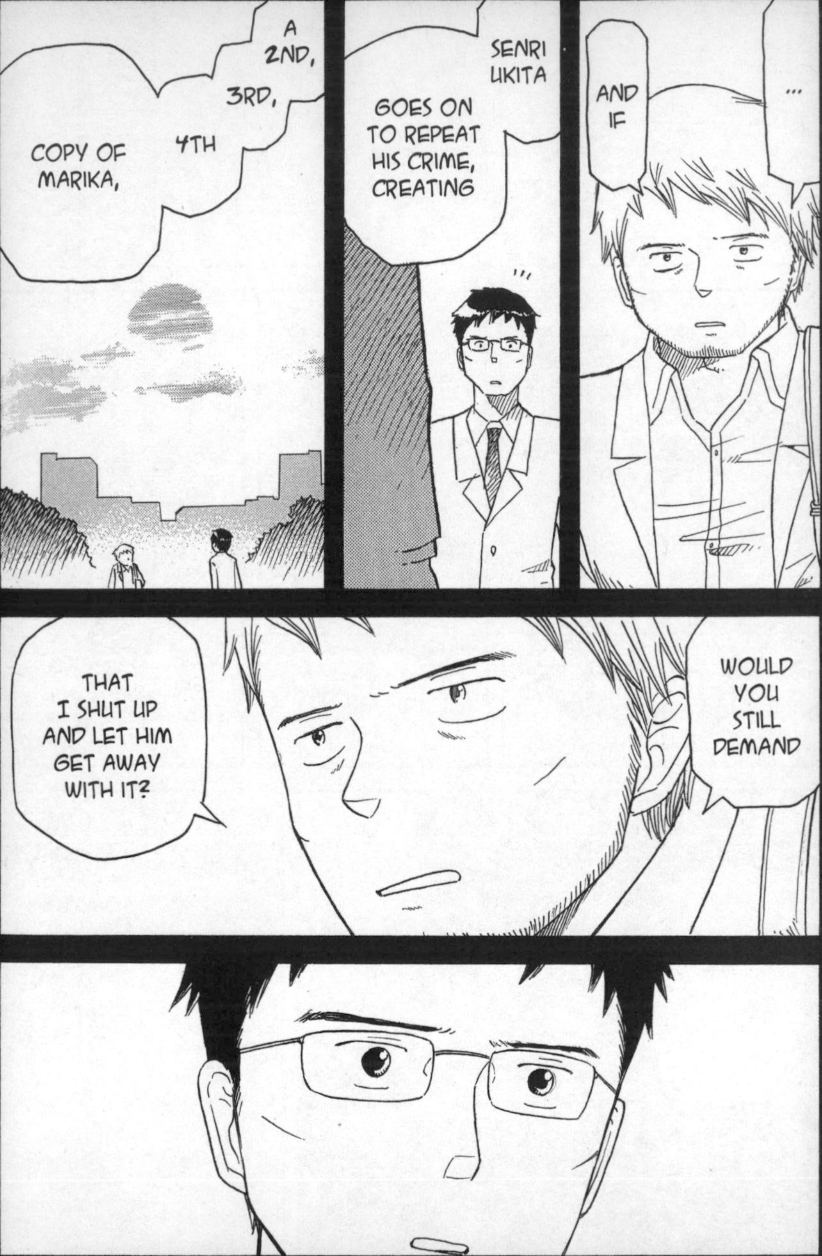
...
AND IF
SENRI UKITA
GOES ON TO REPEAT HIS CRIME, CREATING
A 2ND, 3RD, 4TH COPY OF MARIKA,
WOULD YOU STILL DEMAND
THAT I SHUT UP AND LET HIM GET AWAY WITH IT?

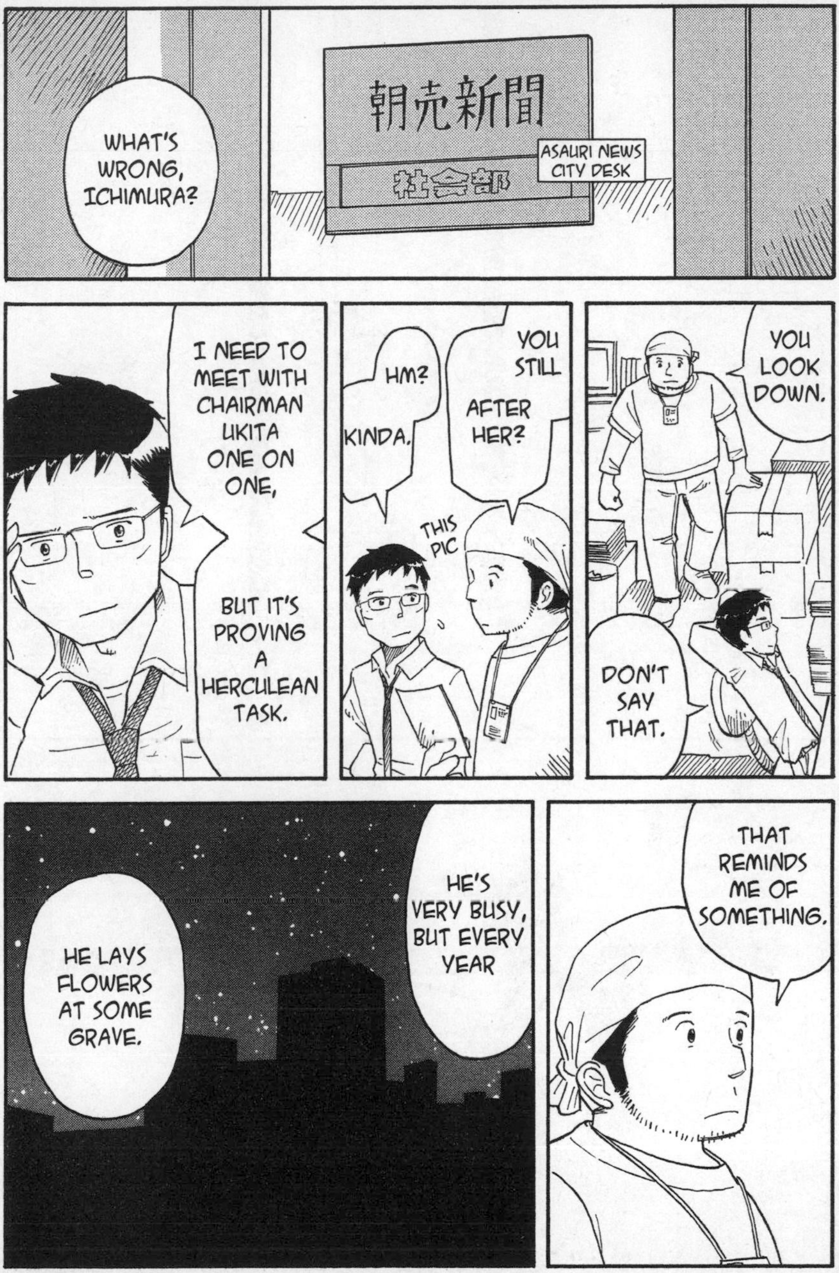
朝売新聞
社会部
ASAURI NEWS CITY DESK
WHAT'S WRONG, ICHIMURA?
YOU LOOK DOWN.
DON'T SAY THAT.
YOU STILL AFTER HER?
HM?
KINDA.
THIS PIC
I NEED TO MEET WITH CHAIRMAN UKITA ONE ON ONE,
BUT IT'S PROVING A HERCULEAN TASK.
THAT REMINDS ME OF SOMETHING.
HE'S VERY BUSY, BUT EVERY YEAR
HE LAYS FLOWERS AT SOME GRAVE.

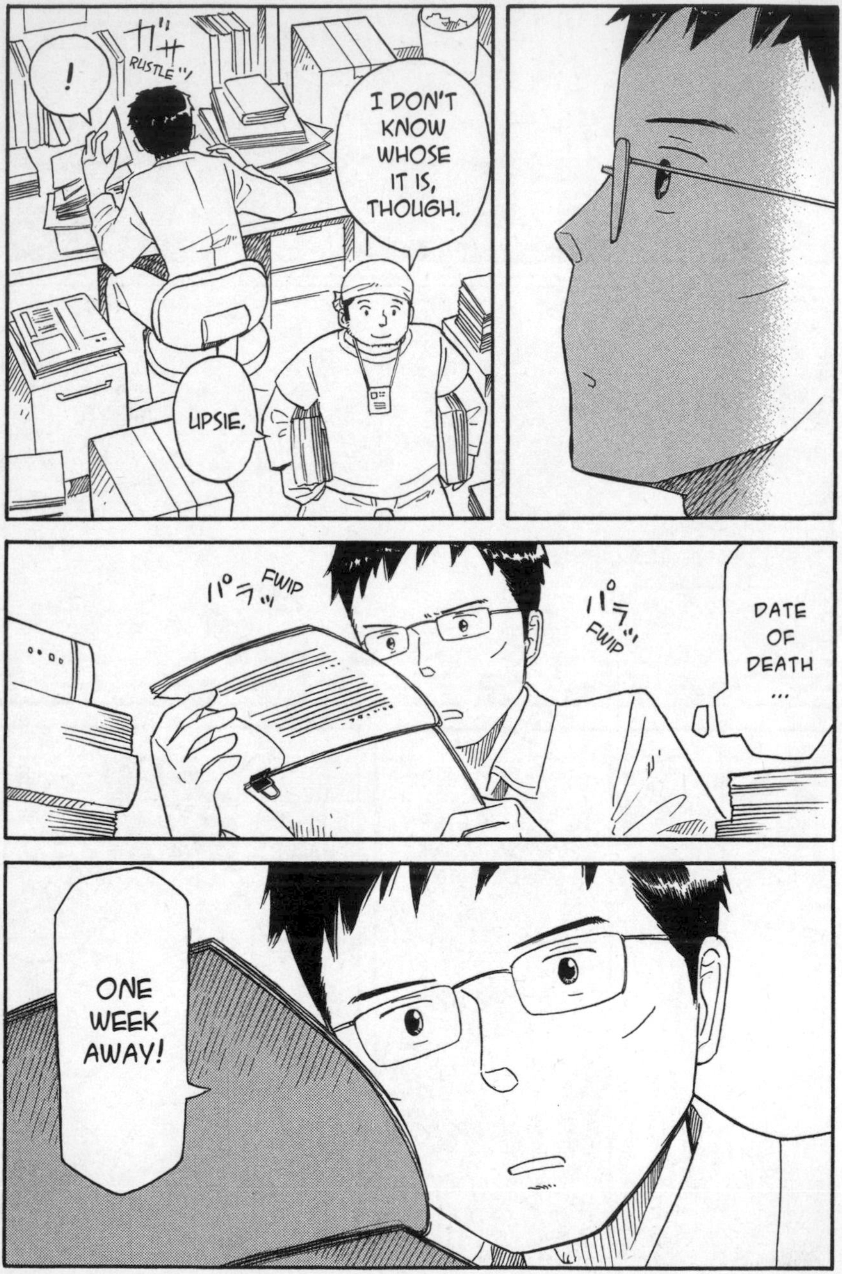
I DON'T KNOW WHOSE IT IS, THOUGH.
ガサ RUSTLE
!
UPSIE.
DATE OF DEATH ...
パラッ FWIP
パラッ FWIP
ONE WEEK AWAY!

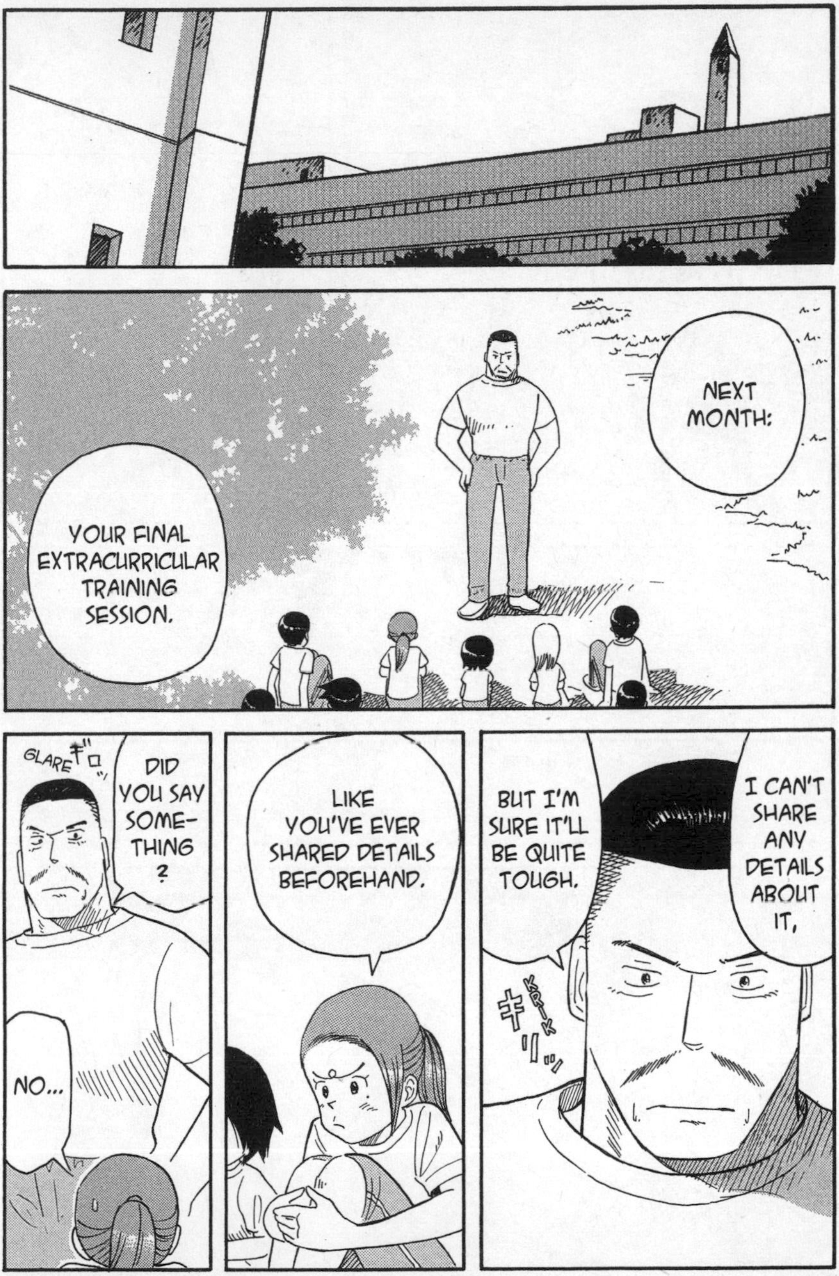
NEXT MONTH:
YOUR FINAL EXTRACURRICULAR TRAINING SESSION.
I CAN'T SHARE ANY DETAILS ABOUT IT,
BUT I'M SURE IT'LL BE QUITE TOUGH.
KRIK
ギリッ
LIKE YOU'VE EVER SHARED DETAILS BEFOREHAND.
GLARE
ギロッ
DID YOU SAY SOMETHING?
NO...

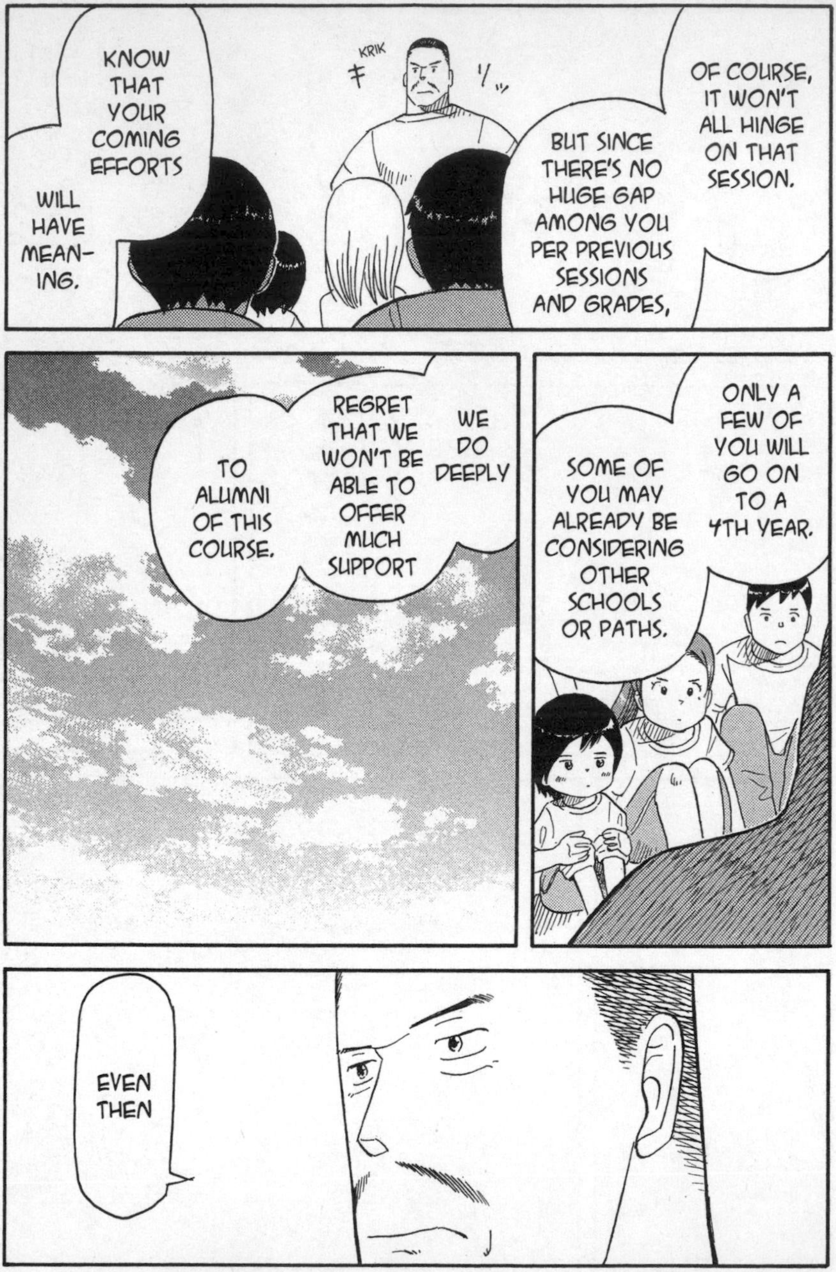
OF COURSE, IT WON'T ALL HINGE ON THAT SESSION.
BUT SINCE THERE'S NO HUGE GAP AMONG YOU PER PREVIOUS SESSIONS AND GRADES,
KRIK
KNOW THAT YOUR COMING EFFORTS
WILL HAVE MEAN-ING.
ONLY A FEW OF YOU WILL GO ON TO A 4TH YEAR.
SOME OF YOU MAY ALREADY BE CONSIDERING OTHER SCHOOLS OR PATHS.
WE DO DEEPLY
REGRET THAT WE WON'T BE ABLE TO OFFER MUCH SUPPORT
TO ALUMNI OF THIS COURSE.
EVEN THEN

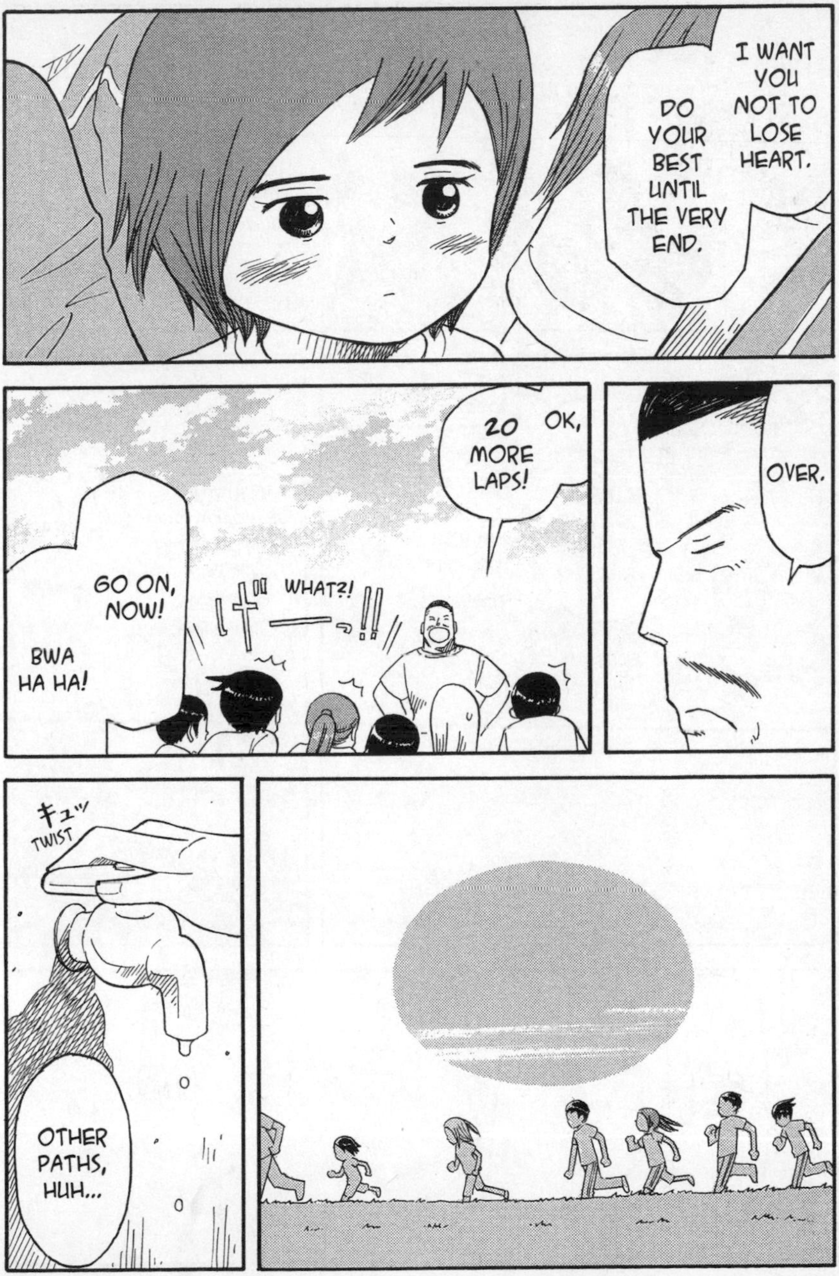
I WANT YOU NOT TO LOSE HEART.
DO YOUR BEST UNTIL THE VERY END.
OVER.
OK, 20 MORE LAPS!
げーっ!!
WHAT?!
GO ON, NOW!
BWA HA HA!
キュッ
TWIST
OTHER PATHS, HUH...

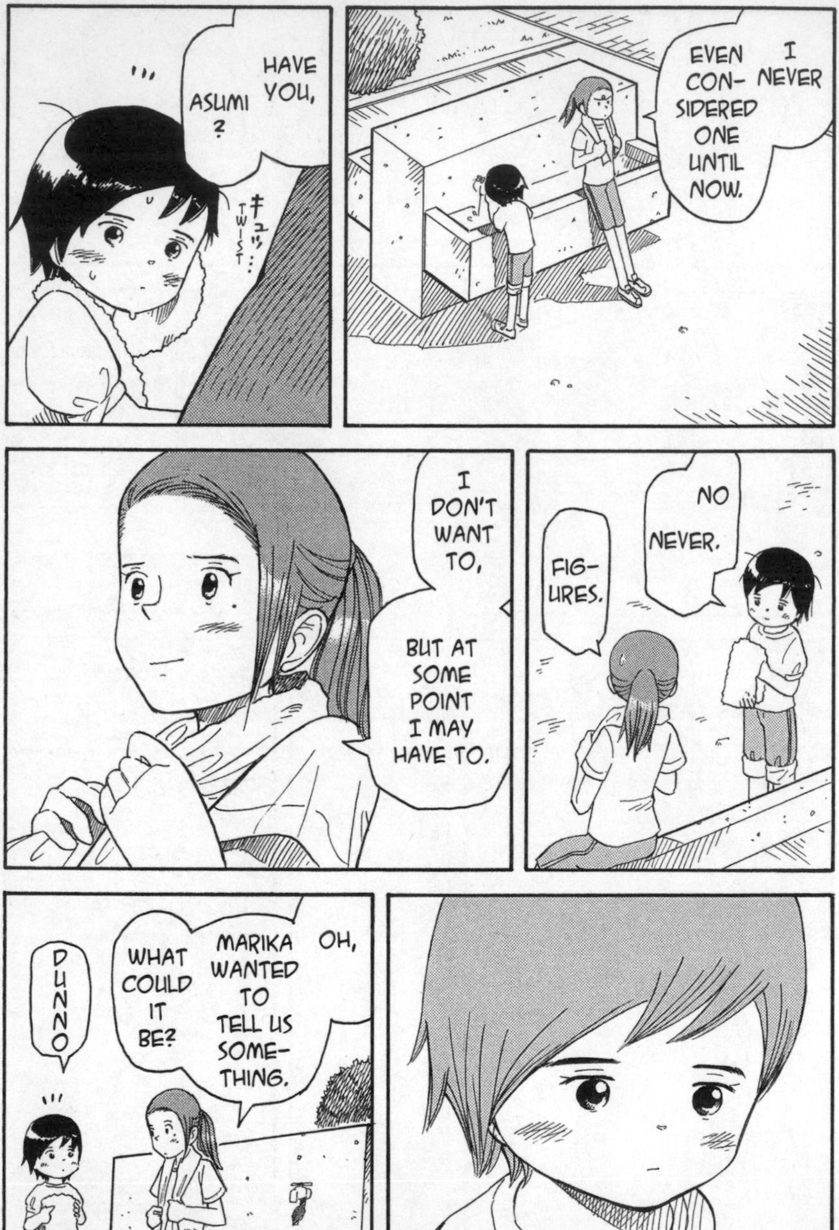
I NEVER EVEN CON-SIDERED ONE UNTIL NOW.
HAVE YOU, ASUMI?
...
キュッ TWIST...
NO NEVER.
FIG-URES.
I DON'T WANT TO,
BUT AT SOME POINT I MAY HAVE TO.
OH, MARIKA WANTED TO TELL US SOME-THING.
WHAT COULD IT BE?
DUNNO

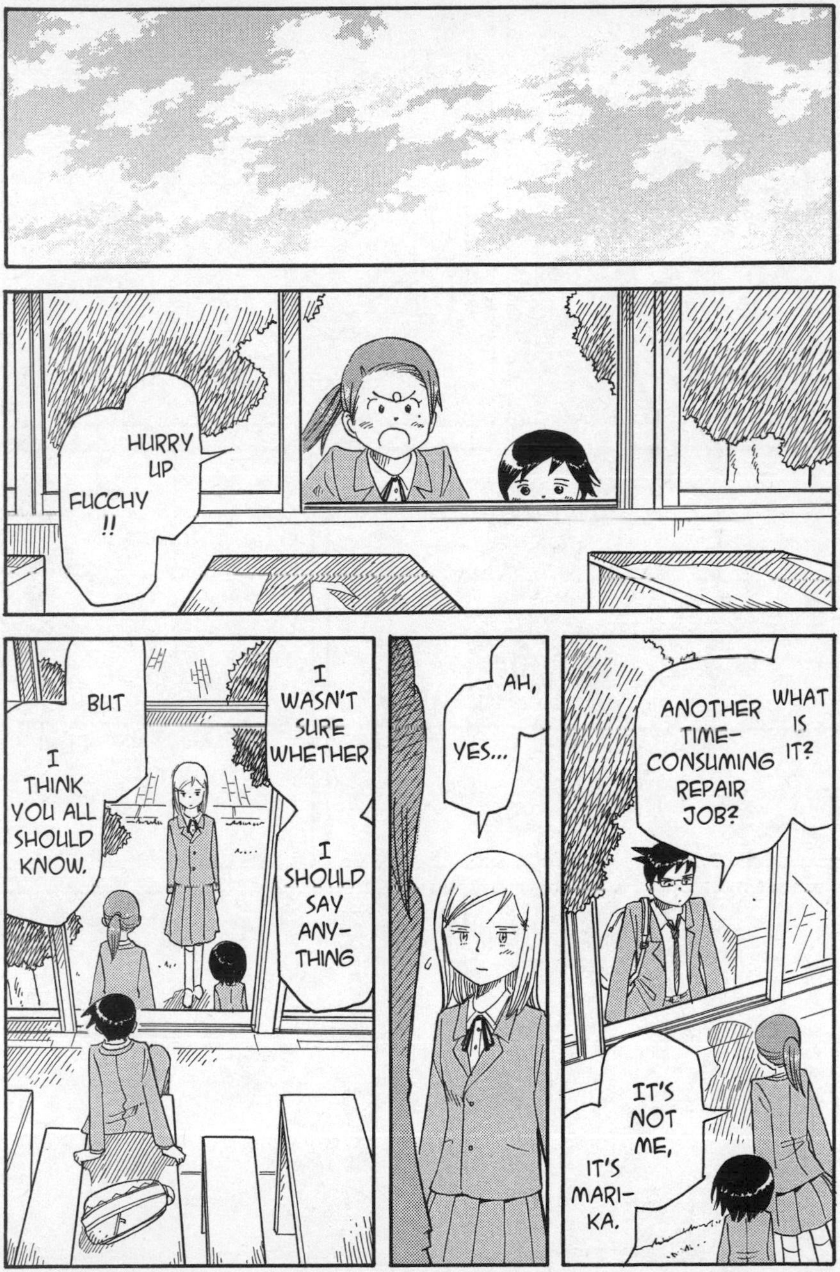
HURRY UP FUCCHY!!
WHAT IS IT?
ANOTHER TIME-CONSUMING REPAIR JOB?
IT'S NOT ME, IT'S MARI-KA.
AH, YES...
I WASN'T SURE WHETHER I SHOULD SAY ANYTHING
BUT I THINK YOU ALL SHOULD KNOW.
...

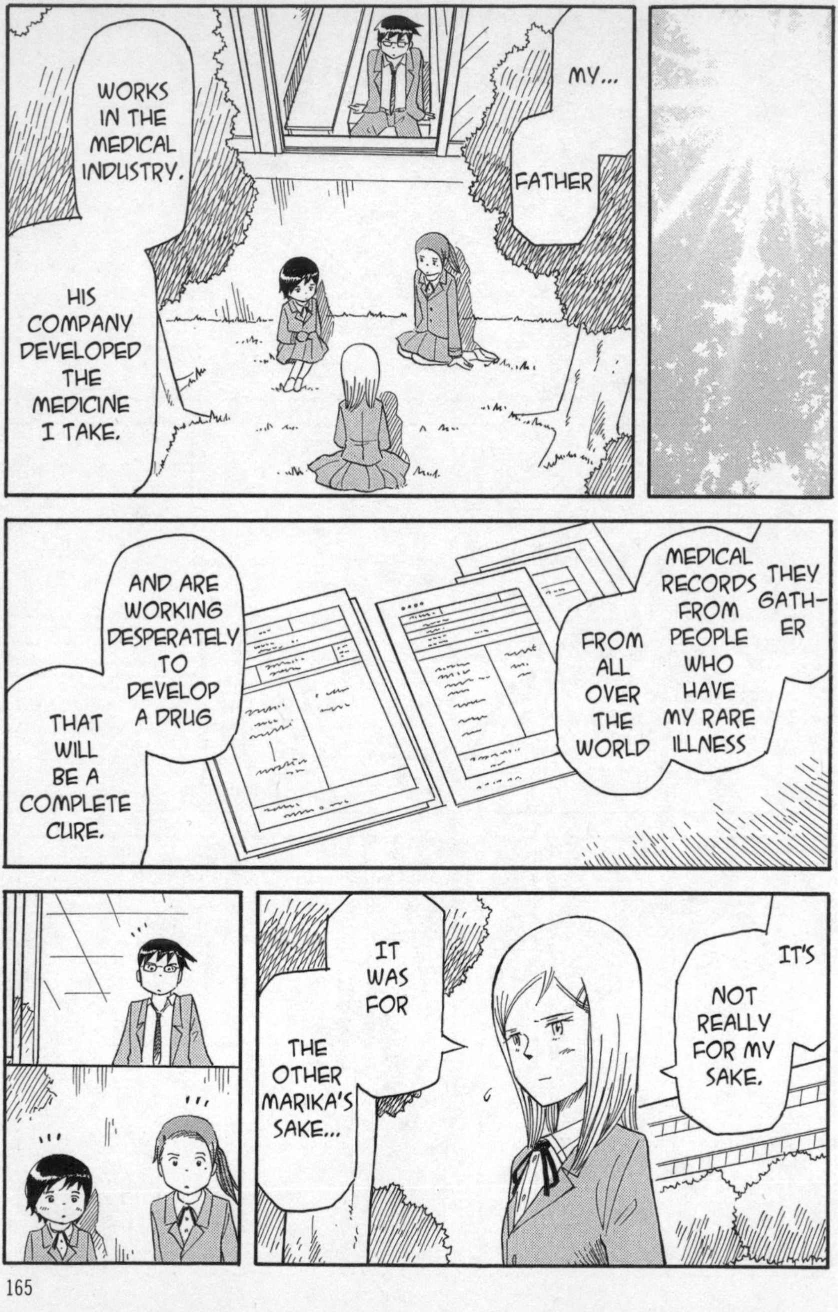
MY...
FATHER
WORKS IN THE MEDICAL INDUSTRY.
HIS COMPANY DEVELOPED THE MEDICINE I TAKE.
THEY GATH-ER
MEDICAL RECORDS FROM PEOPLE WHO HAVE MY RARE ILLNESS
FROM ALL OVER THE WORLD
AND ARE WORKING DESPERATELY TO DEVELOP A DRUG
THAT WILL BE A COMPLETE CURE.
IT'S
NOT REALLY FOR MY SAKE.
IT WAS FOR
THE OTHER MARIKA'S SAKE...

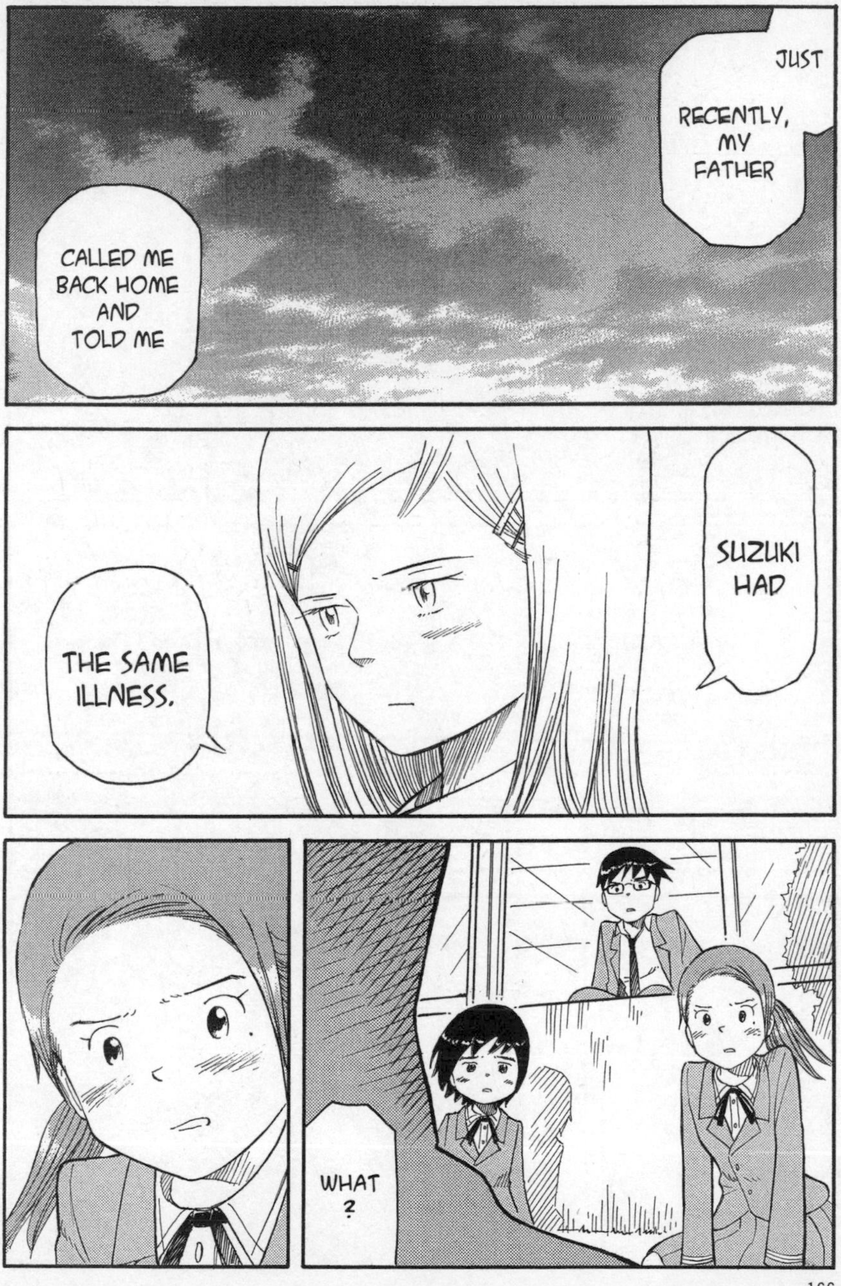
JUST RECENTLY, MY FATHER
CALLED ME BACK HOME AND TOLD ME
SUZUKI HAD
THE SAME ILLNESS.
WHAT?

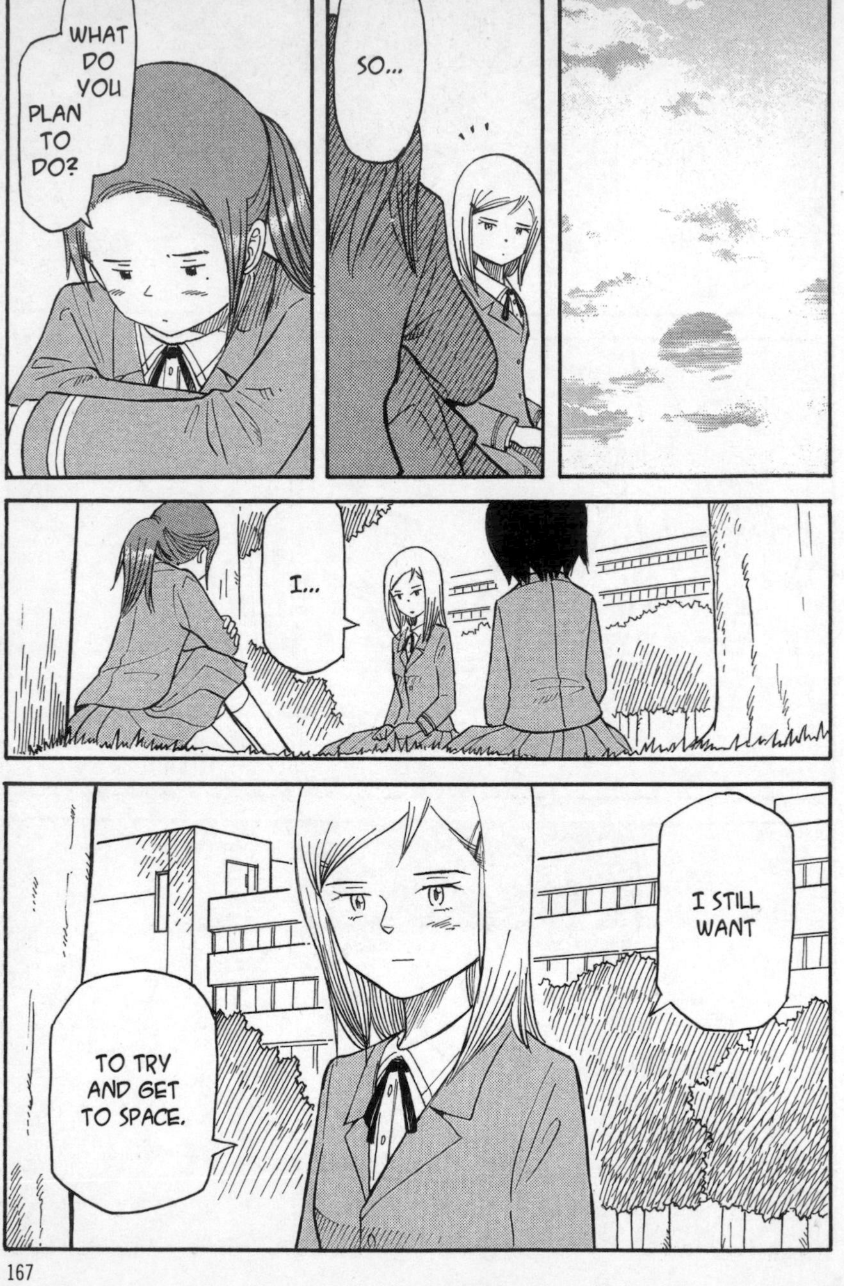
SO...
WHAT DO YOU PLAN TO DO?
I...
I STILL WANT
TO TRY AND GET TO SPACE.

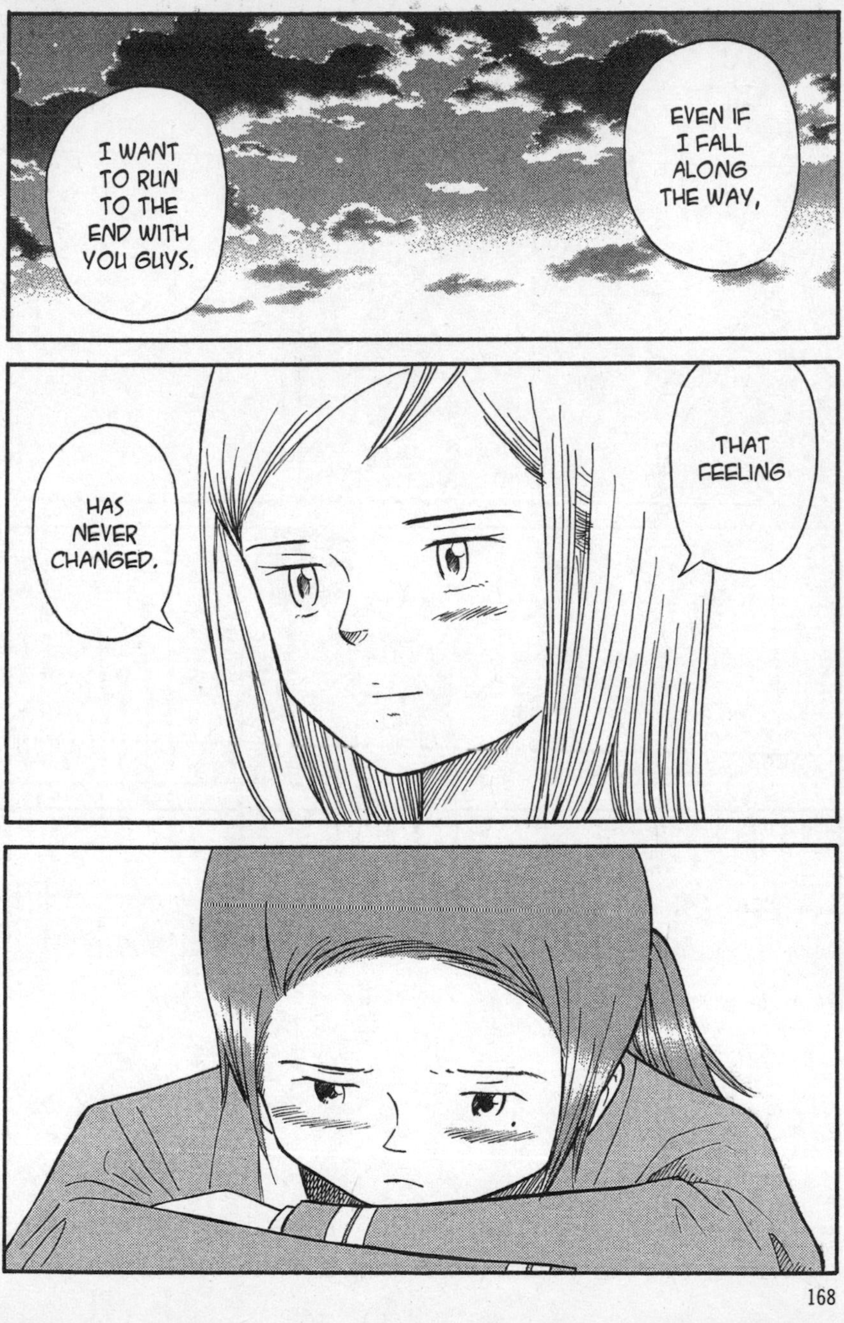
EVEN IF I FALL ALONG THE WAY,
I WANT TO RUN TO THE END WITH YOU GUYS.
THAT FEELING
HAS NEVER CHANGED.

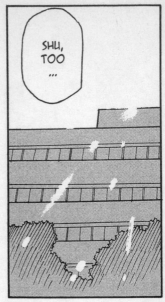

SHU, TOO...

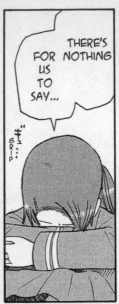

THERE'S NOTHING FOR US TO SAY...

"...GRIP"

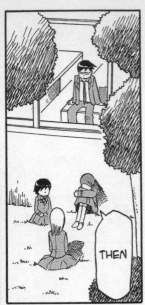

THEN

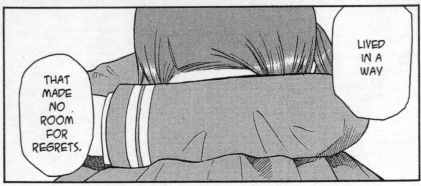

THAT MADE NO ROOM FOR REGRETS.

LIVED IN A WAY

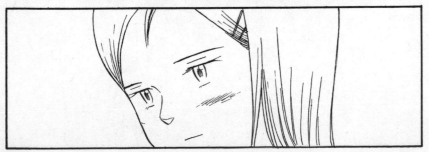

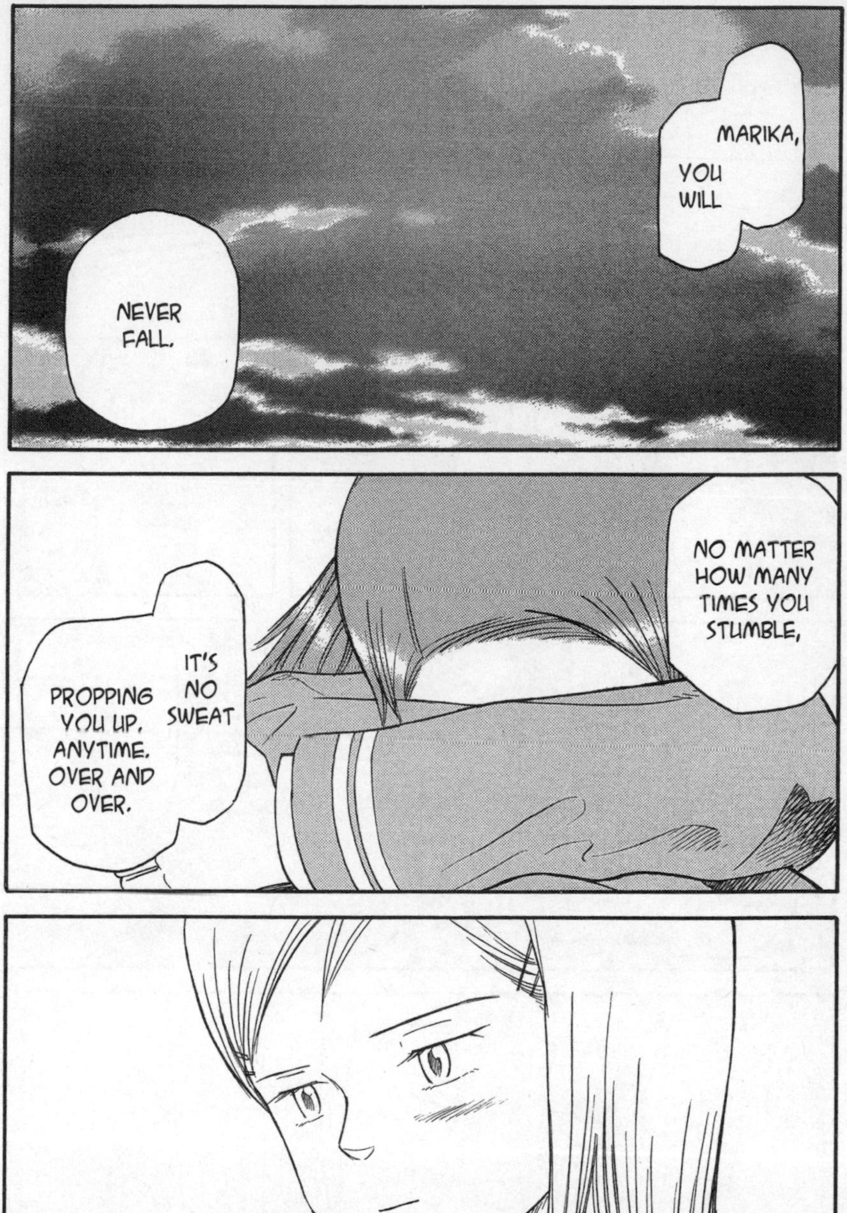
MARIKA, YOU WILL
NEVER FALL.
NO MATTER HOW MANY TIMES YOU STUMBLE,
IT'S NO SWEAT PROPPING YOU UP, ANYTIME. OVER AND OVER.

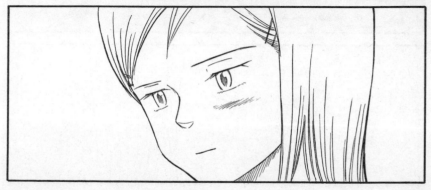

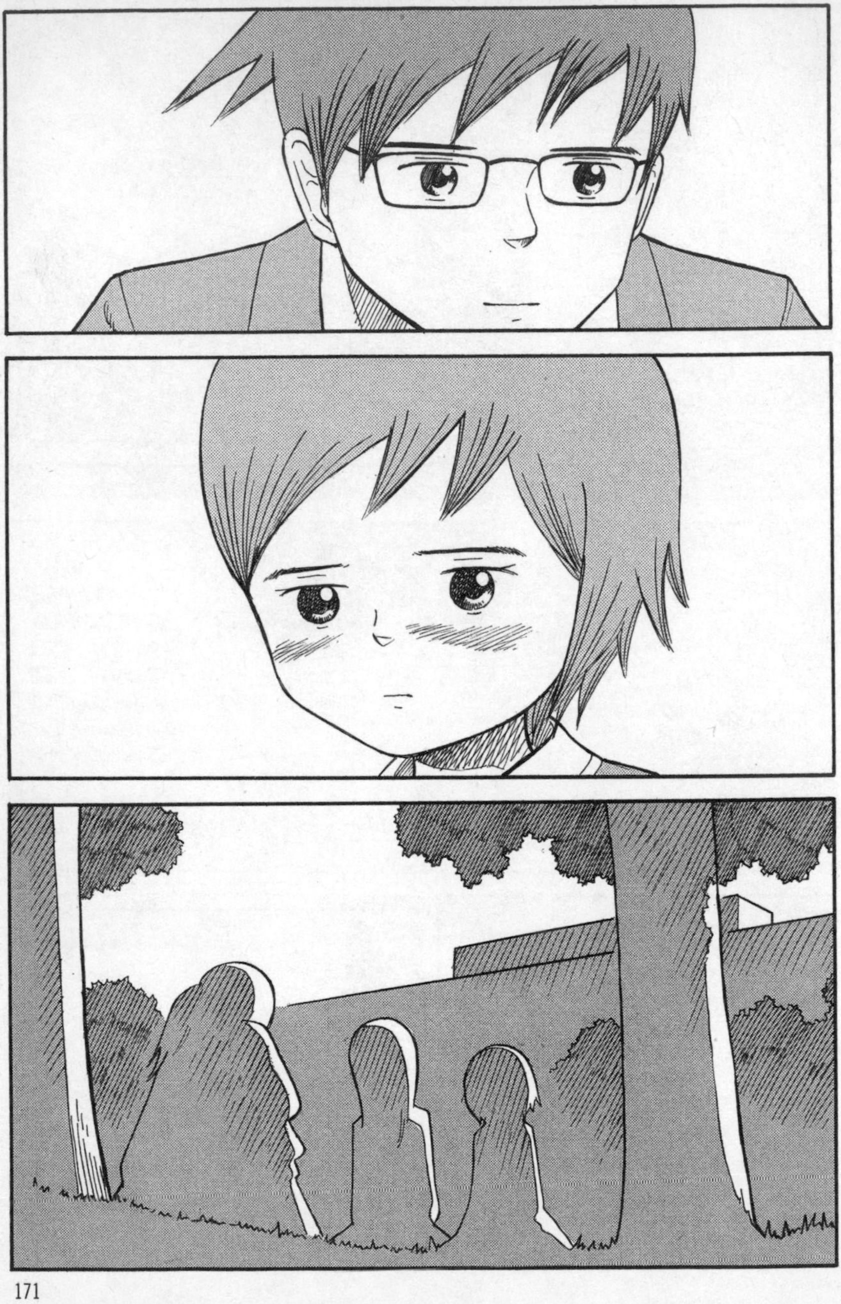

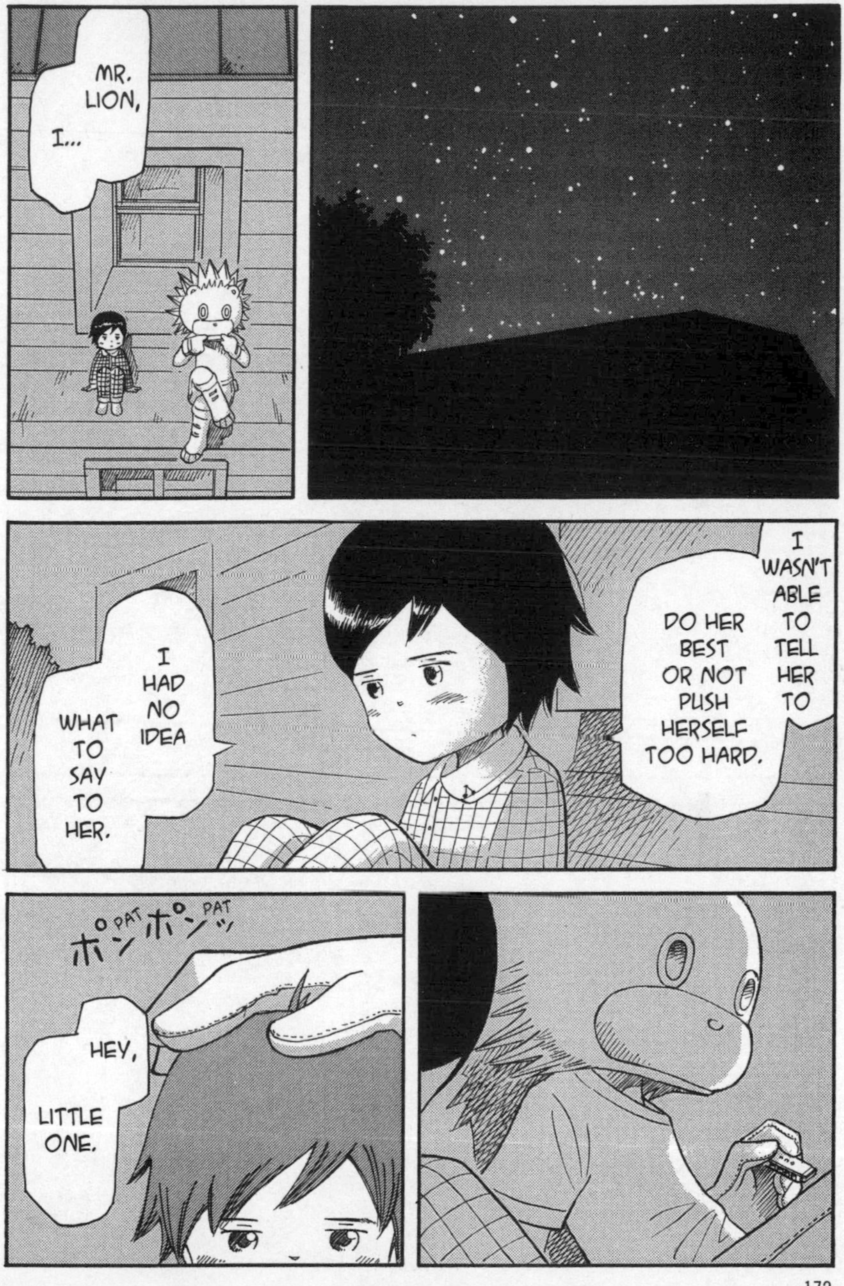
MR. LION, I...
I WASN'T ABLE TO TELL HER TO DO HER BEST OR NOT PUSH HERSELF TOO HARD.
I HAD NO IDEA WHAT TO SAY TO HER.
ポンポンッ PAT PAT
HEY, LITTLE ONE.

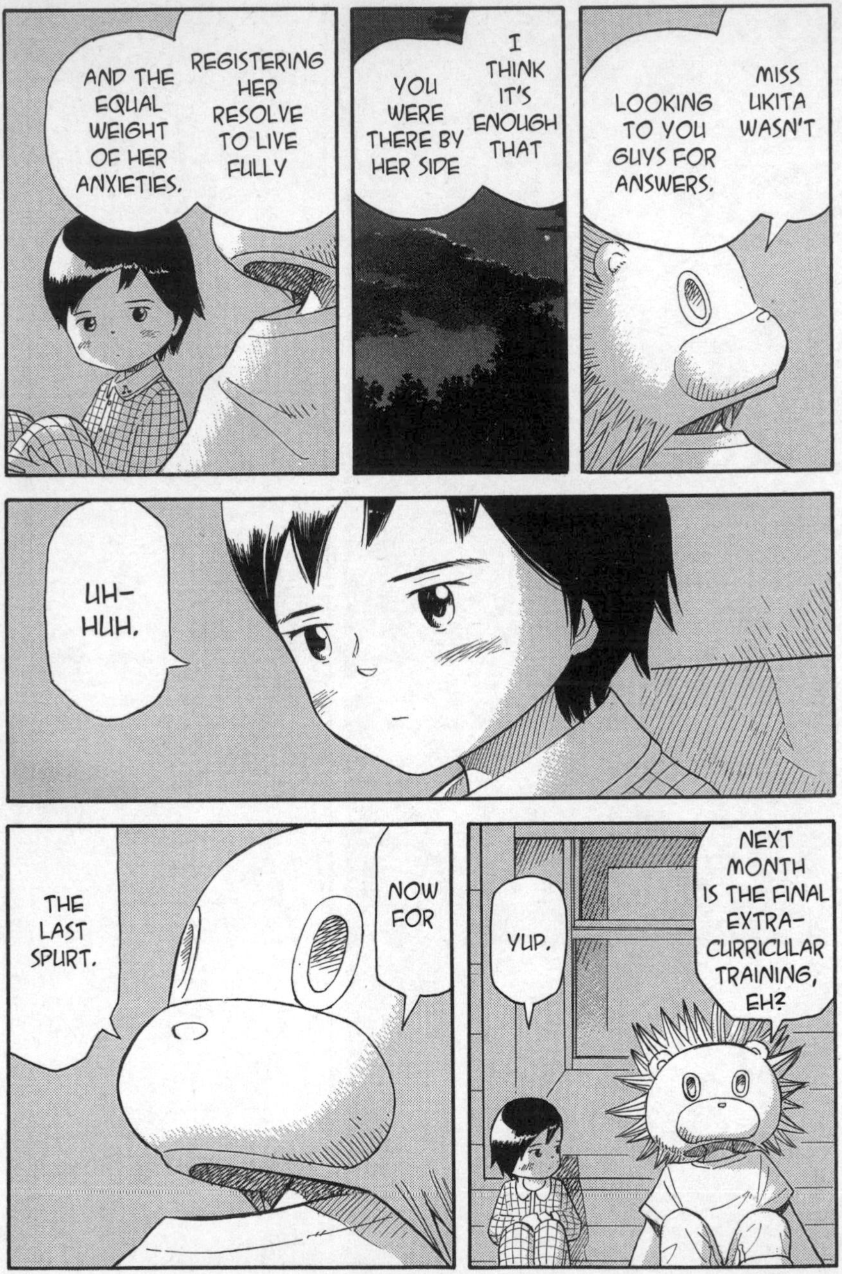
MISS UKITA WASN'T
LOOKING TO YOU GUYS FOR ANSWERS.
I THINK IT'S ENOUGH THAT
YOU WERE THERE BY HER SIDE
REGISTERING HER RESOLVE TO LIVE FULLY
AND THE EQUAL WEIGHT OF HER ANXIETIES.
UH-HUH.
NEXT MONTH IS THE FINAL EXTRA-CURRICULAR TRAINING, EH?
YUP.
NOW FOR
THE LAST SPURT.

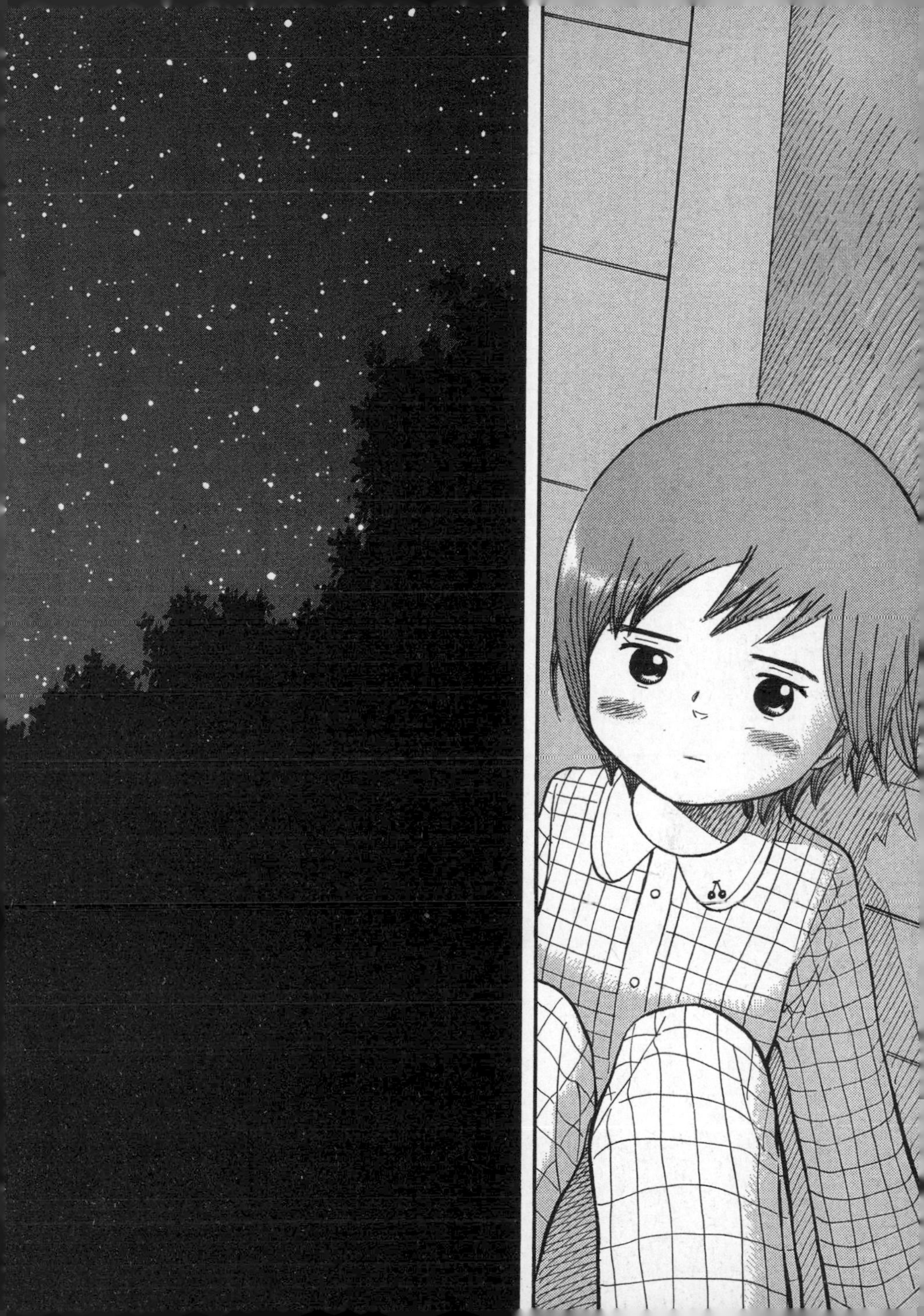

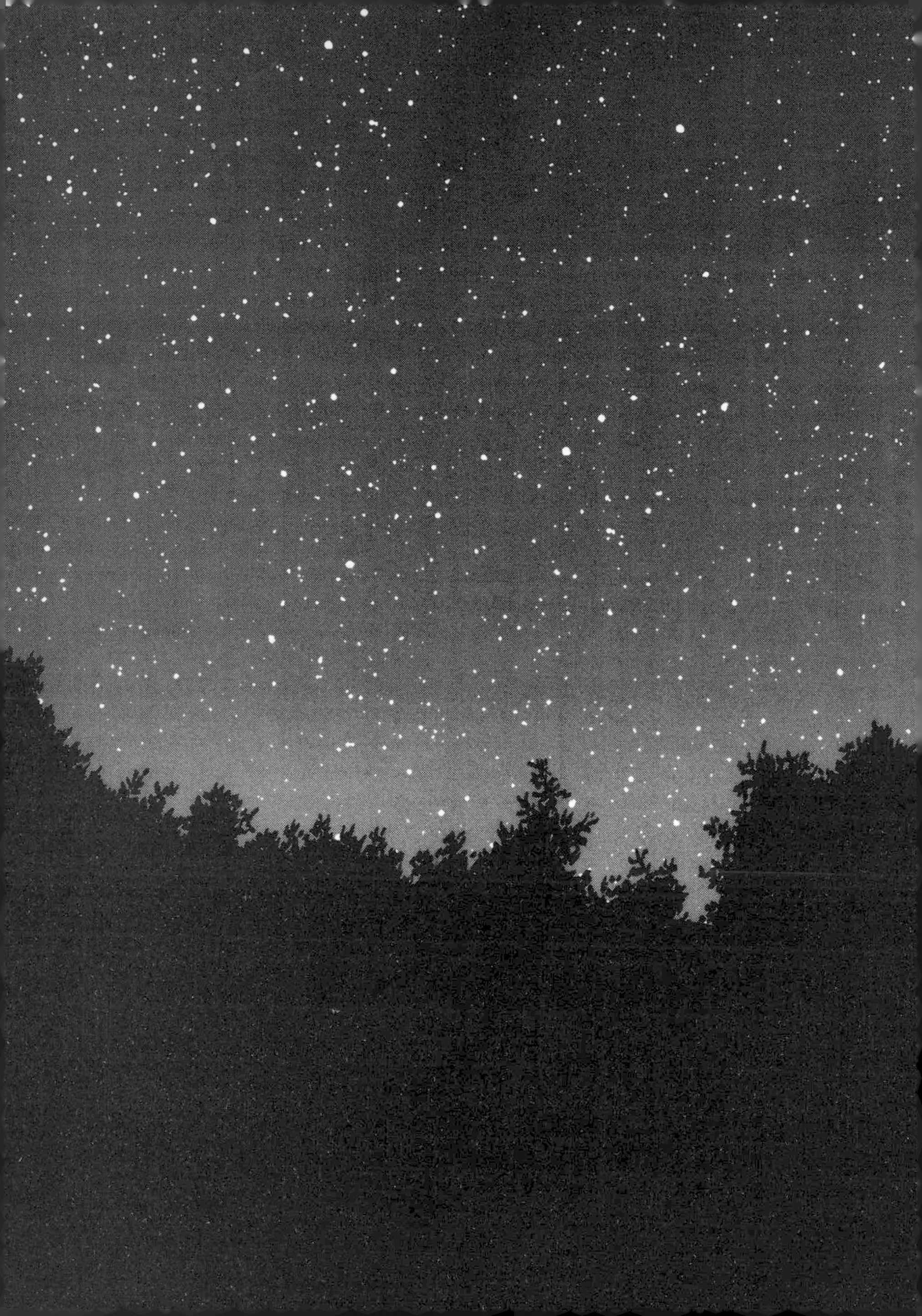

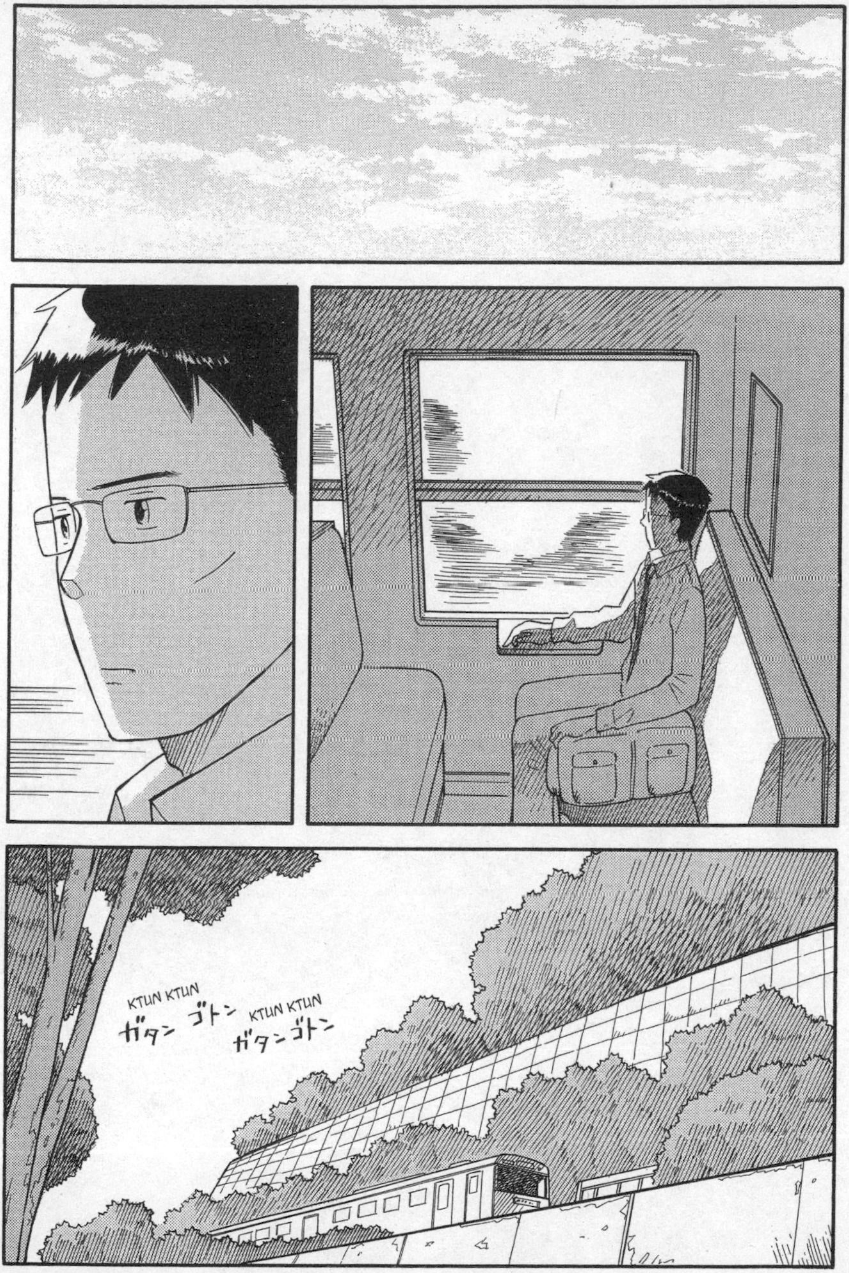
KTUN KTUN
ガタンゴトン
KTUN KTUN
ガタン ゴトン

MISSION:70

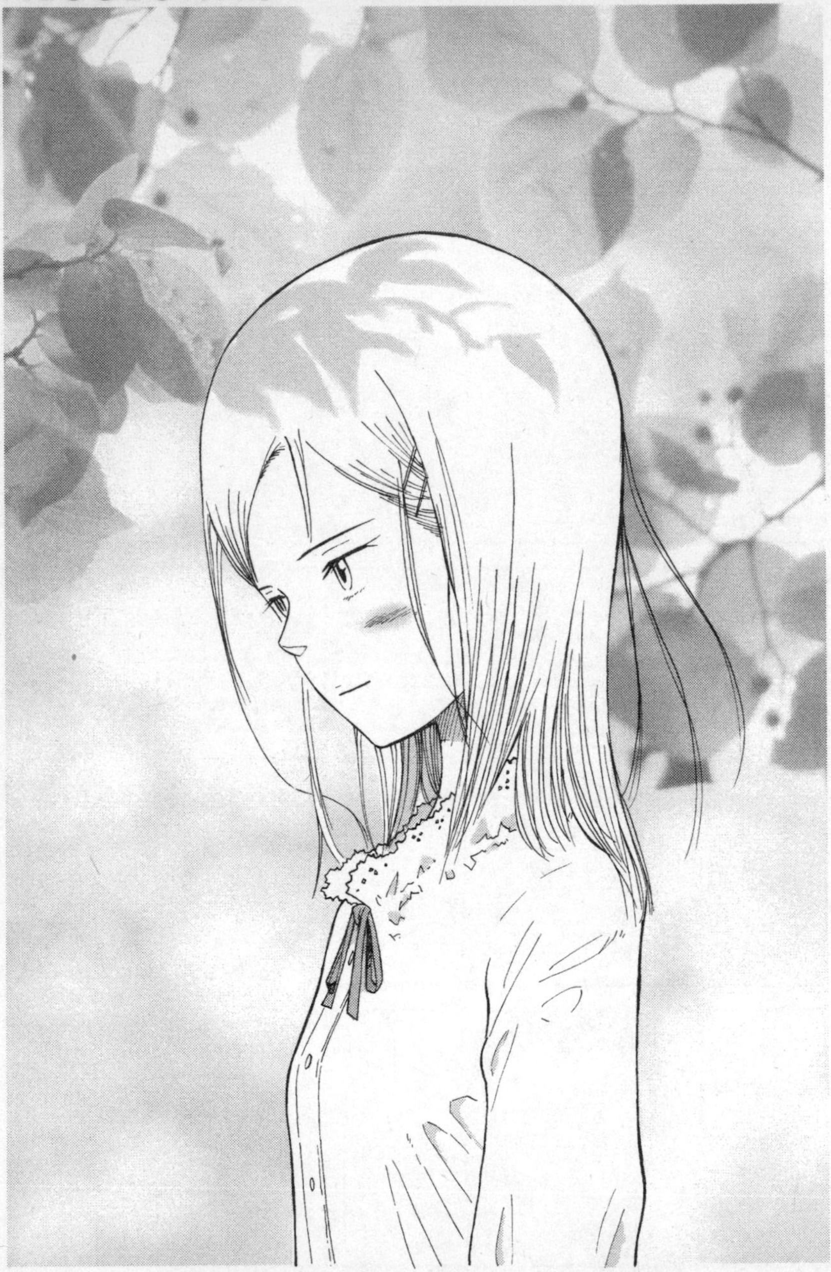

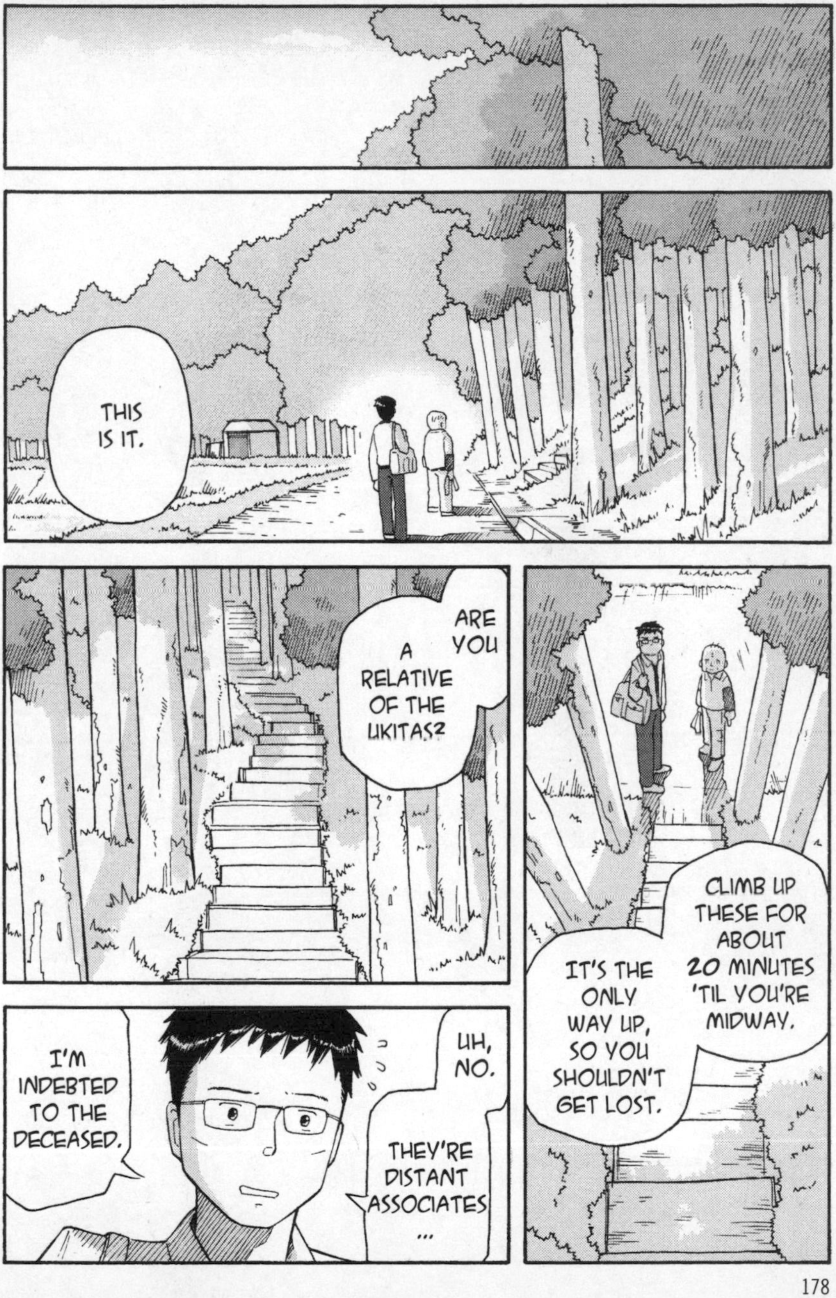
THIS IS IT.
CLIMB UP THESE FOR ABOUT 20 MINUTES 'TIL YOU'RE MIDWAY.
IT'S THE ONLY WAY UP, SO YOU SHOULDN'T GET LOST.
ARE YOU A RELATIVE OF THE UKITAS?
UH, NO.
THEY'RE DISTANT ASSOCIATES ...
I'M INDEBTED TO THE DECEASED.

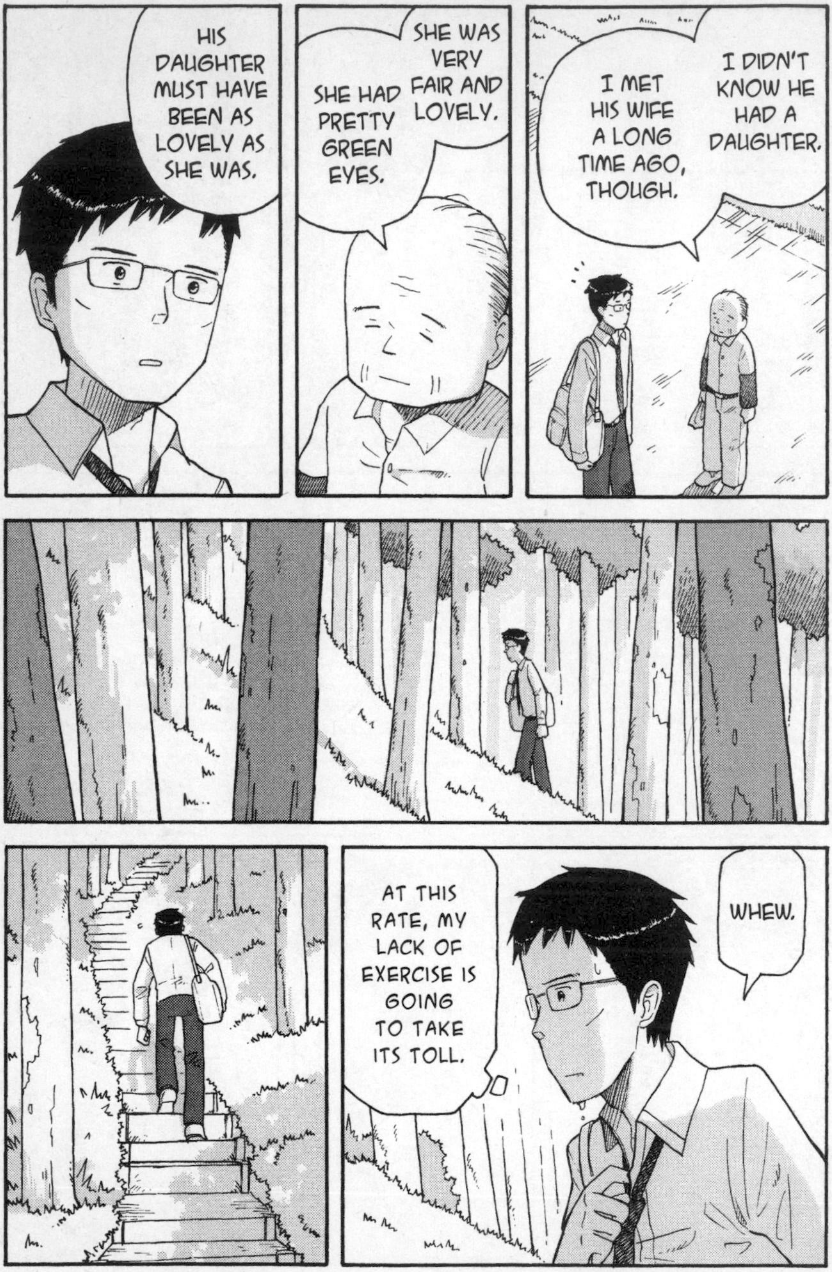
I DIDN'T KNOW HE HAD A DAUGHTER.
I MET HIS WIFE A LONG TIME AGO, THOUGH.
SHE WAS VERY FAIR AND LOVELY.
SHE HAD PRETTY GREEN EYES.
HIS DAUGHTER MUST HAVE BEEN AS LOVELY AS SHE WAS.
WHEW.
AT THIS RATE, MY LACK OF EXERCISE IS GOING TO TAKE ITS TOLL.

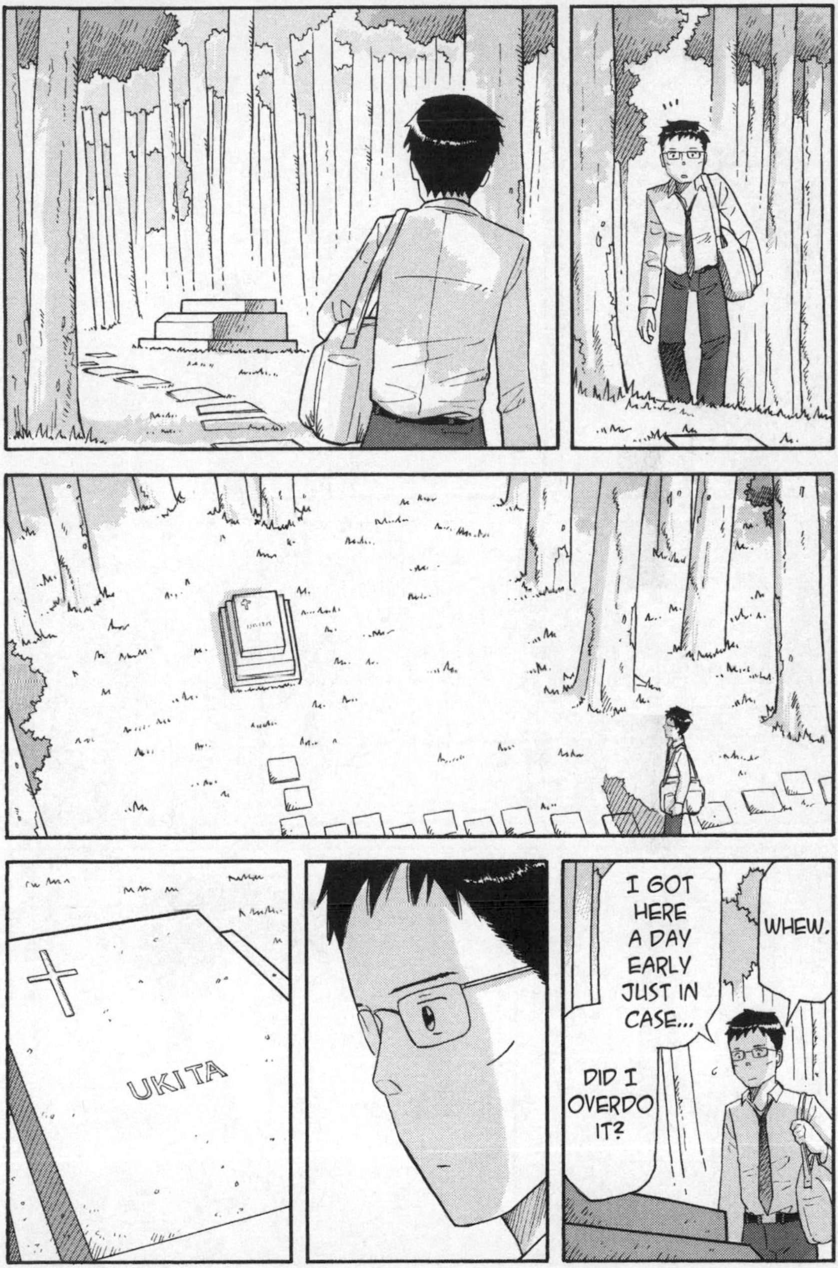
WHEW.
I GOT HERE A DAY EARLY JUST IN CASE...
DID I OVERDO IT?
UKITA

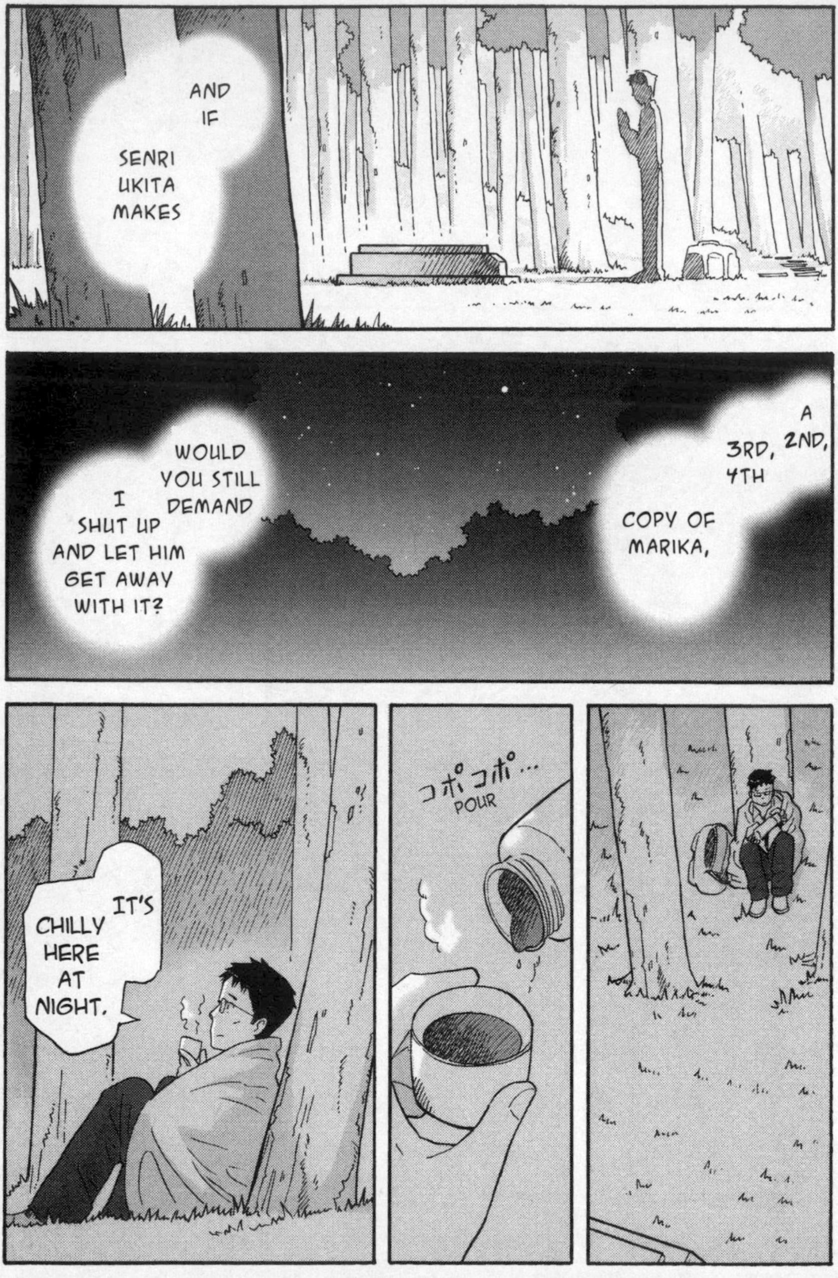
AND IF SENRI UKITA MAKES
A 2ND, 3RD, 4TH COPY OF MARIKA,
WOULD YOU STILL DEMAND I SHUT UP AND LET HIM GET AWAY WITH IT?
コポコポ…
POUR
IT'S CHILLY HERE AT NIGHT.

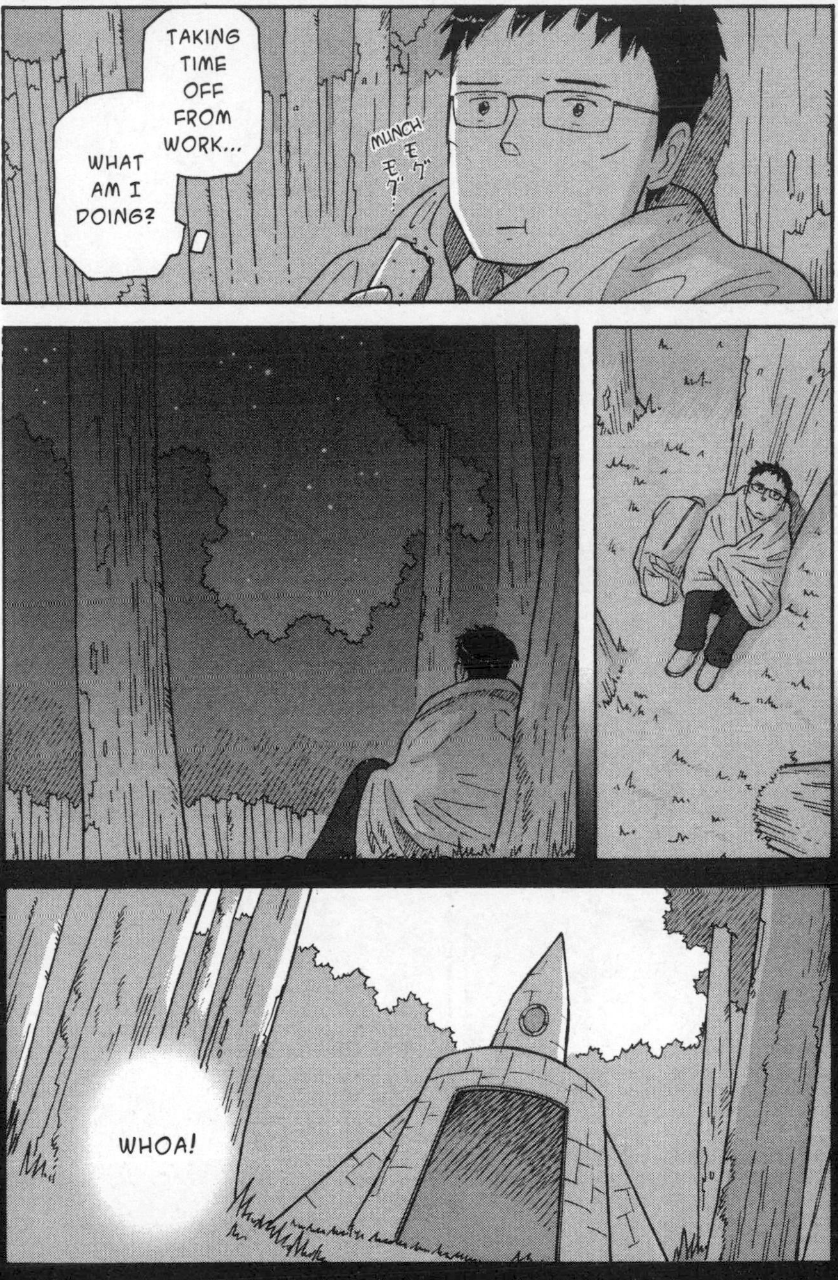
MUNCH
モグモグ
TAKING TIME OFF FROM WORK...
WHAT AM I DOING?
WHOA!

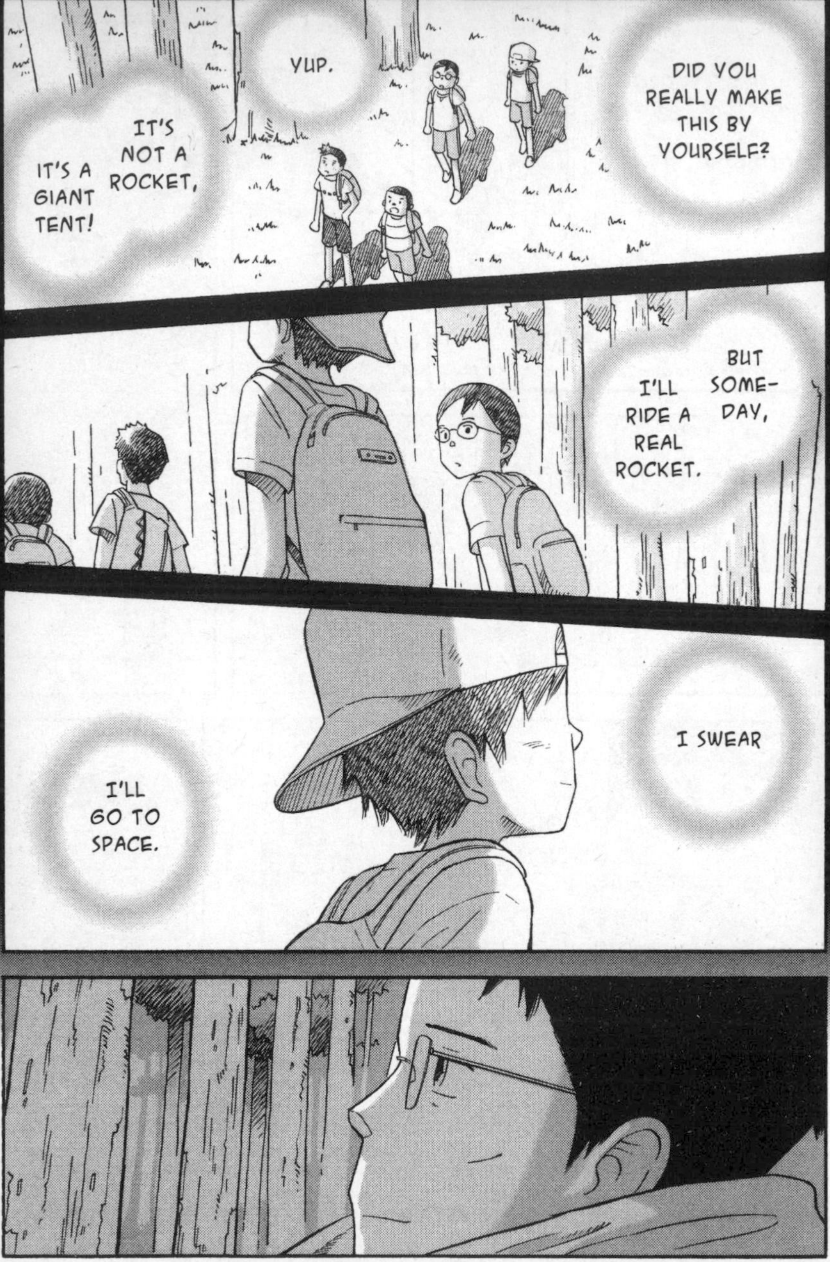

DID YOU REALLY MAKE THIS BY YOURSELF?
YUP.
IT'S NOT A ROCKET,
IT'S A GIANT TENT!
BUT SOME-DAY,
I'LL RIDE A REAL ROCKET.
I SWEAR
I'LL GO TO SPACE.

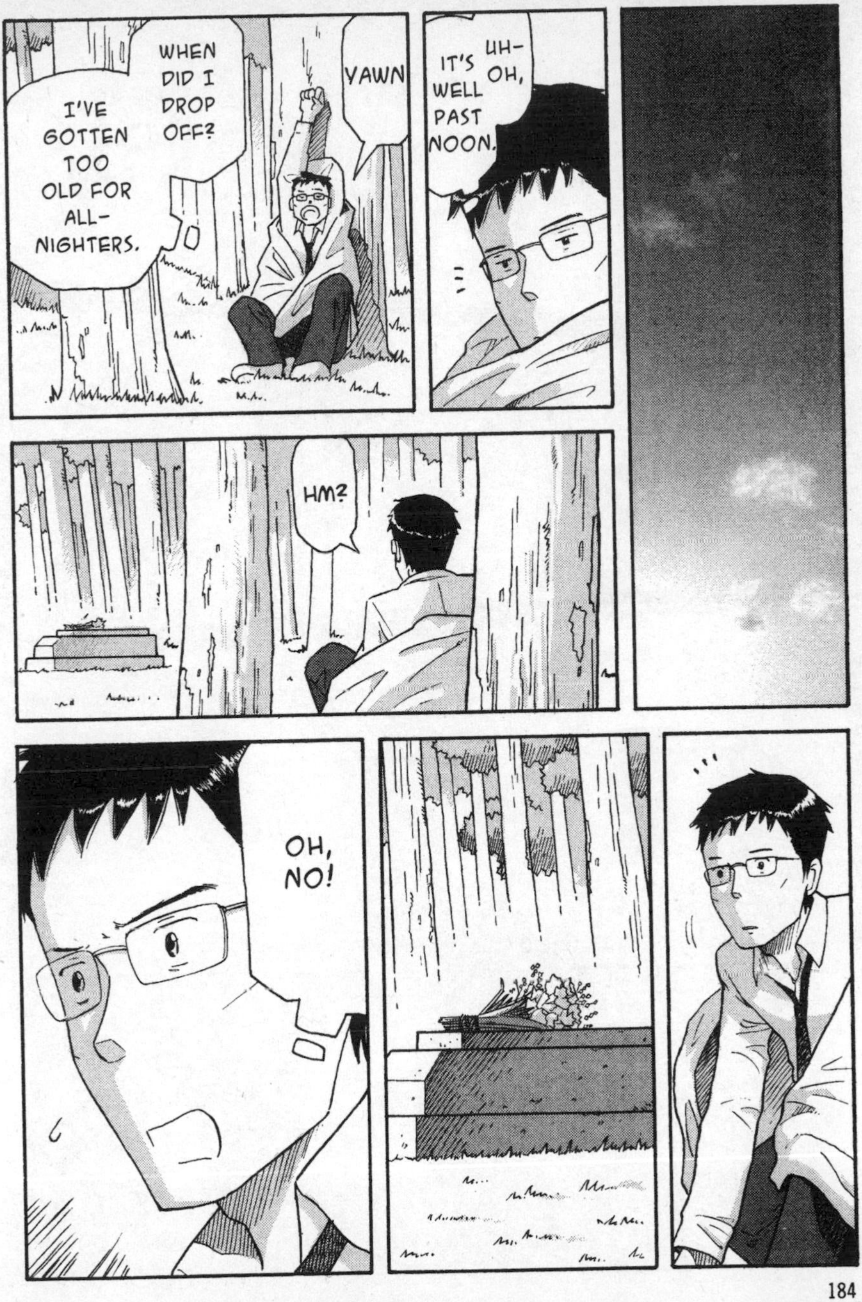
UH-OH, IT'S WELL PAST NOON.
YAWN
WHEN DID I DROP OFF?
I'VE GOTTEN TOO OLD FOR ALL-NIGHTERS.
HM?
OH, NO!

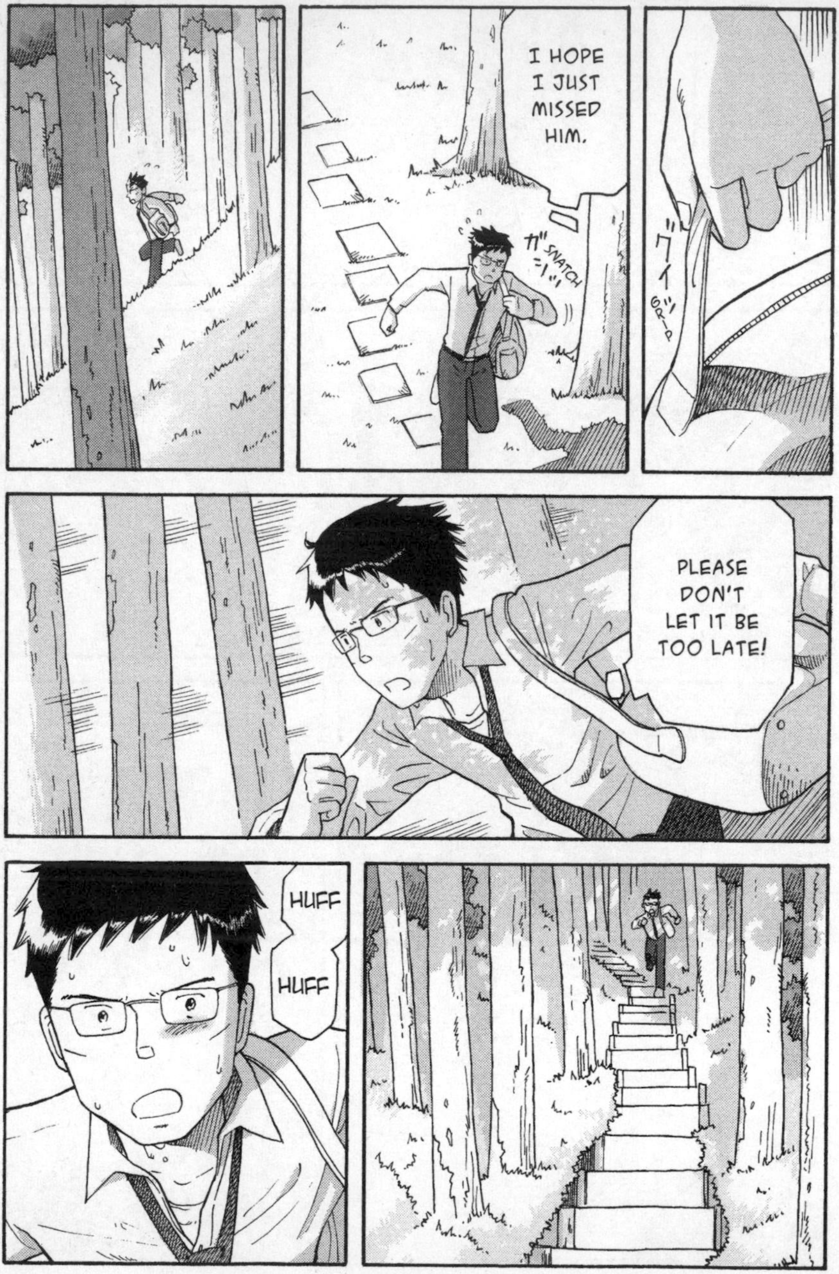
GRIP
I HOPE I JUST MISSED HIM.
SNATCH
PLEASE DON'T LET IT BE TOO LATE!
HUFF
HUFF

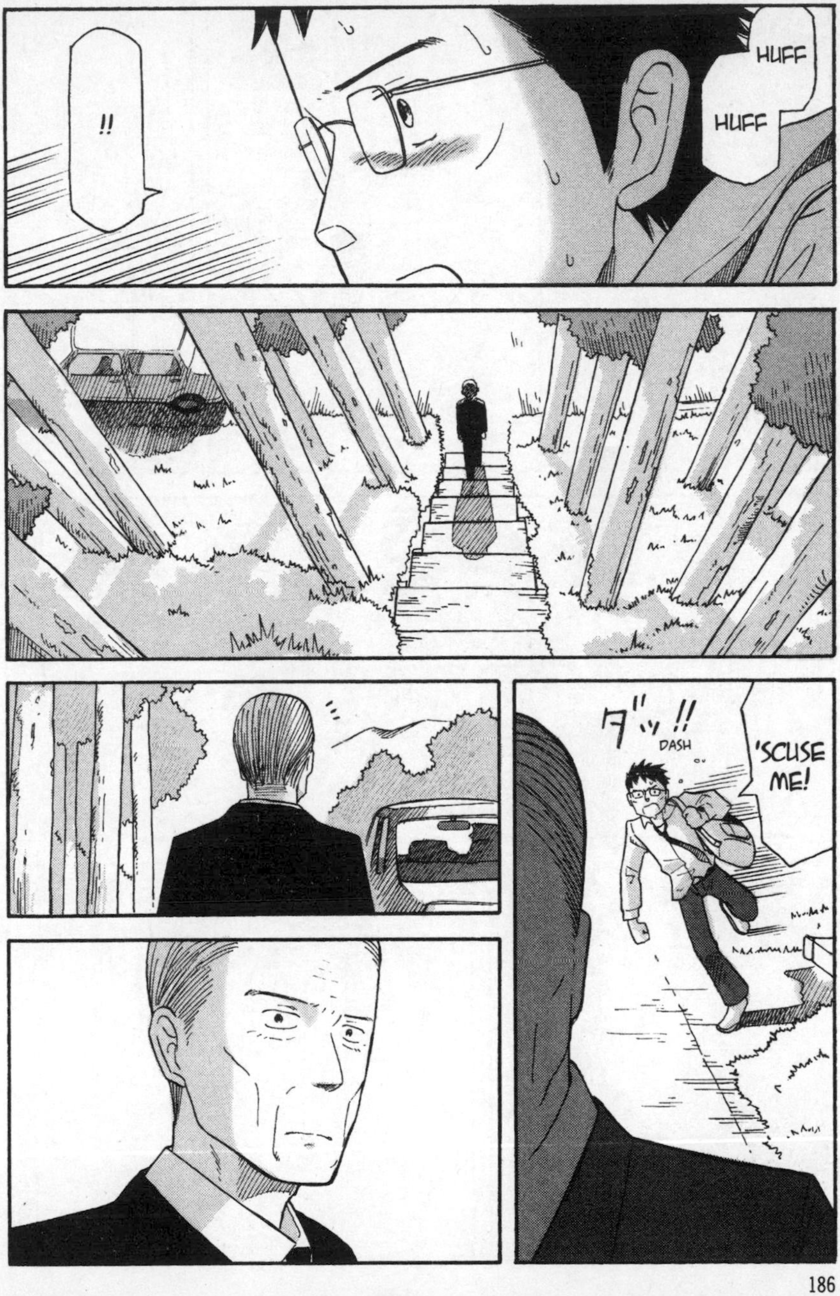
HUFF
HUFF
!!
ダッ!!
DASH
'SCUSE ME!

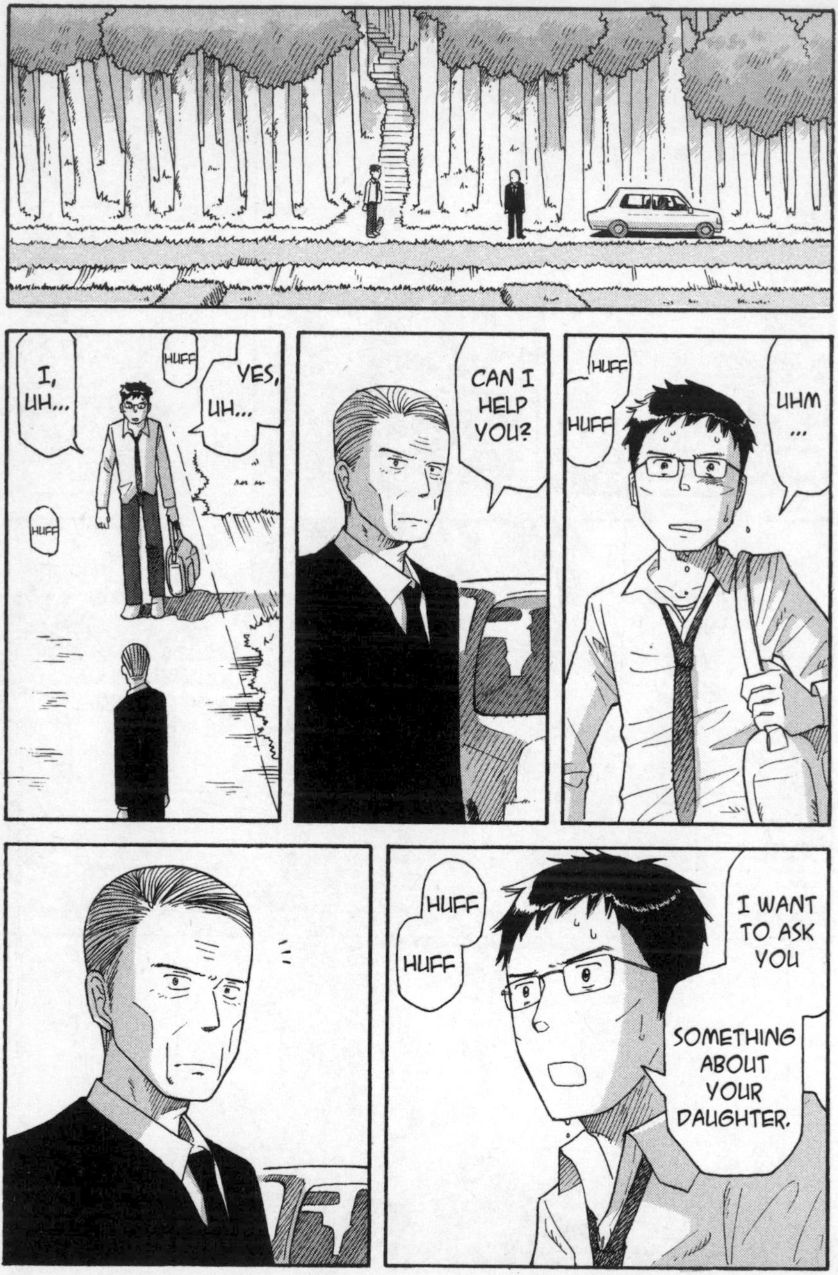
HUFF
HUFF
UHM ...
CAN I HELP YOU?
HUFF
YES, UH...
I, UH...
HUFF
I WANT TO ASK YOU
HUFF
HUFF
SOMETHING ABOUT YOUR DAUGHTER.

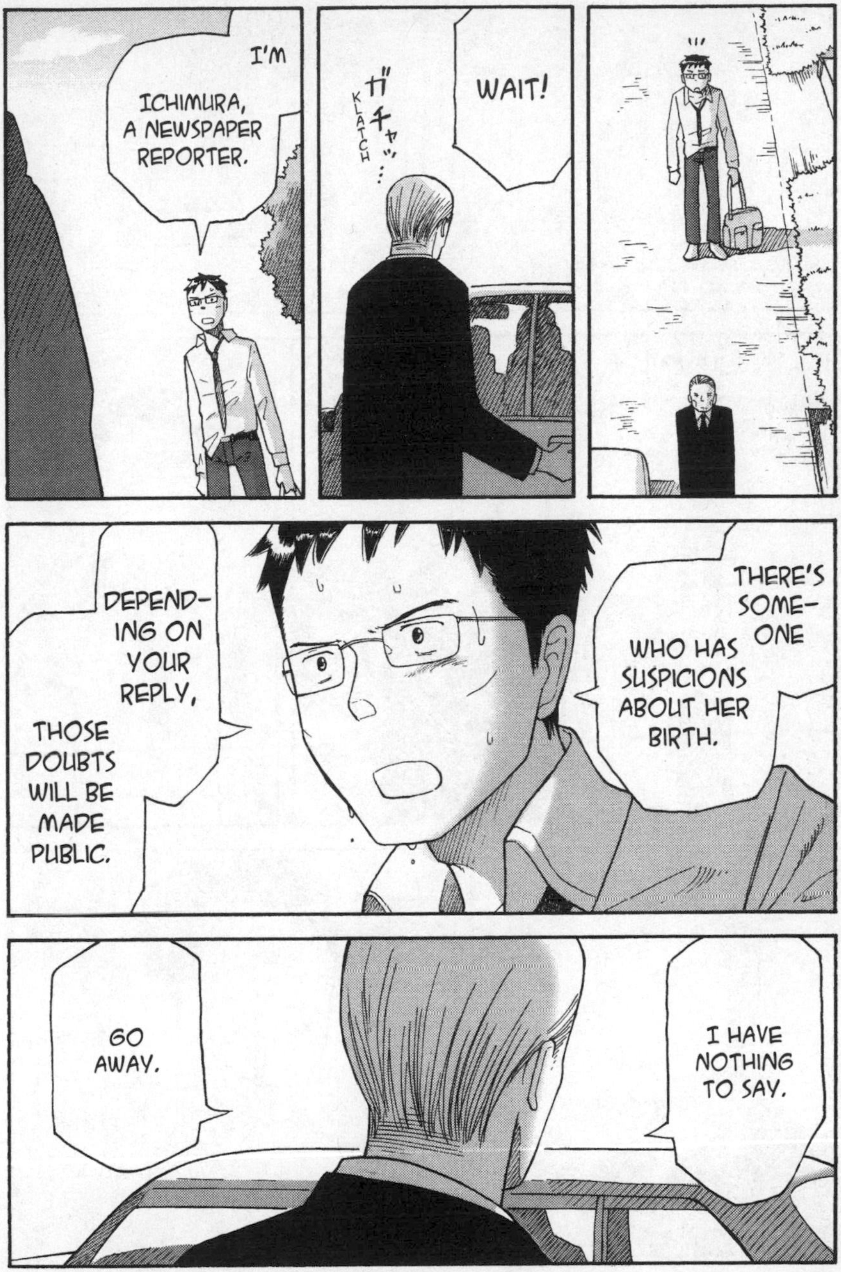
WAIT!
ガチャッ…
KLATCH
I'M ICHIMURA, A NEWSPAPER REPORTER.
THERE'S SOMEONE WHO HAS SUSPICIONS ABOUT HER BIRTH.
DEPENDING ON YOUR REPLY, THOSE DOUBTS WILL BE MADE PUBLIC.
I HAVE NOTHING TO SAY.
GO AWAY.

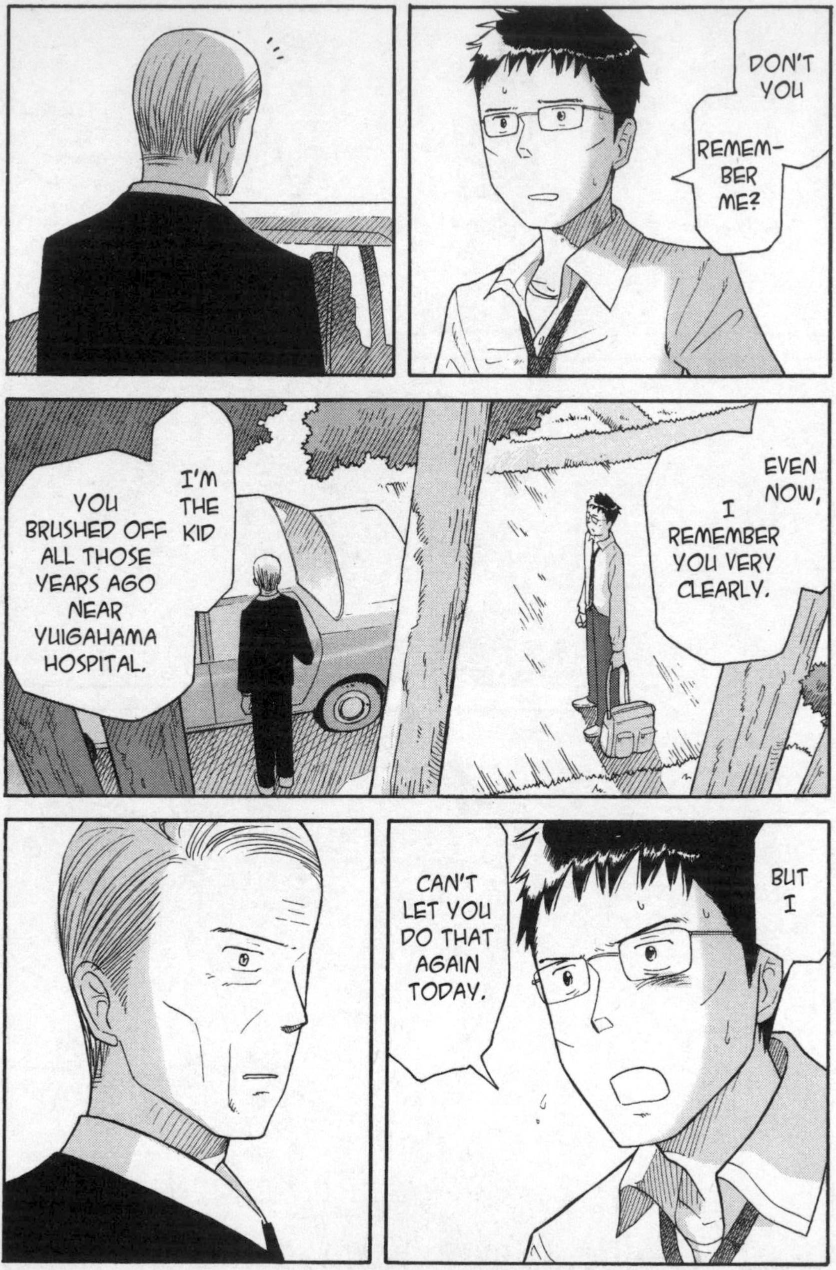
DON'T YOU REMEMBER ME?
EVEN NOW, I REMEMBER YOU VERY CLEARLY.
I'M THE KID YOU BRUSHED OFF ALL THOSE YEARS AGO NEAR YUIGAHAMA HOSPITAL.
BUT I
CAN'T LET YOU DO THAT AGAIN TODAY.

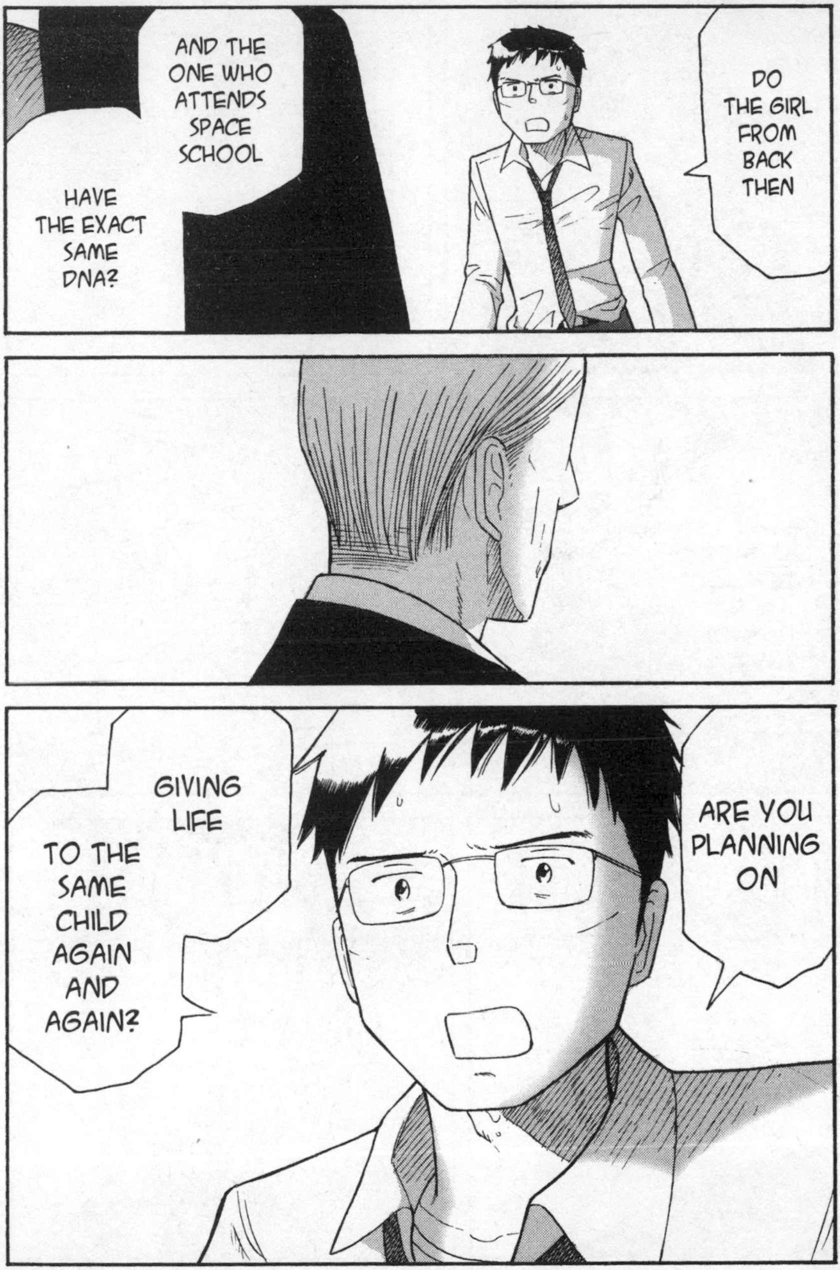
DO THE GIRL FROM BACK THEN
AND THE ONE WHO ATTENDS SPACE SCHOOL
HAVE THE EXACT SAME DNA?
ARE YOU PLANNING ON
GIVING LIFE
TO THE SAME CHILD AGAIN AND AGAIN?

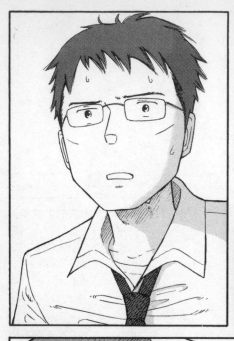
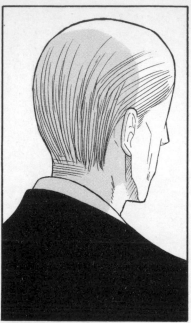
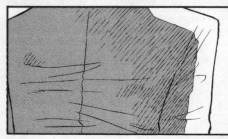
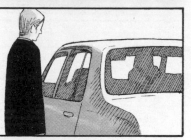
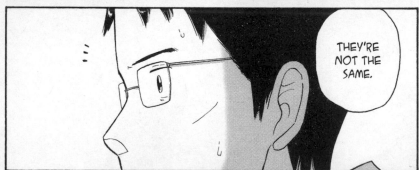

THEY'RE
NOT THE
SAME.

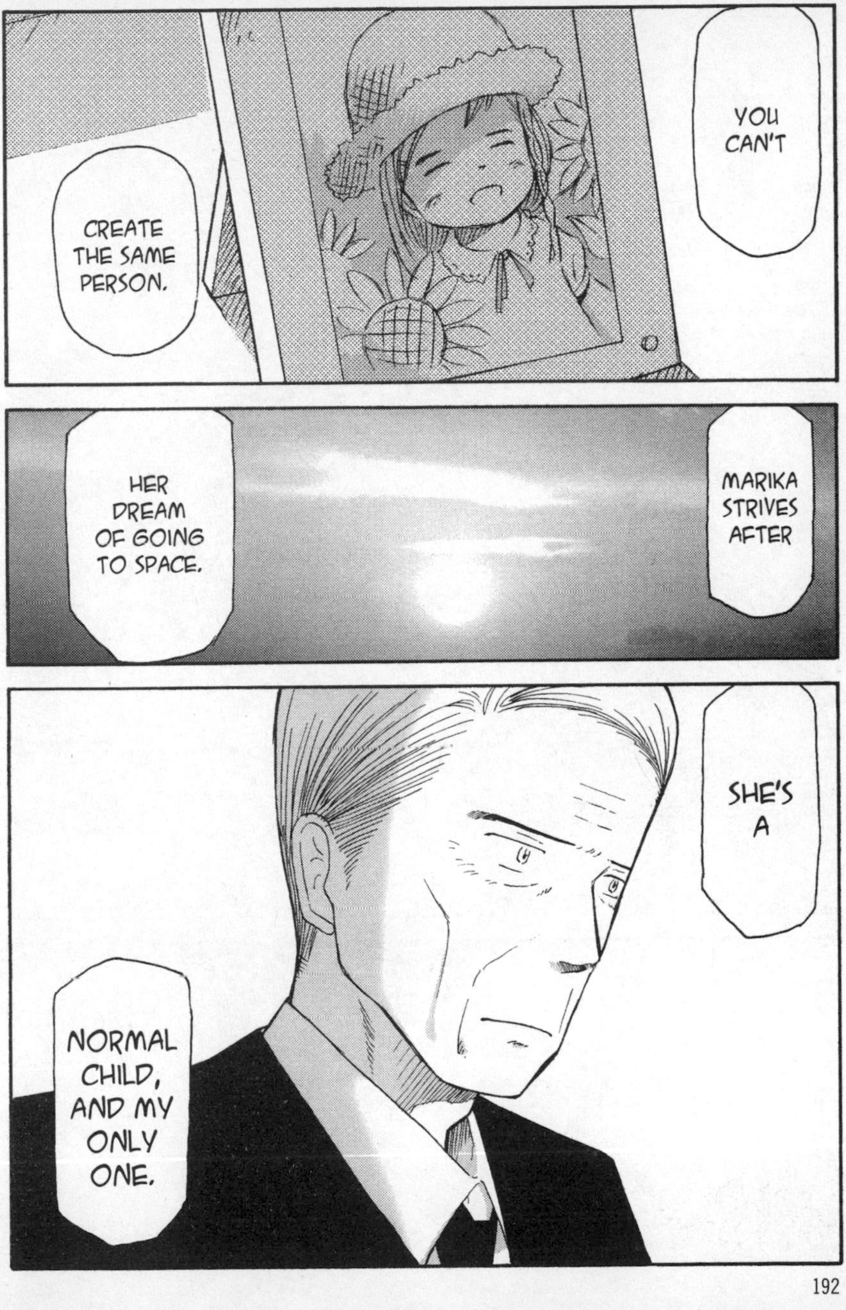
YOU CAN'T
CREATE THE SAME PERSON.
MARIKA STRIVES AFTER
HER DREAM OF GOING TO SPACE.
SHE'S A
NORMAL CHILD, AND MY ONLY ONE.

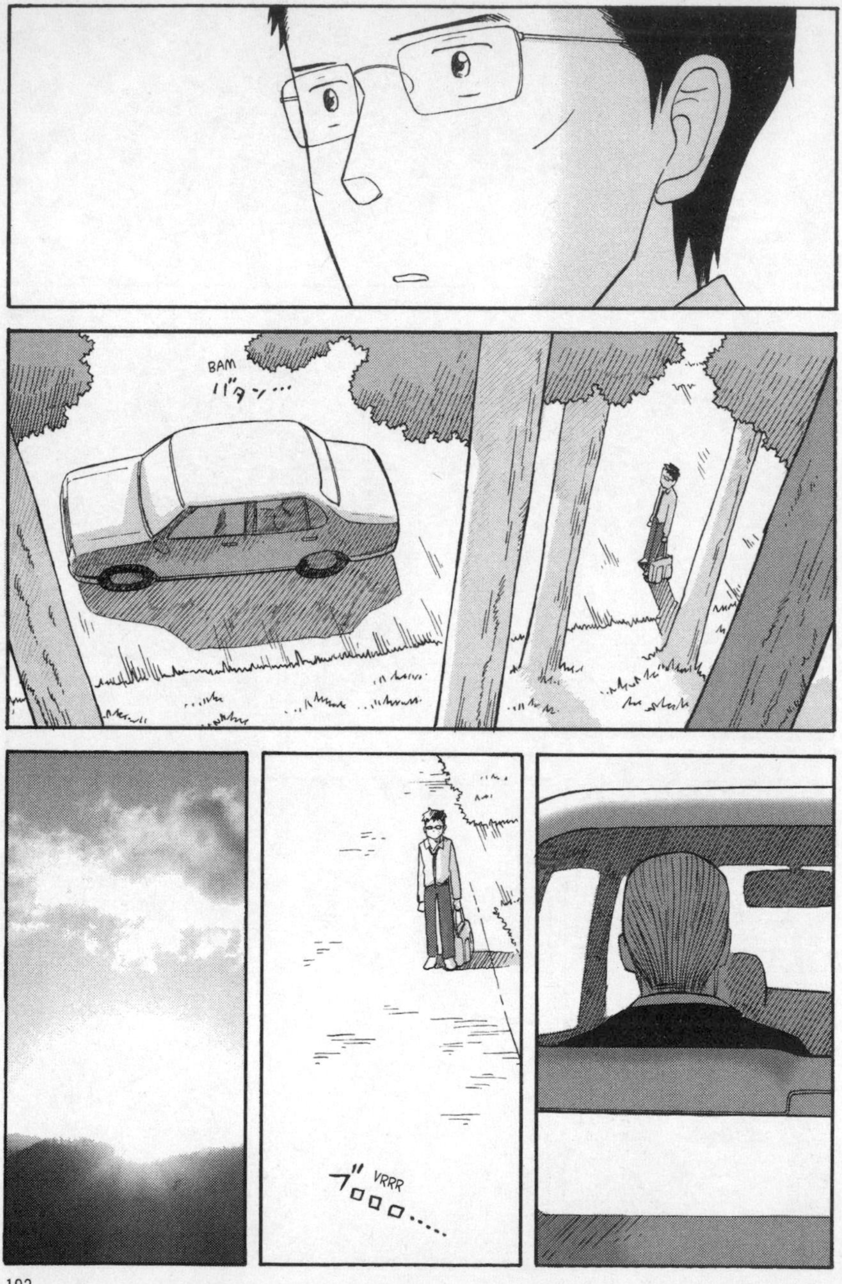
BAM
バタン…
VRRR
ブロロロ……

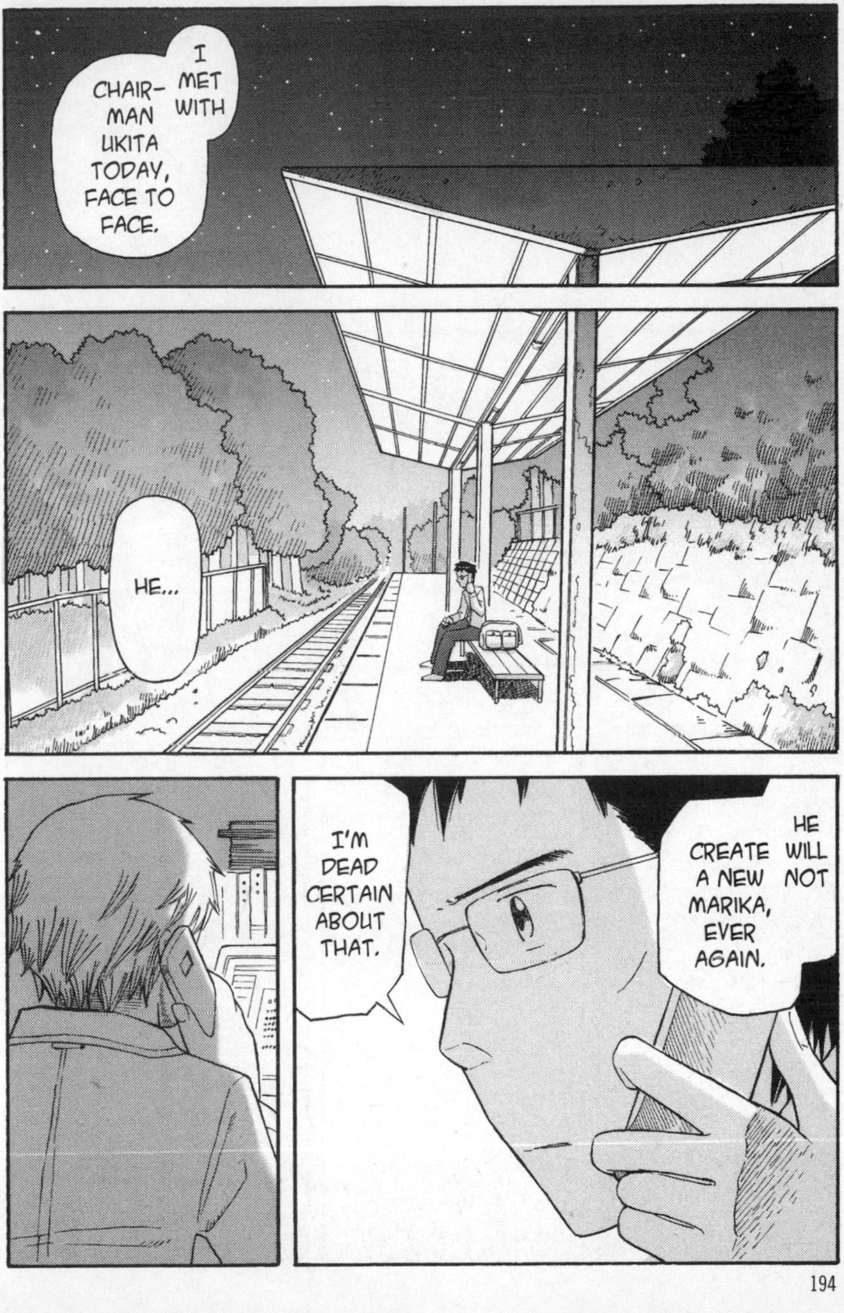
I MET WITH CHAIRMAN UKITA TODAY, FACE TO FACE.
HE...
HE WILL NOT CREATE A NEW MARIKA, EVER AGAIN.
I'M DEAD CERTAIN ABOUT THAT.

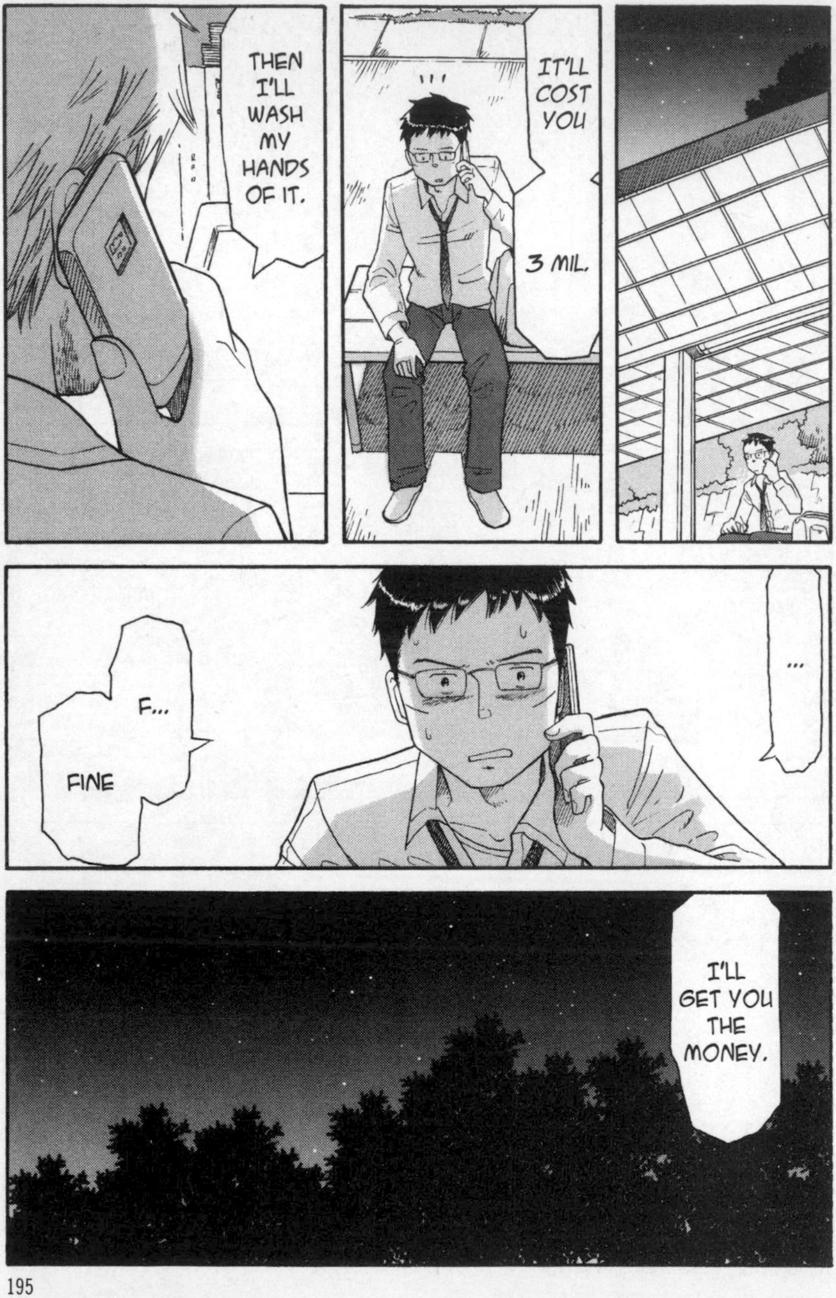
IT'LL COST YOU
3 MIL.
THEN I'LL WASH MY HANDS OF IT.
...
F... FINE
I'LL GET YOU THE MONEY.

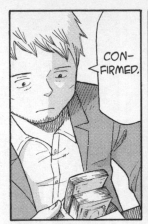

CON-
FIRMED.

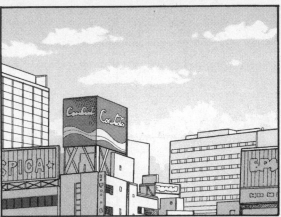

I'LL SEND
A RECEIPT TO
YOUR OFFICE
TOMORROW.

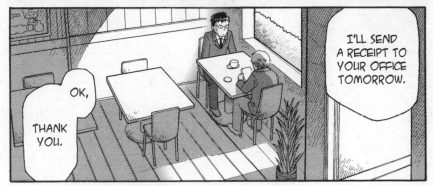

OK,

THANK
YOU.

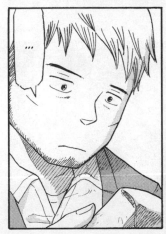

...

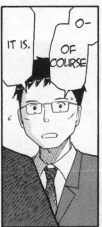

IT IS.

O-
OF
COURSE

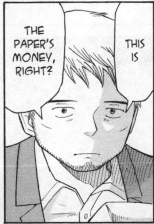

THE
PAPER'S
MONEY,
RIGHT?

THIS
IS

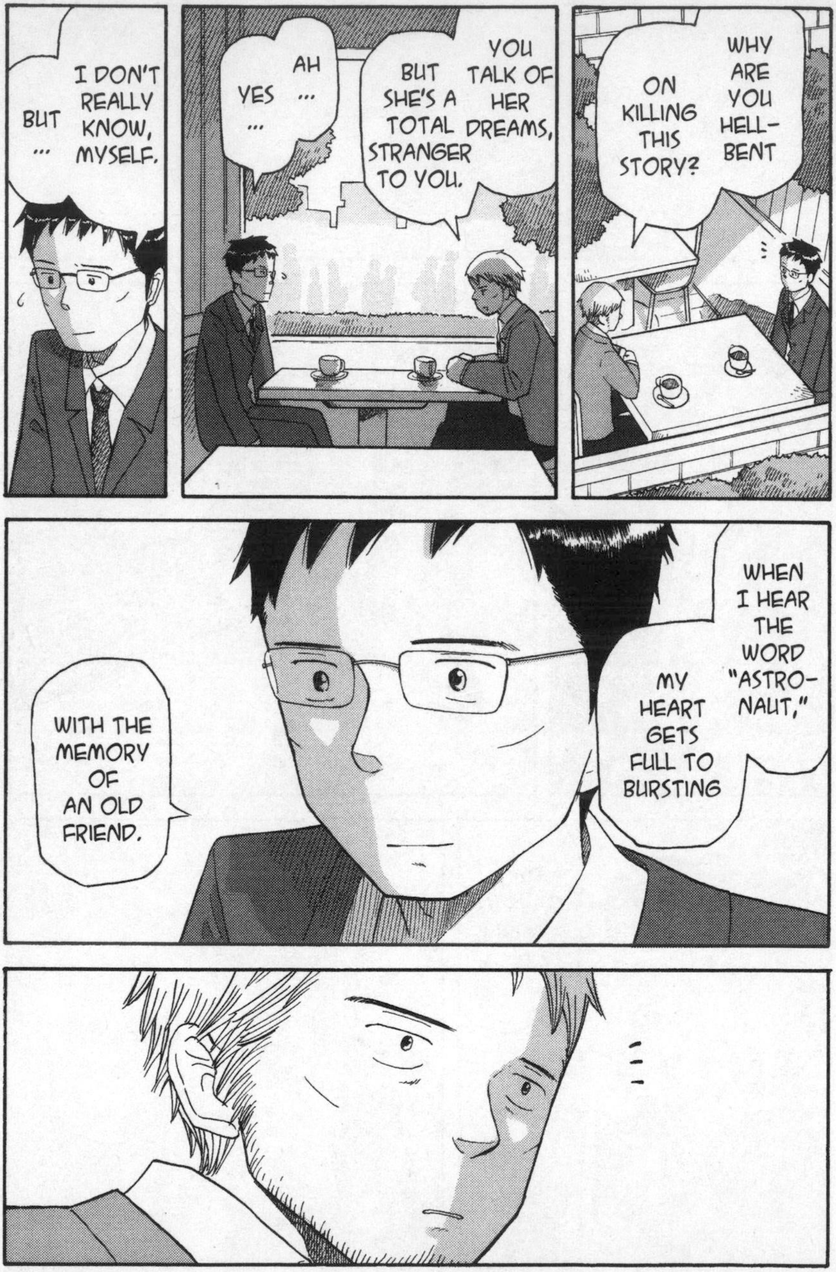
WHY ARE YOU HELL-BENT
ON KILLING THIS STORY?
YOU TALK OF HER DREAMS,
BUT SHE'S A TOTAL STRANGER TO YOU.
AH ...
YES ...
I DON'T REALLY KNOW, MYSELF.
BUT ...
WHEN I HEAR THE WORD "ASTRO-NAUT,"
MY HEART GETS FULL TO BURSTING
WITH THE MEMORY OF AN OLD FRIEND.

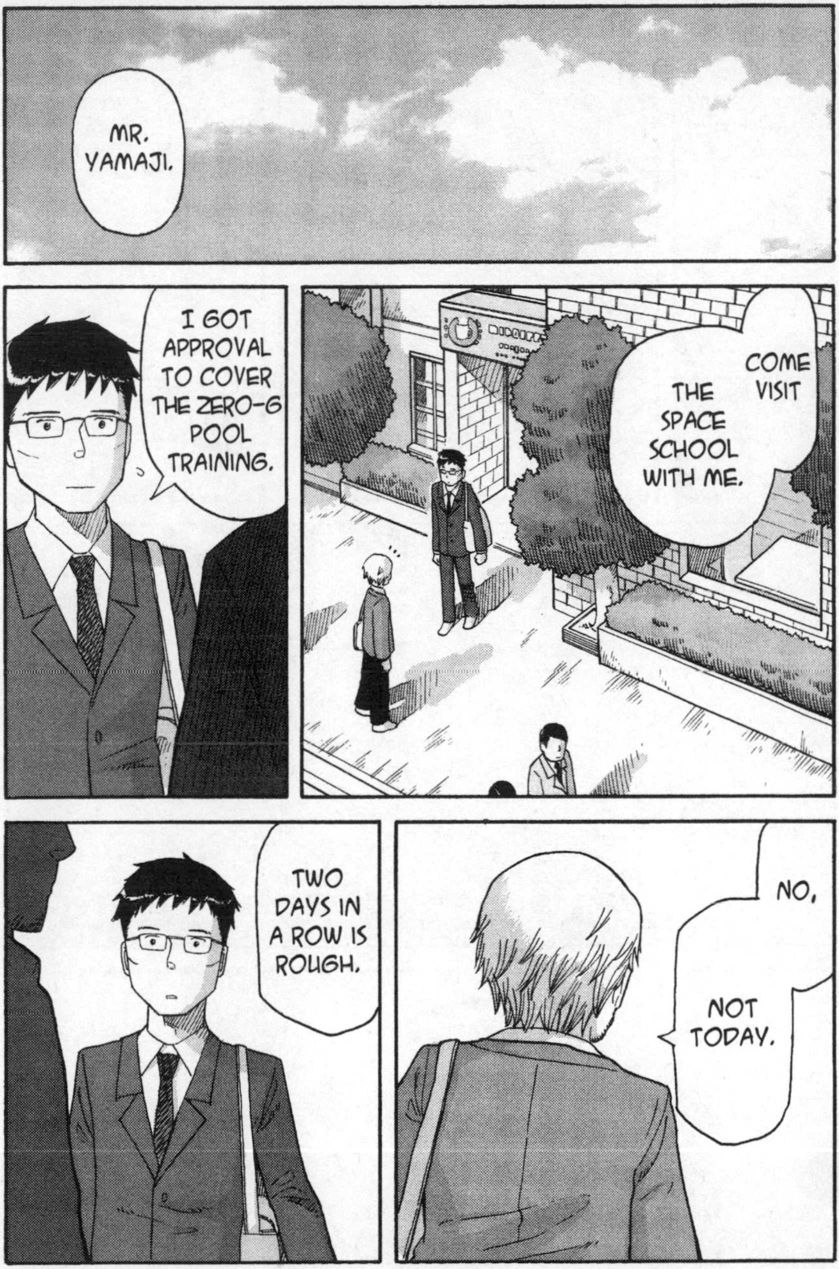
MR. YAMAJI.
COME VISIT THE SPACE SCHOOL WITH ME.
I GOT APPROVAL TO COVER THE ZERO-G POOL TRAINING.
NO,
NOT TODAY.
TWO DAYS IN A ROW IS ROUGH.

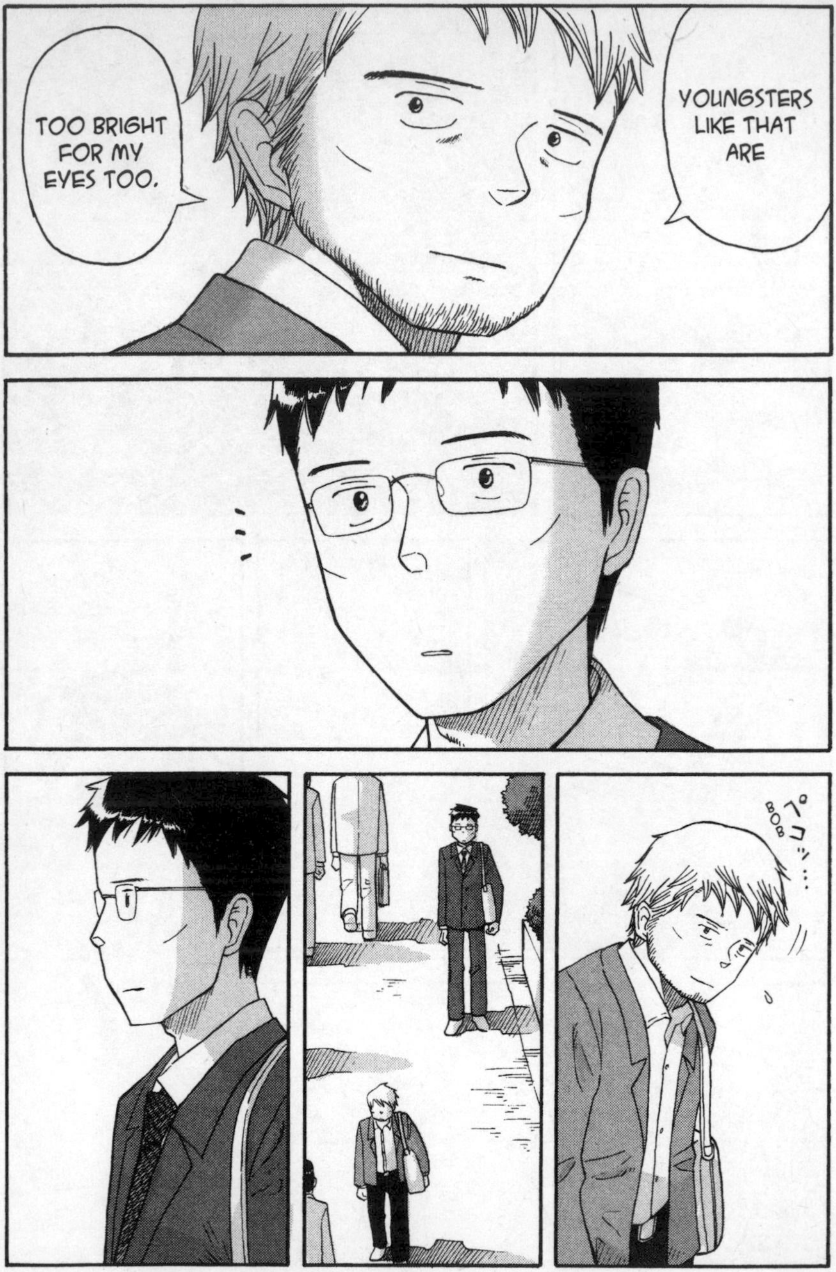
YOUNGSTERS LIKE THAT ARE
TOO BRIGHT FOR MY EYES TOO.
BOB
ペコッ…

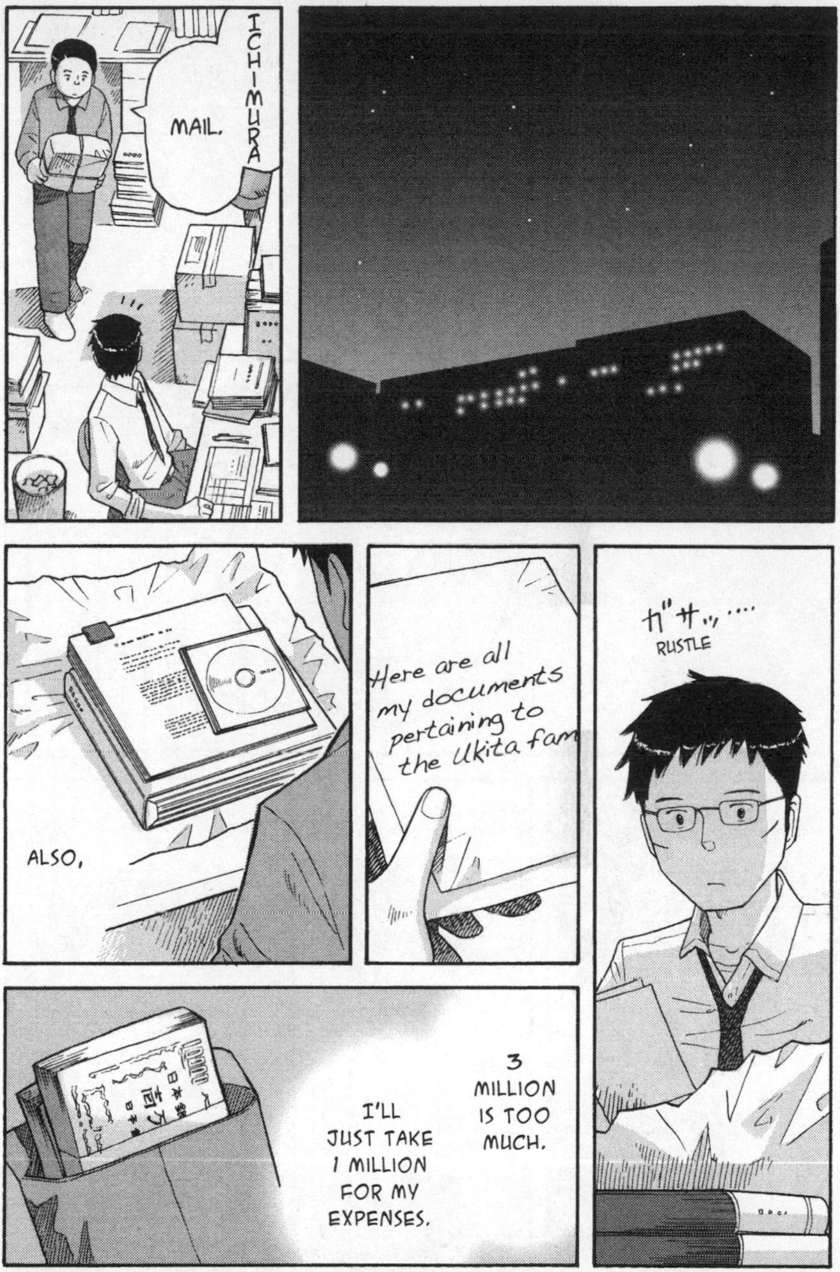
ICHIMURA
MAIL.
ガサッ....
RUSTLE
Here are all my documents pertaining to the Ukita fam
ALSO,
3 MILLION IS TOO MUCH.
I'LL JUST TAKE 1 MILLION FOR MY EXPENSES.

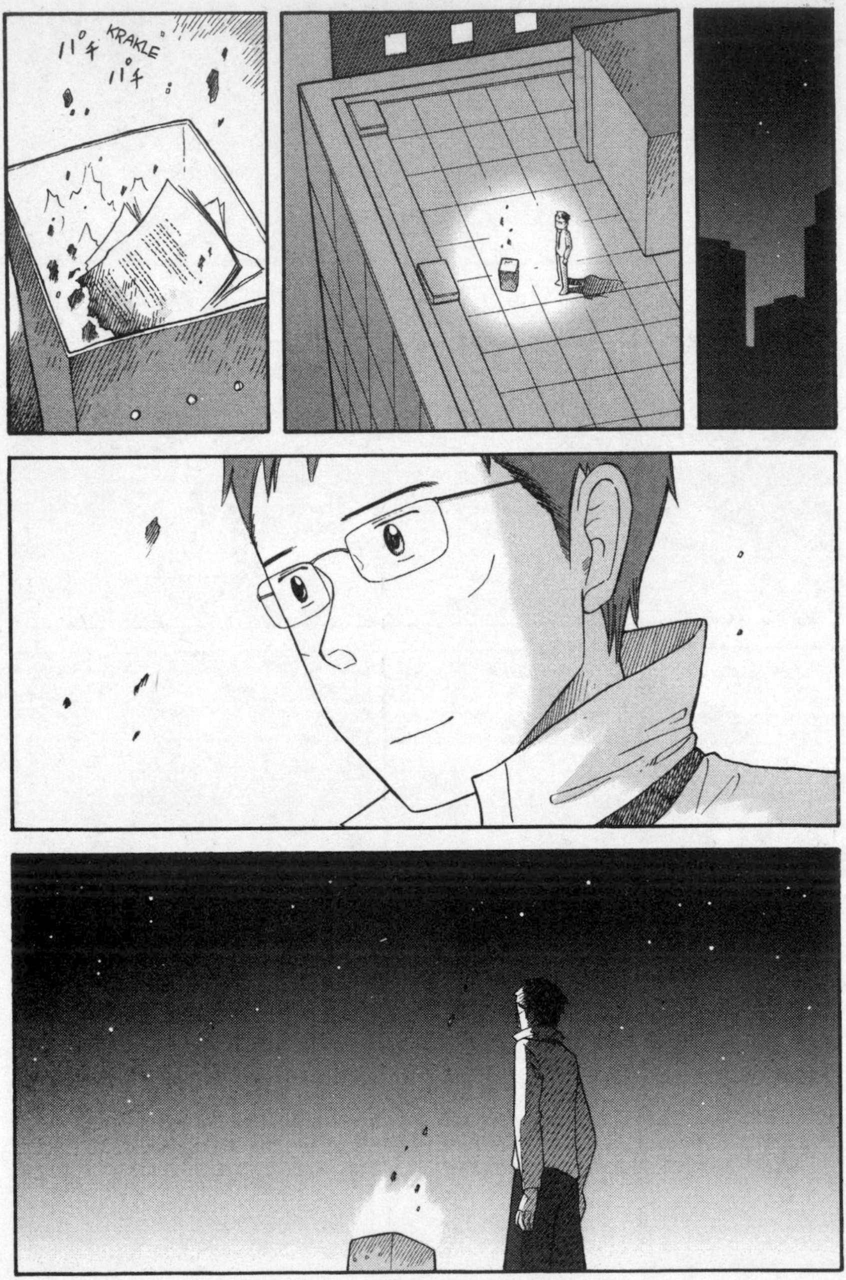
パチ KRAKLE パチ

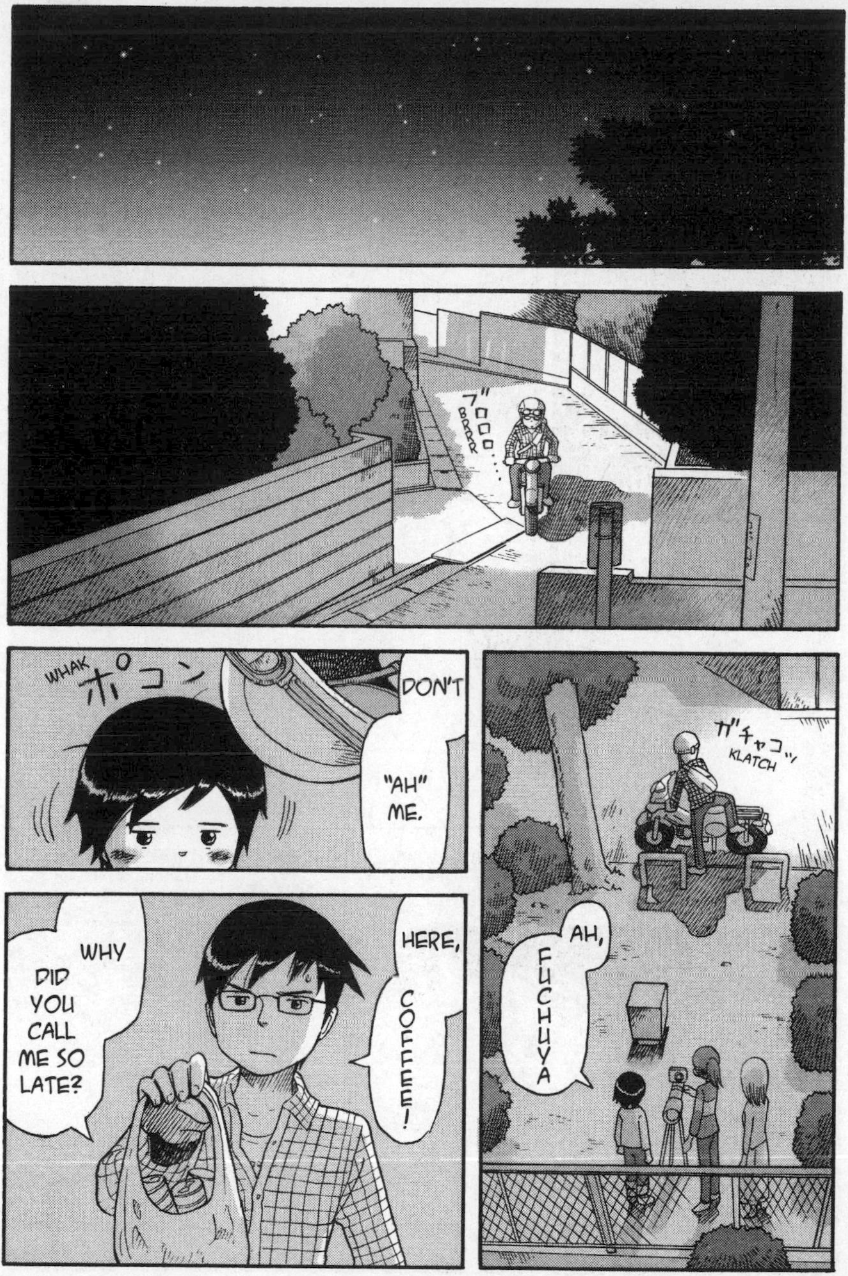

ブロロロ…
BRRRR
ガチャコッ
KLATCH
AH, FUCHUYA
WHAK
ポコン
DON'T "AH" ME.
HERE, COFFEEE!
WHY DID YOU CALL ME SO LATE?

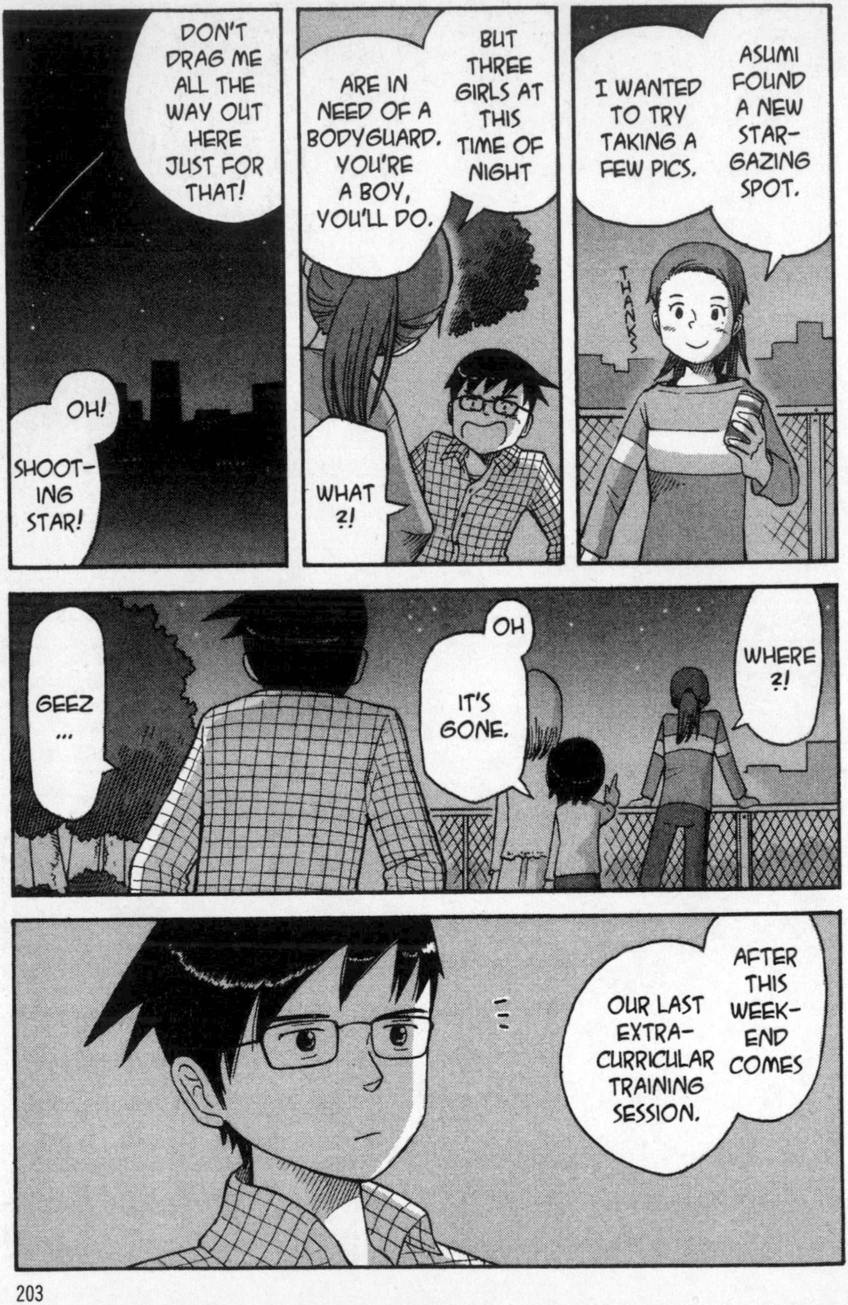
ASUMI FOUND A NEW STAR-GAZING SPOT.
I WANTED TO TRY TAKING A FEW PICS.
THANKS
BUT THREE GIRLS AT THIS TIME OF NIGHT
ARE IN NEED OF A BODYGUARD. YOU'RE A BOY, YOU'LL DO.
WHAT?!
DON'T DRAG ME ALL THE WAY OUT HERE JUST FOR THAT!
OH!
SHOOTING STAR!
WHERE?!
OH
IT'S GONE.
GEEZ...
AFTER THIS WEEKEND COMES
OUR LAST EXTRA-CURRICULAR TRAINING SESSION.
...

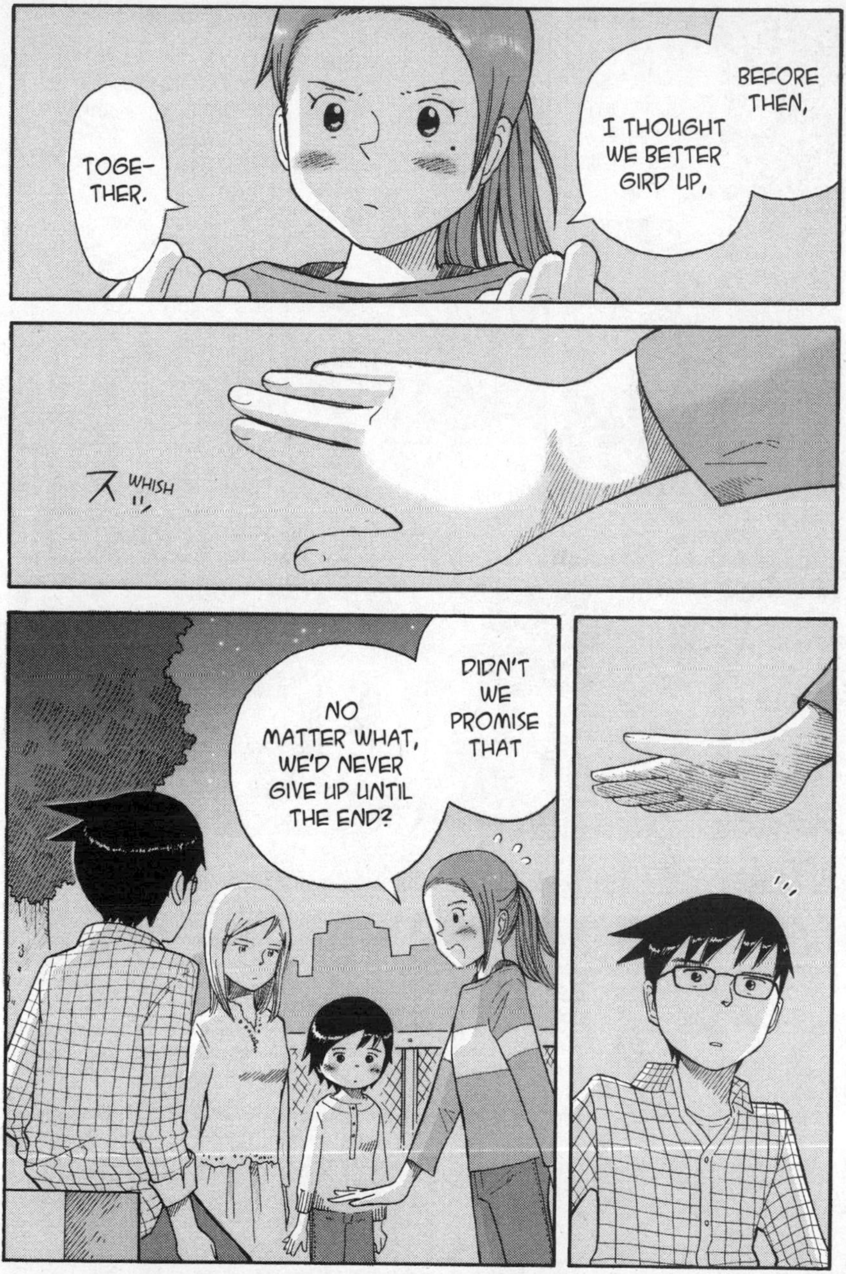
BEFORE THEN,
I THOUGHT WE BETTER GIRD UP,
TOGE-THER.
ス WHISH
DIDN'T WE PROMISE THAT
NO MATTER WHAT, WE'D NEVER GIVE UP UNTIL THE END?

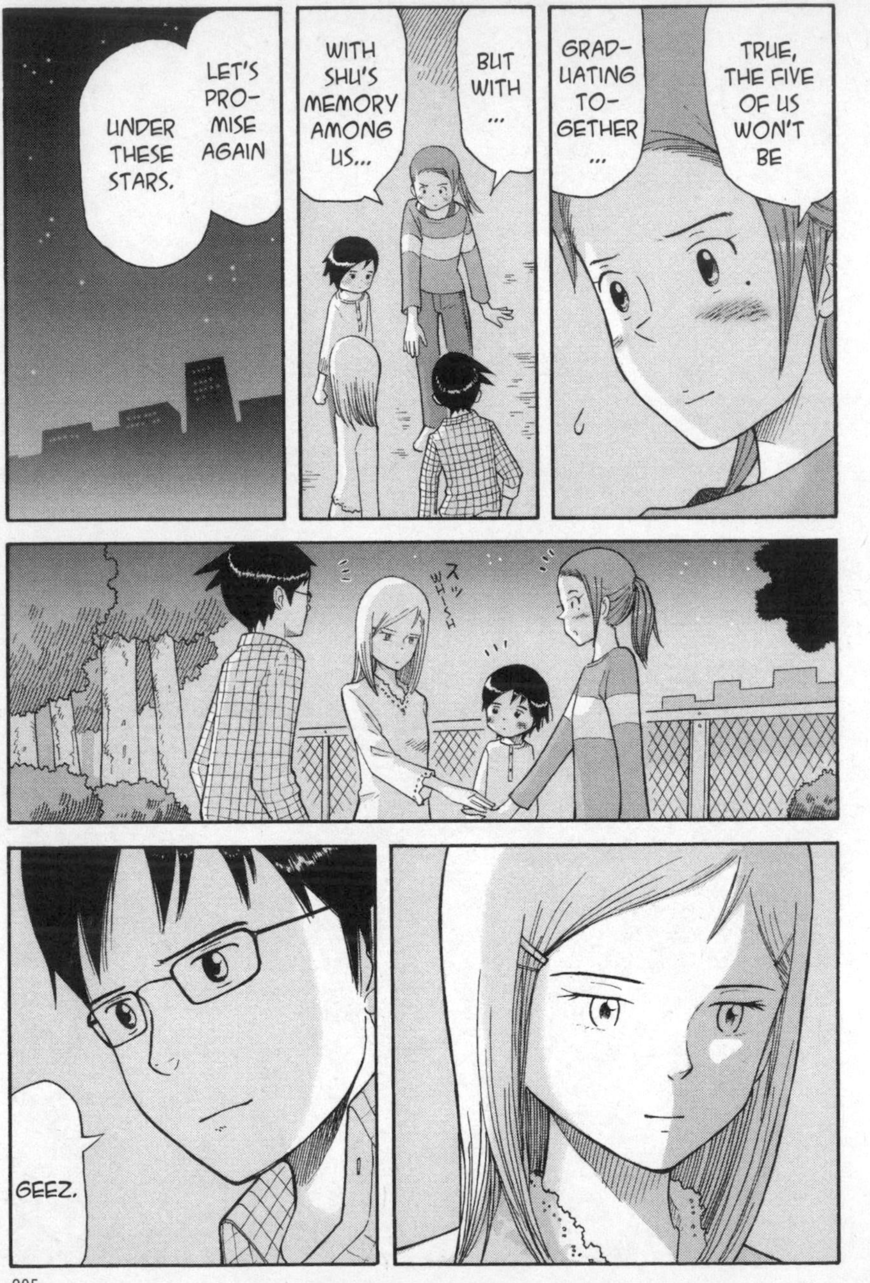
TRUE, THE FIVE OF US WON'T BE
GRAD-UATING TO-GETHER...
BUT WITH...
WITH SHU'S MEMORY AMONG US...
LET'S PRO-MISE AGAIN
UNDER THESE STARS.
スッ WHISH
GEEZ.

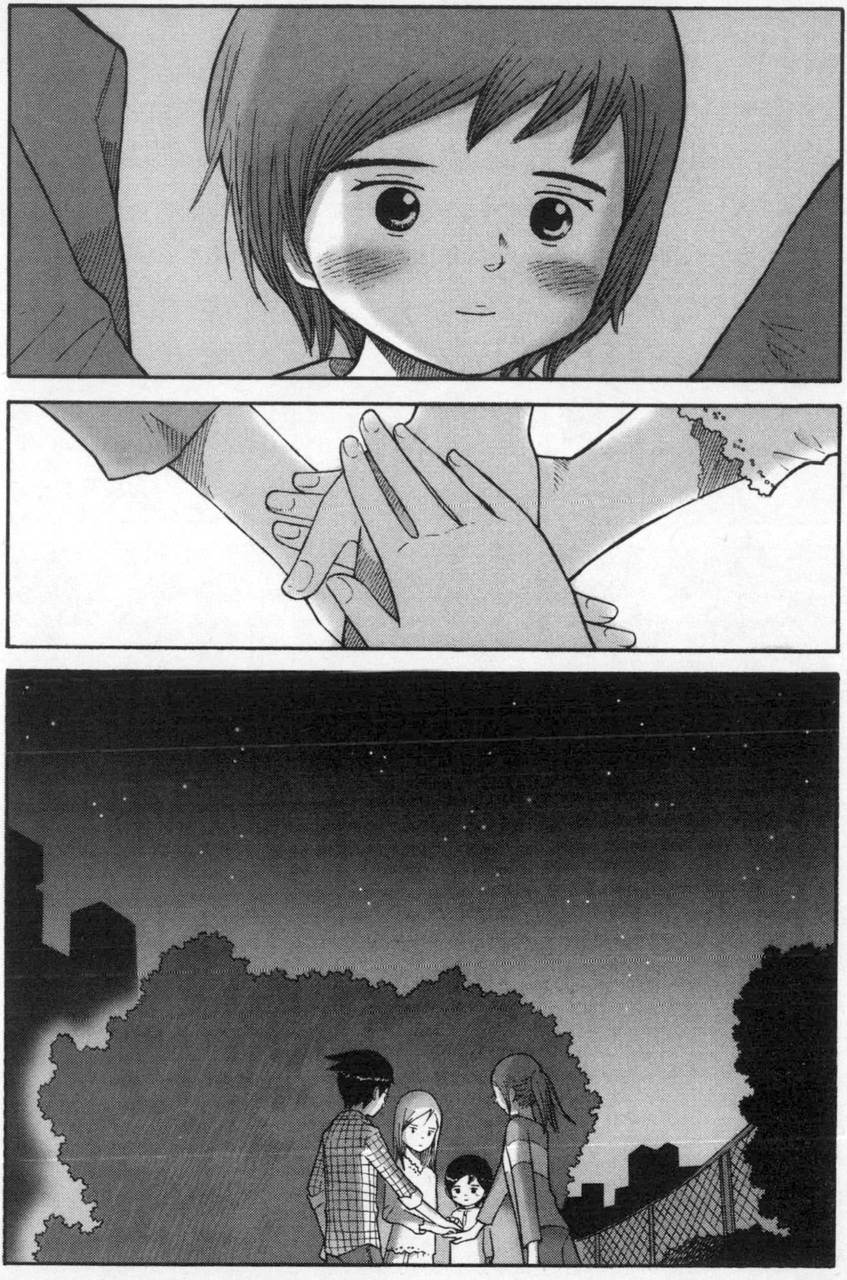

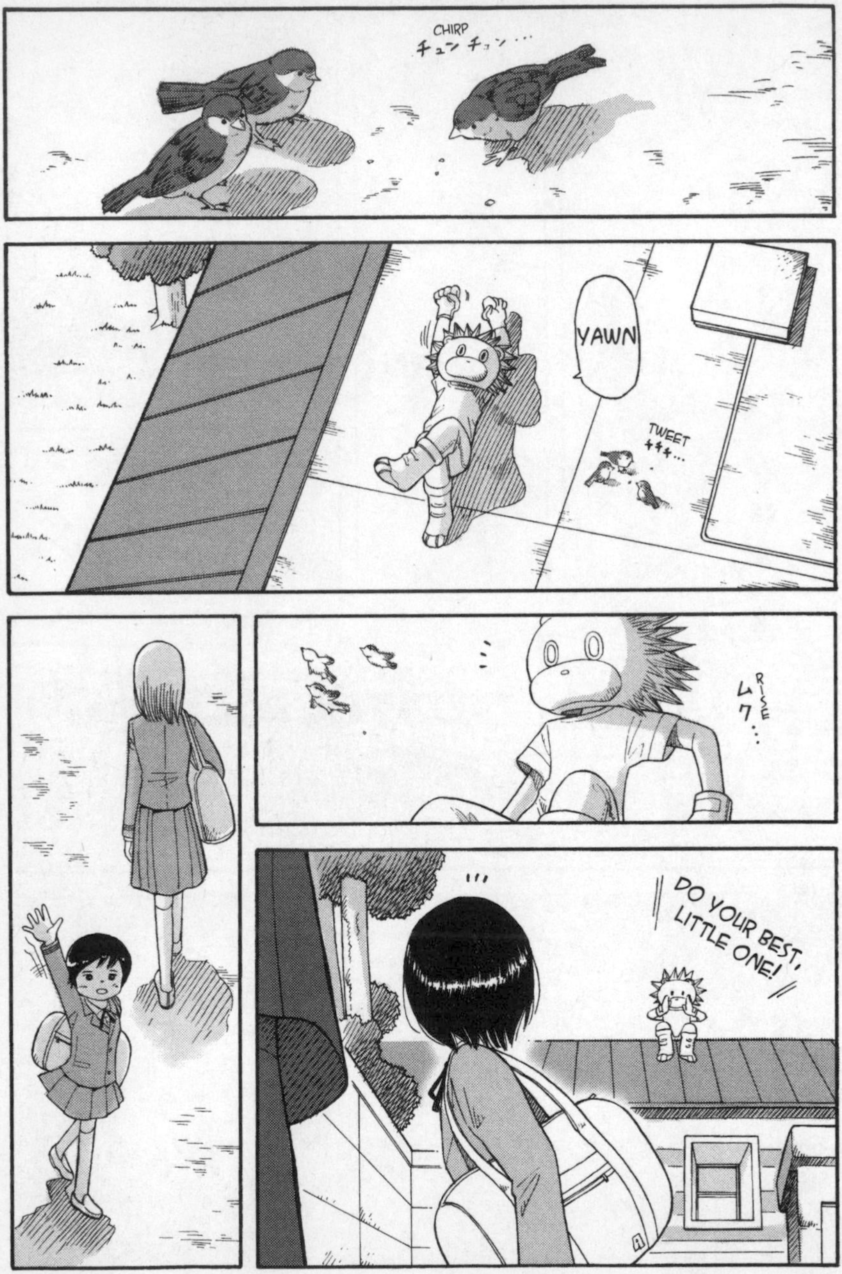
CHIRP
チュンチュン…
YAWN
TWEET
チチチ…
RISE
ムク…
DO YOUR BEST, LITTLE ONE!

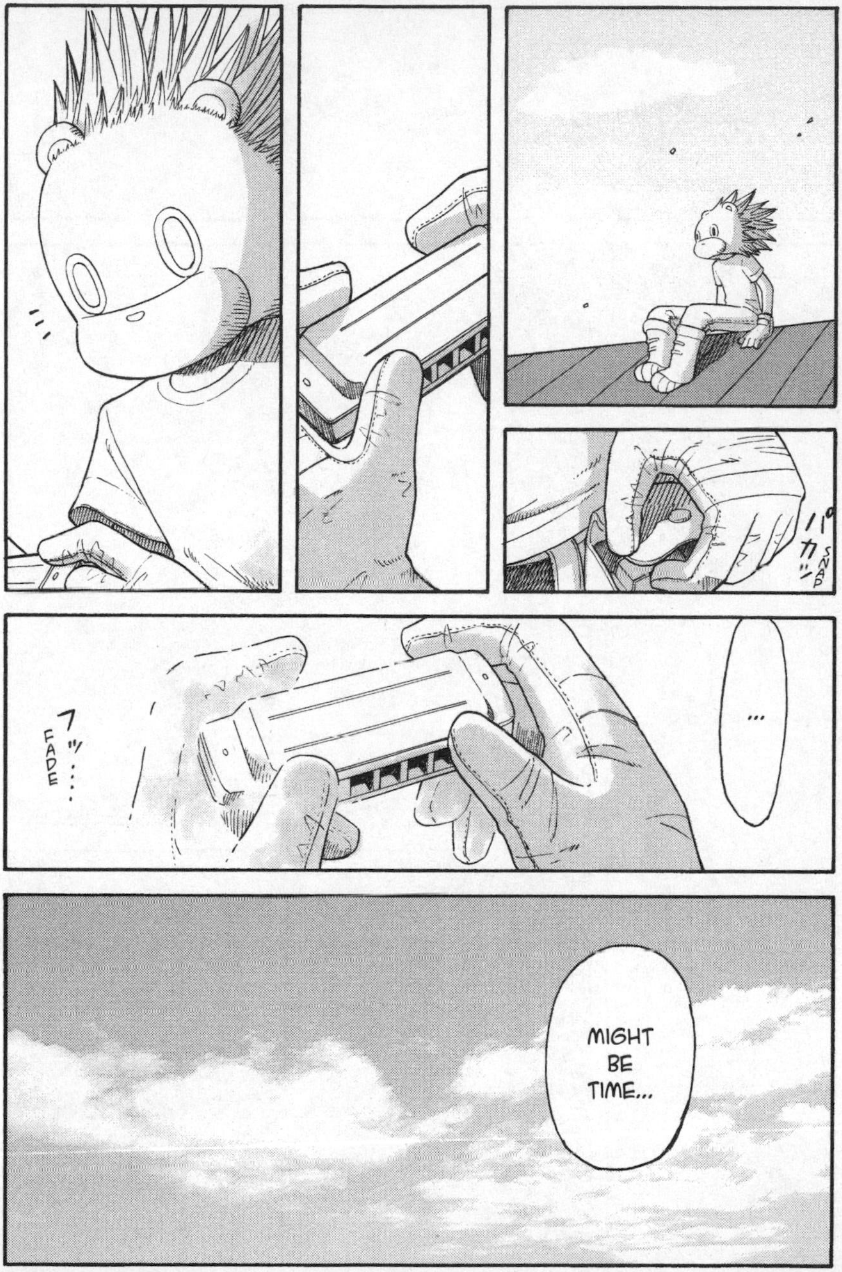

パカッ
SNAP
...
フッ…
FADE
MIGHT BE TIME...

MISSION:71

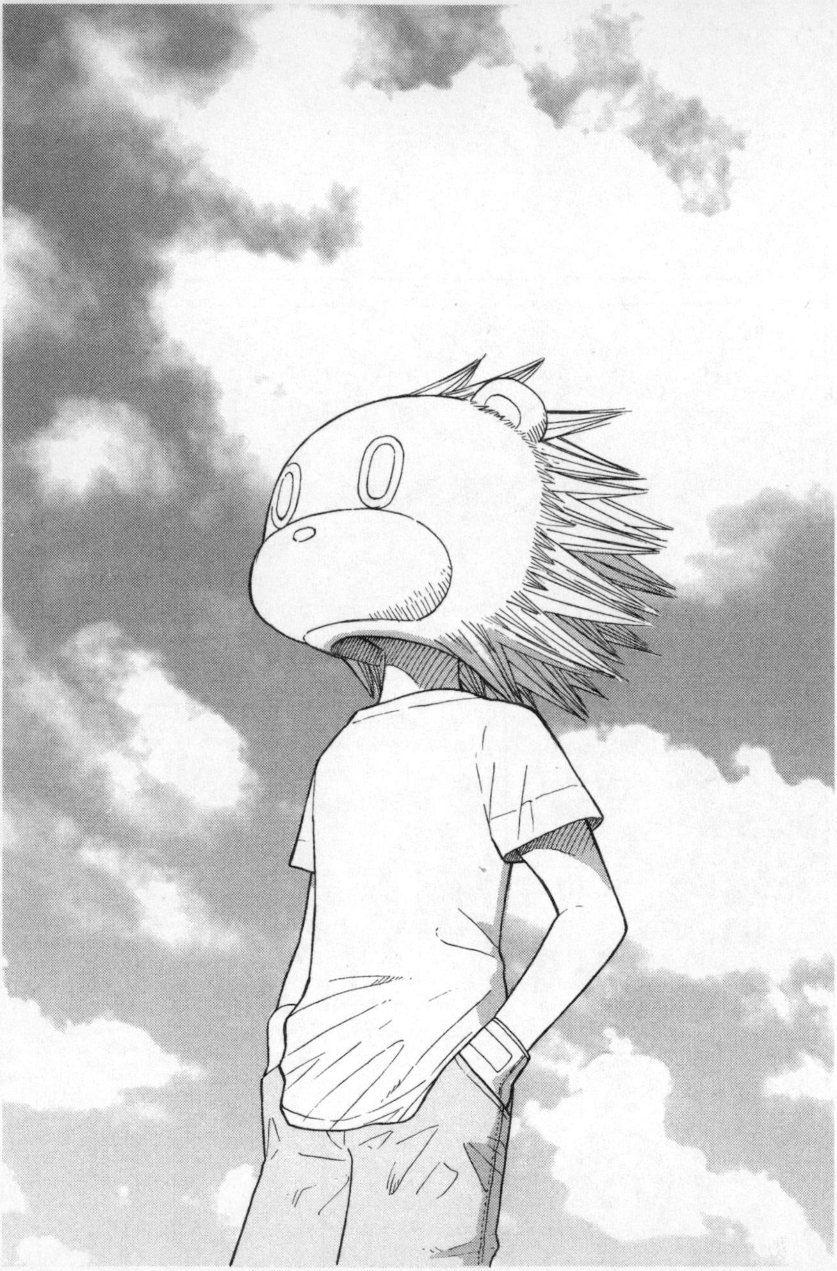

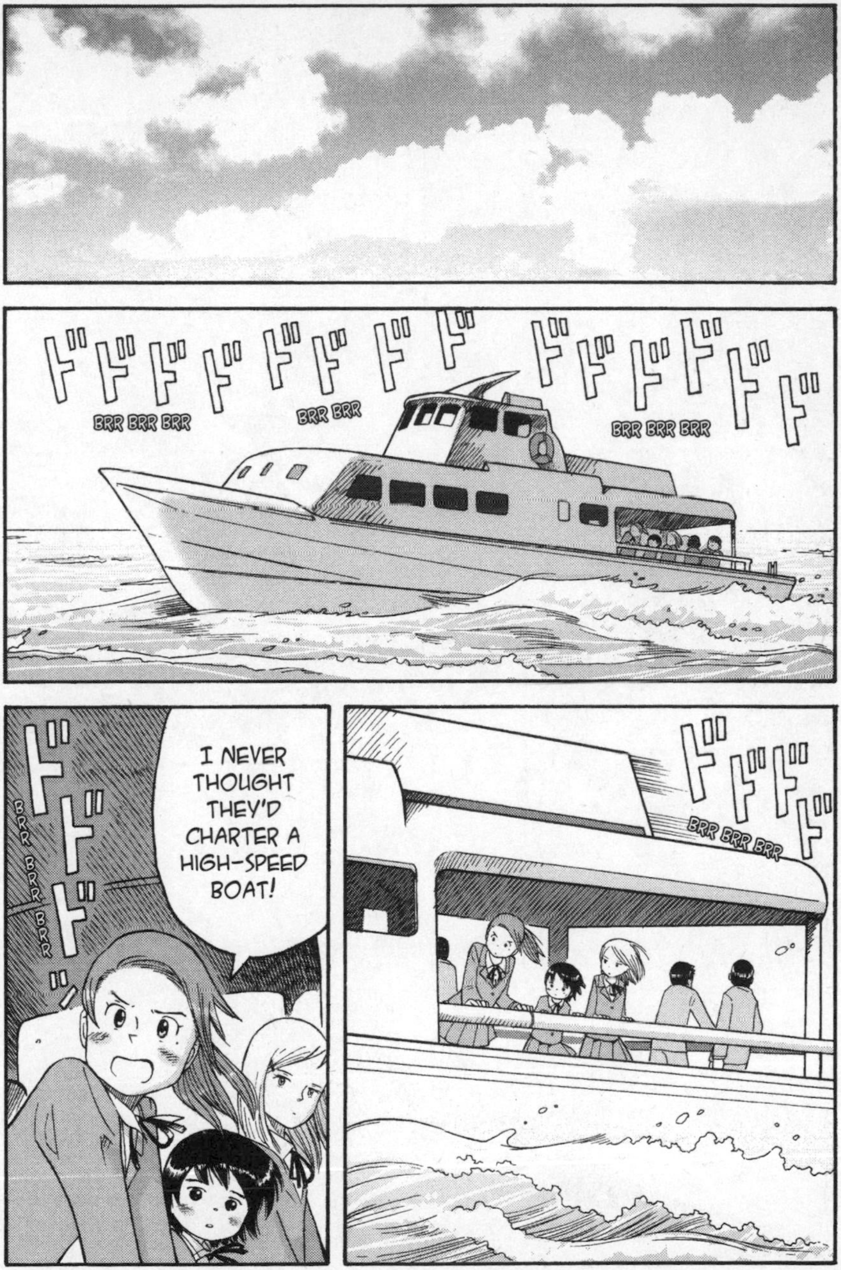
ドドドドドドドドド
BRR BRR BRR
BRR BRR
ドドドドドドド
BRR BRR BRR
ドドドドド
BRR BRR BRR
I NEVER THOUGHT THEY'D CHARTER A HIGH-SPEED BOAT!
ドドド
BRR BRR BRR

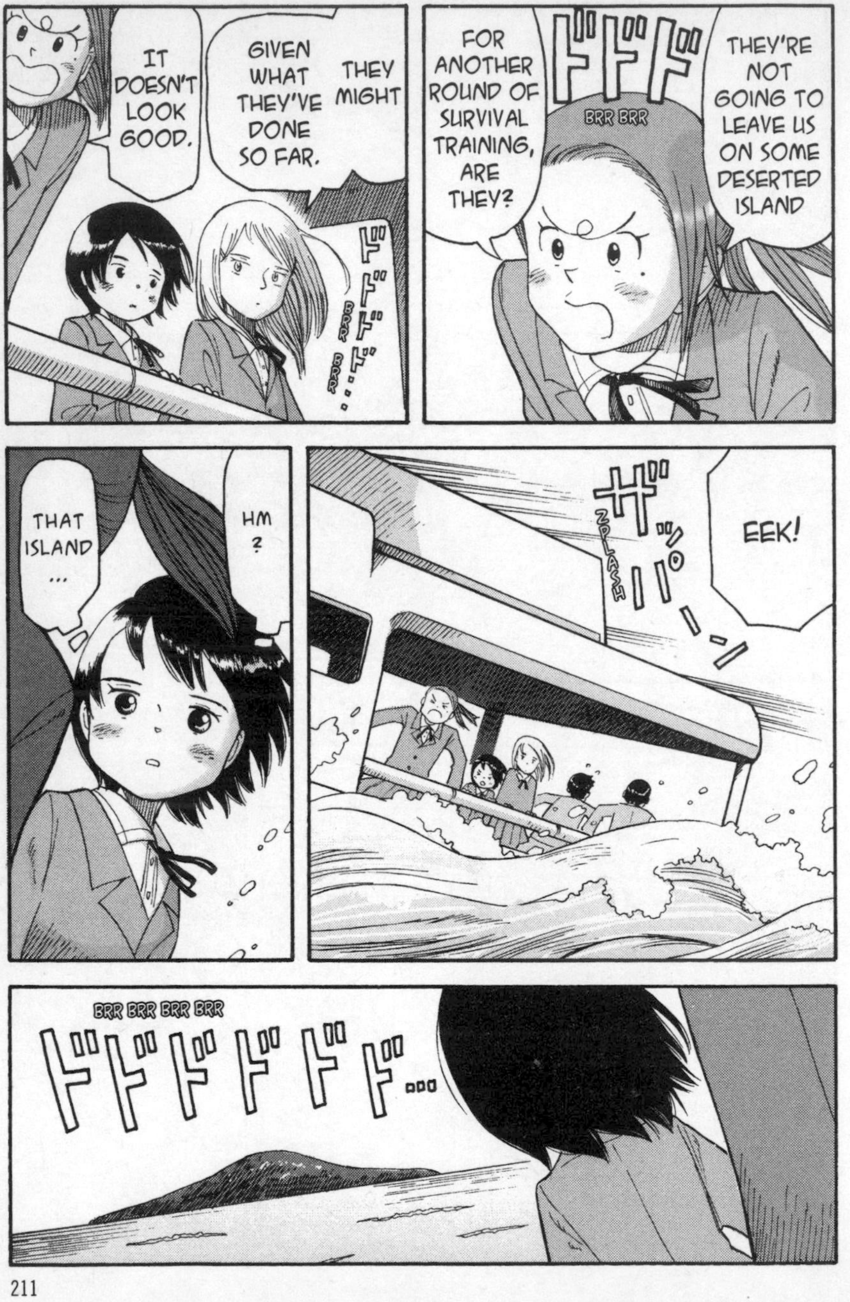
THEY'RE NOT GOING TO LEAVE US ON SOME DESERTED ISLAND
ドドドド
BRR BRR
FOR ANOTHER ROUND OF SURVIVAL TRAINING, ARE THEY?
THEY MIGHT
GIVEN WHAT THEY'VE DONE SO FAR.
IT DOESN'T LOOK GOOD.
ドドドド・・
BRR BRR
EEK!
ザバーン
ZPLASH
HM?
THAT ISLAND...
BRR BRR BRR BRR
ドドドドドド...

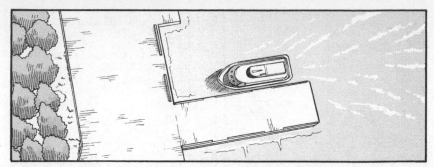

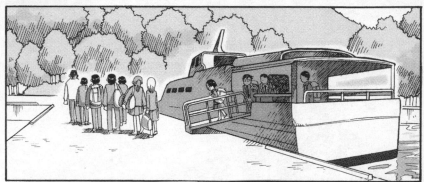

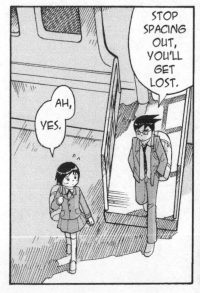

STOP SPACING OUT, YOU'LL GET LOST.

AH, YES.

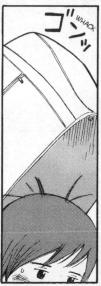

コツン WHACK

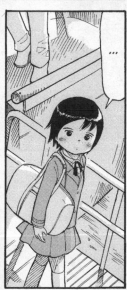

...

212

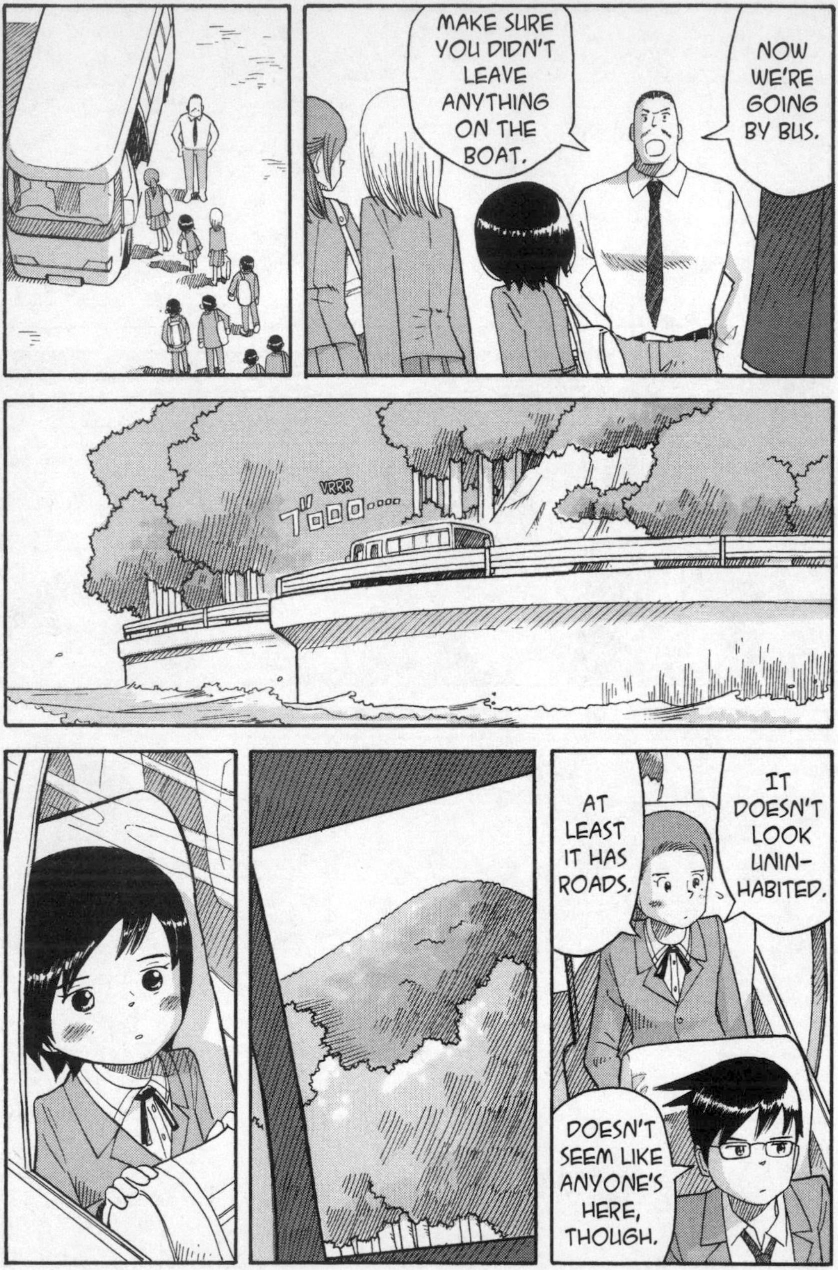
NOW WE'RE GOING BY BUS.
MAKE SURE YOU DIDN'T LEAVE ANYTHING ON THE BOAT.
VRRR
IT DOESN'T LOOK UNIN-HABITED.
AT LEAST IT HAS ROADS.
DOESN'T SEEM LIKE ANYONE'S HERE, THOUGH.

VRRR

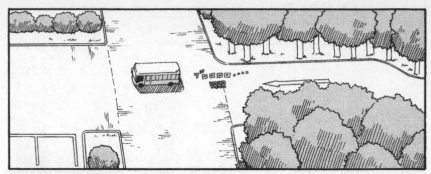

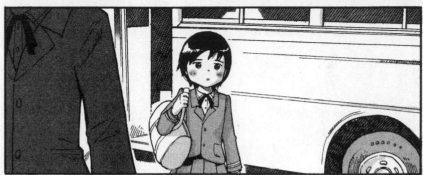

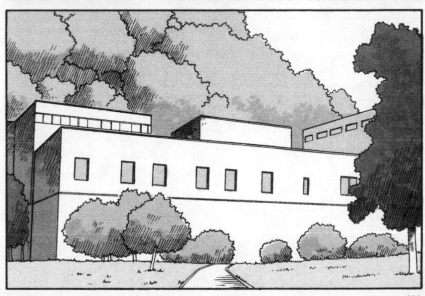

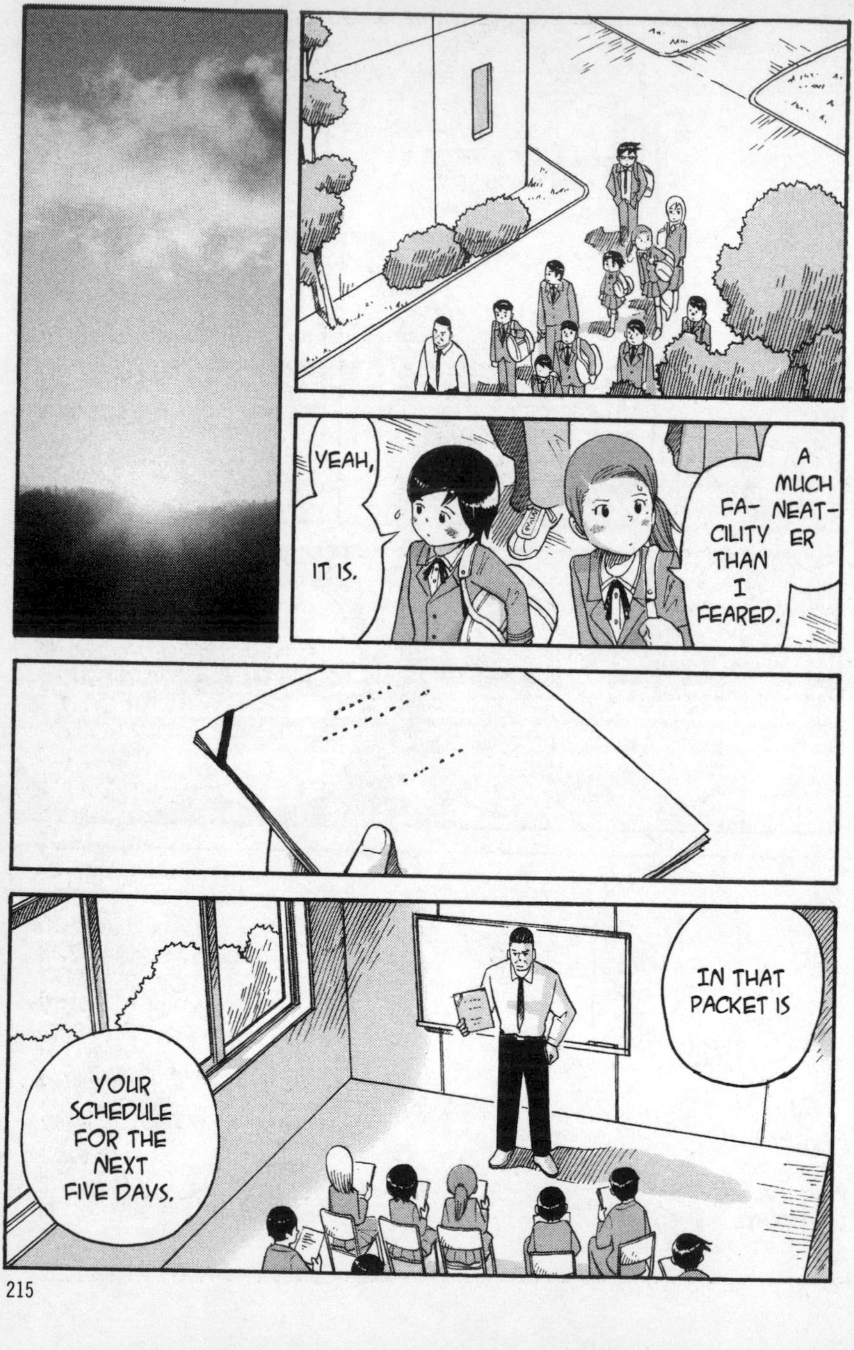
A MUCH NEAT-ER FA-CILITY THAN I FEARED.
YEAH, IT IS.
IN THAT PACKET IS
YOUR SCHEDULE FOR THE NEXT FIVE DAYS.

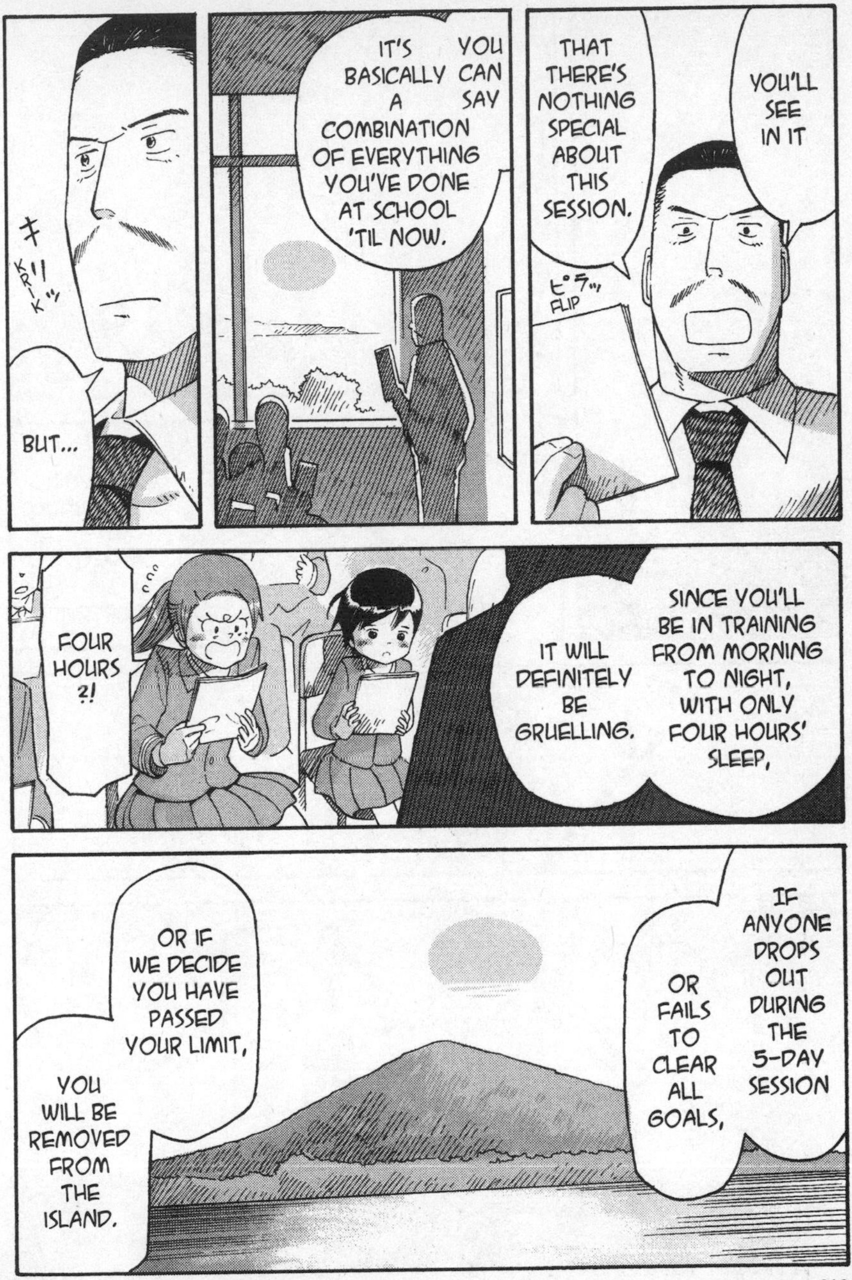
YOU'LL SEE IN IT
THAT THERE'S NOTHING SPECIAL ABOUT THIS SESSION.
ピラッ
FLIP
YOU CAN SAY
IT'S BASICALLY A COMBINATION OF EVERYTHING YOU'VE DONE AT SCHOOL 'TIL NOW.
キリッ
KRIK
BUT...
SINCE YOU'LL BE IN TRAINING FROM MORNING TO NIGHT, WITH ONLY FOUR HOURS' SLEEP,
IT WILL DEFINITELY BE GRUELLING.
FOUR HOURS?!
IF ANYONE DROPS OUT DURING THE 5-DAY SESSION
OR FAILS TO CLEAR ALL GOALS,
OR IF WE DECIDE YOU HAVE PASSED YOUR LIMIT,
YOU WILL BE REMOVED FROM THE ISLAND.

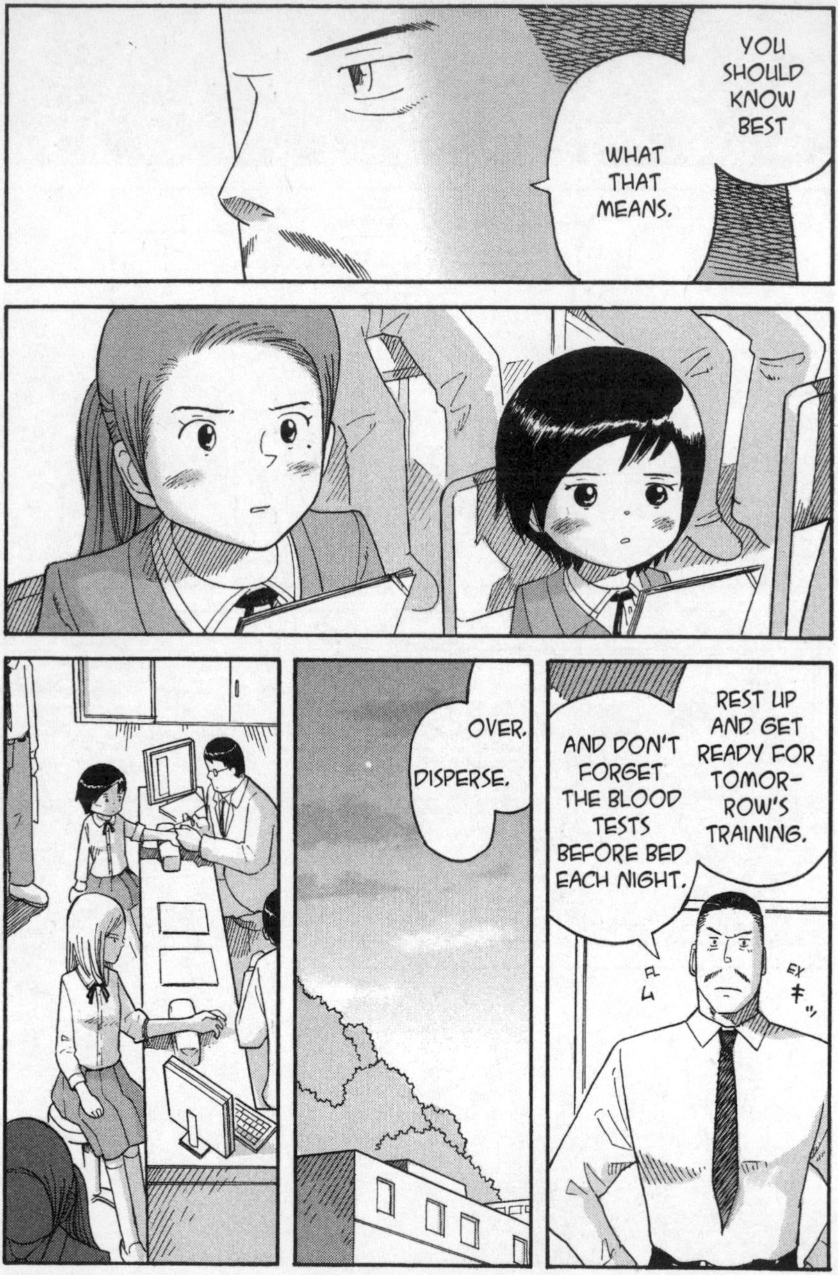
YOU SHOULD KNOW BEST
WHAT THAT MEANS.
REST UP AND GET READY FOR TOMOR-ROW'S TRAINING.
AND DON'T FORGET THE BLOOD TESTS BEFORE BED EACH NIGHT.
ム
キッ
OVER.
DISPERSE.

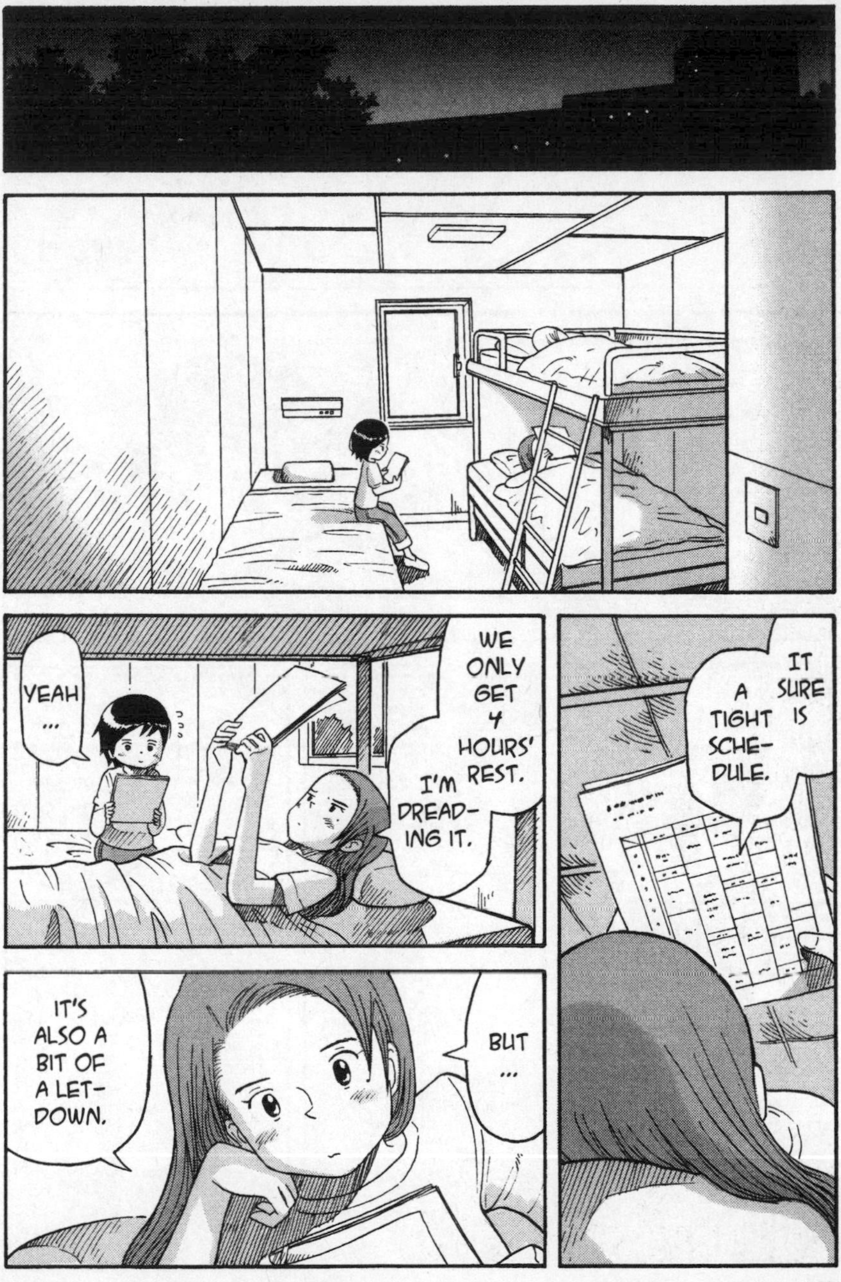
IT SURE IS A TIGHT SCHEDULE.
WE ONLY GET 4 HOURS' REST.
I'M DREADING IT.
YEAH ...
BUT ...
IT'S ALSO A BIT OF A LET-DOWN.

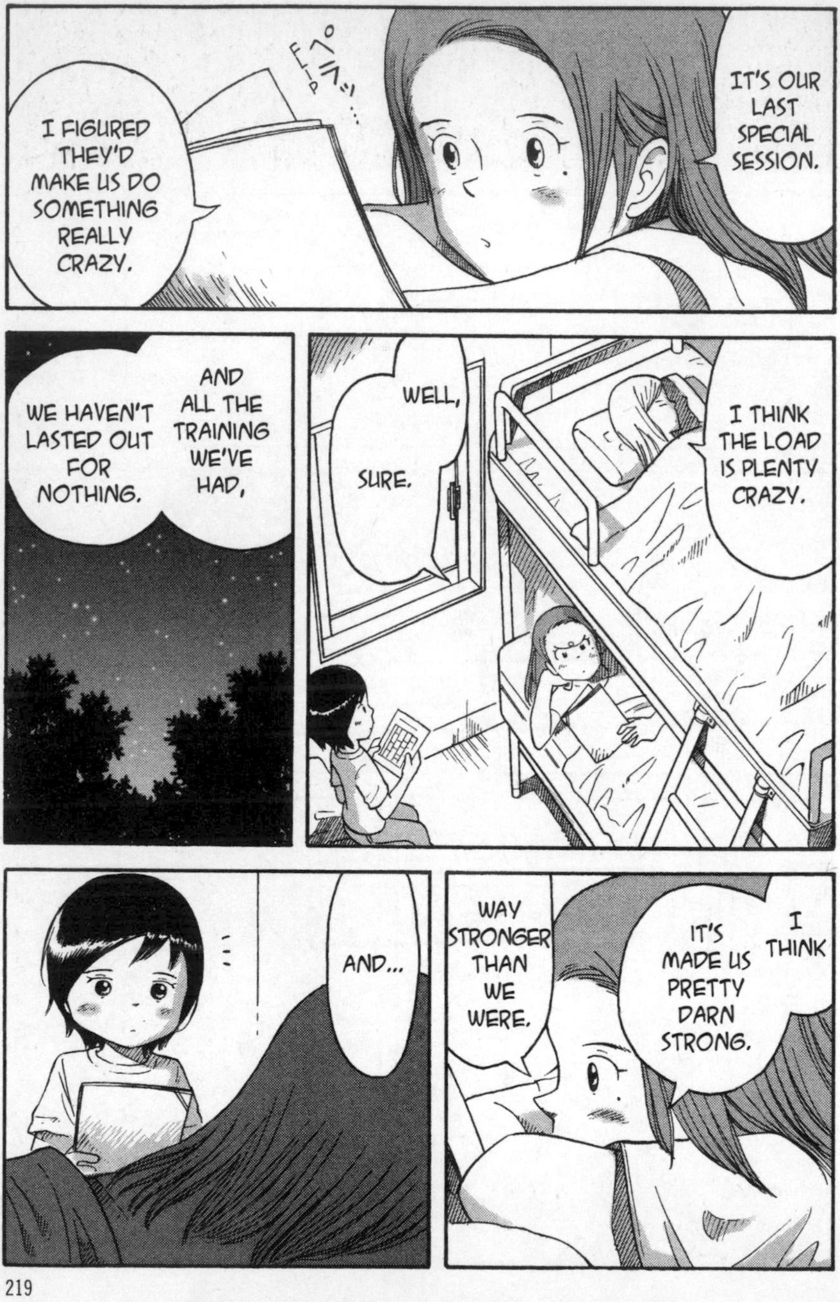
IT'S OUR LAST SPECIAL SESSION.
FLIP
I FIGURED THEY'D MAKE US DO SOMETHING REALLY CRAZY.
I THINK THE LOAD IS PLENTY CRAZY.
WELL,
SURE.
AND ALL THE TRAINING WE'VE HAD,
WE HAVEN'T LASTED OUT FOR NOTHING.
I THINK
IT'S MADE US PRETTY DARN STRONG.
WAY STRONGER THAN WE WERE.
AND...

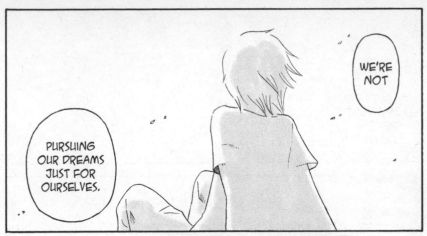

WE'RE NOT
PURSUING OUR DREAMS JUST FOR OURSELVES.
YEAH...
I'VE GOT MORE SPIRIT THAN EVER BEFORE.
DON'T GET TOO SPIRITED AND SPIN YOUR WHEELS.
WHAT DO YOU MEAN.

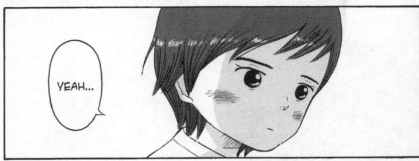

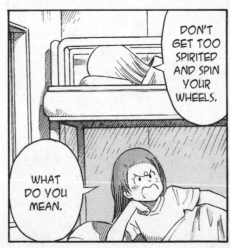

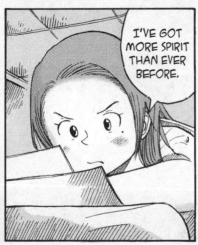

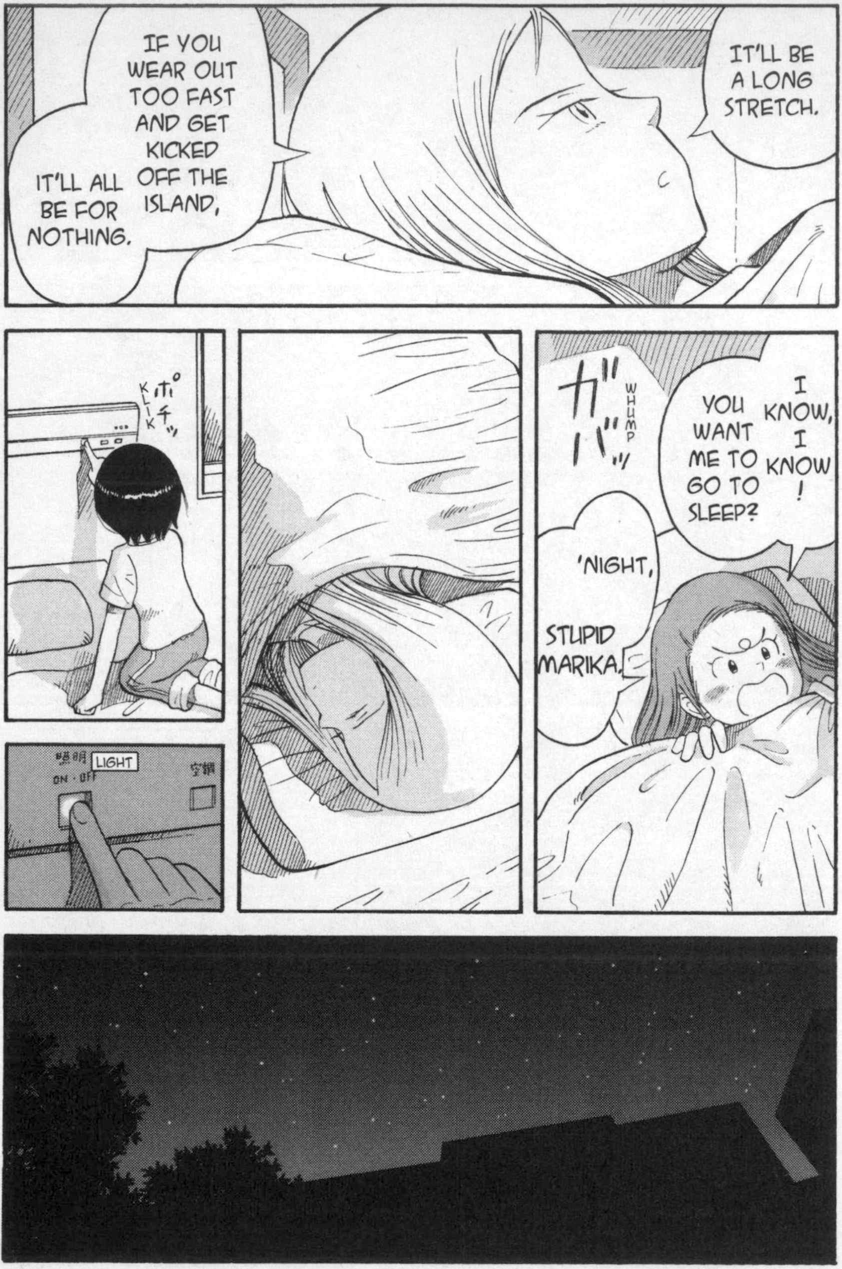
IT'LL BE A LONG STRETCH.
IF YOU WEAR OUT TOO FAST AND GET KICKED OFF THE ISLAND,
IT'LL ALL BE FOR NOTHING.
ガバッ
WHUMP
I KNOW, I KNOW!
YOU WANT ME TO GO TO SLEEP?
'NIGHT,
STUPID MARIKA.
ポチッ
KLIK
照明
LIGHT
ON・OFF
空調

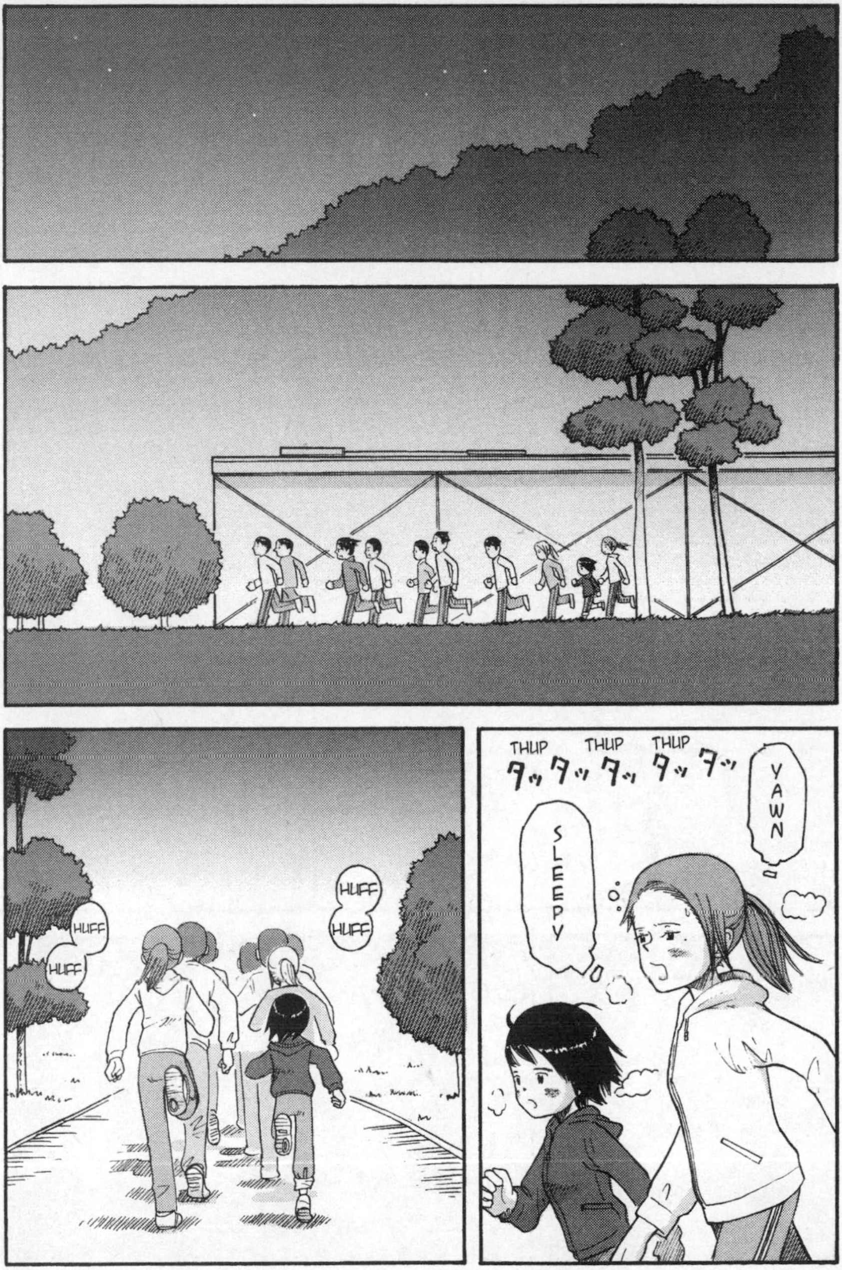
YAWN
THUP THUP THUP
タッタッタッタッタッ
SLEEPY
HUFF HUFF
HUFF HUFF

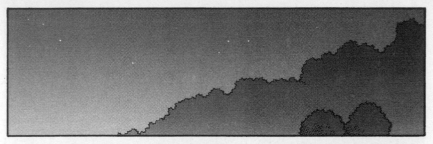

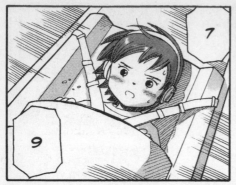

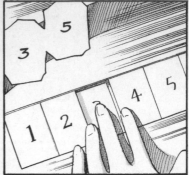

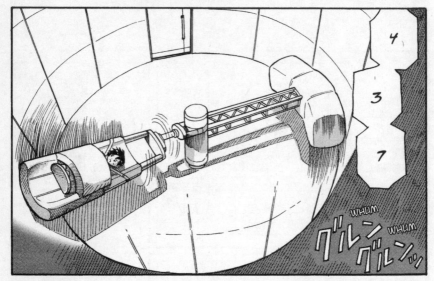

WHUM
WHUM
グルーン
グルーン

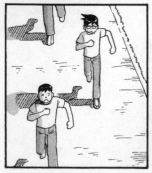

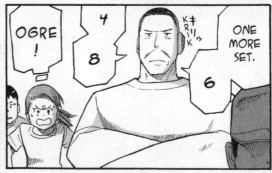

OGRE
!

KRIK
KRIK

ONE
MORE
SET.

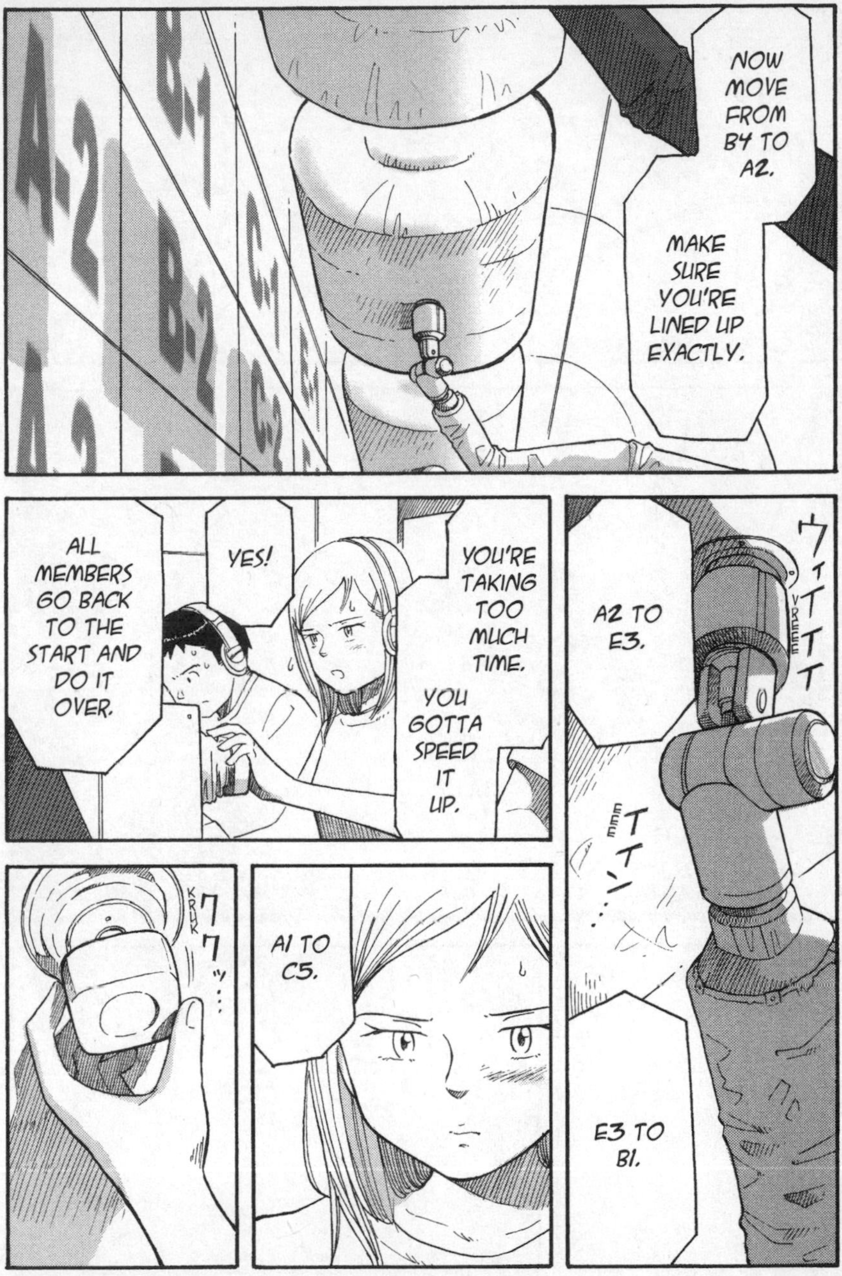
NOW MOVE FROM B4 TO A2.
MAKE SURE YOU'RE LINED UP EXACTLY.
A2 TO E3.
VREEE
EEE
E3 TO B1.
YOU'RE TAKING TOO MUCH TIME.
YOU GOTTA SPEED IT UP.
YES!
ALL MEMBERS GO BACK TO THE START AND DO IT OVER.
A1 TO C5.
KRUK

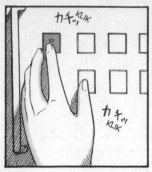

カチッ KLIK

カチッ KLIK

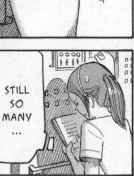

STILL SO MANY ...

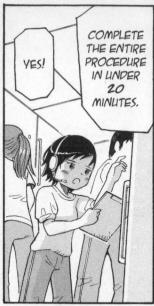

YES!

COMPLETE THE ENTIRE PROCEDURE IN UNDER **20** MINUTES.

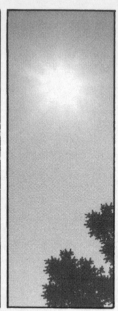

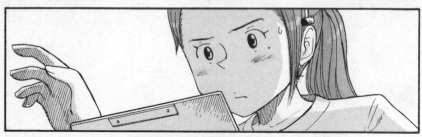

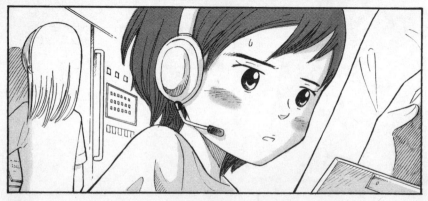

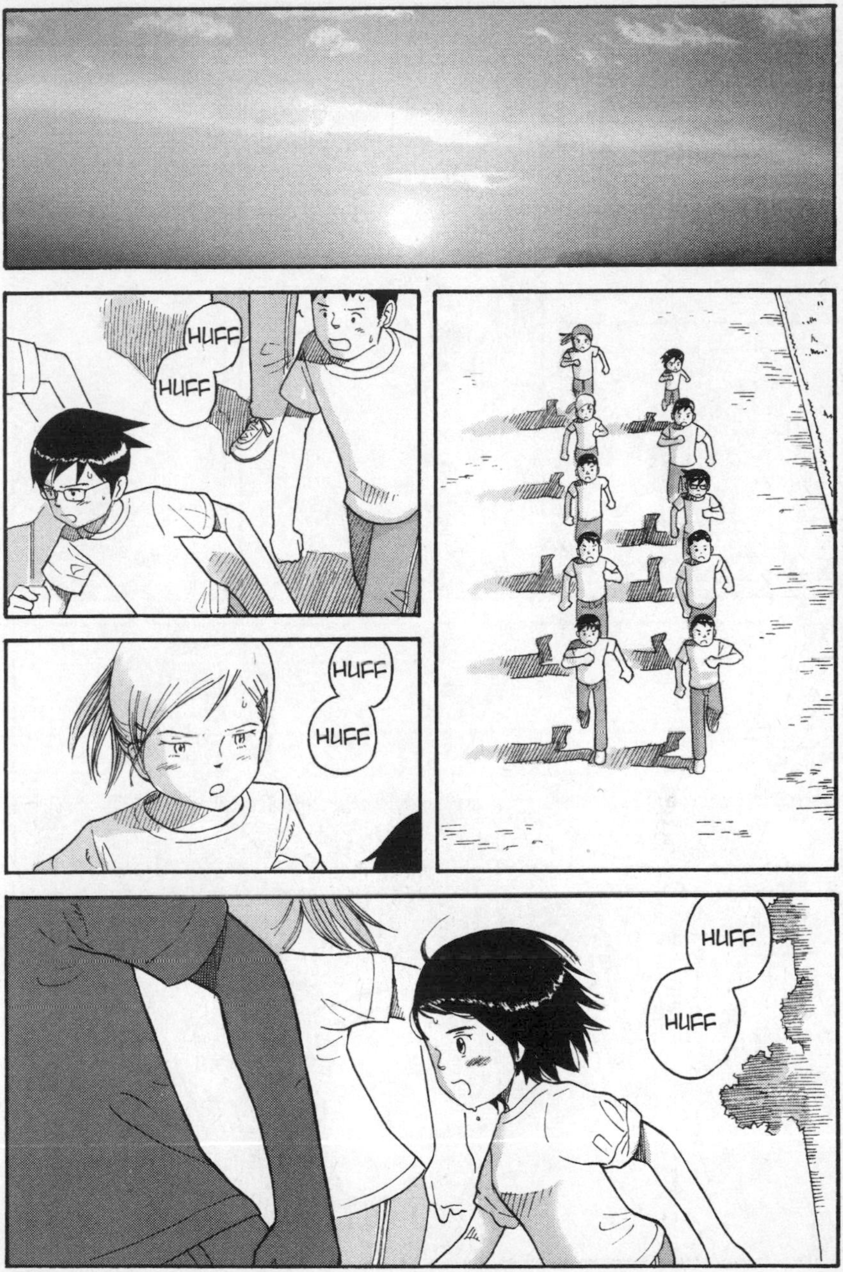
HUFF
HUFF
HUFF
HUFF
HUFF
HUFF

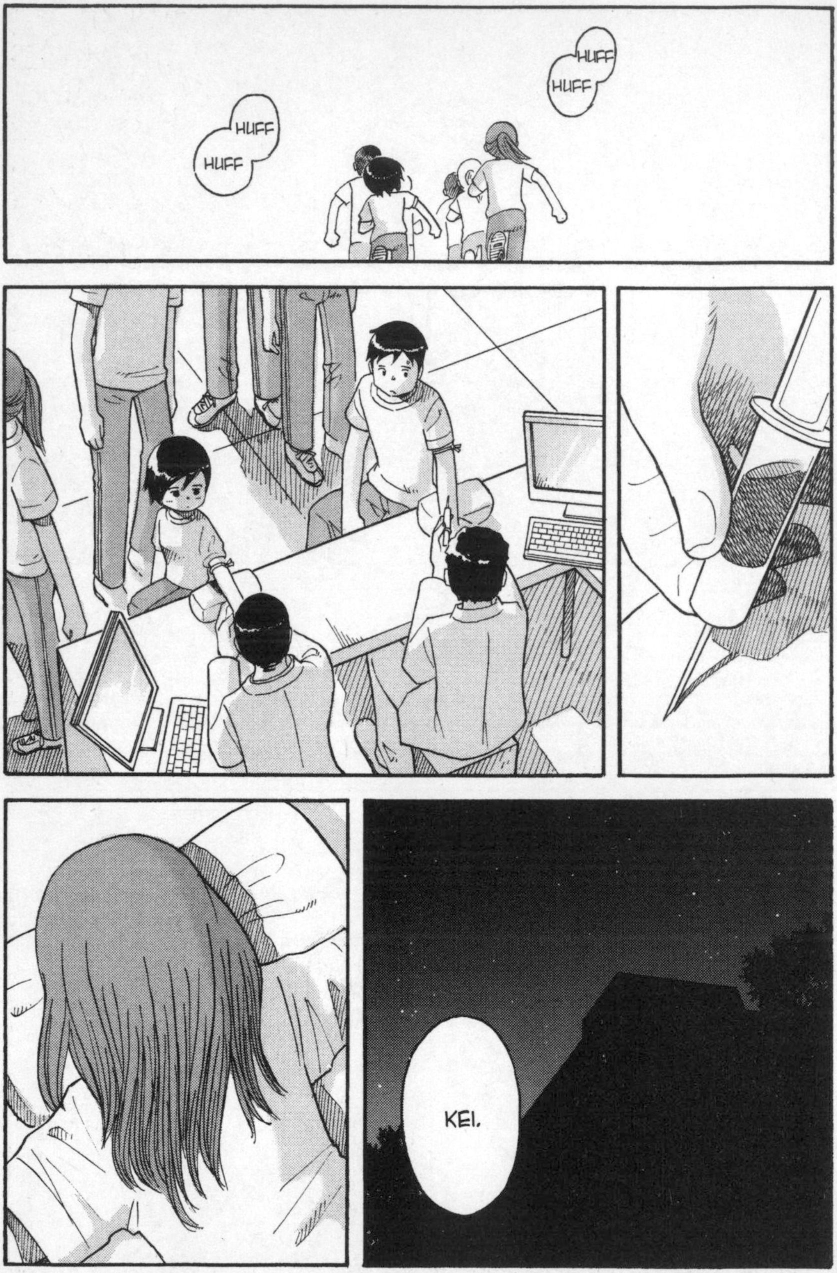
HUFF
HUFF
HUFF
HUFF
KEI.

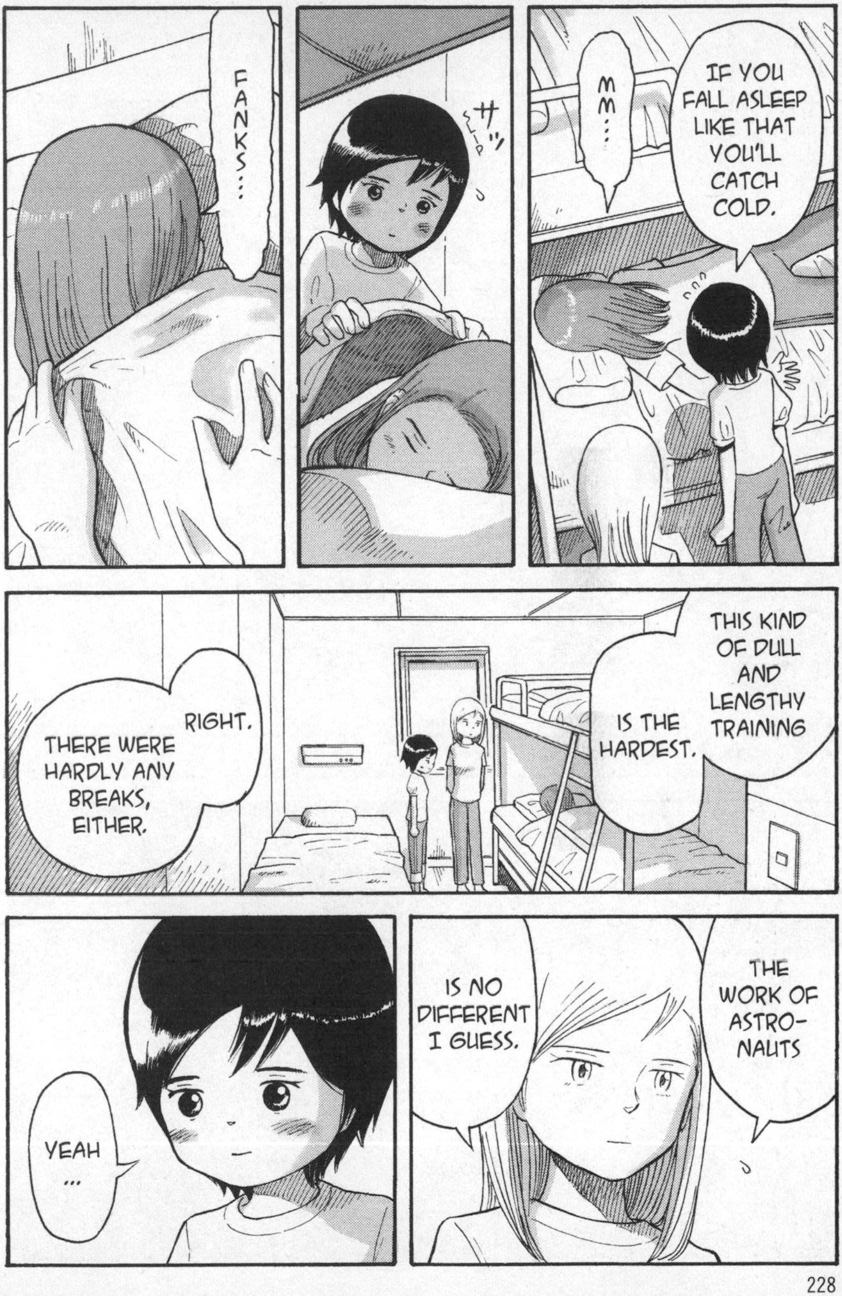
IF YOU FALL ASLEEP LIKE THAT YOU'LL CATCH COLD.
MM...
SLIP
FANKS...
THIS KIND OF DULL AND LENGTHY TRAINING
IS THE HARDEST.
RIGHT.
THERE WERE HARDLY ANY BREAKS, EITHER.
THE WORK OF ASTRO-NAUTS
IS NO DIFFERENT I GUESS.
YEAH ...

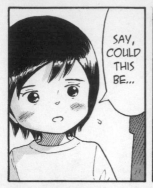

AT ANY RATE, THIS PLACE IS NICE
FOR BEING ON AN EMPTY ISLAND.
AH, YEAH.
SAY, COULD THIS BE...
HEY! YOU STILL AWAKE? GET TO BED
OR YOU'LL BE SORRY IN THE MORNING.
AH, YES.

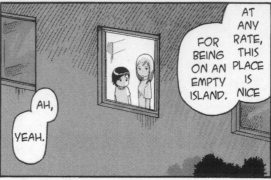

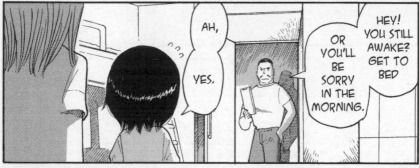

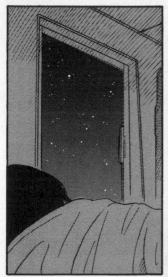

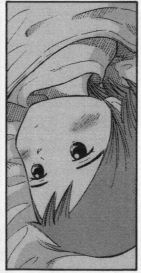

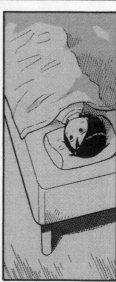

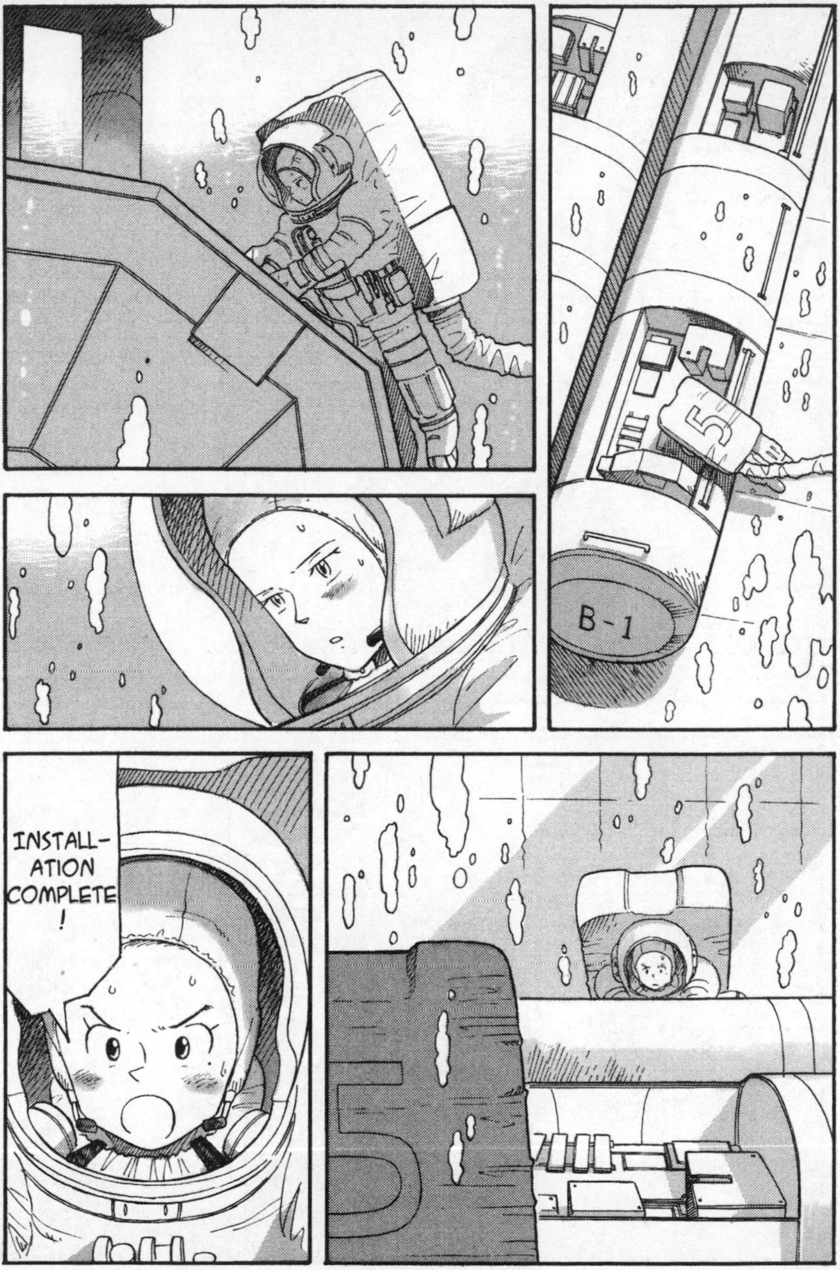
5
B-1
INSTALL-ATION COMPLETE!

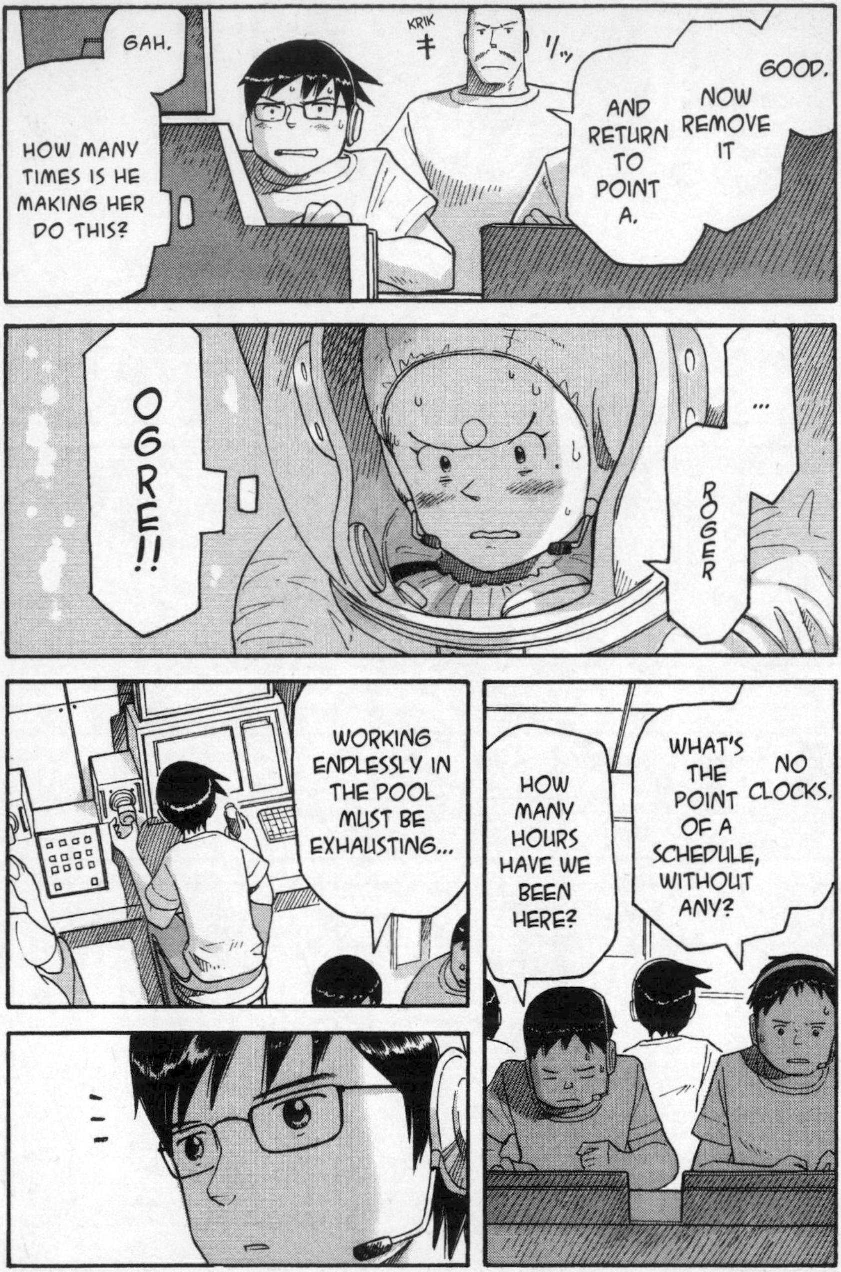
GOOD. NOW REMOVE IT AND RETURN TO POINT A.
KRIK
GAH. HOW MANY TIMES IS HE MAKING HER DO THIS?
...ROGER
OGRE!!
NO CLOCKS. WHAT'S THE POINT OF A SCHEDULE, WITHOUT ANY?
HOW MANY HOURS HAVE WE BEEN HERE?
WORKING ENDLESSLY IN THE POOL MUST BE EXHAUSTING...

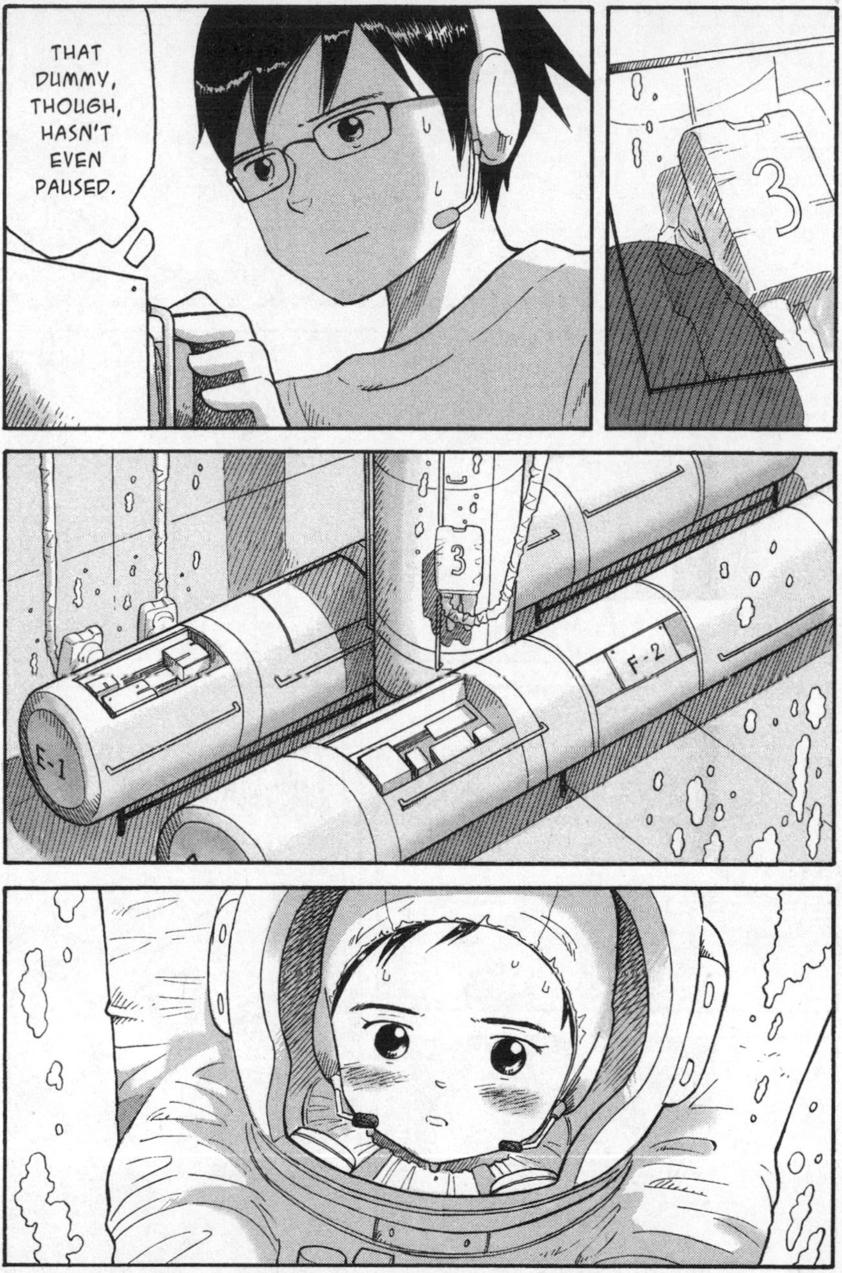
THAT DUMMY, THOUGH, HASN'T EVEN PAUSED.
3
3
F-2
E-1

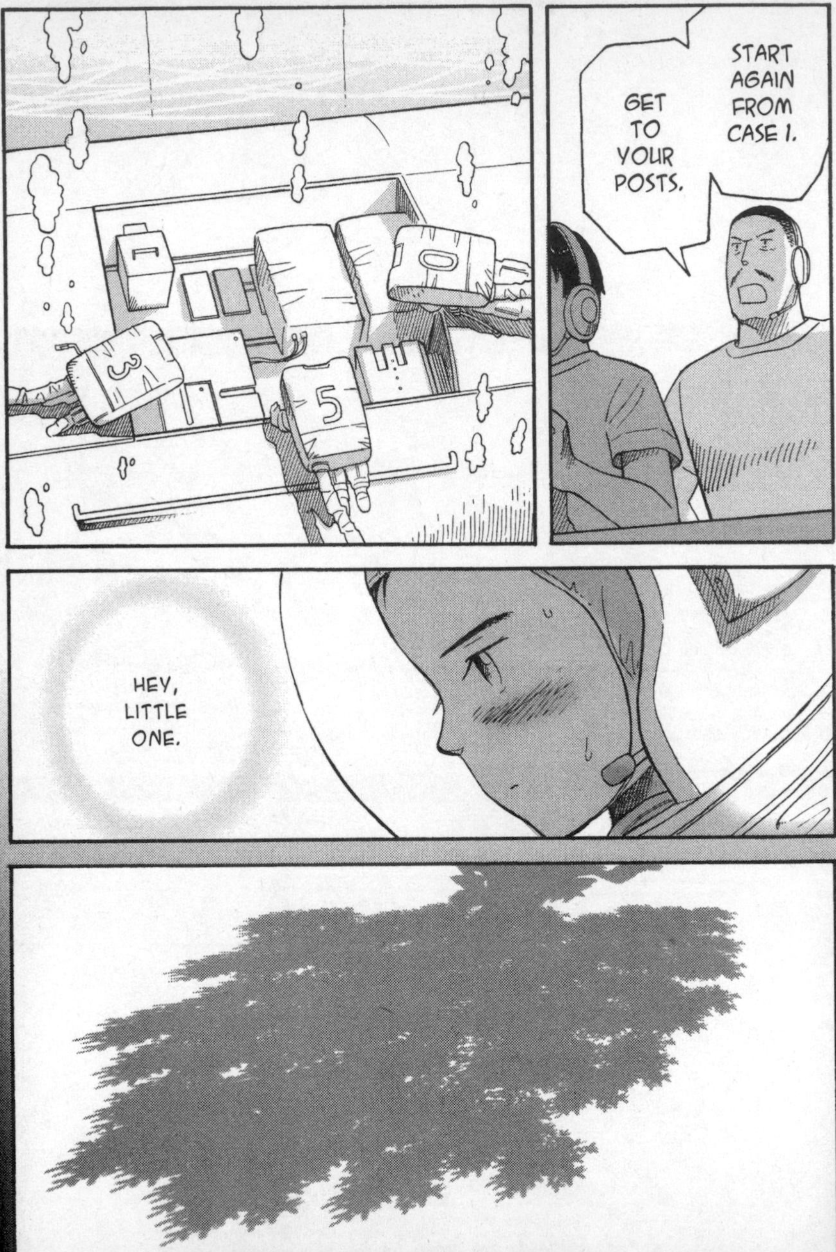
START AGAIN FROM CASE 1.
GET TO YOUR POSTS.
HEY, LITTLE ONE.

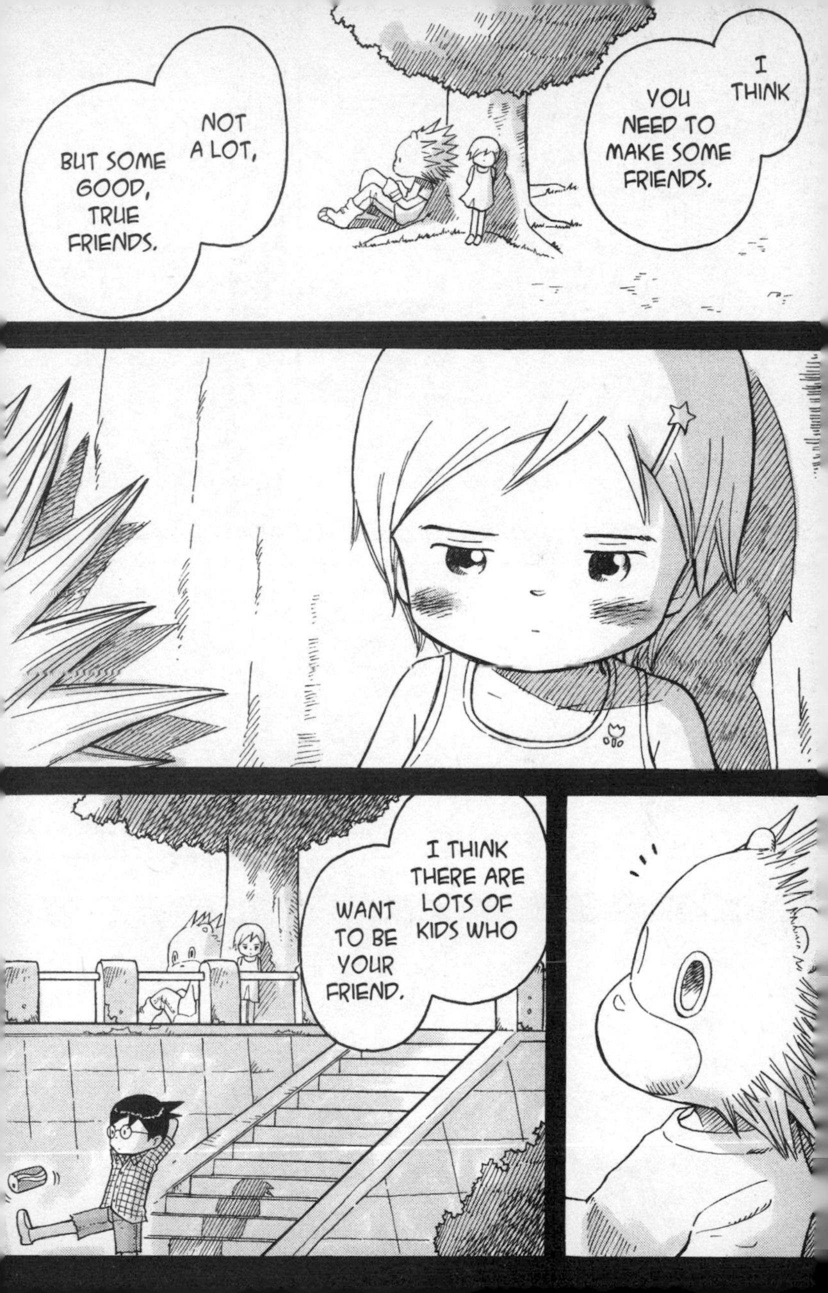
I THINK YOU NEED TO MAKE SOME FRIENDS.
NOT A LOT, BUT SOME GOOD, TRUE FRIENDS.
I THINK THERE ARE LOTS OF KIDS WHO WANT TO BE YOUR FRIEND.

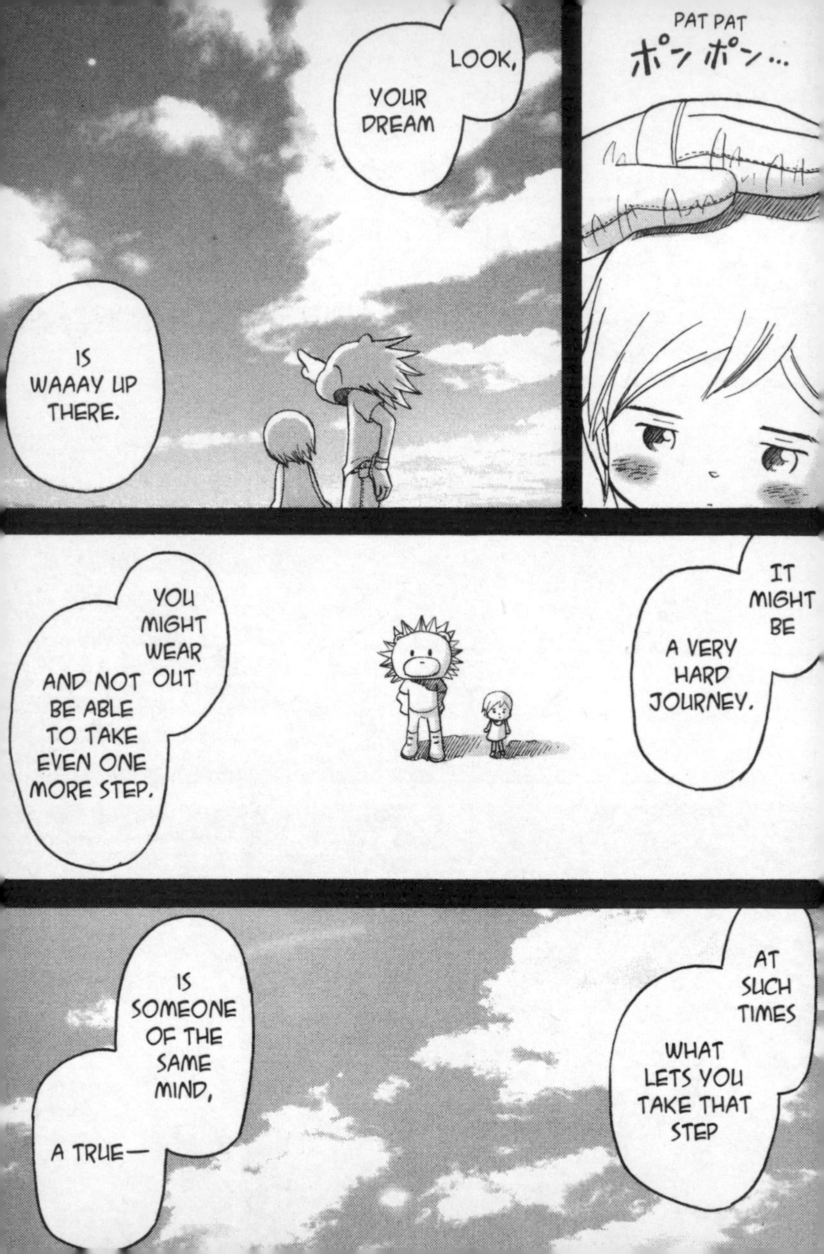
PAT PAT
ポンポン…
LOOK, YOUR DREAM
IS WAAAY UP THERE.
IT MIGHT BE A VERY HARD JOURNEY.
YOU MIGHT WEAR OUT AND NOT BE ABLE TO TAKE EVEN ONE MORE STEP.
AT SUCH TIMES WHAT LETS YOU TAKE THAT STEP
IS SOMEONE OF THE SAME MIND, A TRUE—

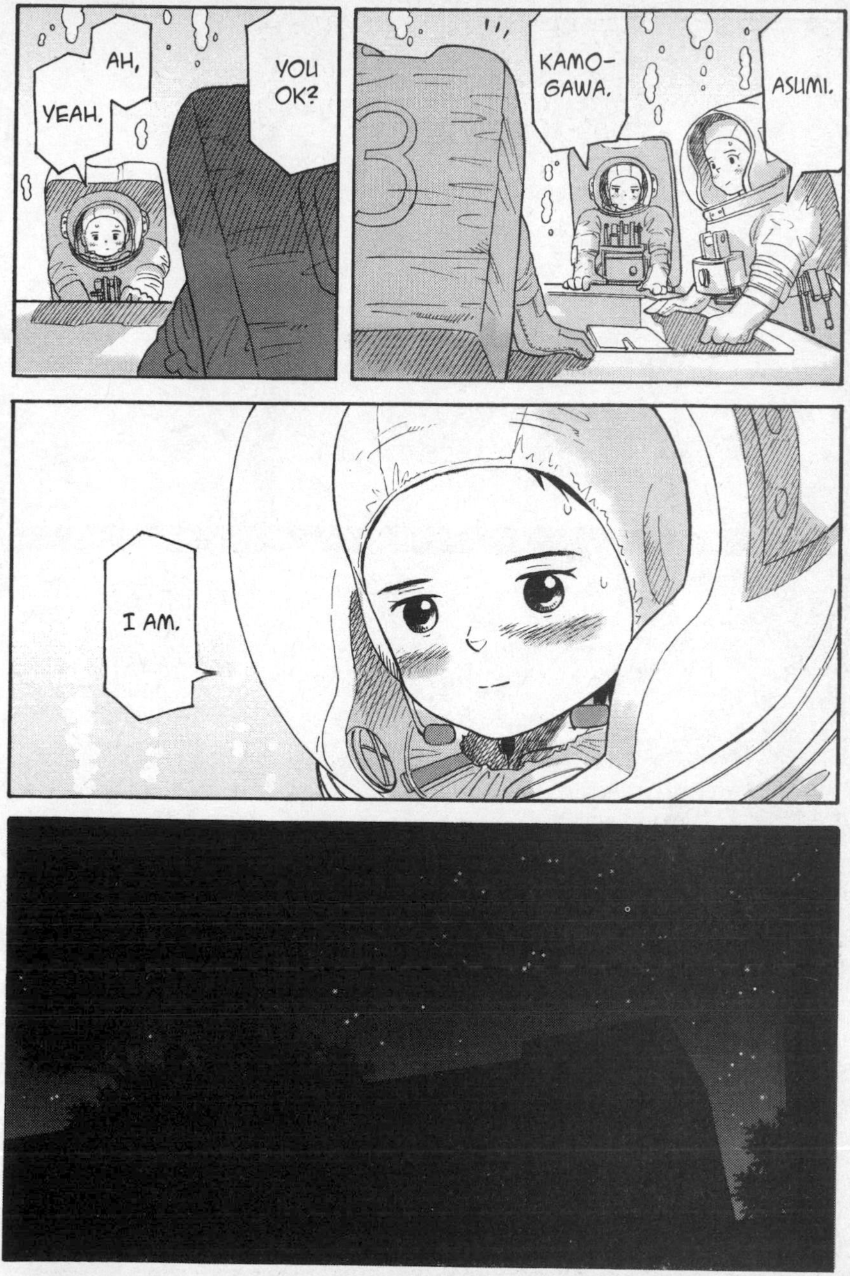

ASUMI.
KAMO-GAWA.
YOU OK?
AH, YEAH.
I AM.

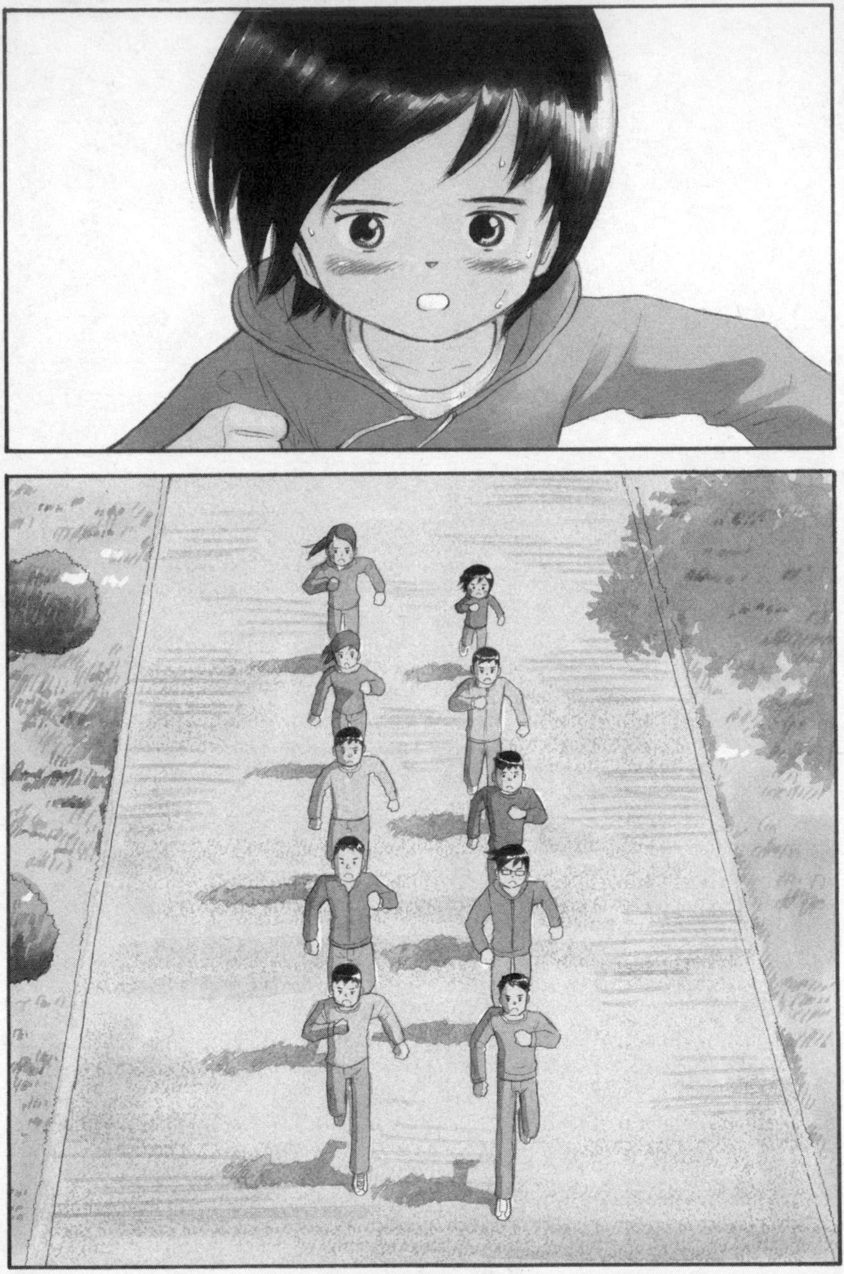

MISSION:72

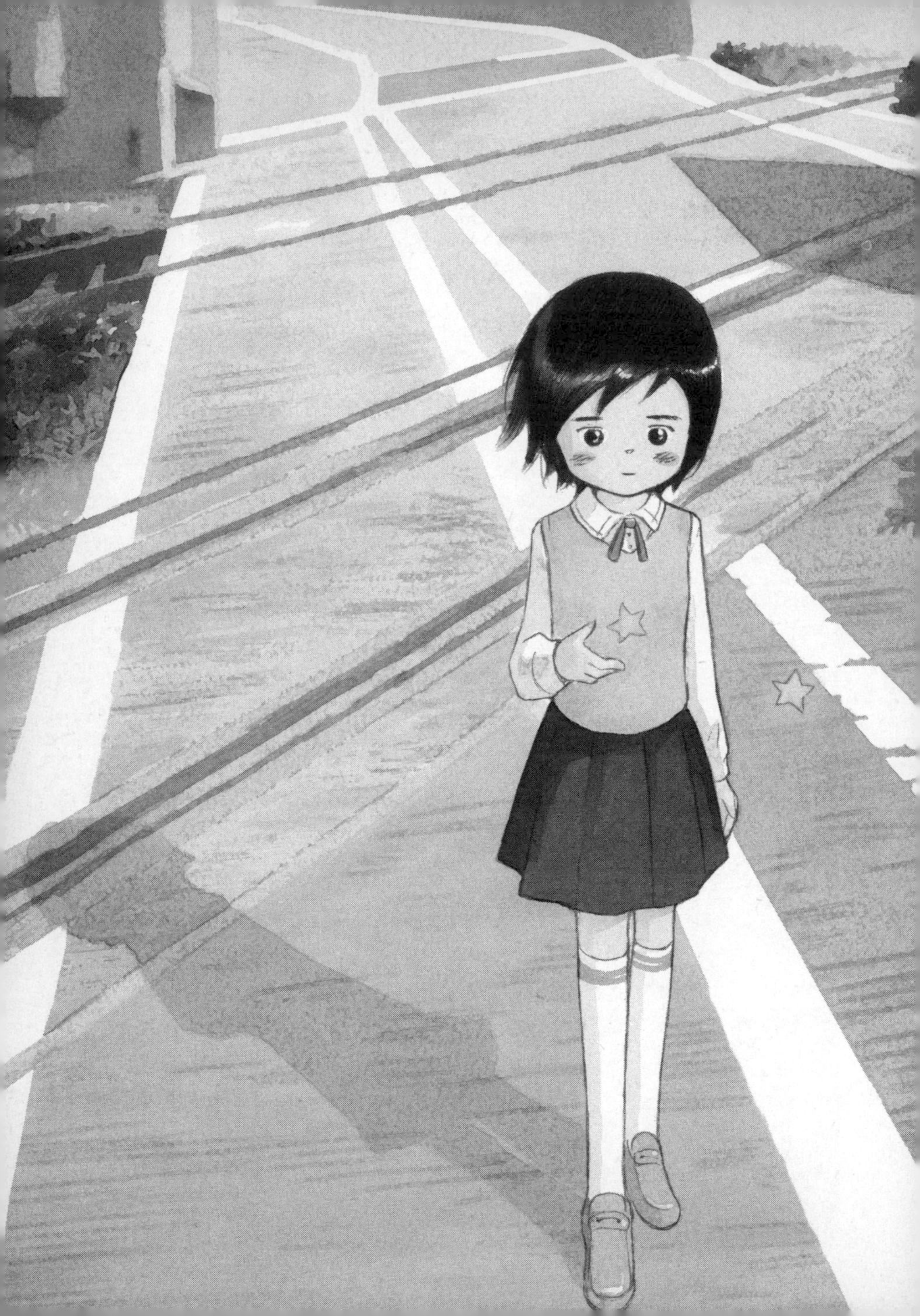

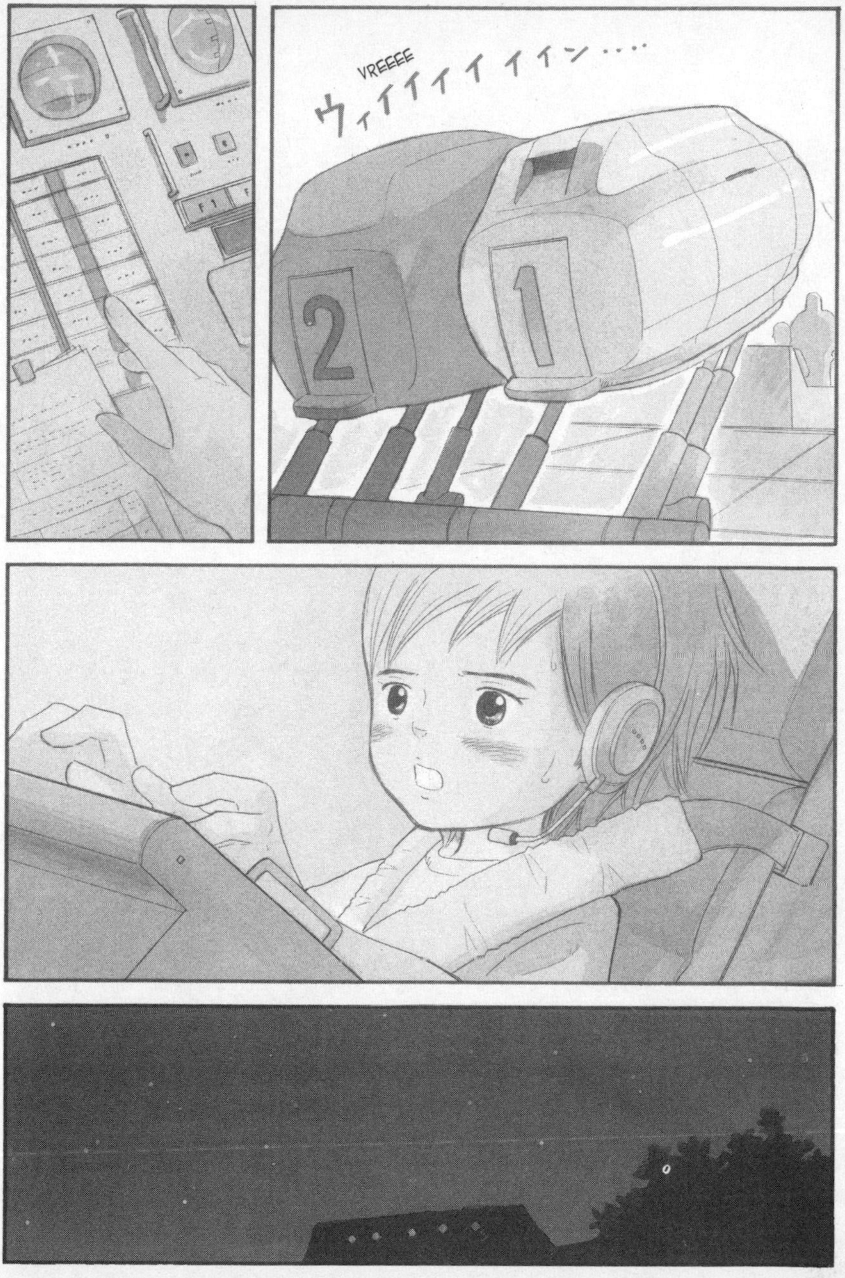
VREEEE
ウィイイイイイン....

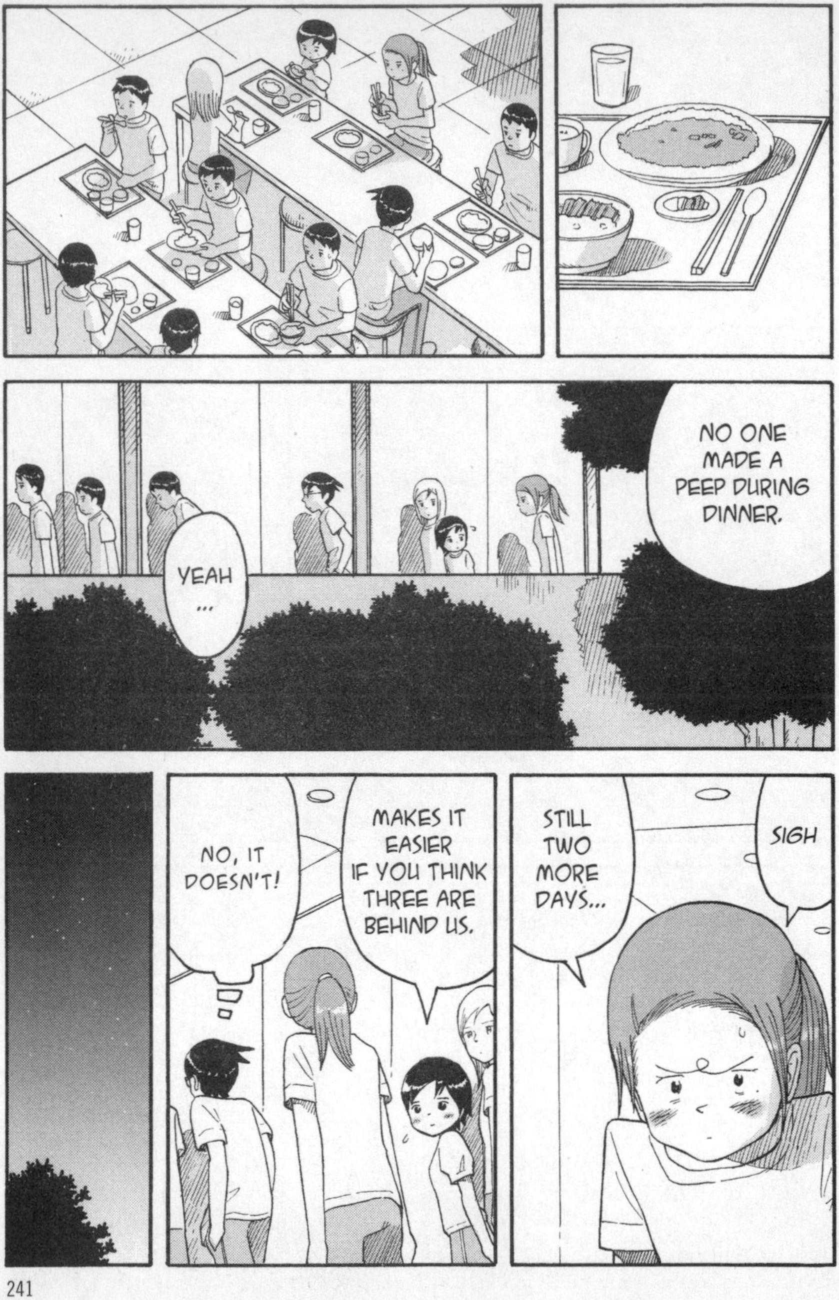
NO ONE MADE A PEEP DURING DINNER.
YEAH ...
SIGH
STILL TWO MORE DAYS...
MAKES IT EASIER IF YOU THINK THREE ARE BEHIND US.
NO, IT DOESN'T!

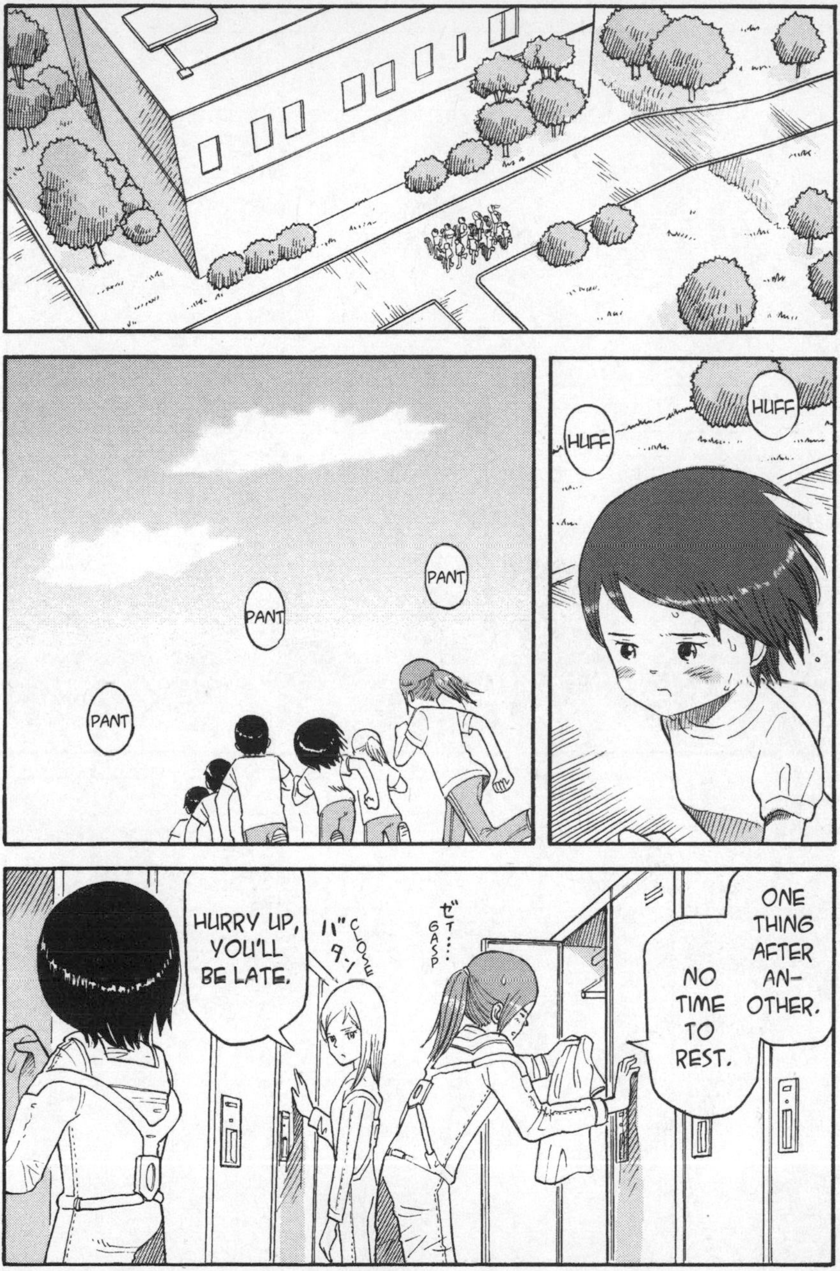
HUFF
HUFF
PANT
PANT
PANT
ONE THING AFTER AN-OTHER.
NO TIME TO REST.
ゼT…
GASP
バタン
CLOSE
HURRY UP, YOU'LL BE LATE.

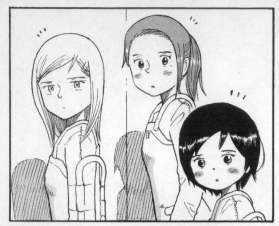
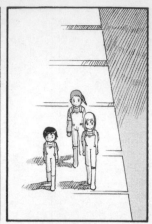
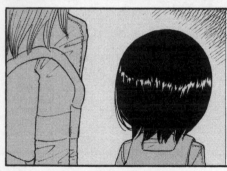
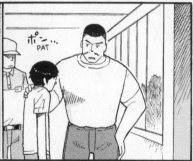

ポン…
PAT

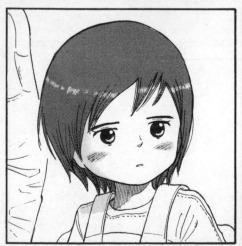
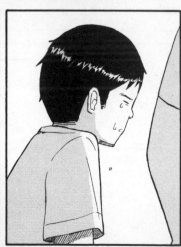

243

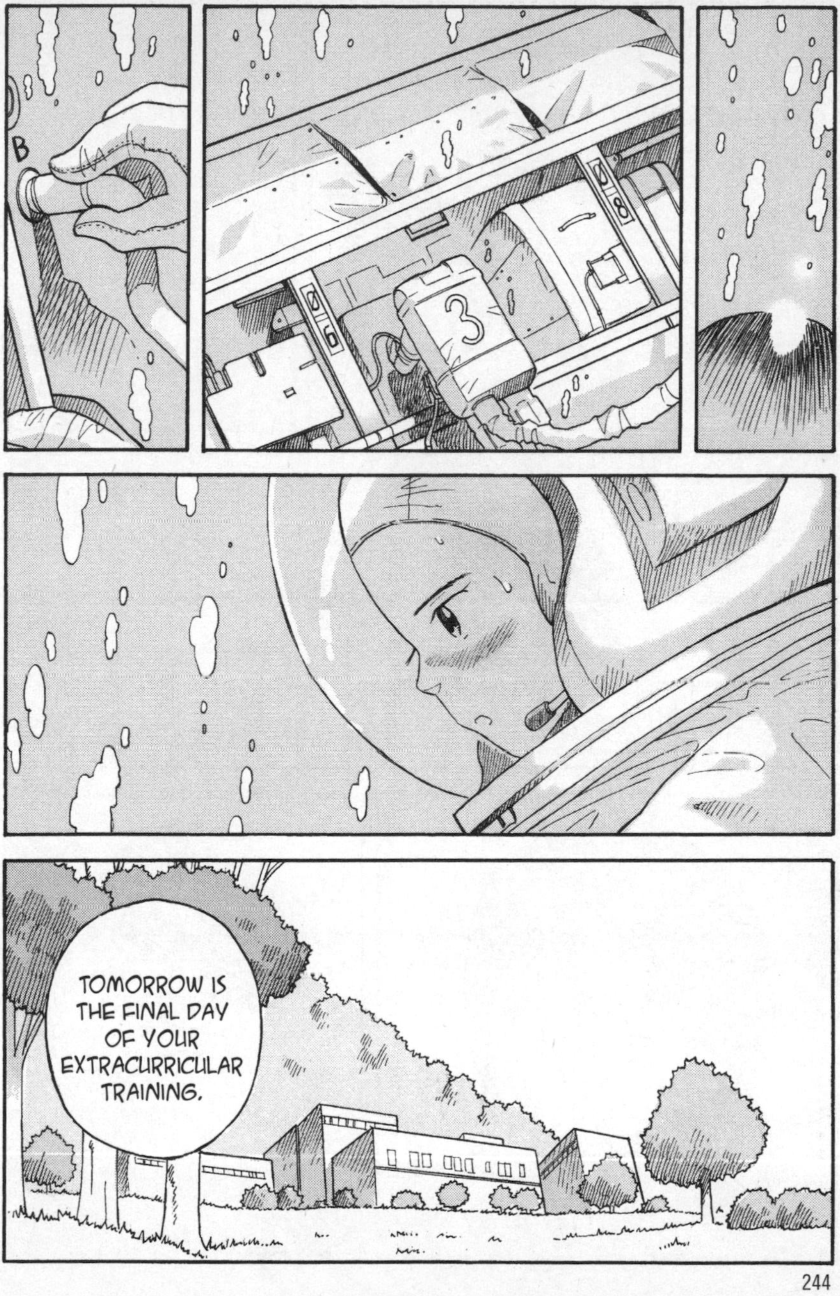
TOMORROW IS THE FINAL DAY OF YOUR EXTRACURRICULAR TRAINING.

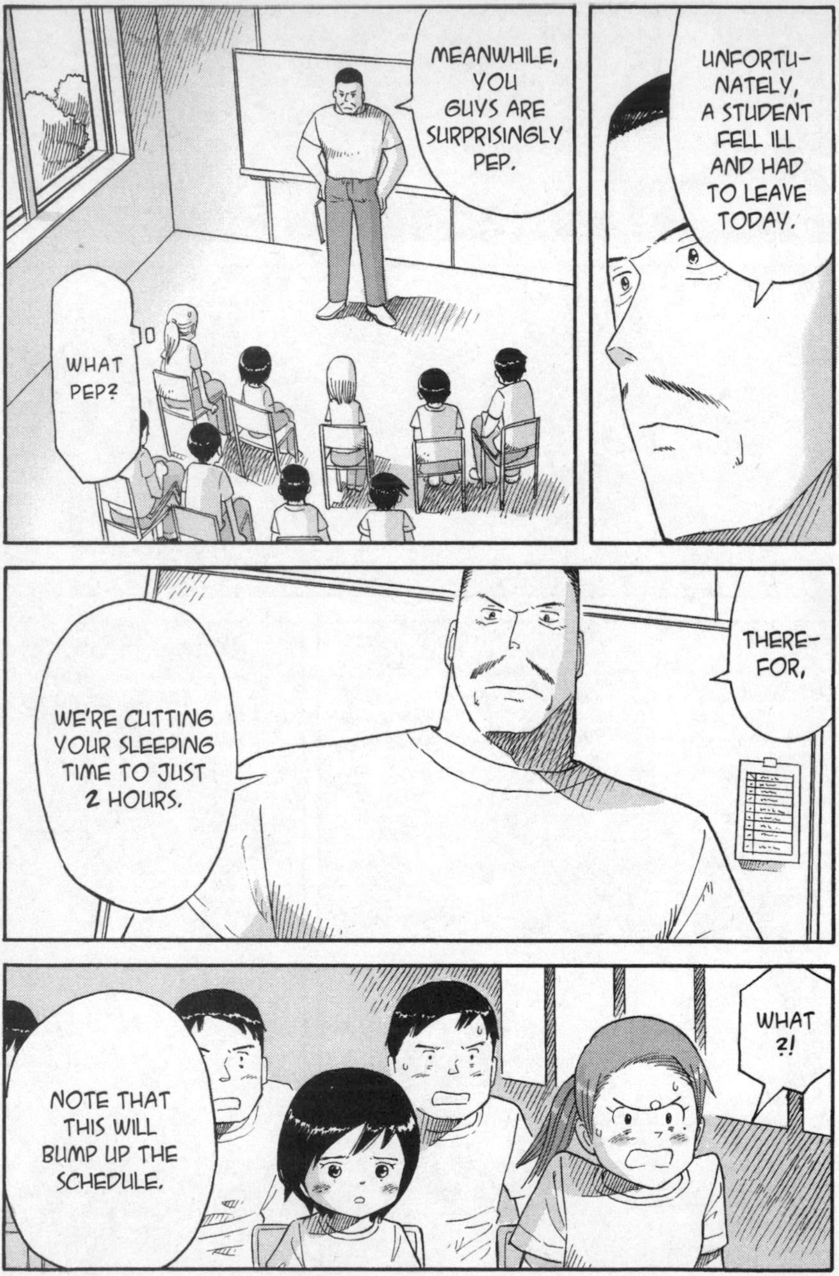
UNFORTU-NATELY, A STUDENT FELL ILL AND HAD TO LEAVE TODAY.
MEANWHILE, YOU GUYS ARE SURPRISINGLY PEP.
WHAT PEP?
THERE-FOR,
WE'RE CUTTING YOUR SLEEPING TIME TO JUST 2 HOURS.
WHAT?!
NOTE THAT THIS WILL BUMP UP THE SCHEDULE.

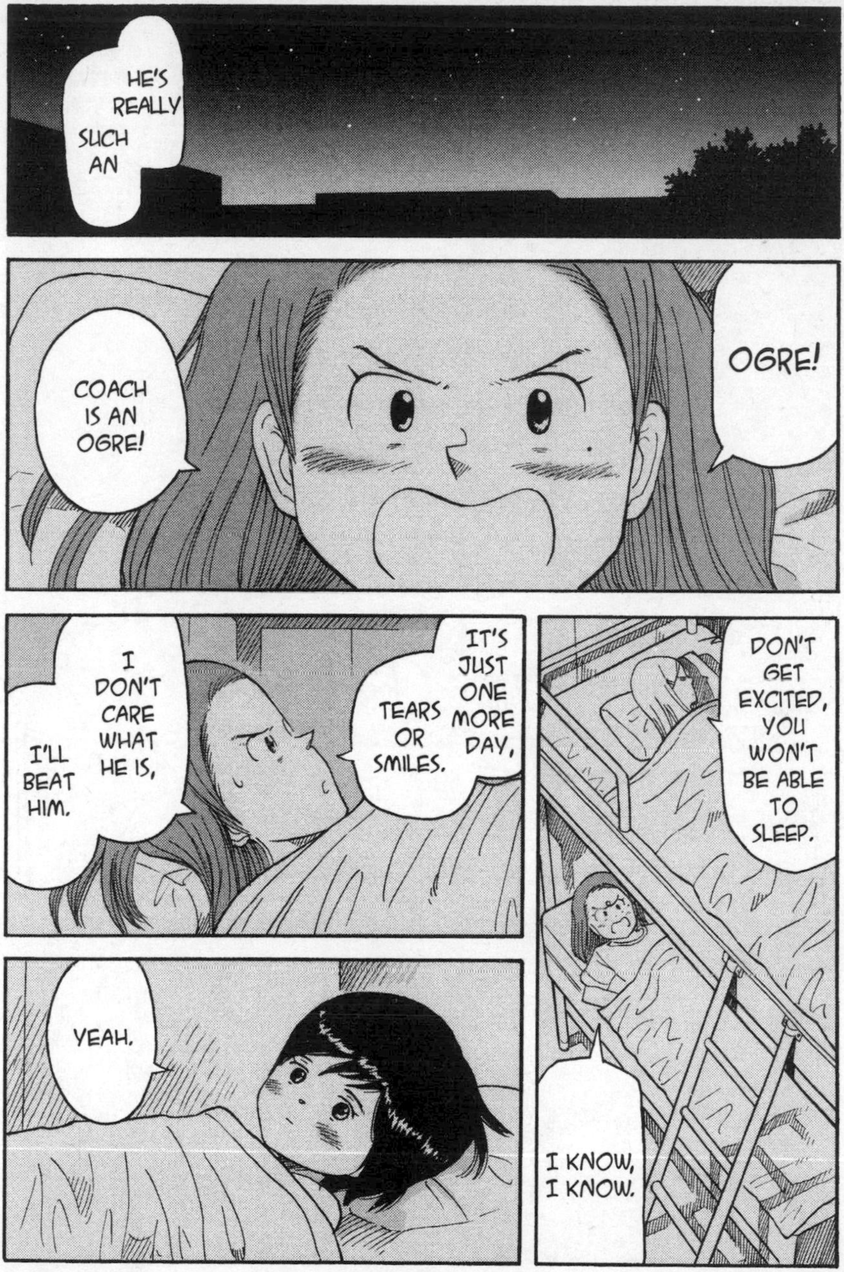
HE'S REALLY SUCH AN
OGRE!
COACH IS AN OGRE!
DON'T GET EXCITED, YOU WON'T BE ABLE TO SLEEP.
I KNOW, I KNOW.
IT'S JUST ONE MORE DAY, TEARS OR SMILES.
I DON'T CARE WHAT HE IS, I'LL BEAT HIM.
YEAH.

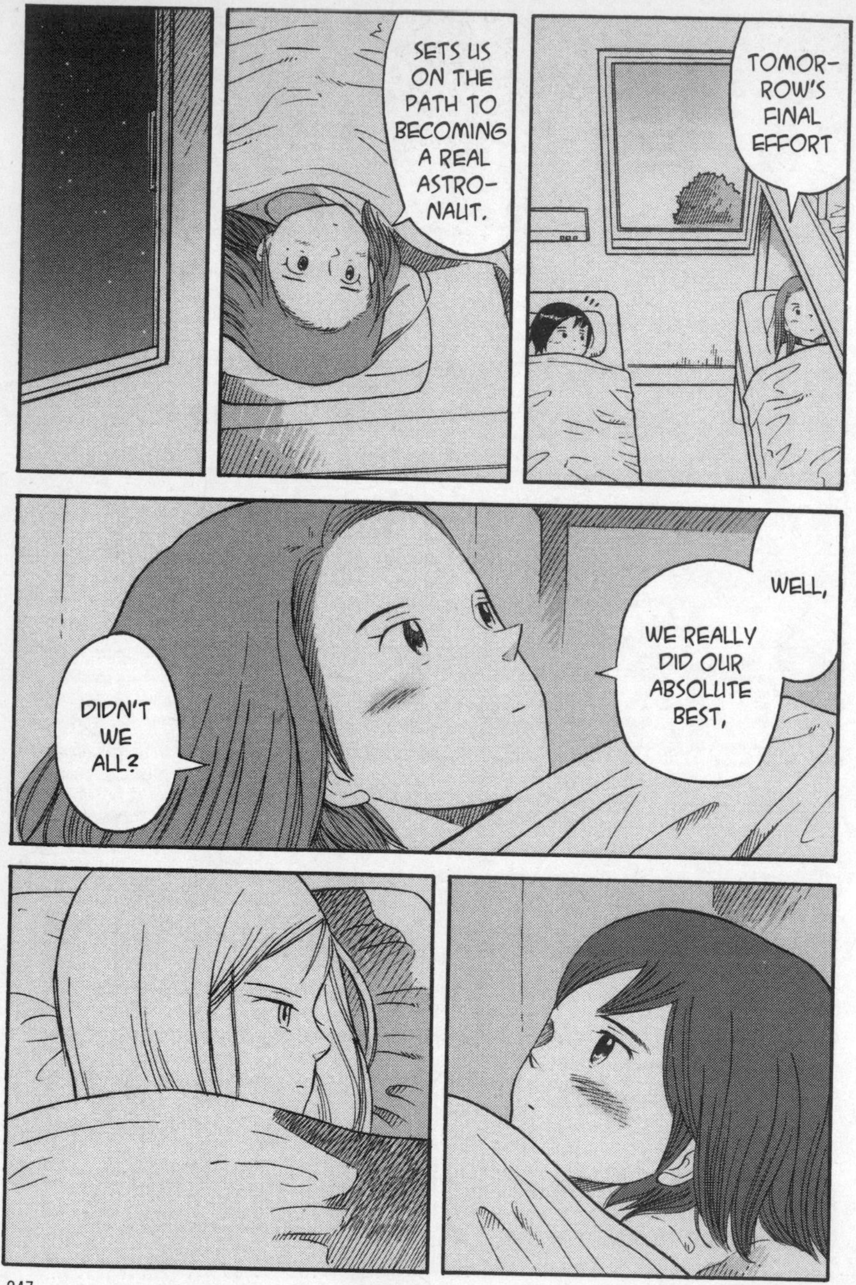
TOMOR-ROW'S FINAL EFFORT
SETS US ON THE PATH TO BECOMING A REAL ASTRO-NAUT.
WELL,
WE REALLY DID OUR ABSOLUTE BEST,
DIDN'T WE ALL?

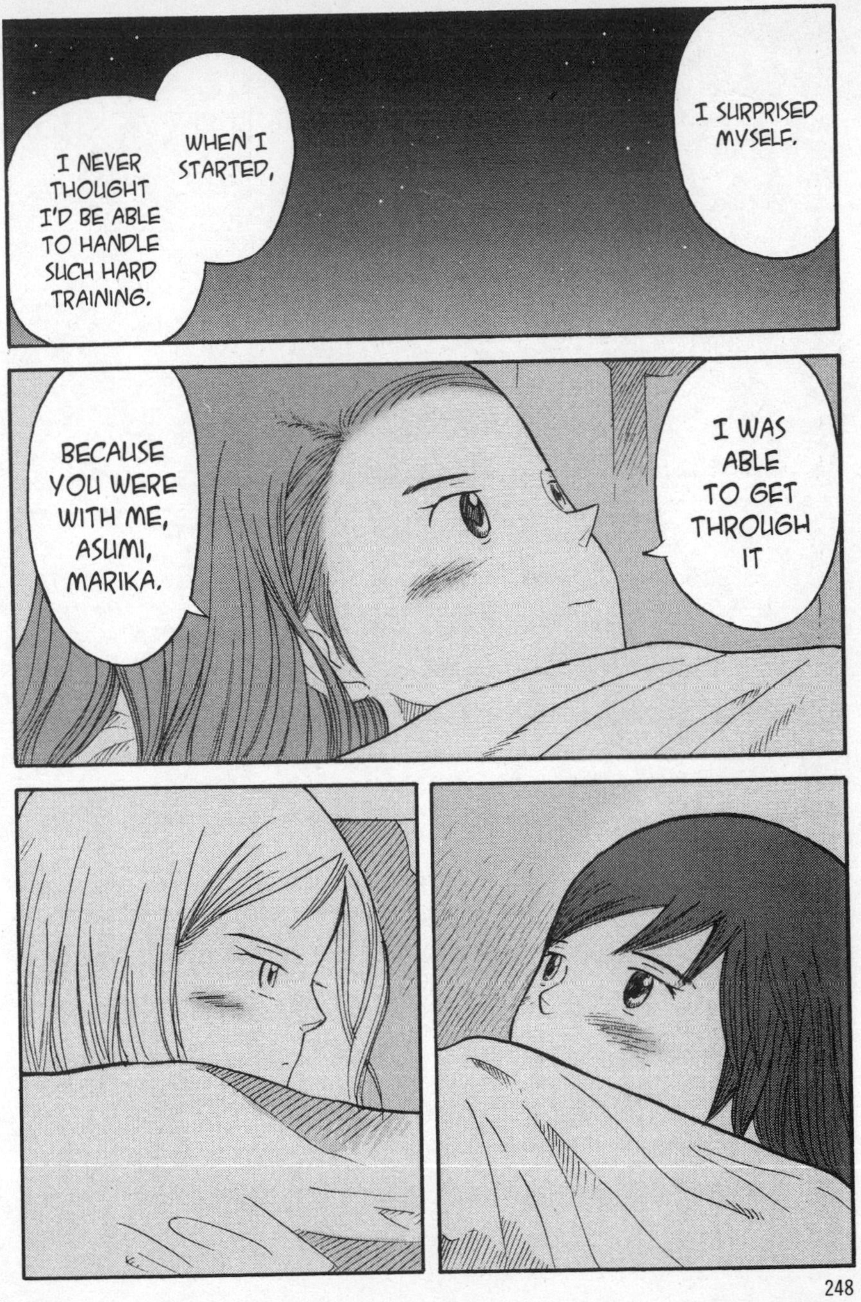
I SURPRISED MYSELF.
WHEN I STARTED,
I NEVER THOUGHT I'D BE ABLE TO HANDLE SUCH HARD TRAINING.
I WAS ABLE TO GET THROUGH IT
BECAUSE YOU WERE WITH ME, ASUMI, MARIKA.

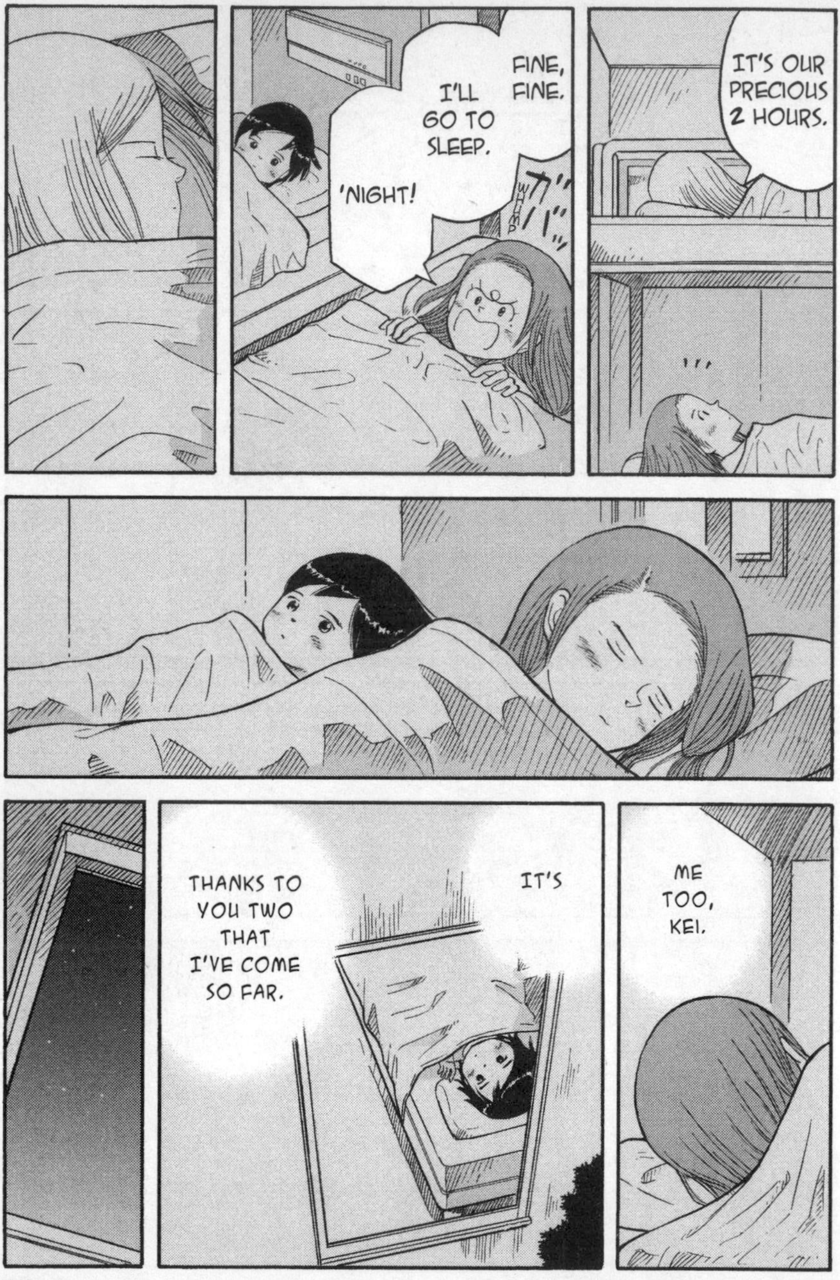
IT'S OUR PRECIOUS 2 HOURS.
...
FINE, FINE.
I'LL GO TO SLEEP.
'NIGHT!
WHUMP
ME TOO, KEI.
IT'S
THANKS TO YOU TWO THAT I'VE COME SO FAR.

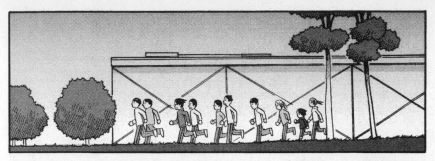

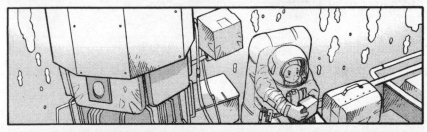

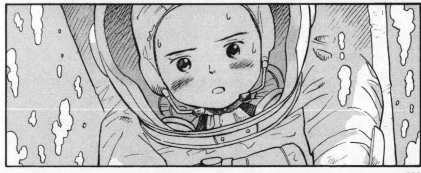

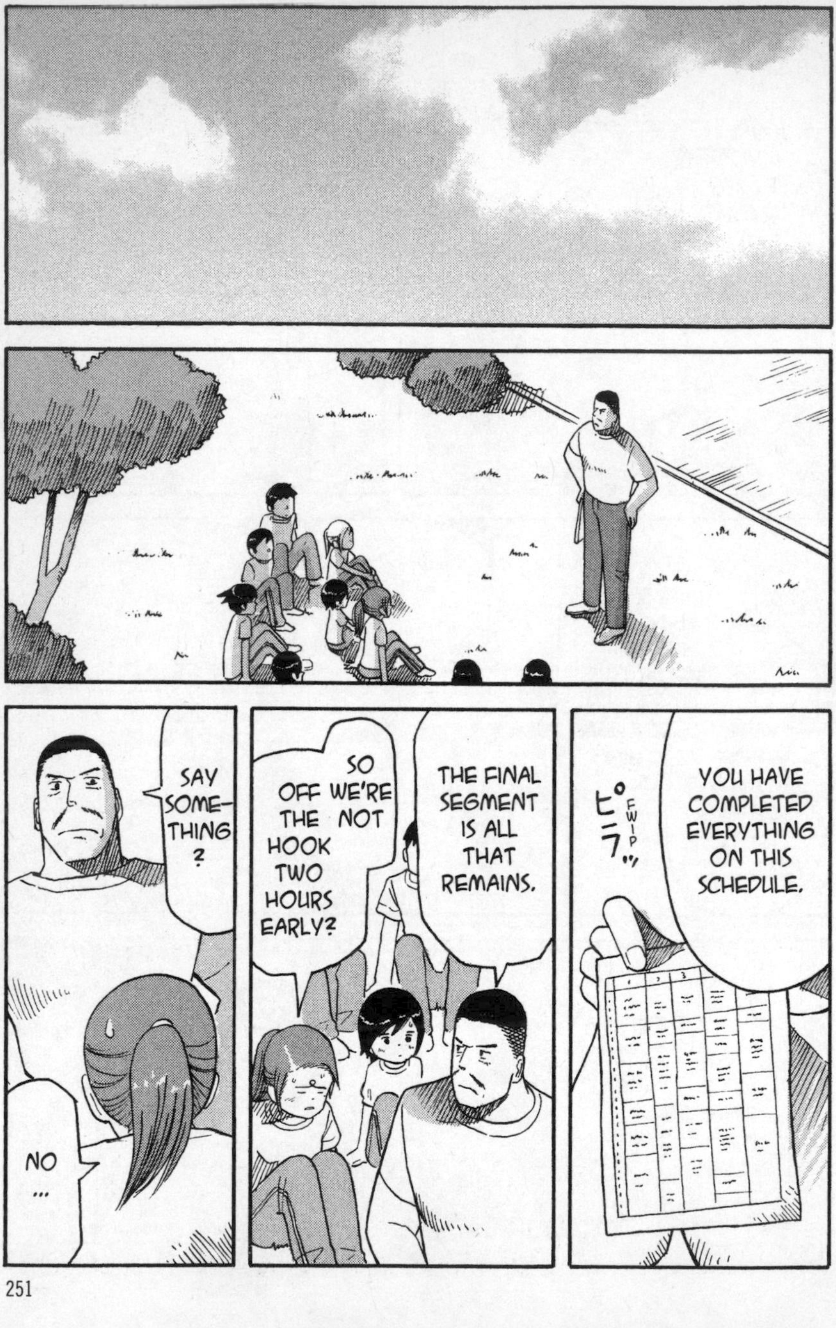
ピラ…
FWIP
YOU HAVE COMPLETED EVERYTHING ON THIS SCHEDULE.
THE FINAL SEGMENT IS ALL THAT REMAINS.
SO WE'RE NOT OFF THE HOOK TWO HOURS EARLY?
SAY SOME-THING?
NO...

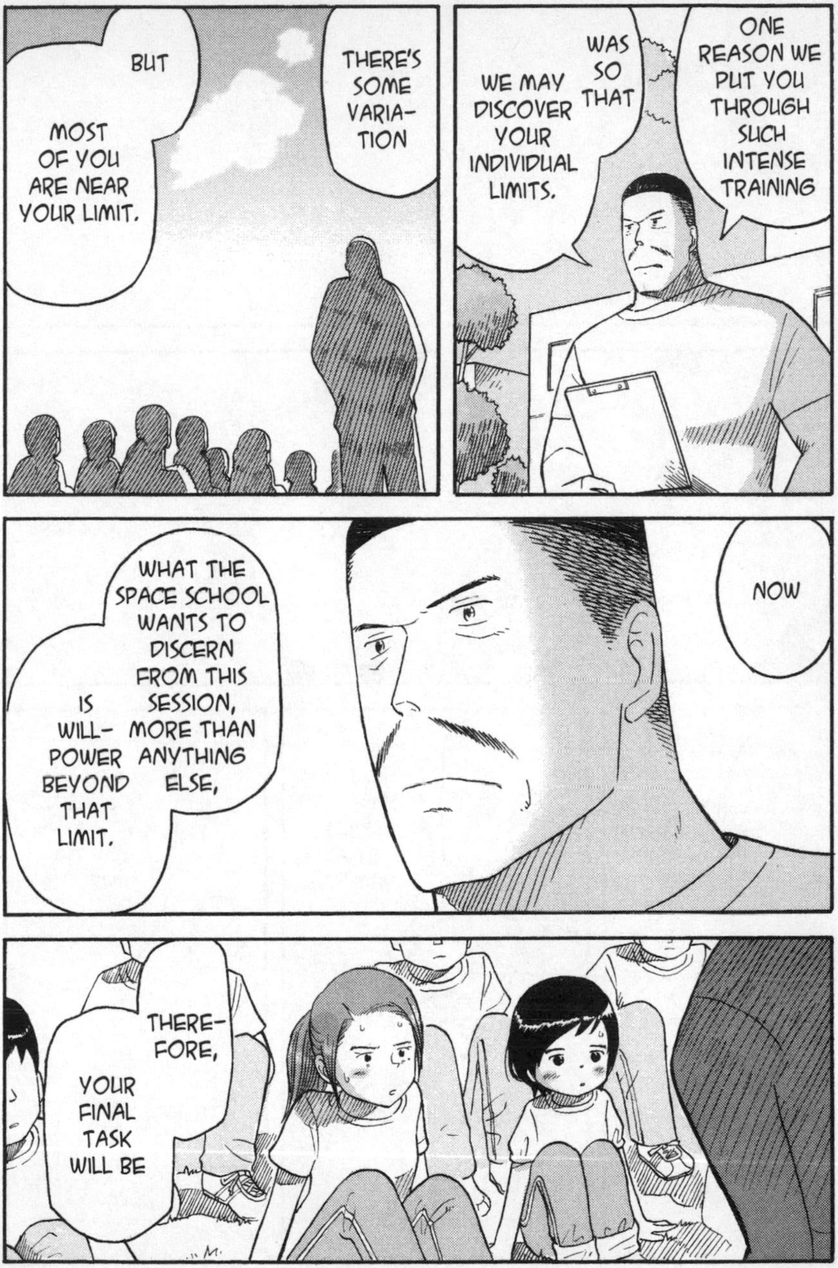

ONE REASON WE PUT YOU THROUGH SUCH INTENSE TRAINING
WAS SO THAT
WE MAY DISCOVER YOUR INDIVIDUAL LIMITS.
THERE'S SOME VARIATION
BUT
MOST OF YOU ARE NEAR YOUR LIMIT.
NOW
WHAT THE SPACE SCHOOL WANTS TO DISCERN FROM THIS SESSION, MORE THAN ANYTHING ELSE,
IS WILL-POWER BEYOND THAT LIMIT.
THERE-FORE,
YOUR FINAL TASK WILL BE

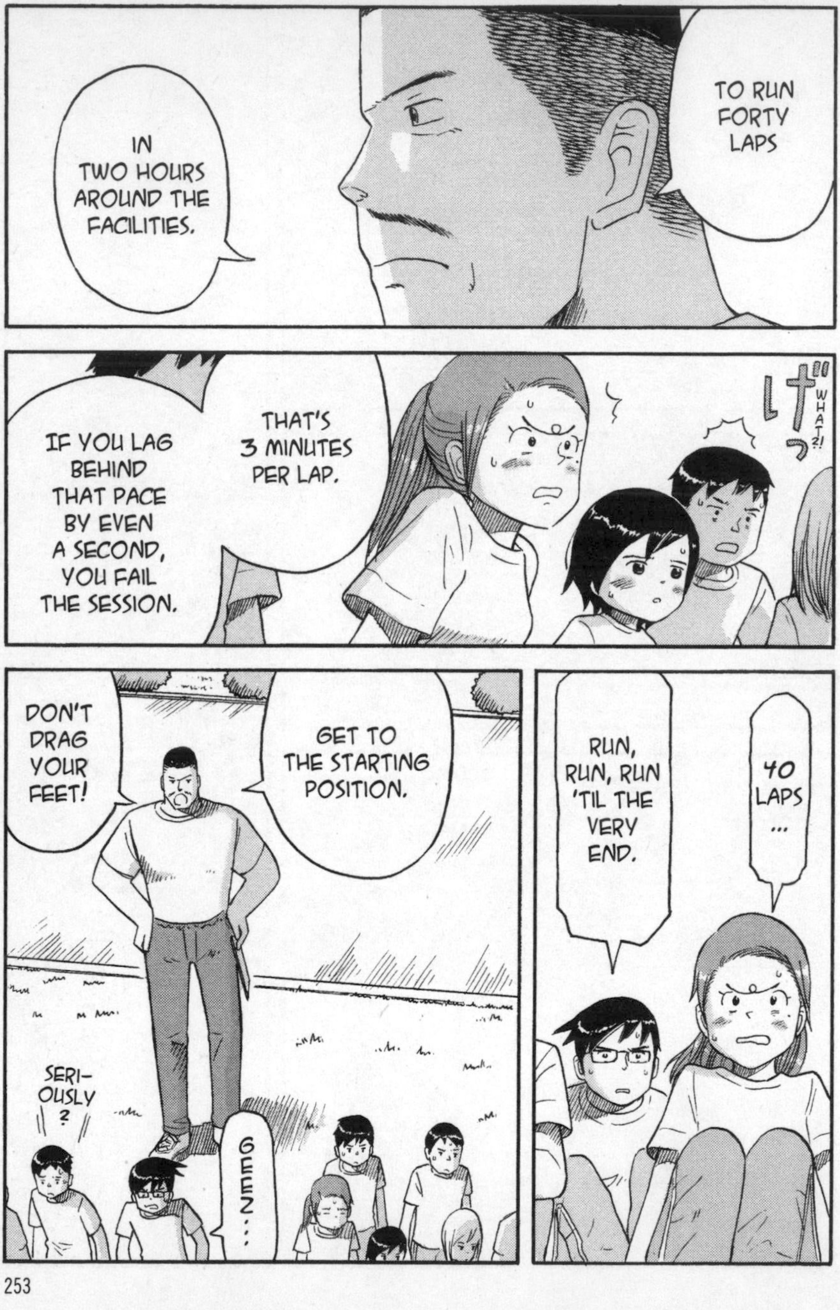
TO RUN FORTY LAPS
IN TWO HOURS AROUND THE FACILITIES.
げっ
WHAT?!
THAT'S 3 MINUTES PER LAP.
IF YOU LAG BEHIND THAT PACE BY EVEN A SECOND, YOU FAIL THE SESSION.
40 LAPS ...
RUN, RUN, RUN 'TIL THE VERY END.
GET TO THE STARTING POSITION.
DON'T DRAG YOUR FEET!
GEEZ...
SERI-OUSLY?

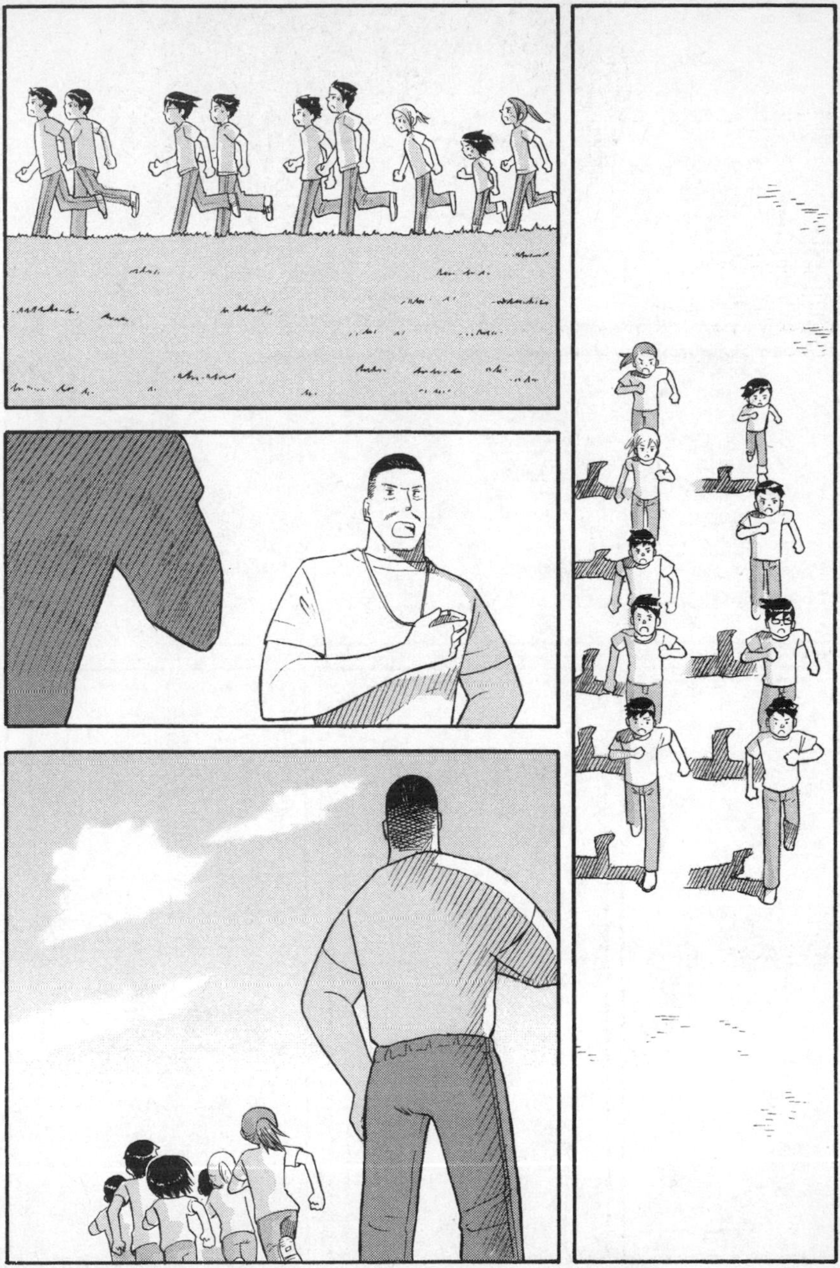

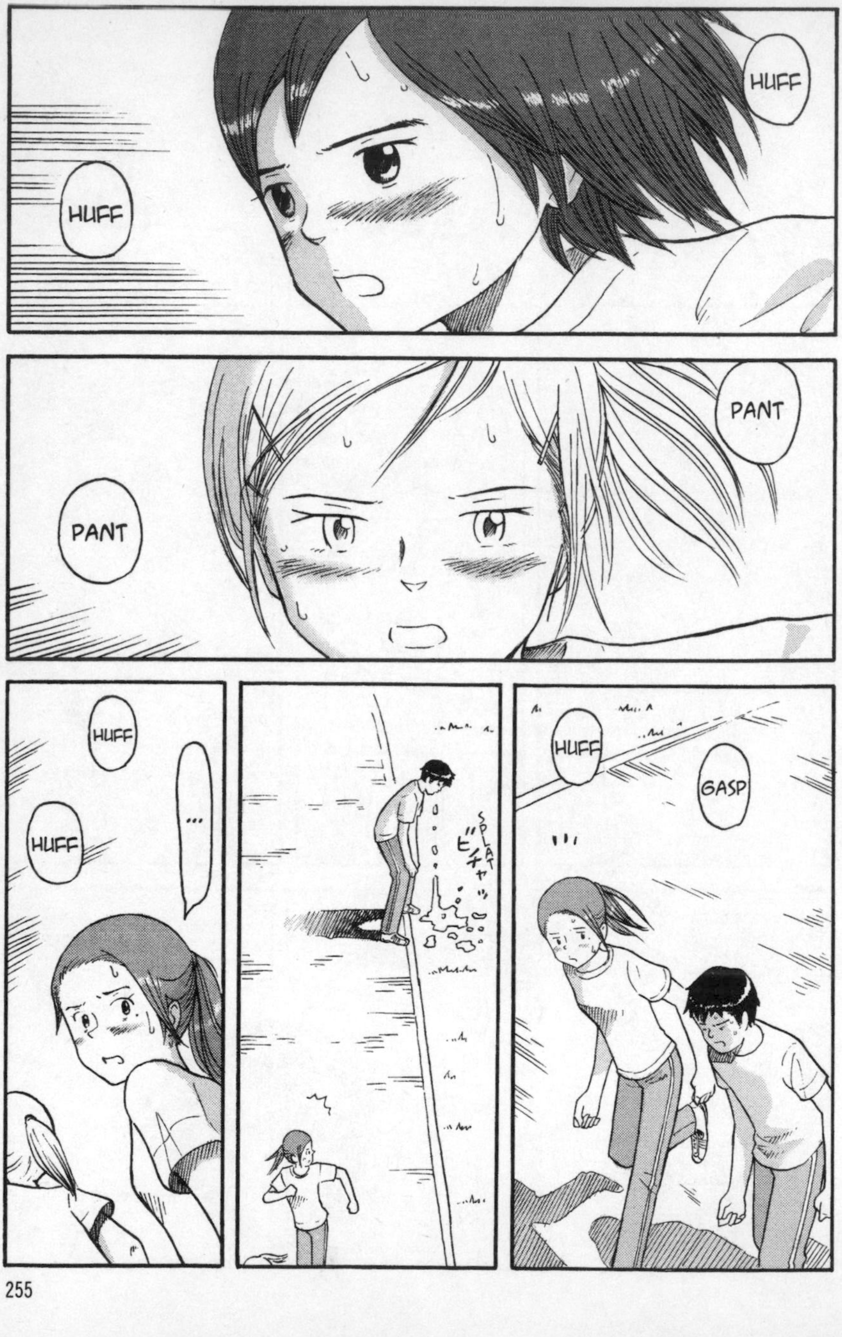
HUFF
HUFF
PANT
PANT
HUFF
GASP
SPLAT
ビチャッ
HUFF
HUFF
...

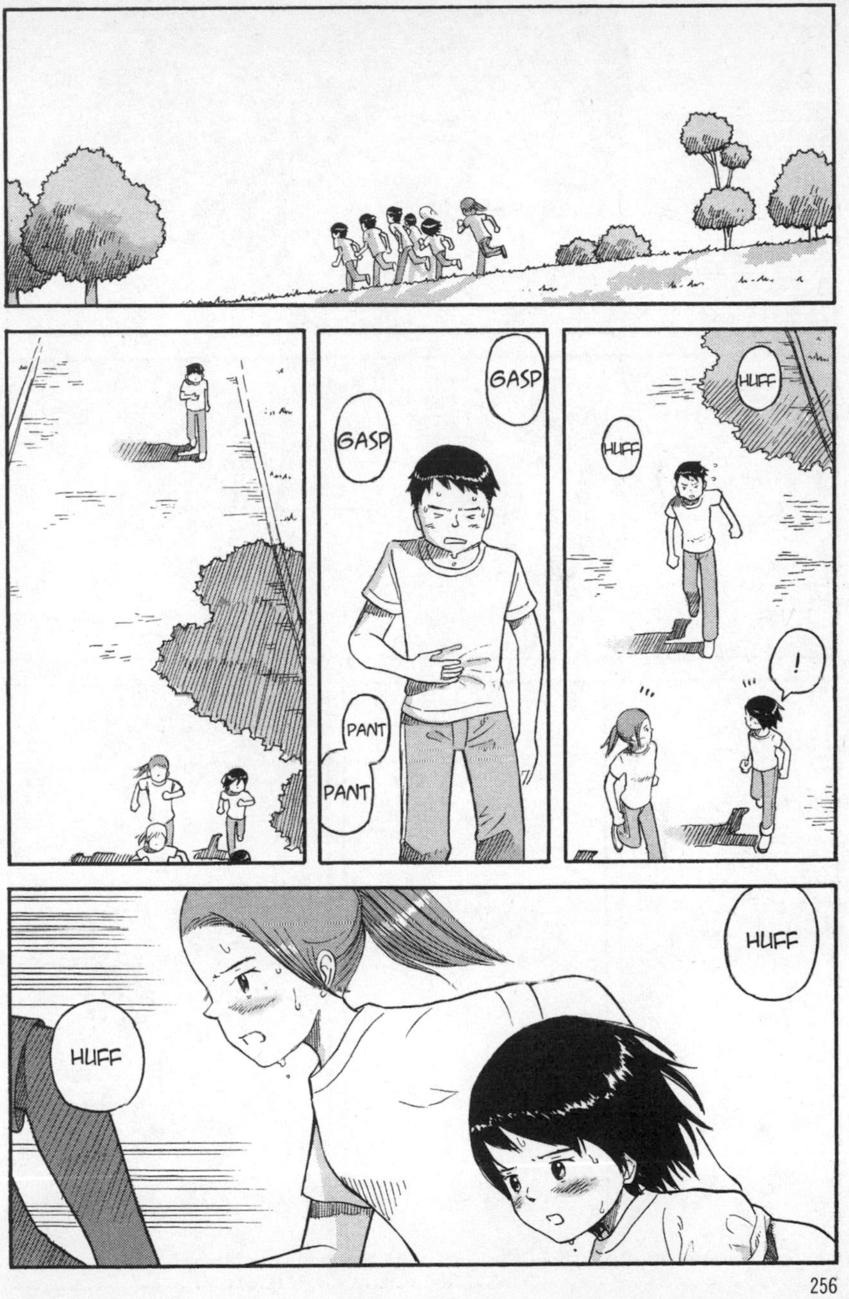
HUFF
HUFF
!
GASP
GASP
PANT
PANT
HUFF
HUFF

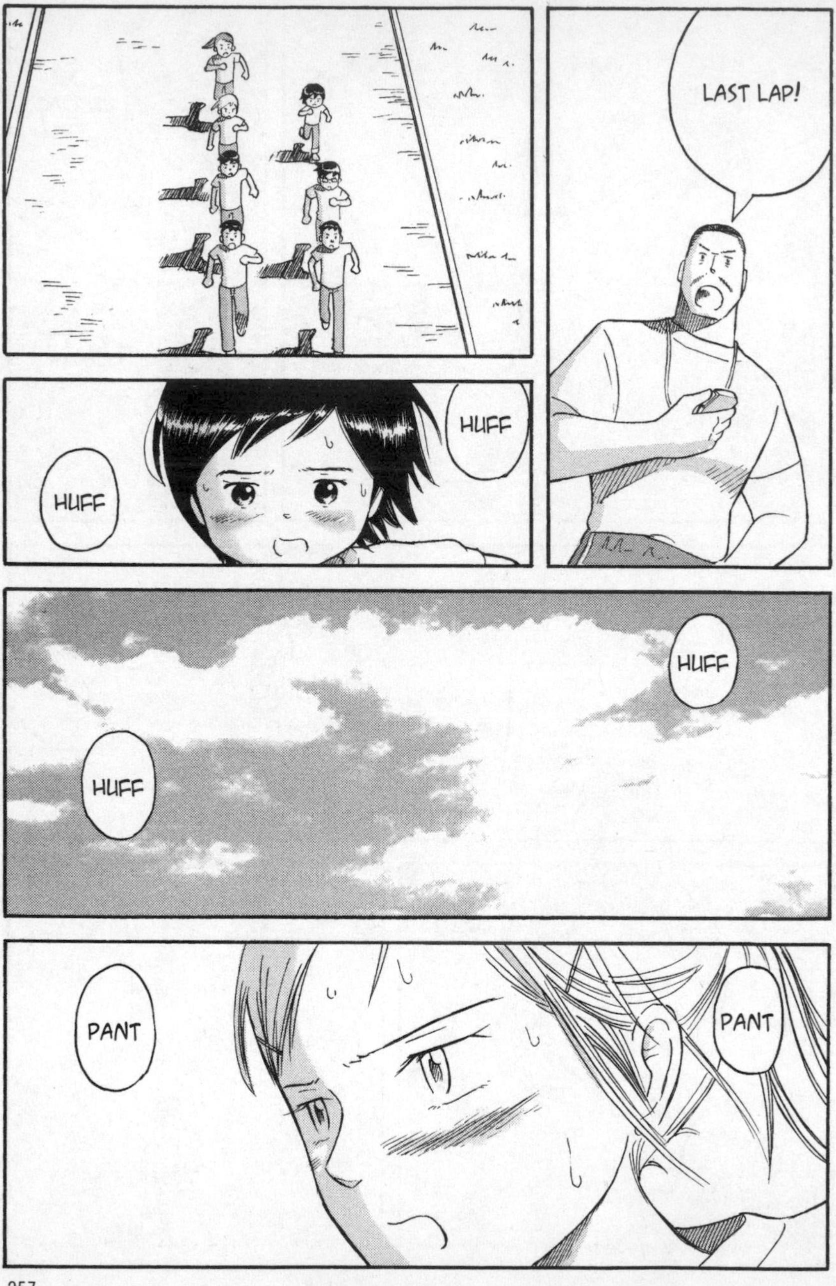
LAST LAP!
HUFF
HUFF
HUFF
HUFF
PANT
PANT

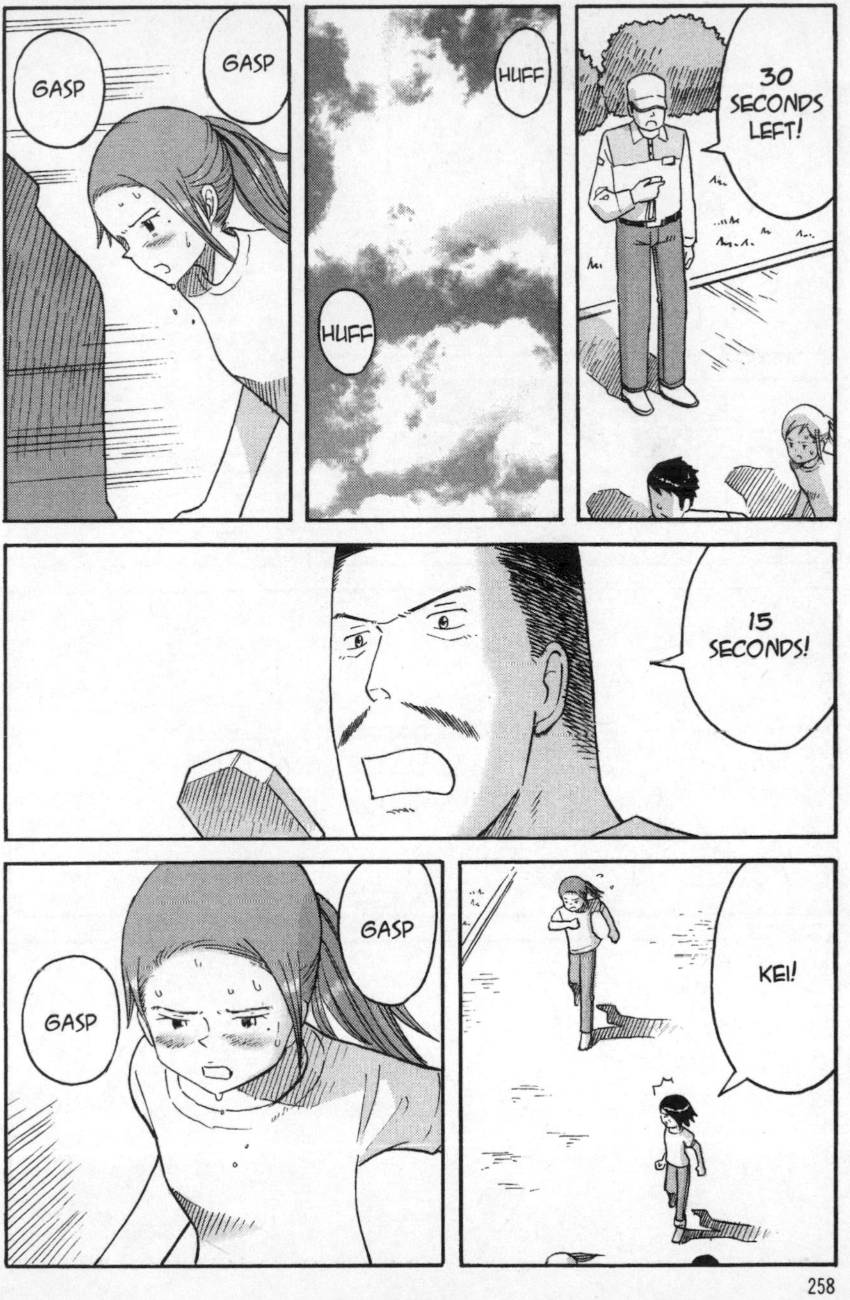
30 SECONDS LEFT!
HUFF
HUFF
GASP
GASP
15 SECONDS!
KEI!
GASP
GASP

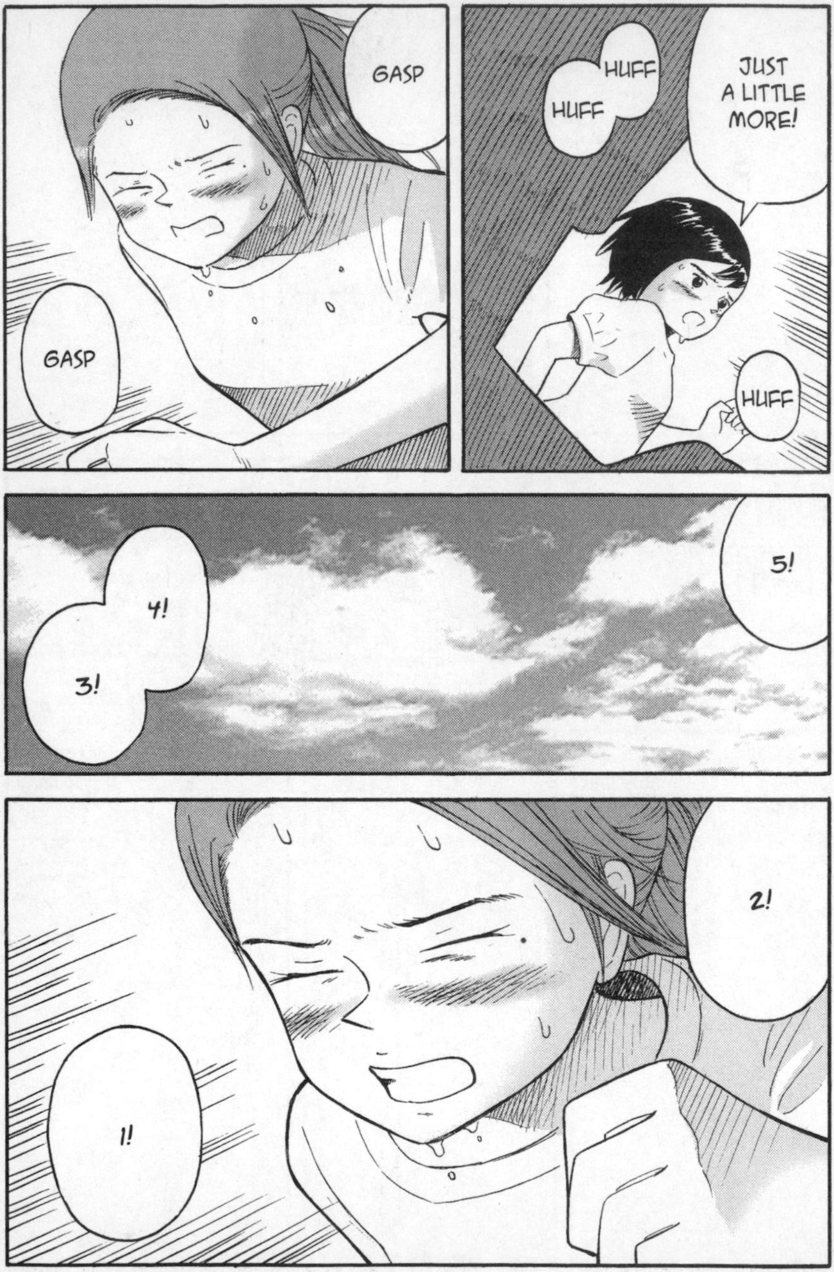
JUST A LITTLE MORE!
HUFF HUFF
HUFF
GASP
GASP
5!
4!
3!
2!
1!

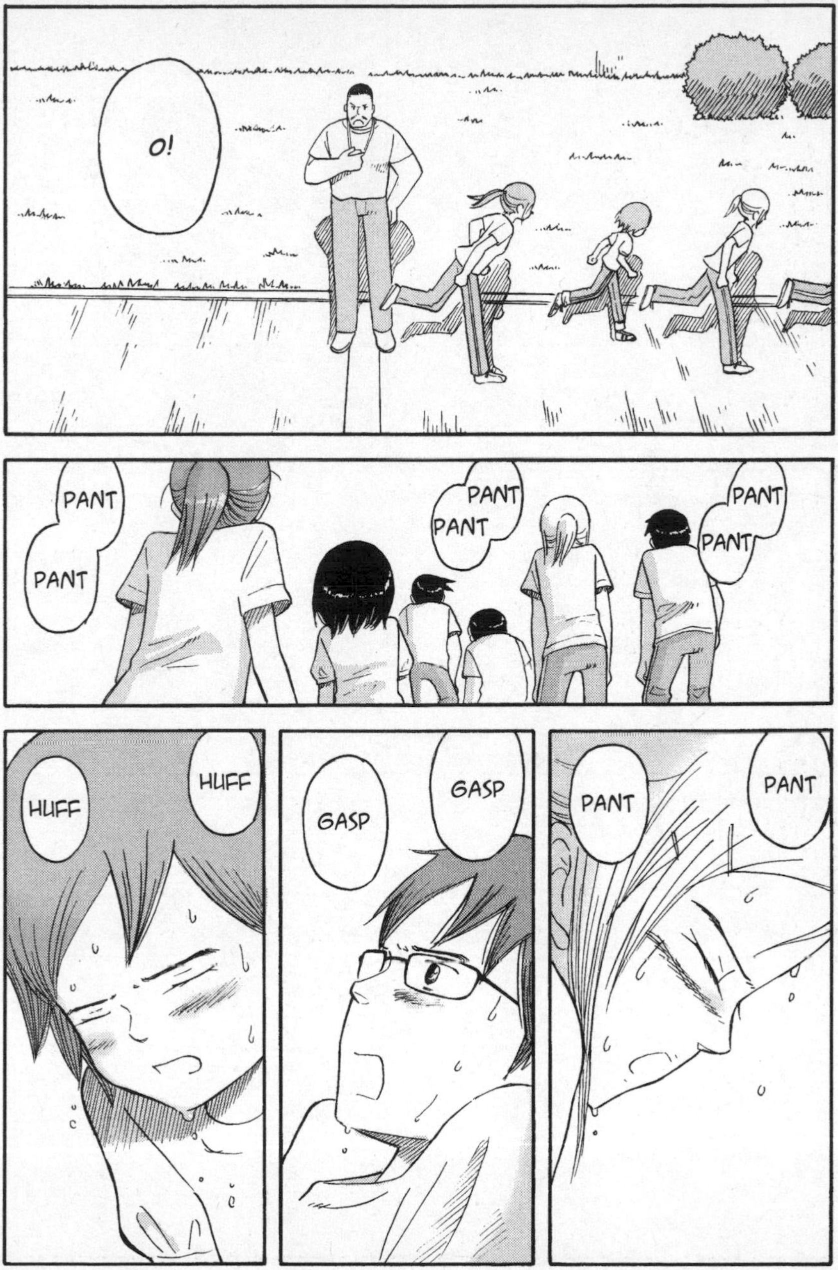
O!
PANT
PANT
PANT
PANT
PANT
PANT
PANT
PANT
GASP
GASP
HUFF
HUFF

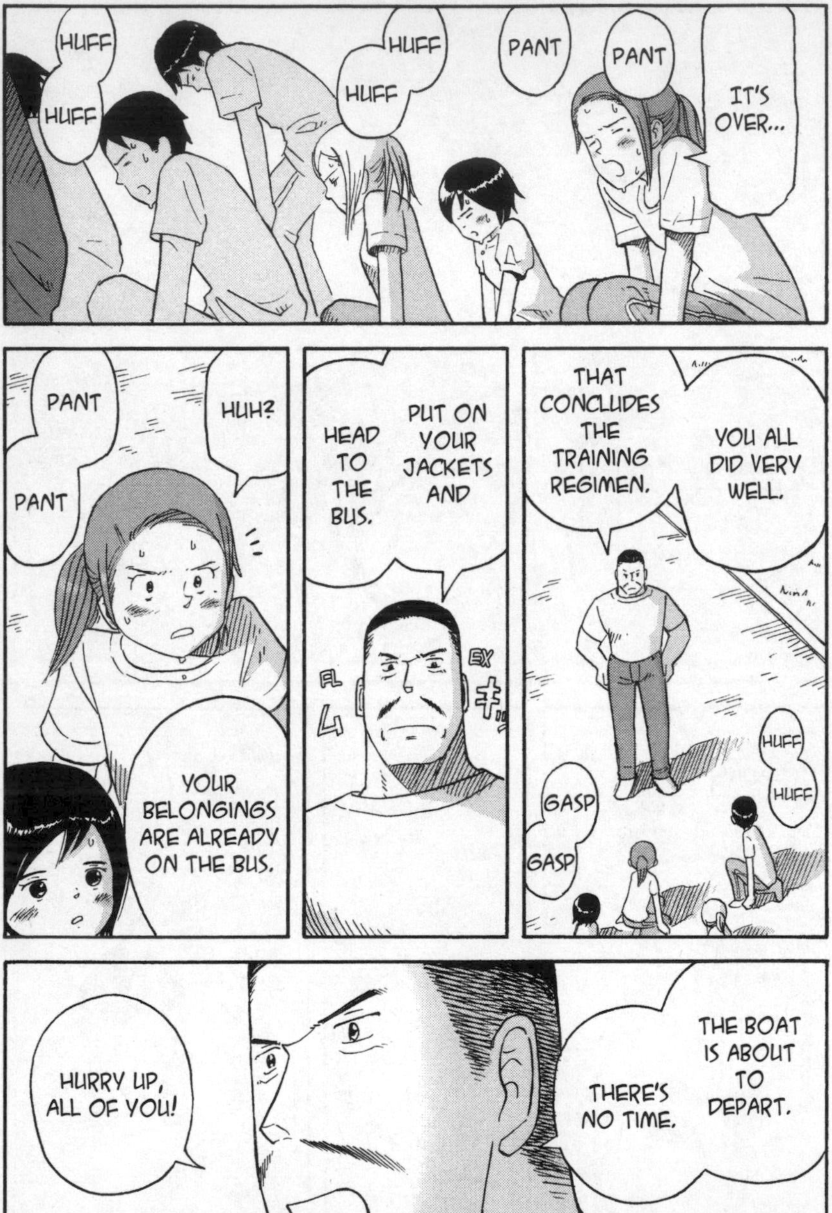
IT'S OVER...
PANT
PANT
HUFF
HUFF
HUFF
HUFF
THAT CONCLUDES THE TRAINING REGIMEN.
YOU ALL DID VERY WELL.
HUFF
HUFF
GASP
GASP
PUT ON YOUR JACKETS AND
HEAD TO THE BUS.
HUH?
PANT
PANT
YOUR BELONGINGS ARE ALREADY ON THE BUS.
THE BOAT IS ABOUT TO DEPART.
THERE'S NO TIME.
HURRY UP, ALL OF YOU!

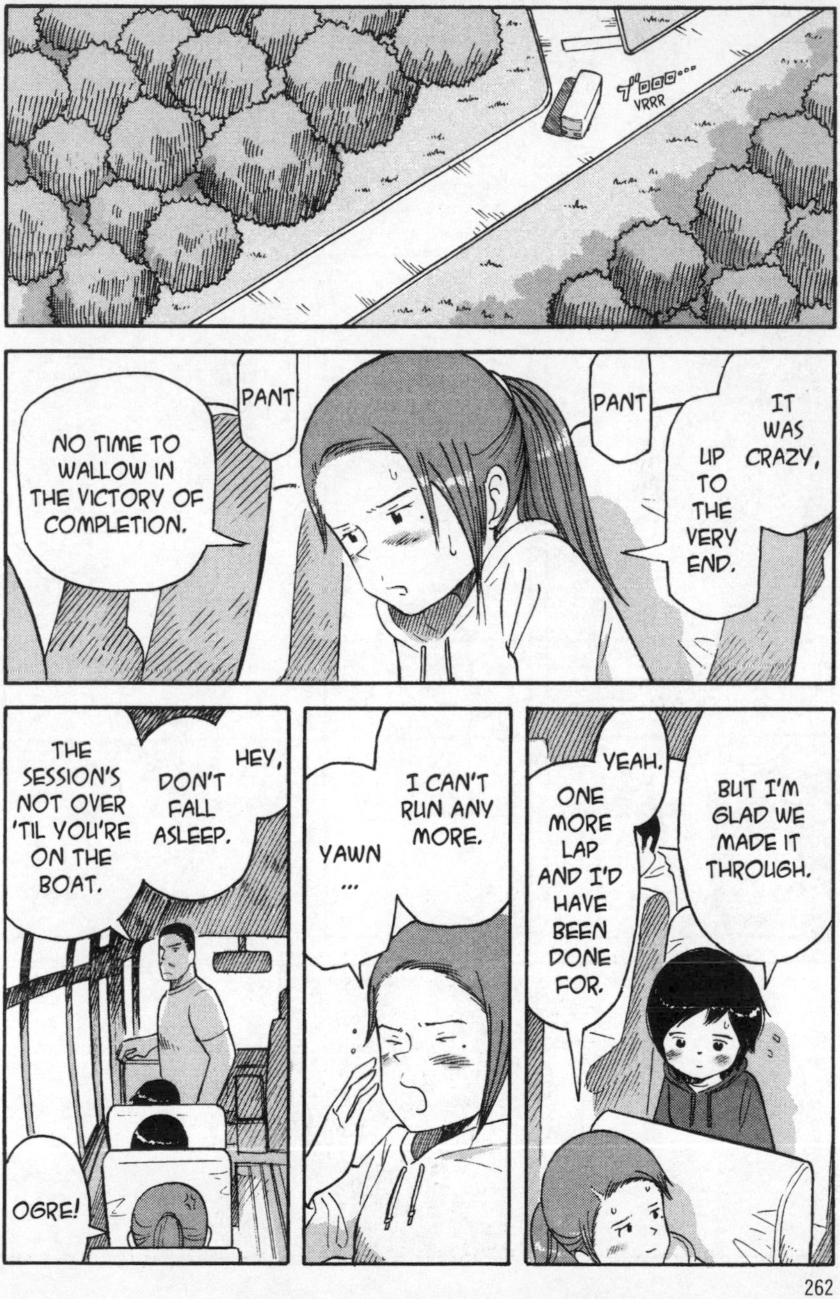
VRRR
PANT
IT WAS CRAZY, UP TO THE VERY END.
PANT
NO TIME TO WALLOW IN THE VICTORY OF COMPLETION.
YEAH. ONE MORE LAP AND I'D HAVE BEEN DONE FOR.
BUT I'M GLAD WE MADE IT THROUGH.
I CAN'T RUN ANY MORE.
YAWN ...
HEY, DON'T FALL ASLEEP.
THE SESSION'S NOT OVER 'TIL YOU'RE ON THE BOAT.
OGRE!

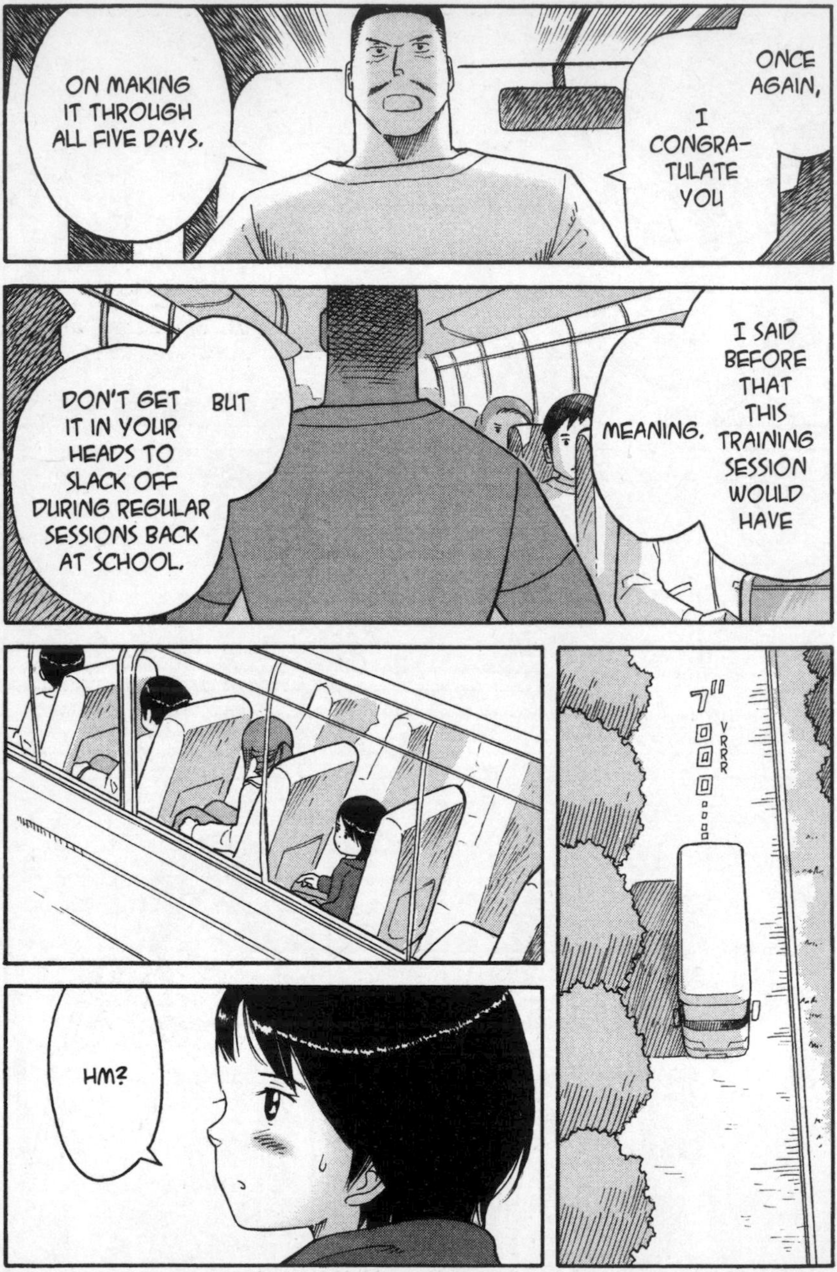
ONCE AGAIN, I CONGRATULATE YOU
ON MAKING IT THROUGH ALL FIVE DAYS.
I SAID BEFORE THAT THIS TRAINING SESSION WOULD HAVE MEANING.
BUT DON'T GET IT IN YOUR HEADS TO SLACK OFF DURING REGULAR SESSIONS BACK AT SCHOOL.
ブロロロ....
VRRR
HM?

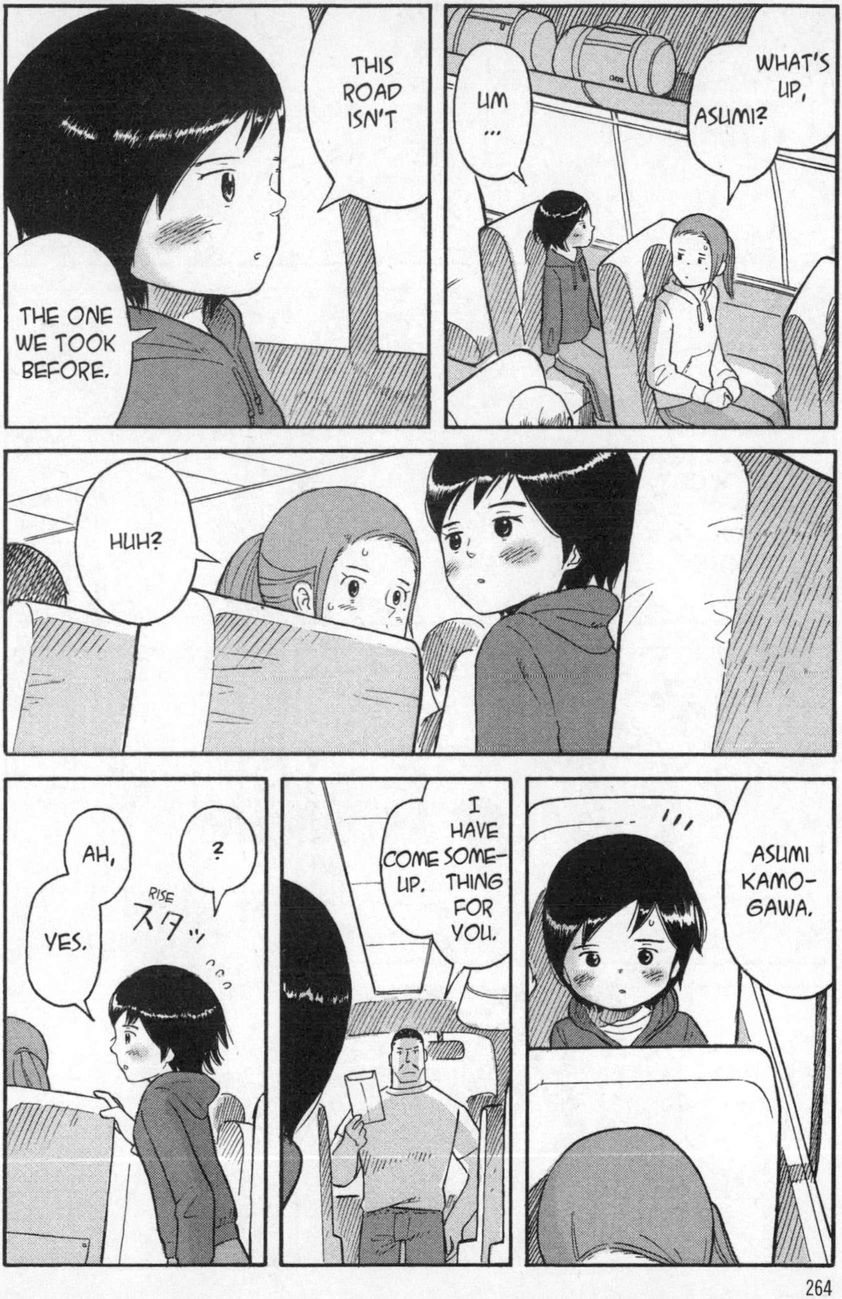
WHAT'S UP, ASUMI?
UM ...
THIS ROAD ISN'T
THE ONE WE TOOK BEFORE.
HUH?
ASUMI KAMOGAWA.
I HAVE SOMETHING FOR YOU.
COME UP.
?
AH, YES.
RISE
スタッ

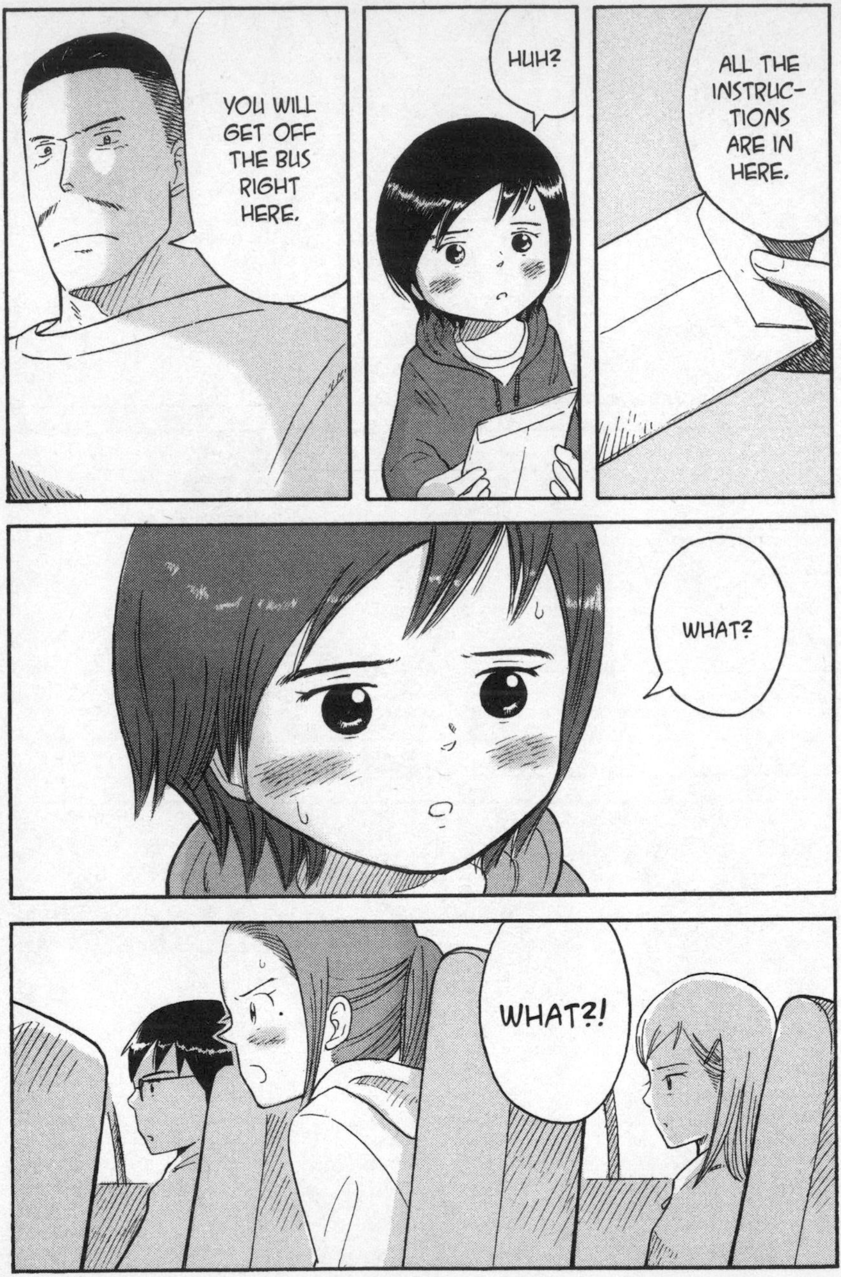
ALL THE INSTRUC-TIONS ARE IN HERE.
HUH?
YOU WILL GET OFF THE BUS RIGHT HERE.
WHAT?
WHAT?!

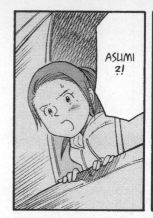

ASUMI
?!

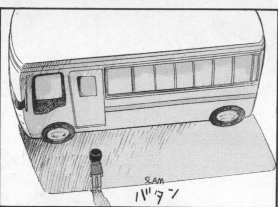

SLAM
バタン

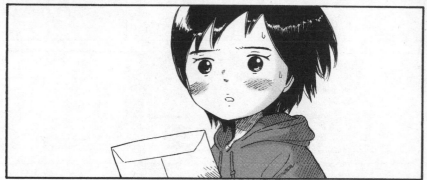

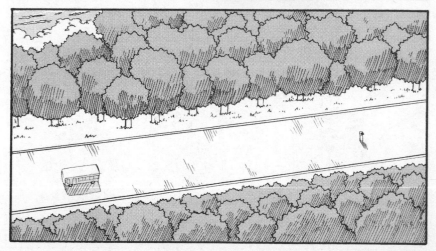

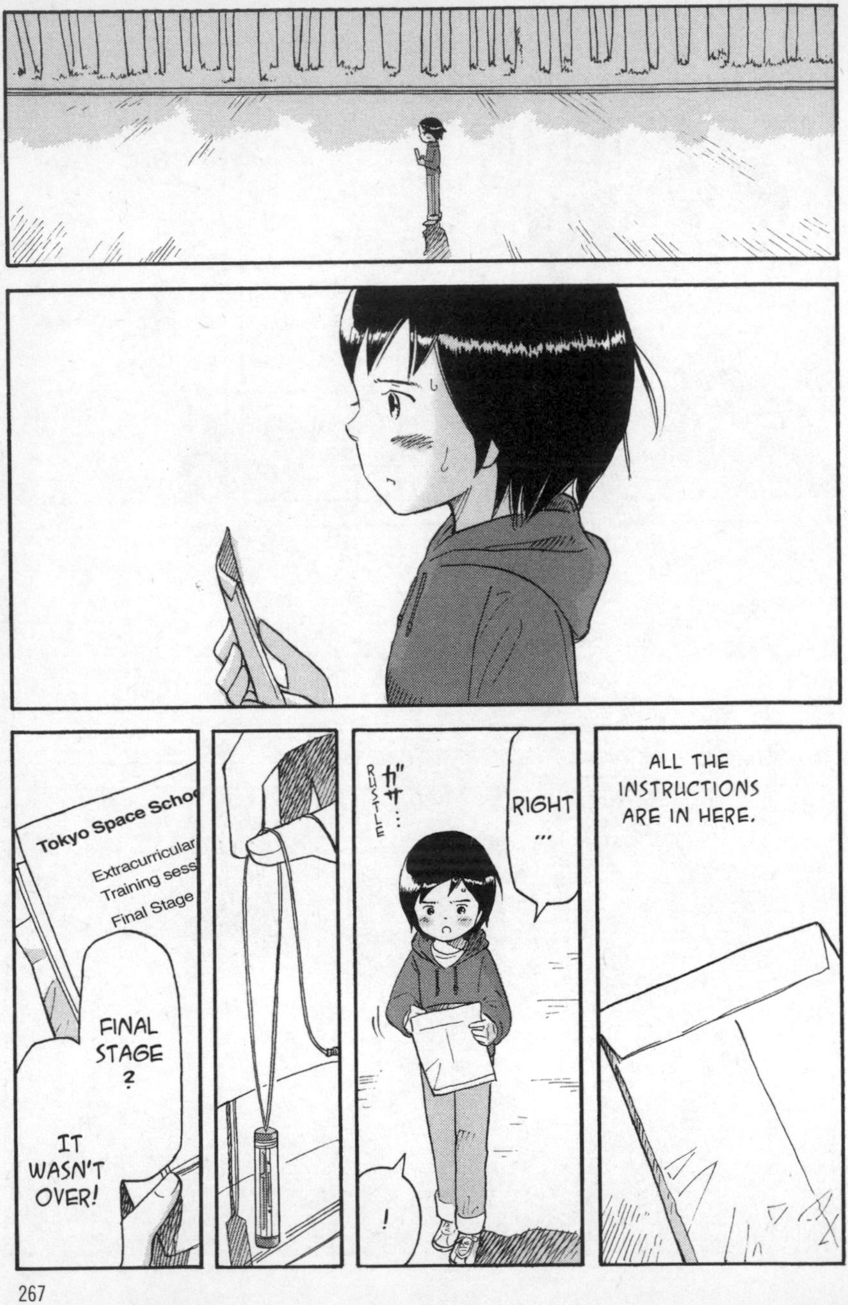
ALL THE INSTRUCTIONS ARE IN HERE.
RIGHT ...
ガサ…
RUSTLE
!
Tokyo Space Scho
Extracurricular
Training sessi
Final Stage
FINAL STAGE ?
IT WASN'T OVER!

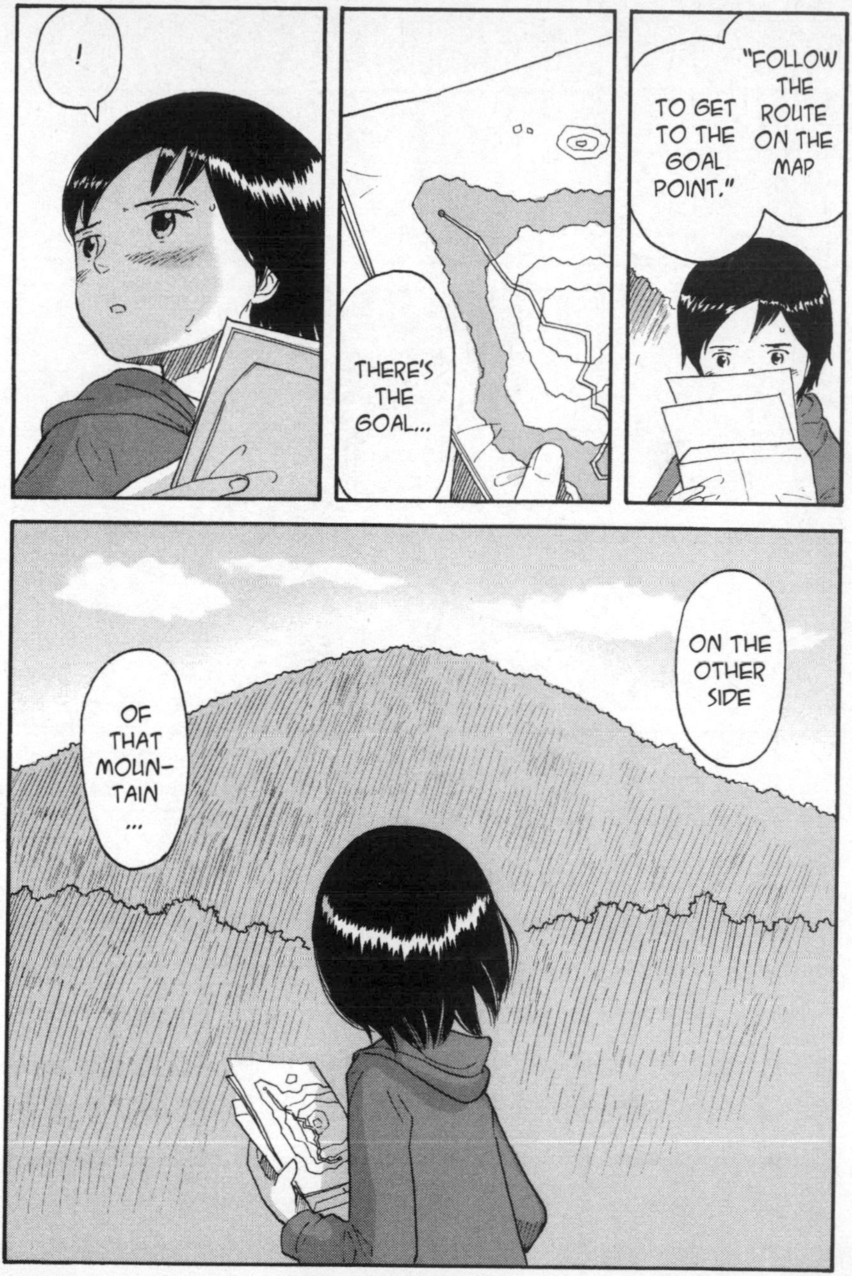
"FOLLOW THE ROUTE ON THE MAP
TO GET TO THE GOAL POINT."
THERE'S THE GOAL...
!
ON THE OTHER SIDE
OF THAT MOUN-TAIN ...

MISSION:73

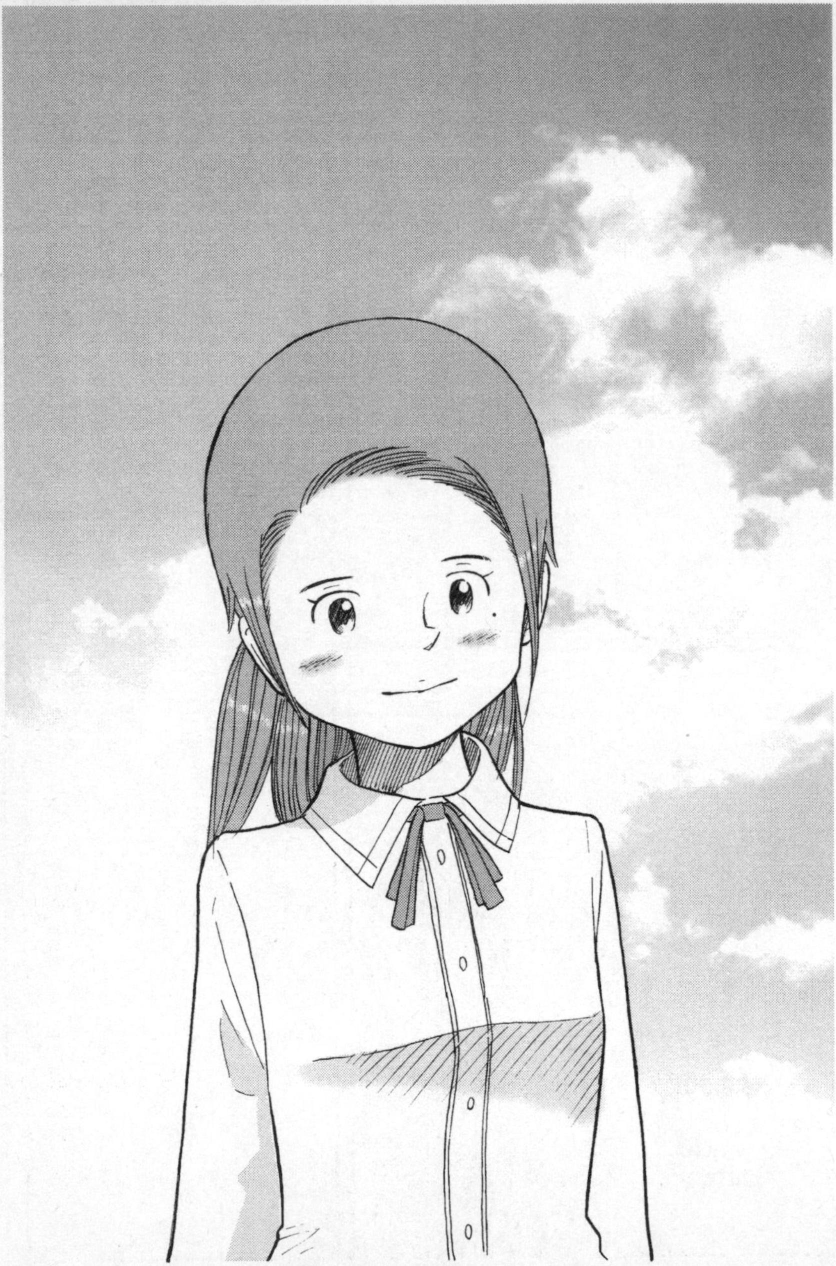

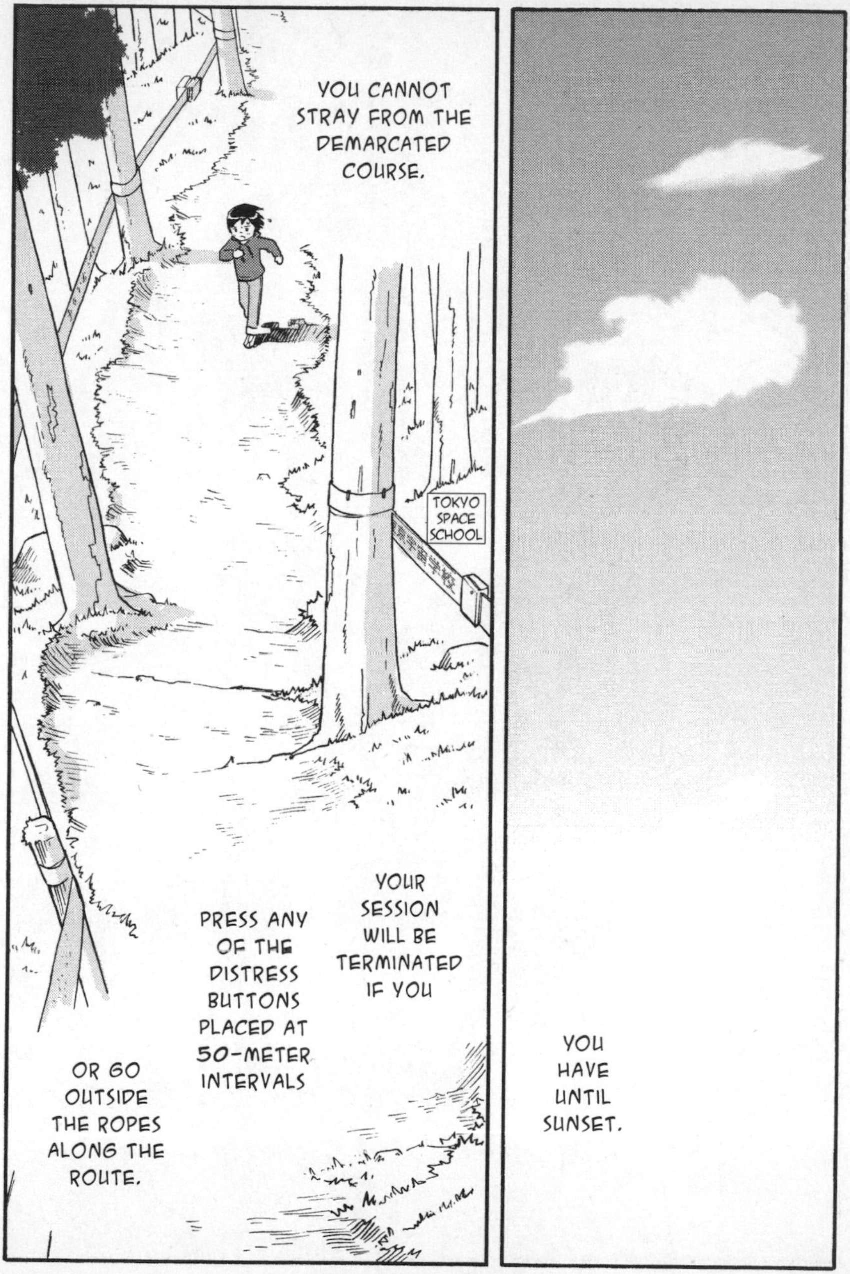
YOU HAVE UNTIL SUNSET.
YOU CANNOT STRAY FROM THE DEMARCATED COURSE.
TOKYO SPACE SCHOOL
YOUR SESSION WILL BE TERMINATED IF YOU
PRESS ANY OF THE DISTRESS BUTTONS PLACED AT 50-METER INTERVALS
OR GO OUTSIDE THE ROPES ALONG THE ROUTE.

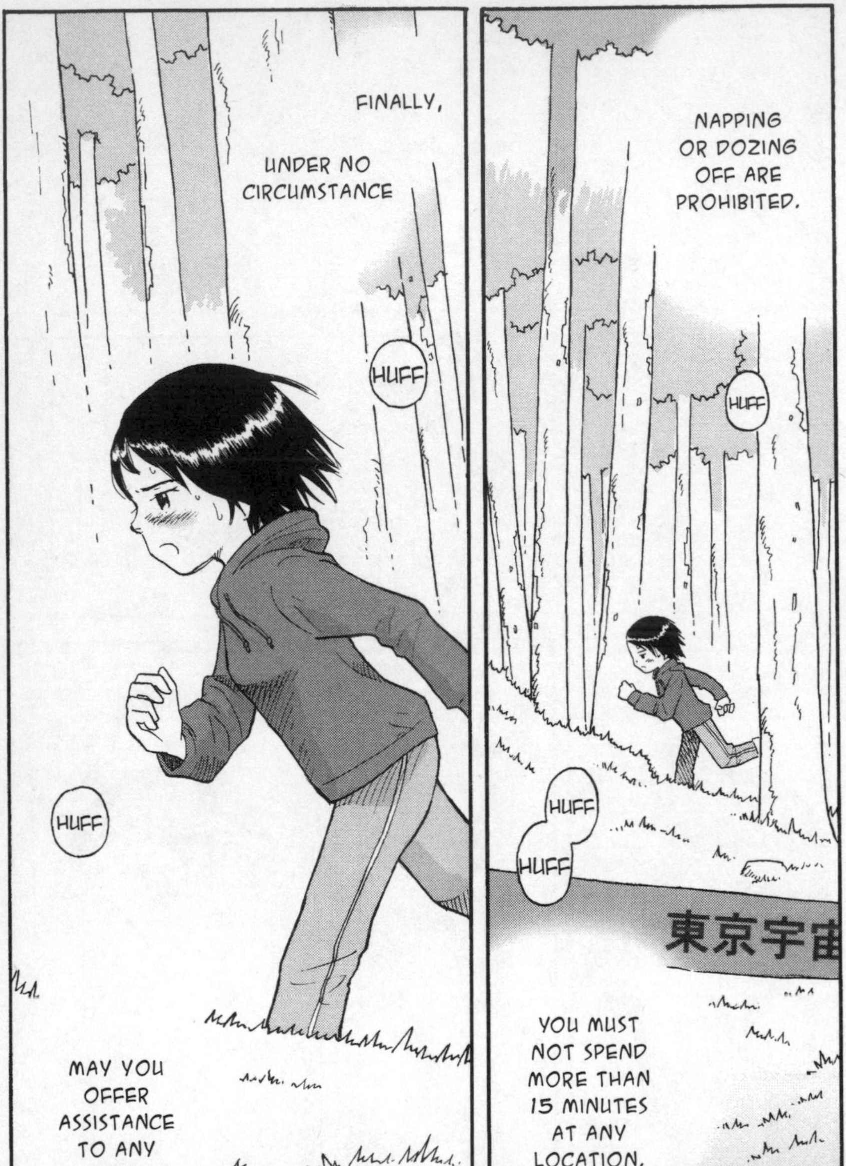
NAPPING OR DOZING OFF ARE PROHIBITED.
HUFF
HUFF
HUFF
東京宇宙
YOU MUST NOT SPEND MORE THAN 15 MINUTES AT ANY LOCATION.
FINALLY,
UNDER NO CIRCUMSTANCE
HUFF
HUFF
MAY YOU OFFER ASSISTANCE TO ANY OTHER STUDENT.

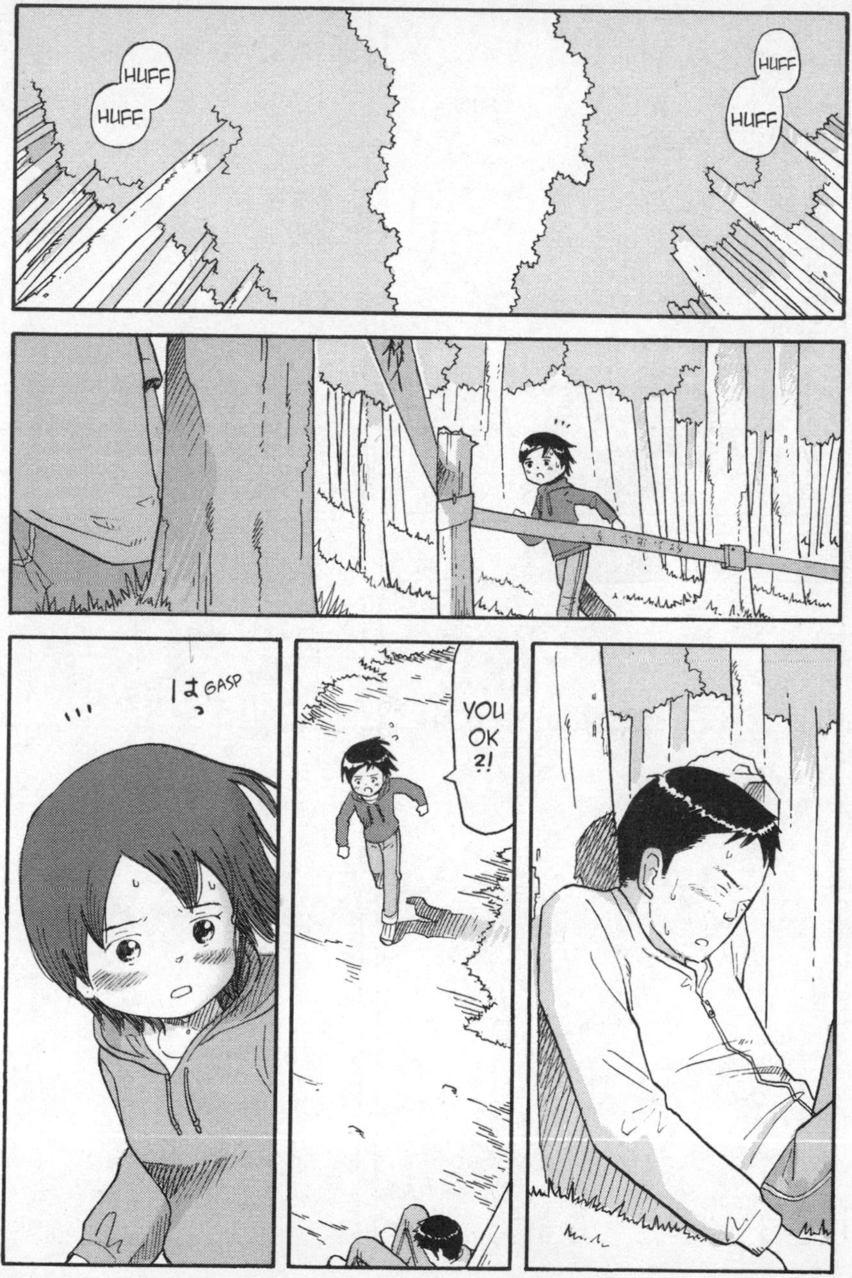
HUFF
HUFF
HUFF
HUFF
YOU OK ?!
はっ GASP

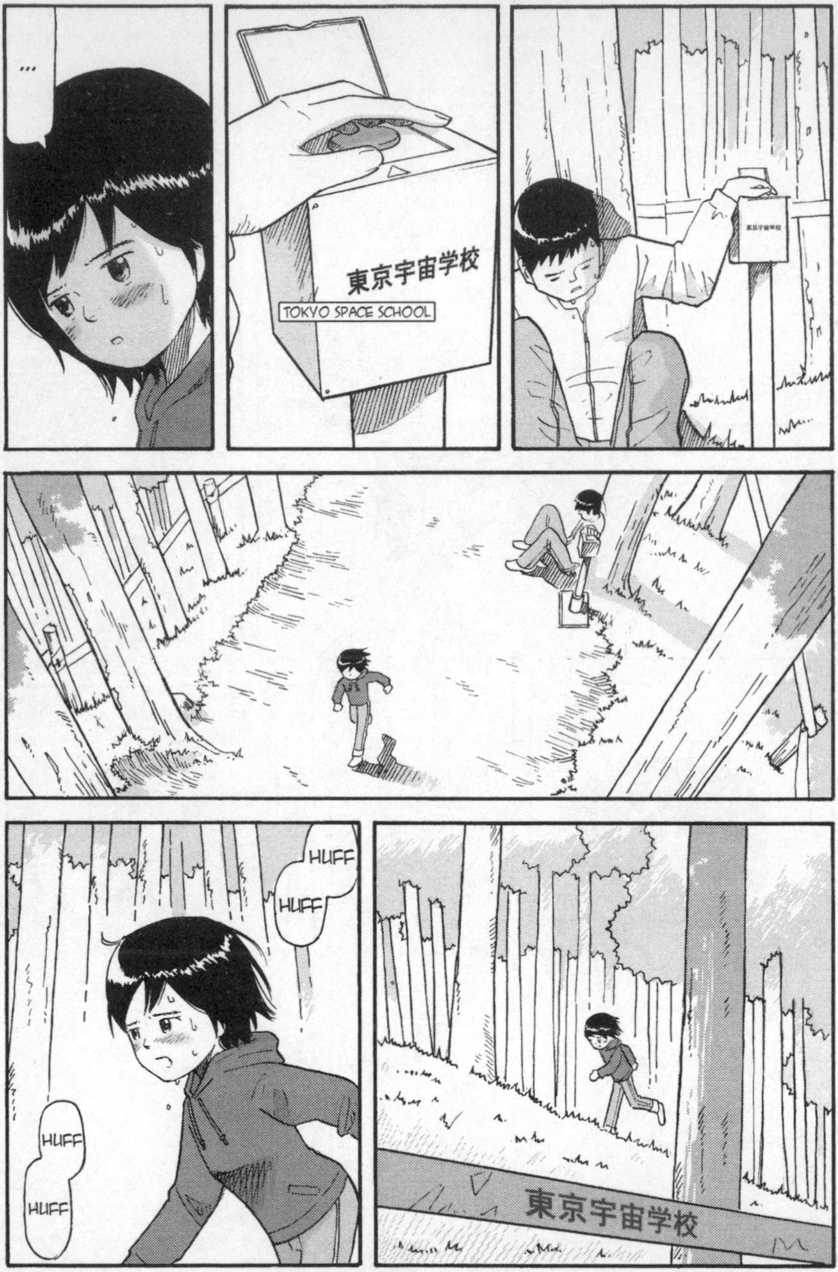
東京宇宙学校
TOKYO SPACE SCHOOL
...
東京宇宙学校
HUFF
HUFF
HUFF
HUFF

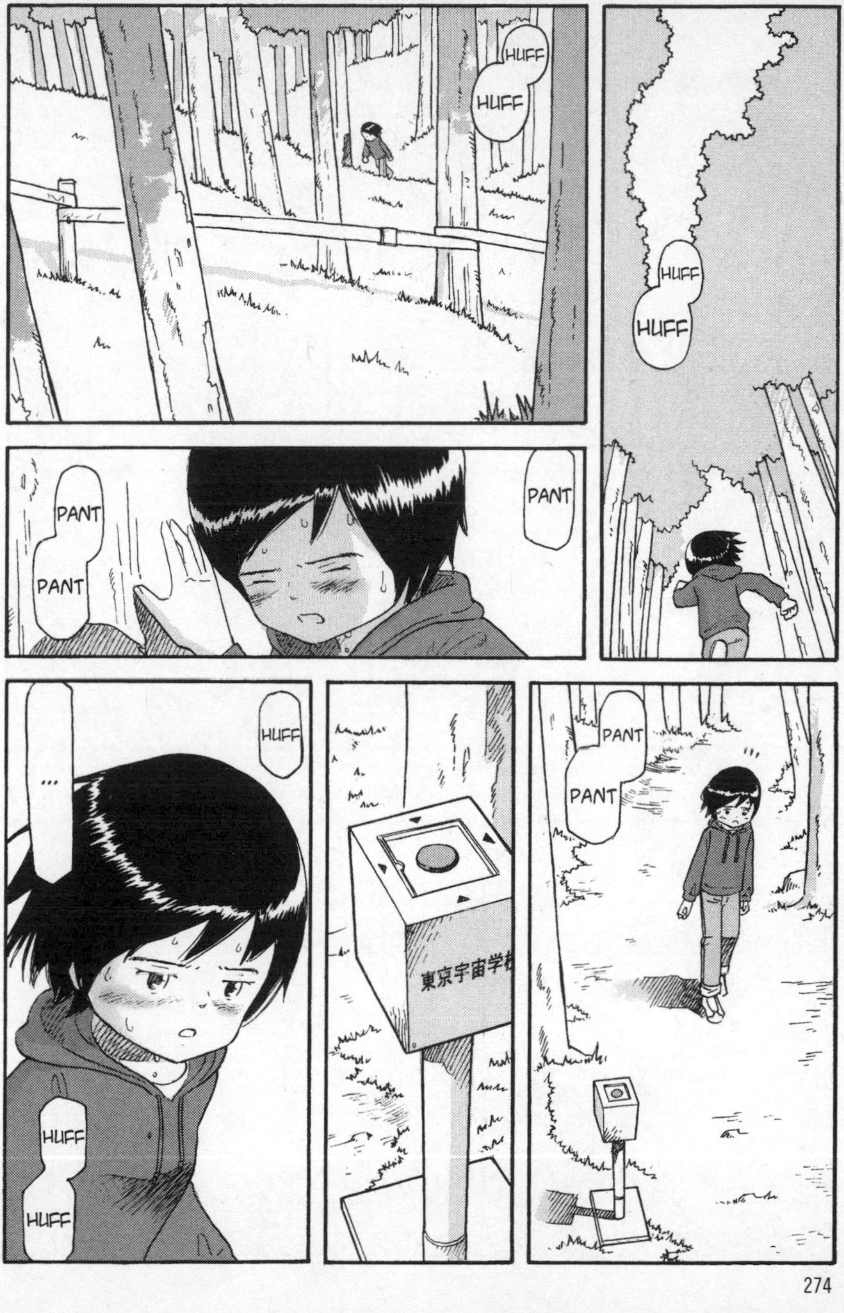
HUFF
HUFF
HUFF
HUFF
PANT
PANT
PANT
PANT
PANT
東京宇宙学
HUFF
...
HUFF
HUFF

PANT
PANT
PANT
PANT
PANT
PANT

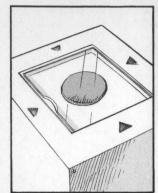

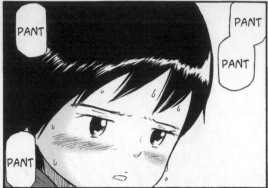

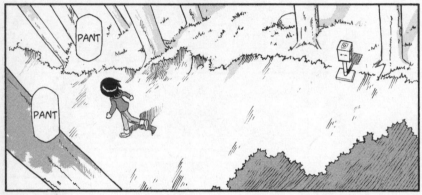

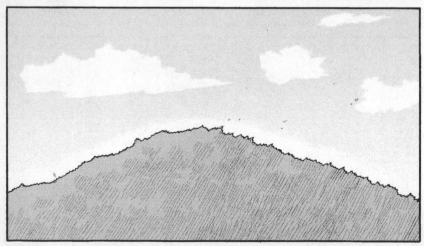

GASP
GASP
OOPS...
ふらっ
TOTTER
OF COURSE
THEY WOULDN'T JUST END IT...
GASP
GASP
ドスンッ
WHUMP
GASP
GASP
GASP
GASP

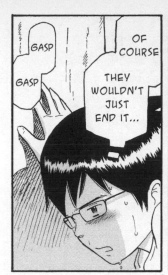

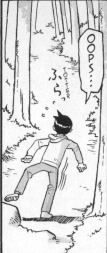

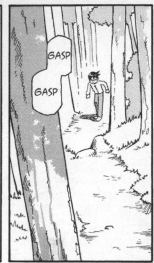

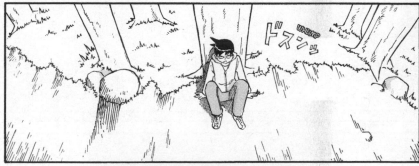

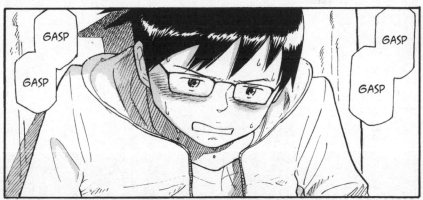

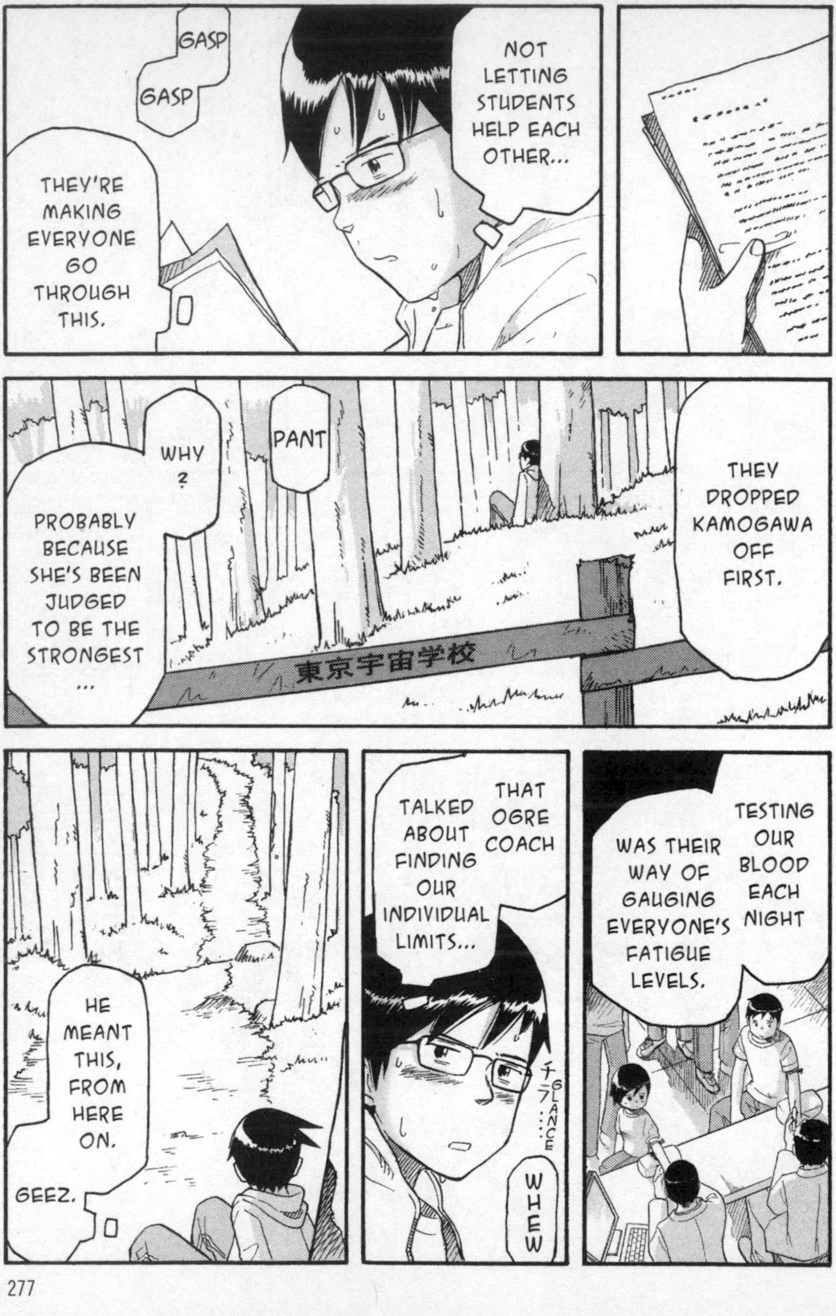
NOT LETTING STUDENTS HELP EACH OTHER...
GASP
GASP
THEY'RE MAKING EVERYONE GO THROUGH THIS.
THEY DROPPED KAMOGAWA OFF FIRST.
PANT
WHY?
PROBABLY BECAUSE SHE'S BEEN JUDGED TO BE THE STRONGEST...
東京宇宙学校
TESTING OUR BLOOD EACH NIGHT
WAS THEIR WAY OF GAUGING EVERYONE'S FATIGUE LEVELS.
THAT OGRE COACH
TALKED ABOUT FINDING OUR INDIVIDUAL LIMITS...
チラ…
GLANCE
WHEW
HE MEANT THIS, FROM HERE ON.
GEEZ.

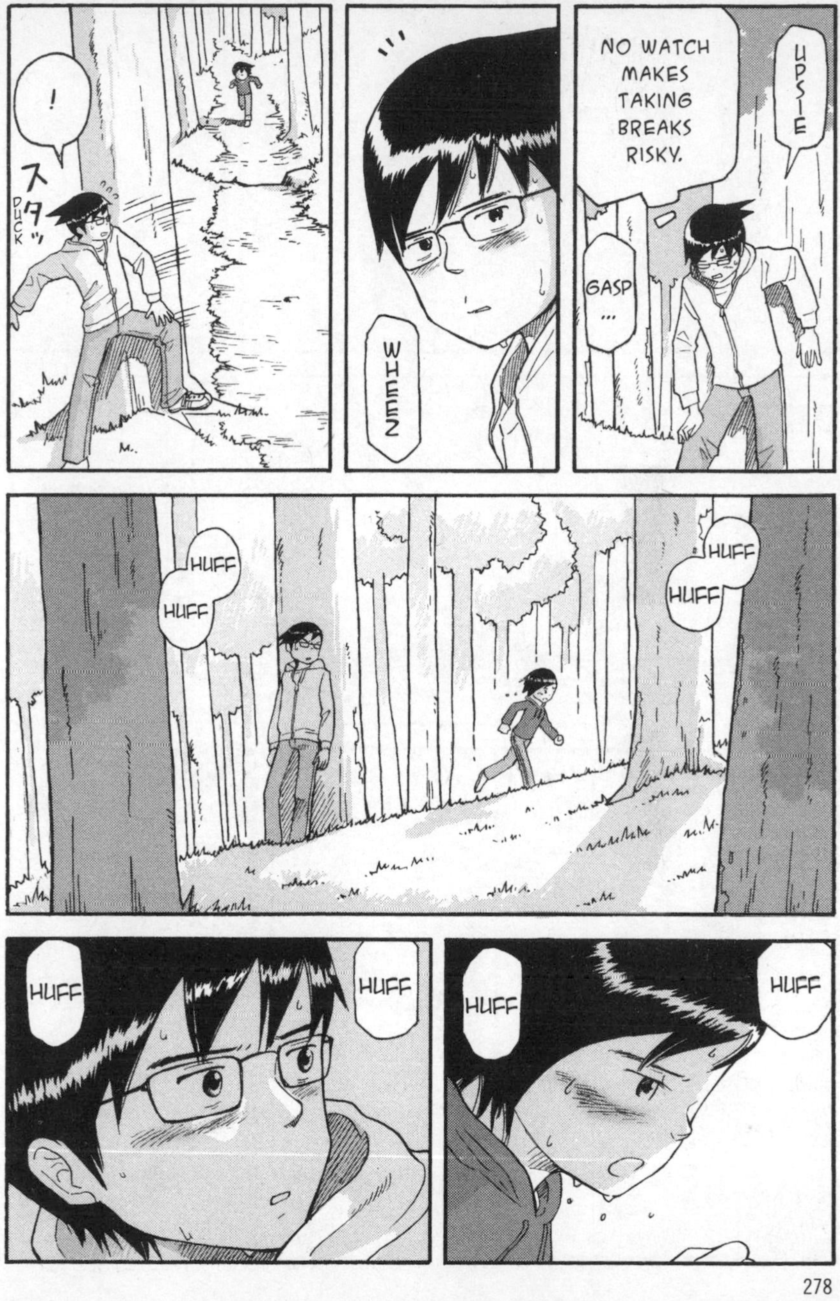
UPSIE
NO WATCH MAKES TAKING BREAKS RISKY.
GASP ...
WHEEZ
!
スタッ
DUCK
HUFF
HUFF
HUFF
HUFF
HUFF
HUFF
HUFF
HUFF

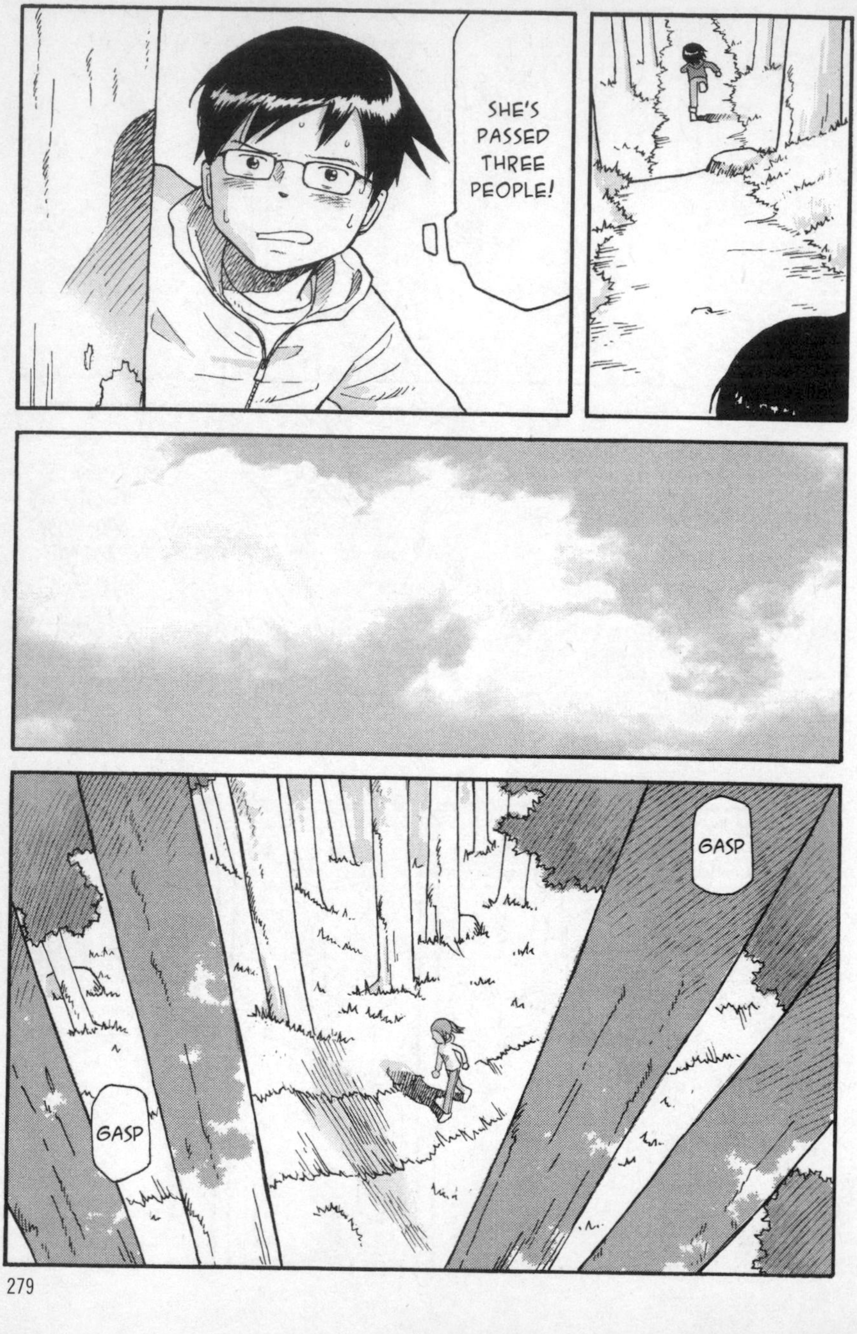
SHE'S PASSED THREE PEOPLE!
GASP
GASP

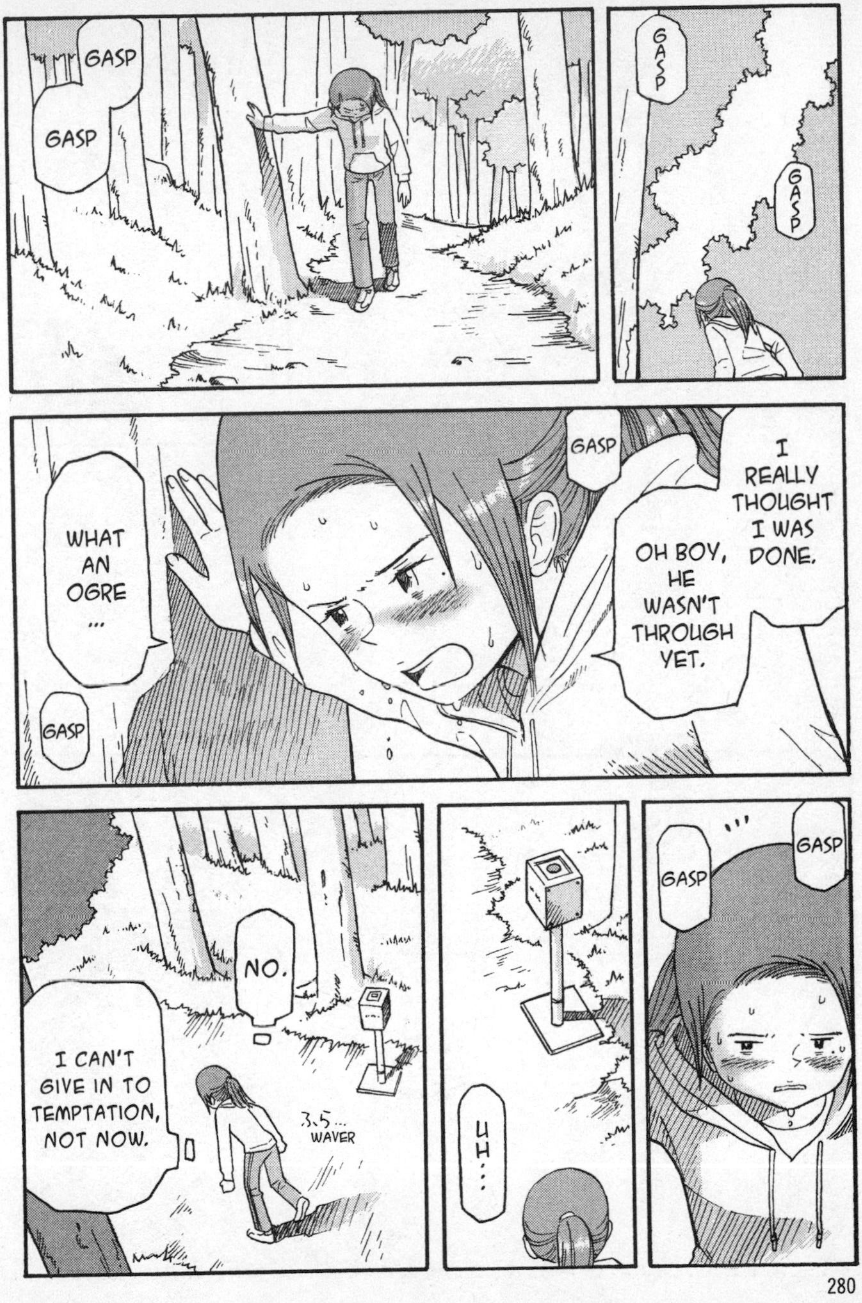
GASP
GASP
GASP
GASP
I REALLY THOUGHT I WAS DONE.
GASP
OH BOY, HE WASN'T THROUGH YET.
WHAT AN OGRE ...
GASP
...
GASP
GASP
UH...
NO.
I CAN'T GIVE IN TO TEMPTATION, NOT NOW.
WAVER

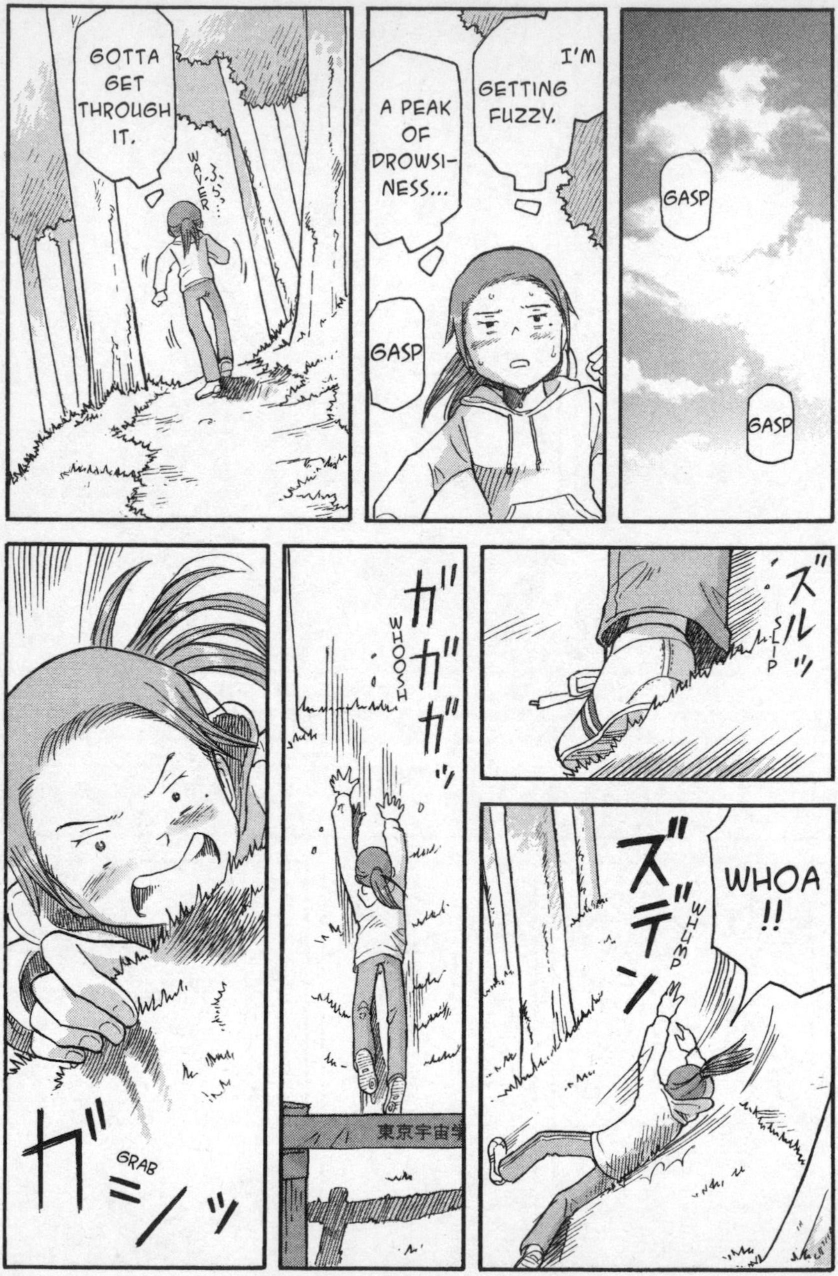
GASP
GASP
I'M GETTING FUZZY.
A PEAK OF DROWSINESS...
GASP
GOTTA GET THROUGH IT.
WAVER
ズルッ
SLIP
ズデン
WHUMP
WHOA!!
ガガガッ
WHOOSH
東京宇宙学
ガシッ
GRAB

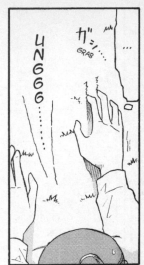

ズズズ…
SLIDE
ガシッ…
GRAB
…
UNGGG……
MY ARMS...
ARE GIVING OUT...
GASP
GASP
I JUST BARELY STAYED WITHIN THE ROPES...
BUT IF I STAYED THIS WAY, THAT'LL DISQUALIFY ME...
東京宇宙学
ガシッ
GRAB
UHN...
GASP
GASP

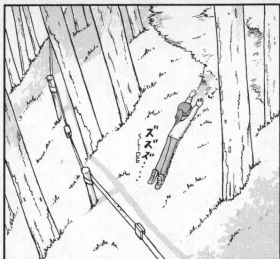

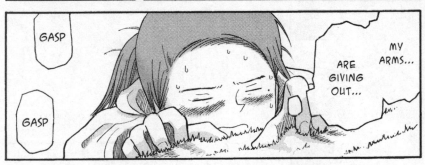

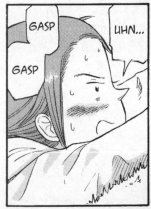

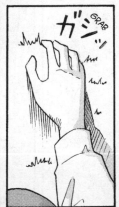

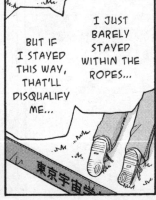

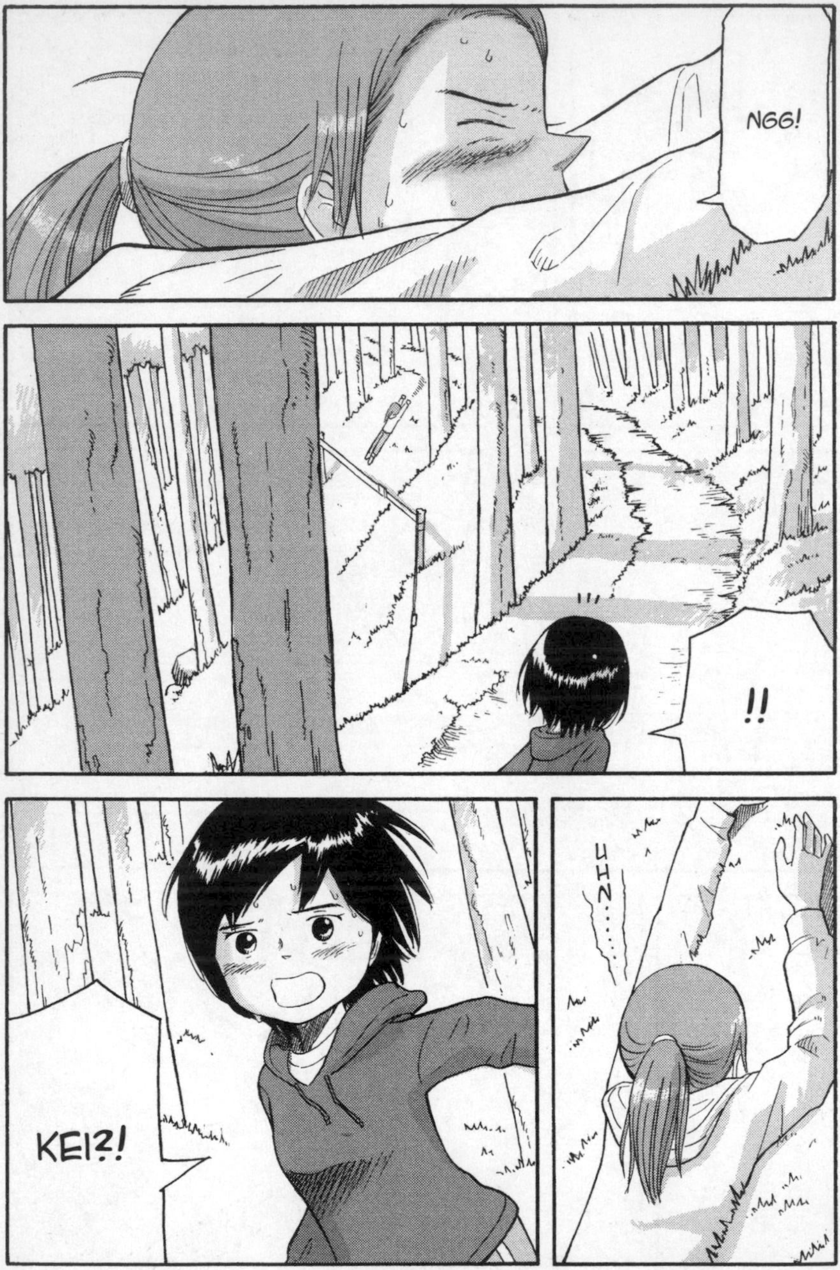
NGG!
!!
UHN......
KEI?!

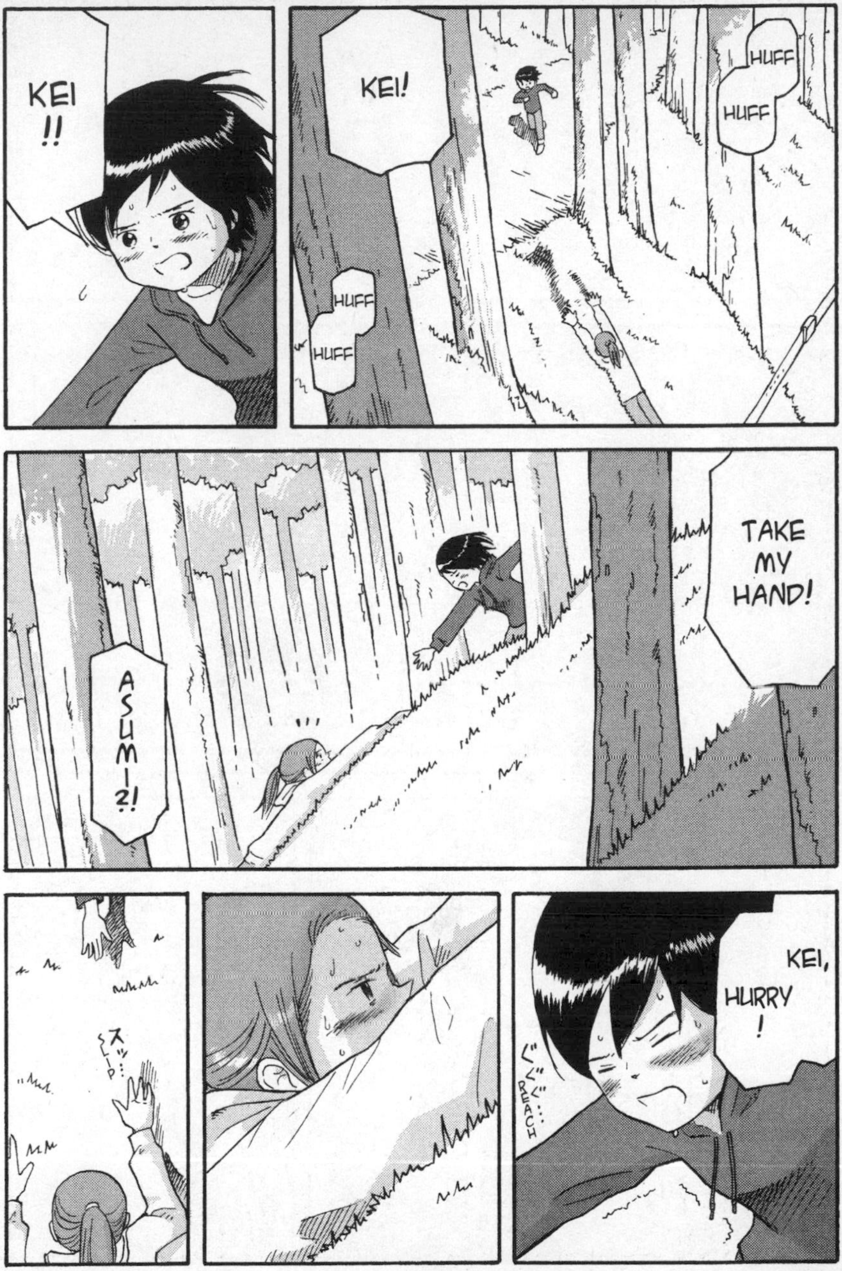
HUFF
HUFF
KEI!
HUFF
HUFF
KEI !!
TAKE MY HAND!
ASUMI?!
KEI, HURRY!
ぐぐぐ…
REACH
スッ…
SLIP

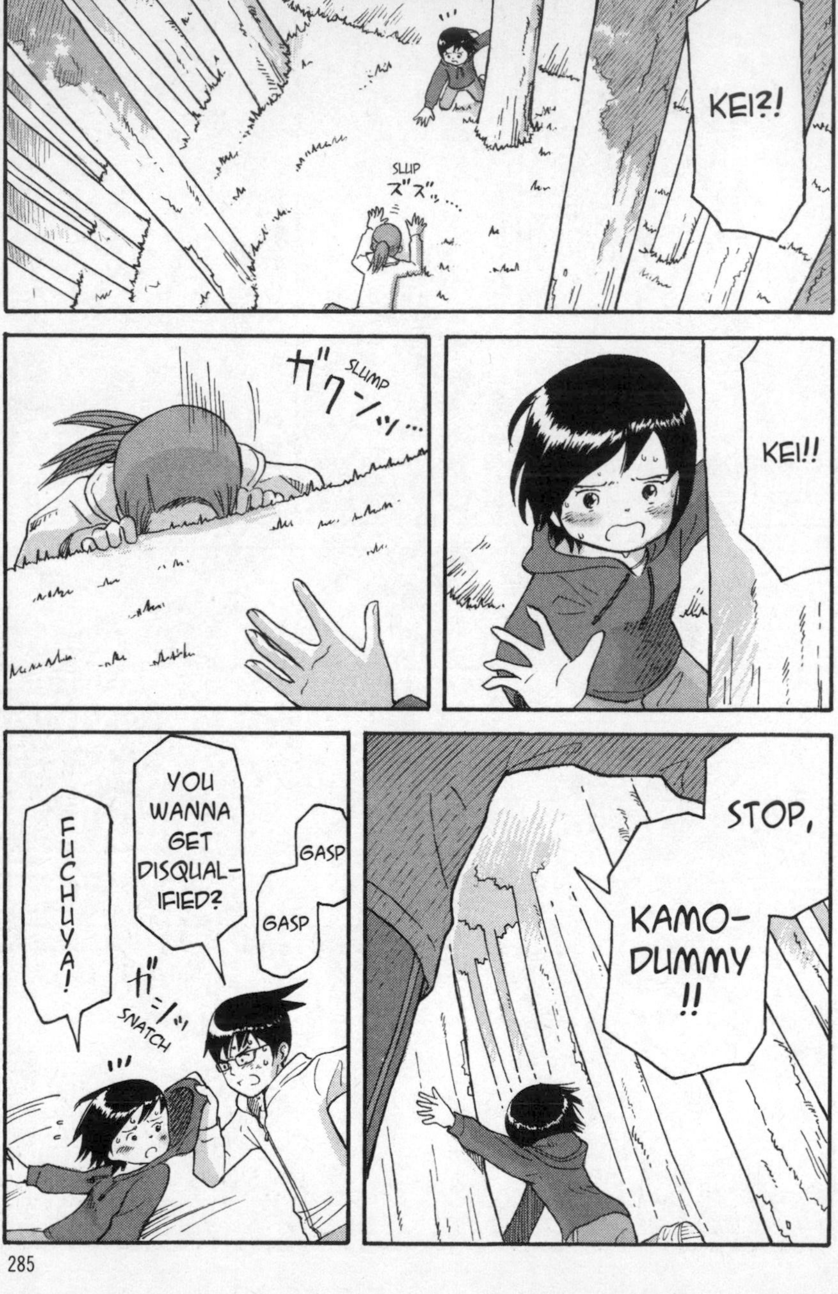
KEI?!
SLUP
ズズッ….
KEI!!
SLUMP
ガクンッ…
STOP,
KAMO-DUMMY!!
GASP
GASP
YOU WANNA GET DISQUAL-IFIED?
FUCHUYA!
ガシッ
SNATCH

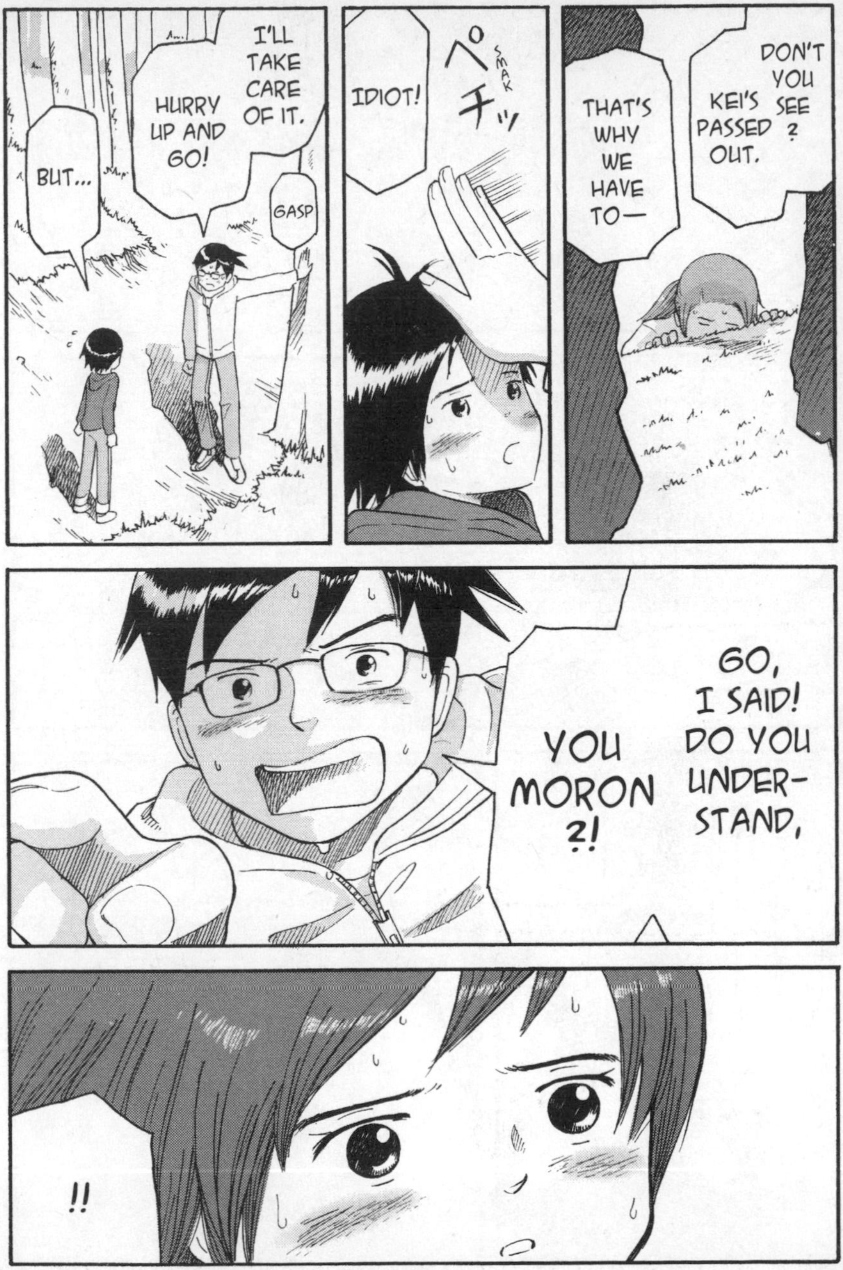
DON'T YOU SEE? KEI'S PASSED OUT.
THAT'S WHY WE HAVE TO—
SMAK
ペチッ
IDIOT!
I'LL TAKE CARE OF IT.
HURRY UP AND GO!
GASP
BUT...
GO, I SAID! DO YOU UNDERSTAND,
YOU MORON ?!
!!

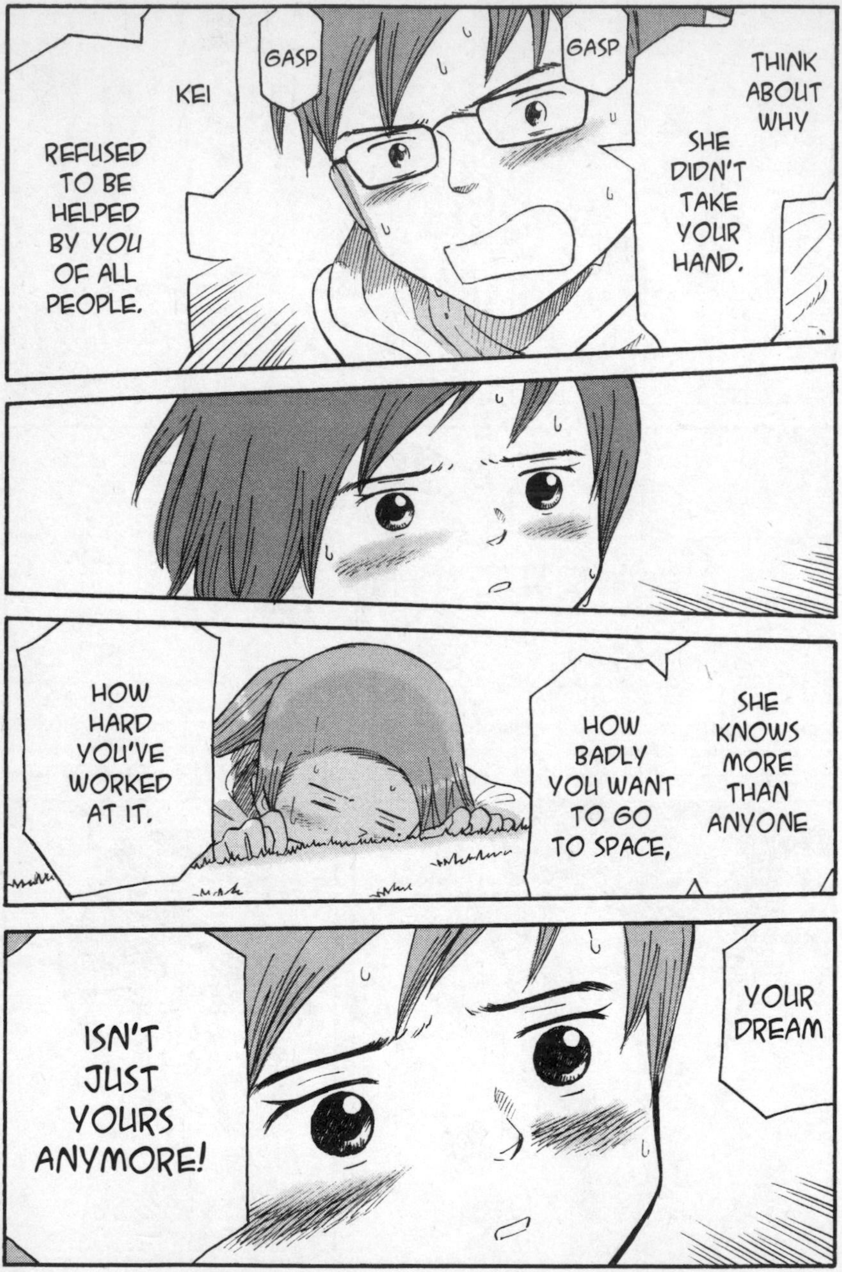
THINK ABOUT WHY
SHE DIDN'T TAKE YOUR HAND.
GASP
GASP
KEI
REFUSED TO BE HELPED BY YOU OF ALL PEOPLE.
SHE KNOWS MORE THAN ANYONE
HOW BADLY YOU WANT TO GO TO SPACE,
HOW HARD YOU'VE WORKED AT IT.
YOUR DREAM
ISN'T JUST YOURS ANYMORE!

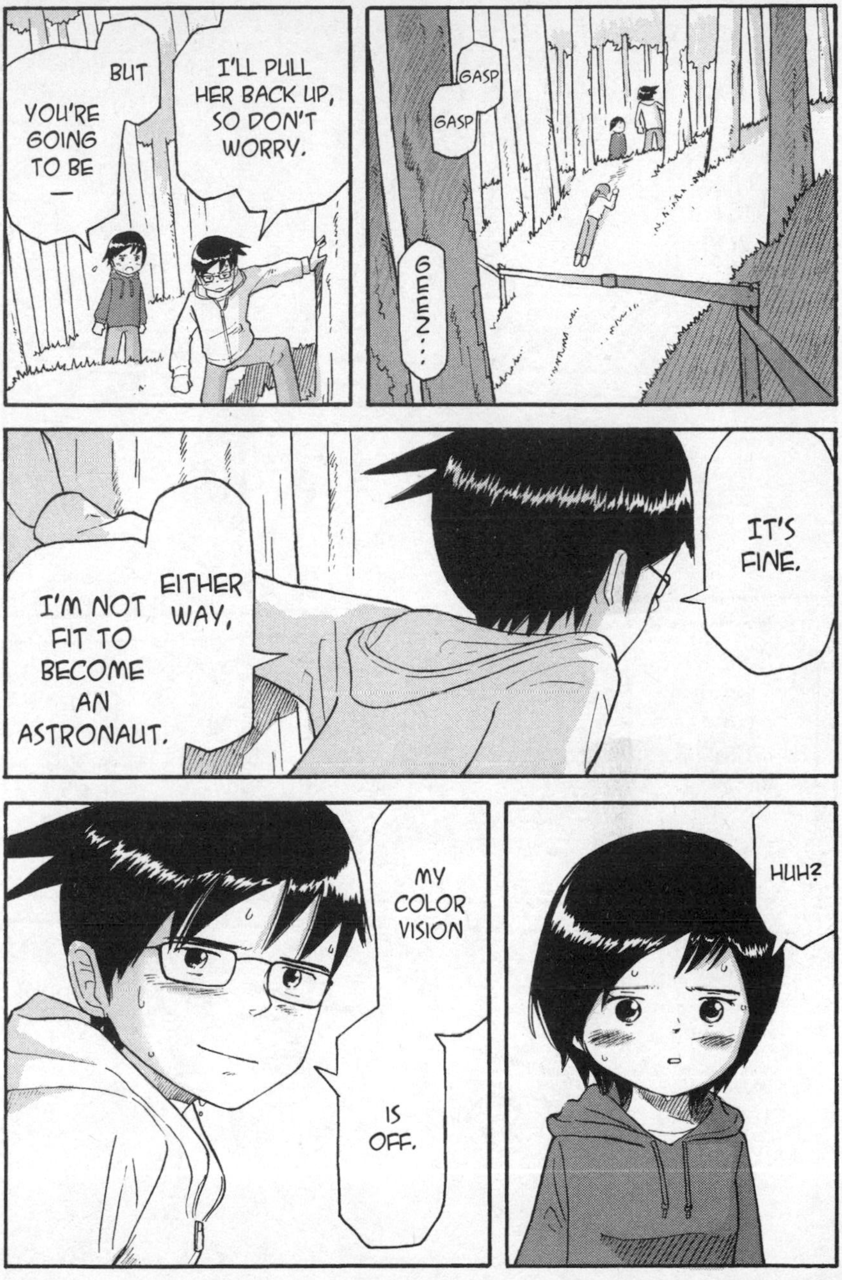
GASP
GASP
GEEZ...
I'LL PULL HER BACK UP, SO DON'T WORRY.
BUT YOU'RE GOING TO BE —
IT'S FINE.
EITHER WAY, I'M NOT FIT TO BECOME AN ASTRONAUT.
HUH?
MY COLOR VISION IS OFF.

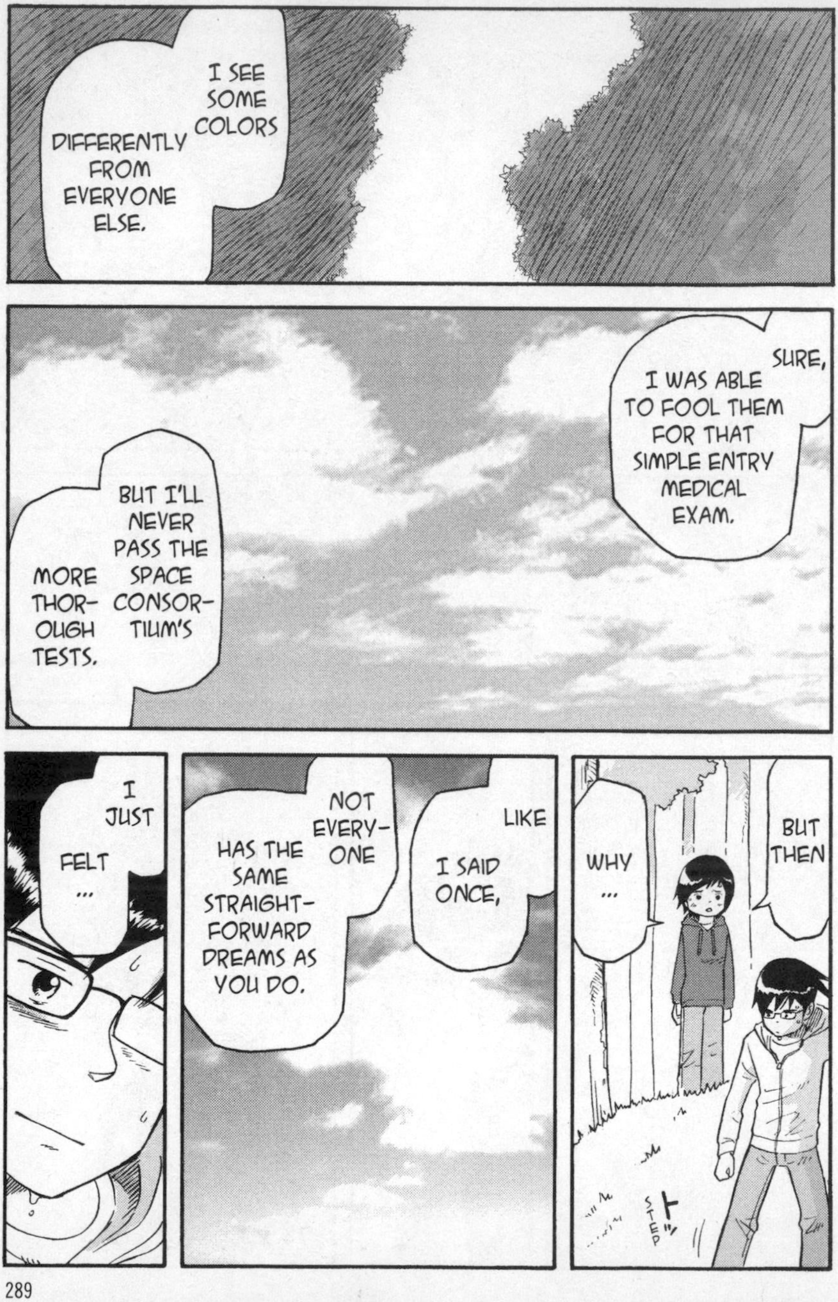
I SEE SOME COLORS DIFFERENTLY FROM EVERYONE ELSE.
SURE, I WAS ABLE TO FOOL THEM FOR THAT SIMPLE ENTRY MEDICAL EXAM.
BUT I'LL NEVER PASS THE SPACE CONSORTIUM'S MORE THOROUGH TESTS.
BUT THEN
WHY ...
STEP
LIKE I SAID ONCE,
NOT EVERYONE HAS THE SAME STRAIGHTFORWARD DREAMS AS YOU DO.
I JUST FELT ...

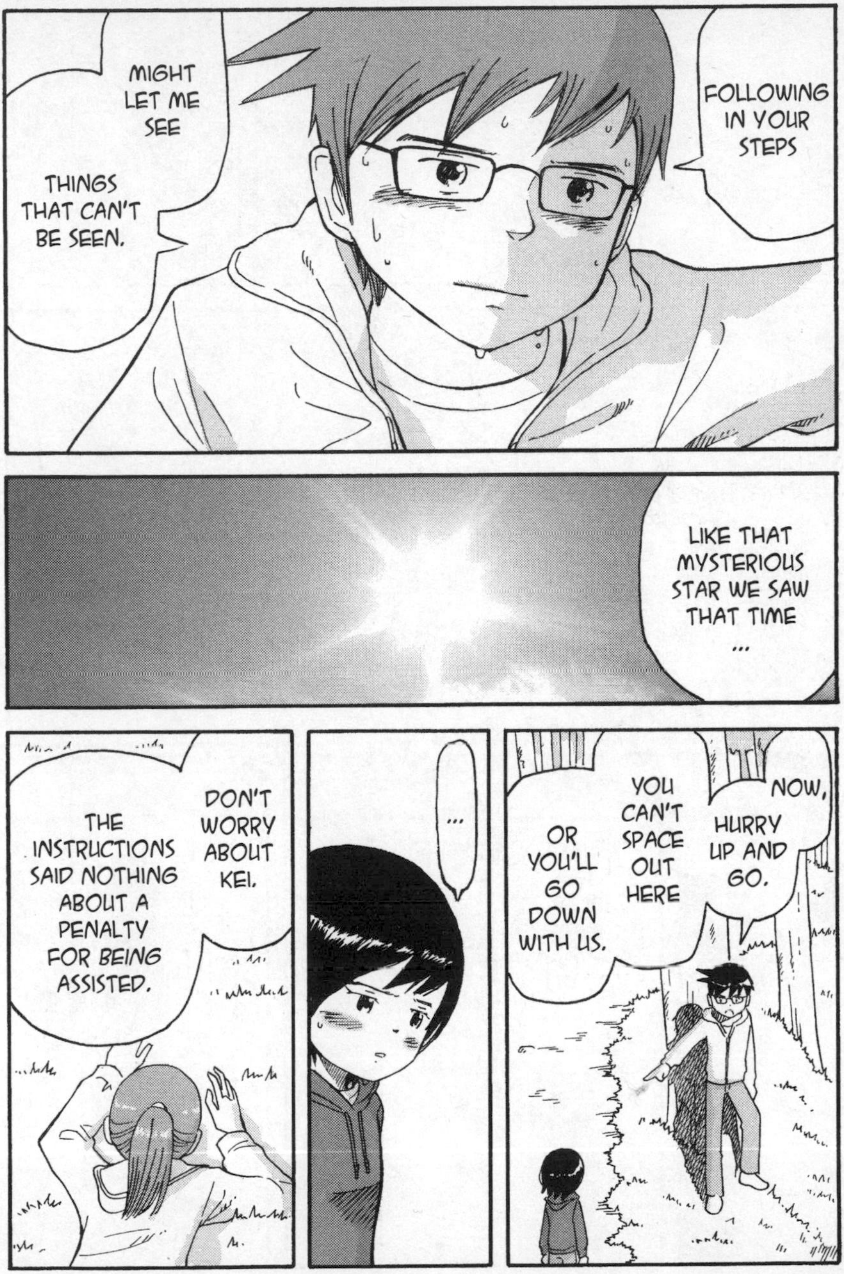
FOLLOWING IN YOUR STEPS
MIGHT LET ME SEE
THINGS THAT CAN'T BE SEEN.
LIKE THAT MYSTERIOUS STAR WE SAW THAT TIME ...
NOW, HURRY UP AND GO.
YOU CAN'T SPACE OUT HERE
OR YOU'LL GO DOWN WITH US.
...
DON'T WORRY ABOUT KEI.
THE INSTRUCTIONS SAID NOTHING ABOUT A PENALTY FOR BEING ASSISTED.

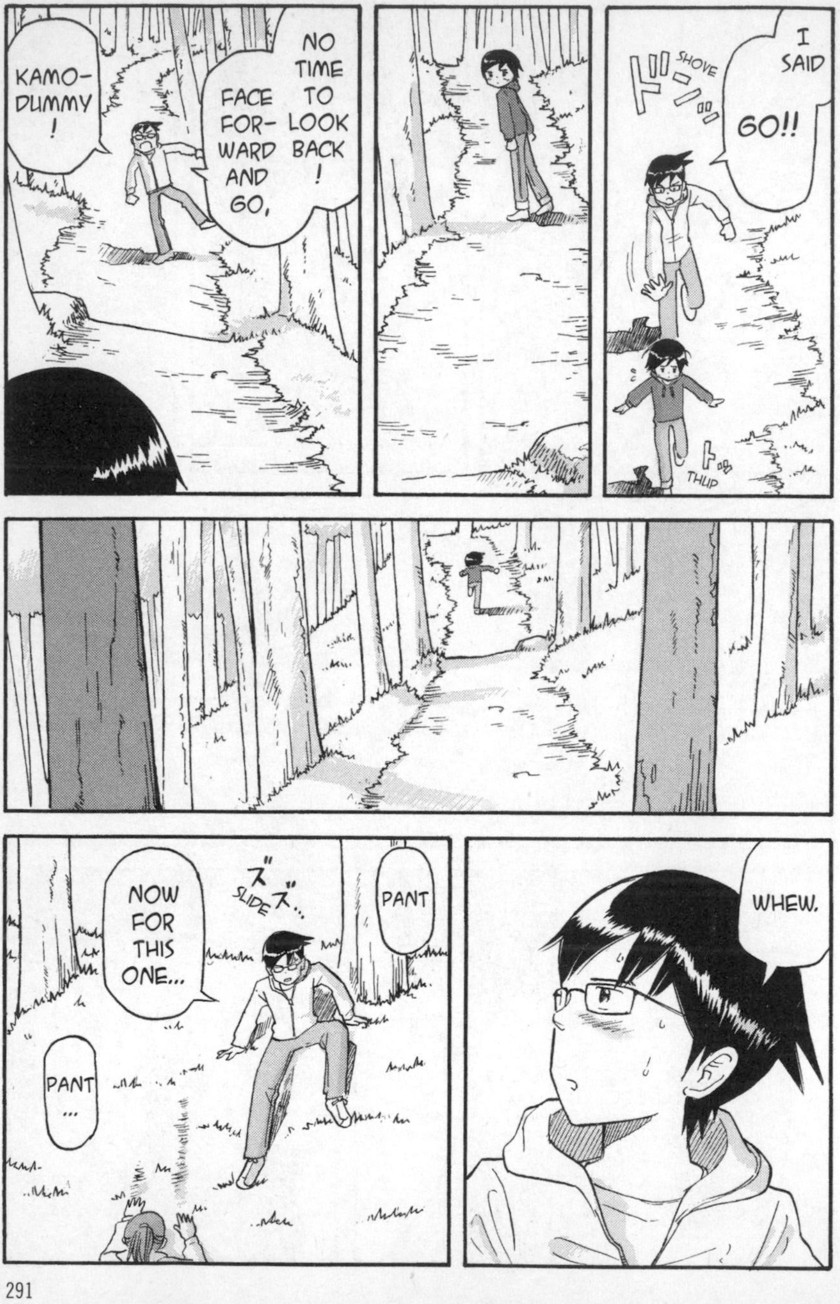
I SAID GO!!
SHOVE
THLIP
NO TIME TO LOOK BACK!
FACE FOR-WARD AND GO,
KAMO-DUMMY!
WHEW.
PANT
SLIDE
NOW FOR THIS ONE...
PANT ...

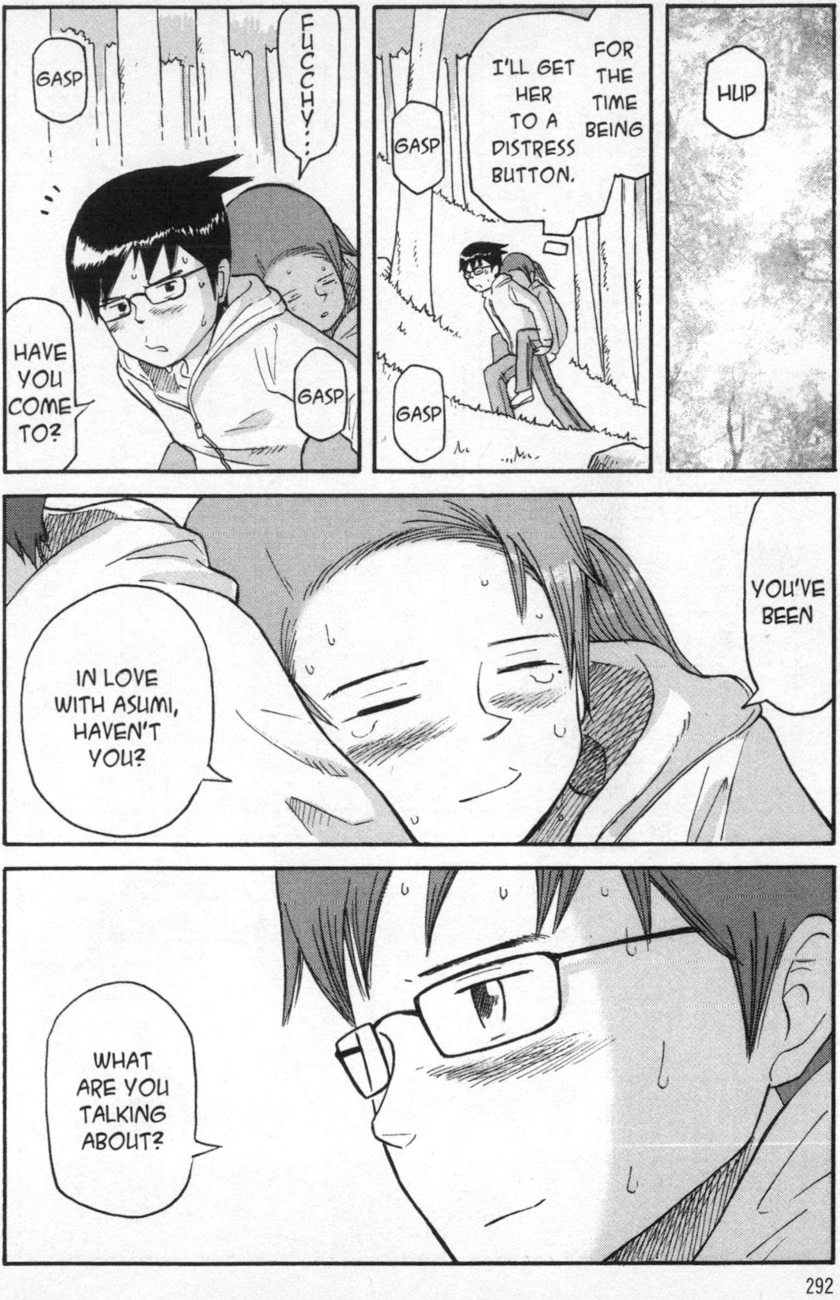
HUP
FOR THE TIME BEING
I'LL GET HER TO A DISTRESS BUTTON.
GASP
GASP
FUCCHY...
GASP
GASP
HAVE YOU COME TO?
YOU'VE BEEN
IN LOVE WITH ASUMI, HAVEN'T YOU?
WHAT ARE YOU TALKING ABOUT?

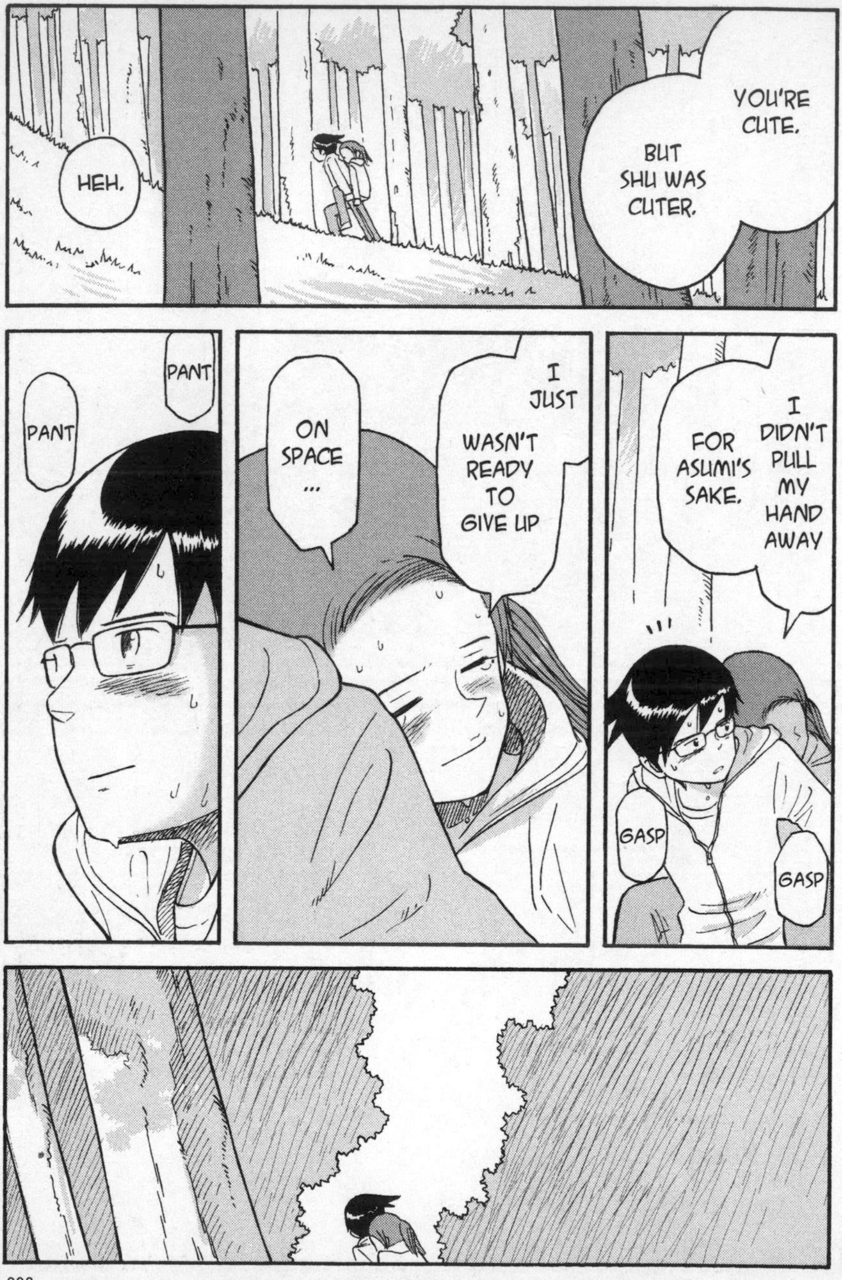
YOU'RE CUTE.
BUT SHU WAS CUTER.
HEH.
I DIDN'T PULL MY HAND AWAY
FOR ASUMI'S SAKE.
GASP
GASP
I JUST WASN'T READY TO GIVE UP
ON SPACE ...
PANT
PANT

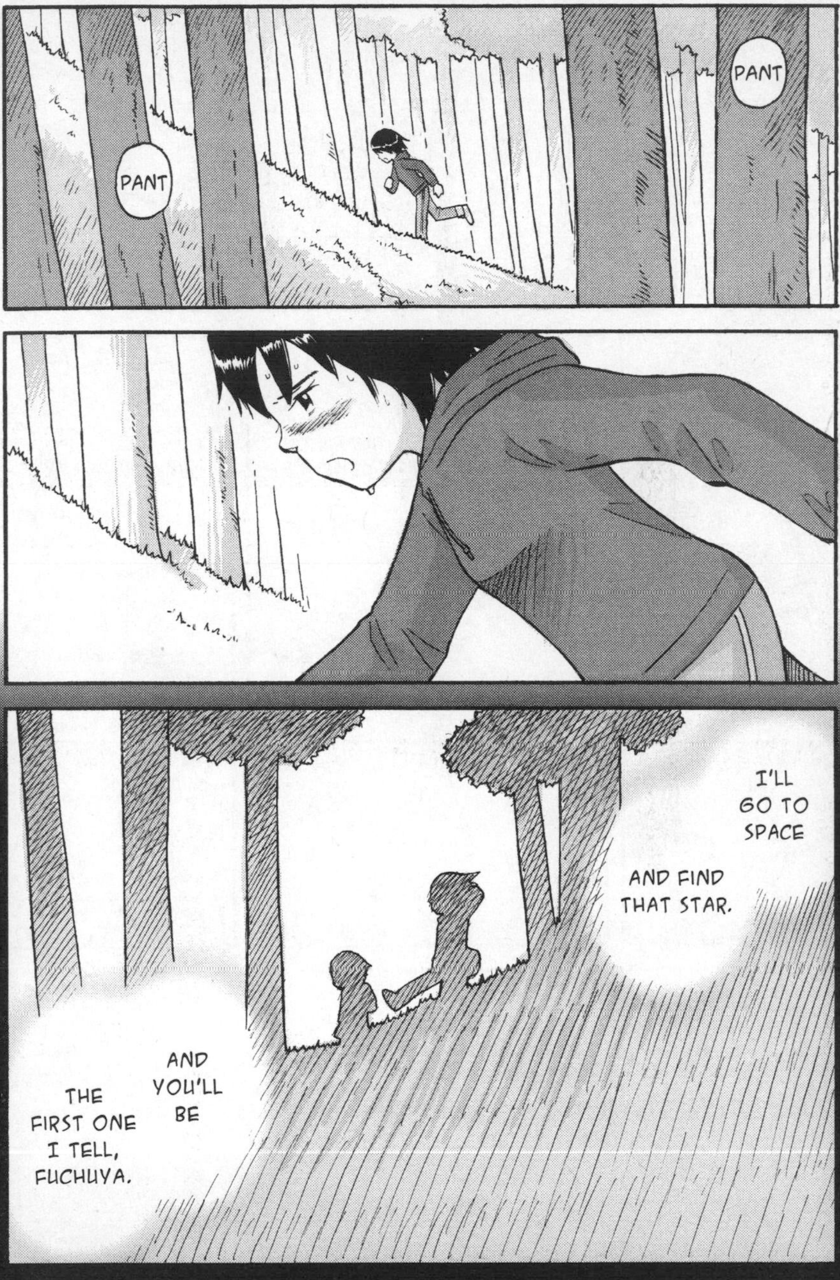
PANT
PANT
I'LL GO TO SPACE
AND FIND THAT STAR.
AND YOU'LL BE
THE FIRST ONE I TELL, FUCHUYA.

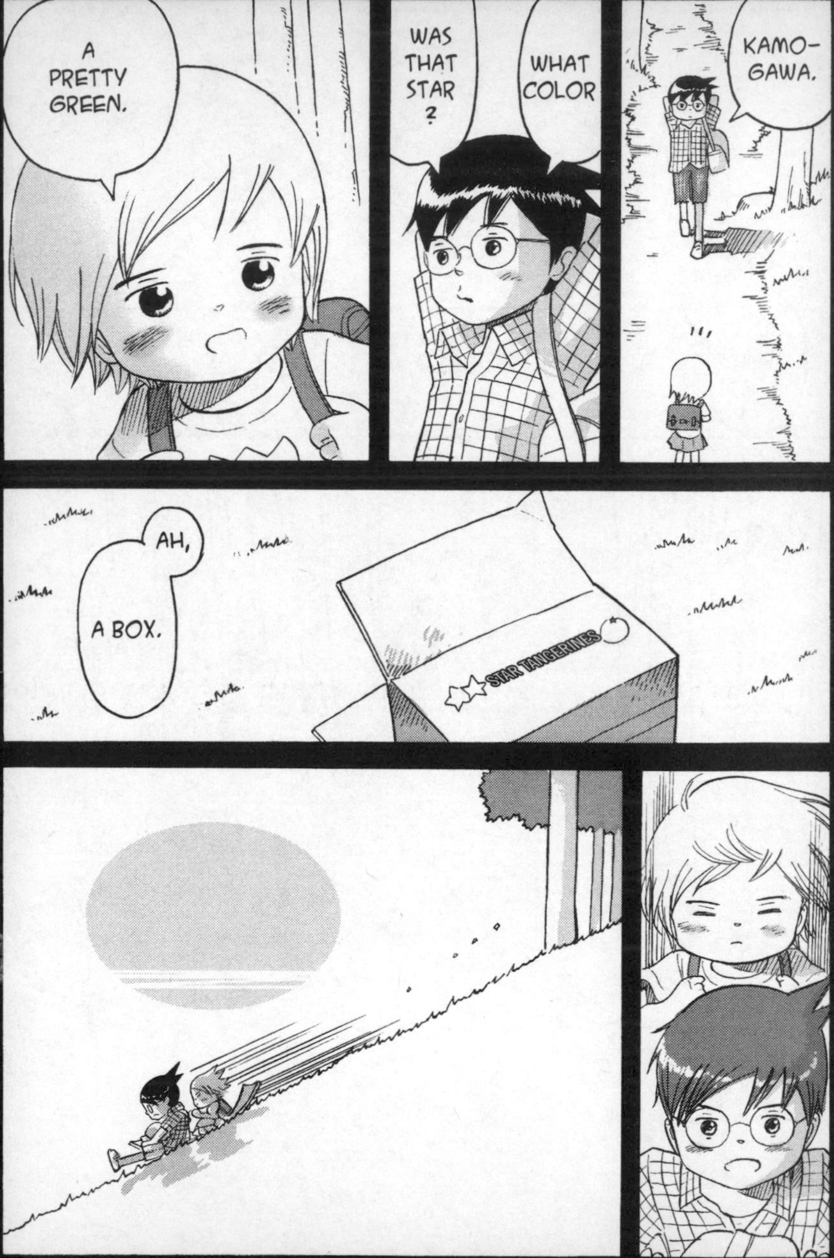
KAMO-GAWA.
WHAT COLOR
WAS THAT STAR?
A PRETTY GREEN.
AH,
A BOX.
STAR TANGERINES

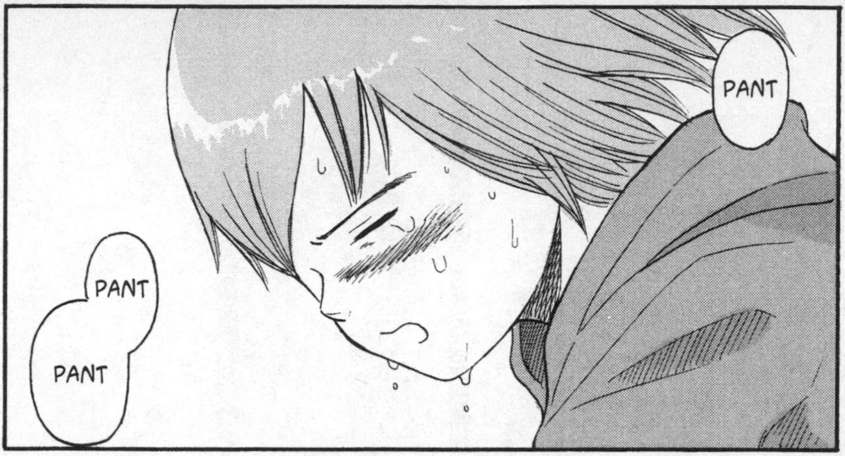
PANT
PANT
PANT
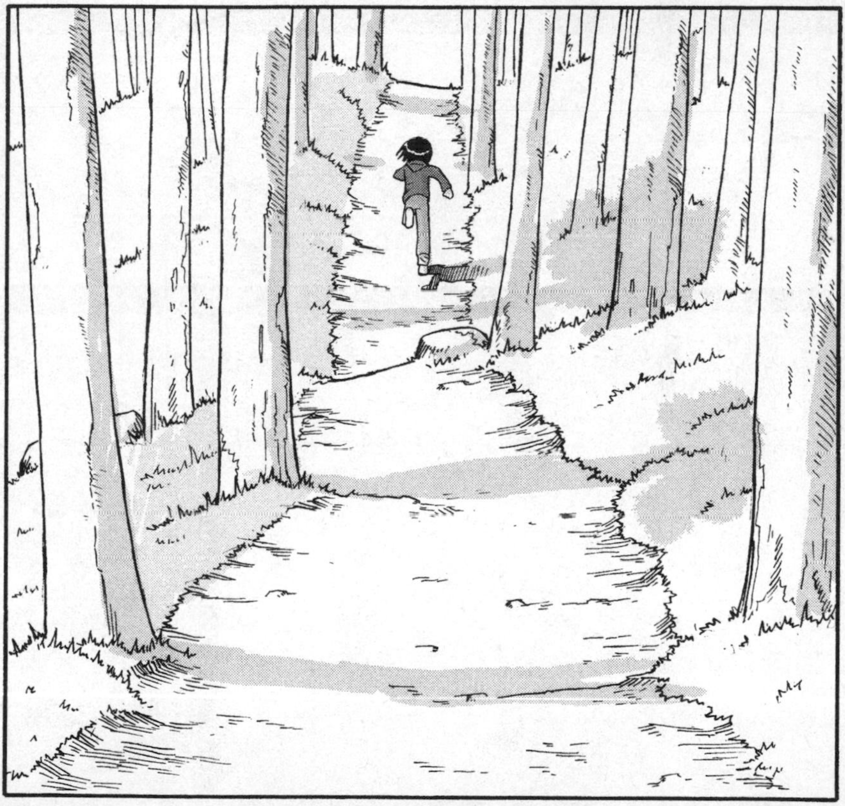

MISSION:74

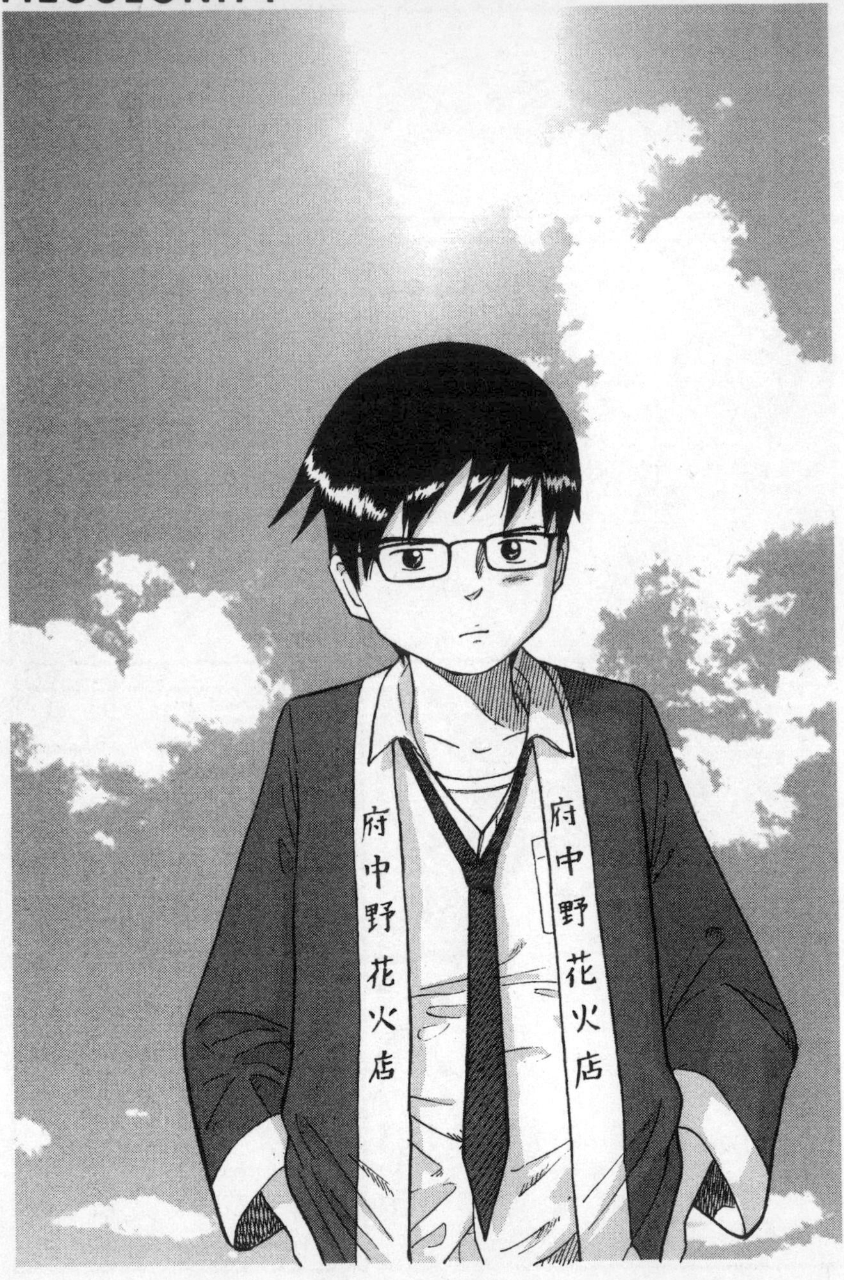
府中野花火店
府中野花火店

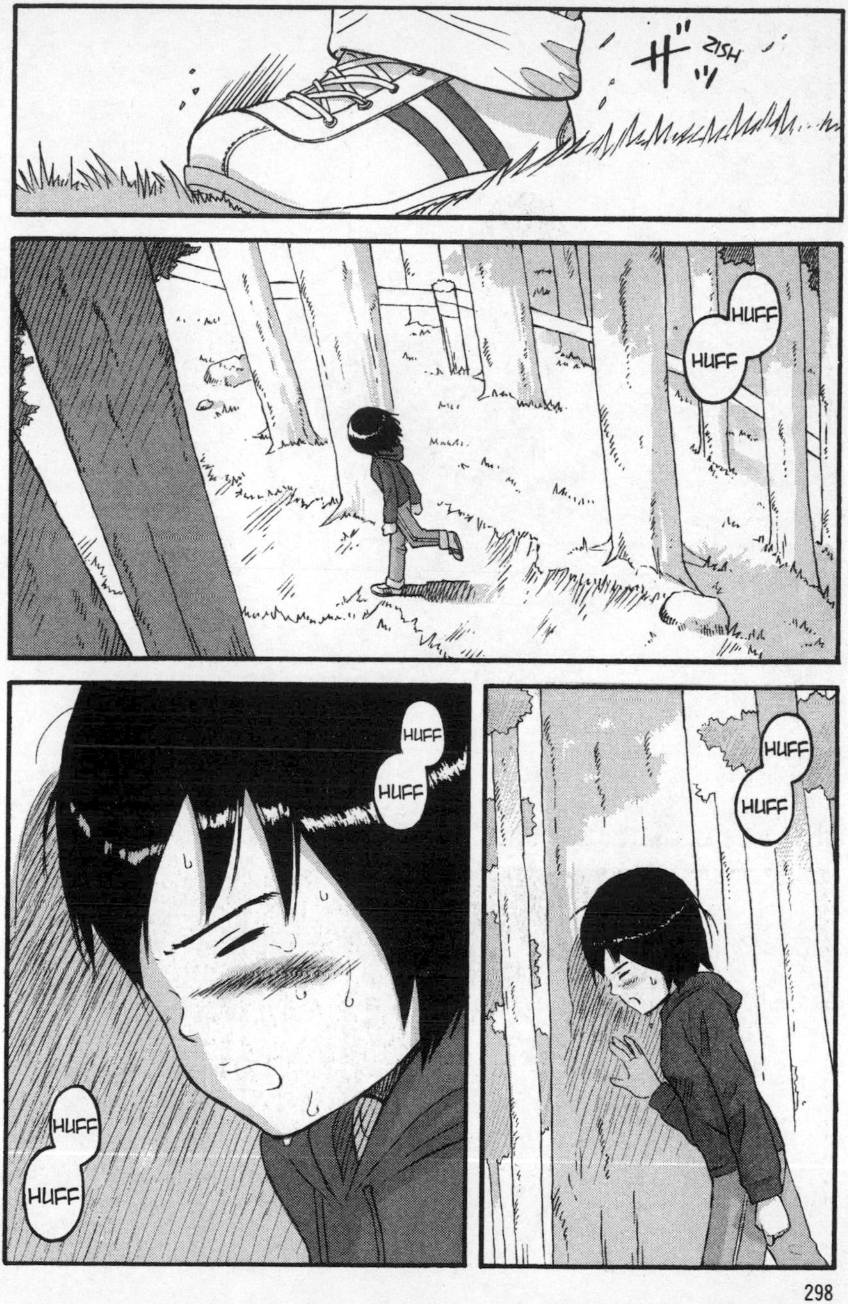
ザッ
ZISH
HUFF
HUFF
HUFF
HUFF
HUFF
HUFF
HUFF
HUFF

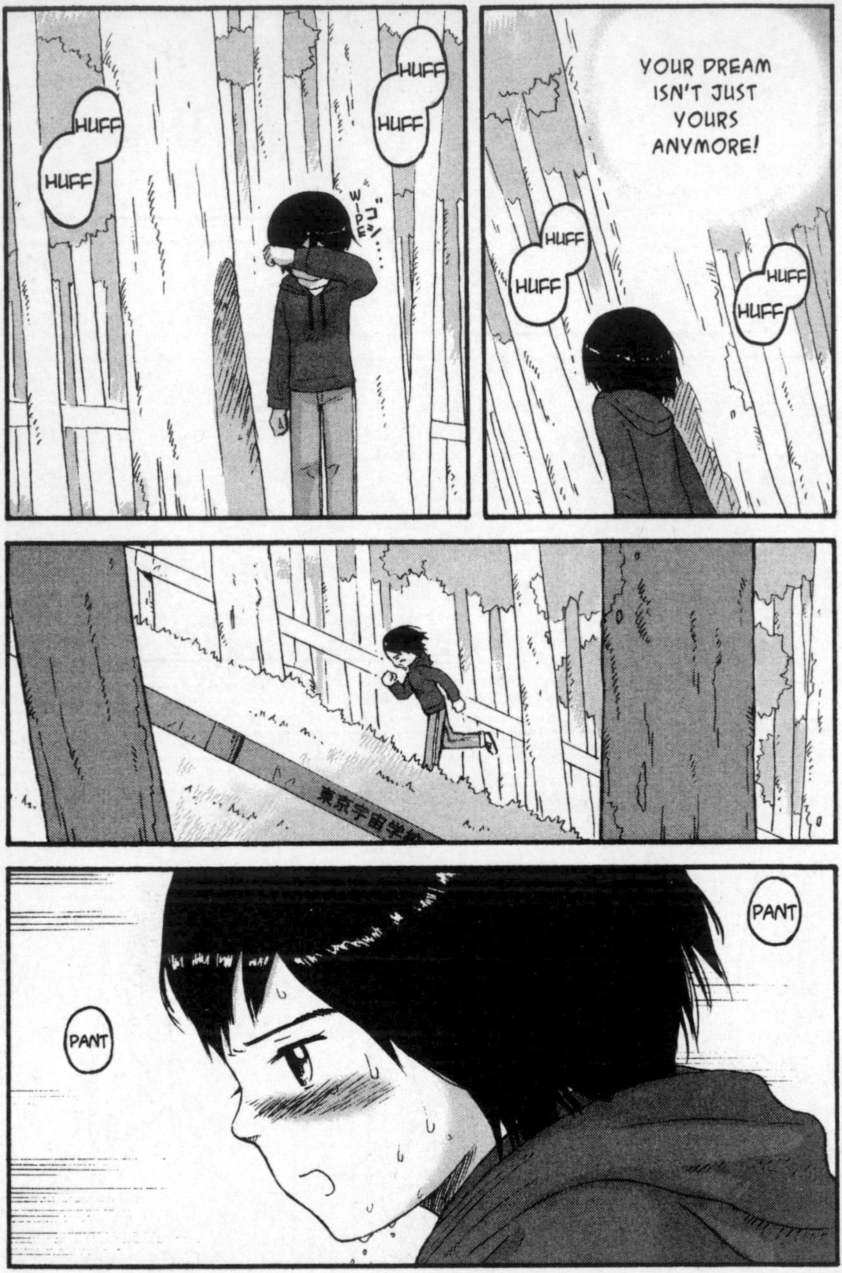
YOUR DREAM ISN'T JUST YOURS ANYMORE!
HUFF HUFF
HUFF HUFF
HUFF HUFF
WIPE
HUFF HUFF
PANT
PANT

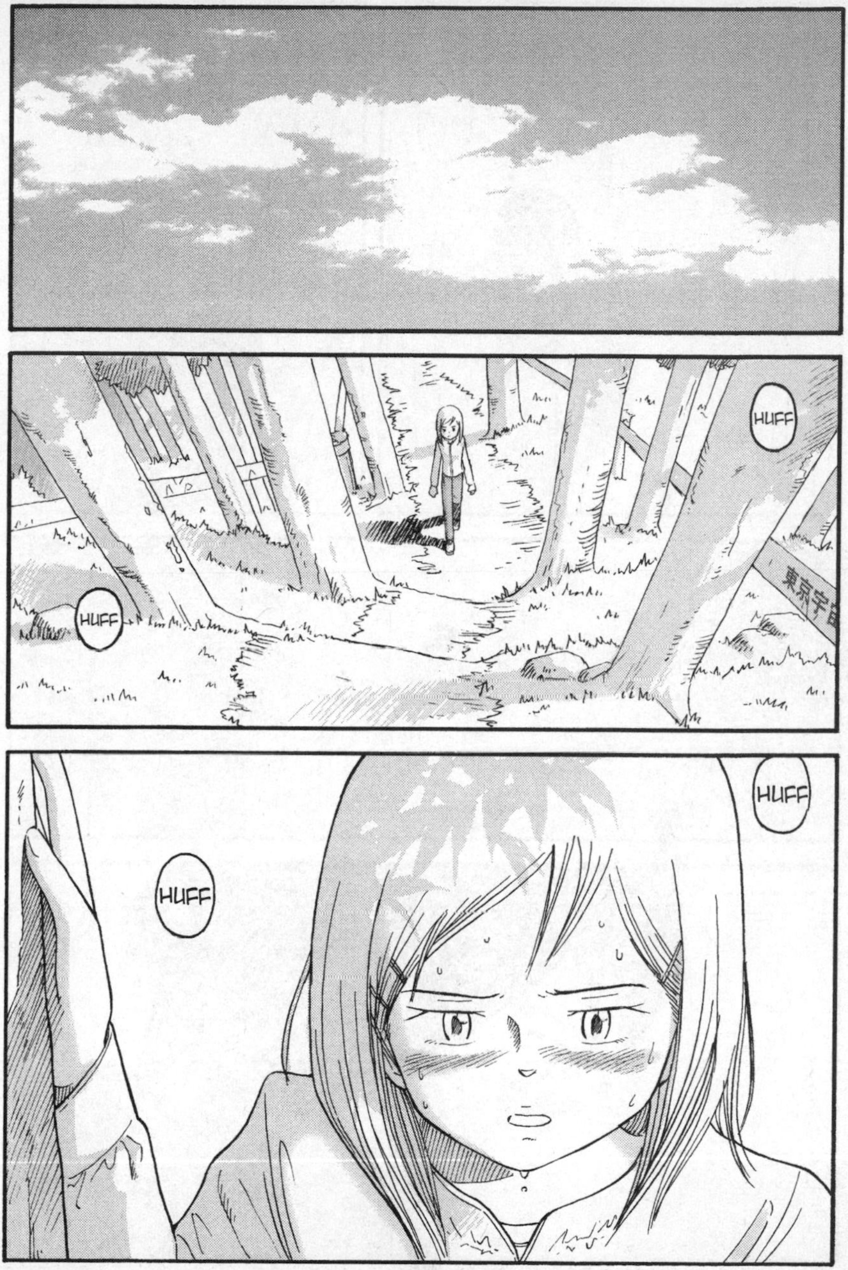
HUFF
東京宇
HUFF
HUFF
HUFF

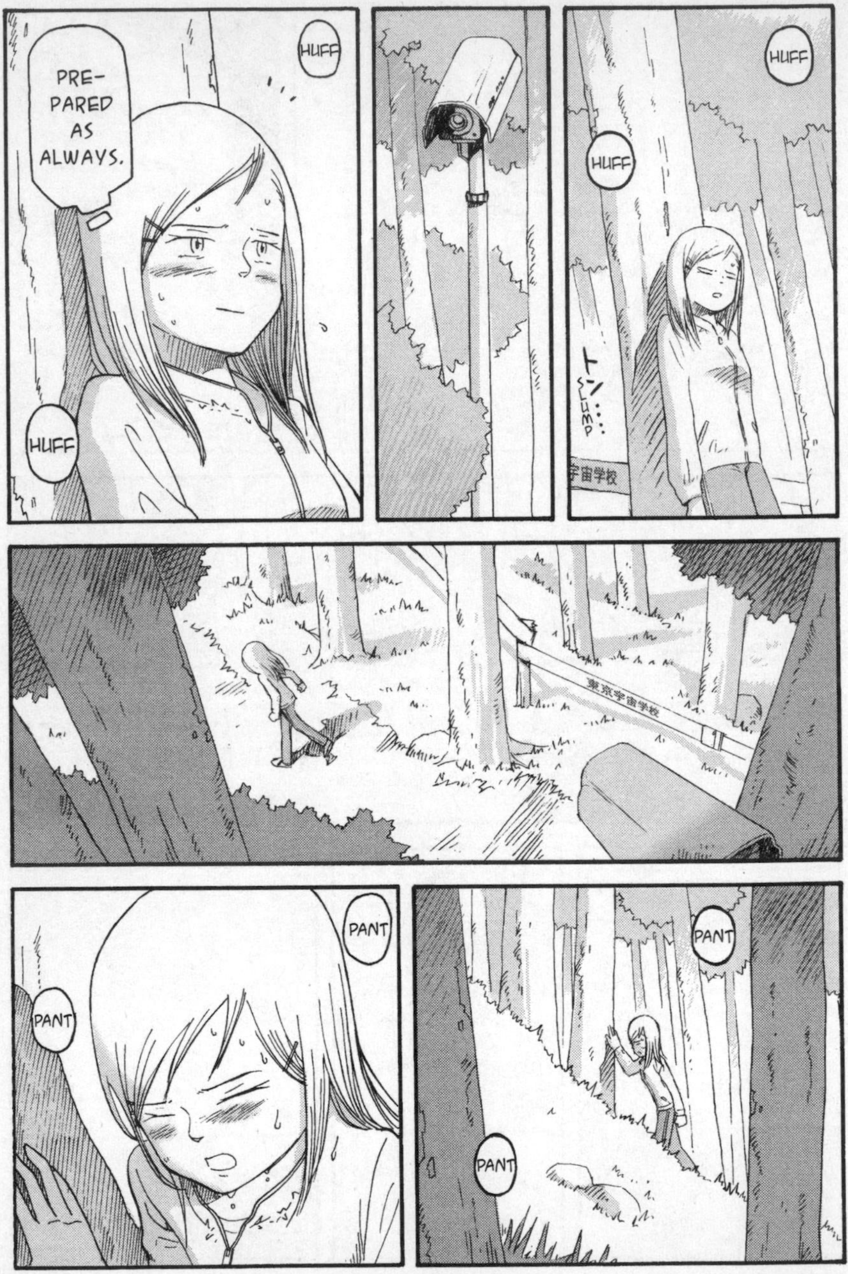
HUFF
HUFF
SLUMP...
宇宙学校
HUFF
PRE-PARED AS ALWAYS.
...
HUFF
東京宇宙学校
PANT
PANT
PANT
PANT

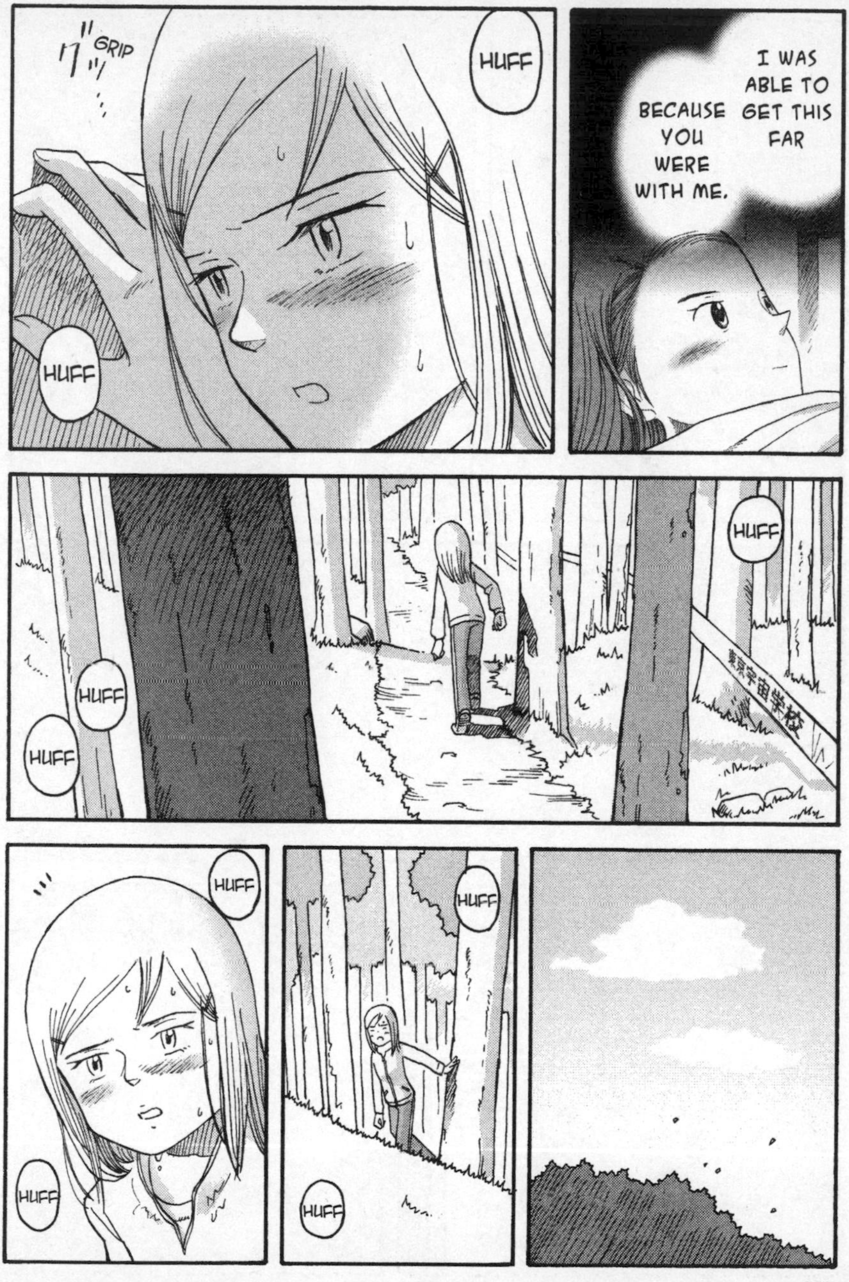
I WAS ABLE TO GET THIS FAR
BECAUSE YOU WERE WITH ME.
HUFF
GRIP
HUFF
HUFF
東京宇宙学校
HUFF
HUFF
HUFF
HUFF
HUFF
HUFF

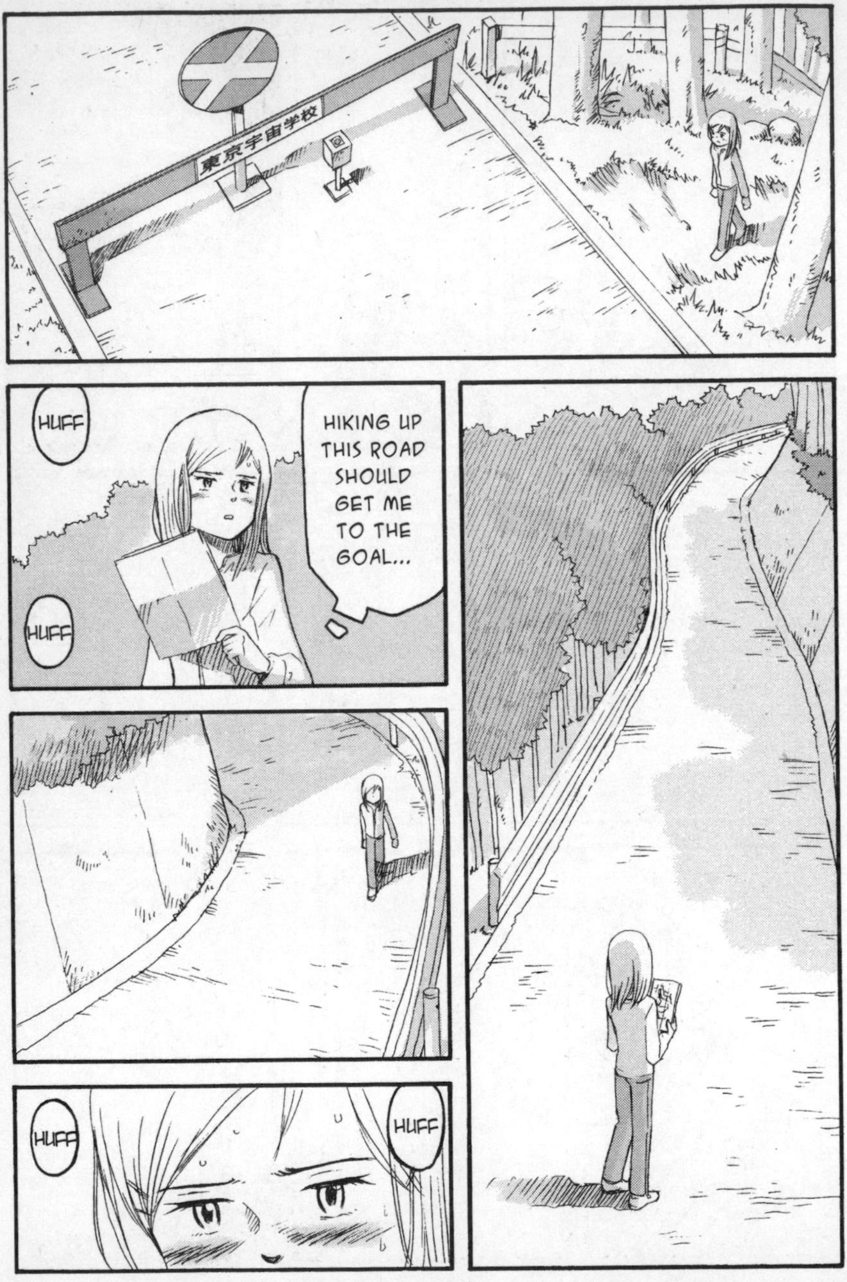
東京宇宙学校
HIKING UP THIS ROAD SHOULD GET ME TO THE GOAL...
HUFF
HUFF
HUFF
HUFF

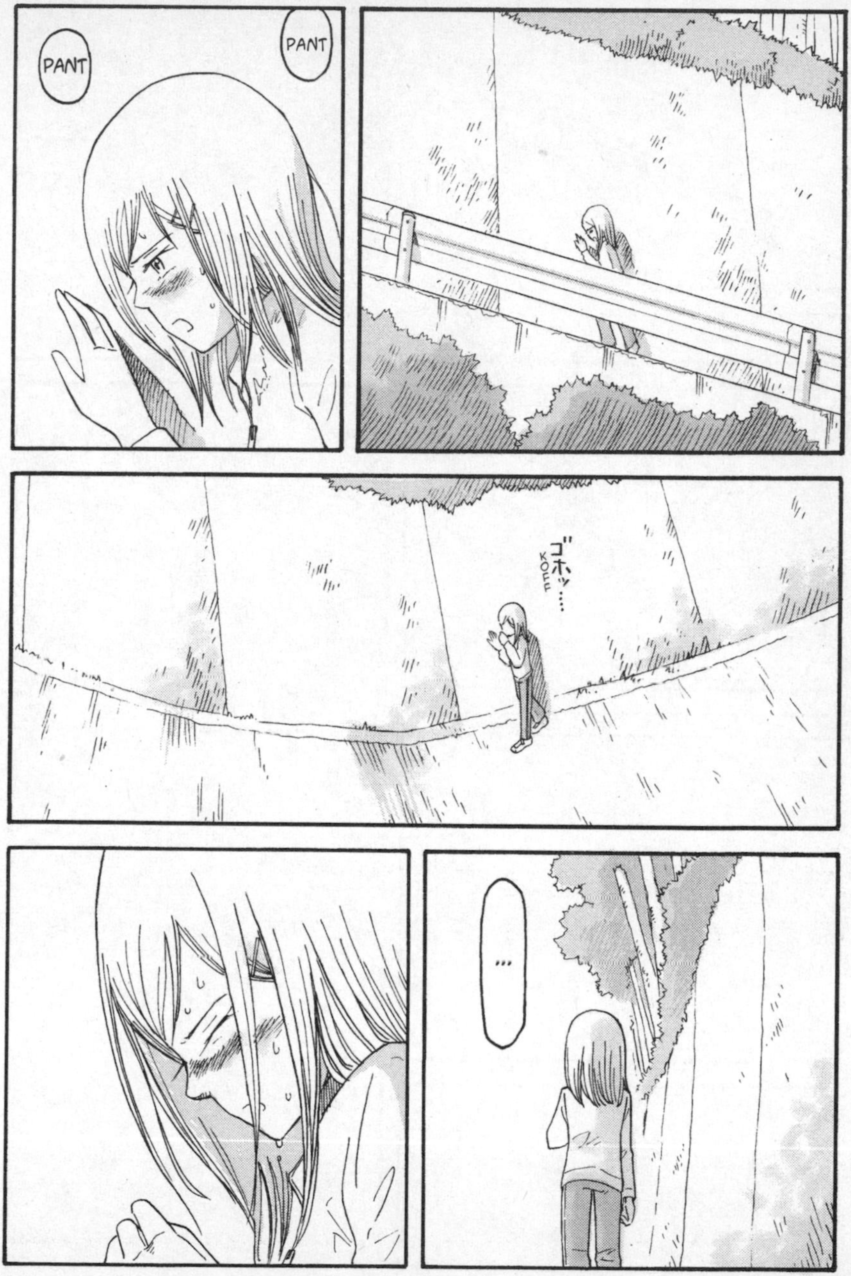
PANT
PANT
ゴホッ…
KOFF
...

ゴホッ
KOFF
ゴホッ
KOFF
ゴホッ
KOFF
ゴホッ…
KOFF

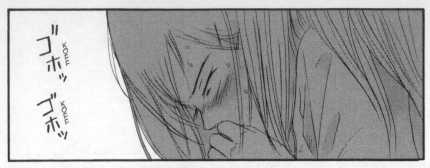

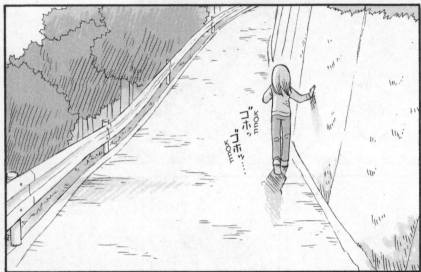

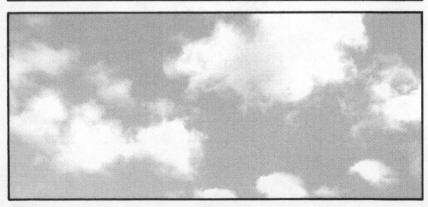

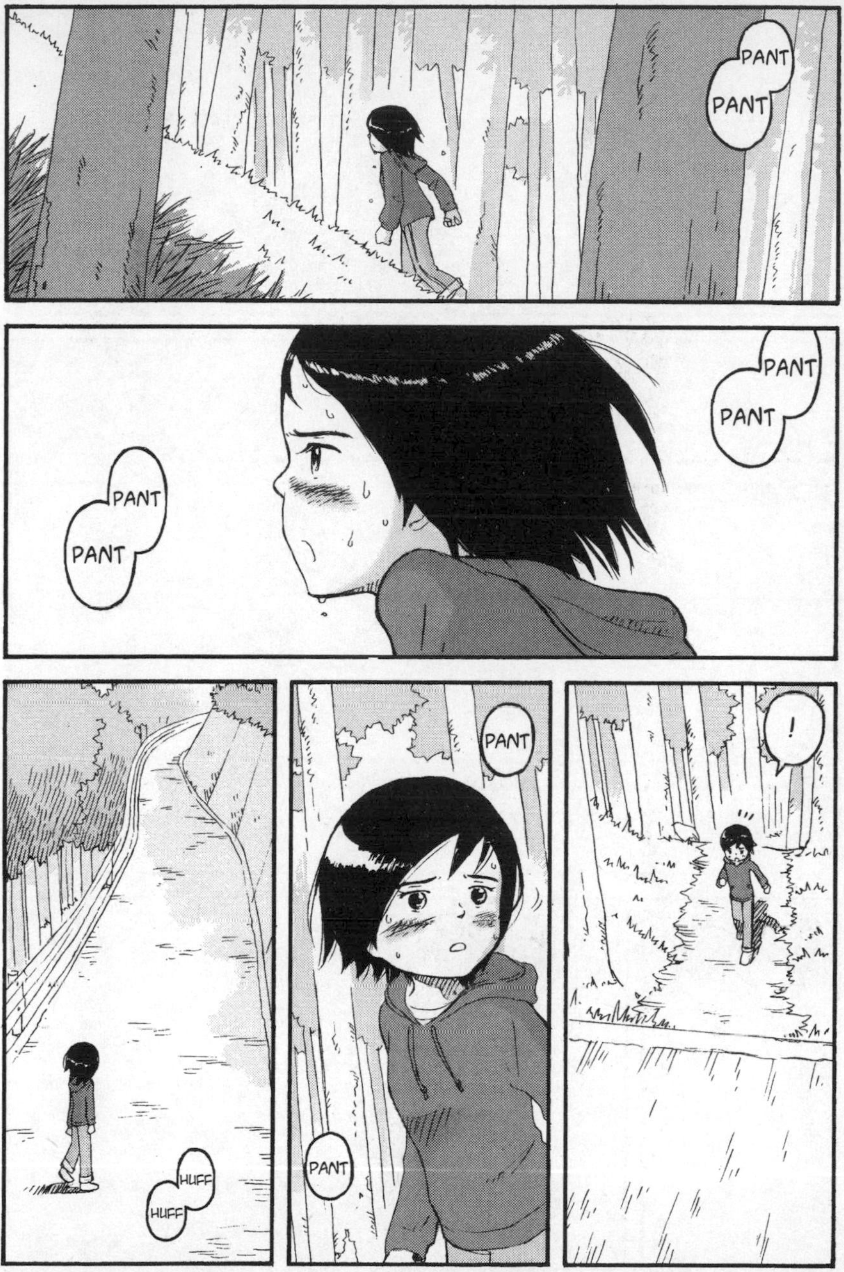
PANT
PANT
PANT
PANT
PANT
PANT
!
PANT
PANT
HUFF
HUFF

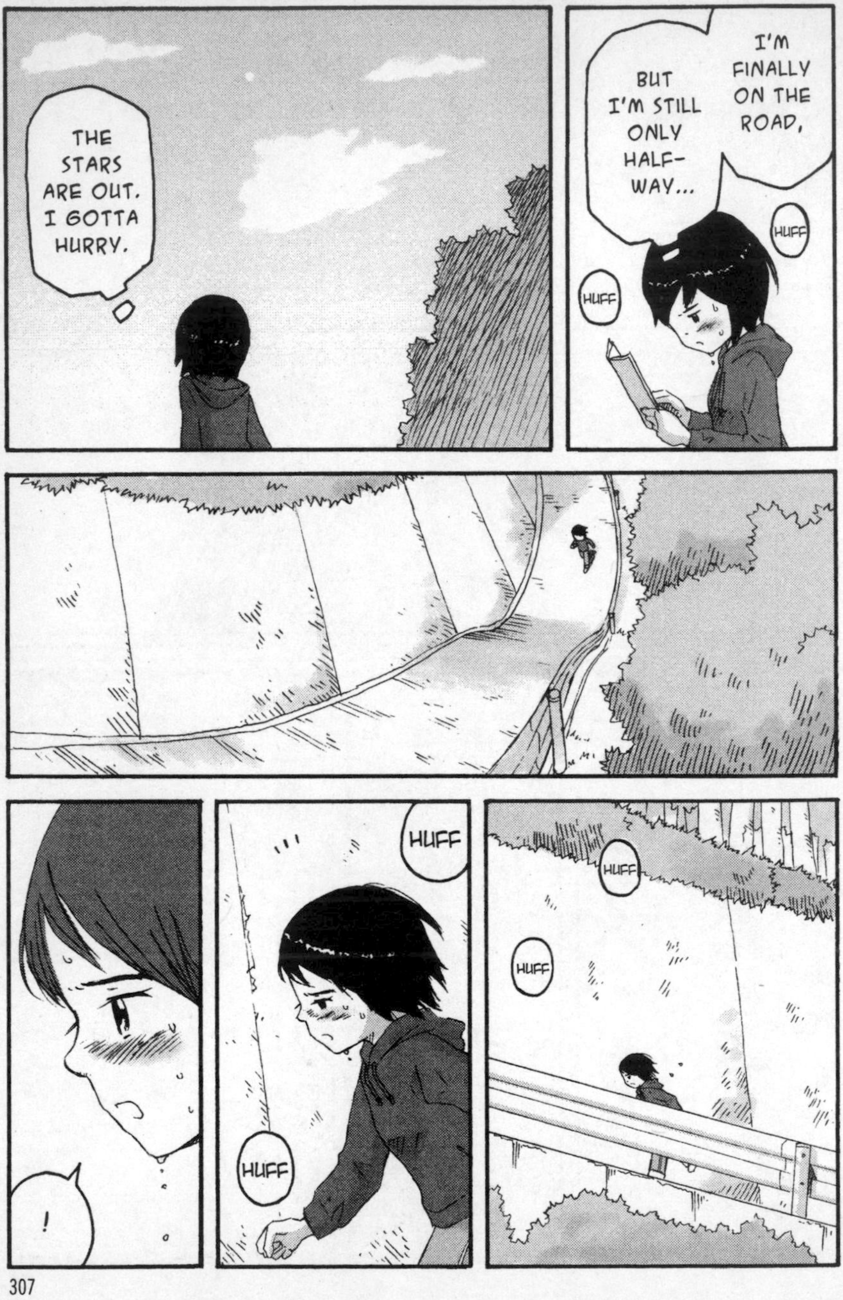
I'M FINALLY ON THE ROAD,
BUT I'M STILL ONLY HALF-WAY...
HUFF
HUFF
THE STARS ARE OUT. I GOTTA HURRY.
HUFF
HUFF
HUFF
HUFF
!

MARIKA ?!
!
HUFF
HUFF
HUFF
HUFF
MISS KAMO-GAWA?
WIPE
......
ARE YOU OK ?!
HUFF
HUFF
HUFF
HUFF

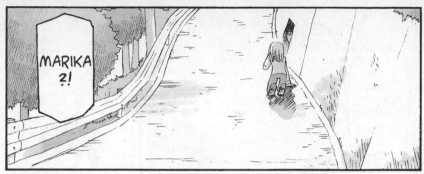

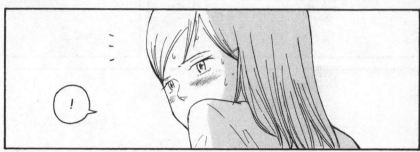

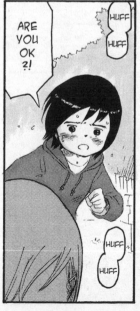

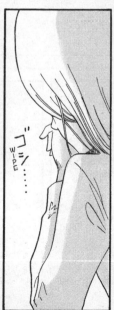

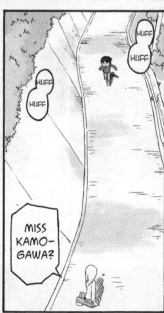

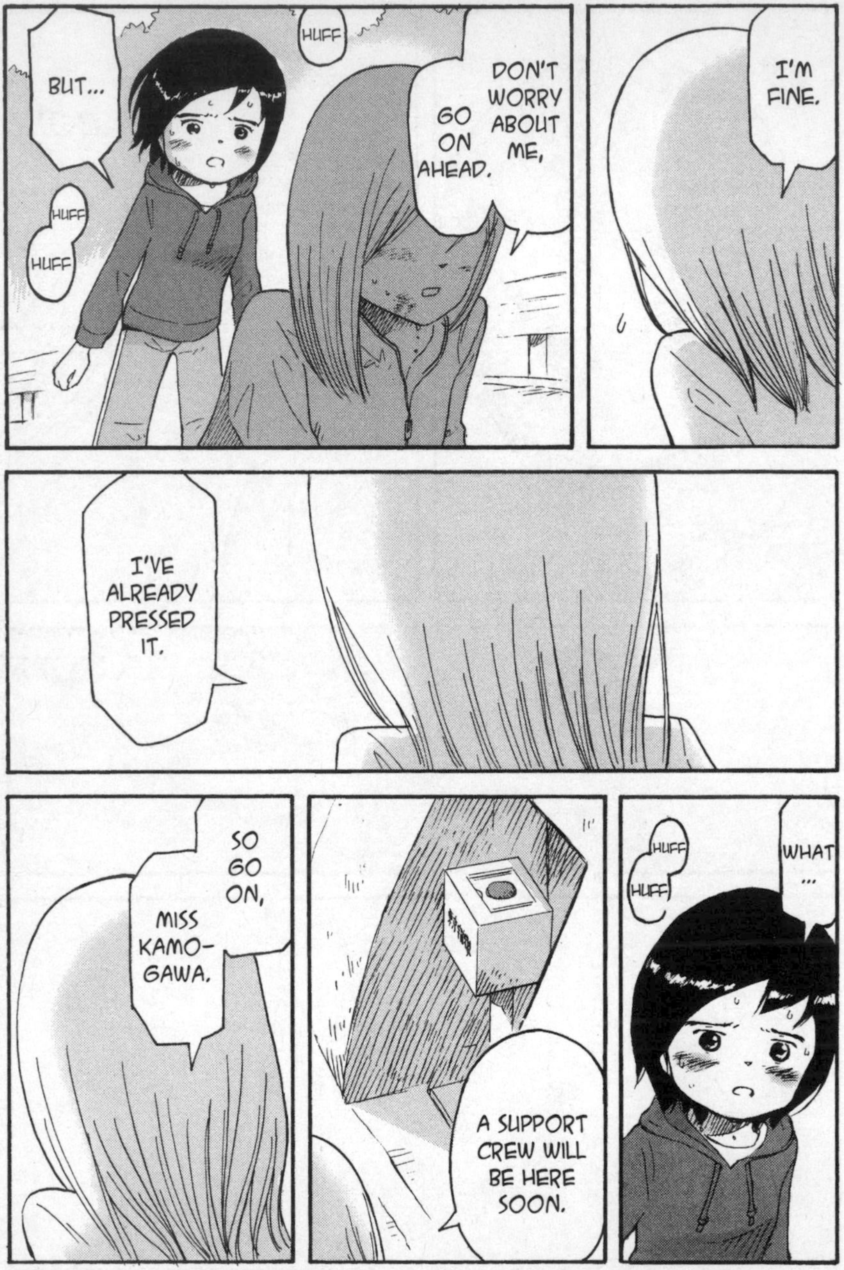
I'M FINE.
HUFF
DON'T WORRY ABOUT ME, GO ON AHEAD.
BUT...
HUFF
HUFF
I'VE ALREADY PRESSED IT.
WHAT ...
HUFF
HUFF
A SUPPORT CREW WILL BE HERE SOON.
SO GO ON, MISS KAMO-GAWA.

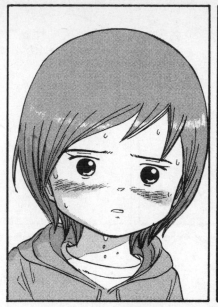

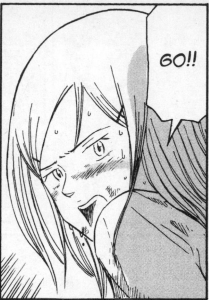

GO!!

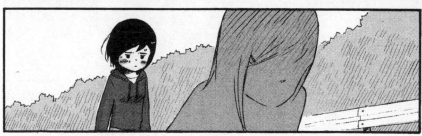

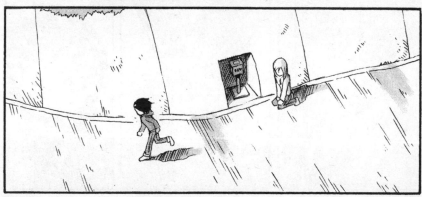

HUFF
HUFF
PANT
PANT
PANT
PANT
PANT
PANT
PANT
PANT

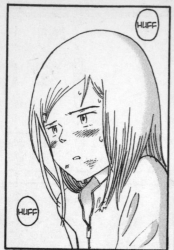

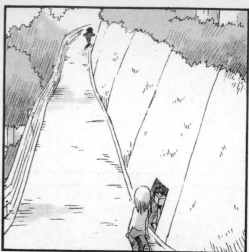

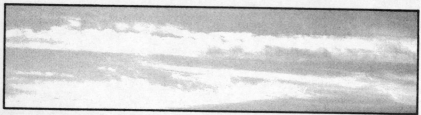

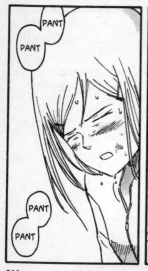

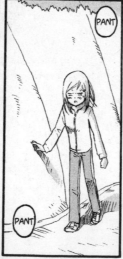

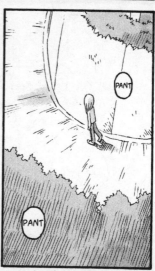

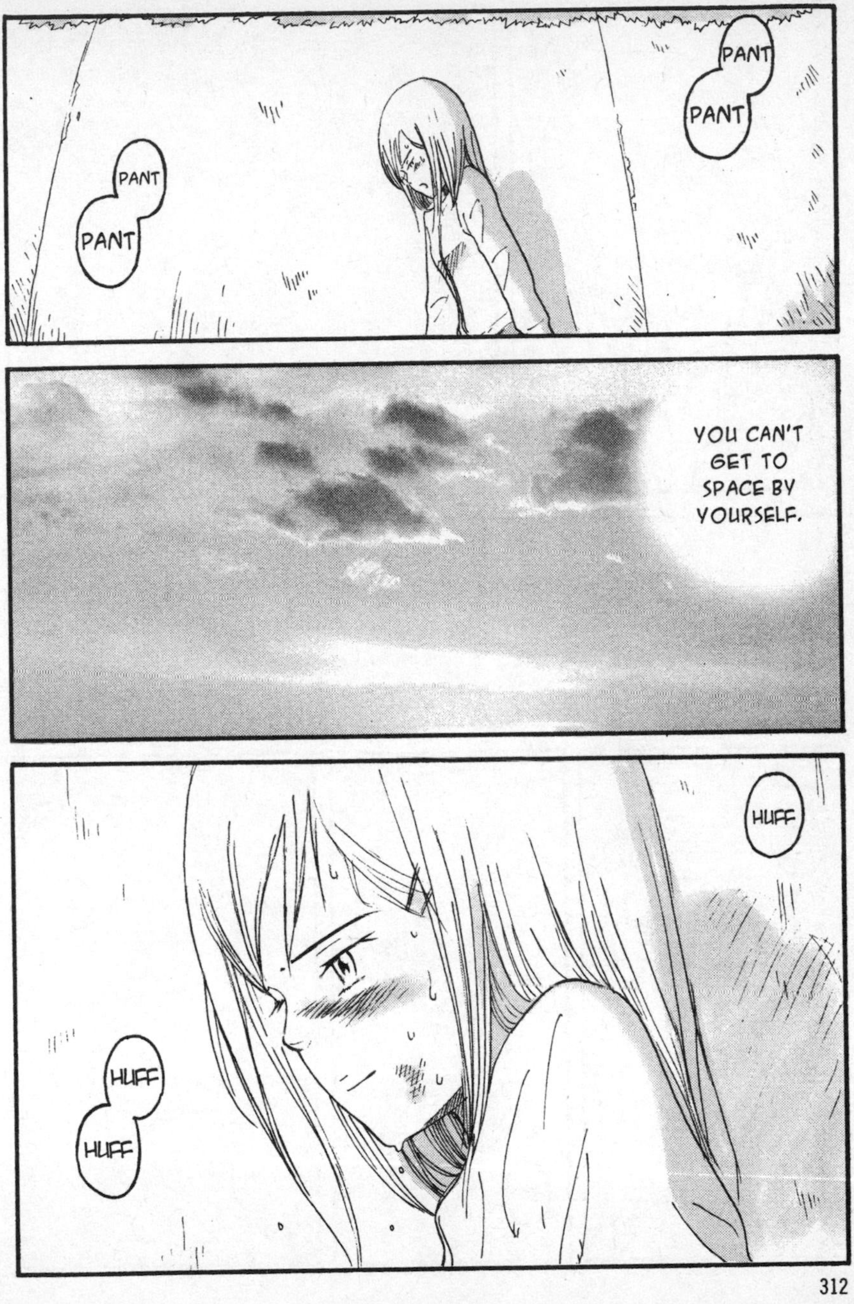
PANT
PANT
PANT
PANT
YOU CAN'T GET TO SPACE BY YOURSELF.
HUFF
HUFF
HUFF

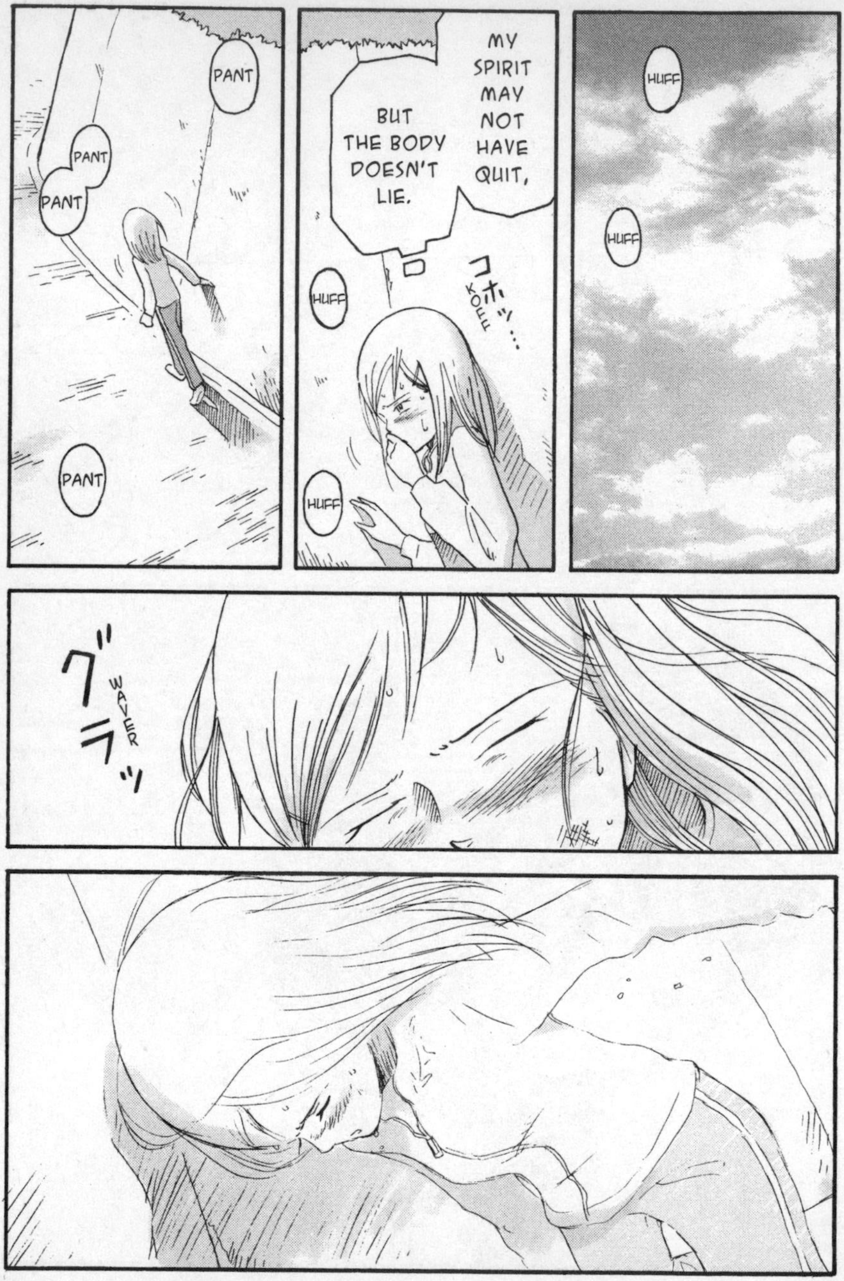
HUFF
HUFF
MY SPIRIT MAY NOT HAVE QUIT,
BUT THE BODY DOESN'T LIE.
コホッ…
KOFF
HUFF
HUFF
PANT
PANT
PANT
PANT
グラッ
WAVER

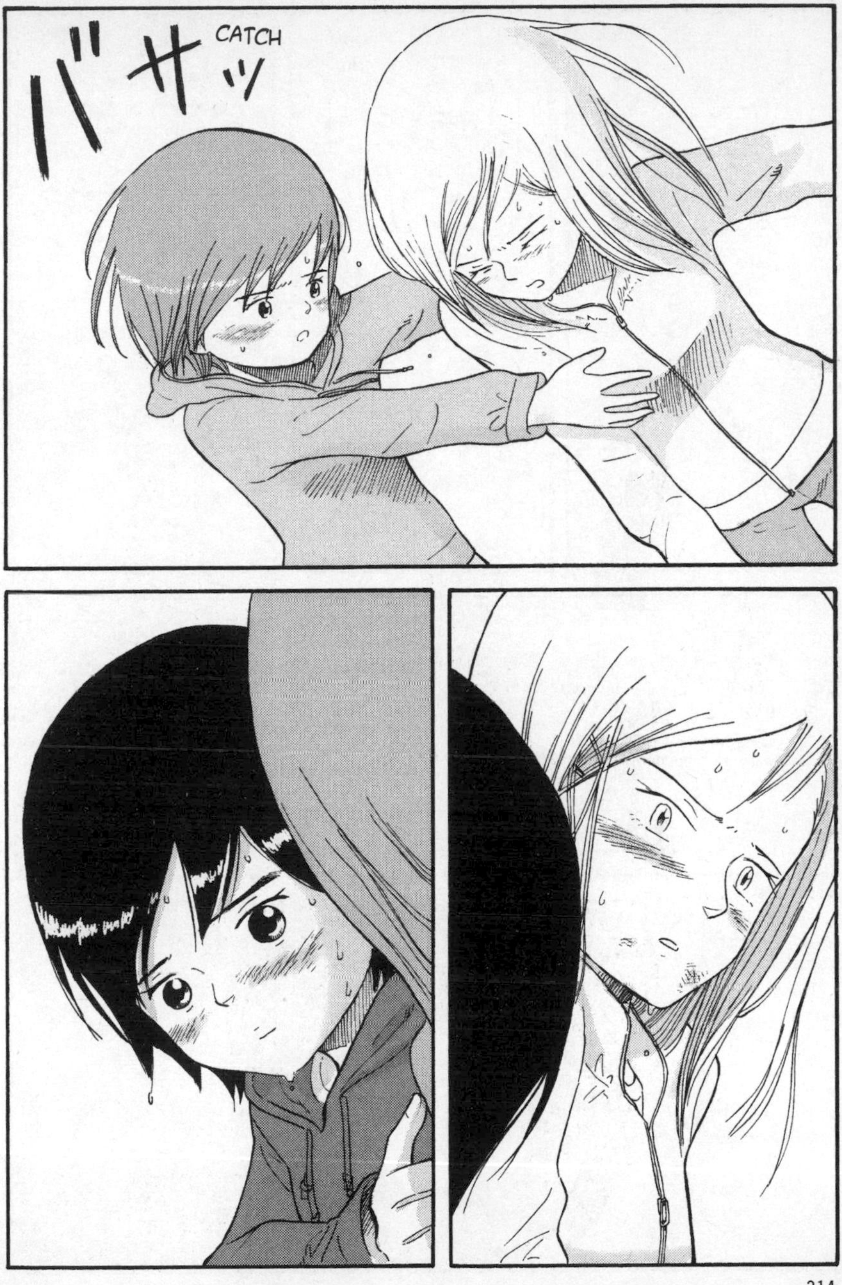
バサッ
CATCH

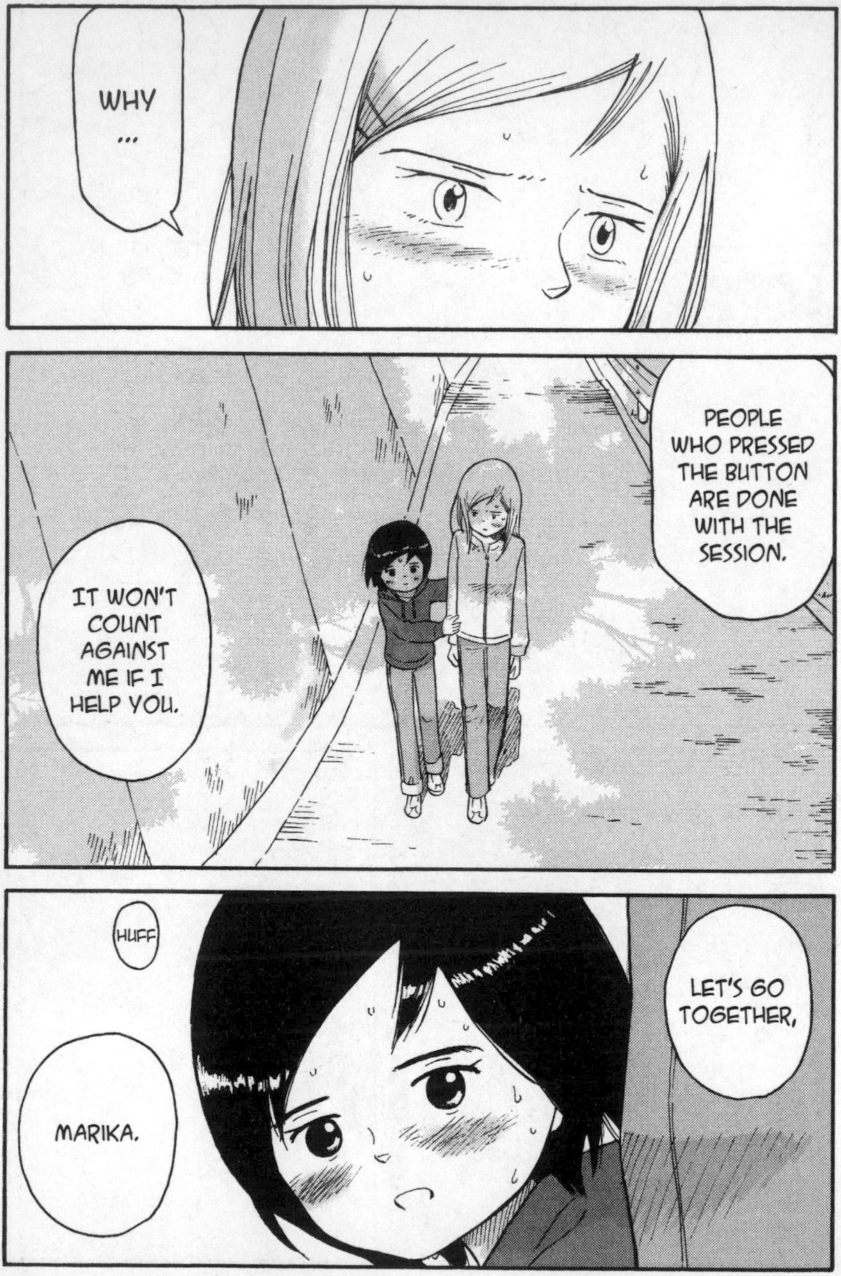
WHY ...
PEOPLE WHO PRESSED THE BUTTON ARE DONE WITH THE SESSION.
IT WON'T COUNT AGAINST ME IF I HELP YOU.
LET'S GO TOGETHER,
HUFF
MARIKA.

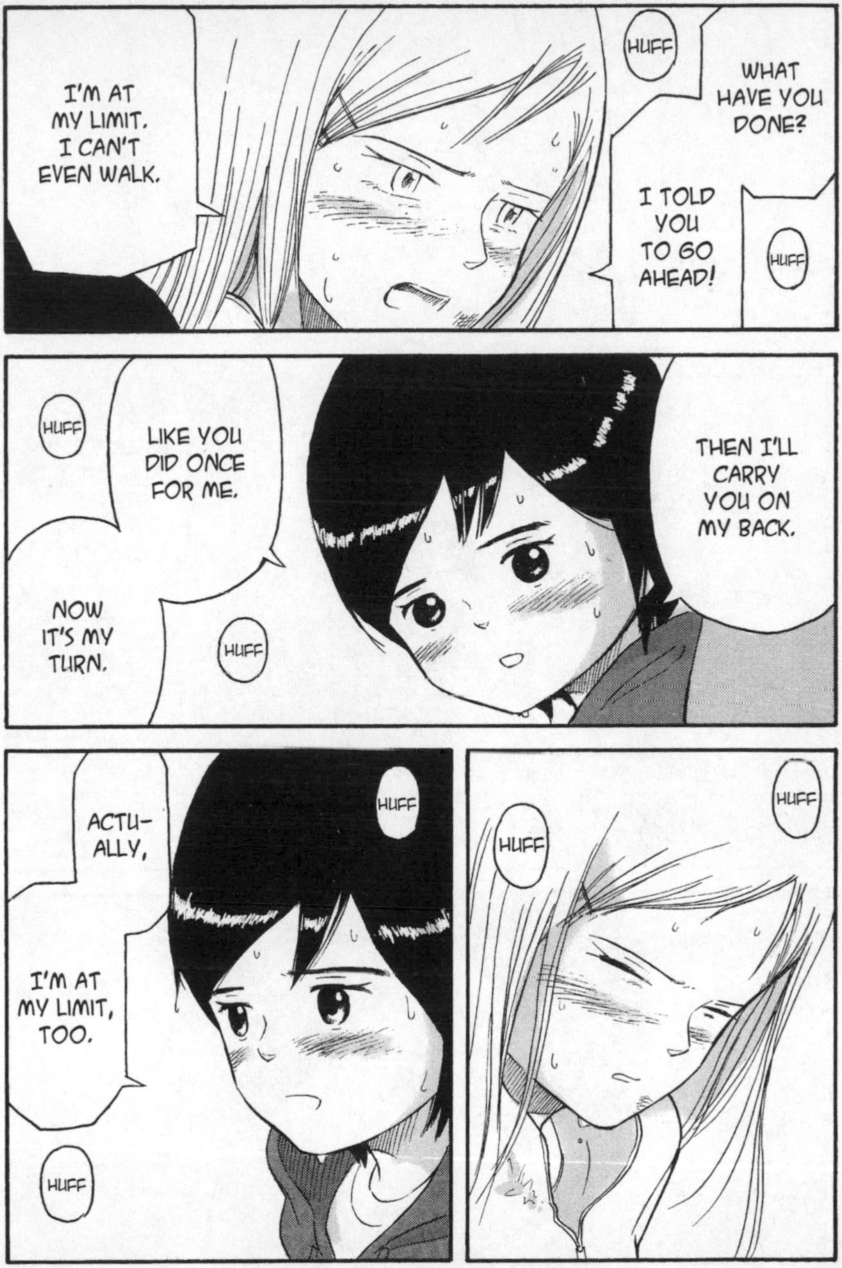
HUFF
WHAT HAVE YOU DONE?
I TOLD YOU TO GO AHEAD!
HUFF
I'M AT MY LIMIT. I CAN'T EVEN WALK.
THEN I'LL CARRY YOU ON MY BACK.
LIKE YOU DID ONCE FOR ME.
HUFF
HUFF
NOW IT'S MY TURN.
HUFF
HUFF
HUFF
ACTU- ALLY,
I'M AT MY LIMIT, TOO.
HUFF

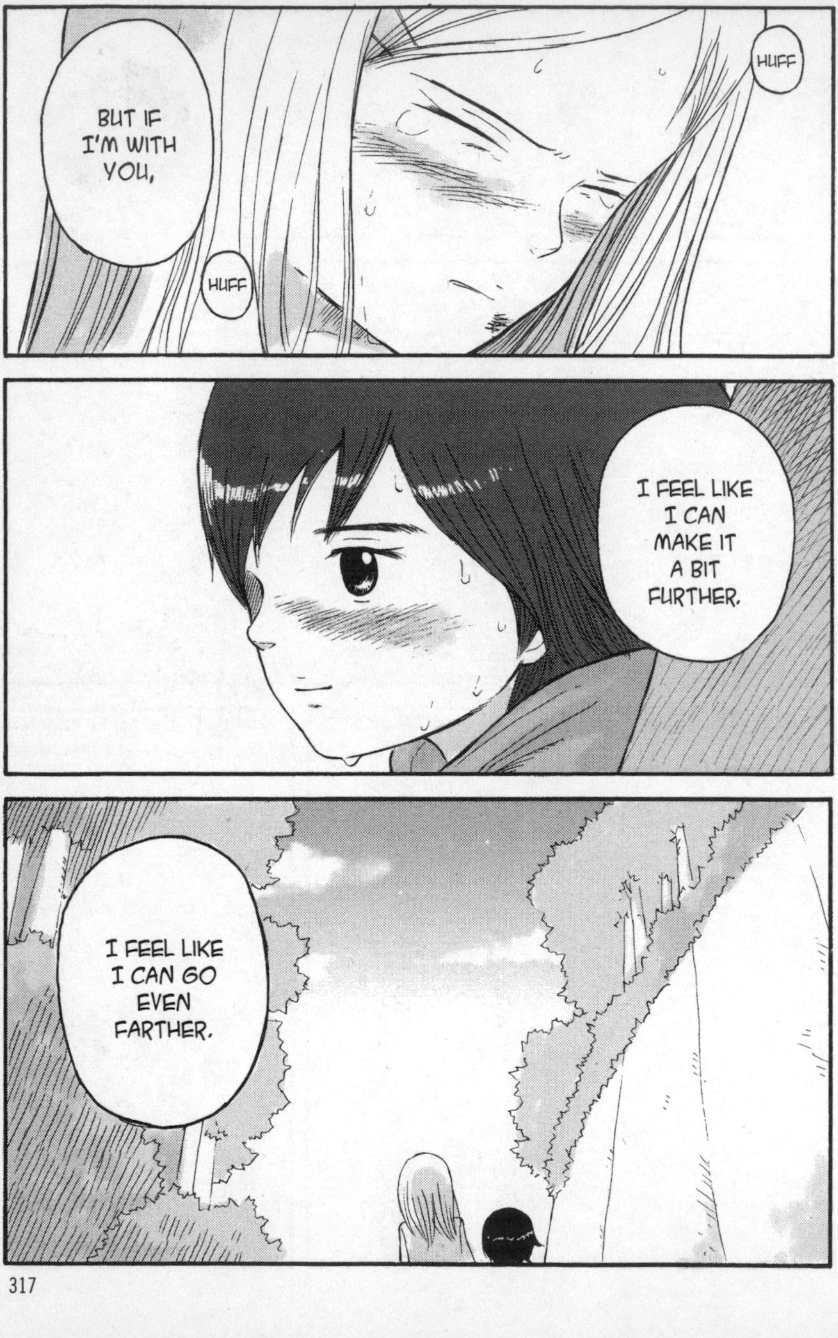
HUFF
BUT IF I'M WITH YOU,
HUFF
I FEEL LIKE I CAN MAKE IT A BIT FURTHER.
I FEEL LIKE I CAN GO EVEN FARTHER.

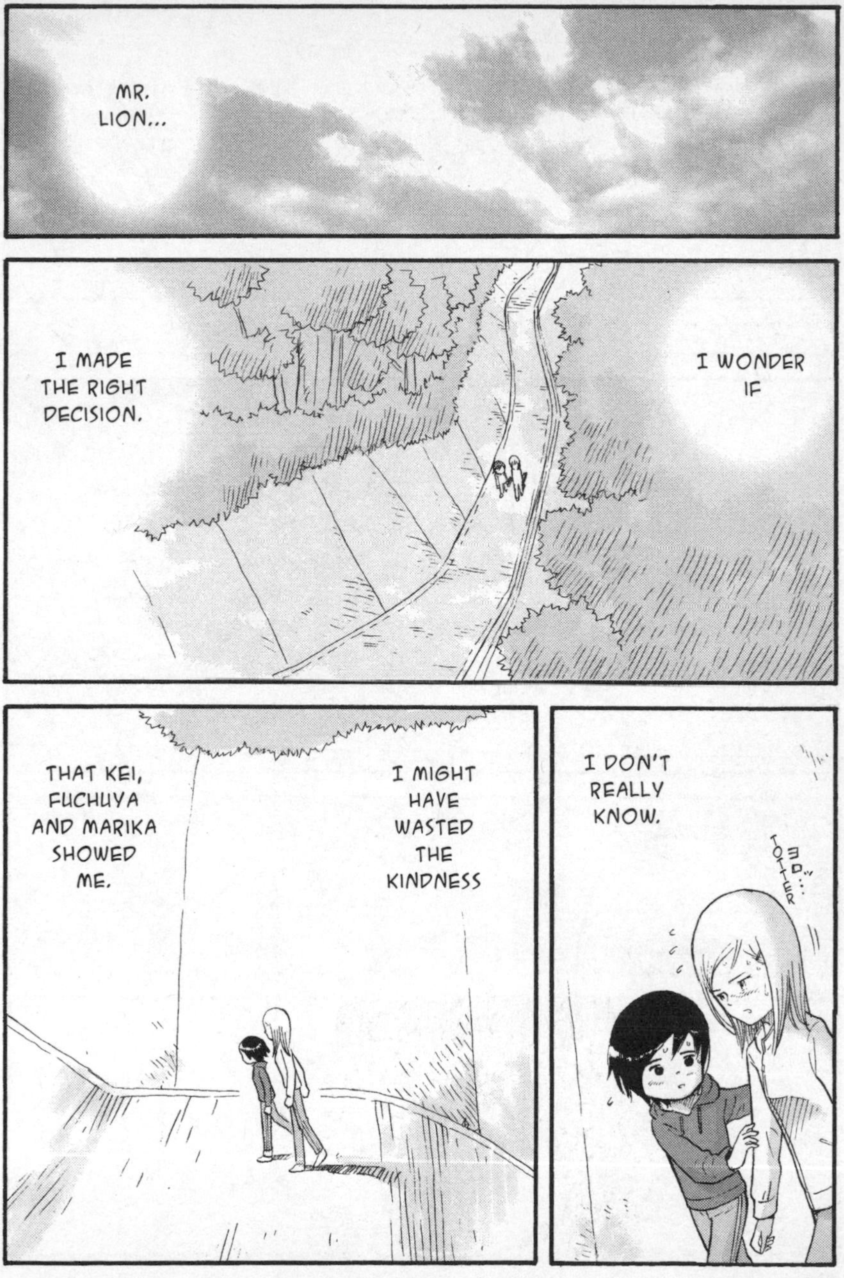
MR. LION...
I WONDER IF
I MADE THE RIGHT DECISION.
I DON'T REALLY KNOW.
TOTTER...
I MIGHT HAVE WASTED THE KINDNESS
THAT KEI, FUCHUYA AND MARIKA SHOWED ME.

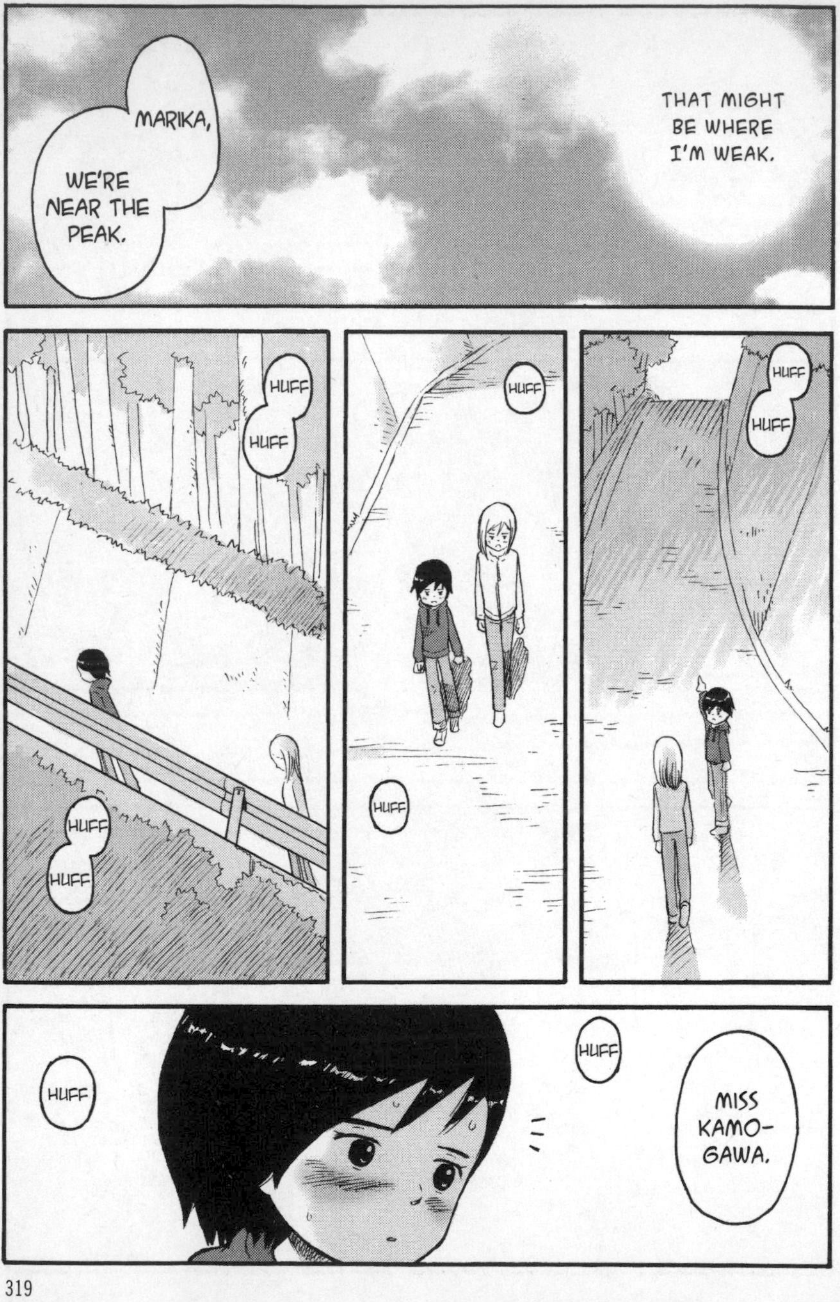
THAT MIGHT BE WHERE I'M WEAK.
MARIKA,
WE'RE NEAR THE PEAK.
HUFF
HUFF
HUFF
HUFF
HUFF
HUFF
HUFF
HUFF
MISS KAMO-GAWA.
HUFF
HUFF

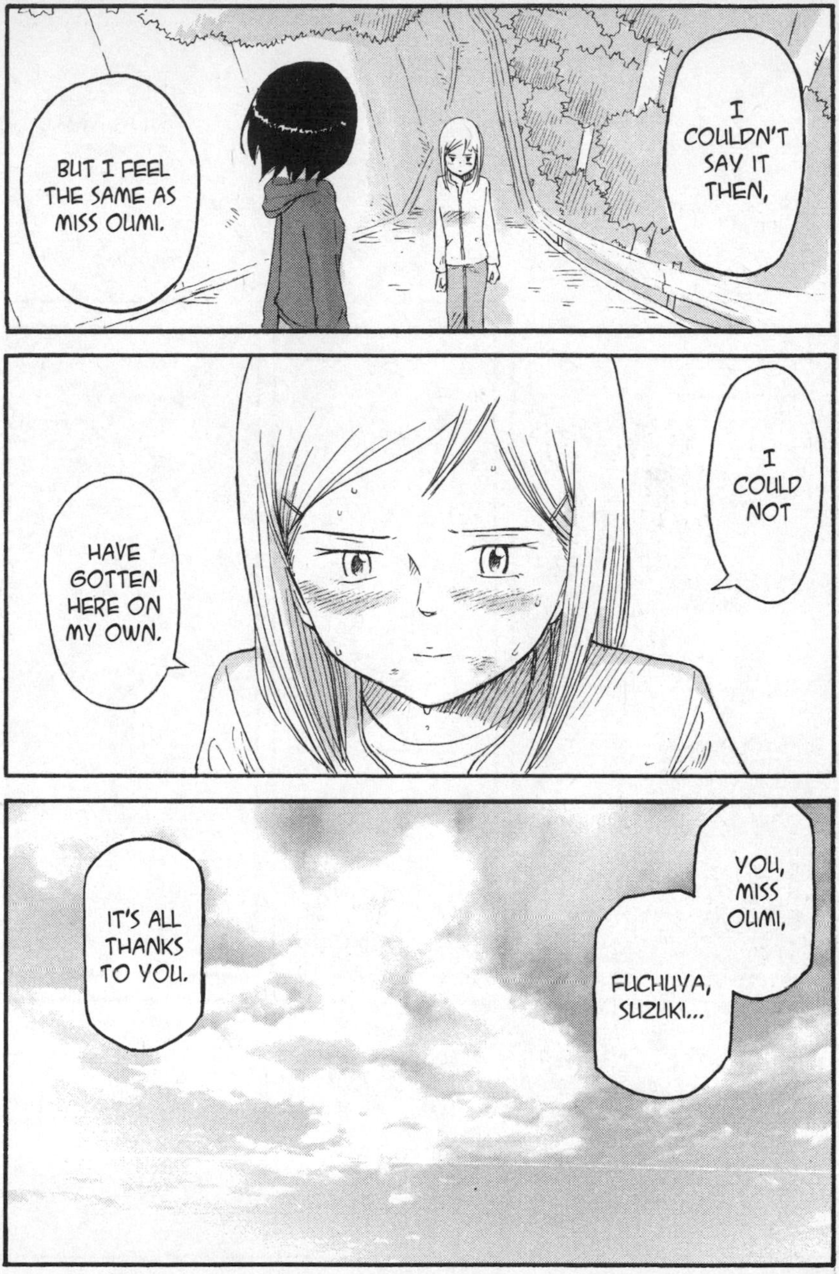
I COULDN'T SAY IT THEN,
BUT I FEEL THE SAME AS MISS OUMI.
I COULD NOT
HAVE GOTTEN HERE ON MY OWN.
YOU, MISS OUMI,
FUCHUYA, SUZUKI...
IT'S ALL THANKS TO YOU.

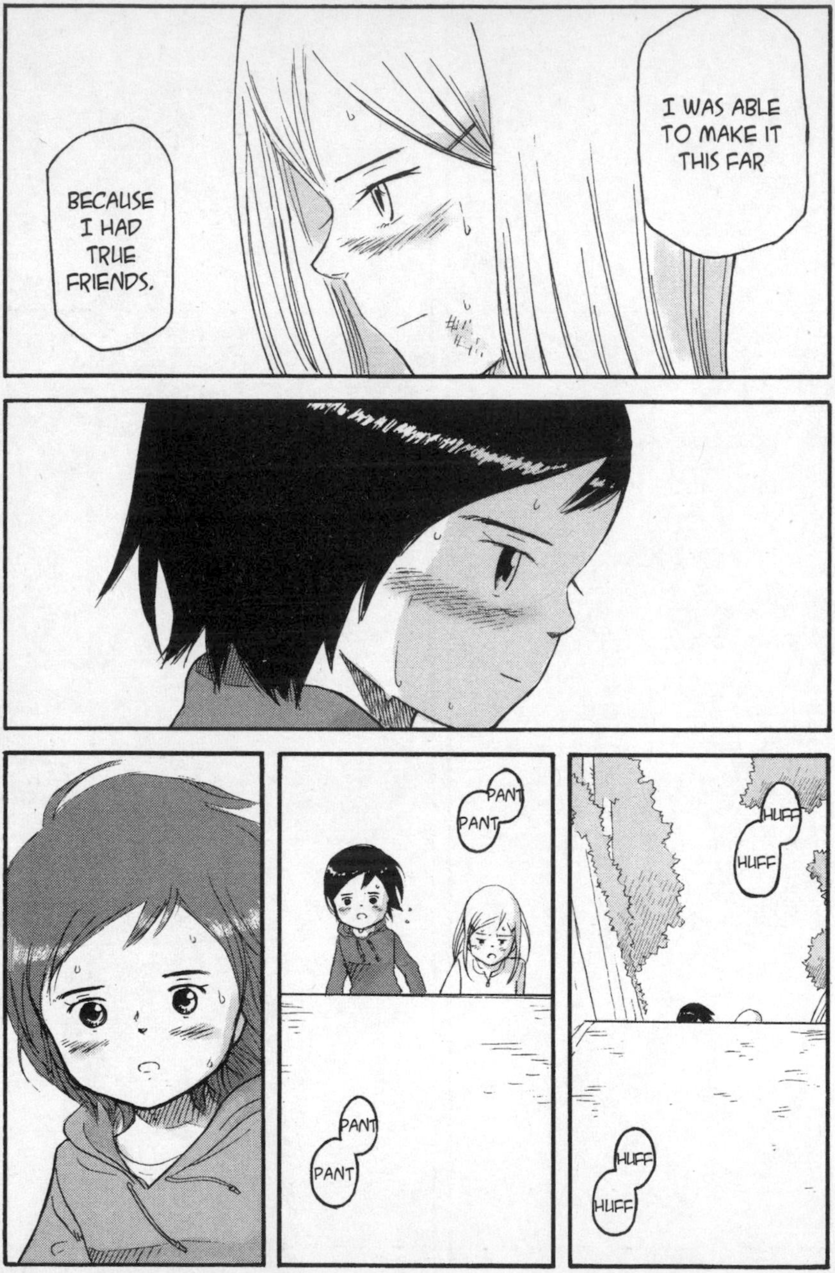

I WAS ABLE TO MAKE IT THIS FAR
BECAUSE I HAD TRUE FRIENDS.
HUFF
HUFF
HUFF
HUFF
PANT
PANT
PANT
PANT

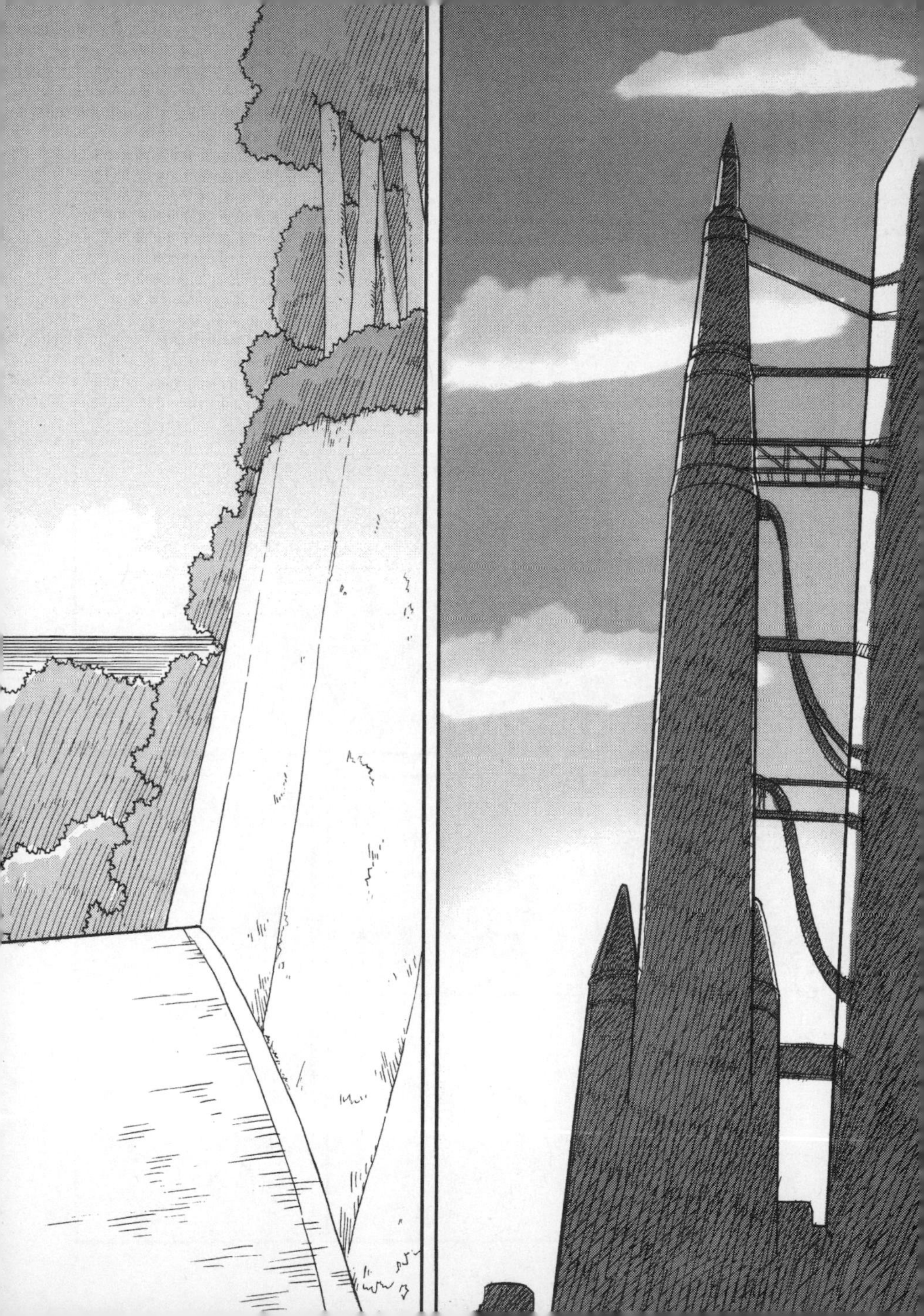

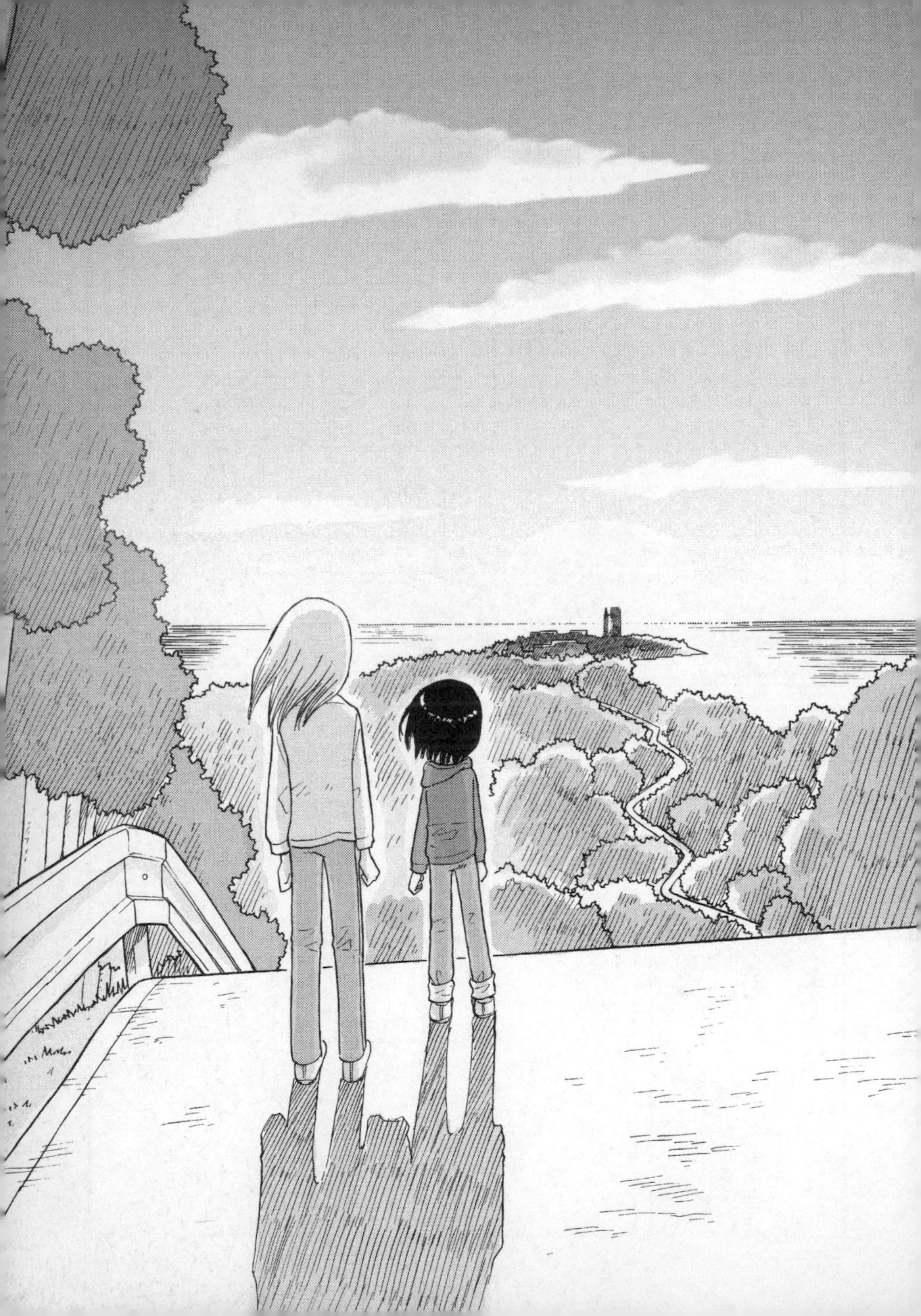

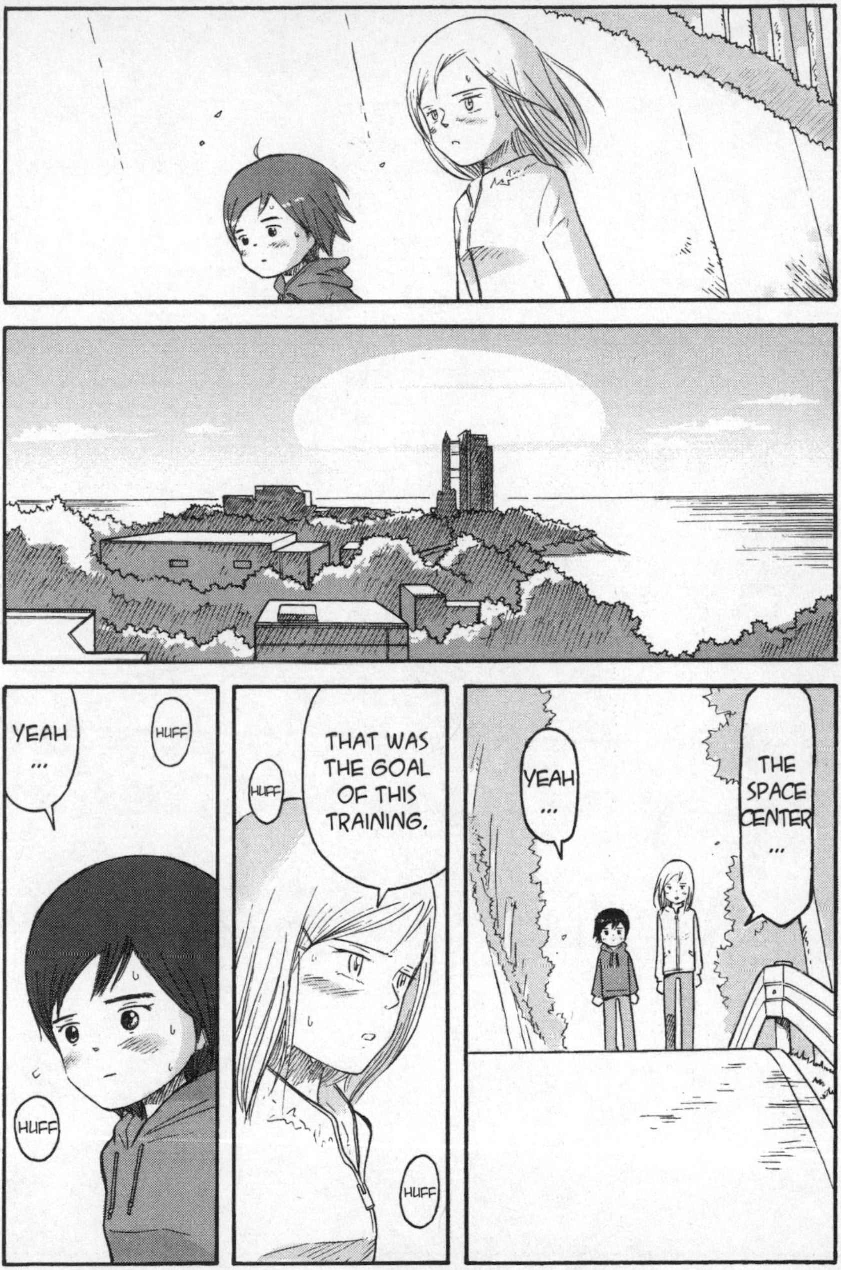
THE SPACE CENTER ...
YEAH ...
THAT WAS THE GOAL OF THIS TRAINING.
HUFF
HUFF
HUFF
YEAH ...
HUFF

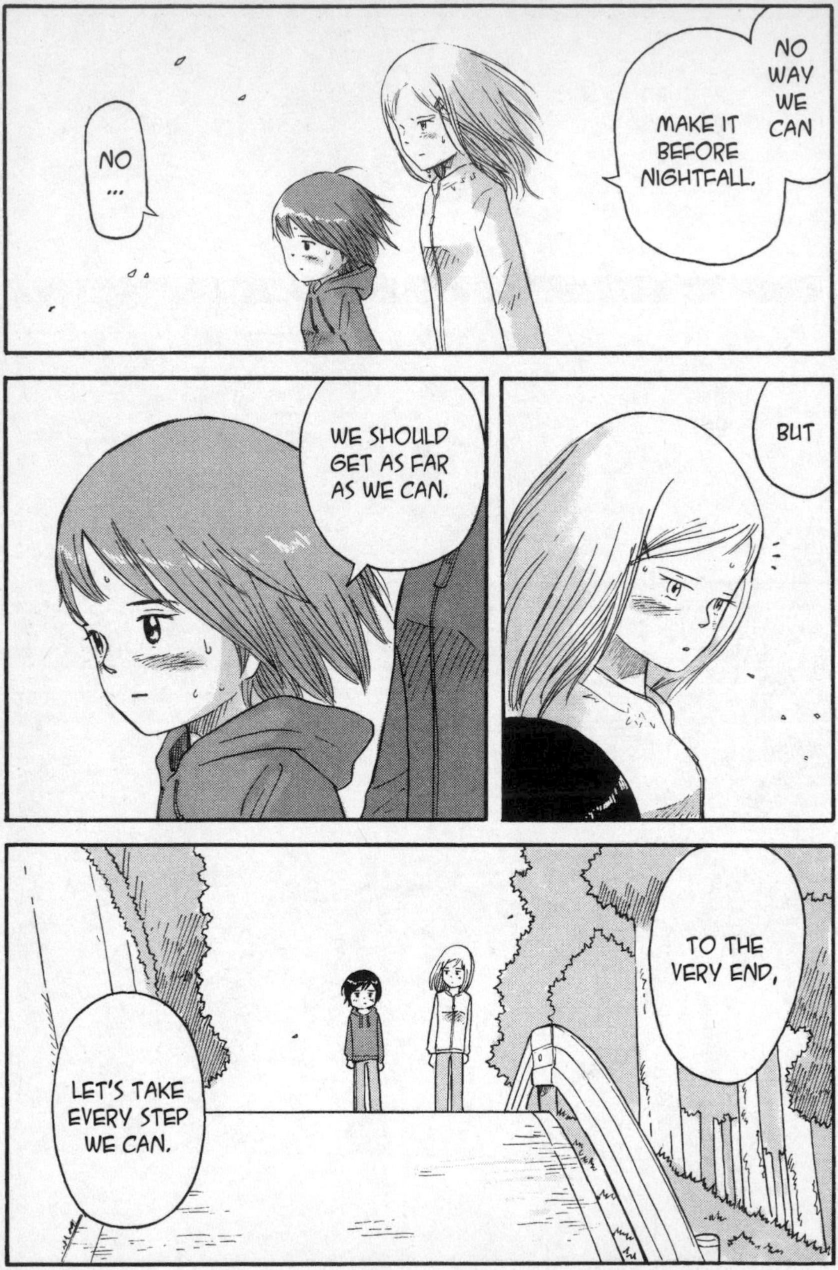
NO WAY WE CAN MAKE IT BEFORE NIGHTFALL.
NO ...
BUT
WE SHOULD GET AS FAR AS WE CAN.
TO THE VERY END,
LET'S TAKE EVERY STEP WE CAN.

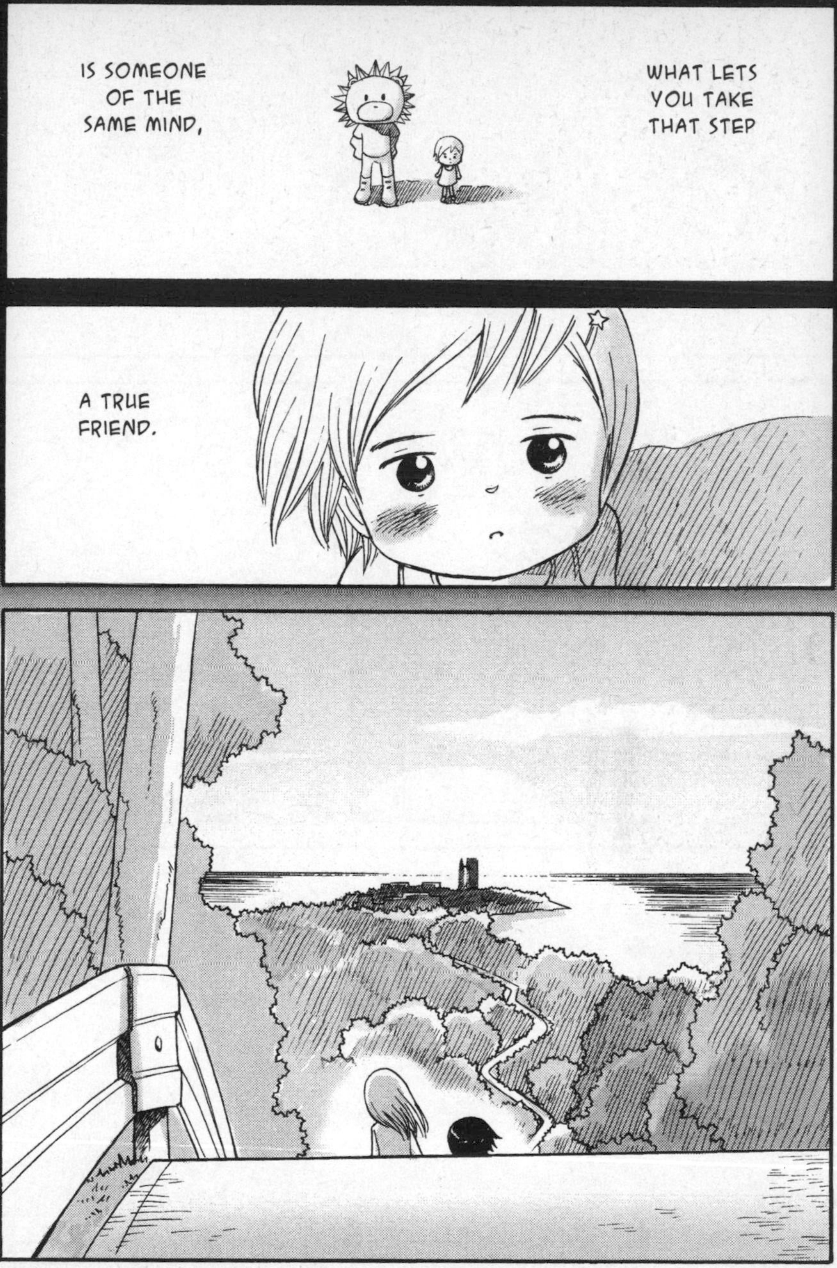
WHAT LETS YOU TAKE THAT STEP
IS SOMEONE OF THE SAME MIND,
A TRUE FRIEND.

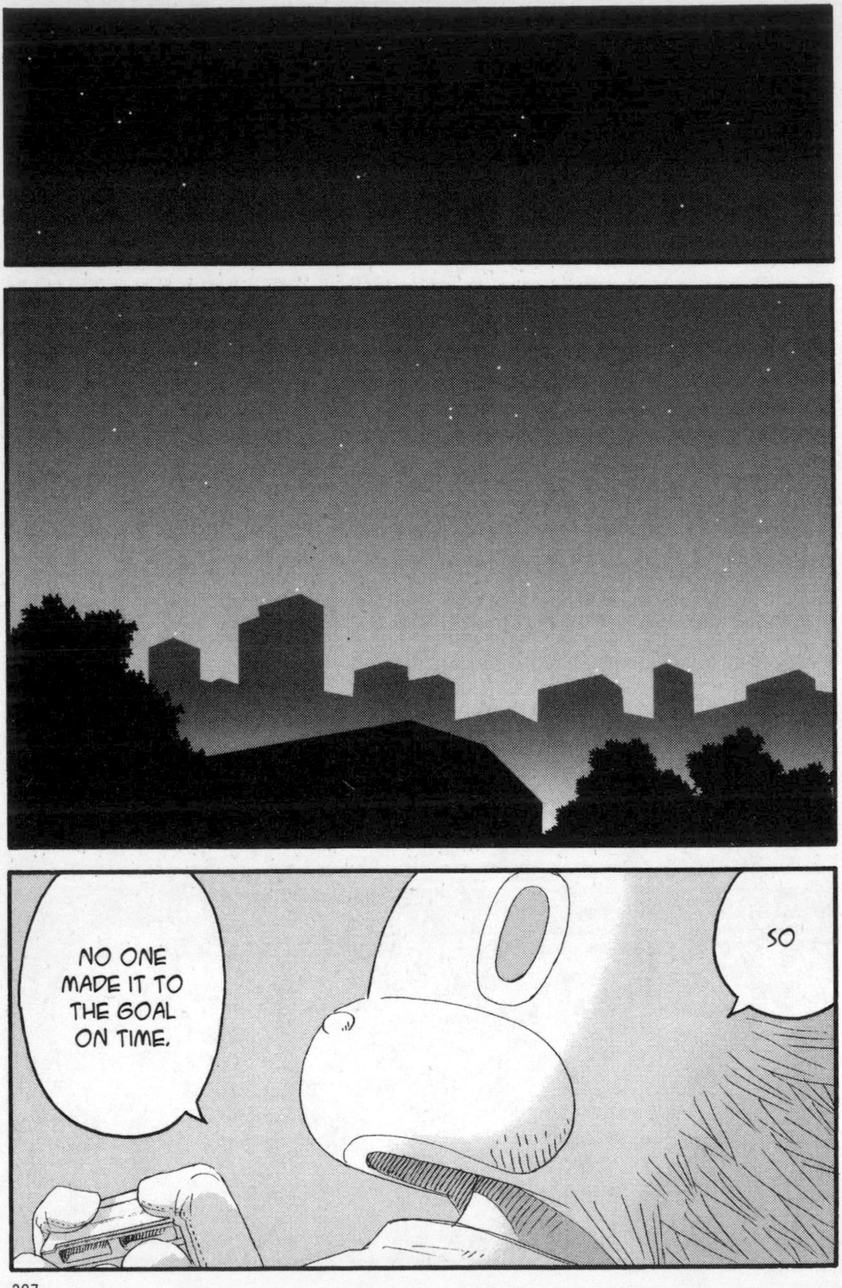
SO
NO ONE MADE IT TO THE GOAL ON TIME.

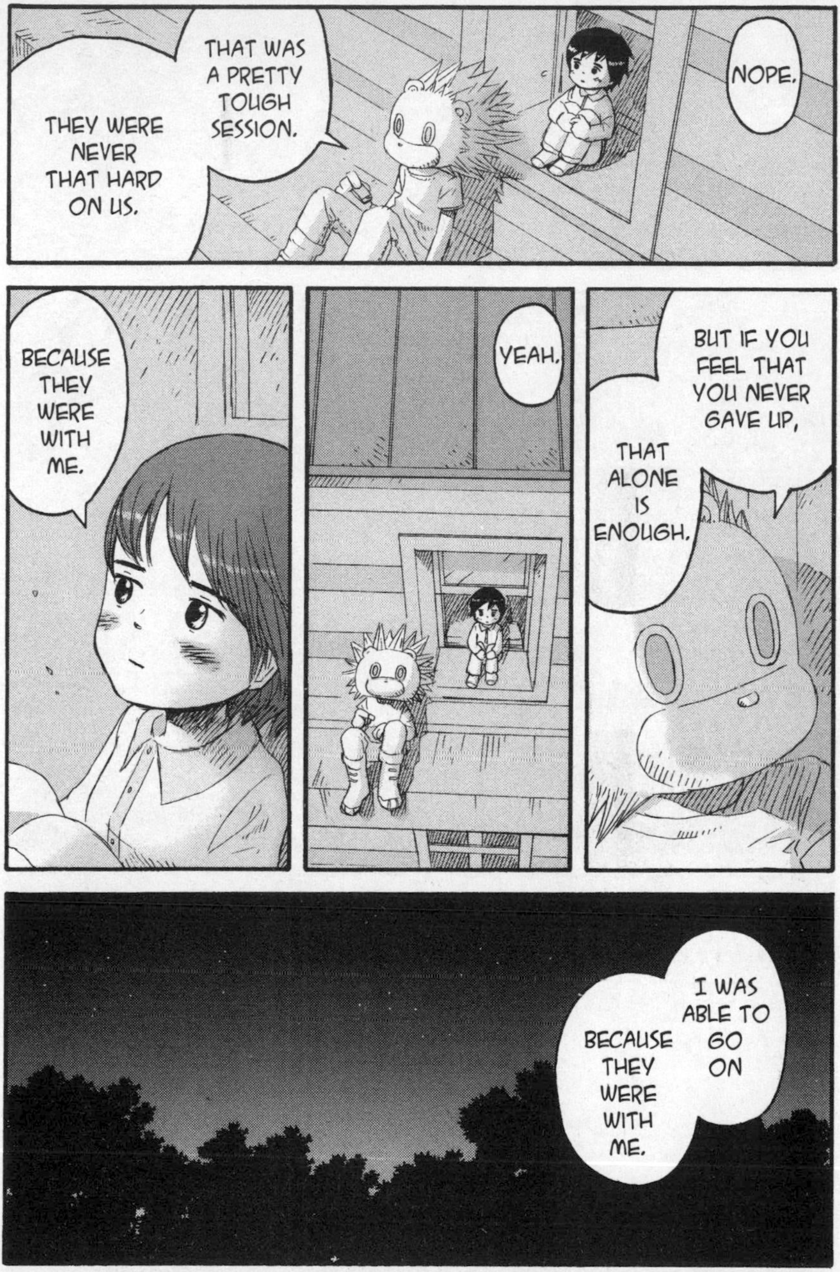
NOPE.
THAT WAS A PRETTY TOUGH SESSION.
THEY WERE NEVER THAT HARD ON US.
BUT IF YOU FEEL THAT YOU NEVER GAVE UP,
THAT ALONE IS ENOUGH.
YEAH.
BECAUSE THEY WERE WITH ME.
I WAS ABLE TO GO ON
BECAUSE THEY WERE WITH ME.

MISSION:75

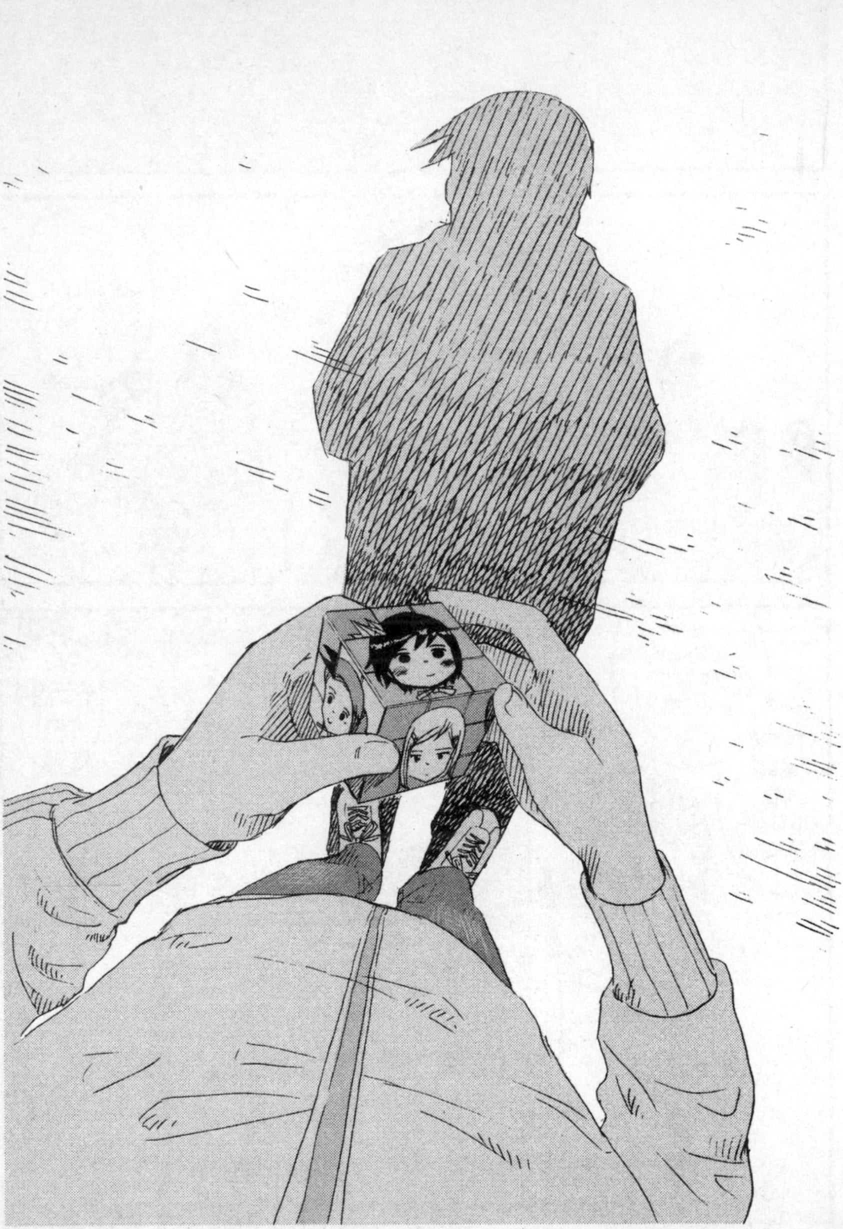

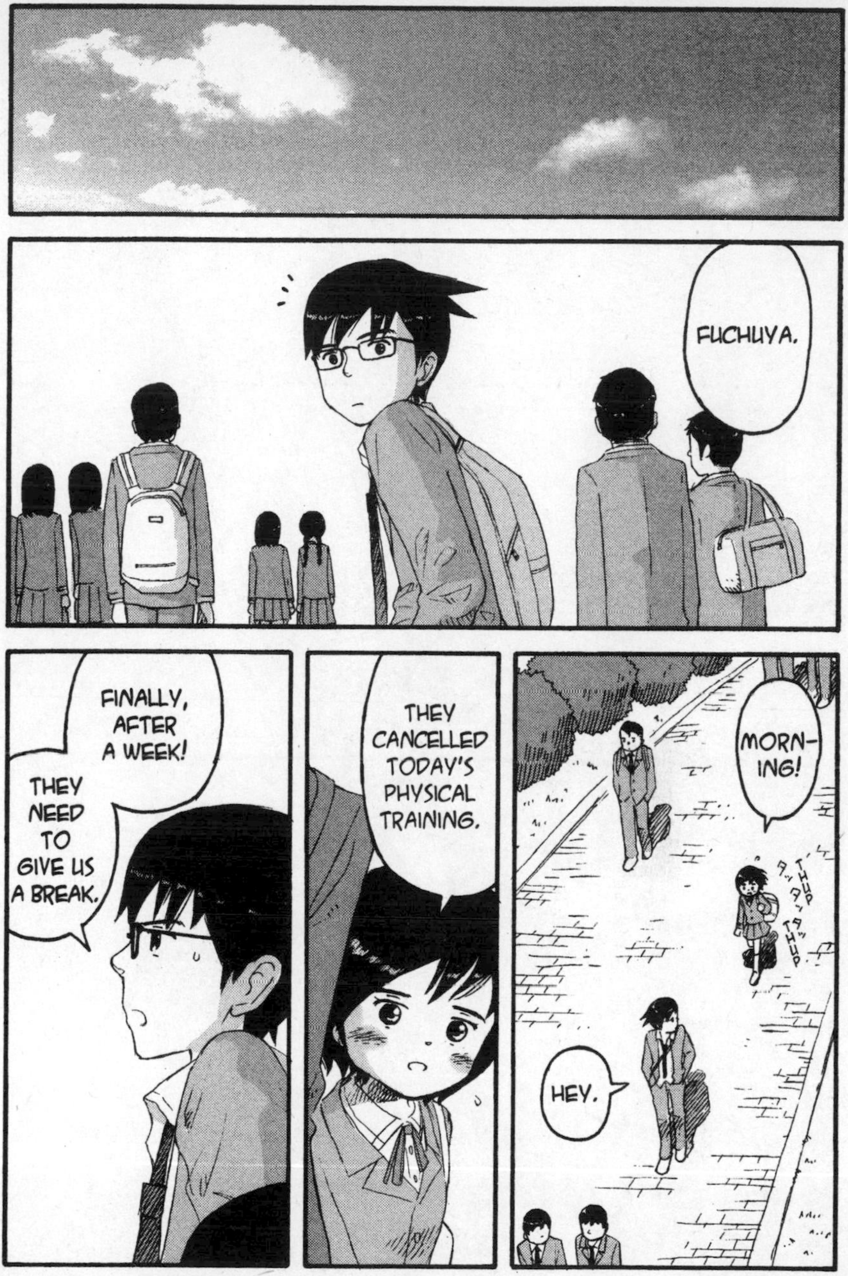
FUCHUYA.
MORN-
ING!
THUP
THUP
HEY.
THEY CANCELLED TODAY'S PHYSICAL TRAINING.
FINALLY, AFTER A WEEK!
THEY NEED TO GIVE US A BREAK.

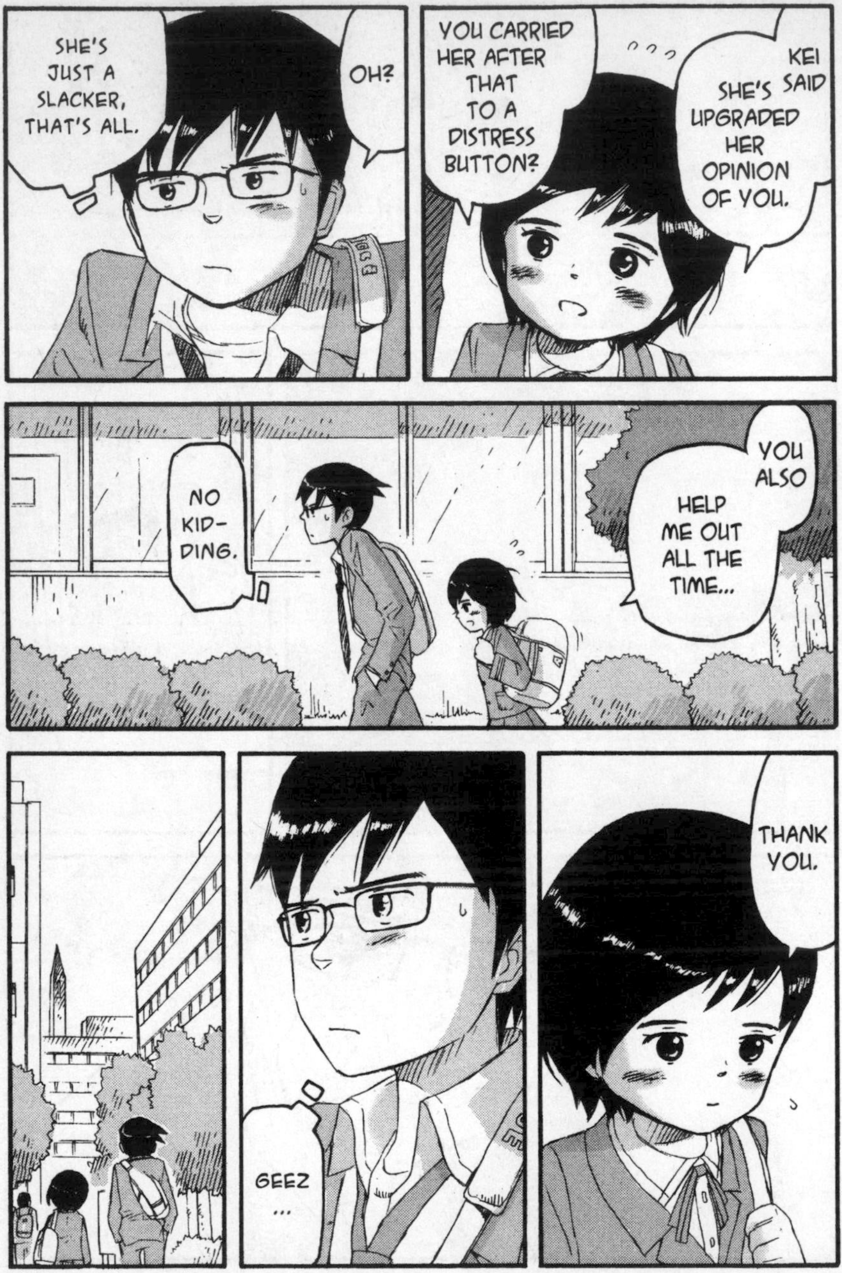
KEI SAID SHE'S UPGRADED HER OPINION OF YOU.
YOU CARRIED HER AFTER THAT TO A DISTRESS BUTTON?
OH?
SHE'S JUST A SLACKER, THAT'S ALL.
YOU ALSO HELP ME OUT ALL THE TIME...
NO KID-DING.
THANK YOU.
GEEZ ...

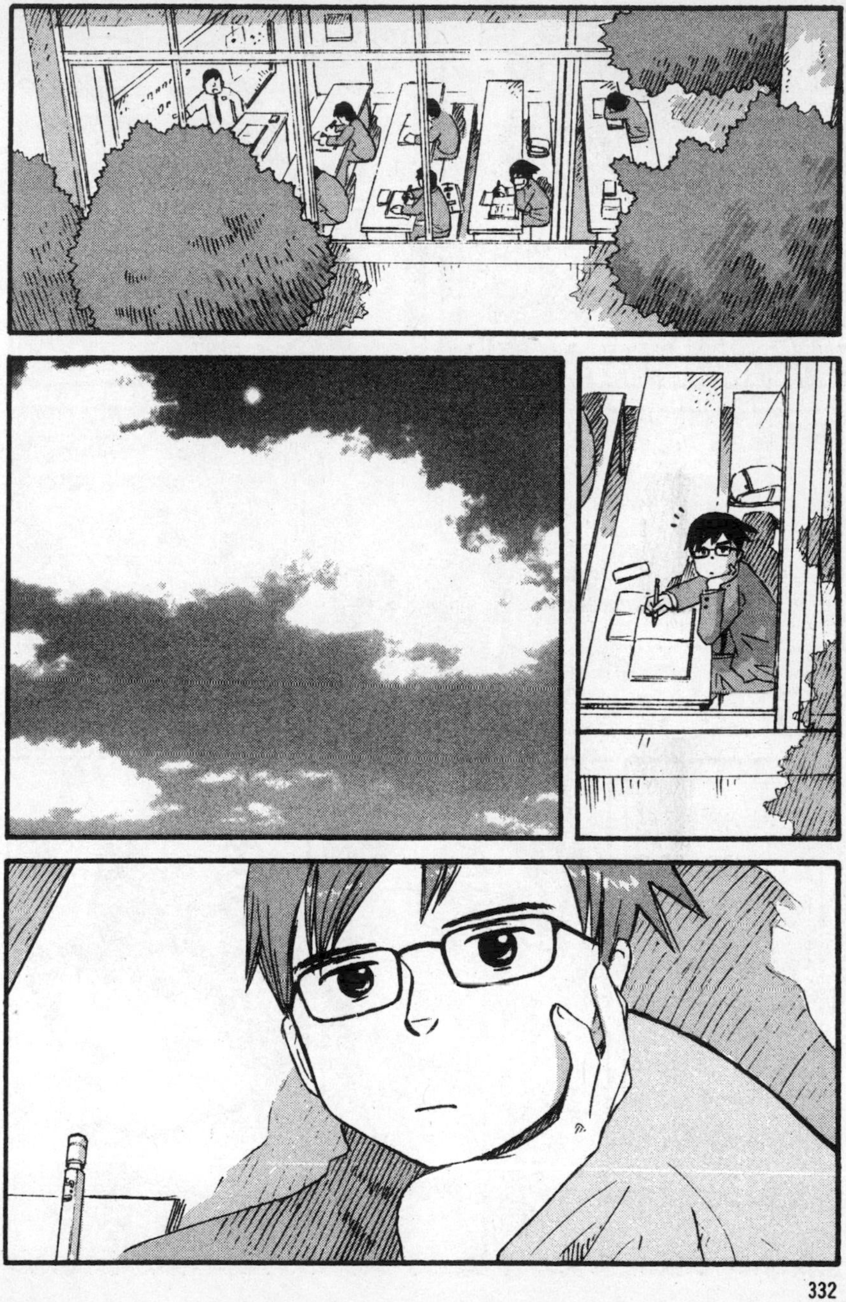

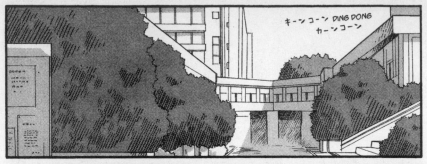

キーンコーン DING DONG
カーンコーン

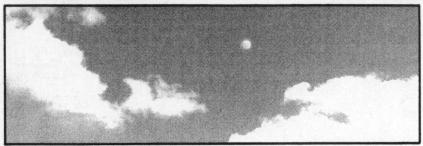

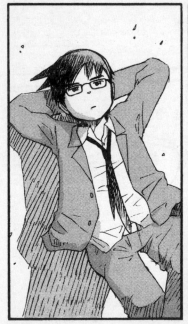

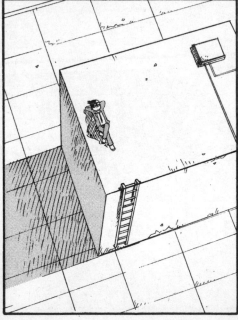

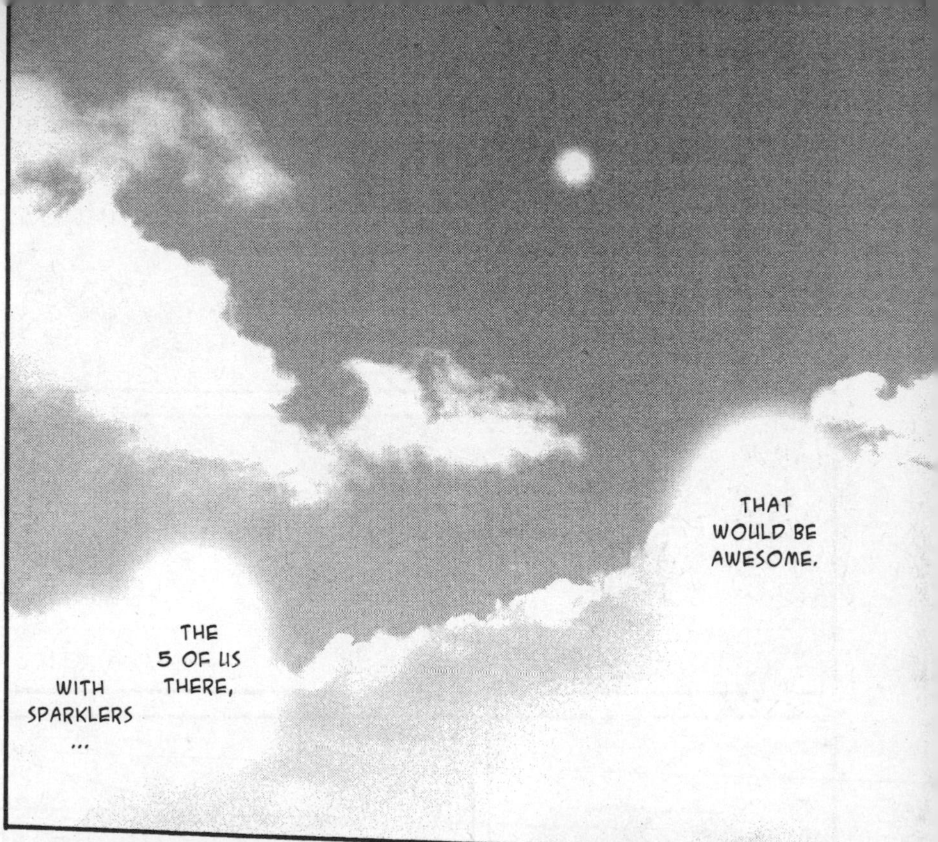
THAT WOULD BE AWESOME.
THE 5 OF US THERE,
WITH SPARKLERS ...

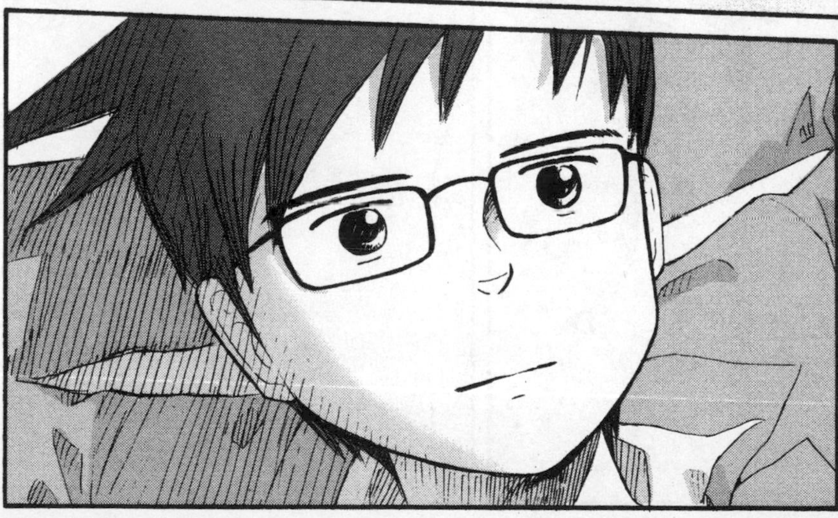

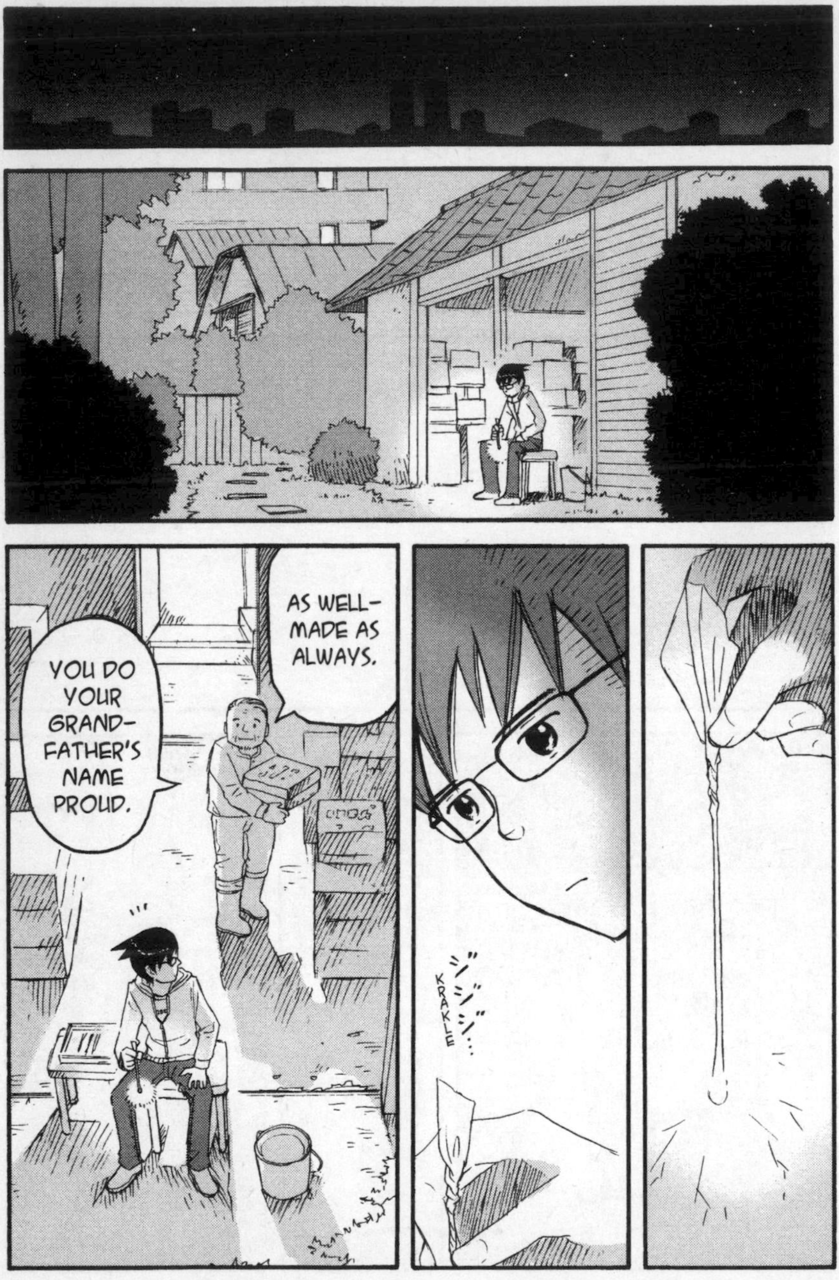
KRAKLE
AS WELL-MADE AS ALWAYS.
YOU DO YOUR GRANDFATHER'S NAME PROUD.

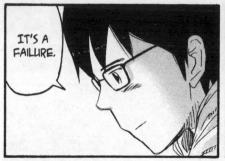

IT'S A FAILURE.

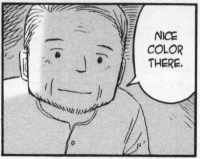

NICE COLOR THERE.

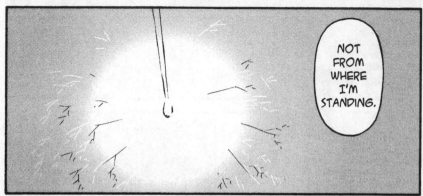

NOT FROM WHERE I'M STANDING.

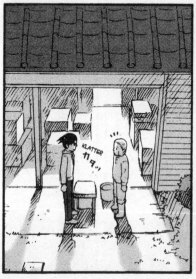

KLATTER カタッ

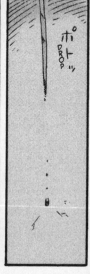

ポトッ
DROP
ポトッ

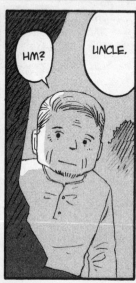

HM?

UNCLE.

336

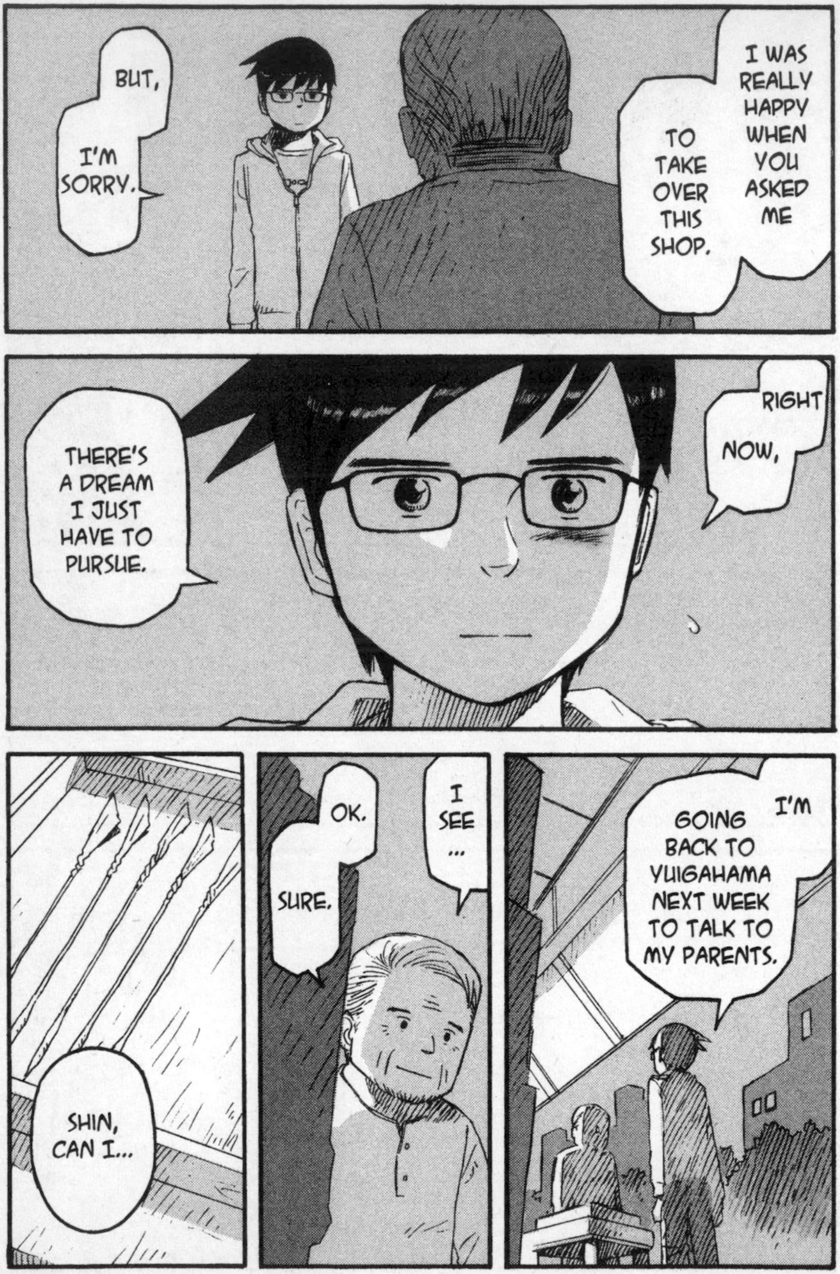
I WAS REALLY HAPPY WHEN YOU ASKED ME
TO TAKE OVER THIS SHOP.
BUT,
I'M SORRY.
RIGHT NOW,
THERE'S A DREAM I JUST HAVE TO PURSUE.
I'M GOING BACK TO YUIGAHAMA NEXT WEEK TO TALK TO MY PARENTS.
I SEE ...
OK.
SURE.
SHIN, CAN I...

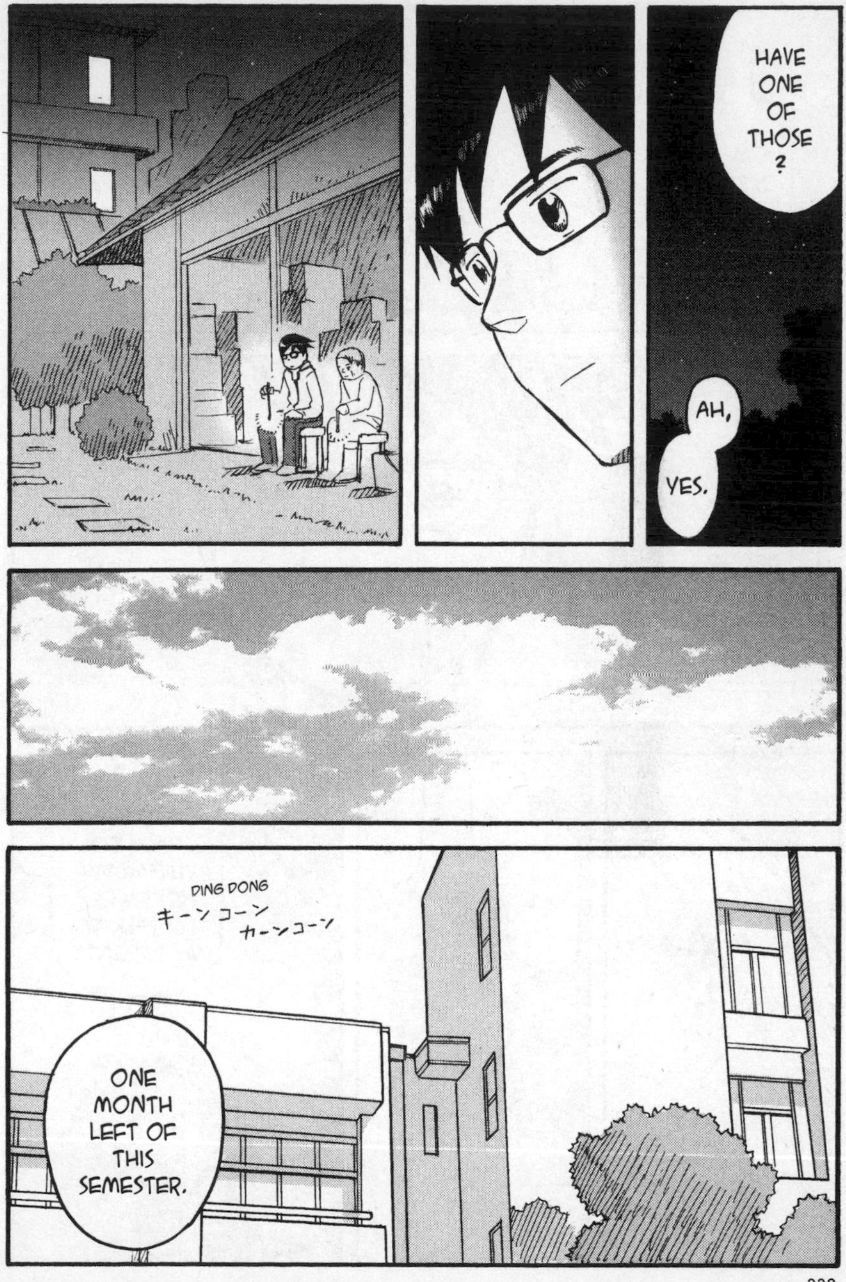
HAVE ONE OF THOSE?
AH,
YES.
DING DONG
キーンコーン
カーンコーン
ONE MONTH LEFT OF THIS SEMESTER.

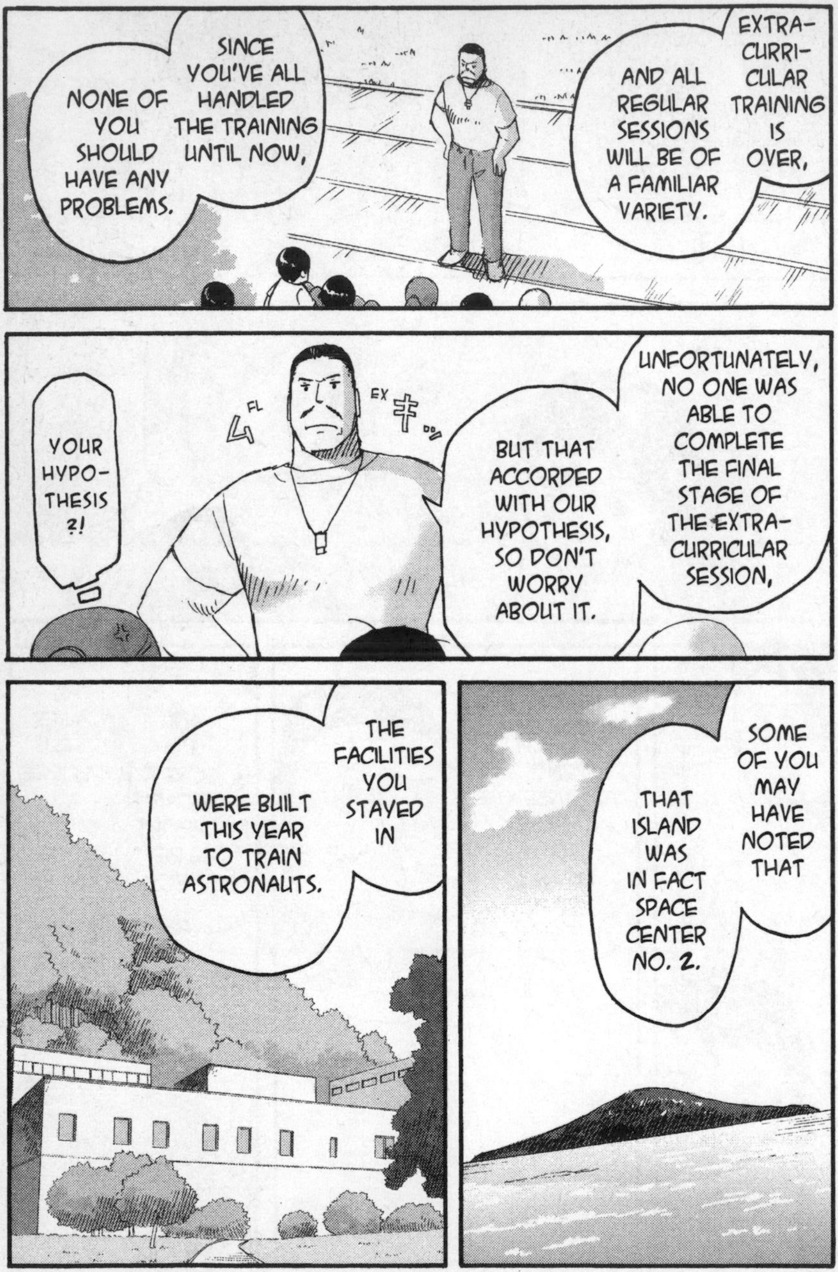
EXTRA-CURRICULAR TRAINING IS OVER,
AND ALL REGULAR SESSIONS WILL BE OF A FAMILIAR VARIETY.
SINCE YOU'VE ALL HANDLED THE TRAINING UNTIL NOW,
NONE OF YOU SHOULD HAVE ANY PROBLEMS.
UNFORTUNATELY, NO ONE WAS ABLE TO COMPLETE THE FINAL STAGE OF THE EXTRA-CURRICULAR SESSION,
BUT THAT ACCORDED WITH OUR HYPOTHESIS, SO DON'T WORRY ABOUT IT.
EX キ
FL ム
YOUR HYPOTHESIS?!
SOME OF YOU MAY HAVE NOTED THAT
THAT ISLAND WAS IN FACT SPACE CENTER NO. 2.
THE FACILITIES YOU STAYED IN
WERE BUILT THIS YEAR TO TRAIN ASTRONAUTS.

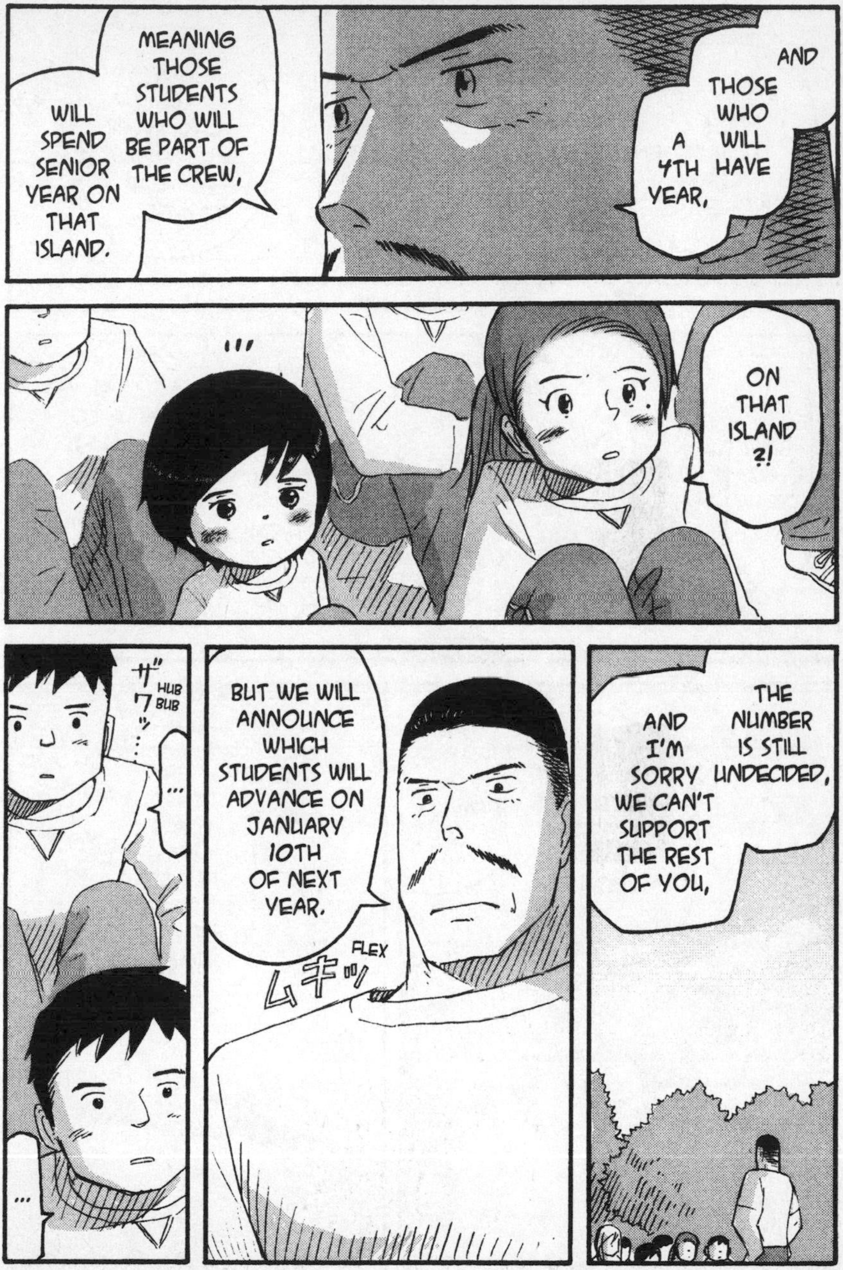
AND THOSE WHO WILL HAVE A 4TH YEAR,
MEANING THOSE STUDENTS WHO WILL BE PART OF THE CREW,
WILL SPEND SENIOR YEAR ON THAT ISLAND.
ON THAT ISLAND ?!
THE NUMBER IS STILL UNDECIDED,
AND I'M SORRY WE CAN'T SUPPORT THE REST OF YOU,
BUT WE WILL ANNOUNCE WHICH STUDENTS WILL ADVANCE ON JANUARY 10TH OF NEXT YEAR.
ムキッ
FLEX
ザワッ
HUB BUB
...
...

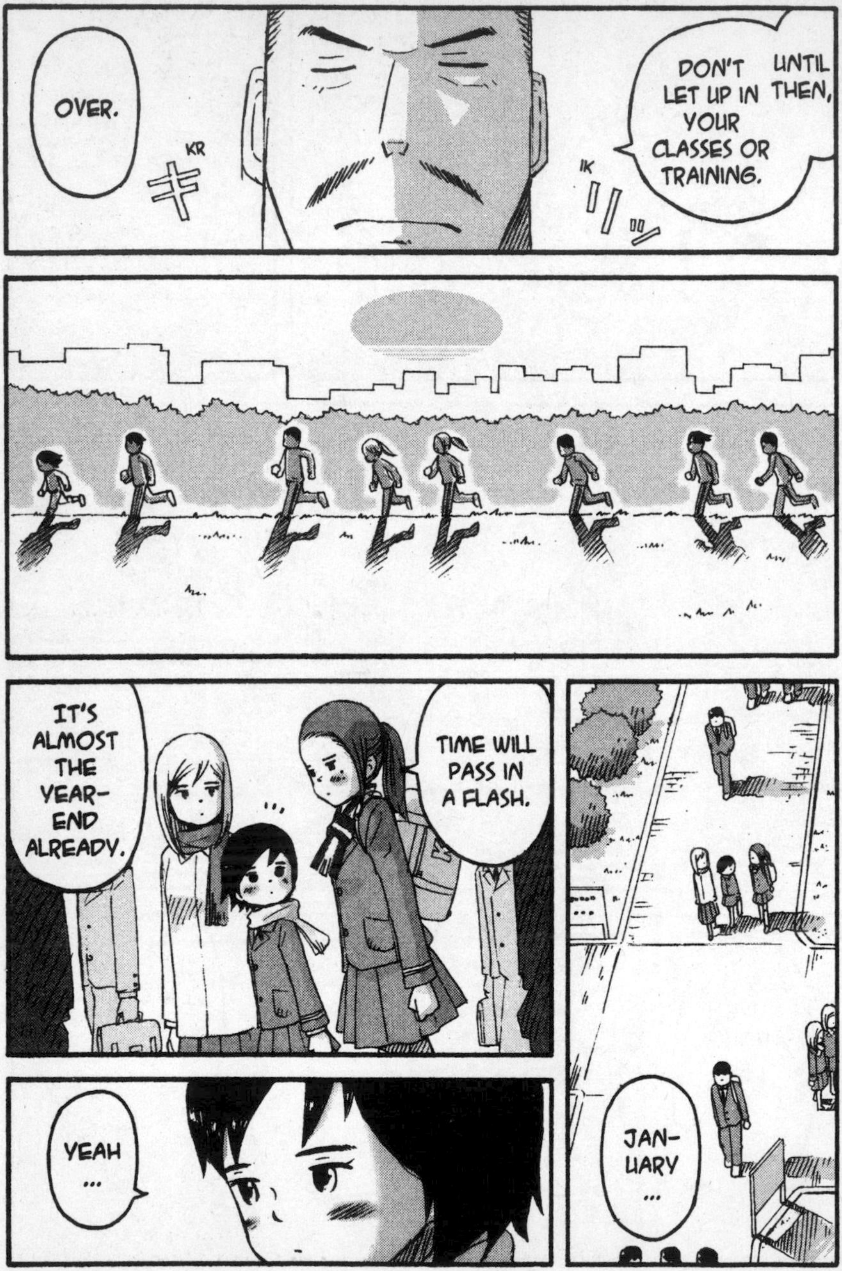

UNTIL THEN, DON'T LET UP IN YOUR CLASSES OR TRAINING.
IK
KR
OVER.
JAN-UARY ...
TIME WILL PASS IN A FLASH.
IT'S ALMOST THE YEAR-END ALREADY.
YEAH ...

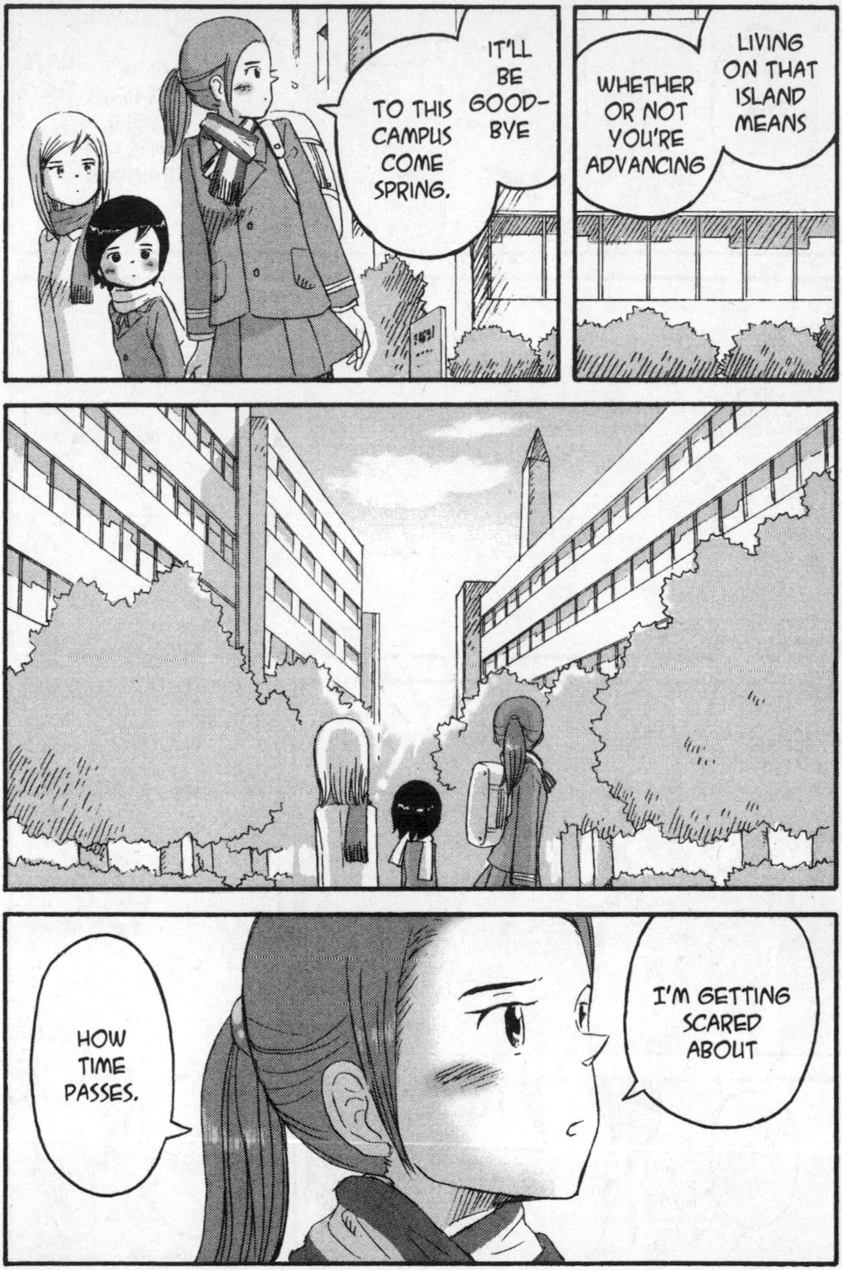
LIVING ON THAT ISLAND MEANS
WHETHER OR NOT YOU'RE ADVANCING
IT'LL BE GOOD-BYE
TO THIS CAMPUS COME SPRING.
I'M GETTING SCARED ABOUT
HOW TIME PASSES.

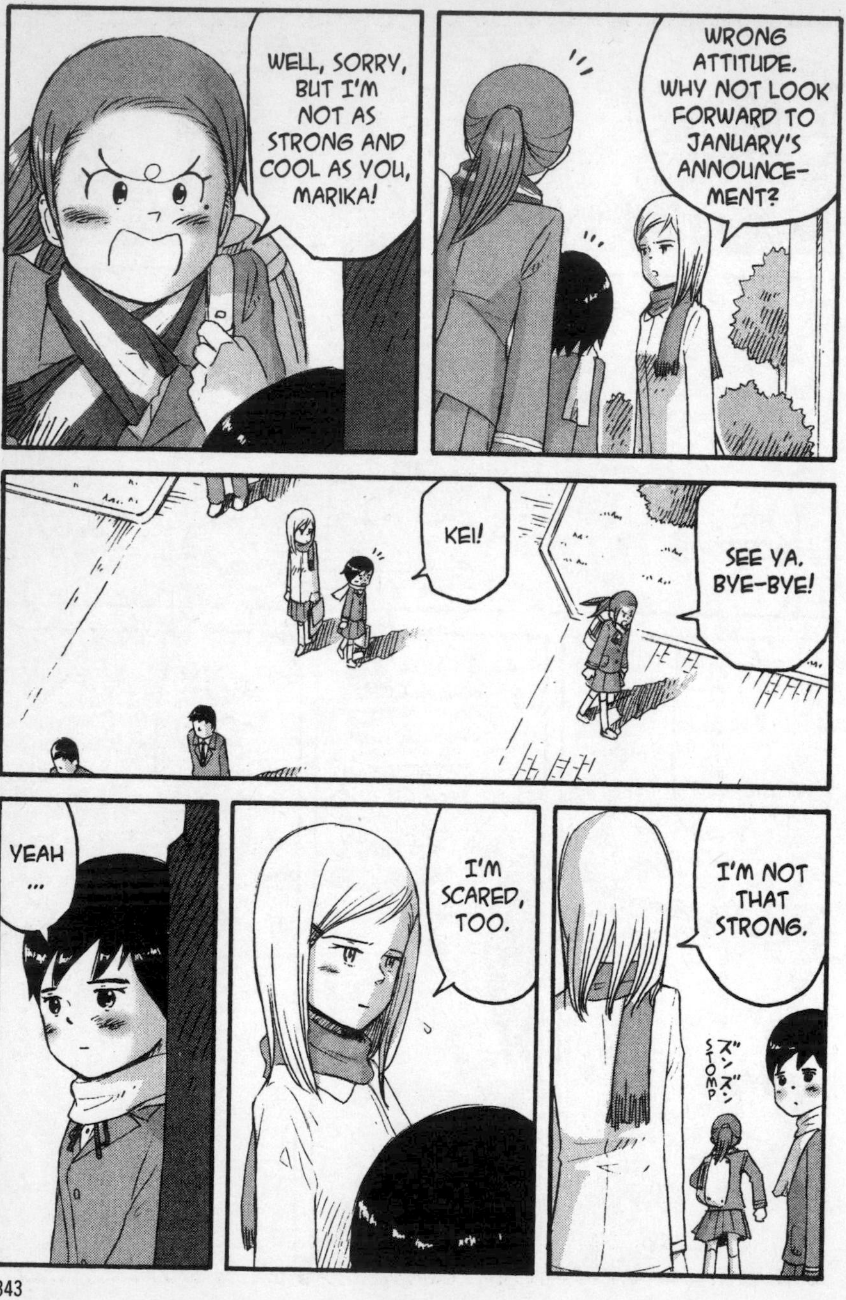
WRONG ATTITUDE. WHY NOT LOOK FORWARD TO JANUARY'S ANNOUNCEMENT?
WELL, SORRY, BUT I'M NOT AS STRONG AND COOL AS YOU, MARIKA!
SEE YA. BYE-BYE!
KEI!
I'M NOT THAT STRONG.
ズンズン
STOMP
I'M SCARED, TOO.
YEAH ...

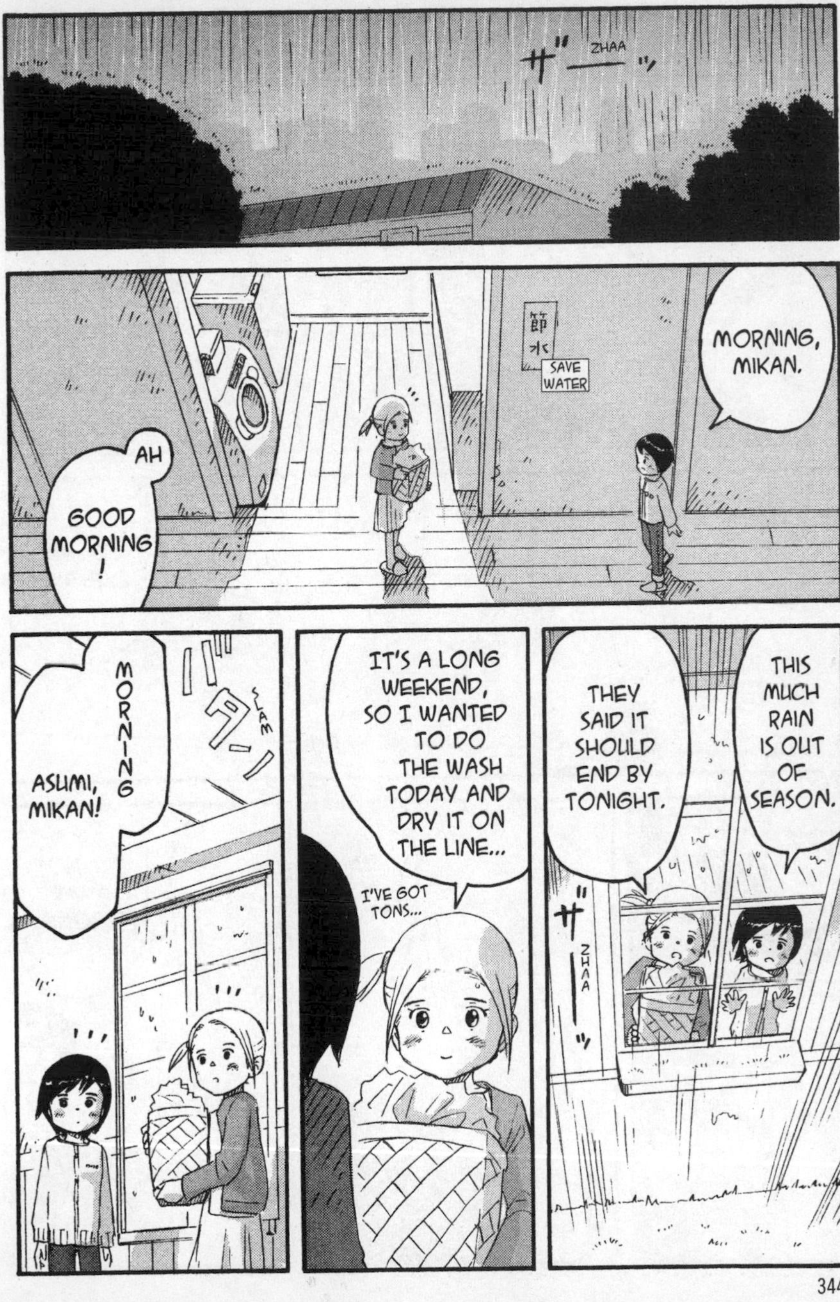
ZHAA
節水
SAVE WATER
MORNING, MIKAN.
AH
GOOD MORNING!
THIS MUCH RAIN IS OUT OF SEASON.
THEY SAID IT SHOULD END BY TONIGHT.
ZHAA
IT'S A LONG WEEKEND, SO I WANTED TO DO THE WASH TODAY AND DRY IT ON THE LINE...
I'VE GOT TONS...
SLAM
MORNING
ASUMI, MIKAN!

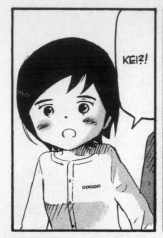

HUFF
HUFF
GAH,
I'M TOTALLY SOAKED.
KEI?!
WHAT'RE YOU DOING HERE SO EARLY,
AND WITH THOSE BAGS?
I'VE DECIDED!
I WILL COM-MUTE TO SCHOOL FROM HERE
UNTIL THE ANNOUNCE-MENT IN JANUARY!

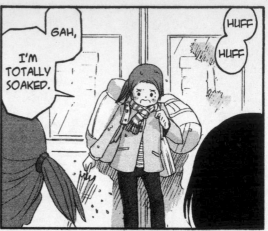

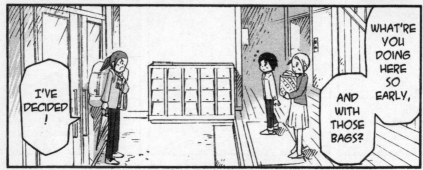

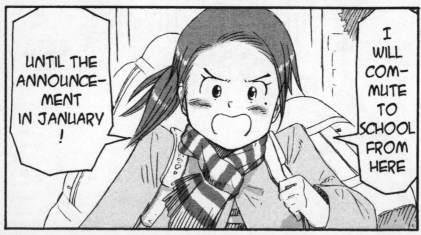

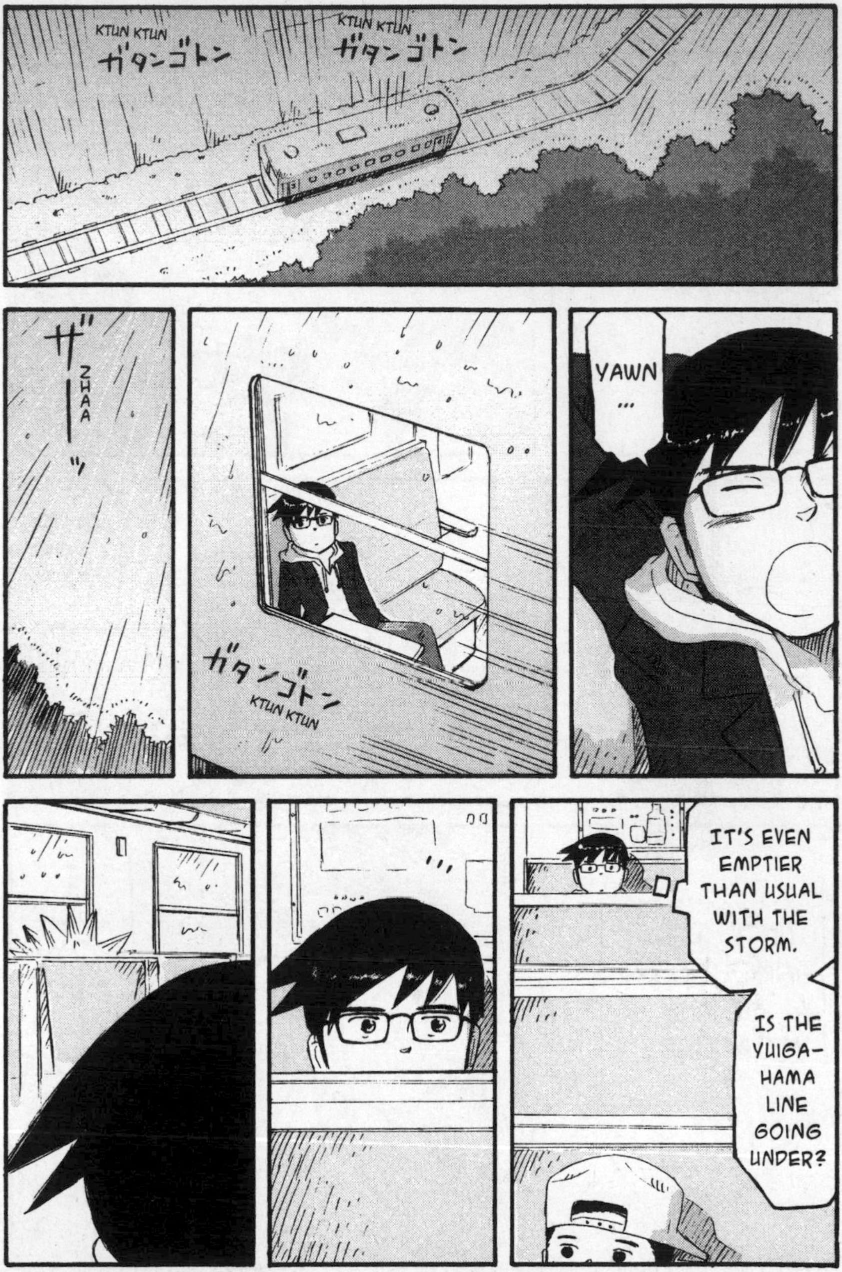
KTUN KTUN
ガタンゴトン
KTUN KTUN
ガタンゴトン
YAWN ...
ガタンゴトン
KTUN KTUN
ザーッ
ZHAA
IT'S EVEN EMPTIER THAN USUAL WITH THE STORM.
IS THE YUIGA-HAMA LINE GOING UNDER?

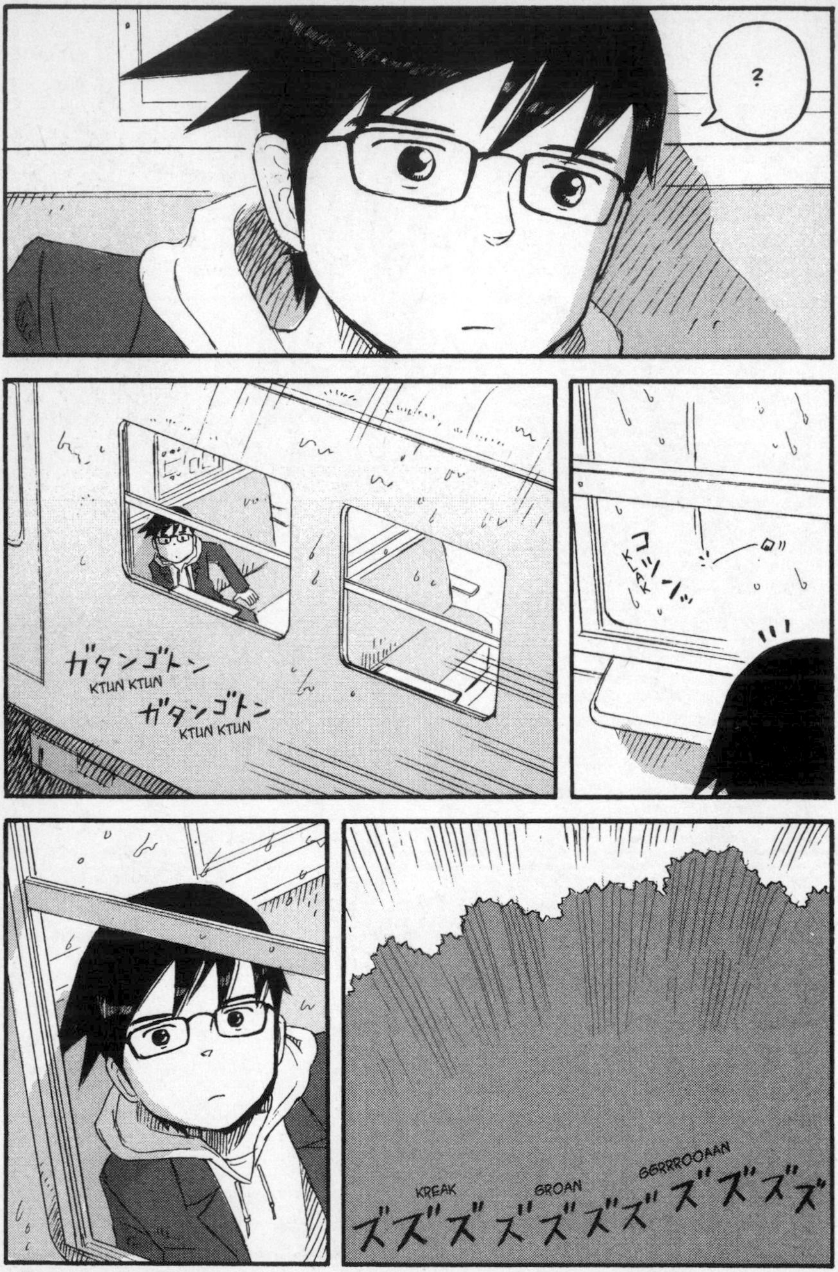
?
コツーン
KLAK
ガタンゴトン
KTUN KTUN
ガタンゴトン
KTUN KTUN
KREAK
GROAN
GRRRROOAAN
ズズズズズズズズズズ

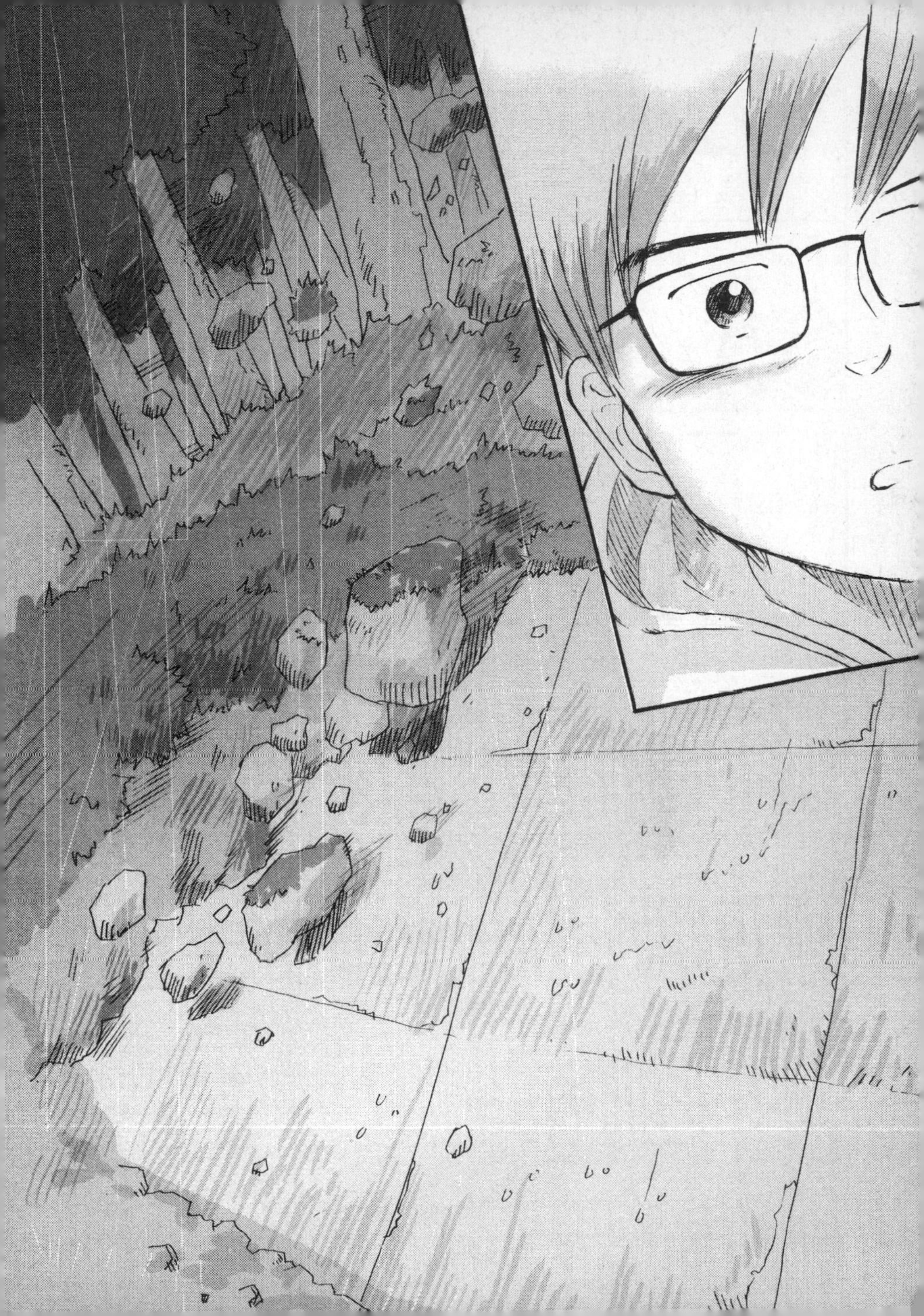

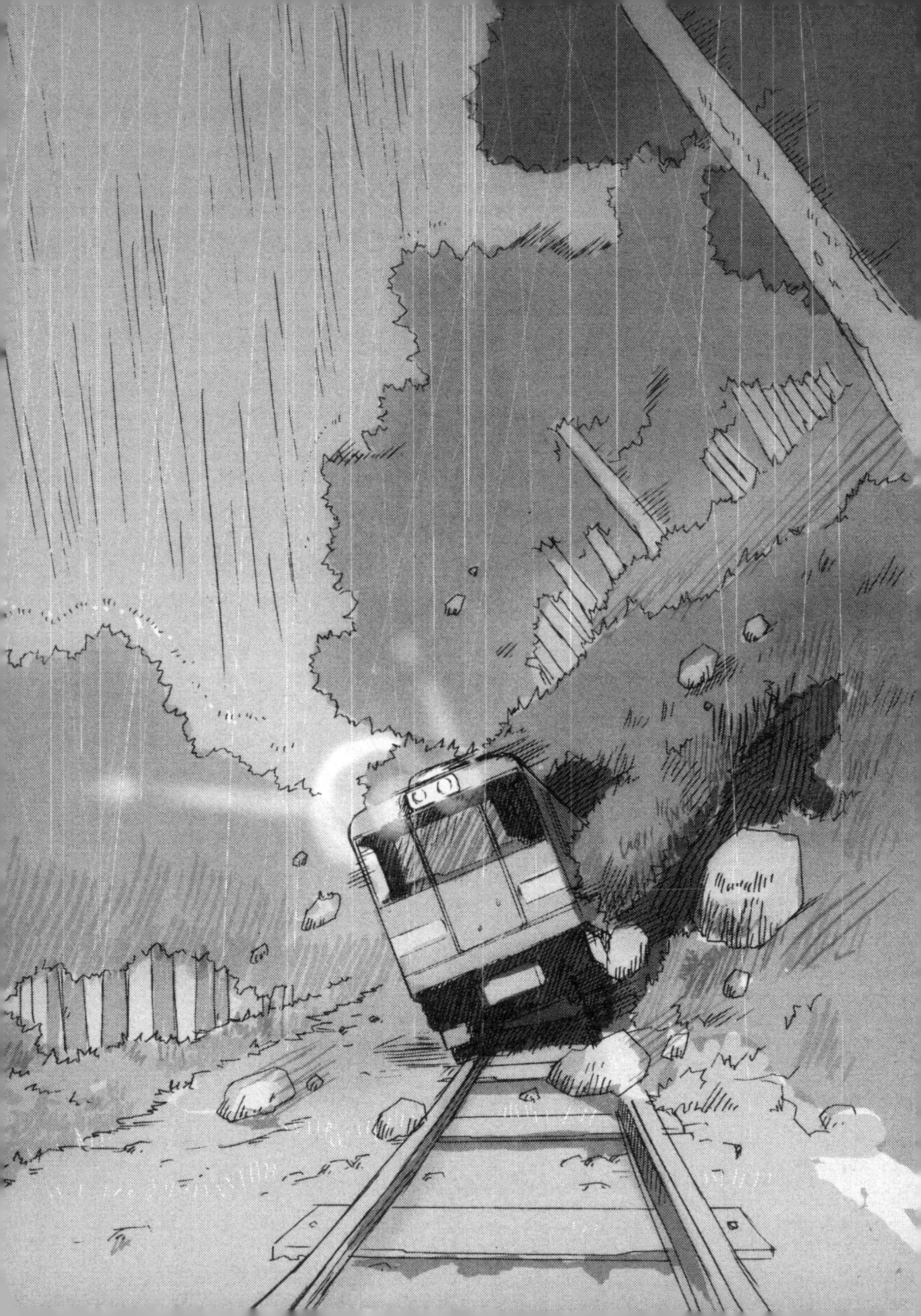

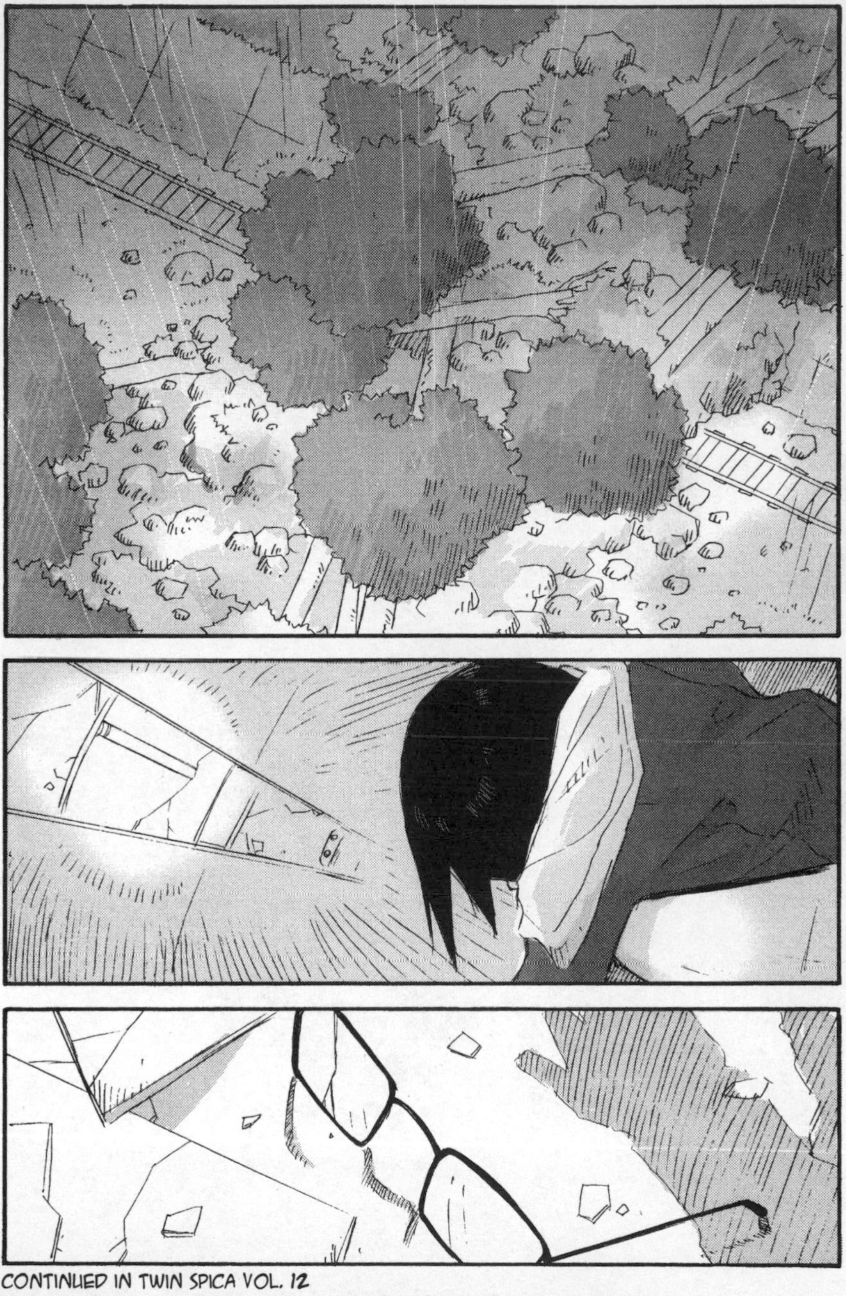

CONTINUED IN TWIN SPICA VOL. 12

ANOTHER SPICA

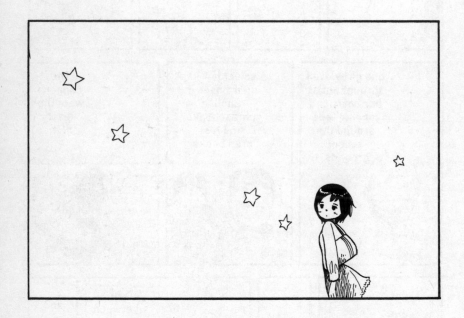

KOU YAGINUMA

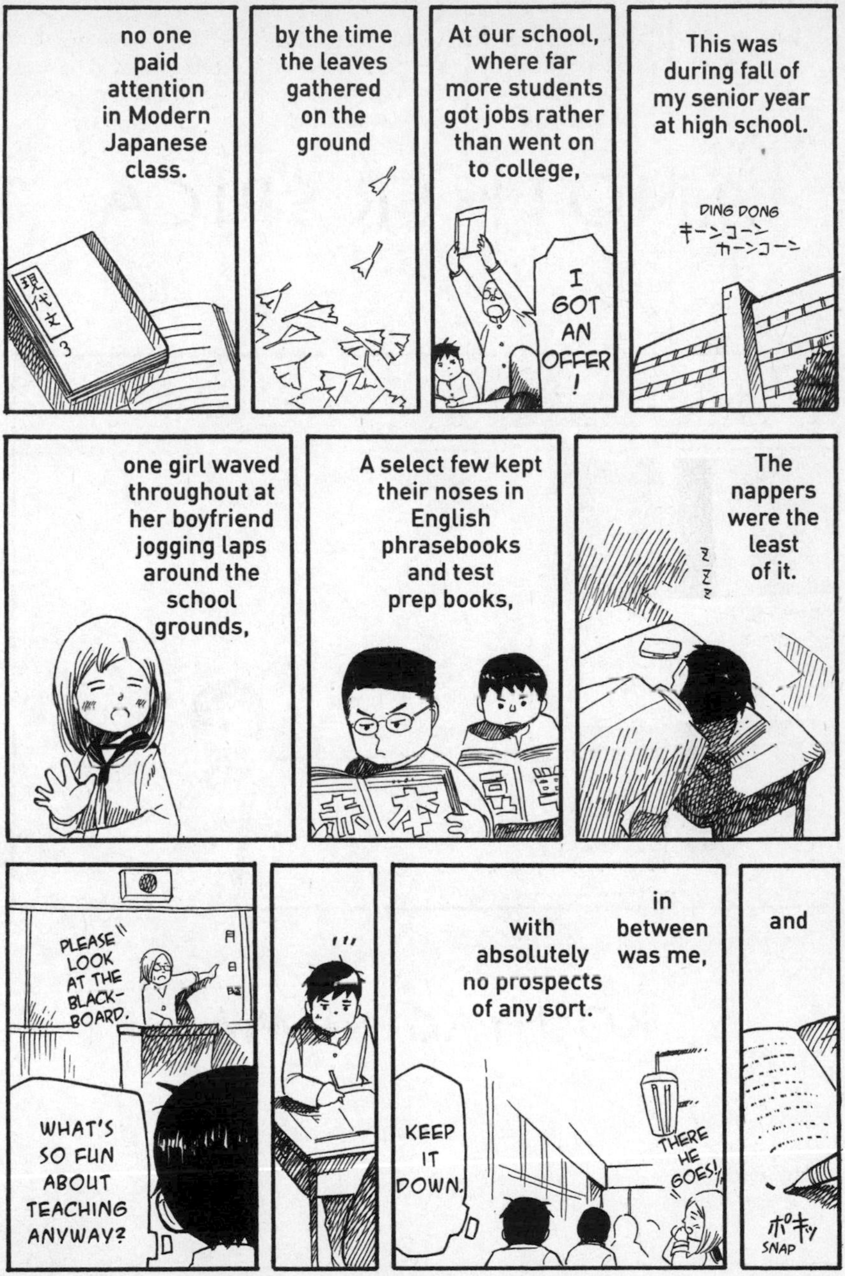
This was during fall of my senior year at high school.
DING DONG
キーンコーン カーンコーン
At our school, where far more students got jobs rather than went on to college,
I GOT AN OFFER!
by the time the leaves gathered on the ground
no one paid attention in Modern Japanese class.
現代文 3
The nappers were the least of it.
Z Z Z
A select few kept their noses in English phrasebooks and test prep books,
赤本
one girl waved throughout at her boyfriend jogging laps around the school grounds,
and
ポキッ
SNAP
in between was me,
with absolutely no prospects of any sort.
THERE HE GOES!
KEEP IT DOWN.
PLEASE LOOK AT THE BLACKBOARD.
WHAT'S SO FUN ABOUT TEACHING ANYWAY?

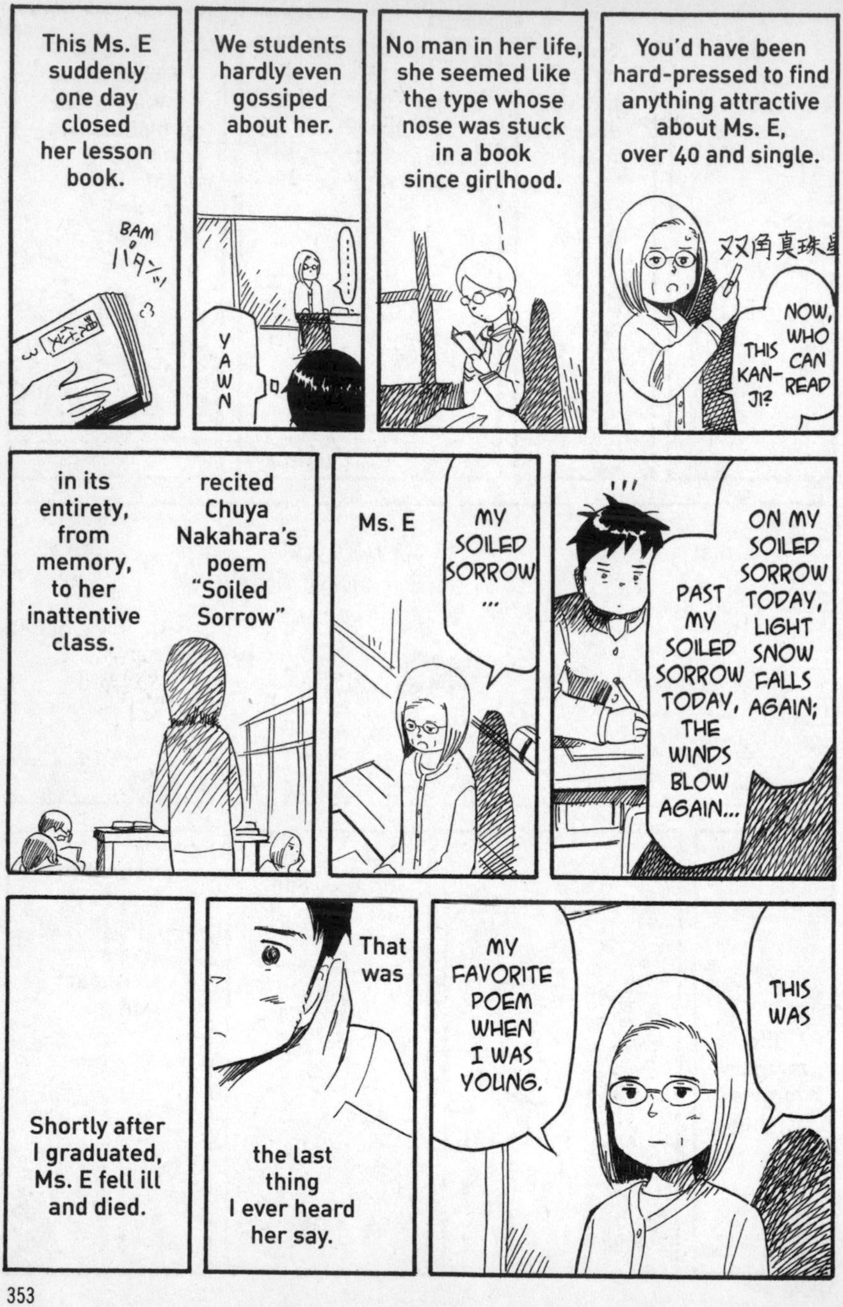
You'd have been hard-pressed to find anything attractive about Ms. E, over 40 and single.
双角真珠
NOW, WHO CAN READ THIS KAN-JI?
No man in her life, she seemed like the type whose nose was stuck in a book since girlhood.
We students hardly even gossiped about her.
......
YAWN
This Ms. E suddenly one day closed her lesson book.
BAM
バタン
ON MY SOILED SORROW TODAY, LIGHT SNOW FALLS AGAIN;
PAST MY SOILED SORROW TODAY, THE WINDS BLOW AGAIN...
MY SOILED SORROW ...
Ms. E
recited Chuya Nakahara's poem "Soiled Sorrow"
in its entirety, from memory, to her inattentive class.
THIS WAS
MY FAVORITE POEM WHEN I WAS YOUNG.
That was
the last thing I ever heard her say.
Shortly after I graduated, Ms. E fell ill and died.

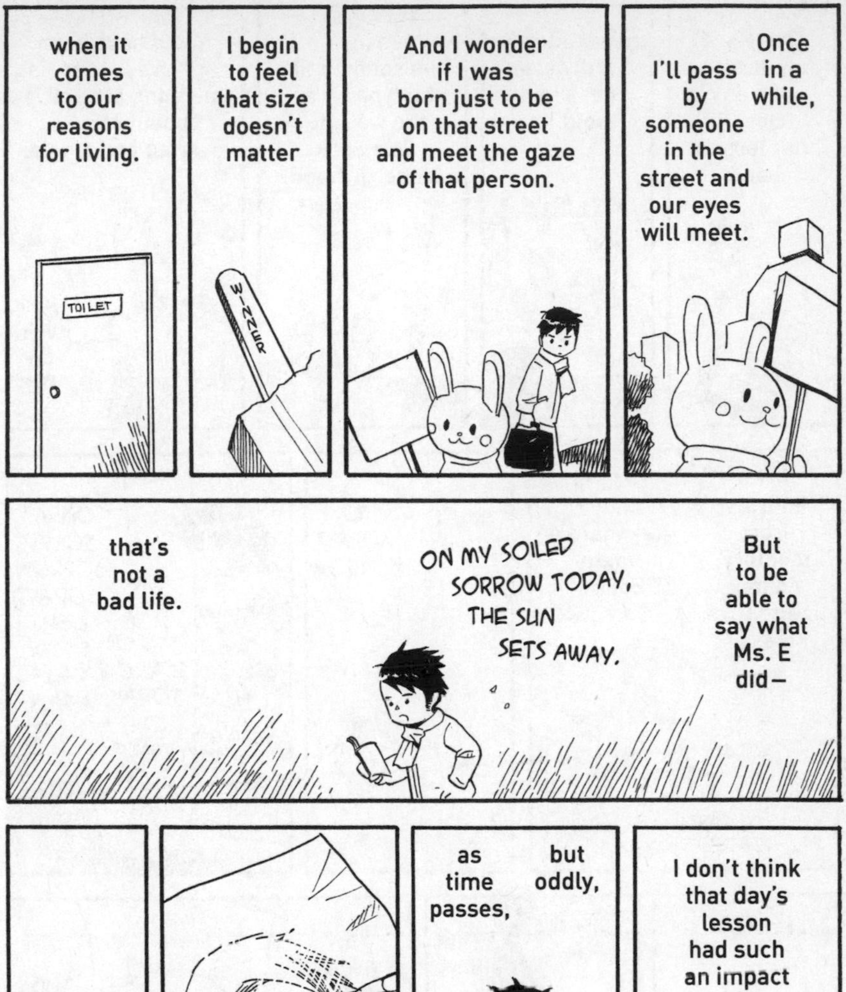
Once in a while,
I'll pass by someone in the street and our eyes will meet.
And I wonder if I was born just to be on that street and meet the gaze of that person.
I begin to feel that size doesn't matter
WINNER
when it comes to our reasons for living.
TOILET
But to be able to say what Ms. E did–
ON MY SOILED SORROW TODAY, THE SUN SETS AWAY.
that's not a bad life.
I don't think that day's lesson had such an impact on me,
but oddly,
as time passes,
the memory grows brighter.

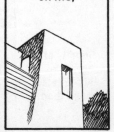

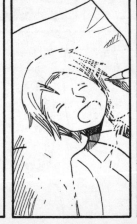

THE END

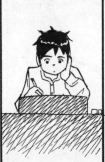

ANOTHER SPICA

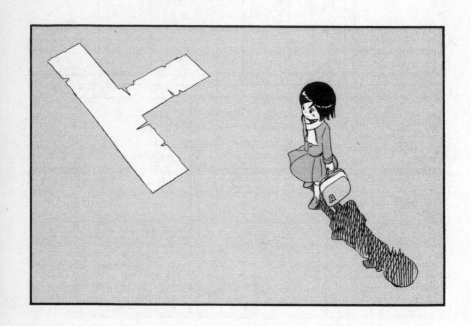

KOU YAGINUMA

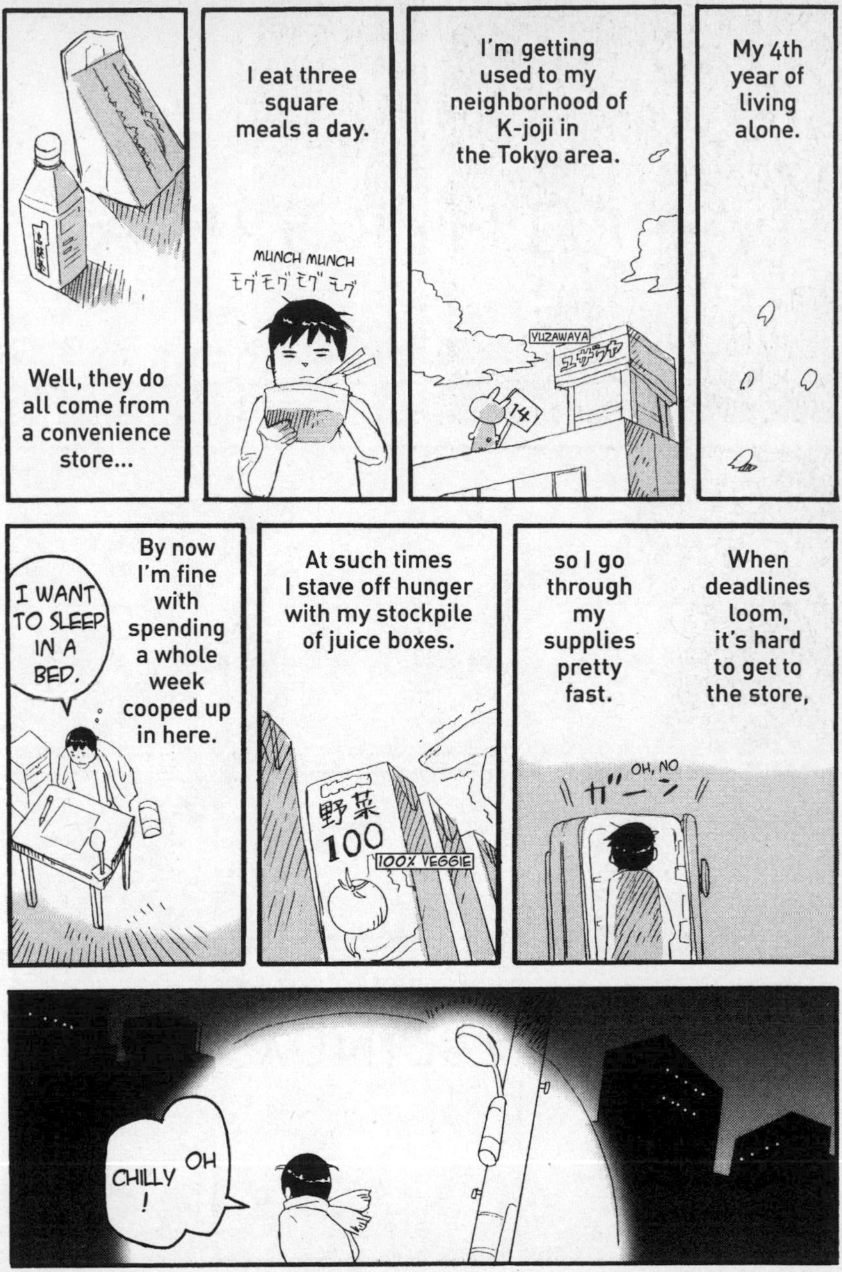
My 4th year of living alone.
I'm getting used to my neighborhood of K-joji in the Tokyo area.
YUZAWAYA
ユザワヤ
14
I eat three square meals a day.
MUNCH MUNCH
モグモグモグモグ
Well, they do all come from a convenience store...
When deadlines loom, it's hard to get to the store,
so I go through my supplies pretty fast.
OH, NO
ガーン
At such times I stave off hunger with my stockpile of juice boxes.
野菜100
100% VEGGIE
By now I'm fine with spending a whole week cooped up in here.
I WANT TO SLEEP IN A BED.
OH CHILLY!

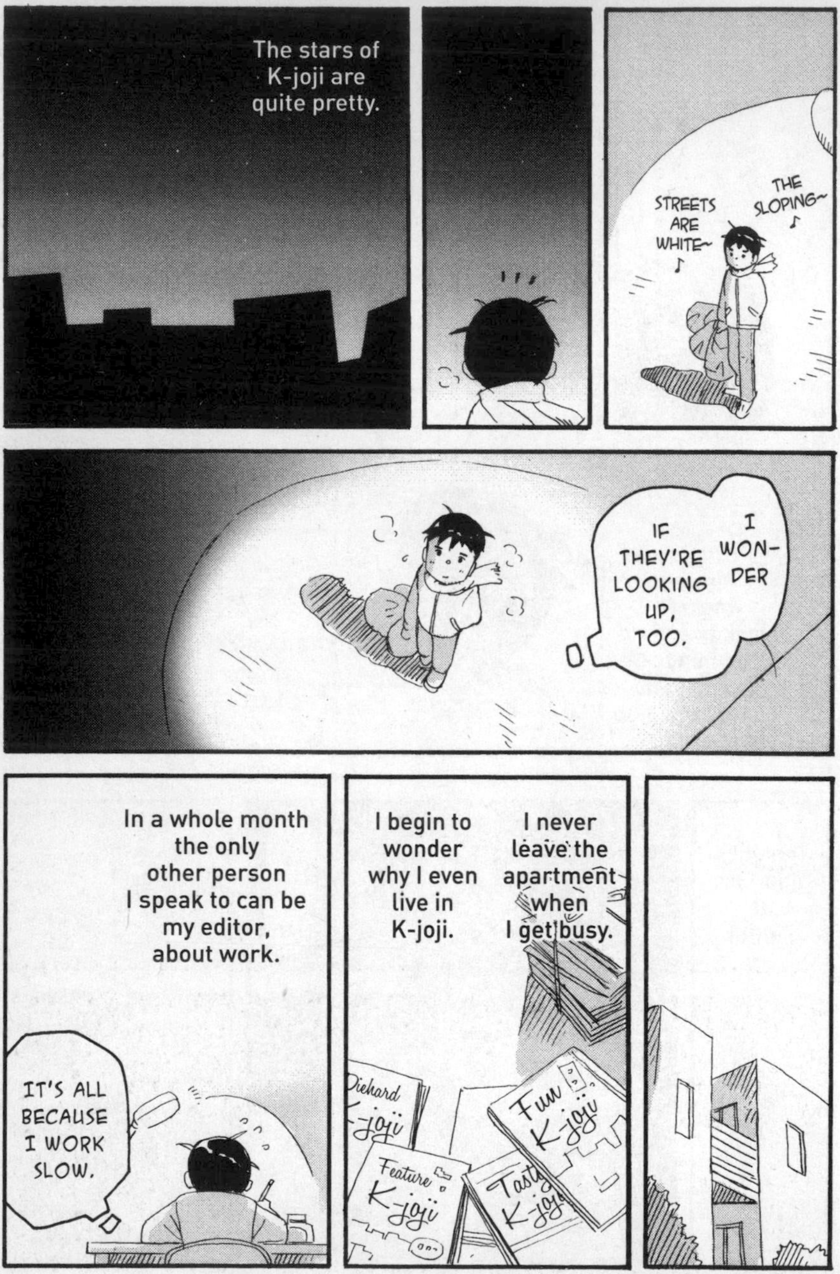
THE SLOPING~ ♪
STREETS ARE WHITE~ ♪
The stars of K-joji are quite pretty.
I WONDER IF THEY'RE LOOKING UP, TOO.
I never leave the apartment when I get busy.
I begin to wonder why I even live in K-joji.
Fun K-joji
Diehard K-joji
Feature K-joji
In a whole month the only other person I speak to can be my editor, about work.
IT'S ALL BECAUSE I WORK SLOW.

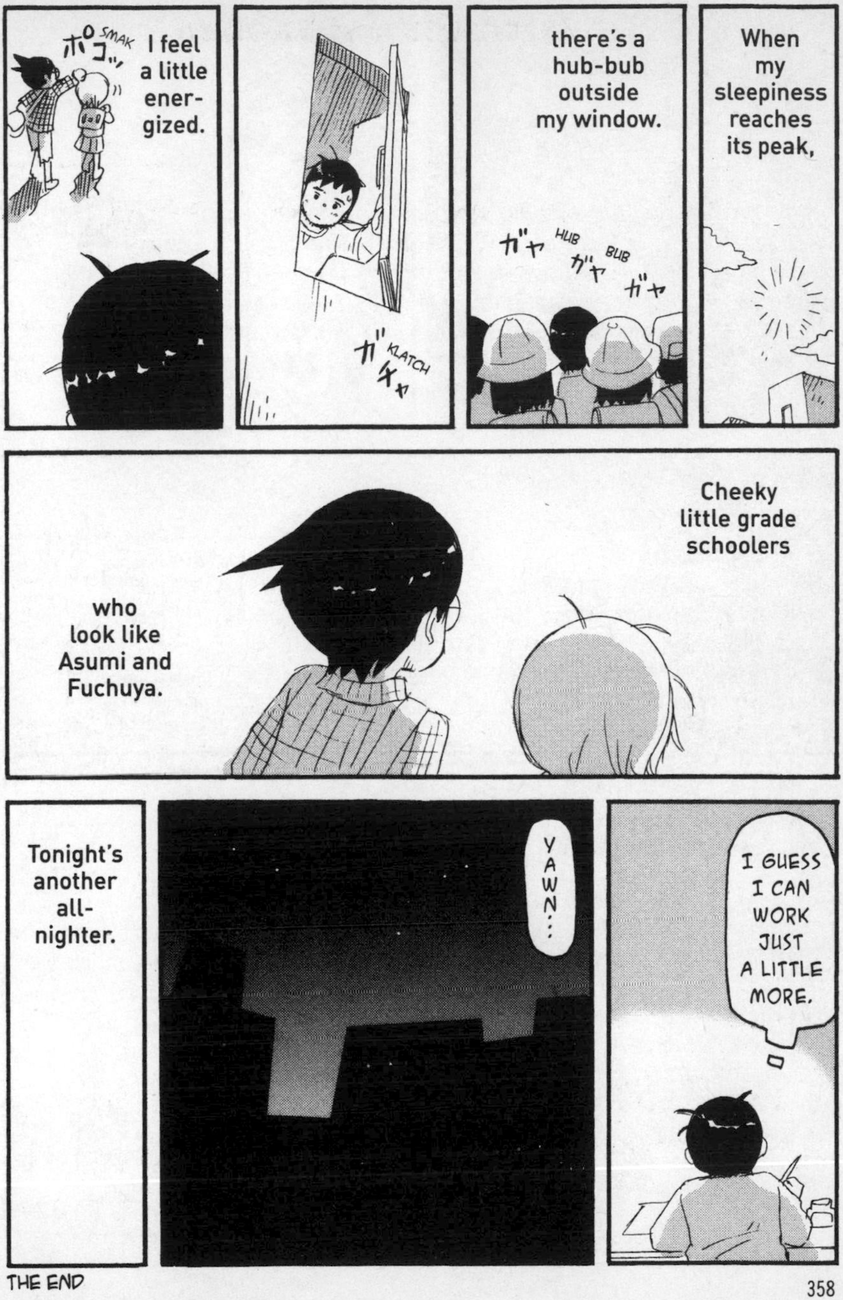
When my sleepiness reaches its peak,
there's a hub-bub outside my window.
ガヤ HUB
ガヤ BUB
ガヤ
ガチャ KLATCH
I feel a little ener-gized.
ポコッ SMAK
Cheeky little grade schoolers
who look like Asumi and Fuchuya.
I GUESS I CAN WORK JUST A LITTLE MORE.
YAWN...
Tonight's another all-nighter.

THE END

Notes on the Translation

P. 29

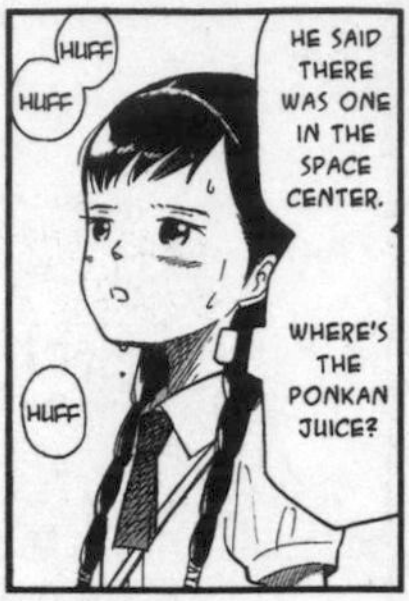
HE SAID THERE WAS ONE IN THE SPACE CENTER.
HUFF
HUFF
WHERE'S THE PONKAN JUICE?
HUFF

Though of the tangerine family, the *ponkan* or "mandarin orange" grows to the size of an orange. Said to originally be from India, today the fruit is mostly grown in Southeast Asia. Warmer regions in both Japan and the United States, however, are also capable of cultivating them and do so.

P. 353

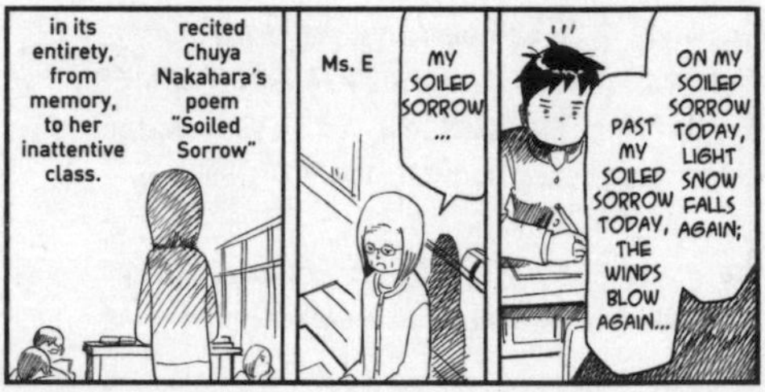
ON MY SOILED SORROW TODAY, LIGHT SNOW FALLS AGAIN;
PAST MY SOILED SORROW TODAY, THE WINDS BLOW AGAIN...
MY SOILED SORROW ...
Ms. E
recited Chuya Nakahara's poem "Soiled Sorrow"
in its entirety, from memory, to her inattentive class.

The precocious poet who dies young is a figure that seems to be cherished across cultures; it is embodied, in modern Japan, by Chuya Nakahara (1907-37). Like Arthur Rimbaud, his role model, he left an output that is modest in volume but whose reputation only rose since his passing. Sensitive teenagers and seasoned critics alike have continued to hold his workå in high regard to this day.

P. 356

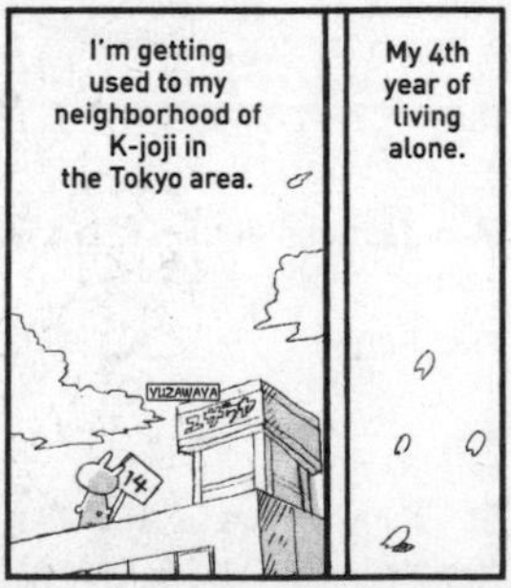
My 4th year of living alone.
I'm getting used to my neighborhood of K-joji in the Tokyo area.
YUZAWAYA

"K-joji" is Kichijoji, an area in the western Tokyo metropolis known for being cultured and hip. It is home to a high concentration of young artists, rather like certain parts of Brooklyn, NY. As the notes to some of the previous volumes pointed out, the stops on train lines serving the area have been used as bit characters' names in the series.

Production - Hiroko Mizuno
           Nicole Dochych
           Tomoe Tsutsumi

Originally published in Japanese as *Futatsu no Supika 13, 14*
by MEDIA FACTORY, Inc., Tokyo, 2007, 2008
Futatsu no Supika first serialized in Gekkan Comic Flapper,
MEDIA FACTORY, Inc., 2001-2009

This is a work of fiction.

ISBN: 978-1-935654-33-9

Manufactured in the United States of America

First Edition

Vertical, Inc.
451 Park Avenue South, 7th Floor
New York, NY 10016
www.vertical-inc.com